# RHÔNE-ALPES

'Take to the fertile slopes above the Rhône to explore a string of
secretive artistic villages. Cliousclat keeps tightly in its shell, protecting
itself from modern encroachments; this is a potters' village where the
houses really are as tightly packed as pieces in a kiln.'

Philippe Barbour

# About the Guide

The **full-colour introduction** gives the author's overview of the Rhône-Alpes region, together with suggested **itineraries** and a regional 'where to go' map and **feature** to help you plan your trip.

Illuminating and entertaining **cultural chapters** on regional history, food, wine and everyday life give you a rich flavour of the Rhône-Alpes.

**Planning Your Trip** starts with the basics of when to go, getting there and getting around, coupled with other useful information, including a section for disabled travellers. The **Practical A–Z** deals with the **essential information** and **contact details** that you may need while you are away.

The **regional chapters** are arranged in a loose touring order, containing plenty of practical information. The author's top **'Don't Miss'** ✪ **sights** are highlighted at the start of each chapter and there are also **short-tour itineraries**.

A **language and pronunciation guide**, a **glossary** of cultural terms and a comprehensive **index** can be found at the end of the book.

Although everything we list in this guide is **personally recommended**, our author inevitably has his own favourite places to eat and stay. Whenever you see this **Author's Choice** ★ icon beside a listing, you will know that it is a little bit out of the ordinary.

## Hotel Price Guide (*also see* p.53)

| | | |
|---|---|---|
| Luxury | €€€€€ | €230 and above |
| Very expensive | €€€€ | €150–230 |
| Expensive | €€€ | €100–150 |
| Moderate | €€ | €60–100 |
| Inexpensive | € | under €60 |

## Restaurant Price Guide (*also see* p.57)

| | | |
|---|---|---|
| Very expensive | €€€€ | over €60 |
| Expensive | €€€ | €30–60 |
| Moderate | €€ | €15–30 |
| Inexpensive | € | under €15 |

# About the Author

As passionate as the Romantics about the Rhône-Alpes' uplifting ranges and deeply vinous valleys, Philippe Barbour (*philippe.barbour@googlemail.com*) has been enjoying its inexhaustible pleasures for very many years. A great advocate of the glorious variety of France's regions, Philippe is also author of Cadogan's *Brittany* and *Loire* guides, and the main contributor to Cadogan *France*.

**2nd Edition Published 2007**

# INTRODUCING
# THE RHÔNE-ALPES

Sitting on a stray Romanesque capital beside a lavender-surrounded swimming pool, sipping a local Côtes du Rhône wine that tastes of cherries, I'm mulling over how I fell in love with the Rhône-Alpes that so captivated the Romantics, who saw in the region's soaring heights and frightening depths a reflection of man's emotional journey through life. My eyes wander distractedly from this introduction I'm preparing, up the stunning mountainsides that encircle me. Above the olive groves, the terraced apricot orchards give way to densely wooded tops from which the odd limestone scar stands out, a reminder of the geological fights that shaped these dramatic parts.

Over the nearest summit, a pair of birds of prey circle far above. I'm taking a more relaxed attitude to dinner down at my parents' house, in their heavenly semi-ruined, semi-restored hill village at a typically awe-inspiring entrance to one of the Rhône-Alpes' pre-alpine ranges. With their vast, dark reptilian backs and huge teeth for mountains, the peaks of the mountains rise, forbidding yet magnetizing, beyond the fruitful, bountiful Rhône valley (which certainly is not just about industry, as you'll see), outer guardians of France's tallest Alpine ranges.

Olive groves and lavender may only be a feature of the southern Rhône-Alpes, where Drôme and Ardèche meet Provence and Languedoc. But all across this region you'll find nature at its most sensational. It's hard to beat for exhilarating, if often challenging, walking, cycling, or pottering about in the car...or for high-energy sports. And these can be enjoyed summer as well as winter. Paragliding was born in these parts. Bungee-jumping, canyoning, mountaineering, rock-climbing and potholing are much-practised

*Previous page: Cliousclat, Drôme, p.196*

*Above, from top: Drôme landscape; detail, Grignan, p.224*

*Above: Flowers and rooftops, Balazuc, along the Ardèche, p.172*

pursuits across the region. Rivers like the Ardèche and Drôme are famed for their canoeing. The stretches of the Rhône covered in our guidebook have really lovely ports strung along them; that at Valence, for example, boasts the largest inland river marina in the country. You can go windsurfing, sailing or waterskiing on the largest lakes. Aix-les-Bains beside Lac du Bourget, and Thonon-les-Bains by Lac Léman, have even won the accolade of *Station Nautique*, the first inland ports in France to gain the distinction for their exceptional watersports facilities. Incidentally, these two are both also thermal spa resorts, among 15 in the Rhône-Alpes now geared to tourist pamperings. In addition, you may be surprised to learn that the Rhône-Alpes's great lakes offer warmer waters for swimming in summer than any of France's coasts.

Most still think of this region for the most famous concentration of ski resorts in the world, with names like Chamonix, Méribel or Val d'Isère coming instantly to mind, and this guide certainly does not ignore the immensely important Rhône-Alpes snow season: a knowledgeable, practical chapter by ski expert Dave Watts guides independent skiers of all levels to organize their own great winter breaks. But the bulk of the book tells you what you need to know to explore all the corners of this magically beautiful region, in spring, summer and autumn.

What does the Rhône-Alpes consist of exactly? you may be asking. It rises between Burgundy and Provence, covering the northern half of the French Alps and their pre-alpine foothills bound by the Rhône, which cuts a crinkly path round them. North of the great river, the region also takes in the southernmost ridges of the Jura range, and, west of it, the last volcanic slopes of the Massif Central. Larger than Switzerland, it is divided administratively into eight *départements*. Those of the Rhône, Loire and Ardèche lie west of the Rhône. The Ain stands north of it. The Isère and Drôme *départements*, the bulk of the pre-Revolutionary province of Dauphiné, stretch east from the Rhône. The Dauphiné's great neighbouring rival, Savoie, only became French by the vote of the people (well, the men) in 1860, and is divided into the Haute Savoie and Savoie *départements*.

The Rhône-Alpes has plenty of fine vineyards to give Burgundy, immediately to the north, a run for its money. It has the Mediterranean fertility, the Roman ruins, and the lavender too, to challenge the charms of Provence immediately to the south...but without such overwhelming summer crowds. Although land-locked, it even has the splendid coasts of its great lakes to challenge the Côte d'Azur in glamour.

Plus, the Rhône-Alpes has fabulously vibrant and cultured historic towns like Annecy, Lyon and Chambéry. It has small-town markets to make you swoon. It has exquisite hill villages that take you halfway to paradise. Glorious châteaux are peppered across its heights, from east to west and north to south. As if that weren't enough, it has the largest concentration of top restaurants of any French region outside Paris. It has more regional nature parks than any other, too, one national park, plus a portion of a second, and, on top of that, the most famous of all the mountain ranges in Europe, the Massif du Mont Blanc. The Rhône-Alpes is, without a doubt, the most sensational of all French regions.

# Where to Go

We start with the regional capital, **Lyon**, France's splendid second city. A far more august place than little Paris in the Roman centuries, Lyon was even the birthplace of Claudius, the man who conquered England. Many know the city as a gastronomic capital of the French provinces; few realize it was also the birthplace of world cinema, thanks to its Lumière boys, or that it is a World Heritage site.

Just north, either side of the Saône, the rich culinary lowlands of **Bresse and Dombes** face bibulous **Beaujolais**, this flirtatious wine territory flaunting one of the world's most famous wine names. Next we hop over the hills to the **upper reaches of the Loire**, with their magnificent mix of volcanic plains and gorges, stepping quietly round the sinuous, wooded gorges and chestnut terraces of the **Ardèche**. While much of the *département de la Loire* remains enchantingly undiscovered, that of the Ardèche has gained quite a name for its fabulous gorges and caves.

We don't shy away from tackling the thin strip of the **Rhône valley** between Lyon and Provence, as in the midst of the heavy industry that has given such a false image of the whole region, many cultural and viticultural surprises crop up, including a staggering line of medieval castles like vast eagles' eyries. The riverside towns such as Valence, Tournon and Montélimar have been sprucing themselves up, while Vienne conceals one of France's greatest Roman legacies. Then, **east of the Rhône**, we delve into the delicious rolling orchards and valleys of western **Isère** and **Drôme**. Beautiful hill villages come two a penny, many with ruined castle, old church, craftspeople and delightful village inn – but then such places exist all across the Rhône-Alpes.

We head on for the major mountain ranges via the least known stretch of the **Rhône, between Lyon and Lac Léman** (you may know it better as Lake Geneva), but exquisite as a backdrop to a Gothic painting, steep vineyards sweeping down to the water. Here the southern talons of the Jura mountain range stick into the river with savage beauty.

Savoie, an independent, if French-speaking state from medieval times, guarded the vast northwestern Alpine ranges, its foothills bathing their feet in the gorgeous **great lakes** of Annecy, du Bourget and Aiguebelette, towns like Annecy and Aix-les-Bains rising romantically above the watersides. Brooding pre-alpine ranges line up along the border of Savoie and the Dauphiné. Medieval monks found peace in these secretive areas, the Maquisards hiding places in the war. The string of regional nature parks in the **Bauges**, **Chartreuse** and **Vercors** ranges encourage traditions. Great historic cities spread out below, Grenoble the former capital of the Dauphiné, and Chambéry the former capital of Savoie.

*Above, from top:*
*Trompe-l'œil, Presqu'île,*
*Lyon, p.78; Châtillon,*
*Beaujolais, p.120; jazz*
*festival in Roman*
*theatre, Vienne, p.184*

After lounging a while beside Western Europe's largest lake, glamorous **Léman**, we tackle the routes to Europe's tallest, most legendary mountain, **Mont Blanc**. The **Vanoise**, the other range of eternally snow-capped mountains and glaciers wholly within Savoie, is encircled by the huge valleys of the Isère and Arc. Now skiing has conquered its mid-slopes, the Trois Vallées famously offering the most extensive ski *domaine* in the world. But down below, the gritty communities offer history, vibrant Baroque churches swarming with *putti*, plus wild white-water sports in summer.

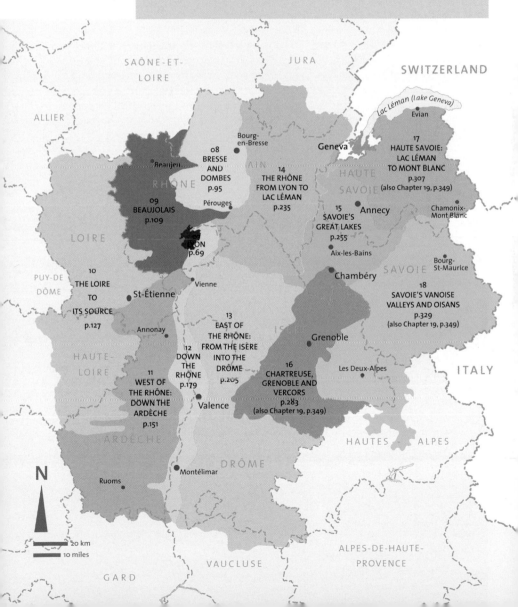

SAÔNE-ET-LOIRE

JURA

SWITZERLAND

ALLIER

*Lac Léman (lake Geneva)*

Evian

Bourg-en-Bresse

Geneva

08
BRESSE AND DOMBES
p.95

Beaujeu

RHÔNE

14
THE RHÔNE FROM LYON TO LAC LÉMAN
p.235

AIN

HAUTE
SAVOIE

17
HAUTE SAVOIE: LAC LÉMAN TO MONT BLANC
p.307
(also Chapter 19, p.349)

09
BEAUJOLAIS
p.109

Pérouges

LYON
p.69

15
SAVOIE'S GREAT LAKES
p.255

Annecy

Chamonix-Mont Blanc

Aix-les-Bains

LOIRE

PUY-DE DÔME

10
THE LOIRE TO ITS SOURCE
p.127

Vienne

St-Étienne

Chambéry

SAVOIE

Bourg-St-Maurice

18
SAVOIE'S VANOISE VALLEYS AND OISANS
p.329
(also Chapter 19, p.349)

Annonay

13
EAST OF THE RHÔNE: FROM THE ISÈRE INTO THE DRÔME
p.205

ISÈRE

Grenoble

12
DOWN THE RHÔNE
p.179

HAUTE-LOIRE

11
WEST OF THE RHÔNE: DOWN THE ARDÈCHE
p.151

16
CHARTREUSE, GRENOBLE AND VERCORS
p.283
(also Chapter 19, p.349)

Les Deux-Alpes

ITALY

Valence

ARDÈCHE

HAUTES ALPES

N

DRÔME

Ruoms

Montélimar

20 km
10 miles

VAUCLUSE

ALPES-DE-HAUTE-PROVENCE

GARD

01

# River Deep

In France, following rivers is often a great way to get to know a region, as so much civilization has been concentrated along them through past centuries. You might not think the **Rhône** the most obvious one to pursue, but it cuts a fabulous path from Lac Léman to Provence, and is nowhere near as dominated by industry as preconceptions would have you believe it: vines and ports thrive along its length, and there are castles, Roman ruins and prehistoric caves to visit along the way.

The second most significant valley in the Rhône-Alpes, and the most dramatic, the **Isère** has carved an awesome, indented path round the Vanoise, to be joined by the mighty Arc, another formidable mountain valley well worth discovering. From Albertville south to Chambéry, you may be surprised to encounter vineyards along the Isère's slopes. Having crossed Grenoble, where it is joined by the Drac, the river emerges from the mountains. The valley beyond offers culinary delights galore before it joins the Rhône.

The stretch of the **Saône** flowing from Burgundy through the northern Rhône-Alpes to Lyon is generally calmer. The culinary-crazed Bresse stretches out on the flats to one side, while wine-mad Beaujolais tries to seduce you with its beautiful curves on the other.

More surprisingly, the region claims large portions of the upper sections of France's longest river, the **Loire**; it parallels the Rhône between Lyon and Provence, flowing in the opposite direction. This is not the tourist-famous Loire valley, but a splendidly secretive section of the river, its broad, bucolic valley hidden from view by long, low mountain ranges peppered with ruined medieval castles.

Confusingly, the Loire's source lies in the *département* of the **Ardèche**, named after one of the most fabulous French rivers, with gorges, caves and villages to take your breath away. The Ardèche river is heavily touristy, but there are other splendid, quieter river valleys to explore, among the best that of the **Drôme**, offering up dreamy villages, the possibility of canoeing by moonlight, and vineyards around Die producing a wine almost as perfumed as the lavender that thrives in this valley.

*Above: Rhône valley skyline from Chapelle de l'Hermitage, Tain-l'Hermitage, p.191*

*Left: Monastery, Loire gorges*

*Above: Montenvers train, Chamonix-Mont Blanc, pp.326–7*

*Opposite page: Mont Aiguille, Trièves-Vercors border, p.302*

# Mountain High

So the Rhône-Alpes boasts the highest peak in Western Europe, Mont Blanc, rising like an otherworldly meringue above the region, often startlingly visible from 100km away and further. But practically the whole of the Rhône-Alpes is covered by magnificent mountain ranges. The Vanoise, with its Ansel Adams-like peaks, is the second grandest, just south of Mont Blanc, and won the honour of being declared France's first national park, in 1963. Europe's highest mountain road pass links it to the Oisans, the Rhône-Alpes's sensational section of the Ecrins, the third great Alpine range in a row, and also a national park.

These areas combined lay claim to the greatest concentration of ski resorts in the world, but we encourage you to explore them outside the winter season, for example in summer, when the cows get buried up to their necks in alpine flowers, munching away to produce divine cheeses like Beaufort, '*Prince des Gruyères*'.

These are just the greatest of the Rhône-Alpes' ranges. In this guide (and in a special itinerary – *see* p.24) we also focus on the formidably beautiful defensive line of the Alpine foothills, or *préalpes*, including the Bauges, Chartreuse and Vercors, as well as on the stunning but more hidden ranges rising north and west of the Rhône: the wonderful high rural havens of the Bugey, Forez and Monts d'Ardèche.

## France's Great Lakes

The Rhône-Alpes may lack any sea coasts, but it makes up for that with the finest lakes in France. In fact, you might dub this the region of France's Great Lakes – think English Lake District, rather than North America. The lakes of Annecy and Aiguebelette, Léman and du Bourget have the drama to match the Côte d'Azur, with some highly glamorous ports and resorts, plus diminutive tracts of beach to fight over. Another very family-friendly, little-known but large lake is Paladru, with Nantua not far behind. Then there are smaller pearls, from a host hidden high in the Alps, via southern Jura gems like Lac Genin, to Issarlès, set in a volcanic crater close to the source of the Loire.

*Above, from top:*
*Lac St-André, p.271;*
*Lac d'Aiguebelette, p.281*

*Above: Choranche cave,*
*Vercors, p.304*

# Going Underground

There's a whole wonderful underground world to explore across
the Rhône-Alpes, just as staggering as the one above ground.
The region in fact puts in a claim to some of the world's deepest-
recorded caves, the Gouffre Mirolda at Samoëns holding second
position at present, at 1,733m. We won't force you down there, but,
without resorting to potholing, you'll find a whole host of great
caverns you can easily visit. That's because so many of the Rhône-
Alpes' ranges beyond the high Alps are made from limestone, a
softish rock that waters have been able to drill through down the
millennia, creating a mass of caves.

*Grottes* are large caverns, sometimes on an immense scale in these parts, while *avens* are vertical natural swallow-holes. One of the finest concentrations of huge caves of both sorts lie beside the sensational Gorges de l'Ardèche, wowing visitors with magical concretions and colours. Across in the Vercors, the Grottes de Choranche, reached via a cliff-hanger of a route, are another of the region's most famous caves, with startling spaghetti-like stalactites.

The caves of the Rhône-Alpes aren't only about natural wonders. They've also provided rich pickings for palaeontologists and archaeologists. Up in the Chartreuse's great Mont Granier, the ursine name of the Caverne des Ours reflects the fact that it contained thousands of bears' bones, having served as a high spot for hibernation over millennia. Humans often used the Rhône-Alpes' caves in prehistoric times, too. The major museum of prehistory beside the Aven d'Orgnac in southern Ardèche covers hundreds of thousands of years of human history. In the very colourful Grotte de Thaïs in the Drôme, a bone with notches was discovered, interpreted as one of the oldest human numerical systems ever found. Just sticking to the Rhône valley between Lyon and Provence, there are smaller caves where many prehistoric human finds have been made; the valley was a favourite spot for mammoth-catching.

*Below: Gorges du Pont du Diable, Chablais, p.317*

Most fabulous of all was the discovery as recently as 1994 of the Grotte Chauvet. Here, expert potholers found the most exceptional array of cave paintings, among the very finest, and oldest, in the world. This cave along the Ardèche river is out of bounds, but there's an excellent film on it, which you can watch at Vallon-Pont-d'Arc.

A number of the region's caves were turned into hideouts in times of war, for example the great caves up in the Vercors range, offering refuge to Resistance fighters; one was even used as a hospital. Many other caves across the region are used for ageing cheeses and wines. The caves at Voiron are claimed as the world's largest liqueur-ageing cellars, for distinctive Chartreuse, the huge, oozing barrels filling the air with a heady scent.

The high Alps are made of harder stuff than the softer limestone ranges, but head up from Chamonix to the Mer de Glace, the most famous glacier in France, and you can enter the cooling ice cave here even in the height of summer.

## Exhilarating Summer Sports...

Mention the French Alps and foreigners automatically think of skiing. But French people know that this is also the greatest area for exciting summer sports. With the Rhône-Alpes, we're talking about the region where paragliding was born... where mountaineering, rock-climbing and mountain-biking are almost as popular as hiking; and where you might even try devalkarting – shooting down a mountainside on a go-kart!

If these aren't exhilarating enough for you, throw yourselves off the Pont de Ponsonnas, one of Europe's largest bungee-jumping sites, over the Drac river.

Rivers bring to mind the possibility not just of canoeing, but also of white-water-rafting and canyoning – the latter a heady mix of demanding sporting disciplines revolving around water. Entering the bowels of the earth, potholers have a field-day in these parts, in recent years famously discovering that staggering cache of hibernating bears' bones in the Chartreuse, and one of the most exceptional sets of prehistoric cave paintings in the world, along the Ardèche (*see* 'Going Underground', opposite).

*Above: Paragliding over Lac d'Annecy, pp.262–5*

## ...and Relaxing in the Rhône-Alpes

You can experience a great deal of exhilaration in the Rhône-Alpes, but you can also enjoy relaxing pursuits or even indulge in a good pampering. More genteel sports are easy to practise in the region: hiking, golfing, horse-riding and donkey-trekking among them. Sailing is possible on the biggest lakes, or, for a really soft option, this is very *pédalo* paradise.

Some of you might consider swirling wine round the glass in a *dégustation* more your cup of tea than your body being spun round by thermals or rapids. Remember, there are not just the Rhône valley vineyards to entice you, but also bibulous Beaujolais and stunning, more mountainous wine routes (*see* the wine itinerary that follows). Or seek still more fragrant peace in the lavender fields of the southern Ardèche and Drôme.

*Above: Lavender field
near Die, Drôme, p.222*

*Below: Spa,
Aix-les-Bains, pp.274–6*

*Right: Casino,
Aix-les-Bains, p.275*

The Rhône-Alpes is also one of France's most important thermal spa destinations. It's nothing new; the Romans got there first in most cases, for example at Aix-les-Bains, with its substantial ancient remains. In recent times, the curative waters were mainly used by the French national health service. But in the last ten years or so, many have been converting themselves to serve a clientele in search of wellbeing breaks, and creating more luxurious facilities. There are 15 such thermal towns, some with distinct specialities, for example Evian, concentrating on mothers and babies, or Brides-les-Bains, catering to slimmers.

In addition, there are man-made spa centres springing up all around. A handful of top hotels now offer the swishest of facilities, including Georges Blanc in Vonnas, or Les Fermes de Marie at Megève. The brand-new Hilton with its ultra-trendy Buddha spa in Evian, and the Lyon Métropole on the banks of the Saône, boast of having some of the largest urban spas in Europe. For something simpler but just as magical, innumerable addresses we've selected have the most gorgeous pools, stunning mountain ranges providing contemplative backdrops.

*Above: Bridge, Lyon, pp.69–94*

# Rich City Life

In a region where nature is so clearly at its most sensational, where picturesque villages lie round every corner, and the small towns seduce visitors with their country markets, remember that there are great historic towns and cities to visit, too. Several of these are cheap-flight destinations, or on TGV fast train routes. Lyon holds pride of place, a city of international standing and sights, starting with its no less than three Roman theatres. It's also the place where cinema was invented, and where the first film of all time was shot.

Annecy is generally considered the most beautiful city of the French Alps. Chambéry, former capital of Savoie, puts on a great show, its near-neighbour Aix-les-Bains making a good double act. Grenoble may have the image of an uncompromisingly contemporary technological city, but it turns out to be a vibrant, cultured place packed with excitement, going from early Christian sights to contemporary art. Other Rhône-Alpes towns with famous names, like Evian, Montélimar and Valence, have benefited from very successful facelifts recently. Even gritty miners' city St-Etienne has created stylish museums at the cutting edge, and its satellite, Firminy, has just completed the bold construction of one of Le Corbusier's most avant-garde church designs, an exciting architectural achievement.

*Clockwise from top:
Palais de l'Isle, Annecy,
p.259; cathedral,
Vienne, p.186; cloister,
Bourg-en-Bresse, p.101*

# Itineraries

## The Best of the Rhône-Alpes: a Roller-Coaster Fortnight

*See the relevant touring chapter pages for our recommendations for accommodation and restaurants*

**Day 1** Arrive in the World Heritage city of **Lyon** for a taste of the Rhône-Alpes' fantastic capital, spreading over the hills where Rhône and Saône meet. Stay in Lyon, perhaps taking a Saône cruise for a relaxing sightseeing tour.

**Day 2** Race to **Lac Léman** by motorway, then slow down completely to explore the lakeside, taking in exquisite villages like **Nernier** and **Yvoire** and the glamorous ports of **Thonon** and **Evian**. Consider a boat trip, or a dip. Pick a hotel by the lake.

**Day 3** Take one of the beautiful Alpine valleys south – the **Dranse de Morzine** has the greatest number of attractions – to join the **Arve valley** leading to **Chamonix**, standing dramatically below Mont Blanc. Stay nearby.

**Day 4** Make sure you've booked a trip up **Mont Blanc**'s flanks, by cable-car or train, well in advance; or plan a walking day. Stay in the same hotel as on Day 3, or head for idyllic Lac d'Annecy for two nights there.

**Day 5** **Lac d'Annecy** is France's most magical lake; get out on it with a mini-cruise...or on a *pédalo*! The gorgeous town of **Annecy** has lots of choices for hotels and restaurants, but **Talloires** is an even more heavenly resort.

**Day 6** Make for the belvederes and the Abbaye de Hautecombe looking down on **Lac du Bourget**. Continue to **Aix-les-Bains**, a town of two halves, the contemporary port down below, the historic quarters up the slope – book a spa pampering well in advance if that appeals. Stay either in Aix or Chambéry.

**Day 7** Explore Savoie's historic capital, **Chambéry**, in the morning, then take the motorway for an afternoon in high-energy **Grenoble**. If you prefer countryside, concentrate on the dramatic **Chartreuse** range between the two. Some of Grenoble's best hotels lie outside the centre, but the city's heart has a real buzz.

**Day 8** Rush by motorway to the Rhône above Valence to make this a wine-tasting day. Shoe-lovers may not resist a stop at shoe-making **Romans**. Then split your time between **Tain-l'Hermitage** and **Tournon**, twin towns facing each other on the Rhône, in the heart of the finest northern **Côtes du Rhône wine territory**. Stay in a Rhône-side hotel.

*Opposite page: Abbaye d'Aulps, Chablais, Haute Savoie, p.317*

*Above, from top: Chambéry, pp.277–81; bubble cars, Grenoble, p.298*

**01 Introduction | Itineraries**

*Above: Marina, Valence, p.194*

*Below, from top: Morning hilltops, Ardèche; wine cellar, Château de la Chaize, Odenas, Beaujolais, p.116*

**Day 9** Head south, either discovering more vineyards, perhaps visiting **Valence** and **Montélimar** along the way, or consider the quieter routes just east, taking you through the **Drôme's** beautiful hills via **Crest** and **Dieulefit** to **Grignan**, one of the prettiest, most artistic hill stops, with a grand château and lovely hotels and restaurants.

**Day 10** Cross the Rhône for the **Ardèche gorges**, starting at **St-Martin-d'Ardèche**. The *corniche* road with its head-spinning views follows the river's north bank, with amazing caves hiding out here. Canoeists set off from **Vallon-Pont-d'Arc**. Find a bed for the night in one of the beautiful Ardèche villages just north.

**Day 11** Explore **Aubenas** or **Vals** before taking the winding way up to **Mont Gerbier-de-Jonc**, at the source of the Loire, set among old volcanic heights with vast views. Seek a room at a rustic inn.

**Day 12** Set off early to explore the upper reaches of the Loire and the pilgrimage town of **Le Puy-en-Velay**, where you can stay for a traditional lentil lunch. Continue north following the Loire almost to St-Etienne; just before, branch west for the **Forez**. Book another deeply rural retreat here.

**Day 13** The slopes roads through the Forez offer enchanting stops and viewpoints. Descend back down into the Loire plain to stay around **Montrond** or **St-Galmier**.

**Day 14** Get off to an early start to make the most of a day in the **Beaujolais**, northwest of Lyon. The entirely vine-covered hills and gorgeous villages make this one of the most glorious viticultural landscapes in France. Take in some cellars. Eat and sleep amidst the vineyards. Then make your way easily back to Lyon.

Above: Wine cellar;
Beaujolais; grapes

## A Sensational Rhône-Alpes Wine Itinerary

*For a week or fortnight; just double the time in each wine area to turn this into a more relaxing tour.*

**Day 1** Start by **Lac Léman**, and the gentle vineyards around **Thonon** and the **Château de Ripaille**.

**Day 2** Head down the motorway to **Chambéry** to discover Savoie's gorgeous **Apremont** and **Chignin vineyards**, lying dramatically under Mont Granier.

**Day 3** Join the Rhône west of **Lac du Bourget** to enjoy the stunning **Marestel** and **Chautagne vineyards**. Lunch at **Seyssel**, then discover the blissful, secretive **Bugey wine territory** just across the river.

**Day 4** Cross north above Lyon for the famous **Beaujolais** hills, completely covered with vines. Take in some of the top ten *crus* villages in northern Beaujolais on the first day here.

**Day 5** On the second day in Beaujolais, explore the golden-stoned wine villages in the south.

*Wine aficionados in search of hidden regions can devote an extra day or two to exploring the **Côte Roannaise** and **Côtes du Forez** vineyards along the volcanic upper Loire.*

**Day 6** Now make for the northern **Côtes du Rhône vineyards** just south of Lyon, between Vienne and Valence. Follow the west bank of the Rhône, in the Ardèche, for famously exclusive riverside vineyards such as **Côte Rôtie**, **Condrieu** and **St-Joseph**. At Tournon, cross to **Tain-l'Hermitage** for the famed Drôme-side **Hermitage** and **Crozes-Hermitage** *appellations* that spread some way over the hills.

**Day 7** Skip further south down the Rhône to discover the Côtes du Rhône below **Montélimar**. Ardèche-side, there are sweet pockets of vineyards. The Drôme side of the Rhône offers a really wide expanse of vineyards, including the **Coteaux du Tricastin** and **Côtes du Rhône Villages**.

*If you have more days to keep on tasting, this last area may be the place to spend more time, the vines stretching as far east as **Nyons**, offering a host of good Côtes du Rhône cellars. Even the **Baronnies** hills still further east produce some tasty, more obscure wines. Venture a little north to **Die** in the Drôme valley, to enjoy the sweet-scented sparkling **Clairette** territories. As to the **Château de Suze-la-Rousse** down on the Drôme's border with Provence, it's home to the **Université du Vin** (see p.226) which is a prestigious educational wine centre, with courses possible in English for small groups of amateur wine-tasters – so contact them if some serious wine studying with friends in stunning surroundings sounds at all appealing!*

## Mountain Ranges and Regional Nature Parks

*For a week or fortnight's itinerary. Days 1–6 keep you quite a way west of the Rhône; days 7–14 cover the pre-alpine ranges well east of the river. If you only have one week, simply choose the ranges one side or the other of the Rhône.*

*PNR indicates a Parc Naturel Régional, or regional nature park.*

**Days 1 and 2**  Make for the Rhône-Alpes' northwest corner, bordering Auvergne. Explore the **Monts de la Madeleine** west of Roanne. The **Forez** range that follows on has remained superbly unspoilt, with glorious villages, views and little sights all along its length.

**Days 3 and 4**  The **Pilat** (PNR) range is still surprisingly rural, lying so very close to industrial St-Etienne. It's small, so, on Day 4, slip over into **northern Ardèche**.

**Days 5 and 6**  The **Monts d'Ardèche** (PNR) take you into the untouristy parts of the **southern Ardèche**, although the area encompasses the well-known source of the Loire at Mont Gerbier-de-Jonc. Explore the chestnut-terraced territory of the north the first day; the second day, wander into the more remote southern half of the park.

**Days 7 and 8**  The easiest route across from the Monts d'Ardèche to the Baronnies range goes from Aubenas to Nyons, crossing the Rhône at Viviers. From **Nyons**, there's a beautiful loop to follow round the bounteous **Baronnies**. From **Buis**, explore the **Ouvèze valley** to the east. Finish further north in the **Diois hills** around **Die**.

**Days 9 and 10**  The road up from Die into the **Vercors** (PNR) is alarming, but you then arrive on a gentle high plateau. However, the Second World War stories, the big caves and the hair-raising Goulets roads provide real chills.

**Days 11 and 12**  The **Chartreuse** (PNR) is intimately linked with the rigorous Carthusian order founded here, but the monastic buildings give the area an appealing sense of calm. Other highlights include the great toothy mountains marking either end of the range, **Mont Granier** in the north, the **Dent de Crolles** in the south, while Fort St-Eynard spies on Grenoble from a great height.

**Days 13 and 14**  **Les Bauges** (PNR) is a quietly sensational range. Vines cling to some of its outer slopes. Penetrate the forested interior to find interesting crafts alive in the old villages. Here you'll feel a world away from all the glamour of the Alpine lakes and resorts either side!

*Above, from top: Sunflowers, Grignan, p.224; chestnut trees, Ardèche; landscape, Drôme*

# CONTENTS

## Maps and Plans

## Reference

# History and Culture

02

## The Prehistoric Rhône-Alpes

Are you sitting tight? We start with a lightning-fast introduction to the millions of years of geological melodrama that led to the sensational natural rollercoaster you'll enjoy in the Rhône-Alpes. The granite edges of the **Massif Central** in the west are much older than the **Alps** in the east, emerging several hundreds of millions of years ago. The relatively youthful Alps arose in the last 100 million years, with the clash of tectonic plates. The previous era's seabed was pushed into the air, forming limestone mountains: north of the upper Rhône, the Jura ridges; further south, the pre-alps, or Alpine foothills.

As the last Ice Age ended, from around 20,000 years ago, meltwaters filled natural depressions, forming the region's most stunning **lakes**, like Léman, Annecy and du Bourget. While the crystalline Alpine mountains proved hard to penetrate, waters cut easily into the limestone ranges, creating vast networks of **underground caverns**, from the Bugey up north to the Ardèche down south, many of which you can visit. Archaeologists have found a treasure trove of remains in them. Places like the Musée de l'Ours in the Chartreuse and Orgnac's Musée de la Préhistoire in the Ardèche cover the traces, while at the Grotte de Thaïs in the Drôme a bone carved with notches counts among the earliest-known examples of a human numerical system. The Rhône valley itself is lined with little museums of prehistory. A fabulous cache of prehistoric art was discovered in the Grotte Chauvet beside the Ardèche as recently as the mid-1990s, a one-off find in the region, rivalling Lascaux in brilliance, and around 30,000 years old. Neolithic communities (*c.* 5000 BC to 2000 BC) left the odd trace, for example by the big lakes.

## Celts Settle; Hannibal Passes Through

While Greeks set up their colony of Marseille at the mouth of the Rhône around 600 BC, bringing olives and vines, Celtic tribes established themselves further north across what would become known as **Gaul**. Celts and Greeks traded by river. The other side of the Alps, Rome grew impressively, and threateningly. Their main rivals for a time were the Carthaginians in North Africa, whose greatest general, **Hannibal**, led history's most famous expedition through the Alps, in 218 BC – with war-trained elephants, to take Rome by surprise. Until archaeologists unearth the confirmatory pachyderm poo, people can only speculate which way they went, but the Col du Petit St-Bernard, Mont Cenis and Buis-les-Baronnies put in claims to seeing the amazing army pass by.

The Romans beat off Hannibal, and in the 120s BC took southern Gaul, creating their much-loved province of **Provence**, just south of what is now the Rhône-Alpes region. Caesar, in his *Conquest of Gaul*, claimed he stepped north at the request of one tribe in the Rhône-Alpes, the Aedui, to oust the pillaging Helvetii (from Switzerland). So began a very long, strong connection between Italy and the Rhône-Alpes. Forget Paris's unimportant little predecessor Lutetia, **Lugdunum (Lyon)**, founded by the Romans in 43 BC, swiftly grew into the most significant city in Gaul. Roman emperors were even born in the town, including Claudius (he who conquered Britain) and Caracalla. Nearby **Vienne** competed in trade and boasts an almost finer Roman legacy. The Roman remains at **Aix-les-Bains** recall how classical Italians loved to take a restorative bath.

## Early Christianity and the Dark Ages

Frightening numbers of early Christian martyrs were killed in Lyon, but the city also claims to have had one of the first churches in Gaul. Then Roman Emperor **Constantine**, in his 313 Edict of Milan, made across the Alps, officially accepted Christianity. Bishops were established in the main regional cities. Grenoble has a rare vestige of a 5th-century baptistry, where new converts were fully immersed. Le Puy-en-Velay early became devoted to the Virgin Mary.

As the Roman Empire disintegrated in the 5th century, tribes from the east moved in, the **Burgondes** to Sabaudia ('Land of the Fir', later Savoie), pressing on to Lyon, but then kicked out by the **Franks** in 534. Gaul was turning into **France**. Despite the terrible fighting, major monasteries emerged. Few remains of the Frankish **Merovingian period** (*c.* AD 500–751) have been found, but for a riveting if unreliable romp of a read through these times, try Gregory of Tours' *History of the Franks*.

After the Arab, or **Saracen**, invasions of southern France were beaten back in the 8th century, the **Carolingian dynasty** (AD 751–987) took some control of Western Europe. **Charlemagne**, their great unifying figure, crowned the first Holy Roman Emperor in 800, created the system of rule by counts over his vast territories. Fragments of primitive late Carolingian churches and carving survive here and there.

## The Medieval Period

At the new millennium, the Rhône formed part of the western boundary of the association of lands ruled by the Holy Roman Emperors. The French **Capetian dynasty** (987–1328) supplanted the Carolingians, but remained rather irrelevant to the regions in the Rhône-Alpes. Here, quasi-independent noble families amassed large territories. In the 11th century, **Humbert aux Blanches Mains** ('White Hands' – he was supposedly very pure; or was it that he ruled over eternally white mountains?) was made first ever count of **Savoie** by the then Holy Roman Emperor in recompense for ousting the rebellious bishop of St-Jean-de-Maurienne, who had tried to break free from imperial power. **Guigues le Vieux**, Comte d'Albon, came by lands closer to the Rhône, the beginnings of Savoie's mighty neighbour, the **Dauphiné**. West of the Rhône, the little lords of the **Forez** and **Beaujolais**, and the bishops of the **Velay** and **Vivarais**, lined up as holders of power.

Typically for the times, fighting and marriage were employed by the regional lords to change the power politics and boundaries down the ensuing medieval centuries. Through to the 15th century, medieval castles went up to oversee river fords and tolls, or on strategic high spots surveying vast tracts. The brutal keeps of the Romanesque 11th and 12th centuries were often enlarged and embellished in the Gothic period from the mid-12th to the 15th century, turning into châteaux.

The other great holders of power in medieval times were the varied branches of the **Catholic Church**. These too have left a great Romanesque and Gothic architectural legacy in cathedrals, churches and monasteries. Outside the cities, memorable examples of Romanesque sights around the Rhône-Alpes include Charlieu and St-Romain-le-Puy by the Loire, Cruas beside the Rhône, Die and St-Chef in the Dauphiné, or Hautecombe and Allinges in Savoie. Lyon saw its archbishops strengthen their grip on the city and its surroundings, and from 1079 they received the honorific but imposing title of Primate of Gaul.

Cluny, and then the more severe **Cistercian** order, spread their influence south from Burgundy into the Rhône-Alpes, while **Franciscans** and **Dominicans** settled in the big cities. Certain holy figures within the region focused on founding new orders devoted to prayer and work, or to charitable causes, including **St Bernard de Menthon** (so closely associated with the lovable mountain-rescue dogs – *see* p.41) and **St Bruno**, from Cologne, who set up his highly ascetic hermitage, later to become the **Chartreuse** (or Carthusian) **monastery**, in the range of the same name.

On the international scene, **Pope Urban II** dropped in on Lyon in 1095 on his European tour whipping up support for the First Crusade. In fact, Lyon became the popes' number one stop in medieval Europe outside Italy. With the Crusades, relics flowed back from the Middle East to inspire veneration in a credulous population.

Protesters emerged against the Catholic Church's wealth and materialism. Lyon merchant **Pierre Valdo** caused a stink in the 12th century with his reforming **Pauvres de Lyon** (or **Vaudois**, or **Waldensians**), seen by some historians as precursors of the Protestants, trying to get back to the purer messages of the New Testament.

## Major Medieval Counts

Back with the competing regional counts, the **Guigues** had major ambitions. By now based in Grenoble, they controlled passes around this strategic city. Guigues IV gained the nickname of **Dauphin** (Dolphin, but probably from some contraction of a typical hyperbole such as *'Dieu fin'* – 'made fine by the grace of God') early in the 12th century. This nickname stuck, their lands becoming known as the **Dauphiné**.

As to the counts of **Savoie**, they took on the title of **Portiers des Alpes**, 'gatekeepers of the Alps', controlling the major passes of the northwest corner of the whole Alpine arc. **Count Thomas I** bought the town of **Chambéry** in the 13th century, later to be promoted to Savoie's regional capital. His descendants were major European players, such as **Pierre II** – for whom, incidentally, the Savoy Palace in London (now site of the Savoy Hotel) was built. Many in this Savoyard dynasty carried the name Amédée. In 1272, **Amédée V** managed, by marriage, to acquire the house of Savoie's most westerly territories, stretching to the Bresse. Dauphins and Savoyards fought over their pre-alpine frontiers; two Dauphins even died in the bloody skirmishes.

The **Capetians** stepped in on the Rhône-Alpes scene when belligerent king **Philippe le Bel** took a firm grip of the French frontiers in the early 14th century. He helped orchestrate the move of the papacy from strife-torn Rome to Avignon (just down the Rhône from this region), where it remained for much of the century, although **Pope Clement V** was in fact crowned pontiff in Lyon. Philippe exploited his control of the papacy to attack the **Knights Templars**, massively wealthy bankers for the Crusades, bringing them to their knees on trumped-up charges. A new order, the **Hospitallers of St John**, took over their role. Lyon and the Lyonnais fell under more direct French royal control from 1312, its merchants gaining important powers.

Philippe le Bel's descendants seemed cursed. By 1328 there were no direct heirs, so English king **Edward III** laid his claim to the French throne, against the new Valois dynasty, beginning the **Hundred Years War**. Most of the Rhône-Alpes lay on the sidelines, although western territories were affected. The Valois gained an important foothold east of the Rhône when they purchased the Dauphiné in 1349 from **Dauphin Humbert II**, who had overstretched himself with crusading dreams, although he did create a Conseil Delphinal and the university of Grenoble. From then on, the heir to the French throne would be known as the *Dauphin* (equivalent to the English heir becoming Prince of Wales). At the same time, the catastrophic **Black Death** swept across France from 1348, the first wave of devastating plague.

## Extravagant 15th-Century Late-Gothic Expansion

Out west, the powerful **Bourbon family** from central France took control of the Roannais and Forez along the Loire. In the east, the house of Savoie was reaching the height of its power. **Count Amédée VII** bought the county of Nice from the Grimaldis in 1388, securing an outlet to the Mediterranean.

In 1416, Savoie's lords became mightier dukes by order of the Holy Roman Emperor Sigismund. The first duke, **Amédée VIII**, extended Savoyard territories to their furthest limits in 1419, going from Neuchâtel (in Switzerland) to Nice and taking in the Piedmont Alps to the east. He sought to retire to his Château de Ripaille, but the **Great Papal Schism** resulted in his being elected **anti-pope Felix V** in 1439. Resigning nine years later, he helped end the dreadful division in the Church of Rome. In 1453, the house of Savoie came by one of Christianity's most famous and disputed relics, a cloth said to have been Christ's burial shroud, kept at Chambéry. The city of **Geneva** lay within the gift of the dukes through the 15th century, its area, the Genevois, repeatedly given as an *appanage* (a lordly territory for a son to rule over). Here, **Annecy** grew into one of Savoie's most spectacular towns.

In the Dauphiné, one royal *Dauphin*, the future **Louis XI** of France, oversaw the creation of a university at Valence and the powerful Dauphiné *Parlement* in Grenoble (a regional law court run by aristrocrats, not a representative parliament). He also encouraged Lyon's great fairs, among the most vibrant in Europe, as well as new industries – silk-making, printing and banking, of major significance for centuries. Louis XI took **Charlotte de Savoie** as his second wife, one of several powerful women from that noble house who were to exercise influence on the French monarchy. Their eldest daughter, Anne de France, became **Anne de Beaujeu**, after the capital of the Beaujolais area, when she married Pierre II de Bourbon. Unlucky Marguerite of Austria was rejected for Louis XI's heir, Charles VIII, and then married Philibert le Beau of Savoie, who promptly died. She saw to her mother-in-law Marguerite de Bourbon's wishes, though, that the run-down abbey of Brou be restored, and commissioned some of the most exquisite tombs in Europe.

Not just major towns received fine Gothic edifices through this period, but also smaller centres, remarkable ones going from Ambierle or St-Bonnet-le-Château out west to Abondance, Bonneval or Lanslebourg far to the east, with countless stunning fortified villages (Pérouges the most famous) built in between.

## Italian Wars and Wars of Religion

Charles VIII and his successors, Louis XII and François I, became obsessed by Italy, going on mad dashes across the Alps to assert inheritance claims there, a famous Grenoblois, **Pierre Terrail de Bayard**, serving all three courageously. **Charles VIII**'s foray almost ended in disaster, but his troops dragged back a lot of booty. Still in the mood for conquest as he returned, he is credited with initiating the first recorded mountaineering adventure in France, of the Vercors' inaccessible Mont Aiguille.

**François I**, son of Charles d'Angoulême and Louise de Savoie, king of France from 1515 to 1547, proved more than a match for Henry VIII of England, but was outdone by **Charles of Habsburg**, the last becoming both Holy Roman Emperor and King of Spain. Bellicose François wasted a fortune on disastrous Italian campaigns, twisting the arms of Lyon's bankers into lending him money; Lyon even acquired the dubious nickname of *Capitale des Guerres*. At the same time, many city merchants prospered as the crown encouraged national industry at the expense of foreign imports. However, disaster struck at the Battle of Pavia in Italy in 1525 – François was captured by troops of the Holy Roman Empire and ransomed at massive expense.

Following Luther's rabid declarations on Church reform from 1519, Savoie was split by **Protestantism** spreading rapidly from Geneva. François' troops stepped in occupying much of the region from 1536. West of the Rhône, François put down his upstart cousin, the **Duc de Bourbon**, confiscating his territories. So Forez and Beaujolais came under the crown. But religious matters were about to slide out of control in France. Already in the 1530s, François I had been enraged to find a paper pouring scorn on the Catholic Mass pinned to his door. It had been prepared by two Protestant Lyonnais, from the safety of Switzerland. The severe Protestant Huguenots recruited increasing numbers, despite persecution. More playfully, **François Rabelais**, practising as a doctor in Lyon, published his fiendishly clever but bawdy giant satires at the city fairs of the 1530s, *Gargantua* and *Pantagruel* counting among the most significant French works of the 16th century. Under the extravagant farce, he advocated moderation.

The Catholic Church tried to put its house in order mid-century with its **Counter-Reformation**, agreed at the Councils of Trent. **Claude d'Urfé** represented France at one meeting, and when he had his château, the Bastie d'Urfé by the Loire, remodelled in Italian Renaissance style, it incorporated symbols emphasizing the Catholic doctrine. The more fanatical **Cardinal François de Tournon**, who had helped negotiate François I's release after his capture at Pavia, successfully pressed the king into signing an order for the extermination of further Vaudois. The cardinal also set up a Catholic college of major influence in the family's home town of Tournon on the Rhône.

François I's first son, also called François, died in Tournon after catching a cold, so **Henri II** and his wife **Catherine de' Medici** succeeded. France entered a war with the Holy Roman Empire, Henri II's troops humiliated by an army led by **Duke Emmanuel-Philibert of Savoie**. By the Treaty of Cateau-Cambresis of 1559, Savoie regained its independence, but the duke moved his capital to Turin, along with the holy shroud.

Inside France, religious hell broke out. In the Rhône-Alpes' lands, Protestantism had taken firm root in Lyon and across the Dauphiné and Ardèche, as well as in Savoie. The authorities tried to eradicate it increasingly viciously. The first full outbreak of the French **Wars of Religion** occurred in 1562, devastating bouts following over four decades. Two superlative histories, Emmanuel Le Roy Ladurie's *Le Carnaval de Romans* (a better read than his better-known *Montaillou*), and Nathalie Zemon-Davis' *Society and Culture in Early Modern France*, analyze the situation in the Rhône-Alpes.

Divided Lyon was one of the places to suffer most from the 1572 **St Bartholomew's Day massacre** of Protestants. But the numbers who died were tiny compared with the legions wiped out by the dreaded plague. In 1577, the Dauphiné got a strong Protestant leader in **Lesdiguières**, close to the head of the Huguenot side, **Henri de Navarre**, who would emerge triumphant. From Savoie, **Duke Charles-Emmanuel** harboured major ambitions, however. But Henri de Navarre took the crown as **Henri IV**, the first of France's Bourbon monarchs (1589–1789, restored 1815–1848). Lesdiguières, appointed Lieutenant General in the Dauphiné, defeated the obstreperous Charles-Emmanuel in the early 1590s, and built a great **castle** at **Vizille**.

## The Ancien Régime

Henri IV sought reconciliation, famously, by converting to Catholicism, and protecting limited Protestant rights by the 1598 **Edict of Nantes**; Privas in the Ardèche was one designated safe haven. In 1601 Henri IV dealt once and for all with troublesome Charles-Emmanuel, taking the north of Savoie, from the Bresse to the Gex; the treaty was signed in Lyon, where the dapper Henri had married the stormy Marie de' Medici the previous year.

In Savoie, the most significant figure of the early 17th century was **François de Sales**, a charismatic religious man from a local lordly family, born at the Château de Thorens. He converted recalcitrant parts of Savoie back to the fold and set up the new **Order of the Visitation** in **Annecy**. With Geneva in Protestant hands, the Genevois Catholic head sat in this other splendid lakeside city, François de Sales becoming bishop. Architecture and art counted among the weapons Catholicism used to win back the populace. Savoie, in particular, saw a plethora of new church buildings or lavish redecoration in Baroque style, underlining stories of the Bible, saints and sacraments, all encircled by pink *putti*. Several good museums explain this Baroque propaganda. Other zealous regional Catholic missionaries included **St Vincent de Paul** and **St Régis**. Among the competing branches of the Church in the Ancien Régime, the powerful **Jesuits** had a major base in Lyon, which produced the most famous Jesuit architect, **Père Martellange**, while **Louis XIV**'s most famous confessor, **Père Lachaise**, taught there. Protestant persecution grew. Louis XIV's **Revocation of the Edict of Nantes** of 1685 cancelled Protestant rights, forcing many skilled Huguenots to head into exile.

Politically, Savoie had fallen under the thumb of the bullying French kings Louis through the 17th century. In 1713, with the European reshuffle at the end of Louis XIV's warring reign, **Victor-Amédée II** of Savoie gained territories as new King of Piedmont and Sicily, but was slightly downgraded in 1718, to King of Piedmont and Sardinia, hence the confusing historical reference in Savoie to the '*Etats Sardes*' from this period on. The lords of Savoie ruled quite independently for most of the 18th century, although Spanish troops caused havoc during the **War of Austrian Succession** (1740–48). In architecture, the neoclassical style dominated, known as the *style sarde* in Savoie.

Royal-appointed *intendants* oversaw the French regions through the 18th century. Industry around the Rhône Valley boomed, notably in **silk-making**, the mills powered by mountain waters, while vast numbers of workers made the looms clatter in Lyon. The city was at the forefront in many domains. Industrial developments began to completely transform the Rhône valley and the fast-expanding city of **St-Etienne**.

On an elevating note, at **Annonay** in the early 1780s, the **Montgolfier brothers** gave birth to the possibility of manned flight with their great balloons. Capping that, in 1786 **Balmat and Paccard** became the first men to reach the summit of Mont Blanc by foot, a sensational achievement for the time. More stirring still for French society, two explosive 18th-century authors were based in the region for some time. **Voltaire**'s cutting criticisms of French injustice enflamed the monarchy. Repeatedly forced into exile, he held intellectual court at his Château de Ferney on the Swiss frontier. **Rousseau**, born in Geneva, ran away from an unhappy apprenticeship there to Annecy, then Chambéry, his tearful journey and the formation of his world-shattering ideas on liberty, justice, education and the general will charted both in his autobiographical *Confessions* and in his novels, several of which feature the Rhône-Alpes region.

## Revolution and Napoleon

The ideas behind the **French Revolution** spread fast. The monarchy reacted repressively towards reform, even if suggested by aristocrats. When it tried to shut the protesting regional *Parlements*, this provoked reaction, notably in Grenoble: in the **Journée des Tuiles** in June 1788, protesters threw roof tiles at royal troops. Historians interpret this as a first rumble of Revolution. The three Dauphiné Estates (clergy, nobility and people) met at **Vizille**, calling for a national meeting of the French Estates. A **National Assembly** was formed in 1789, one regional representative the *bon vivant* **Brillat-Savarin**, later to pen a philosophical classic on French gastronomy, *La Physiologie du goût*. Grenoble boy Henri Beyle recorded his impressions of the Revolution there before transforming into the great novelist **Stendhal**.

In fact, the Revolutionary period passed off relatively peacefully across the region, although not in Lyon. As part of France's Revolutionary wars with its neighbours, **General Montesquiou** took control of Savoie for the Republic. The Revolution created the administrative French *départements* (or counties), with Savoie briefly being made the *département du Mont Blanc*. By 1793, the rabid **Jacobins** were in power in Paris. One of their followers, fanatical **Joseph Chalier**, tried to install his Terror in Lyon. Powerful merchants, supported by the people, executed him instead. In reaction, **Robespierre** had Lyon terribly punished. The Château de Vizille, now converted into an excellent Museum of the Revolution, tells of the complex stages in the upheaval, through the arts. The Loire-side textile town of Roanne also displays Revolutionary ceramics, the plates declaring their politics with slogans.

**Napoleon** spent some early officer days in Valence, before being sent to help crush a silk-workers' revolt in Lyon. Dispatched to Egypt to disrupt British trade, he employed **Champollion**, a little genius from Grenoble, to crack the language code of the *Rosetta Stone*. Back in Europe, Napoleon rapidly took control of much of Italy; Pope Pius VI was dragged to France, dying in Valence. Assuming total power at the end of the century, Bonaparte appreciated Lyon's grandeur. But his megalomania went to his head with such horrors as his Russian campaign, and he was forced into exile on Elba. The irrepressible mastermind rose one more time in 1815, coming up from the Med via Grenoble on a road still known as the **Route Napoléon**, along which he raised crucial support. The resurgence was short-lived, ending with Waterloo in 1815; the monarchies were restored in France and Savoie with **Louis XVIII**

and **Victor-Emmanuel I**. Napoleon's family had briefly enjoyed taking the waters of Aix-les-Bains. But the best-remembered French visitor here around this time was the sickly Romantic poet **Lamartine**, embarked on a tragic love affair.

## The Chaotic Course to the Belle Epoque

French society was so disturbed by Revolutionary and Napoleonic upheavals that the confused new monarchs found it hard to hold the reins – **Charles X** was removed in the **1830 July Revolution** and **Louis-Philippe** in the Europe-wide **1848 Revolution**, both punished for their authoritarianism. Austrian troops occupied large parts of Italy, but Savoie kept its independence. Under **Victor-Emmanuel I**, then **Charles-Félix**, huge fortifications went up to guard against invasions. The French fortified strategic points too, for example the vertiginous Fort l'Ecluse before Geneva, and Grenoble's heights. With restoration came extravagant nostalgia in the arts. Charles-Félix ordered the most ostentatious **neo-Gothic** redecoration of the family mausoleum of the **abbey of Hautecombe**. Chambéry's cathedral and Ste-Chapelle received similar treatment.

Industrial advances were cracking on apace along the Rhône, a powerhouse of French progress, albeit at the expense of the workers. In Lyon, **Joseph Jacquard** invented a fiendishly fiddly but time-saving punch-card weaving loom. The workers suffered dreadfully, and rebelled periodically, including when their Beaujolais rations were cut. Laurent Mourguet's satirical **Guignol** puppet shows brought a little light relief. The Lyonnais manufacturers farmed out increasing amounts of weaving work around the Rhône-Alpes, recalled in countless museums.

The French Church looked to boost its image after the Revolution's battering, with **Jean Vianney**, a superstitious priest at **Ars** in the Dombes, outrageously pushed as a model of piety, followed by child-shepherds from a remote part of the Isère claiming to have witnessed an apparition of the Virgin; the pilgrimage to **Notre-Dame-de-la-Salette** was born. These remain among the most important pilgrimage sites in France.

No miracle could save weaving in the Rhône-Alpes, sent into dramatic decline by a fatal combination of silkworm illness, foreign competition and the invention of artificial materials. France's **vineyards** would then be devastated by a series of illnesses, especially phylloxera, although a Beaujolais man, Victor Pulliat, largely remedied this disaster, by advocating the grafting of American stock.

The **Second Empire** (1852–70) under **Napoleon III** proved an age of technological advances. **Aristide Bergès** was among the first to capture mountain water power, on the Isère, generating hydroelectricity on a grand scale. It was a period of great shopping too, the emperor opening Lyon's Rue Impériale, with its palatial emporia and banks.

In Italy, largely occupied by Austrian troops, the Italians fought for an independent state. The able Piedmont politician **Cavour** (a descendant of the Savoyard de Sales family) and Savoie's ruler, **King Victor-Emmanuel II** of Sardinia, negotiated with Napoleon III. In exchange for military help, France received Savoie (and Nice) in 1860. Savoie's men voted almost unanimously to join France, by 130,533 to 235, in a somewhat rigged vote. Another result: Victor-Emmanuel II became the first King of Italy. But it ended in tears for Napoleon III, provoked by

Bismarck into attacking more powerful Prussia, whose armies walked into France. While the **Third Republic** was born, to last until the First World War, the bishop of Lyon ordered the extravaganza of **Notre-Dame de Fourvière** from Bossan, this Marian shrine still receiving one million pilgrims a year.

More light-heartedly, the French **skiing** industry first took off at Chamrousse near Grenoble in 1878, when Henri Duhamel bought a pair of Scandinavian skis at a Paris exhibition and went home to try them out. The fashion caught on rapidly. The crack French mountain troops, the *Chasseurs Alpins*, encouraged competitions. Sickly and fashionable aristocrats headed for newly glamorous, exotic **spa resorts**, Queen Victoria the most famous visitor to Aix-les-Bains. Less formally, a humble postman, one Facteur Cheval, at Hauterives in the Drôme, created a celebrated work of *architecture naïve*, the **Palais Idéal du Facteur Cheval**.

The **Belle Epoque** at the turn from the 19th to the 20th century saw brilliant inventors at work in the region. However, when Lyon hosted the major International Fair of 1894, it witnessed the traumatic assassination of French president **Sadi Carnot** by anarchist Santo Caserio, who was in turn guillotined in the city. Joyously, the next year, the **Lumière brothers** gave birth to **cinema** in Lyon (*see* p.42), which, with Paris, was also at the forefront of the automobile age, nostalgically recalled at the Château de Rochetaillée. Work began in 1909 on the **Route des Grandes Alpes**, a 700km engineering feat of a road linking Lac Léman with the Mediterranean coast via Europe's highest mountain passes.

Meanwhile, the Drôme had given France its first president of peasant stock, **Emile Loubet**. Under his term of office, the cornerstones of the tolerant, secular French Republic were put in place. As to Lyon's socialist mayor **Edouard Herriot**, he became a major French figure through the first half of the century. In town, he called on progressive architect **Tony Garnier** to develop social housing.

## The Two World Wars

The **First World War** front lay well north of the Rhône-Alpes, but men from across France served in the atrocious trenches. A massive arrival of American troops was vital in ending the conflict, many black US soldiers stationed for a time in Lyon. After the horrors of the 'Great War', the first **Winter Olympics** took place in 1924 at Chamonix and the comedy classic *Clochemerle* (*see* p.42) put Beaujolais centre-stage. But France was paranoid about German aggression, and in the 1930s the massive forts of the **Maginot line** extended as far as the Alps – you can visit one in the Arc valley.

Such defences proved totally ineffective, as Germany conquered France with ignominious ease in June 1940 in the **Second World War**. Rule was first split, the Nazis in northern France, the French collaborationist puppet government led by **Marshal Pétain** overseeing the southern half from Vichy, just west of the Rhône-Alpes. **Lyon** rapidly developed as capital of the southern movements of **Resistance**, with many of the most important figures based in the city. **Jean Moulin** came to unify the diverse strands, working closely with **Charles de Gaulle** from late 1941.

In November 1942, the Nazis occupied most of France after the Allies had gained a foothold across in North Africa. The Italians, allies of the Germans, if less fearsome, had been given control of France's alpine territories. The **Gestapo** set up in Lyon under **Klaus Barbie**. While the vast majority of the population did nothing to act against its occupiers, a proportion collaborated to varying degrees. Disastrously, Moulin was caught in Lyon in July 1943, but by then he had already helped ensure that de Gaulle's camp was established to take over power come the Allied victory.

The German mass call-up forcing young Frenchmen to go to work in Germany caused many to join **Resistance groups**. These grew significantly in ranges such as the Vercors, Chartreuse and Aravis. Resistance fighters were also defiant around Oyonnax and Nantua. As 1944 advanced, the Nazis resorted to desperate and heavy-handed atrocities to flush them out. Compelling if harrowing museums recall the war in the region, notably in Grenoble, Nantua, the Vercors and Izieu, the last remembering the hidden Jewish schoolchildren tragically caught here. Major industrial towns like Lyon inevitably suffered from bombardments. That city was finally liberated in September 1944.

## Speeding into the New Tourist Age

After the Allied victory, Charles de Gaulle encouraged French self-reliance. Vast dams, among the largest in Europe, were built to provide electricity. **Nuclear power** was pushed, to meet the country's massive need for energy, the Rhône seeing huge-funnelled *centrales nucléaires* pop up at regular intervals. One of the first prestigious ventures in Western European partnership, **CERN**, at the forefront in nuclear particle physics research, opened on the border with Switzerland.

Attention also turned to **tourism**, a mass of **ski resorts** rising fast. Courchevel was begun as early as 1946. Bold projects followed at the likes of Les Arcs, La Plagne and Tignes up the Isère. At the time, these provided architectural excitement aplenty, and exhilaration for millions. Resorts also went up respecting traditional forms a little more, like Méribel, La Clusaz, La Rosière, and most recently, smart Ste-Foy-Tarentaise. On top of the annual thrill of the ski season, the Winter Olympics were held at Grenoble in 1968. Towns like this and Lyon boomed industrially, but their first-rate cultural legacies remained curiously unknown. Meanwhile, one of the most famous, if controversial, of all modern architects, **Le Corbusier**, designed civic buildings for Firminy near St-Etienne.

**Conservation** became a concern. Annecy early took action to clean up France's most beautiful, but also terribly polluted great lake. Following the Italian lead, France's first **national park**, the Vanoise, adjoining that of Gran Paradiso, was created in 1963, in good part to protect the endangered European ibex, although the remit broadened to protecting the environment generally. The new division of the French regions occurred in the 1970s, and the Rhône-Alpes region was created then as one of the new administrative entities. Plans developed for **regional nature parks**, to safeguard exceptionally beautiful traditional areas with balanced policies of conservation and development. It is odd, though, that, unlike the tallest mountains of the other continents, **Mont Blanc** hasn't received protected status, while little can stop Savoie's great glaciers receding, faced by planetary warming.

Meanwhile, the motorway and TGV train networks extended across the region, facilitating access down the Rhône and along the furthest Alpine valleys. The first ever TGV train service in fact opened between Paris and Lyon in 1981.

The last King of Italy, **Humbert II**, was buried at Hautecombe in 1983. However, he Second World War reared its head again in ugly fashion after the extradition of Klaus Barbie from Bolivia, where the American authorities had allowed him to 'vanish' in 1951, after he had briefly served them in their fight with Communism. The pope visited the area in 1986, the year before the traumatic trial in Lyon; Barbie was found guilty of crimes against humanity and died in gaol.

Strangely, the popular image stuck of the Rhône-Alpes as a region dominated by industry on the economic side, and mass ski resorts on the tourist side. You'll soon find out how terribly misleading this is. Major industry is largely confined to a few sections of valleys, and, along with innumerable, gorgeous semi-crumbling, semi-restored hill villages, the historic towns and cities in fact prove irresistible.

Wealthy **Lyon**, despite pouring money into culture and the beautification of its splendid centre, was long bypassed by French tourists. Former French prime minister **Raymond Barre** became the city's mayor from 1995 to 2001. During this time Lyon hosted a G7 world economic summit, became headquarters of Interpol (the international crime-fighting agency), and was declared a World Heritage Site; French people suddenly became much more aware of its exceptional 2,000-year legacy, and foreigners are now catching on. Modern developments by famous architects such as **Jean Nouvel** and **Renzo Piano** have been going up recently.

The region has other splendid dynamic cities like Annecy, Chambéry and Grenoble. Albertville held the Winter Olympics in 1992, while exciting mountain towns such as Chamonix and Megève remain perennial favourites. Valence and Montélimar down the Rhône have really smartened themselves up. Even St-Etienne, with its gritty mining and industrial past, has been declared a *Ville d'Art et d'Histoire*, in recognition, especially, of a clutch of fine museums, notably one on modern art. The old spa towns like Aix-les-Bains, Brides-les-Bains or Vals-les-Bains, long reliant on French health service patients, have transformed recently to offer tourists a good pampering. Poshest of all, **Evian** hosted the 2003 G8 summit meeting of advanced industrial countries – a huge police cordon forced the anti-globalization protesters to stay the other, Swiss, side of Lac Léman.

The big centres, as across France, were affected by the **race riots** of 2005. But for tourists this is an exceptionally welcoming region, offering a great mix of exhilarating cities and sports and of some of the most peaceful villages and countryside. Not just such engaged activists but any visitor can appreciate the fact that, along with a plethora of museums and passionately-run smaller *écomusées*, the Rhône-Alpes has seen the creation of far more regional nature parks than any other French region, accompanied by thoughtful, intelligent ecological centres such as the Ecopôle du Forez by the Loire, the Maison du Marais de Lavours in the Bugey, Terre Vivante in the Trièves, Les Jardins de l'Eau du Pré Curieux at Evian. A vibrant region, rather than one pickled in the past, it now even offers great cinema, theatre and jazz in some of its oldest historic venues, like the Roman theatres of Lyon and Vienne.

# Topics

03

# The Taming of the Rhône

'A raging bull racing down from the Alps,' was the memorable way France's most famous 19th-century historian, Jules Michelet, described the awesome, muscular River Rhône. It starts its crazed course just the other side of the Swiss St Gotthard pass from the Rhine, rushing first for Lac Léman, splashing into it on the far eastern side and leaving it in the far west, via Geneva. It then takes sharp turns to Lyon before the final frenzied gallop to the Mediterranean. Between Geneva and Provence, other temperamental waters join forces with it, the Isère and the Drôme from the east, and, from the north, the Jura's Ain and Burgundy's Saône. In the west, seasonally frantic then calm torrents plunge down to it from the Massif Central.

The Rhône remained, until recent times, a wild creature, on whose bucking back the intrepid traded, the Celts and the Greeks starting the serious business, the Romans leaving a stunning legacy. Gymnastically perched castles vividly recall the importance of frontier tolls in medieval times. Through the Ancien Régime, the Rhône remained beyond man's control, although, in 1783, Claude de Jouffray d'Abbans' *Pyroscaphe*, one of the world's earliest steam-powered boats, managed to go upriver at Lyon, 'moving without any animal power'! From the 19th century, more assertive efforts were made to straddle the Rhône's back. Marc Seguin of Annonay (great-nephew of the famous Montgolfier brothers – *see* right) designed the earliest French suspension bridges, the first one spanning the Rhône in 1825.

Water power then began to be exploited for hydroelectricity, although much of the pioneering work on this so-called 'white coal' was carried out by Aristide Bergès along the Isère, the second most important river in the Rhône-Alpes. However, the potential of the Rhône was soon put to great use, nearby Bellegarde putting in a claim to have been the first French town to get public lighting. But the river was really only properly tamed after the Compagnie Nationale du Rhône was set up in 1934, controlling navigation, irrigation and, above all, hydroelectricity. A string of vast dams went up, most memorably the Barrage de Génissiat, built around the Second World War, and then the largest dam in Europe. Seeking to reassert French national independence, after the war, Charles de Gaulle led France along the route of nuclear power stations, building a string along the Rhône. The raging bull stood in chains, somewhat scarred, well and truly harnessed for heavy-duty work.

You may not think tourism and the Rhône go hand in hand. But it's not just about industry. There are stunning castles and vineyards, museums recalling riverside culture back to prehistoric times, gorgeous villages, and riverside towns that have recently given themselves a good dusting down. The ports have been smartened up and offer cruises, or even waterskiing, plus the summer spectacle of river-jousting, as well as more peaceable activities like fishing. As for the choice of hotels and restaurants along the Rhône, it's superlative.

Bourg-St-Andéol on the region's southern river frontier conceals a rare Gallo-Roman relief showing an athletic young man overcoming a formidable bull, a religious sculpture of the Mithraic cult, but well symbolizing the centuries-old struggle with the raging Rhône. How times have changed. Stretches have even been completed of the Véloroute, to allow you to cycle happily side by side with the great beast right from Geneva to the Mediterranean.

# Alpine Heroes Take On Mont Blanc

Heading over to tackle Europe's highest peak, one of the Alps' greatest heroes, St Bernard, is said to have been born at the dramatic Château de Menthon on Lac d'Annecy. Legend has it he slipped out of his bedroom window the night before his wedding, to avoid his arranged marriage. Supposedly spirited off by an angel, he did not simply devote himself to the religious life around Aosta (in Italy), but also famously set up two monasteries, at the Great St-Bernard and Little St-Bernard passes, the latter on the Rhône-Alpes' Italian border just south of Mont Blanc, protecting travellers from both the elements and bandits. In popular images, Bernard was depicted stamping on the devil; he is certainly credited with making the Alps much more secure for pilgrimage and trade. The Bernardine order created the breed of big dogs named after him, for Alpine rescues, and Pope Pius XI declared him patron saint of mountaineers.

While the Petit St-Bernard pass allowed travellers to sidestep Mont Blanc, the greatest adventurers in French *alpinisme* took on the highest summit on the continent, at 4,808m. Some claim a group of Englishmen put Chamonix on the map in the 1740s. Summit fever certainly gripped the village from 1760, when Monsieur de Saussure offered a reward to the first person to get to the top of Mont Blanc, then also known as the Montagne Maudite (the Cursed Mountain). Locals Paccard and Balmat were the first to succeed, in 1786, as statues of their rather maddened-looking figures recall in Chamonix. De Saussure followed the following year, as did Colonel Beaufroy, the first Englishman. There's some dispute over the first woman to climb Mont Blanc: Marie Paradis reached the top in 1809, but was carried much of the way by friends, so the honour goes to Henriette d'Angerville.

# Why Annonay Celebrates a Lot of Hot Air

Just before the end of the Ancien Régime, one of the most significant flights of all time took place at Annonay, thanks to the two brothers, Joseph and Etienne de Montgolfier, who are credited with pioneering hot-air ballooning. The story goes that Joseph began to experiment with the elevating possibilities of hot air after he'd noticed the way his shirt flew up as he tried to dry it over a fire. Late in 1782, he and his brother carried out secretive experiments, lighting fires under the balloons they made from paper and cloth. Rumour spread that they were dabbling in sorcery, but in early June 1783 they held a public demonstration of their invention on Annonay's Place des Cordeliers. The balloon miraculously rose high into the air. Competition hotted up, and proceedings moved to Lyon and Paris. The Montgolfiers organized the first flight with live creatures, for Louis XIV's court – a cockerel, a duck and a sheep beat the first men into the air, Pilâtre de Rozier and the Marquis d'Arlandes making the first successful recorded manned flight of all time on 21 November 1783. But what about the curious commemorative plate in Annonay's museum depicting a tragic Madame Blanchard apparently making an ill-fated balloon trip in 1782, and dying in the process? Nowadays Annonay celebrates hot-air ballooning with its annual early June celebrations, while local companies can organize balloon trips in this cradle of flight.

# Lyon Suburb Sees Birth of World Cinema

Few people realize that cinema was invented in Lyon. Painter-turned-photo-portraitist Antoine Lumière laid the foundations for the Lumière boys' revolution in photography and the moving image. His sons Auguste and Louis were born in the Franche-Comté's capital Besançon, in 1862 and 1864 respectively. The family moved to Lyon in 1870; inventive, sociable Antoine set up his successful studio near Place Bellecour, and his sons received a fine scientific education at the Martinière school.

Louis was the truly innovative one. At just 17, he invented a technique for instant photography, a major breakthrough. The family built a factory to manufacture these *Etiquette Bleue* films on an industrial scale. And at the start of the 20th century Louis devised autochrome plates for colour photography. In between times he came up with the invention for which he is internationally celebrated – the cinematograph. The patent was registered in February 1895 for this machine that captured moving images on the famed transparent strip with its perforated edges. It gave birth to perhaps the greatest artistic industry of the 20th century: cinema film. Lyon puts on great cinematic events throughout the year, including at the Villa Lumière, one of the sumptuous houses the family built on their fortune, now a museum. Annecy has become another important centre of cinema, with several festivals and a permanent exhibition on the attempts to capture moving images before cinema came into existence; its delightful displays allow you to experiment with the variety of machines dreamt up by pioneering inventors like Joseph Plateau, Emile Reynaud or Etienne Jules Marey. The Rhône-Alpes has also adopted a policy of encouraging and backing French films set in the region.

## *Clochemerle* – Poking Fun at the Beaujolais

The main joy of touring Beaujolais is exploring its sleepy wine villages, but one of France's comedy classics turns the petty dramas of a fictional one into a national crisis. In October 1922, Barthélemy Piéchut, Clochemerle's ambitious fox of a mayor, and its biggest vineyard-owner, decides to build a magnificent new edifice, a *Grand Projet* well before President Mitterrand's. Piéchut announces his plan to his right-hand man, the over-earnest teacher Ernest Tafardel, whose lecturing and bad breath the mayor exploits as powerful weapons against his village adversaries. His big idea? A splendid embodiment of the Republican ideals of liberty, equality and fraternity: a communal urinal. He provocatively places it next to the church, within view of the ultra-Catholic, bitter old spinster, the *aride* Justine Putet (roughly translated, Justine Tart), one of Gabriel Chevallier's most viciously drawn caricatures.

The battle isn't just over a urinal. The community is split between liberal Republican and conservative religious factions, and between those who can't resist the pleasures of the flesh and those who want to take their jealous revenge on the unbridled. Such is the brilliance of the comedy, you can't help taking pleasure in all the unhappy tales, in which wine and vineyard inheritance play a large part. Even the village priest Ponosse is profoundly affected by Beaujolais wine, his nose 'a hue somewhere between the violet worn by canons of the Church and a cardinal's purple'! To discover the farcical denouement, read this delicious satire yourselves.

# Food and Drink

04

# Regional Cuisine

Jesus is a sausage in food-obsessed Lyon – a sign of how important the culinary is in this region, and how it's treated with both seriousness and good humour. From the chicken-crazed Bresse in the north to the olive- and truffle-mad Drôme in the south; from the mountain chestnuts transformed into divine *marrons glacés* in the Ardèche out west, via the delectable ravioli, walnuts and St-Marcellin cheese of the middle Isère, over to the densely flavoured cheeses and hams of Savoie in the east – this region serves up some of the finest produce in France. It can also put on lots of frogs' legs, tripe and brains to upset the sensibilities of soft Anglo-Saxons. The region further spawned Brillat-Savarin, which may sound like a French dish that comes with a complicated sauce, but who turns out to have been a brilliant 19th-century *bon vivant* whose philosophizing book on the culinary, *La Physiologie du goût*, is still regarded as a classic. 'Tell me what you eat and I will tell you what you are' is one of his more famous quotes.

The Rhône-Alpes boasts the highest number of stellar chefs outside Paris. In fact, in 1938, Fernand Point of La Pyramide in Rhône-side Vienne became the first in France to achieve hallowed Michelin three-star status. Famous names like Georges Blanc, Paul Bocuse, Alain Chapel, the Troisgros, and Marc Veyrat have followed suit. In 2007, Sophie Pic of Valence's famed family restaurant became the only woman to hold Michelin three-star status in some time. Before these super-talented chefs, however, a formidable array of women restaurateurs in the region's capital, *les mères de Lyon*, made the reputation of that city's culinary establishments.

Traditional Lyon cuisine is copious but not overly sophisticated. Back with that Jésus, it's an exceptionally fat *saucisson* with whitened skin, supposedly looking like a baby wrapped in swaddling clothes! You'll find a huge array of this and other *saucissons* (notably Rosette and Cervelas), plus *quenelles* (*see* below), cheese, fruit, vegetables and wines in Lyon's renowned markets. Greater Lyon also boasts an amazing 2,000 restaurants!

In terms of **meats**, the Lyonnais are pork crazy, and will eat virtually any edible portion of an animal, sometimes under a heavily disguised name – tripe, for example, is served up as '*tablier du sapeur*' ('fireman's apron')! The love of *charcuterie* can be a little daunting, to be sampled in the typical little family-run *bouchon* restaurants. Even the traditional Lyonnais elevenses, *mâchons*, involves mountains of *charcuterie* washed down with a glass of red wine.

To satisfy demand, the provenance of the pigs is rather less certain than that of the pampered *poulets de Bresse*, the most highly regarded chickens in France (*see* p.97). Meadow-grazing lamb from the south can be another treat. In many areas, proud traditions of mountain *charcuterie* are continued – look out for free-range products such as *jambon à l'ancienne* ham, special *saucissons*, and sausages like *diots*, served in a wine sauce. *Caillettes* are minced meat balls from the Ardèche, mixed with spinach or chard. Plenty of game is caught in the region's woods, but quite a lot of fowl is now specially reared. *Pintadeaux de la Drôme*, guineafowl fed on mountain herbs, have their own *appellation d'origine contrôlée*. Pigeon can also be particularly delicious.

The region's large lakes produce decent amounts of **fish**, although many lake fish and even frogs' legs have to be imported these days. *Féra* (white fish also known as *lavaret* or *corégone*) is the fine-flavoured and exclusive emblematic fish of the big lakes, often served mashed in a *brandade*. *Omble chevalier* (char) has a reputation for its good taste. *Lotte* (monkfish) is quite rare, but *perche* common, while little *perchettes* are fried whole. The lakes yield good salmon and trout, the latter also found in mountain rivers. Down among the Dombes and Forez lakes where carp are reared, frogs' legs are a traditional fast-food speciality! The region's waters yield tasty crayfish too. *Quenelles*, a rather strange concoction – a white dumpling sausage made with cream, egg whites, flour and, most commonly, *brochet* (pike) – can be stodgy, but should ideally be as light as a soufflé. The town of Nantua is known for its *quenelles* in crayfish sauce.

Sticking to the savoury, the *tanche* **olives** of Nyons in the Drôme count among the finest in France, with their own *appellation d'origine contrôlée*. Their oil sells at golden prices. Just west, around Grignan and Richerenches, lie France's most prolific **truffle**-producing territories. The southern Ardèche also comes up with these delicacies. Turning to commoner tubers and **vegetables**, potatoes are prepared in various ways, fried in *matafans*, grated in *farçons* or *farcements*, or baked in chunky layers with cream and garlic in *gratin Dauphinois*, the region's *pommes de terre* dish par excellence. Polenta, a savoury maize cake, is popular both in Savoie and the Bresse. Splendid vegetables flourish in the valleys, providing all the ingredients for a superb ratatouille, with local herbs to add flavour. Autumn brings wild mushrooms out onto the menus.

The region produces sensational **cheeses**. Cows, sheep and goats are sent into the higher pastures with the *transhumance* at the beginning of the summer season. The dense Alpine meadows ring with *clarines*, the bells of the Abondance, Montbéliard and Tarine cows, in the warm season. Brillat-Savarin declared Beaufort (*see* p.333) prince of the *gruyères*, the hard mountain cheeses. Its rival, Comté, named after the Franche-Comté or Jura region north of Lac Léman, is produced on the region's frontier. Abondance is another superlative hard *fromage*. The smaller round Tommes come in a variety of styles, Tome des Bauges standing out for its quality, as well as having just one 'm'. Moving to softer varieties, quick-ripening Reblochon has a very long history (*see* p.322), and Vacherin makes a gooey treat. Most internationally famous of all in the Savoie cheese stakes are fondues and *raclettes*, absolutely delicious dishes of melted cheese, the mix of Emmental, Beaufort and Comté in fondues often flavoured with local wines, garlic and nutmeg, while simpler *raclette* comes with *charcuterie* and potatoes. Reblochon turns up baked with bacon, potatoes and cream in *tartiflette*, or fried with potatoes and onions in *péla*. In the south of the region, goats' cheese reigns, going from soft, gentle *chèvre frais* to more pungent, hard, aged circles. *Picodons* of the Drôme come from herds grazing in the herb-filled hills. *Ravioles de Royans*, the most delicate of all ravioli, filled with goat's cheese and herbs, cook in just a couple of minutes. The region's blue cheeses tend to be gentle and include Bleu de Bresse, Bleu de Gex, Bleu de Sassenage, and Fourme de Montbrison, plus rare Bleu de Termignon.

**Walnuts** thrive along the middle Isère in particular, long granted their own *appellation d'origine contrôlée*. **Chestnuts** (*see* p.161) were the paupers' staple in the

Ardèche in times past. Now they are king, transformed into *marrons glacés*, and other delicious, sticky preserves like *crème de marrons*. Ardèche chestnuts have recently been awarded their own *appellation d'origine contrôlée* too. Countless desserts in these parts incorporate them. The heavenly Mont Blanc pudding (a favourite of the decadent Borgias) consists of a large meringue filled with chestnut purée, topped by a mountain of whipped cream. Ice-cream variations carry the same name. Fantastic **fruit** proliferates around the Rhône valley, the quality of the peaches, nectarines, cherries and apricots superlative, with exceptional juice and flavour. Berries come to the fore in the summer Alps.

Regional **cake** specialities include *gâteau de Savoie*, a light sponge, and brioche or *pogne*, often with bright red lumps of praline (nuts caramelized in sugar). The Rhône-Alpes has fine *pâtissiers* galore, and some of the best French **chocolate**-makers, the most famous Bernachon in Lyon, Pralus around the Loire, Weiss, based in St-Etienne, and Valrhôna, the best known internationally, its name indicating that it is made in the Vallée du Rhône (*see* p.190). Incidentally, it was a *chocolatier* from Chambéry, Louis Dufour, who is credited with inventing the chocolate truffle, back in December 1895, when he realized he didn't have quite enough cocoa to satisfy all his customers, so he came up with a delicious new creation by adding whipped cream. But the region's most widely known confection is **nougat** from Montélimar (*see* pp.196–7).

## World-famous Wines, Liqueurs and Waters

> *Le vigneron monte à sa vigne, du bord de l'eau jusqu'au cielao.*
> *('The winemaker climbs to his vines from the water's edge to the sky.')*
> from a local *vignerons*' song along the Rhône valley.

Vines act like mountaineers in parts of the Rhône-Alpes, struggling up madly steep slopes, be it in the vineyards of the northern Côtes du Rhône, or the very unexpected *vignobles* of Savoie or the Bugey. In other parts, they spread out luxuriantly in the sun, most memorably in the Beaujolais in the north, or in the Côtes du Rhône and Coteaux du Tricastin down south. All the region's vineyards look gorgeous, and are wonderful to explore (*see* Itinerary, p.23).

In the northwest, the Beaujolais, Côtes Roannaises, Côtes du Forez and Coteaux du Lyonnais produce light-coloured, easy-drinking ruby wines from the single, gamay grape variety. The main grape variety for the deeper, fuller bodied reds in the northern Côtes du Rhône is syrah, that in the south grenache, with mourvèdre, cinsault or carignan added. For the whites, viognier is king in the northern Côtes du Rhône, roussanne and marsanne noble varieties, while in the south, grenache blanc, clairette and bourboulenc are the main players. More unusual, highly perfumed varieties dominate in higher climes, like altesse, clairette, jacquère, roussette and roussanne in the whites, and mondeuse in the reds. Rather good perfumed sparkling wines are made at St-Péray on the Rhône, around Die in the Drôme and in the Bugey .

In short, the Rhône-Alpes turns out to be a highly surprising and exhilarating region for wine-lovers, and because visiting vineyards is so closely tied with touring, we've included more detailed explanations on the region's main wines in the touring chapters. Special wine boxes cover Beaujolais, the northern Côtes du Rhône, Clairette de Die, the Coteaux du Tricastin and the more southerly Côtes du Rhônes. Further paragraphs mention the smaller *appellations d'origine contrôlée* dotted around the place.

Potent **liqueurs** made with a complex concoction of mountain herbs are a heady speciality of the region. Chartreuse is the most famous, a blend of over 100 herbs, coming in bright yellow or green varieties. Simpler but equally brash-looking Génépi, based on a special plant picked high in the Alps, is popular across Savoie. Among the orchards of the Rhône valley, you'll find excellent distillers of fruit, and nut, liqueurs. To cleanse the palate and clear the head, the region produces some of the most famous of bottled **waters**, Evian and Badoit (the latter from St-Galmier), leaders in still and sparkling respectively, although you'll find lots of other local brands around.

## French Menu Reader

### Hors d'œuvres et Soupes (Entremeses)

*assiette assortie* mixed cold hors-d'œuvre
*bisque* shellfish soup
*bouchées* mini vol-au-vents
*bouillon* broth
*charcuterie* mixed cold meats
*consommé* clear soup
*crudités* raw vegetable platter
*potage* thick vegetable soup
*tourrain* garlic and bread soup
*velouté* thick smooth soup, often fish or chicken

### Poissons et Coquillages (Crustacés) (Fish and Shellfish)

*aiglefin* little haddock
*alose* shad
*anguille* eel
*bar* sea bass
*barbue* brill
*baudroie* anglerfish
*belons* flat oysters
*bigorneau* winkle
*blanchailles* whitebait
*brème* bream
*brochet* pike
*bulot* whelk
*cabillaud* cod
*calmar* squid
*carrelet* plaice
*colin* hake
*coquillages* shellfish
*coquilles St-Jacques* scallops
*crevettes grises/roses* shrimp/prawns
*daurade* bream
*écrevisse* freshwater crayfish
*escargots* snails
*espadon* swordfish
*esturgeon* sturgeon
*flétan* halibut
*friture* deep-fried fish
*fruits de mer* seafood
*gambas* giant prawns
*gigot de mer* a large fish cooked whole
*grondin* red gurnard
*hareng* herring
*homard* lobster
*huîtres* oysters
*lamproie* lamprey
*langouste* spiny Mediterranean lobster
*langoustines* Norwegian lobsters (often called Dublin Bay prawns or scampi)
*limande* lemon sole
*lotte* monkfish
*loup (de mer)* sea bass
*maquereau* mackerel
*merlan* whiting
*morue* salt cod
*moules* mussels
*omble* chevalier
*oursin* sea urchin
*pagel* sea bream
*palourdes* clams
*poulpe* octopus
*raie* skate
*rascasse* scorpion fish
*rouget* red mullet
*saumon* salmon
*sole (meunière)* sole (with butter, lemon and parsley)
*St-Pierre* John Dory
*telline* tiny clam
*truite* trout
*truite saumonée* salmon trout
*thon* tuna

## Viandes et Volailles
## (Meat and Poultry)

*agneau* lamb
*aloyau* sirloin
*andouillette* chitterling (tripe) sausage
*biftek* beef steak
*blanc* breast or white meat
*blanquette* stew of white meat
*bœuf* beef
*boudin blanc* sausage of white meat
*boudin noir* black pudding
*brochette* on a skewer
*caille* quail
*canard, caneton* duck, duckling
*carré* the best end of a cutlet or chop
*cassoulet* bean and meat stew
*cervelle* brains
*chapon* capon
*châteaubriand* porterhouse steak
*cheval* horsemeat
*chevreau* kid
*civet* meat (usually game) stew, in wine and
  blood sauce
*confit* meat cooked in its own fat
*côte, côtelette* chop, cutlet
*crépinette* small sausage
*cuisse* thigh or leg
*dinde, dindon* turkey
*épaule* shoulder
*estouffade* marinated meat stew
*faux-filet* sirloin
*foie* liver
*frais de veau* veal testicles
*fricadelle* meatball
*gésier* gizzard
*gibier* game
*gigot* leg of lamb
*graisse* or *gras* fat
*grillade* grilled meat, often a mixed grill
*jarret* knuckle
*langue* tongue
*lapereau* young rabbit
*lapin* rabbit
*lard (lardons)* bacon (diced bacon)
*lièvre* hare
*magret de canard* breast of duck
*marcassin* young wild boar
*merguez* spicy red sausage
*moelle* bone marrow
*mouton* mutton
*navarin* lamb stew with root vegetables
*noix de veau* topside of veal
*oie* goose
*os* bone
*perdreau* (or *perdrix*) partridge
*petit salé* salt pork
*pieds* trotters
*pintade* guinea fowl

*pot au feu* meat and vegetable stew
*poulet* chicken
*poussin* baby chicken
*quenelles* poached meat or fish dumplings
*queue de bœuf* oxtail
*ris (de veau)* sweetbreads (veal)
*rognons* kidneys
*rosbif* roast beef
*rôti* roast
*sanglier* wild boar
*saucisson* dry sausage, like salami
*selle (d'agneau)* saddle (of lamb)
*steak tartare* raw minced beef with egg yolk
*suprême de volaille* fillet of chicken breast
*tête (de veau)* (calf's) head
*tournedos* thick round slice of beef fillet
*veau* veal
*venaison* venison

## Légumes, Herbes, etc.
## (Vegetables, Herbs, etc.)

*ail* garlic
*aïoli* garlic mayonnaise
*artichaut* artichoke
*asperges* asparagus
*aubergine* aubergine (US eggplant)
*avocat* avocado
*basilic* basil
*betterave* beetroot
*cannelle* cinnamon
*cèpes* ceps, wild boletus mushrooms
*champignons* mushrooms
*chanterelles* wild yellow mushrooms
*chicorée* curly endive
*chou* cabbage
*choucroute* sauerkraut
*chou-fleur* cauliflower
*ciboulette* chives
*citrouille* pumpkin
*clou de girofle* clove
*concombre* cucumber
*cornichons* gherkins
*cresson* watercress
*échalote* shallot
*endive* chicory (endive)
*épinards* spinach
*estragon* tarragon
*fenouil* fennel
*fèves* broad (fava) beans
*flageolets* white beans
*fleurs de courgette* courgette blossoms
*genièvre* juniper
*gingembre* ginger
*haricots (rouges, blancs)* beans (kidney, white)
*haricots verts* green (French) beans
*jardinière* with diced garden vegetables
*laurier* bay leaf
*lavande* lavender
*lentilles* lentils

maïs (épis de) sweetcorn (on the cob)
menthe mint
mesclun salad of various leaves
morilles morel mushrooms
moutarde mustard
navet turnip
oignon onion
oseille sorrel
panais parsnip
persil parsley
petits pois peas
piment pimento
pissenlits dandelion greens
poireau leek
pois chiches chickpeas
pois mange-tout sugar peas or mangetout
poivron sweet pepper (capsicum)
pomme de terre potato
potiron pumpkin
primeurs young vegetables
radis radishes
raifort horseradish
riz rice
romarin rosemary
roquette rocket
safran saffron
salade verte green salad
salsifis salsify
sarrasin buckwheat
sarriette savory
sauge sage
seigle rye
serpolet wild thyme
thym thyme
truffes truffles

### Fruits et Noix (Fruit and Nuts)
abricot apricot
amandes almonds
ananas pineapple
bigarreaux black cherries
brugnon nectarine
cacahouètes peanuts
cassis blackcurrant
cerise cherry
citron lemon
citron vert lime
coing quince
fraise (des bois) strawberry (wild)
framboise raspberry
grenade pomegranate
groseille redcurrant
mandarine tangerine
mangue mango
marron chestnut
mirabelles mirabelle plums
mûre (sauvage) mulberry, blackberry
myrtille bilberry
noisette hazelnut

noix walnut
noix de cajou cashew
noix de coco coconut
pamplemousse grapefruit
pastèque watermelon
pêche (blanche) peach (white)
pignons pine nuts
poire pear
pomme apple
prune plum
pruneau prune
raisins (secs) grapes (raisins)
reine-claude greengage plum

### Desserts
bavarois mousse or custard in a mould
bombe ice-cream dessert in a round mould
chausson turnover
clafoutis batter fruit pudding, often cherry
compote stewed fruit
corbeille de fruits basket of fruit
coulis thick fruit sauce
coupe ice-cream: a scoop or in cup
crème anglaise egg custard
gaufre waffle
génoise rich sponge cake
glace ice-cream
miel honey
œufs à la neige meringue on a bed of custard
pain d'épice gingerbread
sablé shortbread
savarin a filled cake, shaped like a ring

### Cooking Terms and Sauces
aigre-doux sweet and sour
aiguillette thin slice
à l'anglaise boiled
à la bordelaise cooked in wine and diced
  vegetables (usually)
à la diable in spicy mustard sauce
à la grecque cooked in olive oil and lemon
à la jardinière with garden vegetables
à la provençale tomatoes, garlic and olive oil
allumettes strips of puff pastry
à point medium (for steak)
au feu de bois cooked over a wood fire
au four baked
auvergnat with sausage, bacon and cabbage
barquette pastry boat
beignets fritters
béarnaise sauce of egg yolks, shallots and
  white wine
bien cuit well-done (for steak)
bleu very rare (for steak)
bordelaise red wine, bone marrow and
  shallot sauce
broche roasted on a spit
chaud hot
cru raw

*cuit* cooked
*émincé* thinly sliced
*en croûte* cooked in a pastry crust
*en papillote* baked in buttered paper
*épices* spices
*farci* stuffed
*feuilleté* flaky pastry
*flambé* set aflame with alcohol
*forestière* with bacon and mushrooms
*fourré* stuffed
*frit* fried
*froid* cold
*fumé* smoked
*galantine* cooked food served in cold jelly
*galette* flaky pastry case or pancake
*garni* with vegetables
*(au) gratin* topped with browned cheese and breadcrumbs
*haché* minced
*marmite* casserole
*médaillon* round piece
*mornay* cheese sauce
*pané* breaded
*pâte* pastry; pasta
*pâte brisée* shortcrust pastry
*pâte à chou* choux pastry
*pâte feuilletée* flaky or puff pastry
*paupiette* rolled and filled thin slices of fish or meat
*parmentier* with potatoes
*pavé* slab
*poché* poached
*pommes allumettes* thin chips (fries)
*raclette* melted cheese with potatoes, onions and pickles
*saignant* rare steak
*salé* salted
*sucré* sweet
*timbale* pie cooked in a dome-shaped mould
*tranche* slice
*véronique* green grape, wine and cream sauce

## Miscellaneous

*addition* bill (check)
*carte* menu
*couteau* knife

*cuillère* spoon
*formule à €12* €12 set menu
*fourchette* fork
*menu* set menu
*poivre* pepper
*sel* salt

## Snacks

*chips* crisps (chips)
*crêpe* thin pancake
*croque-madame* toasted ham and cheese sandwich with fried egg
*croque-monsieur* toasted ham and cheese sandwich
*croustade* small savoury pastry
*frites* chips (French fries)
*pissaladière* a kind of pizza with onions, anchovies, etc.
*sandwich canapé* open sandwich

## Boissons (Drinks)

*bière (pression)* beer (draught)
*(demie) bouteille* bottle (half)
*brut* dry
*citron pressé/orange pressée* fresh lemon or orange juice, often served with sugar and a jug of water
*doux* sweet (wine)
*eau-de-vie* brandy
*eau potable* drinking water
*glaçons* ice cubes
*infusion* or *tisane (camomille, verveine, tilleul, menthe)* herbal tea (camomile, verbena, lime (linden) flower, mint)
*lait* milk
*menthe à l'eau* peppermint cordial in water
*moelleux* semi-dry
*mousseux* sparkling (wine)
*pichet* pitcher
*pression* draught
*sec* dry
*sirop d'orange/de citron* orange/lemon squash
*verre* glass
*vin blanc/rosé/rouge* white/rosé/red wine

# Planning
# Your Trip

05

## Average Temperatures in °C (°F)

|  | Jan | Feb | Mar | April | May | June | July | Aug | Sept | Oct | Nov | Dec |
|---|---|---|---|---|---|---|---|---|---|---|---|---|
| **Grenoble** | 3 (37) | 3 (37) | 8 (45) | 14 (56) | 16 (61) | 22 (71) | 27 (81) | 26 (79) | 22 (71) | 16 (61) | 11 (51) | 6 (42) |
| **Lyon** | 7 (44) | 6 (42) | 11 (51) | 16 (61) | 17 (63) | 25 (77) | 27 (81) | 27 (81) | 24 (75) | 17 (63) | 10 (50) | 8 (45) |

## When to Go

### Climate

The Rhône-Alpes has the biggest variation in altitude of any region in Europe, going roughly from sea level to 4,808m on Mont Blanc. The climate therefore varies a good deal. The lower parts of the region spreading out from the Rhône generally have easy climates, reflected in their exceptional agricultural fertility (although snow can fall on their heights as late as April). Spring brings out spectacular orchard blossoms. Summers are lovely, sunny and very warm across the region, but the heights offer much-appreciated cooler air. The southern Ardèche and Drôme benefit from clement climates similar to Languedoc and Provence. September is normally the month for the grape harvest.

Autumns are warm and enchanting, with vines and trees changing colour.

In the Alps the ski season lasts, for the highest resorts, from December to April. The smaller pre-alpine resorts and little ones west of the Rhône have much shorter, more weather-dependent seasons. In the high mountains, May and Oct–Nov are quiet, tourist possibilities more limited. The high Alpine summer season essentially runs mid-June to mid-Sept, June being best for stunning flower-filled meadows.

For weather information, see tourist office websites, or the general *www.meteo.fr*.

### Festivals and Events

The box below covers major events. For the plethora of smaller festivals across the region, see local tourist office websites.

### Calendar of Events

**January**

**Valloire**: Ice-sculpting contest, **t** 04 79 59 03 96, *info@valloire.net* (15–18).

**Richerenches**: *La Messe de la Truffe*, to celebrate France's largest truffle market (18).

**February**

**Evian**: Eurocarnaval, *www.eviantourism.com*.

**Nyons**: *Fête de l'Alicolique*, celebrates the olive oil harvest, **t** 04 75 26 10 35.

**March**

**Grenoble**: Grenoble Jazz Festival, over 15 days, *www.jazzgrenoble.com*.

**Vallon-Pont-d'Arc**: *Raid Nature*, running, canoeing, biking and hiking race (Easter).

**April**

**Ardèche and Drôme**: *De Ferme en Ferme*, culinary festival (last weekend of month).

**Chambéry**: *Grande Braderie*, big flea market on the last Sunday, **t** 04 79 33 42 47.

**May**

**Evian**: Musical Stopovers, music festival (6–9), **t** 04 50 26 85 00, *www.royalparcevian.com*.

**St-Etienne**: Festival of Words and Music (over 2nd fortnight), **t** 04 77 25 01 13.

**June**

**Annonay**: Hot-air balloon festival, **t** 04 75 33 24 51.

**Ardèche**: Ardéchoise cycling race, *www.ardechoise.com*.

**Chambéry**: *Estivales du Château*. Start of programme of major, free outdoor concerts in the castle courtyard, lasting through to Aug.

**Drôme**: Transhumance: sheep are taken up to pasture (3rd week), *www.drometourisme.com*.

**Lyon**: *Festival Les Nuits de Fourvière*, Roman open-air theatre (mid-June–mid-Sept), **t** 04 72 32 00 00, *www.nuits-de-fourviere.org*.

**Portes du Soleil**: Mountain-biking festival for all (end June–beginning July).

**Valence**: *Fête des Canaux*.

**July**

The **Tour de France** always passes through the region in July; see *www.letour.fr*.

**Ain**: *Fête des Fours à Pain*.

**Aix-les-Bains**: *Aquascenies*, 3-day lake festival.

**Chambéry**: International Folklore Festival.

**Château de Grignan**: *Fêtes Nocturnes*, theatre.

**Grenoble**: *Cabaret Frappé*, several weeks of outdoor free and paying concerts and events.

**Loire**: Musical Summer, *www.loire.fr.*
**Montélimar**: *Couleur Lavande* (lavender festival), *www.montelimar-tourisme.*
**Saou**: Mozart Festival, t 04 75 76 02 02.
**St-Donat-sur-l'Herbasse**: Bach Organ Festival.
**Vienne**: *Festival de Jazz*, *www.jazzavienne.com.* One of France's most fabulous international jazz festivals, the main venue being the Rhône-side Roman theatre.

## August

**Aix-les-Bains**: *Navig'Aix*, gathering of boats and dinghies, *www.aixlesbains.com.*
**Annecy**: Lake Festival, *www.lac-annecy.com.*
**Chamonix**: Mountain Guides' Festival, wild celebrations on their days off (14–15 Aug).
**Talloires**: *Les Pyroconcerts de Talloires*, dramatic free lakeside concerts (end Aug), *www.talloires-lac-annecy.com.*

## September

The *Journées du Patrimoine* (mid-month) is open house for hundreds of historic venues.
*La Coupe Icare*, a major paragliding competition, is often held at **St-Hilaire-du-Touvet**, *www.coupe-icare.org.*
**Ambronay**: Classical music festival, *www.fest-ambronay.com.*

**Lyon**: *Biennale d'Art Contemporain*, art festival (odd years); *Biennale de la Danse*, dance festival (even years), *www.biennale-of-lyon.org.*

## October

**Annecy**: *Retour des Alpages* (2nd Sat).
**Ardèche chestnut towns**: *Les Castagnades,* celebrations on a favourite culinary theme.

## November

**Beaujeu**: Beaujolais Nouveau launch, a great wine festival (3rd Thurs), t 04 74 07 27 50.
**Grenoble**: Music Festival (38ème Rugissants) (end of Nov).
**St-Etienne**: *Massenet Biennale*, celebrates the 19th-century composer (odd years); Biennale Design Festival (even years), t 04 77 47 88 05, *www.institutdesign.com.*

## December

Christmas markets are held in many of the Rhône-Alpes' main towns and villages.
**Lyon**: Festival of Lights: with exceptional illuminations around town (5–8).
**Val Thorens** and **L'Alpe d'Huez**: Andros Trophy: car competitions on ice.
**Bourg, Montrevel** and **Pont-de-Vaux**: *Les Glorieuses de Bresse,* fiercely fought-over and celebrated chicken competitions, *www.glorieusesdebresse.com.*

# Tourist Information

France has some of the world's best tourist information services. For information on the whole region, contact the very well organized **Comité Régional du Tourisme (CRT) Rhône-Alpes**, 104 Route de Paris, 69260 Charbonnières-les-Bains, t 04 72 59 21 59, *www.rhonealpes-tourisme.com.*

Most of the Rhône-Alpes' eight *départements* (or counties) have their own **Comité Départemental du Tourisme** or **CDT**, offering masses of more specific information on their area. Many have translated their websites into English. Savoie and Haute Savoie have recently joined forces as Savoie Mont Blanc. For the most detailed, local tourist information, contact the town or area *offices de tourisme* listed in the touring chapters.

## *Département* Tourist Boards

**CDT Ain**, 34 Rue Général Delestraint, B.P.78, 01002 Bourg-en-Bresse, t 04 74 32 31 30, *www.ain-tourisme.com.*

**CDT Ardèche**, 4 Cours du Palais, 07000 Privas Cedex, t 04 75 64 04 66, *www.ardeche-guide.com.*

**CDT Drôme**, 8 Rue Baudin, B.P. 531, 26005 Valence Cedex, t 04 75 82 19 26, *www.ladrometourisme.com.*

**CDT Isère**, 14 Rue de la République, B.P.227, 38019 Grenoble, t 04 76 54 34 36, *www.isere-tourisme.com.*

**CDT Loire**, 5 Place Jean Jaurès, 42021 St-Etienne Cedex 01, t 04 77 43 24 42, *www.loire.fr.*

**CDT Rhône**, 35 Rue St-Jean, 69005 Lyon, t 04 72 56 70 40, *www.rhonetourisme.com.*

**Savoie Mont Blanc**, 24 Bd de la Colonne, 73025 Chambéry Cedex, t 04 79 85 12 45, *www.savoie-mont-blanc.com.*

## French Tourist Offices Abroad

The main website is *www.franceguide.com.*
**UK**: 178 Piccadilly, London W1J 9AL, t 09068 244 123.

**Ireland**: 10 Suffolk St, Dublin 1, t (01) 635 1008.

**USA**: 16th Floor, 444 Madison Av, NY 10022, t (212) 838 7800; 676 N. Michigan Av, Chicago, IL 60611, t (312) 751 7800; 9454 Wilshire Bd, Beverly Hills, CA 90212, t (310) 271 6695.

**Canada**: 1981 Avenue McGill College, Suite 490, Montréal, Québec, t (514) 288 4264.

**Australia**: Level 20, 25 Bligh Street, Sydney, NSW 2000, t (02) 9231 5244.

## Embassies and Consulates

### Foreign Embassies, etc. in France

**UK**: 24 Rue Childebert, Lyon, t 04 72 77 81 70, www.amb-grandebretagne.fr.

**Ireland**: 4 Rue Rude, 75016 Paris, t 01 44 17 67 00, www.irlgov.ie/irishembassy/France.htm.

**USA**: 16 Rue de la République, 69002 Lyon, t 04 78 38 33 03, www.amb-usa.fr.

**Canada**: 21 Rue Bourgelat, 69002 Lyon, t 04 72 77 64 07, www.amb-canada.fr.

### French Embassies, etc. Abroad

**UK**: 58 Knightsbridge, London SW1X 7JT, t (020) 7073 1000, www.ambafrance-uk.org; 21 Cromwell Rd, London SW7 2EN, t (020) 7073 1200, www.consulfrance-londres.org (for visas); 11 Randolph Crescent, Edinburgh EH3 7TT, t (0131) 225 7954, www.consulfrance-edimbourg.org.

**Ireland**: 36 Ailesbury Rd, Ballsbridge, Dublin 4, t (01) 277 5000, www.ambafrance.ie.

**USA**: 4101 Reservoir Rd NW, Washington, DC 20007-2185, t (202) 944 6195, www.ambafrance-us.org; 205 North Michigan Avenue, Suite 3700, Chicago, IL 60601, t (312) 327 5200, www.consulfrance-chicago.org; 10990 Wilshire Bd, Suite 300, Los Angeles, CA 90024, t (310) 235 3200, www.consulfrance-losangeles.org; 934 Fifth Av, New York, NY 10021, t (212) 606 3600, www.consulfrance-newyork.org. There are also French consulates in Atlanta, Boston, Houston, Miami, New Orleans and San Francisco.

## Entry Formalities

### Passports and Visas

Holders of **EU, US, Canadian, Australian, New Zealand and Israeli** passports do not need a visa to enter France for stays of up to three months; most other nationals do. Apply at your nearest French consulate or embassy. The most convenient visa is the *visa de circulation*, allowing for multiple stays of three months over a three-year period. If you intend to stay for longer, the law says that non-EU citizens need a *carte de séjour*.

Non-EU citizens had best apply for an extended visa prior to leaving home – a complicated procedure requiring proof of income, etc. You can't get a *carte de séjour* without the visa.

### Customs

**EU citizens** over the age of 17 do not have to declare goods imported into France for personal use if they have paid duty on them in the country of origin. In theory, you can buy as much as you like to take home, provided you can prove the purchase is for your own use. In practice, Customs will be more likely to ask questions if you buy in bulk, e.g. more than 3,200 cigarettes or 400 cigarillos, 200 cigars or 3kg of tobacco; plus 10 litres of spirits, 90 litres of wine and 110 litres of beer. Travellers caught importing any of the above for resale will have the goods seized along with the vehicle they travelled in, and could face imprisonment for up to seven years.

Travellers from **outside the EU** must pay duty on goods worth more than €175 that they import into France.

Travellers from the USA are allowed to take home, duty-free, goods to the value of $400, including 200 cigarettes or 100 cigars; plus one litre of alcohol. You're not allowed to bring back absinthe or Cuban cigars. Canadians can bring home $300 worth of goods in a year, plus their tobacco and alcohol allowances.

**French Customs**, www.douane.gouv.fr.

**UK Customs**, t 0845 010 9000, www.hmce.gov.uk.

**US Customs**, t (202) 354 1000, www.customs.gov. Seek advice.

## Disabled Travellers

When it comes to providing access for all, France isn't exactly in the vanguard, but things are beginning to change, especially in newer buildings, and national organizations are becoming more helpful too. All TGVs are equipped for wheelchair passengers – contact Rail Europe in the UK or USA (see p.58) or the SNCF in France (see p.59) for details; alternatively you can ask for an assistant to accompany you on your journey (although you will have to pay).

The Channel Tunnel is a good way to travel by car; on Eurotunnel trains passengers stay in their vehicles, while Eurostar has a special area reserved for wheelchair users and their assistants (who can travel at reduced rates, t 08705 186 186 for more information).

## Disability Organizations

### In France
**Association des Paralysés de France**, 22 Rue du Père-Guérin, 75013 Paris, t 01 44 16 83 83, www.apf.asso.fr. Offices in all départements.
**Comité National Français de Liaison pour la Réadaptation des Handicapés**, 236 bis Rue Tolbiac, 75013 Paris, t 01 53 80 66 63. Access information and guides to French regions.

### In the UK
**Can Be Done**, t (020) 8907 2400, www.canbedone.co.uk. Specialist holidays.
**Holiday Care Service**, The Hawkins Suite, Enham Place, Enham, Alamein, Andover SP11 6JS, t 0845 124 9974, www.holidaycare.org.uk. Publishes an information sheet on holidays for disabled and older people (£5).
**RADAR** (Royal Association for Disability and Rehabilitation), 12 City Forum, 250 City Rd, London EC1V 8AF, t (020) 7250 3222, www.radar.org.uk.

### In the USA
**Alternative Leisure Co.**, 165 Middlesex Turnpike, Suite 206, Bedford, MA 01730, t (718) 275 0023, www.alctrips.com.
**Mobility International USA**, 132 E Broadway, Suite 343, Eugene, Oregon, 97401, t/TTY (541) 343 1284, www.miusa.org.
**SATH** (Society for Accessible Travel and Hospitality), 347 5th Ave, Suite 610, New York, NY 10016, t (212) 447 7284, www.sath.org.

### Other Useful Contacts
**Access Ability**, www.access-ability.co.uk.
**Access-Able Travel Source**, www.access-able.com. A database of information.
**Emerging Horizons**, www.emerginghorizons.com. An international subscription-based on-line (or mailed) quarterly travel newsletter.

Ferry companies offer special assistance if contacted beforehand. Vehicles modified for disabled people are charged reduced tolls on *autoroutes*. For more information contact the **Ministère des Transports**, 246 Boulevard St Germain, 75007 Paris, t 01 40 81 21 22, www.transports.equipement.gouv.fr.

*Gîtes accessibles aux personnes handi-capées*, published by **Gîtes de France**, lists self-catering (see www.gites-de-france.fr). Hotels with facilities for the disabled are listed in Michelin's *Red Guide to France*.

The Rhône-Alpes has been gathering together useful information on disabled access across the region; you may find details on the website, or ask for the brochure 'Tourisme et Handicap', listing places and sights with special disabled facilities. On www.rhonealpes-tourisme.com there are useful sections on accessible skiing and other sports and activities.

## Insurance and EHIC Cards

Citizens of the EU who bring along their **European Health Insurance Card** (EHIC – apply online at www.ehic.org.uk, or pick up a form from a post office) are entitled to the same health services as French citizens. This means paying up front for medical care and prescriptions, then up to 75–80 per cent of the costs are reimbursed later. As an alternative, consider a **travel insurance** policy, covering theft and losses and offering 100 per cent medical refund; check to see if it covers extra expenses if you get bogged down in airport or train strikes. Beware that accidents resulting from sports are rarely covered by ordinary insurance. Canadians are usually covered in France by their provincial health coverage; Americans and others should check their individual policies.

## Money and Banks

**Euros** come in denominations of €500, 200, 100, 50, 20, 10 and 5 (banknotes) and €2, €1, 50 cents, 20 cents, 10 cents, 5 cents, 2 cents and 1 cent (coins). For the latest **exchange rates**, see www.xe.com/ucc.

French **banks** are generally open Mon–Fri 8.30am–12.30pm (or 9–12 noon) and 1.30–4pm. Some branches open on Saturdays, in which case they will close Monday. All banks close on public holidays. Banks displaying the 'Change' sign will exchange foreign currency, generally at better rates than *bureaux de change* (and far better than at railway stations and in hotels), but the cheapest places to exchange cash are the main post offices. Travellers' cheques are the safest way of carrying money, but there can be problems getting them exchanged. Very rarely will you be able to use travellers' cheques directly in payments, as you would in the USA.

The widespread presence of **ATM cash-points** often makes using them with a **credit or debit card** the most convenient – and sometimes most economical – way of getting money. The fees can still work out better than bank commission rates. Major **credit cards** such as Visa and MasterCard are very widely accepted in France, but American Express and Diners Club less so. In smaller hotels and restaurants, especially in rural areas, and *chambres d'hôtes* (B&Bs), owners may not accept cards, so do not rely entirely on them.

All French plastic now works on the **chip-and-pin** system. Some self-service petrol stations and bridge toll booths may reject foreign cards.

# Getting There

## By Air

The region's major international airports are at Lyon and Geneva (just across the border in Switzerland). Chambéry/Aix-les-Bains and Grenoble also have direct flights from the UK, while Nîmes and Avignon airports lie not far south. The airlines offering flights to these places are detailed in the box below, although not all of these services operate year-round, so check. Also compare prices; don't assume the no-frills operators will always be cheapest. Bargain tickets are also available from student travel and flight-only agencies. For the best offers, check the Sunday newspapers as well as websites.

**Lyon St-Exupéry International Airport**, t 04 72 22 72 21, *www.lyonairport.com*.

**Geneva Cointrin International Airport**, t (41) 22 717 71 11, *www.gva.ch*.

There are frequent flights from many parts of North America to Paris, from where you can travel on to Rhône-Alpes by train (*see* p.57 and p.59). It can sometimes be cheaper to fly to London and get a direct flight on from there, so compare prices.

## Airline Carriers

### UK and Ireland

Routes change frequently. The Rhône-Alpes regional tourist board keeps up-to-date lists.

**Aer Lingus, t** IR 0818 365 000, *www.aerlingus. com*. Dublin to Lyon and Geneva.

**Air France, t** 08701 42 43 43, *www.airfrance. com*. London Heathrow to Lyon.

**bmiBaby**, *www.bmibaby.com*. To Geneva from Birmingham, Cardiff, Manchester, Nottingham.

**British Airways, t** 0870 850 9850, *www.ba.com*. To Lyon from Heathrow, Birmingham and Manchester; to Geneva from London City, Gatwick, Heathrow and Manchester.

**easyJet, t** 0905 821 0905, *www.easyjet.com*. To Lyon from Stansted; to Grenoble from Gatwick, Luton and Bristol; to Geneva from Gatwick, Luton, Stansted, Belfast, Bournemouth, Bristol, East Midlands, Edinburgh, Glasgow, Liverpool and Newcastle.

**Flybe, t** 0871 700 0535, *www.flybe.com*. Exeter, Birmingham and Norwich to Chambéry/Aix-les-Bains and Geneva, plus Exeter to Avignon.

**Flyglobespan, t** 08705 561522, *www.flyglobe span.com*. Edinburgh to Chambéry/Aix-les-Bains and Geneva.

**Jet2, t** 0871 226 1737, *www.jet2.com*. Leeds-Bradford or Manchester to Chambéry/Aix-les-Bains and Geneva, and from Newcastle to Chambéry.

**Ryanair, t** UK 0871 246 0000, t IR 0818 30 30 30, *www.ryanair.com*. Grenoble from Stansted, Dublin, Glasgow, Liverpool and Nottingham. Look also at flights to Nîmes.

**Swiss International Airlines, t** 0845 601 0956, *www.swiss.com/uk*. Geneva from Heathrow and London City airport.

**ThomsonFly**, *www.thomsonfly.com*. Grenoble from Bournemouth, Coventry and Nottingham.

### USA and Canada

For services to Paris and London, except for Air Transat.

**Air Canada**, Canada/USA t 888 247 2262, *www.aircanada.com*.

**Air France**, USA t 1-800 237 2747, Canada t 1-800 667 2747, *www.airfrance.com*.

Air Transat, *www.airtransat.com*. Direct flights to Lyon from Montréal or Toronto, May–Oct.

American Airlines, t 1-800 433 7300, *www.aa.com*.

British Airways, t 800 247 9297, *www.ba.com*.

Continental, t USA 1-800 231 0856; t Canada 1 800 525 0280 *www.continental.com*.

Delta, USA/Canada t 800 221 1212, *www.delta.com*.

Northwest Airlines, t 1-800 225 2525, *www.nwa.com*.

United Airlines, t 1-800 538 2929, t 1-800 674 46 80 (toll free), *www.united.com*.

## Students, Discounts and Special Deals

### UK and Ireland

Students with ID cards can get reductions on flights, trains and admissions.

Budget Travel, 134 Lower Baggot St, Dublin 2, t (01) 631 1100, *www.budgettravel.ie*.

Club Travel, 30 Lower Abbey St, Dublin 1, t (01) 435 0016 within Eire, *www.clubtravel.ie*.

Europe Student Travel, 6 Campden St, London W8, t (020) 7727 7647. A small travel agent catering to non-students too.

STA Travel, 117 Euston Rd, London NW1 2SX, t 0870 166 2603, *www.statravel.co.uk*. Many other branches in the UK.

Trailfinders, 194 Kensington High St, London W8, t 0845 050 5940/t (020) 7937 1234, *www.trailfinders.com*.

United Travel, 2 Old Dublin Rd, Stillorgan, Co. Dublin, t (01) 215 9300, *www.unitedtravel.ie*.

USIT Now, 19–21 Aston Quay, Dublin 2, t (01) 602 1904, and other branches in Ireland, *www.usitnow.ie*.

*www.cheapflights.co.uk*
*www.ebookers.co.uk*
*www.expedia.co.uk*
*www.flightcentre.com*
*www.icelolly.com*
*www.lastminute.com*
*www.opodo.co.uk*
*www.traveljungle.co.uk*
*www.travelocity.com*

### USA and Canada

Try the small ads in newspaper travel pages. Numerous travel clubs and agencies also specialize in discount fares, but they may require you to pay an annual membership fee.

Airhitch, 481 Eighth Avenue Suite 1771, New York, NY 10001-1820, t (212) 247 4482, 1-877-AIRHITCH, *www.airhitch.org*.

STA Travel, 205E 42nd Street, New York, NY 10017, t (212) 627 3111/822 2700, or t 800 781 4040, *www.statravel.com*.

Travel Cuts, 187 College St, Toronto, Ontario M5T 1P7, t (416) 979 2406, *www.travelcuts.com*. Canada's largest student specialists. In the USA, t 1-800 592 2887, *www.travelcuts.com/us*

*www.traveldiscounts.com*, USA t (408) 813 1111. Members get special rates.

*www.eurovacations.com*
*www.expedia.com*
*www.orbitz.com*
*www.smartertravel.com*
*www.traveldiscounts.com*

## By Train

The **Eurostar** from London or Ashford to France, followed by the TGV, is a very civilized way to travel to the Rhône-Alpes. For the cheapest fares, book at least 21 days in advance or include a Saturday night in your stay. Promotional fares are often available at off-peak times. Take the Eurostar from London to Lille or Paris Gare du Nord. In Lille you simply need to change platform for rapid services to the Rhône-Alpes TGV stations; in Paris, you need to cross from Gare du Nord to Gare de Lyon for the TGV – allow one hour for this.

In summer, Eurostar runs a once-weekly direct service to Avignon, just south of the Rhône-Alpes. The winter snow train runs Fri eves Jan–April from London or Ashford to Chambéry, Albertville, Moûtiers, Aime-la-Plagne and Bourg-St-Maurice, with buses to La Plagne, Courchevel, Les Arcs, Méribel and Tignes.

If you plan to take some long train trips, it may be worth investing in a **rail pass** (*see www.raileurope.co.uk/railpasses*), although France has now pulled out of the Euro Domino scheme. Other alternatives for **European residents** of at least 6 months include the **Inter-Rail** pass, offering 16 days' unlimited travel through France, Belgium, the Netherlands and Luxembourg (Zone E) from around £160 (under-26s) or £225 (26 or over). They include 50% discounted fares on some cross-Channel ferries plus reduced fares on Eurostars. Cards are not valid on UK trains.

Passes for **North Americans** include the **France Railpass**, giving 4 days' unlimited travel throughout the country in any one month for around $240–280 including special rates on Eurostar and an option to purchase 6 extra days. The equivalent **France Youthpass** for under-26s costs around $175–200. There's also the 6-day **Rail 'n' Drive** pass, giving 2 days' unlimited 1st-class rail travel through France and 2 days' car rental from $265. Also for non-Europeans, the **Eurail Pass** allows unlimited 1st-class travel through 17 European countries for 15, 21, 30, 60 or 90 days; it saves the hassle of buying numerous tickets but will only pay for itself if you use it a lot; a 15-day Eurail Pass costs around $620, a 21-day pass $795, 30 days $995, 2 months $1,400, 3 months $1,750. A 15-day **Eurail Pass Youth** for under-26s costs around $400 but is for 2nd-class travel only. The **Eurail Pass Flexi** allows first-class travel for any 10 days or 15 days in a 2-month period for around $725 or $950 respectively. All include discounted fares on Eurostar.

There are other combinations of passes available, such as for couples travelling together. See the Rail Europe website for full details and up-to-date prices. **Rail Europe** handles bookings for all services, including Eurostar and Motorail, sells rail passes and acts for other continental rail companies. The German railways website *www.deutsche-bahn.co.uk* has a useful English-language journey planner and ticket-booking service for all of Europe. You can book tickets online on the French railways website *www.sncf.com*, available in French and English, and have them sent to addresses outside France.

**Rail Europe (UK)**, 178 Piccadilly, London W1, **t** 08708 371 371, *www.raileurope.co.uk*.

**Rail Europe (USA and Canada), t** 877 257 2887 (US), or **t** 800 361 RAIL (Canada), *www.raileurope.com*.

**Eurostar, t** 08705 186 186, *www.eurostar.com*. *www.seat61.com*. Independent website.

## By Coach

**Eurolines** operates regular cheap coach services from London to Paris, Lyon, Chambéry, Grenoble and Chamonix. Book 30 days in advance for cheaper return tickets to Paris. The journey to Paris takes 8hrs; Lyon 14hrs 15mins; Chambéry 14hrs 30mins; Grenoble 15hrs 45mins; Chamonix 19hrs.

There are discounts for pensioners, under-26s, and under-12s.

**National Express Eurolines, t** 08705 808080, *www.nationalexpress.com/eurolines*.

## By Car

Crossing to France by ferry – or by the competing car-carrying Channel Tunnel – has many advantages for anyone travelling from Britain, especially with children: you can take your own car, and as much baggage as you can fit in your vehicle; children aged 4–15 often get reduced rates, and under-4s go free.

To get to the Rhône-Alpes you then have a fairly long drive; as a guide, the distance from Calais to Lyon is 750km (466 miles), a journey taking around 6½hrs. For information on driving in France, *see* p.59.

## By Car and Train

Putting a car on a **Eurotunnel** train through the Channel Tunnel is the fastest way to France from Britain, taking only 35mins, with up to 4 departures an hour, and avoiding weather problems. Fares start from around £125 for a standard return in low season, rising substantially in summer and high seasons. The price for all tickets is per car.

**Eurotunnel, t** 08705 35 35 35, *www.eurotunnel.com*.

## By Car and Sea

The downside of ferry travel can be the cost – fares are often expensive in peak season.

## Ferry Operators

See also *www.ferrybooker.com* for both ferry and Eurotunnel bookings.

**Brittany Ferries, t** 08709 076103, *www.brittanyferries.com*.

**Condor Ferries, t** 0870 243 5140, *www.condorferries.co.uk*.

**Irish Ferries, t** 08705 17 17 17, *www.irishferries.com*.

**Norfolkline, t** 08708 70 10 20, *www.norfolkline.com*.

**P&O Ferries, t** 08705 980 333, *www.poferries.com*.

**SeaFrance, t** 0870 443 1653, *www.seafrance.com*.

**Speed Ferries, t** 0870 22 00 570, *www.speedferries.com*.

**Transmanche, t** 0870 420 1267, *www.transmanche.ferries.org, www.transmanche.tbreaks.com*.

The competition with Eurotunnel is fierce, though, with many deals to be had. All the companies prefer you to book online, and give discounts if you do – but phone first to ask for details of the cheapest fares available.

# Getting Around

## By Air

Regular Air France services fly from Paris to Lyon, Grenoble and Geneva. For reservations from within France, t 0820 820 820.

## By Train

**SNCF nationwide information number, t 08 92 35 35 35** (€0.50/min), *www.sncf.com*.

Travelling by rail in France is a joy: French Railways (**SNCF**) trains are sensibly priced, clean...and they move. The sleek **TGVs** (*trains à grande vitesse*) allow you to nip from Paris to Lyon in a mere 2hrs. **Inter-City** trains are also efficient; Geneva–Lyon takes 1hr 50mins. Off the main lines, there's also a decent network of local trains, though in some areas **SNCF buses** have replaced train routes. Train and bus services are linked.

**Fares** are reasonable, with discounts sometimes available. If you plan on making only a few long hauls, an **Inter-Rail pass** or **France Railpass** (*see* p.57) bought before you leave home will save you money. Other possible discounts, aimed mainly at French residents but which may just fit your circumstances, can be obtained once in France and hinge on the exact time of your departure: for non-TGV trains, SNCF fares vary according to whether you travel in **blue** off-peak periods (*période bleue*) or **white** (*blanche, or période de pointe*) periods (usually Friday and Sunday evenings and national holidays). *Découverte* discounts are free but only available on tickets booked in advance, and annual *cartes* must be paid for. Check them out on *www.voyages-sncf.com*. NB: Before boarding a train, you must stamp (*composter*) your **ticket** in the orange machines by the platform entrances. This date-stamps your ticket.

## By Bus

The Rhône-Alpes has a good network of bus services. Find detailed, up-to-date timetables on the various *département* websites; the web addresses are given near the start of each touring chapter. In towns, '*gare routière*' indicates the bus station.

## By Car

Drivers must carry their **driving licence**, **vehicle registration** and up-to-date **insurance** papers in the car with them. Those with a driving licence from any EU country, the USA, Canada or Australia don't need an international licence. If taking a car to France, make sure you're properly insured. It's also advisable to have **breakdown assistance**.

Cars from the UK or Ireland require **headlamp adjusters**. French law also requires you to carry spare **bulbs** for the car's main lights, and a **warning triangle**, to be placed 50m behind the car if you break down.

**Speed limits** are 130kph/80mph on *autoroutes* (toll motorways); 110kph/69mph on main highways; 90kph/55mph on other roads; and 50kph/30mph in urban areas. **Fines** for speeding, payable on the spot, are high (from €200), and can be astronomical (up to €4,500) if you fail a breathalyser test. Avoid drinking alcohol when driving.

If you wind up in an **accident**, the procedure is to fill out and sign a *constat amiable*. If your French isn't sufficient to deal with this, hold off until you find someone to translate for you. If you have a **breakdown**, it is best to telephone the police (**t** 17).

A few important points to note when driving in France. First, watch out for *priorité à droite* in towns and villages, an archaic system whereby traffic coming from streets to your right, unless halted by a stop sign and/or a thick white line, has right of way. However, this doesn't apply at roundabouts, where you give way to cars already on it. Secondly, French drivers rarely respect pedestrian crossings.

**Petrol** stations can be scarce in rural areas; many keep shop hours, and are shut at night, on Sunday afternoons, on Mondays, or for lunch. Unleaded fuel is *sans plomb*, and diesel may be called *gazole* or *gasoil*. The cheapest places to buy fuel are generally supermarket stations; the most expensive are on motorways. Many stations are self-service out of hours, but don't always accept foreign credit

## Car Hire

### UK

**Avis, t** 0870 606 0100, *www.avis.co.uk.*
**Budget, t** 0844 581 2231, *www.budget.co.uk.*
**Europcar, t** 0845 722 2525, *www.europcar.co.uk.*
**Hertz, t** 08708 44 88 44, *www.hertz.co.uk.*
**Thrifty, t** (01494) 751 600, *www.thrifty.co.uk.*
**National Citer,** *www.citer.com.*
**Sixt,** *www.sixt.com.*

### USA and Canada

**Auto Europe, t** 1 888 223 5555,
*www.autoeurope.com.*
**Avis, t** 800 331 1212, **t** 800 331 2323 (hearing-impaired), *www.avis.com.*
**Europcar, t** 877 940 6900, *www.europcar.com.*
**Europe by Car, t** 800 223 1516,
*www.europebycar.com.*
**Hertz, t** 800 654 3131 (USA), **t** 800 654 3001 (international toll free), *www.hertz.com.*

cards. Motorway toll stations are generally staffed, and you can pay by cash or card.

**Route planners:** *www.mappy.com,*
*www.rac.co.uk, www.theaa.com.*

**Autoroute information:** *www.asf.fr,*
*www.autoroutes.fr, www.route.equipement.*
*gouv.fr, www.equipement.gouv.fr.*

**Road and traffic information:** *www.bison-fute.equipement.gouv.fr.* Site of the French National Traffic Centre, with information on all aspects of driving in France.

## Hiring a Car

Car hire is relatively expensive. If you're travelling from North America, there are big pluses to booking a car in advance through one of the major agencies or online booking services, or looking for a fly-drive travel package with car included. All the major car hire chains operate in France.

The minimum age for hiring a car in France is around 21 to 25, and the maximum around 70. For an instant online price comparison, log on to *www.autosabroad.com*, or call **t** 08700 66 77 88.

## By Bicycle

Cycling signals as much pain as pleasure in largely mountainous Rhône-Alpes. However, loads of people love the challenge – one of

the hazards of driving in the region is suddenly coming upon bands of cyclists pumping up the kinds of inclines for which most people require escalators! Do wear helmets. Theft is not uncommon, so make sure your insurance covers your bike or the one you hire.

Getting your own bike to France from the UK and Ireland is fairly easy: Air France, British Airways and some ferry operators will carry them for free. On Eurostar, bikes travel in the guards' vans, with advance reservation and an extra charge. From the USA or Australia most airlines will carry them as long as they're boxed and included in your total baggage weight. Certain French trains (*autotrains*, with a bicycle symbol in the timetable) carry bikes for free; otherwise you have to send them as registered luggage and pay a fee, with delivery 'guaranteed' within 48 hours (delays are common). To find out which trains accept bikes, check the SNCF website, *www.sncf.com.*

You can hire bikes at most SNCF stations and in major towns, and you can usually drop your bike off at another station. Private firms hire mountain bikes (VTTs or *vélos tout terrain*) and racing bikes. Rates should be around €9 a day, with a deposit of up to €80 or the yielding of a credit card number. Most towns have cycle paths and shelters, and hire points in some car parks.

The region is renowned for mountain-biking, unsurprisingly. There are specialist trails in all the ranges. In the high Alps, many resorts allow bikes to be carried up the mountainsides on the mechanical lifts that operate in summer. Tourist offices can supply specialist touring guides, and the official French IGN mapping agency (*www.ign.fr*) publishes maps for cyclists.

**Fédération Française de Cyclotourisme,**
**t** 01 56 20 88 88, *www.ffct.org.* Maps and cycling information in France.

**Cyclists' Touring Club, t** 0870 873 0060,
*www.ctc.org.uk.* Information in Britain.

## On Foot

With some 4,000km of clearly marked long-distance footpaths or *sentiers de Grande Randonnée* (**GRs**), and a fantastic variety of landscapes, the Rhône-Alpes is a superb region for serious walking. GR paths are indicated by red-and-white striped signs. The shorter *Petites Randonnées* (**PRs**) are usually signalled by single yellow or green stripes, *sentiers de Grande Randonnée de Pays* (**GRPs**) by a red and yellow stripe. They are lovingly maintained by the Fédération Française de la Randonnée Pédestre, which produces excellent guides (*topoguides*) to many GR paths. The best maps for walking in France are the IGN's 1:25,000 Série Bleue and Top 25 series.

**Fédération Française de la Randonnée Pédestre (FFRP)**, 14 Rue Riquet, 75019 Paris, **t** 01 44 89 93 93, *www.ffrp.asso.fr*.

**Institut Géographique National (IGN)**, 136 bis Rue de Grenelle, 75007 Paris, **t** 01 43 98 80 00, *www.ign.fr*. Maps can be ordered online.

# Where to Stay

For **spas**, *see* p.67.

## Hotels

We have selected very special hotels in our touring chapters, from top-of-the-range luxury establishments, via delightful, more moderately priced addresses, to characterful places for those on a tighter budget.

Hotel **price ranges** in this guide (*see* box, below) are based on average rates for a double room, with bathroom. In hotels these do not include breakfast, but this is included with the basic price in all *chambres d'hôtes*.

Most hotels have a range of rooms and prices. The categories in this guide don't include luxury suites, but most top French hotels have them, so ask. Most two-star hotel rooms have en suite showers and toilets, while one-stars have rooms with or without.

French hotels charge for the room, not per person, so families can travel pretty cheaply. People travelling alone don't get such a good deal: **single rooms** are quite rare, and usually cost two-thirds of the price of a double. Try to book ahead; it's advisable for any hotel, and essential for hot spots in high season.

Hotel **restaurants** are often high quality, and many hotels offer good-value half-board or full-board deals (in summer, some insist on it). Hotel **umbrella associations**, such as the traditional, family-run Logis de France (*www.logis-de-france.fr*), the more upmarket Relais du Silence (*www.relais-du-silence.com*), the charming Châteaux & Hôtels de France (*www.chateauxhotels.com*), or the prestigious Relais et Châteaux (*www.relais chateaux.fr*), promote independently owned hotels and their restaurants.

## Chambres d'Hôtes

*Chambres d'hôtes*, the French equivalent of B&B, are very popular. They offer different qualities from hotels, being homely and personal. They tend to be better value, but cannot offer the same range of facilities as hotels. Book well in advance, especially for French holiday times (Easter and July–Aug). Many can offer staying guests a *table d'hôte* evening meal, if reserved in advance.

Tourist offices keep lists of local *chambres d'hôtes*, but are not allowed to recommend specific ones. Most country *chambres d'hôtes* are affiliated to the same **Gîtes de France** organization as self-catering *gîtes* (*see* below). It classifies *chambres d'hôtes* with one to four *épis* (ears of corn). Another umbrella organization is **Clévacances** (*see* below), which has more B&Bs in towns.

## Gîtes and Self-catering

All short-term rented accommodation with its own facilities comes under the French term *gîte*. Most but not all are affiliated to the **Fédération Nationale des Gîtes de France** (*www.gites-de-france.fr*), whose yellow and green symbol is familiar in every part of the country. The other umbrella organization here too is **Clévacances**. *Gîte* furnishings vary enormously, from opulent to very basic. Both Gîtes de France and Clévacances publish guides and have central booking services, or can be contacted through tourist offices.

**Maison des Gîtes de France Rhône-Alpes**, 1 Rue Général Plessier, 69002 Lyon, **t** 04 72 77 17 55, *www.gites-de-france-rhone-alpes.com*.

**Fédération Nationale des Locations Clévacances**, 54 Bd de l'Embouchure, BP 2166, 31022 Toulouse, **t** 05 61 13 55 66, *www.clevacances.com*.

## Hotel Price Categories

| | | |
|---|---|---|
| *luxury* | €€€€€ | €230 + |
| *very expensive* | €€€€ | €150–230 |
| *expensive* | €€€ | €100–150 |
| *moderate* | €€ | €60–100 |
| *inexpensive* | € | below €60 |

**Brittany Ferries, t** 08705 360 360, *www.brittanyferries.com*. Agent for Gîtes de France.

**Villas International,** 4340 Redwood Highway, Suite D309, San Rafael, CA94903, **t** 1-800 221 2260, *www.villasintl.com*.

## Camping

There is a very good choice of campsites in Rhône-Alpes, from four-star luxury sites with swimming pools, restaurants and loads of space, to one-star sites with basic facilities. Virtually every town and village has a no-frills municipal campsite. Camping on farms is popular too, and tends to be cheaper; most are designated as *Campings à la Ferme* by Gîtes de France (*see* p.61). Rhône-Alpes Tourisme has an official website with a vast range of sites and offers (*www.camping-rhonealpes.co.uk*), while a nationwide guide, the *Guide Officiel Camping-caravaning*, is available in most French bookshops. In summer, book your plot in advance, as even out-of-the-way sites fill up quickly.

# Specialist Tour Operators

## Cookery

*See* also Nicolas Le Bec, p.93, and Château de la Motte, p.133.

**La Cuisine de Savoie,** Hôtel Million, 73200 Albertville, **t** 04 79 32 25 15, *www.hotelmillion.com*. Prestigious establishment running week-long courses in English for small groups.

**Institut Paul Bocuse, t** 04 72 18 02 20, *www.institutpaulbocuse.com*. Offers four cuisine and culture courses in a 19th-century château, with a wine-tasting cellar.

**Ecole du Grand Chocolat Valrhôna,** 26600 Tain-l'Hermitage, **t** 04 75 07 90 90, *www.valrhona.com*. Chocolate-making in the Drôme.

## Wine

**Alpes Flaveurs,** *www.alpes-flaveurs.com*. Tours, visits and wine-tasting in the Savoie region.

**Ecole Beaujolaise des Vins,** 210 Bd Vermorel, BP 317, 69661 Villefranche Cedex, **t** 04 74 02 22 18, *www.beaujolais.com*. Courses may be in English.

**Université du Vin,** Suze-la-Rousse, Drôme, **t** 04 75 97 21 30, *www.universite-du-vin.com*. Courses on wine in a great castle, with lectures. Classes in English possible.

**Arblaster and Clarke Wine Tours,** UK **t** (01730) 893 344, *www.winetours.co.uk*. Fantastic tours by leading wine writers and experts.

## Walking/Hiking

**Belle France, t** 0870 405 4056, *www.belle-france.co.uk*. Independent walking, cycling and boating holidays.

**Great Walks of the World,** UK **t** (01935) 810 820, *www.greatwalks.net*. Self-explanatory.

**Ramblers Holidays,** UK **t** (01707) 331 133, *www.ramblersholidays.co.uk*. Organizes Tour du Mont Blanc walking holidays.

**Sherpa Expeditions,** 131a Heston Road, Hounslow, Middlesex TW5 0RF, **t** (020) 8577 2717, *www.sherpaexpeditions.com*. Self-guided or escorted inn-to-inn walking tours around Ardèche or Mont Blanc.

**Sentiers de France, t** 01 45 69 86 46, *www.sentiersdefrance.com*. Self-guided walking tours.

## River Cruising

**Pavillon Saône,** book through H2olidays, Port de Plaisance, 21170 Saint Jean de Losne, France, **t** 03 80 29 13 81, *www.barginginfrance.com*. Sail a hired cruiser down the Saône.

**Peter Deilmann River Cruises,** UK **t** (020) 7436 2931, *www.peter-deilmann-river-cruises.co.uk*. Choice of luxury Rhône and Saône cruises.

**Travel Renaissance Holidays,** 28 South Street, Epsom, Surrey KT18 7PF, **t** (01372) 744 455, *www.travelrenaissance.com*. Luxury Rhône Viking cruises, on boats carrying 50 people or more.

## Golfing

**French Golf Holidays,** UK **t** (01277) 824 100, *www.frenchgolfholidays.com*.

**Golf Par Excellence,** UK **t** (01737) 211 818, *www.golfparexcellence.com*.

## Language Courses

**Le Chalet Français,** Chamonix, **t** 04 50 54 26 88, *www.lechaletfrancais.com*. Lodgings and meals are in a rustic chalet.

**Ecole des Trois Ponts,** Château de Matel, 42300 Roanne, **t** 04 77 71 53 00, *www.3ponts.edu*. Language courses in a lovely setting; also cookery courses in small classes, or combinations.

**Experience Language Ltd.,** 9c Westbourne Terrace, London, **t** 0845 458 0578, *www.experiencelanguage.co.uk*. Intensive, small-group language courses in Lyon or Chamonix.

## Art Holidays

*See* also *www.creative-escapes.co.uk* for photography and travel-writing courses in the Ardèche. *See* also Morestel, p.240.

**Centre Artistique de Piégon, t** 04 75 27 10 43, *www.compu.ch/piegon*. In the southern Drôme. Facilities for solo or group artists.

# Practical A–Z

06

# Conversions: Imperial–Metric

## Length (multiply by)
Inches to centimetres: 2.54
Centimetres to inches: 0.39
Feet to metres: 0.3
Metres to feet: 3.28
Yards to metres: 0.91
Metres to yards: 1.1
Miles to kilometres: 1.61
Kilometres to miles: 0.62

## Area (multiply by)
Inches square to centimetres square: 6.45
Centimetres square to inches square: 0.15
Feet square to metres square: 0.09
Metres square to feet square: 10.76
Miles square to kilometres square: 2.59
Kilometres square to miles square: 0.39
Acres to hectares: 0.40
Hectares to acres: 2.47

## Weight (multiply by)
Ounces to grams: 28.35
Grammes to ounces: 0.035
Pounds to kilograms: 0.45
Kilograms to pounds: 2.2
Stones to kilograms: 6.35
Kilograms to stones: 0.16
Tons (UK) to kilograms: 1,016
Kilograms to tons (UK): 0.0009
1 UK ton (2,240lbs) = 1.12 US tonnes (2,000lbs)

## Volume (multiply by)
Pints (UK) to litres: 0.57
Litres to pints (UK): 1.76
Quarts (UK) to litres: 1.13
Litres to quarts (UK): 0.88
Gallons (UK) to litres: 4.55
Litres to gallons (UK): 0.22
1 UK pint/quart/gallon =
1.2 US pints/quarts/
gallons

## Temperature
Celsius to Fahrenheit:
multiply by 1.8 then
add 32

Fahrenheit to Celsius:
subtract 32 then multiply
by 0.55

# France Information

## Time Differences
**Country:** + 1hr GMT; + 6hrs EST; + 9hrs PCT
**Daylight saving** from last Sun in March
to last Sun in October

## Dialling Codes
*Note: omit first zero of local number*
**France country code** 33
**To France from:** UK, Ireland, New Zealand 00 /
USA, Canada 011 / Australia 0011, then dial 33
and then the number without the initial zero
**From France to:** UK 00 44; Ireland 00 353; USA,
Canada 001; Australia 00 61; New Zealand 00
64 then the number without the initial zero
**Directory enquiries:** 118 000 / 12
**International directory enquiries:** 00 33 12

## Emergency Numbers
**Police:** 17
**Ambulance:** 15
**Fire:** 18

## Embassy Numbers in France
**UK:** 04 91 15 72 10; **Ireland** 01 44 17 67 00;
**USA:** 04 91 54 92 00; **Canada** 04 93 92 93 22;
**Australia** 01 40 59 33 00; **NZ** 01 45 01 43 43

## Shoe Sizes

| Europe | UK | USA |
| --- | --- | --- |
| 35 | 2½ / 3 | 4 |
| 36 | 3 / 3½ | 4½ / 5 |
| 37 | 4 | 5½ / 6 |
| 38 | 5 | 6½ |
| 39 | 5½ / 6 | 7 / 7½ |
| 40 | 6 / 6½ | 8 / 8½ |
| 41 | 7 | 9 / 9½ |
| 42 | 8 | 9½ / 10 |
| 43 | 9 | 10½ |
| 44 | 9½ / 10 | 11 |
| 45 | 10½ | 12 |
| 46 | 11 | 12½ / 13 |

## Women's Clothing

| Europe | UK | USA |
| --- | --- | --- |
| 34 | 6 | 2 |
| 36 | 8 | 4 |
| 38 | 10 | 6 |
| 40 | 12 | 8 |
| 42 | 14 | 10 |
| 44 | 16 | 12 |

## Crime and the Police

**Police t** 17

France is a pretty safe country, but be aware that thieves can target foreigners, especially their cars and holiday homes. Cars with foreign number plates or that are obviously rented can be seen as rich pickings. Be extra careful in cities.

Report thefts to the nearest **Gendarmerie** or, in towns, the **Police Nationale**. They will give you an official statement, required for an insurance claim. If your passport is stolen, contact the police and your consulate. Keep photocopies of passports, driving licences and other important documents; this makes life easier reporting a loss.

By law, the French police can stop anyone and demand to see some ID.

## Eating Out

French restaurants generally serve between noon and 2pm and in the evening from 7 to 10pm, with later summer hours; *brasseries* in the cities often stay open continuously. Service should be included now in all restaurant bills, but you may wish to add a small tip for good service.

This guide has placed restaurants into four price bands (*see* box, below), based on a three-course meal without wine for one person. This is also based on set menus, and does not usually reflect prices of luxurious *menu gastronomique* feasts.

For more information on food, wine and eating in Rhône-Alpes, and some help in ordering, *see* **Food and Drink**, pp.43–50.

## Electricity

The electric current in France is 220 volts. UK and Irish visitors with appliances from home need two-pin European plug adaptors; North Americans with 110v equipment will normally need a voltage transformer as well. Older-style French plug sockets have two round prongs, but there is a new kind of socket with fatter prongs and a third earth prong. Arm yourself with adaptors.

## Health and Emergencies

**Ambulance** (SAMU) **t** 15
**Police and ambulance t** 17
**Fire t** 18

In a medical emergency (*un cas d'urgence médicale*), go to the local hospital (*hôpital*, or *centre hospitalier*, or *hôtel-dieu*). You can also call the local **SOS Médecins** (the number will be in the phone book). Local doctors cover night duty.

The local papers have details of doctors on call (*médecins de service*) and chemists (*pharmacies*) open outside normal hours. If it's not an emergency, **pharmacists** are trained to administer first aid and dispense free advice for minor problems. In rural areas there is always someone on duty if you ring the bell; in cities pharmacies are open on a rotating basis on Sundays and holidays, and addresses are posted in their windows and in the local newspaper.

For information on **EHIC cards** and health and travel **insurance**, *see* p.55.

## Internet

Most towns now have **cybercafés**, and you can often e-mail from the tourist office or your hotel, and from some post offices (using a France Telecom phonecard; *see* p.67).

## National Holidays

Banks, shops, offices and many museums close, but most restaurants stay open.

**1 January** New Year's Day
**Easter Sunday** (Mar or April)
**Easter Monday** (Mar or April)
**1 May** *Fête du Travail* (Labour Day)
**8 May** VE Day, Victory 1945
**Ascension Day** (around mid-May)
**Pentecost (Whitsun)** (end May/early June)
**14 July** Bastille Day
**15 August** Assumption of the Virgin Mary
**1 November** All Saints' Day
**11 November** Remembrance Day (First World War Armistice)
**25 December** Christmas Day

### Restaurant Price Categories

| | | |
|---|---|---|
| *very expensive* | €€€€ | over €60 |
| *expensive* | €€€ | €30–60 |
| *moderate* | €€ | €15–30 |
| *inexpensive* | € | below €15 |

# Opening Hours

While many **shops and supermarkets** are now open continuously Tuesday–Saturday from 9 or 10am to 7 or 7.30pm, businesses in smaller towns still close for lunch from 12 or 12.30pm to 2 or 3pm, or in the summer 4pm. In many towns, Sunday morning is a big shopping period. There are local exceptions, but many shops shut Mondays. **Markets** are usually mornings only, although clothes, flea and antique markets run into the afternoon.

With **museums**, we've done our best to include opening hours in the text, but please note that they do change regularly. Most museums charge admission, between 3 and 10 euros. You can normally get a discount if you have a student ID card, or are an EU citizen under 8 or over 65 years old.

Many **churches** are open every day, but may shut for lunch. Others are closed all day and only open for Mass. Sometimes notes on the door direct you to the *mairie* or priest's house (*presbytère*) where you can pick up the key. There are often admission fees for cloisters, crypts and special chapels.

## Post Offices

**Post offices** (**PTT** or **La Poste**) are easily spotted by their blue bird on yellow logo. Every town has a post office, as does many a village. Main post offices open Mon–Fri 8am–7pm, Sat 8–12 noon; in villages, offices may not open till 9am, often close for lunch, and shut at 4.30–5pm.

Ordinary **stamps** can be bought in any tobacco shop (*tabac*).

## Sports and Activities

Local tourist offices will provide you with fuller information. The regional tourist board site, *www.rhonealpes-tourisme.com*, is also a very useful place to start research, with links for the various sports. In 2007, Lyon and St-Etienne are host cities for the Rugby World Cup. In 2009, Val d'Isère will host the World Skiing Championships.

### Caving (*La Spéléologie*)

There are some exceptional caves to explore here. Some around Samoëns in Haute Savoie count among the deepest in the world. Cavers must be led by a qualified guide. (*See* also *www.ffspeleo.fr*.)

### Climbing (*L'Escalade*)

The Ardèche and the limestone cliffs in the Alpine foothills are much favoured by climbers, as well as the higher ranges; some of the technically toughest climbs can be found near Lyon. For non-experts, the *via ferrata* offers routes prepared with steel cables, fixed ladders and artificial holds. Organizations offer climbing excursions, led by qualified instructors, throughout the area.

### Cycling and Mountain Biking (*Le Vélo ou Vélo Tout Terrain: VTT*)

The Rhône-Alpes has great, often challenging terrain for cycling and mountain biking, with an abundance (around 8,379km) of mountain and valley trails. Areas such as the Dombes, which has long, flat routes, are easy for family outings. At the other end of the scale, for biking junkies, areas such as the Isère, the Vanoise, and Les Portes du Soleil offer challenging downhill routes – ski lifts operate all summer for them. *See* also p.60, Getting Around: By Bicycle', and *www.ffc.fr*.

### Golf (*Le Golf*)

There are over 60 golf courses to putt your way across in the Rhône-Alpes, from high-altitude greens in the Alps, via the banks of the great lakes, to those close to the cities (notably Lyon, Grenoble and Geneva) and along the Rhône and Loire valleys. Club addresses are listed on the regional tourist board website.

### Horse-riding (*L'Equitation*)

Horse-lovers are well catered-for, with over 6,000km of orange-signposted bridle paths; it's a great way to visit the Monts du Forez, for example, or the Maurienne , the Ardèche or the Drôme. 'Horse Hostels' and farms will accommodate you and your steed along the way. Donkeys (*ânes*) offer a gentler alternative in some areas.

Some of the region's 4,000 riding schools offer one-hour rides with a qualified guide (average cost €12 per person) or riding lessons for beginners; longer, all-inclusive excursions and holidays are also available.

**Rhône-Alpes à Cheval**, Maison du Tourisme, 14 Rue de la République, BP 227, 38019 Grenoble cedex, **t** 04 76 42 85 88, *rhone-alpes-a-cheval@wanadoo.fr*.

## Paragliding (*Le Parapente*)

Paragliding was founded in the Rhône-Alpes in 1978, so it's no surprise that 50 paragliding schools are registered in the region. Famous centres include Thollon-les-Mémises by Lac Léman, the Col de la Forclaz above Lac d'Annecy, and St Hilaire du Touvet, near Grenoble, but there are scores of options. Details are available on *www.rhonealpes-tourisme.com*, or contact: **Ligue Rhône-Alpes de Vol Libre**, Chemillieu, 01300 Nattages, **t** 04 79 44 40 78, *www.ffvl.fr*.

## Skiing (*Le Ski*)

The Rhône-Alpes boasts the best skiing in the world – *see* Chapter 19, **Winter Sports**, for specialist advice on organizing your own independent ski trip. Otherwise, the most economical way to join in is to book a package holiday. **Summer skiing** at Les Deux Alpes and Tignes is extremely reliable; that at Alpe d'Huez, La Plagne, Val d'Isère and Val Thorens is more variable according to snow conditions.

Check the tourist board websites for details of the resorts, or contact:

**Fédération Française de Ski**, 50 Rue des Marquisats, 74011 Annecy Cedex, **t** 04 50 51 40 34, *www.ffs.fr*.

## Spas

The region has 15 excellent thermal spa resorts, almost all of which have updated their thermal spa centres in recent times to offer fitness or head-to-toe pampering breaks as well as health treatments. Some have specialities: for example, Brides-les-Bains is known for slimming breaks, Evian for mother-and-baby breaks.

The thermal spa stations are: Aix-les-Bains, Allevard-les-Bains, Brides-les-Bains, Challes-les-Eaux, Divonne-les-Bains, Evian-les-Bains, La Lèchère, Montbrun-les-Bains, Montrond-les-Bains, Neyrac-les-Bains, St-Gervais-les-Bains, St-Laurent-les-Bains, Thonon-les-Bains, Uriage-les-Bains and Vals-les-Bains. For more details, *see* the general index references. Several spas have a **casino** as well.

In addition, many luxury hotels in the region have opened non-thermal spa centres, detailed in the touring chapter boxes.

## Walking (*La Randonnée*)

*See* **Planning Your Trip**, 'Getting Around: On Foot' pp.60–61, first.

Rhône-Alpes is the only region in France where you can go **glacier-walking**. Mont Blanc, the Vanoise, the Rateau and the Grande Rousse range are the main centres. You can walk with a guided group or a private guide, June–Sept; trips usually last two days.

## Water Sports

The glaciers and Alpine rivers of Rhône-Alpes make the region ideal for **white-water sports**: rafting, canoeing, kayaking, white-water swimming, canyoning, tubing (flying downstream on an inflatable doughnut) and hot-dogging (in an inflatable canoe) are all available to the steely-nerved.

You can **sail** on Lakes Annecy, Geneva/Léman and du Bourget (all of which have several sailing schools offering courses at all levels) and hire boats on the Loire, Rhône and Saône. High-altitude sailing is available at Lakes Monteynard and Mont Cenis. The **Ligue de Voile Rhône-Alpes**, **t** 04 79 25 26 89, *www.voile-rhonealpes.org*, publishes booklets

**Waterskiing** can be done on the Rhône, the Saône and Lakes Monteynard, Annecy, du Bourget and Léman (Geneva) between May and October – even for four-year-olds! Contact the **Ligue Rhône-Alpes de Ski Nautique**, **t** 04 79 75 78 49, for a list of clubs.

# Telephones

Most public phone boxes now operate with **phone cards** (*télécartes*) or credit cards, although a few still accept coins. *Télécartes* are sold at post offices, news-stands and *tabacs*. You can also purchase the US-style phonecards which use a PIN-number system.

In this guide, we give telephone numbers as they are used in France. Dial all 10 digits when calling from within the country. Calling from outside France to a French number, the international French code is 33, then you drop the first zero of the 10-digit number. To call from within France to an international number, dial **t** 00, then the country code (UK

44; USA and Canada 1; Ireland 353; Australia 61; New Zealand 64), followed by the area code (minus the first zero for UK numbers) and the number.

For the French operator, dial **t** 13; for **directory enquiries**, dial **t** 118 000 or **t** 12, or see *www.pagesjaunes.fr* (the Yellow Pages website). For international directory enquiries call **t** 33 12.

British and Irish **mobile phones** work in France if they have a roaming facility; check with your service provider. North American cellphones will not work without a triband facility. If you're going to be in France a while and using your mobile a lot, and as long as your mobile is not locked to a UK network, avoid high charges (both outgoing and incoming) by temporarily replacing your UK SIM card with an international one (sold, for example, at *www.0044. co.uk*), or buying a pay-as-you-go phone from a large super-market or phone shop. French mobile numbers begin with **t** 06.

## Time

France is one hour ahead of UK time and six hours ahead of North American Eastern Standard Time, 9 hours ahead of Pacific Coast Time. French summertime (daylight-saving), as in the UK, runs from the last Sunday in March to the last Sunday in October.

## Toilets

The hole-in-the-ground lavatory is still surprisingly common in rural France. Bars and cafés normally don't mind you using their facilities, but it's polite to make a small purchase at the same time. There are some public toilets for which you have to pay, either to get into – those funky, modern oval-shaped street facilities – or to get out of, when there's a caretaker (you should leave them a small tip).

# Lyon

Lyon is a peach of a world heritage city. Founded by the Romans, it expanded across wonderful hills overlooking the peninsula where the rivers Saône and Rhône meet, with fabulous views to the Alps. Lyon eclipsed Paris in its early days; today, it battles it out with Marseille for the title of France's second city.

Forget about images of an industrial town. Lyon's extensive historic centre counts among the most glamorous in Western Europe. The Presqu'île, or peninsula, is now the heart of the city, but interesting quarters radiate out from here – the Roman and Renaissance areas are to the west, while out east is where the Lumière brothers invented cinema for the world. Lyon also claims the finest choice of restaurants in France outside Paris.

# 07

## Don't miss

**①** Roman and Christian monuments enjoying timeless Alpine views
Fourvière hillside **p.72**

**②** A swan's-eye view of Lyon
Saône cruise **p.78**

**③** A cocktail of shopping and culture
Presqu'île **p.78**

**④** A memorable riverside stroll
Rhône east bank **p.88**

**⑤** Cinema's birthplace
Villa Lumière **p.91**

*See map overleaf*

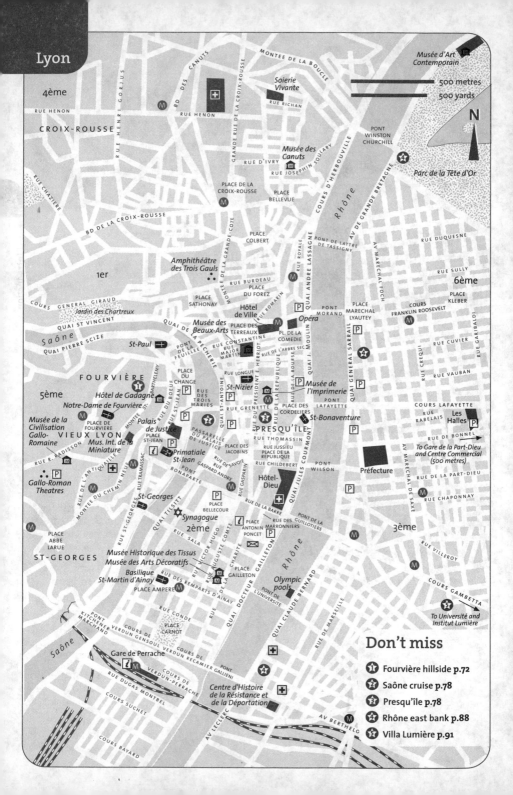

# Lyon

**4ème**

**CROIX-ROUSSE**

Soierie Vivante

Musée des Canuts

PLACE DE LA CROIX-ROUSSE

PLACE BELLEVUE

Musée d'Art Contemporain

500 metres
500 yards

N

PONT WINSTON CHURCHILL

Parc de la Tête d'Or

**6ème**

PLACE KLEBER

**1er**

Amphithéâtre des Trois Gauls

PLACE COLBERT

Jardin des Chartreux

PLACE SATHONAY
PLACE DU FOREZ

Hôtel de Ville

Opéra

PLACE MARECHAL LYAUTEY

COURS FRANKLIN ROOSEVELT

Musée des Beaux-Arts

PLACE DES TERREAUX

PL. DE LA COMEDIE

St-Paul

PLACE DU CHANGE

**FOURVIÈRE**

**5ème**

Hôtel de Gadagne

Notre-Dame de Fourvière

St-Nizier

Musée de l'Imprimerie

COURS LAFAYETTE

Les Halles

St-Bonaventure

**PRESQU'ÎLE**

Musée de la Civilisation Gallo-Romaine

**VIEUX LYON**

Palais de Justice

Mus. Int. de la Miniature

Primatiale St-Jean

PLACE DES JACOBINS

PLACE DE LA RÉPUBLIQUE

Préfecture

To Gare de la Part-Dieu and Centre Commercial (500 metres)

Gallo-Roman Theatres

St-Georges

Hôtel-Dieu

**3ème**

**ST-GEORGES**

PLACE ABBE LARUE

Synagogue

**2ème**

PLACE BELLECOUR

PLACE ANTONIN PONCET

PLACE DES MARRONNIERS

Musée Historique des Tissus
Musée des Arts Décoratifs

Basilique St-Martin d'Ainay

PLACE AMPERE

PLACE GAILLETON

Olympic pools

Gare de Perrache

PLACE CARNOT

To Université and Institut Lumière

Centre d'Histoire de la Résistance et de la Déportation

## Don't miss

**1** Fourvière hillside p.72

**2** Saône cruise p.78

**3** Presqu'île p.78

**4** Rhône east bank p.88

**5** Villa Lumière p.91

# Getting to Lyon

**By air**: Air France, British Airways and easyjet fly to Lyon from London airports, Aer Lingus from Dublin, Air Transat from Montréal and Toronto. BA also offers flights to Lyon from Birmingham and Manchester. Lyon-St-Exupéry **airport** (**t** 04 72 22 72 21, *www.lyon.aeroport.fr*) lies *c.* 25km east of the centre. The winged building rising dramatically beside the terminals is the airport's **TGV station**, designed by Santiago Calatrava, but does not have connections to central Lyon. **Satobus shuttle buses** (**t** 04 72 22 71 27, *www.satobus.com*) leave the airport every 20mins during the day, serving the city's two central railway stations, Lyon-Part-Dieu east of the Rhône, Lyon-Perrache on the Presqu'île. Or there are **taxis**. A separate, regular shuttle bus service links the airport to the **car-hire** area some distance from the terminals; Avis, Budget, Europcar, Hertz, National/Citer and Sixt are among the companies represented.

**By rail**: Lyon was the first French city connected to Paris by fast **TGV**, in 1981, and now has excellent TGV rail links across the country. Also be aware that it can take as little as 5hrs to get from London to Lyon by train: book a Eurostar to Lille-Europe and a TGV from there. Paris is 2hrs from Lyon, Marseille 1hr 30mins.

# Getting around Lyon

Lyon has excellent **metro**, **tram** and **bus** systems (for general info, **Allô TCL**, **t** 08 20 42 70 00, *www.tcl.fr*), useful for the northern and eastern quarters in particular. Use the **cable cars**, known as *ficelles* or *funiculaires*, to get up the steep Fourvière and Croix-Rousse hillsides. A good new way to introduce yourselves to the city centre is with **le Grand Tour** (*www.lyonlegrandtour.com*) open-top tourist buses, offering a hop-on, hop-off service around Fourvière and the Presqu'île.

For **taxis**, try **Lyon International Taxis**, **t** 04 78 88 16 16, or **Allô Taxis**, **t** 04 78 28 23 23, or see the tourist office website for more options. **Rickshaws** serve the centre, run by **Cyclopolitain**, **t** 08 26 10 00 03. Consider **hiring bikes** from the major central car parks (**t** 04 72 41 65 25, *www.lpa.fr*).

For **river cruises**, **Naviginter**, **t** 04 78 42 96 81, *www.naviginter.fr*, runs short trips from Quai des Célestins on the Saône, and dinner cruises from Quai Claude Bernard on the Rhône. If you're feeling flush, splash out on a **Lyon Taxi Boat**, **t** 04 72 56 51 23, operating April–Oct.

Picture a crate of ripening peaches, with all its variety of hues, and you'll have a notion of historic Lyon's irresistible waterside colours. Traditionally, the Saône has been portrayed as the feminine, graceful half of Lyon's river partnership, the Rhône as the masculine, muscular one, as symbolic statues all around town recall. These two splendid rivers (in fact historically both major working waterways) unite at the end of the long, smart central **Presqu'île**, heart of the city, with grand Ancien Régime squares, great arts museums, and superb shops, hotels and restaurants.

Lyon's older historic quarters rise west of the Saône, the churches and mansions of **Vieux Lyon** backed by the steep **Fourvière** hill in which the city's major Roman remains lie semi-hidden. From the 15th century, the place became one of Europe's main silk producers, the makers rattling off pieces in ear-splitting numbers in the **St-Georges** quarter south of the Saône-side cathedral. But in the 19th century the workers crossed onto the **Croix-Rousse** hill above the Presqu'île, only stopping their work to revolt in desperation.

A large swath of central Lyon, from the Roman hill, across the Presqu'île to the high-rise silk-weavers' houses on Croix-Rousse, was declared a UNESCO World Heritage Site in 1998, in recognition of its remarkable legacy going back 2,000 years. On top of that, in its smart eastern suburbs Lyon boasts the site of the first cinema film ever, shot in 1895 by the Lumière brothers outside their home.

## A Note on Lyon's History

Given that it has been the most important city in the region for the last two millennia, Lyon's history takes up large portions, if not the lion's share, of the general **History** chapter of this book, so consider reading that first to gain an understanding of the place. Lyon was, for example, of far greater importance to the Romans and early Christians than insignificant little Paris! However, the touring sections of this chapter do give the historical context you need to appreciate the city to the full.

You might use the different sections as highly enjoyable walking tours, or simply to explore particular sights and areas.

Brash new quarters are racing up now beside the Rhône; this is a vibrant modern city as well as a great historic one. Despite its well-known wartime traumas and problem suburbs, these days Lyon looks very self-confident at its core. The French traditionally stereotype the Lyonnais as arrogant, which is rather unfair, but they *are* particularly proud of their city centre – even certain underground car parks have been turned into art spaces. It's appropriate that lions are a recurring symbol around town – playing on the city's name, but also reflecting its character.

There are even comparisons to be made between Lyon and Paris. Although the Lyon conurbation only has around 1.3 million inhabitants, as against the capital's 9.5 million, like the capital it has plane-lined river quays, *bateaux-mouches* plying its waters, a copy of the top of the Eiffel tower, and a white church glowing on its main hillside, a more central answer to the capital's Sacré Cœur. Plus the city is divided into *arrondissements* like Paris and has a far more comfortable *métro* system. To foreign visitors who may have a completely false notion of the place from its industrial outskirts, Lyon will come as a wonderful surprise, bursting with interest – it turns out to be a giant, juicy peach of a city to savour.

## The Fourvière Hillside and Gallo-Roman Lyon

**Notre-Dame de Fourvière**
*www.fourviere.org;
open daily 8–7*

 **Fourvière hillside**

The bright white **Notre-Dame de Fourvière** church shining on top of the Fourvière hill labours under the illusion that it's a fairytale castle. It is the major landmark in Lyon, visible from many points in the centre; to get your bearings in town, head up to it first. Take either the new Grand Tour tourist bus or the cable car (*funiculaire* or *ficelle*) from beside the cathedral to avoid the cramp-inducing climb via the pedestrian paths; consisting of hundreds of steps, these narrow *montées* pass between hushed walled properties, some still concealing monastic institutions on this long-religious slope nicknamed *la colline qui prie* (the praying hill), although graffiti artists have plastered vacuous messages along the way.

Reaching the broad terrace at the end of the church, you are rewarded with a fine visual map of central Lyon. On clear days the uninterrupted views east as far as Mont Blanc are magnificent. People stare out with reverence, as though still paying homage to Lug, the Celtic sun god after whom the Romans named their new town, Lugdunum, at its foundation in 43 BC. From up here, In one sweeping glance you can take in much of the Rhône-Alpes region.

'A citadel of superstition', one outraged Republican protester branded showy Notre-Dame de Fourvière when it was built. Many a Lyonnais today enjoys referring to it as the upturned elephant, because of the four squat corner towers sticking out above the bulky building. It was ordered by archbishop Monseigneur de Genouilhac just after the Franco-Prussian War of 1870, in gratitude to the Virgin Mary for her supposed role in sparing the city from attack. Conservative Catholics were also appalled by the lavish decorations on this work designed by Pierre Bossan. The ostentatious west front hints at the extravaganza inside. Everywhere there are floral as well as religious details, and of course lions. The interior feels almost Oriental, built on huge Moorish-looking arches. Mosaics cover floor and walls, much of the decoration devoted to the Virgin, illustrating declarations by the Church on her Immaculate Conception, and her status as Mother of God and protectress of France. The crypt is almost on the same scale as the church, albeit in more sober style. Here, the plethora of plaques of *grâces* and *reconnaissances* indicate what a major pilgrimage destination this is, still receiving one million pilgrims a year.

**Musée d'Art Sacré**
*t 04 78 25 13 01, www.*
*lyon-fourviere.com;*
*open April–early Jan*
*daily 10–12.30 and*
*2–5.30; closed mid-*
*Jan–Mar; adm*

There are older places of pilgrimage on the site: the 18th-century **Ancienne Chapelle de la Vierge** houses wildly ornate Baroque altarpieces, and is topped on the outside by a big gilded Virgin. She was added in the 19th century, a work by the popular sculptor Joseph Fabisch, who went on to make the much-venerated Virgin of Lourdes. The adjoining **Musée d'Art Sacré** presents sumptuous religious articles, plus temporary exhibitions. Climb the **basilica observatory** for spectacular views.

**Basilica observatory**
*open April–Sept*
*Wed–Sun 10.30–12 and*
*2–6.30; Oct–Mar Sat,*
*Sun and public hols*
*1.30–5.30; adm*

Close by, a metallic **tower** sticks out like a copy of the top of Paris' Eiffel Tower – which is exactly what it is, but in grey. Erected in 1893 for an ambitious restaurant owner, at 85m (close on 300ft) it now serves as a television transmitter.

Notre-Dame de Fourvière probably occupies the site of the Gallo-Roman forum of Lugdunum, the name Fourvière apparently deriving from *Forum Vetus*, Old Forum. South along the hillside, admire the remnants of two major **Roman theatres** built side by side in a spectacular location facing east. These huge structures were only unearthed in the 1930s, after a band of nuns digging their land struck upon an ancient wall; the city then took over the excavations. The main theatre originally went up around 15 BC, one of the earliest in Gaul; it doubled in size under Hadrian, to seat 10,000. The smaller theatre, or Odeon, dates from around AD 100

**Roman theatres**
*open daily*
*9am–nightfall; free*

07

Lyon | The Fourvière Hillside and Gallo-Roman Lyon

and was used for performances of music and poetry; it could seat 3,000. These theatres now serve as spectacular venues for a rich and varied programme of outdoor summer events, *Les Nuits de Fourvière*. At any time, avoid stumbling on the outsized paving blocks as you soak up the ancient atmosphere.

**Musée de la Civilisation Gallo-Romaine**
*t 04 72 38 49 30, www.musees-gallo-romains.com; open Tues–Sun 10–6; adm, free Thurs*

Roman Lugdunum was substantially excavated throughout the 20th century, many finds ending up in the **Musée de la Civilisation Gallo-Romaine** overlooking the two theatres. Its 1970s concrete layers, designed by the architect Zehrfuss, look a bit drab now, but were sensitively incorporated into the hillside. Although the collections concentrate on Lugdunum's rapid growth into a major Roman political and religious centre, they also cover earlier periods in the Rhône-Alpes region, for instance with the processional chariot from La Côte-St-André dating back to 700 BC. Busts of Lyon's founder, Plancus, and the emperors closely associated with the city, help put faces to the Roman names, and models recreate Lugdunum's grandest buildings. The religious sections include cruder devotional items from the Gaulish tradition, and much finer-figured representations of Roman divinities. Separate areas are devoted to Lugdunum's economic life and craftsmen. Among the mosaics, one of the most spectacular depicts a scene at the Roman circus – you can even see what is described as gladiators' graffiti. Roman finds are still being made: in the 1990s, a new hoard of buried Gallo-Roman treasure was found in the suburb of Vaise, now on show here. The museum also holds temporary exhibitions.

## Vieux Lyon: Medieval and Renaissance Lyon

Squeezed between Fourvière's hillside and the Saône, the cramped streets of Vieux Lyon are lined with great tall mansions, their ground floors often given over to touristy restaurants and boutiques. Gorgeous small squares allow for a little breathing space. This area was home to the massively powerful archbishops of Lyon and their noble aides, the canon-counts.

The most venerable building in Vieux Lyon, the medieval **Primatiale St-Jean**, or Cathedral of St John, turns its muscular, rounded back on the Saône. Its finely chiselled west façade overlooks pretty if sober **Place St-Jean**, on which a copper John the Baptist performs a civilized baptism of Christ, protected beneath a small dome. At the top of the cathedral front is a petalled rose window; below it, although the main statues were torn down by fanatical Protestants, the figures on the carved panels around the portals merely suffered beheadings. The plethora of scenes proves engrossing, told with medieval chivalric verve, and often violence.

Inside, the tall Gothic nave has a simple grandeur, but the place was heavily restored in the 19th century. The swankiest side chapel, with its more elaborate vaulting, was built as the resting place for Charles de Bourbon, long-serving archbishop of Lyon in the 15th century. In the squat Romanesque apse, admire some intense 13th-century stained glass. The transepts, each with their own sets of organ pipes, have bright stained-glass rose windows, one featuring good and bad angels, while the remarkable childlike 16th-century astronomical clock provides unintentional light entertainment with its chimes and God popping out of a cloud like a figure from a Guignol show (*see* overleaf). The treasury conceals smaller marvels. The whole area around the cathedral was once occupied by episcopal buildings, portions of which survive; the notable Romanesque edifice beside the Primatiale, with its diminutive arches and patterned bricks, served as the refectory of the canon-courts, then as a choristers' school.

North of the cathedral lie the most touristy streets of Vieux Lyon. The well renovated, fruity-coloured façades of mansions built for wealthy residents in the 15th and 16th centuries loom over the narrow streets. Take the main artery, **Rue St-Jean**, past dramatic Flamboyant Gothic and Renaissance houses, the arcades of the **Maison des Avocats** most impressive to one side. Visit the **Musée International de la Miniature** and you enter this, one of Vieux Lyon's grandest houses. You also get a chance to climb one of the most elegant staircases typical of the Renaissance quarter. On arrival, however, you have to negotiate the substantial shop on the ground floor. The displays on the floors above prove engrossing, with some hilarious comic pieces, some intriguing behind-the-scenes views of Lyon, some oddities, and some truly artistic bijou creations. At certain times you can watch a craftsman at work.

On along Rue St-Jean, passing the imposing 19th-century former Palais de Justice (*see* p.77), you'll find ethnic eateries, plus touristy places claiming to be real *bouchons* (*see* p.94) and English-style pubs. Don't miss the streets parallel to Rue St-Jean either. **Rue des Trois Maries** is graced by the odd religious statue. Reach **Rue du Bœuf** via broad **Rue Neuve St-Jean**, which serves as an intensely busy square, or try the secretive way to it, via the longest *traboule* in town, taking you through five courtyards from 54 Rue St-Jean to 27 Rue du Bœuf. These *traboules* (perhaps a contraction of the Latin '*transambulare*', 'to walk through') are narrow covered alleys linking the big mansions, offering private paths through the area; while many are now open to the public, they are often dingy and, although the inner courtyards are overseen by picturesque galleries and towers, bins often preside below – greenery might look more fetching. No.16 on Rue du Bœuf conceals Vieux Lyon's most famous soaring stair tower, the arch-windowed **Tour Rose**.

**Musée International de la Miniature**
*t 04 72 00 24 77, www.mimlyon.com; open daily 10–7; adm*

Heading north, Rue St-Jean shimmies through a series of sweet squares teeming with tourist life. **Place de la Baleine** perhaps got its name from whale-meat being shipped in to the nearby quay for Lent; **Place du Gouvernement** was where the Ancien Régime governors were based; and **Place du Change** was where Lyon's currency exchange was set up from the time of the fairs – the 18th-century neoclassical makeover to plans by the architect Soufflot made the building look like an elegant theatre. Since the Revolution, it has doubled as Protestant church and concert venue.

Beyond, the recently restored medieval church of **St-Paul** is signalled by its funnel of a spire, later murals showing the major stages in the saint's life. However, the real local hero is puppeteer Laurent Mourguet, a plaque on Place St-Paul recalling that he lived here from 1795 to 1832. It was after the young Mourguet had lost his job as a silk-worker that he dedicated himself to his puppet passion. At first, he followed the traditional stories of long-established Italian Commedia dell'Arte slapstick, but then he created his own characters, their banter providing working-class commentary on the events of the day. Wide-eyed, cheeky Guignol, with his tight black cap, brown frock coat and long pigtail, had a Chinese air, but chattered away in Lyonnais dialect. His lady friend Madelon grudgingly put up with him. His great mate Gnafron, a red-nosed tippler, was wedded to Beaujolais. The Guignol characters spread across France, and have now become a national institution something akin to Punch and Judy.

The name of **Rue Juiverie**, tucked away south of Place St-Paul, recalls the Jewish community who lived and traded here in the Middle Ages, driven out by the French royal purge in the 14th century. Grand Renaissance houses were built here in the 16th century. The **Bullioud mansion**, the plushest, was designed in part by one of France's most inventive Renaissance architects, the Lyonnais Philibert Delorme. Contorted lions' faces stick out from the later Baroque façade of the **Hôtel des Lions**.

Rue de Gadagne behind Place du Change contains the largest mansion in Vieux Lyon, named after one of the most influential Italian banking families to settle in town, chased out of Florence by the mightier Medicis. 'As rich as Gadagne' would become a catch-phrase in Lyon. The huge rambling Renaissance **Hôtel de Gadagne** has been undergoing a vast renovation recently. When it eventually reopens, its renewed **Musée Historique de Lyon** will offer a major trawl through the city's history, with fine fragments on display, such as the splendid medieval capitals rescued from Ile Barbe abbey, as well as covering major episodes in the city's later life, including the Revolutionary terror; and its **Musée International de la Marionnette** will be devoted to puppets from around the world, although focusing most on Mourguet's Guignol creations.

**Hôtel de Gadagne**
*t 04 72 56 74 06, www. museegadagne.com*

# Along the Banks of the Saône

A string of bridges connects the two banks of the Saône, for charm almost rivalling the Seine in central Paris, although they all had to be rebuilt after being destroyed in the war, while in the last few years, graffiti artists have been left to go mad here.

Stroll south along the plane-lined west bank of the Saône for one of Lyon's most uplifting walks. Along **Quai de Bondy**, the massive **Palais de Bondy** dates from the early 20th century, a Belle Epoque building with striking bas-reliefs, made for exhibitions and performances. Touristy pubs, discos and girlie bars follow in a brash line, but, at expansive **Place Fusseret**, you can enjoy the uplifting view across to the dramatic façade of the church of **St-Nizier** from in front of Lyon's most famous ice-cream parlour, **Nardone**, with its generous terrace set under a huge theatrical mural.

The thick trunks of the plane trees along **Quai Romain Rolland** mirror the 24 huge, sober columns of the 19th-century former **Palais de Justice**. Designed by Baltard, the original extravagant interior decorations remain in place. This building has witnessed traumatic trials for the nation, including those of Klaus Barbie and Italian anarchist assassin Santo Caserio, killer of French president Sadi Carnot in Lyon.

Past the rounded back of the cathedral, the **Palais St-Jean** was the archbishops' palace down the centuries, its complex array of buildings given their present outer forms by Soufflot in the mid-18th century. Along **Quai Fulchiron**, the spire of the church of **St-Georges** protrudes, a cute neo-Gothic number, by the architect Bossan again, although in his opinion it was a 'youthful error'! The clatter of the looms of Lyon's early weavers once rang out in the now comfortably quiet St-Georges quarter. Triangular **Place de la Trinité**, with a cluster of restaurants, has historic connections with Guignol, also recalled in a couple of little museums close by.

Take Passerelle St-Georges, one of many appealing footbridges over the river, to walk up the east bank of the Saône. Along **Quai Tilsitt** the central **synagogue** merges self-effacingly into the row of smart apartment blocks. **Quai St-Antoine** hosts the city's major outdoor food market every morning bar Monday. The most noticeable façade along this quay once housed the Antonin monastic order (*see* p.215); it is now home to the **Théâtre des Ateliers**. Quai de la Pêcherie hosts Lyon's *bouquinistes* , with their funky metallic outdoor bookstalls.

*Bouquinistes*
*open Sat, Sun and hols*

On **Quai St-Vincent**, the Baroque façade of **St-Vincent** looks as if it has been squashed into its strange angle by the bullying buildings shouldering in on either side. Beyond its concave entrance, questionable modern paintings of Christ's story have been added to the cool white neoclassical interior. North of here, a huge, elaborate outdoor *trompe-l'œil* **mural** wraps itself around some of the façades of No.49. Lyon's city council has encouraged many such pieces of public art, but none is more startling than this one, depicting 24 famous figures born around the Rhône and Saône. They go from Emperor Claudius and St Blandine, to the best-known Lyonnais faces today – chef Paul Bocuse, literary TV-star Bernard Pivot, film-maker Bertrand Tavernier and charity worker Abbé Pierre, the last often voted the most admired Frenchman of modern times. Delightful triangular **Place Martinière** offers deep shade just above, plus a small traditional covered market.

**✪ Saône cruise**

From Quai St-Antoine, you can embark on a **cruise up the Saône**, which takes you north as far as the **Ile Barbe**, a wooded island conserving just the faintest memories of Lyon's oldest monastery. The commentary fills you in on the elegant buildings along both banks. The Lyonnais make the most of some delightfully positioned riverside restaurants beside the west bank in particular.

# The Presqu'île de Lyon

**✪ Presqu'île de Lyon**

Back in the very heart of town, cafés spill out across **Place des Terreaux**, big, lively social hub of Lyon's central peninsula, with many splashing fountains; the melodramatic main one is by Bartholdi, better known for his Statue of Liberty. His fleshy female charioteer commands four wildly tugging horses, representing river waters dashing to the sea. Rejected by Bordeaux, Lyon happily took them all on. Smaller jets add a refreshing contemporary twist.

The grandiose **town hall** overlooks proceedings, built in the 17th century to emphasize the merchant city's power, paying homage to King Henri IV, who brought peace to France after the terribly divisive Wars of Religion – he even renounced Protestantism, and married Catholic Marie de' Medici, here in Lyon in 1600, to help unite the country. Grizzled lions rest their paws over some of the windows, while muscular figures of Hercules and Minerva stand silhouetted above the big, jolly equestrian sculpture of Henri IV.

Beyond rises the brazen **opera house**, its classical colonnade and stilted statues topped by a bold modern glass vault, designed by ground-breaking architect Jean Nouvel. It rather resembles a tunnel placed high in the sky. Challenging contemporary sculptures and fountains run along the spacious square sloping up from the opera house, popular with skateboarders.

**Musée des Beaux-Arts**
*t 04 72 10 17 40; open Wed, Thurs and Sat–Mon 10–6, Fri 10–8; closed Tues; adm*

## Musée des Beaux-Arts in the Abbaye St-Pierre

Back on Place des Terreaux, the enormously long-faced classical façade of the fine arts museum soberly calls cultural visitors inside. The Ancien Régime Abbey of Our Ladies of St Peter's (also known as the Palais St-Pierre, it's so grand) long served as something of a posh finishing school for daughters of the regional aristocracy. After the Revolution it was turned into Lyon's fine arts museum, one of the most important in France, wholly refurbished in the 1990s. Before entering, pause in the restful **courtyard**, now a **sculpture garden**; some wag of a curator has transformed this part of the former convent into an outdoor exhibition space dominated by male nudes, some by Rodin. The abbey church has been converted into a great setting for more diverse sculpture. Between the two, in the **entrance hall**, one of the calmest masterpieces of the museum greets you: Perugino's *Ascension*, curiously donated by Pope Pius VII in 1816.

A grand Baroque staircase adorned with trumpeting angels leads up to the main collections. The **first floor** has a whole wing devoted to antiquities, another to medieval sculpture and craft pieces, and a third to sculpture and *objets d'art* from the Renaissance to the 20th century. Highlights among the antiquities include ancient Egyptian temple doors and a sculpture from the Athens Acropolis. Ivories going back to Byzantine and Carolingian times feature among the beautiful sculpture sections. Medieval Europe is represented by splendid church pieces, and a parallel area is devoted to Islamic works. Moving to the French Ancien Régime, enamels depicting biblical scenes stand out. There are non-religious items such as ceramics, glass, clocks and furniture, and the museum has further huge collections of coins and medals.

Allegorical dreamscapes typical of Pierre Puvis de Chavannes, a celebrated 19th-century neoclassical artist from Lyon, decorate the staircase leading to the **second floor**, where the different schools of European painting are well represented. Outstanding Italian works include a Tintoretto, and three Veroneses displaying 'Impressionist' touches well before their time. Bassano's battle scene of 1495, subtitled *Charles VIII receiving the crown of Naples*, illustrates the troubled relationship between France and Italy that affected Lyon so strongly, although apparently no such battle took place!

The French Ancien Régime collections hold surprises such as works by Simon Vouet, an accomplished classical artist who painted an exceptionally modern self-portrait. An amazing pale-faced knight by a Le Nain brother, along with Jacques Stella's unflinching self-portrait, are further masterpieces. Then comes the usual avalanche of large-scale religious scenes, not just from courtly France but also from the mercantile Low Countries. Two major pieces by Rubens are displayed. The Dutch collection has charming small scale landscapes and still lifes too. Eighteenth-century French art hits back with the excesses of rococo, including Boucher's *The Light of the World* and Greuze's *Lady of Charity*.

The sugary mock-historical style of troubadour painting had Lyon's artistic circle on its knees in the early 19th century; Pierre

Révoril and Fleury Richard were among its leading exponents. Then came a wave of Lyon artists influenced by Ingres' neoclassical purity, including the much-loved Hippolyte Flandrin. Flower-painting became another Lyon speciality. The Romantics are represented by regional painters too, but also by bigger, national names: Delacroix with two contrasting pieces, Géricault powerfully stirring the emotions as ever, with his study of maddened envy. The Impressionist works, with a handful of Manets, Monets and Degas, make up the second largest collection in France after Paris' Musée d'Orsay, and form a splendid link to the post-Impressionist 20th-century art movements also represented here.

## Further Down the Presqu'île

Rue Chenavard, Rue Herriot and Rue de la République are Lyon's smartest shopping streets, all heading south from Place des Terreaux. Although remarkable buildings stand out on the Presqu'île, you may notice that many of the mansion blocks look plainer on the outside than in a showier city like Paris, or even Grenoble. Often in Lyon, the wealthy didn't like to display their fortunes on the outside. One particular decorative feature of the town's wealthy blocks, though, is their *lambrequins*, patterned trimmings in wood or iron embellishing the tops of windows.

Look out for some of the Presqu'île's oldest shops along **Rue Paul Chenavard**, which takes you to Place Meissonnier and the pale, narrow Romanesque façade of the former church of **St-Pierre** (now part of the fine arts museum, which has a shop next door). Rue Chenavard continues to the entrance of the sharply spired church of **St-Nizier**, named after a miracle-working 6th-century bishop of Lyon. Its ornate Gothic exterior, including gargoyles, has been scrubbed clean. Go through the striking central Renaissance porch to see the mainly neo-Gothic decoration inside, although *Notre Dame des Grâces* by the great Lyonnais Ancien Régime sculptor Coysevox stands out, along with some major paintings. South, **Rue de Brest** takes over from Rue Chenavard. To the west, don't miss gently curving **Rue Mercière** – with the deep crushed-velvet reds of its tall Renaissance façades, it counts among the most stylish streets on the Presqu'île, with tempting restaurants along it.

The odd grand façade and decorative detail stands out above the idiosyncratic shops at the northern end of **Rue du Président Herriot**, which runs parallel to Rue Chenavard and Rue de Brest. Branch off for Rue Poulaillerie, where the **Musée de l'Imprimerie**, Lyon's well regarded museum of printing, is tucked away in the **Hôtel de la Couronne**. In the courtyard of this lovely Renaissance mansion, a large plaque shows a man and a woman pouring water, representing the city's two rivers, of course. This place served as the town hall before the huge Hôtel de Ville was built on Place des

**Musée de l'Imprimerie**
*t 04 78 37 65 98; open Jan–Dec Wed–Sun 9.30–12 and 2–6; adm*

Terreaux. The museum goes about its business seriously, tracing the history of writing back to its Middle Eastern roots before concentrating on the 15th-century revolution in printing. The place contains a rare Gutenberg Bible (c. 1454). In early printing times, Lyon swiftly grew into the third most important publishing centre in Europe after Venice and Paris. On French history, it is fascinating to see a copy of the original Protestant *Placard Contre la Messe* of 1534. This explosive piece denounced in crude language 'the pope and all his vermin of cardinals, bishops, priest, monks and other cockroaches...' but also argued a very strong case against the Catholic Mass. It was written by a Lyonnais, Antoine Marcourt, from the safety of Protestant Neuchâtel in Switzerland, and was printed by a fellow Lyonnais exile, Pierre de Vingle. One copy was even affixed to the door of King François I's bedroom. In his rage, the monarch supported the persecution of Protestants and, after a second *placard* in January 1535, banned all printing in France for a time. If you tire of the worthy explanatory texts, a whole floor is devoted to fine prints, including Gustave Doré's illustrations of Rabelais' saucy satirical giants' tales, first printed in Lyon, where the author was practising as a doctor.

Back along Rue Herriot, at Place Francisque Regaud, you might stop at the jaded 19th-century extravaganza that is the **Café des Négociants**. Like Rue Mercière and Rue de Brest, Rue Herriot continues down to Place des Jacobins.

Impressively broad **Rue de la République** came into being as Rue Impériale in the mid-19th century, inaugurated by Emperor Napoléon III and Empress Eugénie. It is still lined with grandiose period buildings but is now pedestrianized; the locals refer to it as Rue de la Ré, coming in droves to the department stores that have taken over many of the most ornate addresses. The odd family store has survived, and the street is packed with historic memories. A plaque at No.1 recalls the first ever public cinema screening, organized by the Lumière brothers on 25 January 1896. The major French banks established swanky offices near the top of the street; Crédit Lyonnais, founded in 1863 by Henri Germain, opened here in 1872. French president Sadi Carnot was assassinated in front of it in 1894, while Lyon was hosting an International Fair; a red stone marks the spot where he was stabbed.

**Rue de la Bourse**, parallel to the main shopping artery, contains further grand buildings. The **Ampère secondary school** was previously the Lyon seat of the Catholic Jesuit order. Louis XIV's celebrated confessor, Père Lachaise, taught here, while Père Martellange became the Jesuits' most renowned architect. He had the school's **Chapelle de la Trinité** remodelled from 1617; its Baroque interior, with painted stucco work and Italian marble statues of the main Jesuit saints, has been sumptuously restored.

Back on Rue de la Ré, the palatial **Palais du Commerce**, smothered with columns, medallions and statues, including a racy image of intertwined naked swimmers representing Rhône and Saône, was built to house a stock exchange, chamber of commerce and commercial court, reflecting Second Empire economic dynamism.

**Place des Cordeliers** is the next square where the shopping artery widens out. To one side stands the 14th-century Church of **St-Bonaventure**, once part of an extensive Franciscan monastery. The church has kept its dark Gothic interior; at one end tapestries illustrate Bonaventure's life, including the saintly Franciscan being surprised doing his washing-up as the church authorities come to declare him a cardinal. Following his promotion, he played a significant part in the great Council of Lyon of 1274, working to try and reunite the Churches of East and West, but he died in the city, and was buried here. Chillingly, it is said that the last of the silk-worker rioters of the 1830s were massacred in the elaborate Sacré Cœur chapel.

Further down Rue de la Ré, a few exceptional shops have survived from the 19th century, such as the confectioner Voisin and the jeweller Augis. The main Lyonnais newspapers fought it out in this section, *Le Progrès* the main one to have lasted, although no longer based here. **Place de la République**, with its dynamic, sporty-looking swimming-laned fountain and children's carousel, is still overseen by Second Empire buildings. Also cast an eye over the extravagant façades of Rue Président Carnot, a development from the Belle Epoque. On the last leg of Rue de la République, the **Casino-Kursaal**, Lyon's main Belle Epoque music hall, has long been converted into a big cinema complex, while the **Bellecour Theatre** now houses the major FNAC entertainments store.

**Passage de l'Argue**, a slightly jaded covered gallery of shops, connects the north of Place de la République with **Place des Jacobins**, which bears the nickname of the Dominican monastic order established here in the medieval period, although all trace of the monastery has vanished, replaced in the Second Empire by more commercial grandeur. Figures of four of Lyon's most famous artists preside on the large central fountain. A trio of short, smart shopping streets fan out from the bottom of Place des Jacobins: ultra-chic **Rue Emile Zola**, most inappropriately named, is home to designer clothes shops, jewellers and very posh *pâtisseries*. To the side, **Place des Célestins** carries the title of another medieval religious order whose buildings have long gone, replaced by the swanky Belle Epoque **Célestins theatre**, recently renovated.

Looking enormously vacuous after the intense shopping streets to the north, **Place Bellecour**, one of the largest squares in Europe, measures a staggering 200 by 300 metres and originally served as a military training ground. It occasionally hosts major public gatherings now, but most of the time it feels as if it could do with more action. The lonely figure of an imperial Louis XIV trots across the red gravel square, like a royal out on a solitary early-morning ride. Below his lively statue, the river gods Saône and Rhône recline on lions, works by the accomplished Coustou brothers. Of the two matching pavilions on the south side of the square, one contains Lyon's tourist office; the other holds occasional art exhibitions. The flower stalls bring regular life to this end of the square.

Just east on **Rue des Marronniers**, packed with people and restaurants, you'll find the biggest concentration of *bouchons*. Further major shopping arteries lead south. Broad, mainly pedestrian **Rue Victor Hugo** is full of familiar French and international brand names. Parallel **Rue Auguste Comte** draws wealthy shoppers in search of fine antiques and designer interior decorations, but anyone can get a taste for the luxuries of the high life by visiting the following twin museums on Rue de la Charité.

An old sock is clearly much more significant than simply any old sock when it has managed to survive since ancient Coptic Egyptian times. The splendid **Musée des Tissus** spreads its net very wide indeed, covering not just the famous silks of Lyon but also textile-making across the world, from ancient times to the present. The collections make the massive, modernized 18th-century **Hôtel de Villeroy** burst at the seams. The early Christian Copts were amazingly accomplished weavers, best demonstrated by wonderful funerary cushions celebrating a man's life, and by a masterpiece of cloth depicting fish swimming through shimmering waters. Moving swiftly on, Greek, Roman, early Persian (or Sassanid) and Byzantine periods are also represented. As regards Western Europe, the pieces go back about one thousand years. Perhaps the most remarkable medieval work comes from England: the 14th-century *Tree of Jesse*, utterly seductive with its string of coquettish, finger-pointing kings, and its still more flirtatious-looking Virgin. Back with the Middle East, the Persian and Turkish carpets from the 15th to 17th centuries are exceptional large-scale works, the delicacy of the Persian weaving astounding (look out for the elaborate depiction of Layla's story), while in the Turkish pieces the clarity of design stands out. Lyon's own silk-weaving tradition is splendidly displayed; its golden age came in the 18th century, when no one could match the skill of Philippe de Lassalle, whose cameo textile court portraits look like the most accomplished of paintings.

The neighbouring **Musée des Arts Décoratifs** focuses on Ancien Régime furnishings, but this, too, is a museum on a grand scale, occupying a mansion that retains its period proportions. The place was built for Jean de Lacroix, adviser to Lyon's Cour des Monnaies. He clearly amassed vast amounts of moneys for himself. One portrait shows him looking extremely chipper in fine costume;

**Musée des Tissus**
*t 04 78 38 42 00,*
*www.musee-des-tissus.com; open*
*Jan–Dec Tues–Sun*
*10–5.30; adm*

**Musée des Arts Décoratifs**
*t 04 78 38 42 00;*
*open Tues–Sun 10–12*
*and 2–5.30; adm*

07

Lyon | The Presqu'île de Lyon

many others show cheerful noblemen admiring the décor, all reflected in old mirrors. Splendid ceramics and decorative objects, including a head-spinning number of cartel clocks, stand on the gorgeous furniture. Some of the extravagant interiors have been moved here from other Lyon mansions. One of the most ornate shows scenes of Ovid's wild tales. Another is lined with detailed 19th-century wallpaper illustrating Lyon's riverbanks in that period. The museum is also particularly proud of its silver collections. The place is so stunningly furnished, it's just a shame someone doesn't sit down at one of the countless harpsichords on display and play!

West down Rue Victor Hugo, **Place Ampère** pays its respects to the great Lyonnais scientist (*see* p.122). The restored Romanesque **Basilique St-Martin d'Ainay** nearby formed part of a long-influential Benedictine abbey. The medieval builders incorporated the odd Roman cast-off into the architecture. The place retains enchanting Romanesque decoration, but was heavily restored in the 19th century, Flandrin and Fabisch adding many elements. This area offers a calm corner on the Presqu'île.

Join the Saône's east bank nearby and there's a quite fascinating riverside walk to take further south, peering down on lived-in houseboats, or yachts taking a rest on their journey north. You pass alongside the odd intriguing bar: **La Voile** is one of Lyon's trendiest spots, in summer putting out broad reclining chairs recalling decadent Roman ways. As to the flower-decorated former **La Sucrière** factory, it now serves as one of the major venues for contemporary art shows in Lyon.

Back in the middle of the Presqu'île, the very bustling, slightly seedy **Lyon-Perrache railway station** forms a barrier across the peninsula. Outdoor escalators lead up to it from **Place Carnot**, a refreshingly green garden. Huge statues stand out here; one represents Liberty stroking a big lion – made to celebrate the centenary of the Revolution in which Lyon proved so difficult to tame. Redevelopment is under way on the southern tip of the Presqu'île, a central piece of land, but one long dominated by factories, and rather neglected. The peninsula ends in a razor-sharp tip like a shark's nose. Across the Saône, the sizeable modern **Aquarium du Grand Lyon** overlooks the spit and a cat's cradle of major roads. Inside, enjoy big-screen showings of glamorous undersea adventures, exotic fish, and regional species, including the odd amazing huge catfish caught in the Rhône.

**Aquarium du Grand Lyon**
*t 04 72 66 65 66,*
*www.aquariumlyon.fr;*
*open Tues–Fri 10–6,*
*Sat and Sun*
*10–7; adm*

## The Croix-Rousse Silk-making Slopes

The Croix-Rousse hillside, named after a red stone cross that once stood up there, rises sharply to the north of Place des Terreaux. By the 19th century, the area had become synonymous with the silk trade that had turned this area into a hive of activity, nicknamed, in contrast to prayer-filled Fourvière, *la colline qui travaille*, 'the working hill'. The steepness of the Croix-Rousse slope was only emphasized by the sheer, soaring sides of the tall, severe blocks built specifically to house looms, especially the mind-bogglingly complex but time-saving punch-card machines invented by local man Joseph Jacquard after the Revolution. These, however, did little to improve the lot of the ordinary silk-workers, known as *canuts*. Before the end of the 19th century, silk manufacturing plummeted and the area emptied. The neglected Croix-Rousse hillside is gradually picking up again, although a strange atmosphere reigns, a kind of eerie mourning for the vanished workers.

Before you start up the slope, spare a thought for the 80 Jews who were tragically rounded up in a purge in February 1943 immediately behind Place des Terreaux on **Rue Ste-Catherine**. Virtually all Lyon's silk-making traditions have vanished, just a few specialist companies still producing items for fashion houses and wealthy clients. One studio-shop you can visit, the **Atelier de la Soierie**, tucked into a courtyard just off the start of Rue Romarin, simply prints on silk rather than weaving, but the process is enthusiastically demonstrated.

**Atelier de la Soierie**
*open Mon–Sat*

There is a choice of routes up the Croix-Rousse hillside. If you head up from the western end of Rue Ste-Catherine, pause for a drink at one of the corner cafés on enchanting **Place Sathonay**, although the statue of an unsteady Lyonnais soldier in the middle acts as a warning against overdoing it. Pass via the little lion fountains up to the rather ignored third Roman theatre of Lyon, the **Amphithéâtre des Trois Gaules**. It has come down in the world since it served as the place where representatives of France's 60 Celtic tribes met under early Roman rule, and where St Blandine and other early Christian martyrs were fed to the lions in the 2nd century. The most direct route uphill, however, takes you via the **Montée de la Grande-Côte**, a shopping street presenting a gorgeous array of multicoloured façades with arcaded entrances. Break the unrelenting climb by taking a look at the long, flat perpendicular streets to the side, where you can unearth some original, independent specialist shops and cafés.

Further west along the slope, you get great views down on the Saône from **Place Rouville**, backed by the enormous **Maison Brunet** silk-house, with supposedly as many windows as days of the year, or from the shaded, terraced **Jardin des Chartreux**. Behind it, the school-surrounded, Baroque-domed church of **St-Bruno** has been receiving a major clean-up to lure visitors inside again with its glamorous Italian baldaquin and elaborately framed paintings.

Taking the eastern side of the Croix-Rousse slopes, a scattering of gay spots stand along the streets skirting east round the base of the hillside, extending along Rue Romarin and, across Place Croix Pacquet, into **Rue Royale**. Look along here and **Rue des Petits Feuillants** for atmospheric, trendy little restaurants. **Rue des Fantasques**, a little higher, offers a panoramic option, with spectacular glimpses of rooftops, the Rhône and far beyond.

Up in the streets just west, you'll encounter a mix of bars in what was the heart of the 19th-century silk-making quarters. The Croix-Rousse slope has been smartened up recently, although trendy-to-louche studenty and sleazy pubs and bars still hang around at the base of several blocks. Just before circular Place du Forez, the big **Condition Publique des Soies** on Rue St-Polycarpe was where silk was officially weighed in the 19th century.

The big, sober Ancien Régime church of **St-Polycarpe** dominates the end of the street. Close to it, off Rue Leynaud, **Passage Thiaffait** is the best example of a recently renovated passageway on Croix-Rousse, with cutting-edge designers opening challenging boutiques. **Rue Burdeau** above contains many massive *soyeux* houses; **Place Chardonnet**, along its length, honours Hilaire de Chardonnet with a statue, over-generously, given that he was one of the principal inventors of synthetic textiles, helping to destroy Lyon's traditional silk trade for good. Trendy venues and alternative designer boutiques have opened nearby.

Explore the 19th-century *traboules* or passageways signposted through the neighbourhood – shortcuts (albeit with many steps) to help the *canuts* carry their packages of silk around more easily. The most vertigo-inducing array of stairways is at **Cour des Voraces**, named after the silk-workers' guild that met here. Higher up, quiet, shaded **Place Colbert** offers wonderful views east, which are more unimpeded still on **Place Bellevue**.

An alternative does exist to climbing the Croix-Rousse hillside on foot: take the *métro*, or a *ficelle*, the latter leaving from below the Amphithéâtre des Trois Gaules. Once you've reached the Croix-Rousse plateau, you feel almost as if you've reached a separate big town. **Boulevard de la Croix-Rousse**, the broad, flat main street, hosts amazingly theatrical markets. Jacquard's statue stands in prominent position on **Place de la Croix-Rousse**, where fairs are frequently held. Other principal figures in Lyon's silk-making history stand out on the huge mural nearby.

Continue just a bit further north for Rue d'Ivry, on which stands the **Musée des Canuts**, where you can learn about the life of Lyon's silkworkers in times past and the importance of Jacquard's invention, as well as sometimes witnessing live demonstrations. Its shop sells silks produced in the region. Press a bit further north for Rue Richan where **Soierie Vivante** offers an alternative presentation on silk, together with a local silks boutique, in an old family workshop.

**Musée des Canuts**
*t 04 78 28 62 04; open Tues–Sat 10–6.30, guided visits at 11 and 3.30; adm*

**Soierie Vivante**
*t 04 78 27 17 13, www. soierie-vivante.asso.fr; open Wed–Sat 9–12 and 2–6.30, Tues 2–6.30, demonstrations at 2 and 4 daily; adm*

# Along the Banks of the Rhône

## The West Bank

Grand medical history dominates the Rhône's west bank through central Lyon, although walking along this side of the river you're severely limited by the very busy road and lack of waterside quays.

Heading south from the series of lively squares opening on to the Rhône above the **opera house**, the massive, grandiose façade of the **Hôtel-Dieu** makes by far the biggest impression on this bank, extending almost a quarter of a mile. First founded as a religious hospital in the 12th century, this place became recognized as one of the leading medical centres in Europe, and Rabelais practised here in the 16th century. The architect Soufflot designed the majestic river façade for it in the 18th century. The massive central dome came crashing down in the fight for Lyon's liberation in 1944, its restoration only completed in 1972.

**Musée des Hospices Civils de Lyon**
*t 04 72 41 30 42; open Mon 1–5.30, Tues–Fri 10–12 and 1–5.30, plus Sun in Oct–June 1.30–5.30; adm*

Make your way guiltily past doctors, nurses and patients, then up inside the dome, to visit the quietly fascinating**Musée des Hospices Civils de Lyon** . This covers the history of Lyon's pioneering medicine, for example its early work with the insane, trying baths in the Rhône to calm the patients. It presents pharmaceutical pots, exquisite *bourdaloues* (chamber pots) and historic equipment resembling torture instruments. It even serves as something of a fine arts museum, with its lavish wood-panelled interiors and devotional paintings; the latter were considered an essential part of the cure (or of salvation). Many were rescued from other historic Lyon medical establishments, like the former Hospice de la Charité.

**Place Antonin Poncet**, named after a 19th-century Lyonnais surgeon and connecting the Rhône to Place Bellecour, has a lone old bell tower that stands out mournfully, sole remnant of that pioneering Hospice de la Charité. A ground-breaking venture when set up by wealthy citizens in the 17th century to provide a soup kitchen for the city's poor, it grew into a fully-fledged hospital. In the 1930s a huge, austere **post office** replaced other dilapidated remnants; go inside to see startlingly bright murals on the history of Lyon, with gratuitous nudity thrown in for free. Restaurants with broad terraces line the square's opposite side.

Place Poncet looked rather sterile until recently. The little forest of thin white pillars that has suddenly sprouted up isn't simply an intriguing piece of contemporary art; it's also a **memorial** to what is generally described as Europe's first genocide of the 20th century, the massacre of Armenians by the Turkish authorities between 1915 and 1920. Many refugees came to live by the Rhône (for their story, *see* Valence's Centre Arménien, p.194). Greater Lyon now has a significant Armenian community, numbering some 45,000. But it also has many inhabitants of Turkish descent, some of whom protested at the inauguration in March 2006 of the memorial, which was even daubed in denial graffiti. The stones sticking out from the polished surfaces, as though caught in mid-flight, make onlookers think of terrible martyrdom.

Continuing along the river, you pass the smart modern block of the **Sofitel** hotel that replaced a military hospital. Bill Clinton stayed here during the 1996 G7 summit. The pomposity of the monument to the doctor-turned-influential-late-19th-century-mayor after whom **Place Gailleton** is named may look comical now, but his bust, framed within a triumphal arch, gives focus to this delightful square. Further south, the motorway hogs the Rhône's west bank to the tip of the Presqu'île.

## The East Bank of the Rhône

⭐ East bank of
the Rhône

The Rhône's flat east bank offers a truly splendid city walk, the comfortable riverside route stretching almost unbroken for five kilometres from the traditional Parc de la Tête d'Or in the north to the contemporary Parc de Gerland in the south. This bank is far better geared to *flâneurs* than the west bank; the broad quays on this side have been undergoing a fabulous revamp for the benefit of both walkers and cyclists.

On the north side of the Tête d'Or park, the new Rhône-side **Cité Internationale** quarter has been shooting up at a rate of knots in recent years. The latest addition is the **Palais des Congrès de Lyon**, which should startle participants arriving at this brand-new convention centre; it looks as if a flying saucer has landed in town. Major concerts and events will also be held inside. The smart cloned blocks just back from the Rhône-side path, which has been left a bit wild in parts up here, were designed by Renzo Piano, and provided with sharp flats and hotel, cinema and casino. The

**Musée d'Art
Contemporain**
*t 04 72 69 17 17,
www.moca-lyon.org;
open for exhibitions
only, Wed–Sun
12–7; adm*

somewhat older **Musée d'Art Contemporain** has been swamped by this large lifestyle statement, but the controversial contemporary art it regularly displays still shakes things up. The international **Interpol** headquarters look well protected on the southern end of the new architectural row.

The graceful **Parc de la Tête d'Or**, supposedly named after a story claiming that a golden head of Christ was buried here, was beautifully laid out in the 19th century, although the rose gardens above the deep green lake look a bit brash for British tastes. You might go boating around the string of islands, but be prepared for a shock – one of them (which can also be reached via a pedestrian subway) has a moving war memorial designed by Tony Garnier, dedicated to 10,000 dead; the extraordinary monument shows a dozen men carrying a coffin, the coffin dressed, the men naked. As for the park's free **zoo**, it has been undergoing modernization to give the animals more space. To the south, the **botanical garden** has preserved its grand array of period greenhouses, protecting a prestigious display of plants from across the globe.

Continuing south, you might explore the well-to-do quarters a bit east of the river, grandiose public buildings and Parisian-style apartment blocks interspersed with comfortable squares overseen by substantial 19th-century churches. **Cours Roosevelt** offers the most tempting shopping. Behind the Préfecture stands one of the most central of Lyon's Arab quarters.

The **Halles**, the food-crammed 1970s covered market some way east of Pont Lafayette, is where Lyon's demanding celebrity chefs shop, but also where crowds of Lyonnais come to stock up on fabulous produce, from regional cheeses to some frankly alarming-looking oversized local *saucissons*. Seafood features large too. Although the architecture is underwhelming, foodies and the faint-hearted swoon in front of the mind-boggling array of fine produce. Many shoppers perch at one of the unfussy bars for a tasty light lunch. Among the interesting new buildings nearby, cast an eye over the sleek contemporary **Palais de Justice**, or law courts.

The heart of the modern **Part-Dieu** business and commercial quarter looks more hackneyed now, but major buildings stand out. Unmissable, the **Crédit Lyonnais** skyscraper rises confidently above the rest, like a huge pencil about to write a big fat cheque in the air – the Crédit Lyonnais bankers were found to be acting with a pie-in-the-sky attitude before the company was taken over. The **Auditorium** is the major concert hall, in the shape of a shell. A vacuous piazza stands in front of **Part-Dieu railway station**, encased in polished red buildings. Opposite, domed skylights bring a bit of natural light into the huge, smart, but sterile **Centre Commercial** shopping mall. South behind the university quarter, you can explore Lyon's little Chinese quarter.

The joy of following the eastern riverside route down the Rhône is that you get fabulous views not just across to the Presqu'île, but also up to the buildings on the Fourvière hillside, dramatically lit at night. Riverboats are tied to the bank below **Pont de Lattre de Tassigny**, while the odd fisherman tries his luck. The jaded gardens of **Place Maréchal Lyautey** signal the start of Cours Roosevelt.

Major administrative and university buildings follow behind plane-shaded quays, including the grand **Préfecture**, headquarters for the Rhône *département*. The splendid twin riverside Olympic-sized **open-air swimming pools**, supplied by filtered Rhône water, make one of the most tempting stops in summer to swim and sunbathe. At night, student bars come to life along the broad pavements, while long cruise boats moor below.

Moving to a seriously harrowing subject, the **Centre d'Histoire de la Résistance et de la Déportation** at 14 Avenue Berthelot (east of Pont Gallieni) occupies the characterless yet chilling buildings of

**Centre d'Histoire de la Résistance et de la Déportation**
*t 04 78 72 23 11,*
*chrd@mairie-lyon.fr;*
*open Wed–Sun*
*9–5.30; adm*

07 | Lyon | Along the Banks of the Rhône

## Jean Moulin and Lyon in the Resistance

A plaque at the Centre d'Histoire de la Résistance recalls the thousands of Jews of the *département* of the Rhône tortured, executed and deported from 1942 to 1945. Jews weren't alone in suffering appallingly here, however. At the Ecole de Santé Militaire, numerous Resistance figures were tortured, most notoriously **Jean Moulin**, the movement's most famous figure. Speculation as to how he was captured in the town that became capital of the southern French Resistance dominate memories of Lyon in the war. But extremely important Resistance leaders were at work here before Moulin.

The Lyonnais captain **Henri Frenay** emerges as the most exceptional character among the Lyon-based groups, one of the few Frenchmen to set about resisting the Germans straight after the French defeat of 1940. By summer 1941, he had established an intelligence service and secret army, naming his group the **Mouvement de Libération Nationale**. It began printing its own newspaper, *Vérités* – the Centre emphasizes the importance of such clandestine publications. Frenay organized an alliance with another Resistance group, **Liberté**, run by **François de Menthon**, a right-wing Catholic Lyon law professor. Together, they formed **Combat**, the strongest southern Resistance group. The spikier **Emmanuel d'Astier de la Vigerie**, alias 'The Red Aristocrat', established **Libération**, the second-largest early Resistance group in the southern zone. Several Lyonnais pro-Communists joined him. This group also ran a famous newspaper. A third major Resistance group, **Franc-Tireur**, was also founded in Lyon.

In July 1941 Jean Moulin met Frenay, via an American agent, **Pastor Howard Lee Brooks**. Moulin also met with de Menthon before heading across the Channel in October 1941. In what was surely the most important meeting of all for the French Resistance, Moulin met Charles de Gaulle in London and the two men established the most extraordinary trust, the general-in-exile appointing Moulin as his sole representative in southern France, with the role of uniting the quarrelling Resistance factions.

This led to the foundation of the Resistance's united military wing, the **Armée Secrète**, and the **Mouvements Unis de la Résistance (MUR)**, in January 1943. Crucially, Moulin helped to establish de Gaulle as French leader-in-waiting, as opposed to General Henri Giraud, US president Franklin D. Roosevelt's preferred choice – Roosevelt detested the independent-minded de Gaulle.

However, the Gestapo was rapidly uncovering the Resistance's secret networks. On 21 June 1943 disaster struck in Lyon. Many Resistance leaders had been invited to a secret meeting in Dr Dugoujon's house in Caluire (north of the Croix-Rousse area) to appoint a new military leader for the Armée Secrète. The rendezvous was discovered, and the head of the Gestapo in Lyon, **Klaus Barbie**, came to arrest the group; controversy has raged ever since over whether Moulin was betrayed. Brave to the last, he revealed nothing under torture. At Barbie's trial in Lyon in 1987, he claimed that Moulin threw himself down a stairwell of the Ecole de Santé Militaire to try to kill himself rather than give away information. As for Barbie, he died in a French gaol in 1991.

Even if the majority of Lyonnais did nothing in terms of active collaboration or resistance during the war, most suffered from major food shortages. The most shocking story came from the Vinatier mental hospital: of its 2,890 patients through the conflict, 2,000 died of starvation or exposure.

the town's former military hospital, which the dreaded German Gestapo police force took over as its Lyon headquarters in the Second World War. The vital part played by Lyon in the Resistance is thoroughly covered at this excellent centre, which doesn't shy away from tackling collaboration and other difficult issues.

New buildings are going up fast further south. The **La Mouche** quarter's name acts as a reminder that the famous *bateaux-mouches* so closely associated with the Seine were originally made here in the mid-19th century, by Lyonnais entrepreneurs who took some up to a Paris Universal Exhibition. The **Parc des 4 Rives** has been recently planted with trees as well as funky contemporary architecture. The staggering former butchers' market, the **Halle Tony Garnier**, from the first half of the 20th century, has been turned into a major concert venue. You might end your walk at **Gerland Park**, home to Lyon's highly successful football team. Lyon's huge commercial docklands stretch away from here.

# Cinema and Invention in the Eastern Quarters

⭐ **Musée Lumière**
*métro line D to Monplaisir-Lumière stop; t 04 78 78 18 95, www.institut-lumiere. org; open Tues–Sun 11–6.30; adm*

Discover how cinema came into being at the **Musée Lumière** on clearly named Rue du Premier Film. This museum occupies the flashy **Villa Lumière**, nicknamed the Château Lumière by locals – you'll see why, and realize what a wealthy family the Lumières became. They were a greatly inventive lot. Antoine, father of Louis and Auguste, built up the family fortune selling photographic equipment before his boys came up with cinema (*see* p.42). Antoine loved planning grand houses to flaunt the family's success and enjoy the latest comforts; this villa was completed in 1902.

The Lumière company kept the property until the 1960s. Over the next decade, most of the other Lumière buildings around here were demolished, including the separate lavish villa which Auguste and Louis' families shared, and most of the factory. But it was here that the first cinema film of all time was shot – arguably the most important minute in the history of the moving image, showing the rather banal if engaging sight of Lumière company workers leaving at the end of their day. You can view this film, and many of the other earliest Lumière shorts, in the villa's basement. Although silent, they are accompanied by a delightful modern commentary. But at the start of your visit this museum puts the Lumière brothers' invention in period context, focusing first on pre-cinema attempts to produce moving images. The competition was stiff, the Lumières' greatest rival the American Thomas Edison. After inventing cinematography, the Lumières sent out company photographers to shoot images around the world, now on display in the sumptuous bedrooms. The centre puts on major cinematic events in the one factory building left. Joyously, this is the very building in front of which the first film of all time was shot.

*Musée d'Art Africain*
*nearest métro stop Garibaldi, t 04 78 61 60 98, http://perso. wanadoo.fr/musafrique; open Wed–Sun 2–6; adm*

Back along the great long, straight boulevards into central Lyon from Monplaisir, the **Musée d'Art Africain** at 150 Cours Gambetta holds collections on Black African societies.

*Musée Urbain Tony Garnier*
*t 04 78 75 16 75, www.museeurbaintony garnier.com; open Tues–Sun 2–6 (Sat in Mar–Oct 11–7); visits to the museum flat at 3, 4 and 5; adm; outdoor murals free*

Not too far south of both the above, the **Musée Urbain Tony Garnier** celebrates an influential 20th-century Lyonnais architect. Embracing modernity early on, Garnier conceived a highly regarded model industrial city. The Lyon authorities employed him on major projects from 1905. A firm believer in providing good-quality housing for the poor, he planned one of the first large-scale low-cost social housing estates in France, the **Cité des Anciens Etats**, built between 1929 and 1933, rebaptized the **Cité Tony Garnier**. A visitor centre introduces Garnier's work; the guided tour takes you inside one of the ground-breaking apartments; while outdoors 24 huge murals recall Garnier's main projects. The area is now named the **Quartier des Etats-Unis** – a US military camp was set up here in the First World War – to commemorate the crucial role American troops played in ending that appalling conflict.

## Tourist Information in Lyon

(i) **Lyon >**
*Place Bellecour, 69002 Lyon, **t** 04 72 77 69 69, www.lyon-france.com.*

The **tourist office** organizes themed guided tours, has a souvenir shop, and can book hotels (**t** 04 72 77 72 50). With a good-value **Lyon City Card**, valid for one, two or three days, you get free public transport, a free river cruise, and reductions or even free access to some museums, guided tours, concerts and the rare shop.

## Shopping in Lyon

(★) **La Cour des Loges >>**

(★) **La Villa Florentine >>**

The **Presqu'ile** between Place des Terreaux and Place Carnot is major shopping territory. Big brand-name and department stores stand along **Rue de la République** and **Rue Victor Hugo**. For the greatest concentration of luxury and fashion boutiques, plus one or two superlative food shops, explore the so-called **Carré d'Or**, or 'Golden Square', between Place des Jacobins, Place de la République, Place des Céléstins and Place Bellecour. For upmarket antiques and interior decoration, start with **Rue Auguste Comte** and **Rue de la Charité**. **Quai de la Pêcherie** by the Saône is interesting for stylish household goods.

On the lower slopes of **Croix-Rousse** hillside, seek out trendy new designers and quirky shops. **Vieux Lyon** across the Saône is more touristy, with lots of souvenir shops, Guignol puppet stores and the odd interesting boutique, several ethnic. One or two also specialize in silks.

East of the Rhône, foodies flock to the modern **Halles** (covered market). **Part-Dieu** has a huge typical international mall. For more stylish options east of the river, including the reputed Bernachon chocolate shop, try **Cours Roosevelt**.

## Markets

For food, the best are the daily Saône-side **Quai St-Antoine** displays, and the huge market stretching along **Bd de la Croix-Rousse**. The Sunday morning craft market on **Quai Rolland** west of the Saône is quite a delight.

On the east side of Parc de la Tête d'Or, the **Cité des Antiquaires** antiques market is open Thurs, Sat and Sun 10–7 *(10–1 in summer)*.

## Where to Stay in Lyon

**Lyon** ✉ **69000**

*Arrondissement* numbers are given after the street addresses. Change the final zero of the basic Lyon postcode for the *arrondissement* postcodes.

****La Cour des Loges**, 2 Rue du Bœuf, 5e, **t** 04 72 77 44 44, *www.courdesloges. com* (€€€€€). Rival of Villa Florentine, but far below it in the Renaissance quarter, offering a stunning mix of historic architecture and modern design, including Lyon silks. Exclusive restaurant (€€€€); trendy bar.

****La Villa Florentine**, 25 Montée St-Barthélémy, 5e, **t** 04 72 56 56 56, *www.villaflorentine.com* (€€€€€). Exclusive location high on Fourvière hill, in a former convent converted into an Italianate delight. Pool. Enjoy the views from the excellent restaurant, **Les Terrasses de Lyon** (€€€€; *open eves only Mon–Sat*).

*****Lyon Métropole**, 85 Quai J.Gillet, 4e, **t** 04 72 10 44 44, *www.lyonmetropole-concorde.com* (€€€€€). This 1980s hotel on the east bank of the Saône some way north of the centre has big, bright rooms between the river and its Olympic-sized pool. It claims to have the largest urban spa in Europe. Facilities include a large indoor pool and a hydrojet course. It also has 10 tennis courts. The terrace of the brasserie-style restaurant (€€) oversees the outdoor pool.

**Collège Hôtel >**

**\*\*\*Collège Hôtel**, 5 Place St-Paul, 5ᵉ, t 04 72 10 05 05, *www.college-hotel. com* (€€€). Exciting bright block turned new hotel, at the northern end of Vieux Lyon. Trendy, well-appointed, air-conditioned, deliberately slightly clinical but amusing rooms. Some have lovely terraces, those on the higher floors spectacular views over Vieux Lyon's roofs.

**\*\*\*Phénix Hôtel**, 7 Quai Bondy, 5ᵉ, t 04 78 28 24 24, *www.lephenix.warwick hotels.com* (€€€). In a beautiful Saône-side Renaissance building, a historic hotel that has been receiving guests since the 16th century. The rooms, some with fireplaces, have been renovated with style; air-conditioning.

**Auberge de l'Ile >>**

**\*\*\*Beaux-Arts**, 75 Rue du Président Herriot, 2ᵉ, t 04 78 38 09 50, *www. accorhotels.com* (€€€). Art Deco features, plus a few rooms decorated by contemporary artists.

**\*\*\*Carlton**, 4 Rue Jussieu, 2ᵉ, t 04 78 42 56 51, *www.accorhotels.com* (€€€). Its glamorous dome stands out in the Presqu'île's shopping district. The rooms have opulent old-fashioned style; some are moderately priced.

**\*\*\*Globe et Cécil**, 21 Rue Gasparin, 2ᵉ, t 04 78 42 58 95, *www.globeetcecil. com* (€€€). A stylish place where the rooms have individual touches.

**Nicolas Le Bec >>**

**\*\*\*Grand Hôtel des Terreaux**, 16 Rue Lanterne, 1ᵉʳ, t 04 78 27 04 10, *www. hotel-lyon.fr* (€€€–€€). Smartly renovated rooms in a classic central address, a tiny, cooling pool cleverly tucked in by the breakfast area.

**\*\*\*Hôtel des Artistes**, 8 Rue G. André, 2ᵉ, t 04 78 42 04 88, *www.hoteldes artistes.fr* (€€). Bright, quite simple charm by the Théâtre des Célestins.

**Pierre Orsi >>**

**\*\*Hôtel Bayard**, 23 Place Bellecour, 2ᵉ, t 04 78 37 39 64, *www.hotelbayard. com* (€€). Very central, with character and quirky décor.

**\*\*L'Elysée**, 92 Rue du Président Herriot, 2ᵉ, t 04 78 42 03 15, *www. elysee-hotel.com* (€€). Appealing, cosy little rooms at this traditional option.

**\*\*Au Patio de Morand**, 99 Rue de Créqui, 6ᵉ, t 04 78 52 62 62, *www. hotel-morand.fr* (€€). Enchanting, intimate, fresh rooms set around a peachy little courtyard close to the best shopping east of the Rhône.

**\*\*Hôtel du Théâtre**, 10 Rue de Savoie, 2ᵉ, t 04 78 42 33 32, *www.hoteldu theatre.online.fr* (€€). Good value, stylish, some rooms with nice views.

## Eating Out in Lyon

Greater Lyon's most famous restaurant, named after its world-renowned chef, Paul Bocuse, great patrician of French postwar cuisine, stands by the Saône below the Mont d'Or some 12km north of town, so you'll find its details on p.126. But 'Monsieur Paul' and his team have also opened up simpler, high-quality, good-value satellite brasseries around Lyon in recent years, each specializing in a different cuisine; *see* L'Ouest and Le Sud below, plus *www.bocuse.fr* .

**Auberge de l'Ile**, Ile Barbe, 9ᵉ, t 04 78 83 99 49 (€€€€–€€€). On its exclusive island up the Saône, an exceptional restaurant in historic buildings, serving exquisite seasonal dishes. *Closed Sun and Mon, and most Aug.*

**Léon de Lyon**, 1 Rue Pléney, 1ᵉʳ, t 04 72 10 11 12 (€€€€–€€€). Superb traditional regional cuisine in a warm, panelled, classic restaurant on the Presqu'île below Place des Terreaux. *Closed Sun and Mon, early May and most Aug.*

**Nicolas Le Bec**, 14 Rue Grolée, 2ᵉ, t 04 78 42 15 00, *www.nicolaslebec.com* (€€€€–€€€). The up-and-coming name in Lyon cuisine, the very inventive young chef here creating waves in his stylish contemporary restaurant. As so often with the big names, the lunchtime menus can be half the price of dinner. The chef also runs cookery classes. *Closed Sun and Mon.*

**Pierre Orsi**, 3 Place Kléber, 6ᵉ, t 04 78 89 57 68 (€€€€–€€€). Another classic luxury Lyon restaurant, just south of the Parc de la Tête d'Or, in a splendid historic house with rose-surrounded terrace. *Closed Sun and Mon.*

**L'Arc en Ciel**, 129 Rue Servient, 3ᵉ, t 04 78 63 55 00 (€€€€–€€€). Part of the Radisson Part-Dieu hotel, in a sensational location at the top of Lyon's tallest building, the Crédit Lyonnais skyscraper. Good food to accompany the great views and décor.

*Closed Sat lunch and Sun, and mid-July–mid-Aug.*

**Bistrot de Lyon**, 64 Rue Mercière, 2ᵉ, t 04 78 38 47 47 (€€). Traditional Lyonnais produce, plus a wide range of seafood, in a very atmospheric if jaded Belle Epoque setting.

**Brasserie Georges 1836**, 30 Cours de Verdun-Perrache, 2ᵉ, t 04 72 56 54 54 (€€). Huge, bustling theatre of a Lyonnais culinary institution behind Perrache station, the smart waiters putting on poised performances 24 hours a day.

⭐ **Les Muses de l'Opera** >

**Les Muses de l'Opéra**, 7th floor of the Opera House, 1 Place de la Comédie, 1ᵉʳ, t 04 72 00 45 58 (€€). Extraordinary opera-house rooftop location.

⭐ **L'Ouest** >

**L'Ouest**, 1 Quai du Commerce, 9ᵉ, t 04 37 64 64 64 (€€). Some way north up the Saône, in the up-coming Vaise district on the west bank, one of Paul Bocuse's stable, a stylish brasserie with a generous terrace, serving spicier, more exotic cuisine.

**Le Sud**, 11 Place Antonin Poncet, 2ᵉ, t 04 72 77 80 00 (€€). Another Paul Bocuse creation, offering flavoursome Mediterranean cooking, French brasserie style and efficiency, and a terrace just off Place Bellecour.

**Le Vivarais**, 1 Place Gailleton, 2ᵉ, t 04 78 37 85 15 (€€). For a smart meal on a lovely Presqu'île Rhône-side square. A still life animal may watch over you as you try regional specialities. *Closed Sat lunch and Sun, and most Aug.*

### Bouchons

*Bouchons* are Lyon's lively, unfussy little family-run restaurants serving simple, stocky regional food (including lots of offal) and wine at moderate prices. A *bouchon* is normally a cork in French, but these restaurants specific to Lyon got their name from the first one being set up in stables behind the old town hall where horses were rubbed down, '*bouchonné*' in French.

**Bouchon du Musée**, 2 Rue des Forces, 2ᵉ, t 04 78 37 71 54 (€€). The original one, simple and buzzing; the traditional fare includes tripe.

**Au Petit Bouchon Chez Georges**, 8 Rue Garet, 1ᵉʳ, t 04 78 28 30 46 (€€). Some of the best *bouchon* fare in a delightful atmosphere. *Closed Sat, Sun and Aug.*

**Café des Fédérations**, 8 Rue Major Martin, 1ᵉʳ, t 04 78 28 26 00 (€€). Excellent hearty cuisine and atmosphere, overseen by a genial host and some alarmingly large *saucissons*. *Closed weekends, and late July–Aug.*

## Culture, Nightlife and Events in Lyon

For listings of what's on, try the tourist office's *www.lyon-france.com*; *Lyon City News* is its useful regular magazine. *Le Petit Bulletin* is a good free listings magazine that's widely available. Then there's *Lyon Poche*.

In this highly cultured city, Lyon's **Roman theatres** count among its most dramatic stages in summer, hosting a whole array of events in the *Nuits de Fourvière* programme. There are numerous other theatre venues, such as the newly restored **Célestins** theatre. Given that Lyon is where world cinema was born, look out for movie events through the year, particularly at the **Institut Lumière**. The **opera house** stages challenging, often brilliant productions. The modern **Auditorium**, home to the Orchestre National de Lyon, presents excellent music programmes. The **Halle Tony Garnier** makes a huge atmospheric venue for pop concerts. The latest major venue is the flying-saucer **Palais des Congrès** (*see* p.88).

Further concert and theatre venues are peppered across the city. For dance, look at **Maison de la Danse**. Lyon hosts major cultural **Biennales**, the next ones on contemporary art in 2007 and 2009, dance and marionettes in 2008 and 2010.

You can swim in the twin Olympic-sized **outdoor pools** on the east bank (*see* p.89). A new annual summer attraction is the *Fête des Guinguettes* in mid-July, when the riversides make merry, and a beach is even laid by the Rhône. Lyon is always beautifully lit at night, but puts on spectacular illuminations over several days around 8 Dec, the *Festival des Lumières*.

Some of the liveliest spots for nightlife include the area around the lower slopes of Croix-Rousse and the Rhône's east bank; Vieux Lyon is more touristy.

# Bresse and Dombes

*Lowlands of the Rhône-Alpes, the Bresse and Dombes lie quietly across the Saône river from the ebullient wine-making hills of the Mâconnais and Beaujolais. In these flatlands, however, the culinary arts reach the highest peaks. These areas are famed for excellent restaurants, the Bresse being especially renowned for its white chickens roaming free in lush green fields. Another uplifting sight in these parts is the tombs at Brou's monastery outside capital Bourg-en-Bresse.*

*The Dombes, with its hundreds of lakes, is a haven for migrating birds, but masses of species remain on display year-round in Europe's largest bird park. Quaint brick villages lie scattered across the area; Châtillon-sur-Chalaronne is exceptionally attractive, although the prize for prettiness usually goes to the pebbly and more famous Pérouges.*

## 08

### Don't miss

⭐ **Gambolling with Bressan chickens**
Farms near St-Trivier-de-Courtes **p.99**

⭐ **Bressan culture behind glass**
Musée de la Bresse **p.100**

⭐ **Death exquisitely idealized**
Brou monuments **p.101**

⭐ **A timber-frame extravaganza**
Châtillon-sur-Chalaronne **p.105**

⭐ **Gorgeous pebbly houses**
Pérouges **p.103**

*See map overleaf*

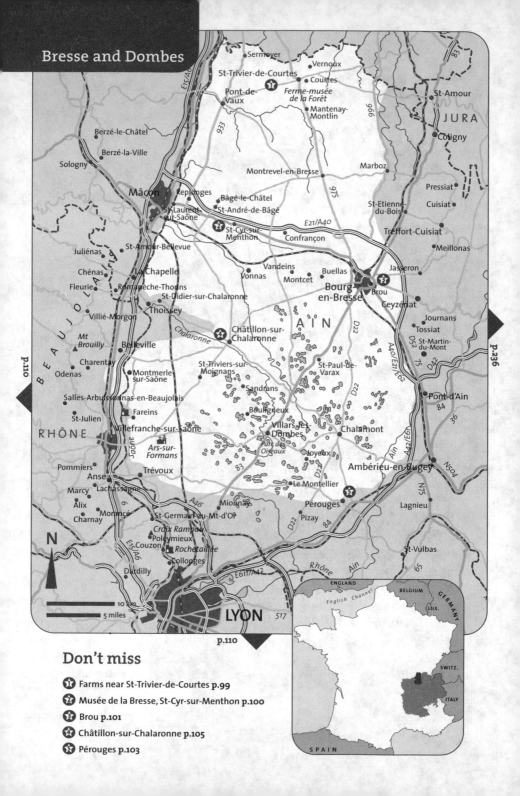

## Don't miss

⭐ Farms near St-Trivier-de-Courtes **p.99**

⭐ Musée de la Bresse, St-Cyr-sur-Menthon **p.100**

⭐ Brou **p.101**

⭐ Châtillon-sur-Chalaronne **p.105**

⭐ Pérouges **p.103**

The Beaujolais hill-dwellers used to refer mockingly to the *ventres jaunes* ('yellow bellies') of the Bresse, curiously boasting of themselves as the *boyaux rouges* ('red guts'). Here, to avoid any disputes, we keep Bresse and Beaujolais apart. The nickname may have related to the Bressans' farming wealth and their supposed habit of keeping their gold tightly in their belts; or perhaps it was a reference to the area's becoming major corn-growing territory when the crop was introduced from the Americas. *Maïs* came to have a thousand and one uses here. For example, the locals made *gaudes*, like polenta; they stored the cobs so as to decorate the exteriors of their farms in extravagant manner; and, in this culinary-mad land, they fed corn to their pampered chickens. Old traditions are upheld, and this is prosperous farming territory, even if a brief outbreak of bird flu in 2006 caused a small flap.

The name Bresse derives from *broussaille* – 'scrubland'; now its fields remain surprisingly green even in summer. Greater Bresse split in two in Carolingian times; the lords of Savoie came by its southern half in the 13th century, but in 1601 King Henri IV of France wrested it from the bellicose Duke Charles-Emmanuel,

## Capering Capons and Culinary Follies

French cookery excels in these flat lands of exceptional culinary traditions – and exceptional establishments too, such as those of Georges Blanc and the late Alain Chapel. It's a delight seeing flocks of white capons gambolling about green fields next to timber-frame farms from which corn-cobs hang in decorative bundles. These chickens are unique, having their own *appellation d'origine contrôlée* (for more information, visit www.pouletbresse.com). Britain's highly acclaimed contemporary chef, Heston Blumenthal, raved about the *poulets de Bresse* in his recent television series and accompanying book, *In Search of Perfection*, declaring them, after a comparative tasting, the chickens with the best flavour, and choosing them for his lesson in cooking the perfect chicken.

In the Bressan fields not all is idyllic, as natural laws still apply and predators such as foxes, weasels and crows kill roughly one third of the birds. When the chicks are about a month old, the males are neutered to remain adolescent capons, and both sexes are left to roam the fields. Along with their natural pickings, they are fed wheat, corn and milk supplements. After 16 weeks, they are usually enclosed and fattened for a fortnight, the female *poulardes* for slightly longer.

Their necks wrung, the birds are wrapped in a tight cloth so that the fat is absorbed more fully into the flesh; a few days later they are elaborately prepared for sale. This process reaches its macabre pinnacle for the big competitions held at Pont-de-Vaux, Montrevel and Bourg-en-Bresse – details include removing the final signs of plumes with tweezers. It is a great honour to win, and Bressan farmers see their highly prized (and highly priced) chickens as symbolic of the French quest for quality – their blue legs, white plumes and red crests even reflecting the colours of the French flag! For farms selling direct, look out for 'Produits de la Ferme' signs.

While the autumn ritual of emptying the Dombes lakes to extract fish is a fairly obvious, if muddy, event, the locals also delight in hunting down frogs – quite an art, even if more and more *grenouilles* on French menus are now imported from Eastern Europe. Rolled in flour, fried rapidly in the pan and served in a garlic butter sauce, frogs' legs are sometimes referred to as the fast food of the area.

For some of the most painstakingly elaborate cuisine in France, try the area's fabled restaurants. The almost legendary but practical-minded Georges Blanc is claimed to have had a special motorway exit made to speed foodies to his fabulous restaurant at Vonnas – a town with a mere 2,000 inhabitants! True or not, it indicates the passion, standards and even folly involved in producing the finest French food.

## Getting to and around Bresse and Dombes

**By air**: Lyon-St-Exupéry **airport** lies just south of the Dombes.

**By rail and bus**: Bourg-en-Bresse has good **rail** links with Lyon and Paris (2hrs by TGV). Mâcon, just in Burgundy, has a TGV stop outside town. For Pérouges, trains from Lyon go to Meximieux; then it's a 15min walk up the hill. For detailed **bus** services, see *www.multitud.org*, or *www.ain.fr*.

along with more mountainous Bugey and Gex to the east (*see* Chapter 14). All were joined together in modern times to create the *département* of Ain, pronounced like the French for one, '*un*'.

The Bresse remains divided between the regions of Burgundy and the Rhône-Alpes. We cover the latter half, centred around its capital, Bourg-en-Bresse. The culinary arts having taken on a predominant role, Bourg is now best known for its Bleu de Bresse cheese, but in the 16th century the building of its great church of Brou turned it into an artistic hotbed.

More than 1,000 lakes lie sprinkled across the Dombes, a flat clay plateau south of the Bresse, a secretive, soggy land between the Saône and Ain rivers. Herons colonize the *étangs* all year, and storks fly freely, while migrating birds love the area. Europe's largest bird centre is home to species from all over the globe. The traditional local culinary staples are lake fish and frogs' legs.

The Romanesque churches dotted around the Dombes show it was well inhabited in early medieval times, when most of the lakes were created. The area retained its semi-independence and regional court through much of the Ancien Régime; Trévoux, just north of Lyon, was its proud if improbable little capital. But it oversaw territories that were mainly dirt-poor, evoked in that brilliantly cutting French film *Ridicule*, which exposed the petty, pitiless court etiquette of Versailles compared with the serious desperation of an impoverished rural community racked by malaria.

Some places in the Dombes knew easier times in centuries past, however, such as the exquisite village of Pérouges. Here, many of the buildings are made of pebbles, but much of the architecture across these clay territories looks markedly different from the rest of the Rhône-Alpes region, as it is in brick and timber. For an architectural display to rival Pérouges, visit timber-frame Châtillon-sur-Chalaronne, happily situated where Bresse and Dombes meet.

# Chicken Runs into the Bresse

For a quietly charming introduction to the Bresse – the first, most northerly section of the Rhône-Alpes region if you arrive along the main routes from the north, down the busy A6 motorway or N6 main road from Paris – make for **St-Trivier-de-Courtes**, a tiny fortified town of traditional Bressan brick.

**① Bressan farms**

In the countryside nearby, look for a rather dispersed flock of fine old **Bressan farms**, a few still proudly displaying their *cheminée sarrasine*, the traditional, extravagant local behatted chimney. Comparisons with minarets are exaggerated, but you can see where they came from. The broad hearth below these chimneys was open on all sides to heat the multi-purpose main room, or *maison chauffure*. Only about 30 original chimneys still exist, but many timber-frame, brick and *pisé* (straw- and earth-covered) buildings survive, although some are in a poor state.

North of St-Trivier-de-Courtes, seek out more delightful typical farms just west of **Vernoux**, with white chickens running about in their fields. Nearby, at **Courtes**, you can visit the **Ferme de la Forêt**

**Ferme de la Forêt**
*t 04 74 30 71 89; open July–Aug daily 10–12 and 2–7; Easter–June and Sept–Oct Sat, Sun and public hols roughly same times, but check; adm*

with its **Ecomusée**. Although not in a forest, it dates back to the 17th century and retains all the elements so distinctive of Bressan architecture. Its rustic museum has real atmosphere.

The D975 leads south towards the capital, Bourg-en-Bresse. **Mantenay-Montlin** along here would be unremarkable were it not for its ten-metre high silver cockerel in front of the church. Nearby **St-Jean-sur-Reyssouze** prides itself on its flowers and its Romanesque church. Near **Montrevel** are two Bressan architectural gems, the traditional **Ferme de Sougey** and the **Manoir de la Charme**. Children and campers enjoy **La Plaine Tonique**, a large lake offering all manner of aquatic pursuits.

**La Plaine Tonique**
*t 04 74 30 80 52, www. laplainetonique.com*

As an alternative to cutting across the Bresse, you might head south via the Saône valley. Coming this way, just north of **Sermoyer**, the first village, the **Site des Charmes** presents an unexpected vista of natural sand dunes. The wide, flat ribbon of land that then extends south beside the river often floods in the wet seasons, and is mainly reserved for market gardening and fishing, although the Resistance laid out makeshift airfields here during the war.

**Pont-de-Vaux**, set back east of the flood-prone plain of the Saône, but linked to the river by a shaded canal, has built a smart new marina. For a leisurely river trip, embark on a day's cruise (*contact the tourist office*) from here to Trévoux. Pont-de-Vaux has long been a thriving market town, its valley position making it a rival to more distant Bourg-en-Bresse; and it is still a popular stop just off the main French route south. The central **Musée Antoine Chintreuil**

**Musée Antoine Chintreuil**
*t 03 85 51 45 65, www.pontdevaux.com; open April–Oct Wed–Mon 2–6; closed Tues; adm*

displays works by a local 19th-century landscape artist, plus ornithological exhibits, for once excluding chickens, although the town goes potty over its December *Concours de Volaille*.

Joined by a venerable old bridge to the imposing southern Burgundian wine centre of Mâcon, **St-Laurent-sur-Saône** has an interesting church housing some vibrant paintings. Turning your back on Burgundy and heading east, the few towers standing at almost-circular **Bâgé-le-Châtel** hint at this little village's brief role as the medieval capital of the Bresse in the 13th century. The main landmark is the church tower, rising to over 100ft. The soaring octagonal tower at neighbouring **St-André-de-Bâgé** recalls that the mighty abbey of Cluny, based across in southern Burgundy, was master here; the large, sober Romanesque edifice conceals lively medieval carvings.

Close to the motorway exit supposedly built for top restaurateur Georges Blanc, the extensive **Musée de la Bresse**, at **St-Cyr-sur-Menthon**, has been turned into the area's main tourist showcase. In one part, the **Domaine des Planons**, a beautiful, traditional farm with double-arcaded galleries, contains an exhibition on traditional farm life and a mini interior *son-et-lumière* presentation. Stables and barns form a further part of the exhibition, and a few animals, including white fowl, of course, bring life to the place. A separate striking sunken contemporary structure has been added in another area to cover aspects of Bresse culture in more detail, with displays on traditional ways and crafts, food and fêtes. The elaborate, colourful decoration Bressan women displayed at festivities was truly remarkable: chains, ribbons, lace and enamel jewellery appeared to be as many weapons in the female armoury to impress. The competition was clearly fierce...as it is between the fine chefs of the area, whose prowess often features in temporary exhibitions. There are also short **trails** to follow round the museum's estate. Farms at the nearby hamlet of **La Mulatière** provide further examples of picturesque Bressan architecture.

The village of **Vonnas**, south by the Veyle river, appears almost entirely devoted to Georges Blanc's famed restaurants and boutiques. There is also a **Musée des Attelages** in a converted old mill, presenting horse-drawn carriages from across Europe, and the trades formerly associated with them. It lies off the central village green, which is almost choked by flowers – the villages of the Ain *département* have become a little *parterre*-potty since the start of the French national flower competitions in the 1950s. At nearby **Vandeins**, an oriental-looking Christ greets you at the church. **Buellas** also has a characterful Romanesque church, its typical porch on wooden pillars known as a *galonnière*.

**②️ Musée de la Bresse**
*t 03 85 36 31 22; open July–Sept Wed–Mon 11–6; April–June and Sept–Oct Thurs–Mon 10–6; adm*

**Musée des Attelages**
*t 04 74 50 09 74; www. vonnas.com/musee.php; open mid-Mar–mid-Nov daily 10–12 and 2–6; adm*

## Bourg-en-Bresse and Brou

Bourg-en-Bresse, capital of the Bresse and, since the Revolution, of the Ain *département*, was through much of the Middle Ages a major outpost of Savoie. Briefly seized by the French king François I, the Bresse was returned to the duke of Savoie in 1559. A huge citadel matching the one at the new, safer Savoyard capital of Turin went up in Bourg to guard against attacks by the French – who laid siege to the citadel in 1600, and then largely demolished it.

Along Bourg's one or two lively shopping streets sloping down the hillside, the odd remarkable old timber-frame house has survived, while the mainly Gothic **church** stands out thanks to the bright Baroque towers added later. In the grand grey interior, the wooden stalls are carved with a joyous collection of saints, aristocratic faces, jesters and fighting dogs and dragons.

These pale alongside the artistic riches of the splendid triple-cloistered **abbey of Brou**, set in a historic suburb a mile east of Bourg. First visit the Flamboyant Gothic **church** signalled by its Burgundian-style, multi-coloured roof; the edifice went up between 1513 and 1532. The abbey's main benefactor, Marguerite of Austria (*see* box, below), is shown with her second husband Philibert de Savoie on the tympanum of the main façade. Beyond the outrageously ornate stone rood screen, the chancel displays sculptures of Marguerite and Philibert in a couple of the most elaborate and dignified tombs in France. The figures are each represented twice in idealized form: above in finery, overseen by classical figures and chubby naked *putti*; and below in death, with Marguerite's body wrapped in a shroud, Philibert's naked, rivalling Michelangelo's *David* in beauty. The tombs were designed by Jean de Bruxelles, the highly flattering main figures executed by the German sculptor Conrad Meit. The couple are depicted again in the splendid stained glass, devoted, somewhat understandably, given Marguerite's bad luck with marriage partners, to the theme of resurrection, and inspired by engravings by Dürer. The wooden stalls below depict intense biblical scenes, while the *putti* playing mischievously under the seats illustrate Man's vices.

Augustinian monks prayed for the lords of the land here up until the Revolution, when the place was just saved from destruction. Two of the cloistered **courtyards** contain further Gothic figures in stone, but the more rustic, cobbled third proves the prettiest. The vaulted main rooms and the cells around these cloisters have been converted into the Ain's main **fine arts museum**.

Medieval religious statues now fill the **refectory** with life. Amazing 16th-century paintings include a Burgundian triptych of

**Abbaye de Brou**
t 04 74 22 83 83, www.
culture.fr/rhone-alpes/
brou; open mid-
June–Sept daily 9–6,
April–mid-June daily
9–12.30 and 2–6;
Oct–Mar daily 9–12
and 2–5; adm

08 Bresse and Dombes | Bourg-en-Bresse and Brou

### Unlucky in Love, Lucky in Death

Marguerite of Austria was a woman of great importance on the European royal scene. One of the best-connected figures of the early 16th century, she was born in 1480, daughter of Holy Roman Emperor Maximilian and Mary of Burgundy, later to become aunt to both Emperor Charles V and King François I of France. Dreadfully unlucky with men, as a girl her engagement was arranged to the future King Charles VIII of France; still in her youth, she was jilted, for political reasons, in favour of Anne of Brittany. In 1497 she married the Infante Juan of Spain, but he died a few months later. Philibert le Beau of Savoie scarcely fared better, killed in a hunting accident three years after their marriage in 1501. Undaunted, Marguerite remained an exceptionally capable figure and became regent of Flanders for the future Emperor Charles V in 1507. At Brou she carried out her mother-in-law Marguerite de Bourbon's wishes and had the abbey rebuilt; she died two years before the church was completed.

St Jerome and a Flemish Christ flanked by utterly miserable angels, while Marguerite and Philibert crop up again, in less idealized fashion, in portraits. Some gruesome pieces feature large, for example one of two monks flagellating themselves, while Gustave Doré's depictions of Dante's *Inferno* looks like a massacre of old men in a gay sauna. But you can also enjoy some less disturbing Dorés and delightful local landscapes by Chintreuil. Utrillo and Utter also left colourful renditions of Rhône-Alpes scenery.

Serene contemporary pieces well suited to the surroundings stand out in the **cloisters** themselves. Local crafts have their place too, particularly in the form of ceramics produced in Meillonnas, a village reputed for its pottery (*see* p.242), situated on the wooded ridge of the **Revermont** that forms the eastern backdrop to Bourg. Incidentally, **Emaux Bressans Jeanvoine** is the one craft shop in Bourg still making the traditional Bressan bead-encrusted enamel jewellery that became particularly fashionable in the Belle Epoque.

An interesting outpost of the Bresse before the Revermont, **St-Etienne-du-Bois**, up the N83, was the cradle of the famous white-plumed Bresse chickens. A couple of stunning old timber-frame houses (which were often deliberately built to be easily transportable) have been moved here, to **La Maison de Pays en Bresse** ; one presents a traditional interior, the other traditional professions in an area that has clung on to Bressan ways – pluckily, it might be said. This cultural centre fights for the proud maintenance of traditions and culture in the Bresse.

**Emaux Bressans Jeanvoine**
*1 Rue Thomas Riboud, Bourg-en-Bresse; open Tues–Sat*

**La Maison de Pays en Bresse**
*t 04 74 30 52 54, www.maisondepaysenbresse.com; open April–Nov Mon–Sat 9.30–6.30 and Sun pm; adm*

ⓘ **St-Trivier-de-Courtes**
*Parc de la Carronière, 01560 St-Trivier-de-Courtes, t 04 74 30 71 89, www.st-trivier-de-courtes.com*

## Market Days in the Bresse

**St-Trivier-de-Courtes:** Mon am.
**Montrevel-en-Bresse:** Tues am.
**Pont-de-Vaux:** Wed am.
**Bâgé-le-Châtel:** Tues am.
**Vonnas:** Thurs am.
**Bourg-en-Bresse:** Wed am and Sat am.

## Activities in the Bresse

The area is very flat, so it offers easy, well-marked **cycling** and **horse-riding**, although Pont-de-Vaux goes mad once a year in August/September time for the **World Quad Bike Championships**. There are two **golf courses** south of Bourg. Saône **river cruises** are possible from Pont-de-Vaux – book via the tourist office. Montrevel's lake is very popular for **water sports** in summer.

## Where to Stay and Eat in the Bresse

**Vernoux** ✉ 01560
**Ferme-Auberge du Grand Colombier**, t 04 74 30 72 00 (€€). Among green, chicken-covered fields, a big renovated Bressan farm restaurant serving hearty fare cooked in its old-style oven. *Only open Thurs, Fri, Sat, and Sun lunch, plus public hols; always book.*

**Montrevel** ✉ 01340
***Hôtel Le Pillebois**, off the D975 between Montrevel and Attignat, t 04 74 25 48 44, www.hotellepillebois.com (€€). Modern, charming, well-priced country hotel, plus pretty restaurant (€€€–€€) and pool. *Restaurant closed Sat lunch and Sun eve.*
**Chez Léa**, 10 Rue d'Etrez, t 04 74 30 80 84 (€€€–€€). A classic, rigorously run, fine roadside stop for creamy Bressan cuisine in a smart dining

room packed with chicken decorations. *Closed Sun eve, Mon (out of season) and Wed, plus mid-Dec–mid-Jan and late June–mid-July.* The chef's sons run the simpler, neighbouring **Le Comptoir**, t 04 74 25 45 53 (€€).

### Sermoyer ✉ 01190
**Le Clos du Châtelet B&B**, t 03 85 51 84 37, *www.leclosduchatelet.com* (€€). On the Burgundy frontier, a magnificent 18th-century property. Delicious *table d'hôte* (€€). Pool.

### Pont-de-Vaux ✉ 01190
**\*\*Le Raisin**, 2 Place Michel Poisat, t 03 85 30 30 97, *hotel.leraisin@wanadoo.fr* (€). A sprawling, popular stop with plain, comfortable, modernish rooms and fine traditional restaurant (€€€–€€). *Closed Jan; restaurant closed Sun pm, Mon, and Tues lunch.*

### Replonges ✉ 01750
**\*\*\*\*La Huchette**, RN79, t 04 85 31 03 55, *www.chateauxhotels.com/huchette* (€€€–€€). Close to Mâcon, slightly dated, but with spacious, comfortable rooms. The beamed restaurant (€€€) has a good reputation. Garden with pool. *Closed part of Nov; restaurant closed Mon, and Tues lunch.*

### Confrançon ✉ 01310
**\*\*\*Auberge La Sarrasine**, RN79 t 03 74 30 25 65, *www.sarrasine.com* (€€€–€€). East of Mâcon on the road to Bourg, a Bressan farm converted into delightful, warm, refined little hotel with air-conditioned rooms. The

restaurant (€€€–€€) focuses on the best local specialities. Garden, pool, plus golf close by. *Restaurant open eves for hotel guests only; closed Wed.*

### St-Cyr-sur-Menthon ✉ 01380
**La Pilleuse B&B**, t 03 85 36 31 97 (€). Two lovely rooms in a hamlet of wonderful traditional Bressan buildings just 300m from the Musée de la Bresse, with a warm welcome.

### Vonnas ✉ 01540
**\*\*\*\*Georges Blanc**, t 04 74 50 90 90, www. *georgesblanc.com* (€€€€€–€€€€). For culinary brilliance plus chic contemporary rooms. A splendid new spa centre including indoor pool was added in 2006. Also outdoor pool and tennis court. *Closed Jan.*

**L'Ancienne Auberge de la Mère Blanc**, t 04 74 50 90 50 (€€€–€€). An extra Blanc inn in Belle Epoque style; offers simpler traditional cuisine. *Closed Jan.*

### Bourg-en-Bresse ✉ 01000
**\*\*\*Hôtel de France**, 19 Place Bernard, t 04 74 23 30 24, *www.grand-hoteldefrance.com* (€€). Central, on a charming square, a stylish stop-off since the early 20th-century. **Chez Blanc**, the attached restaurant, t 04 74 45 29 11 (€€), is a great place to try food from the Georges Blanc school.

**\*\*\*Le Prieuré**, 49 Bd de Brou, t 04 74 22 44 60, *www.hotelduprieure.com* (€€). Most rooms in this smart modern hotel look onto Brou church. Calm garden. There are restaurants near by.

---

*In left margin:*

⭐ **Georges Blanc >>**

ⓘ **Pont-de-Vaux >**
*2 Rue de Lattre de Tassigny, 01190 Pont-de-Vaux, t 03 85 30 30 02, www.pontdevaux.com*

ⓘ **Bourg-en-Bresse >>**
*6 Av Alsace Lorraine, 01005 Bourg-en-Bresse, t 04 74 22 49 40, www.bourg-en-bresse.org*

*In right margin (vertical):* **08 Bresse and Dombes | The Dombes**

---

# The Dombes

Quiet land of so many hundreds of lakes, southwest of Bourg-en-Bresse, the flat plateau of the Dombes extends between the Ain and Saône valleys almost to Lyon. Skirting round the densest region of Dombes lakes, the D22 route south from Bourg follows the Veyle river to **Chalamont**, one of the main centres for the popular tradition of horse-breeding in the Dombes, and preserving a little collection of old houses; at over 300 metres, it is also the highest point in the Dombes.

The D22 leads down to Pérouges. Coming by train from Lyon, you alight at **Meximieux**, a pretty enough little stop in itself. But tourist attention focuses on famously picturesque **Pérouges** up above. One story has it that the place name derives from the settling here

 **Pérouges**

of Romans from Perugia. It shares a defensive hillside position with that Italian city, sitting high on the edge of the Dombes plateau looking over the Ain valley. Today, despite the industrial sprawl from Lyon menacing even places this far away, the fortified village remains pretty well protected by its circle of ramparts, although at some stage it carelessly lost a whole outer ring of walls.

The astonishing, stern **church** was incorporated into the defensive inner ramparts, and even provided with gun holes. The long, tall Gothic interior contains striking wooden statues, including a tender *Madonna* offering protection to a crowd of figures within her cape. Pérouges was bitterly fought over between Savoyards and Dauphinois (to the south), notably in 1468, as recalled in a stirring quote on one gateway taunting the '*coquins*' (rascals) who failed to take the place by siege, even if they did apparently run off with doors and locks! Now the village happily welcomes hordes of visitors via both of its open old **gateways**.

Many of the houses have outside walls made of the same stones as the cobbled streets, as well as parts of timber-frame and brick; many date from the late 15th century, after the siege. The **Place de la Halle**, its splendid houses hung with decorative corn-cobs, lost its covered market to a fire in 1839, but its linden tree dates back to the Revolution, when it was planted as a symbol of liberty. You can peek into several interiors here, as many have been turned into craft shops or restaurants. Take refuge from the main tourist trade in the **Musée du Vieux Pérouges**, which gathers together pieces of local history in two of the grandest houses, one once belonging to the lords of Savoie. Its tower provides wide views of the area.

**Musée du Vieux Pérouges**
*t 04 74 61 00 88;*
*open April–Oct daily 10–12 and 2–6; adm*

The N83 cuts through the heart of the *étangs* of the Dombes and is the most direct route from Bourg-en-Bresse to Lyon. These lakes are all private and many of them are well-hidden. At **St-Paul-de-Varax**, though, the **Etang du Moulin** has an extremely large outdoor pool open to bathers alongside its fish-filled lake popular with anglers. On the **church** front, vestiges of the liveliest Romanesque carvings include an amazing image of a falling angel. The famed Lumière family, inventors of cinema (*see* p.42 and **Lyon**, p.91), had a **château** (*private; on the D17*) here where they shot one of their very first films, the comedy short *Le Jardinier arrosé*.

**Etang du Moulin**
*t 04 74 42 53 30*

The monks at the serious 19th-century Cistercian **Abbaye de Notre-Dame-des-Dombes** were involved in the transformation of the Dombes into a more healthy area at that time, and gave refuge to a number of Jews during the war. The monks have long made *masculine*, a curious mix of fruit jelly and raw meat. Romantically reflected in a lake further south, the ruined tower of **Le Plantay** draws admirers and artists. **Notre-Dame-de-Beaumont**, in its sweet location, overlooks the Chalaronne. Inside, a lovely series of Gothic wall paintings illustrate the life of the Virgin.

**Parc des Oiseaux**
*t 04 74 98 05 54, www.*
*parcdesoiseaux.com;*
*open July–Aug daily*
*9.30–7; May–June and*
*Sept daily 9.30–6.30;*
*Mar–April and Oct–Nov*
*daily 10–4.30; Dec–Feb*
*check by phoning; adm*

**Domaine du Grand Maréchal**
*t 04 74 24 54 96*

 **Châtillon-sur-Chalaronne**

**Musée du Train Miniature**
*t 04 74 55 03 54, www.*
*trainchatillon.com;*
*open mid-June–mid-*
*Sept and French school*
*hols Tues–Sun 10–12*
*and 2–7; otherwise just*
*Sat and Sun same*
*times; adm*

**Hospital**
*open as Musée*
*Traditions et Vie,*
*see overleaf*

Wild birds are attracted in huge numbers to the Dombes, but at the popular **Parc des Oiseaux** near **Villars-les-Dombes** birds from across the world, including even condors, are kept behind bars. Herons, storks and other 'locals' are free to fly rather tauntingly outside, but the modern aviaries, presenting some 400 species, are truly spacious. There are also observatories, a large hatching house explaining the park's breeding programme, and snack bars. Starting out from Villars-les-Dombes, the **Route des Etangs de la Dombes** in fact consists of two marked road circuits, discreetly signalling points of interest along the way.

Southeast, **Joyeux** offers a pretty picture of a typical Dombes village, while its 19th-century **castle** was one of a whole pack built then as hunting lodges for wealthy Lyonnais. Just south, the keep of the **Château de Montellier** typifies the medieval strongholds of the area, constructed on mounds known by the curious name of *poyps*. In the 14th century, this one was headquarters of the Thoire-et-Villars family, overlords of huge territories stretching from the Saône to Lac Léman; their possessions were later sold to the house of Savoie. Northwest of Villars towards Châtillon, from the road through the village of **Bouligneux**, you can spot one of the most impressive brick castles of the Dombes, set beside a lake; tomb effigies of the local lords lie in the church. **Sandrans** has another characteristic *poyp*, and offers horse-carriage rides from the **Domaine du Grand Maréchal**.

A forest of wooden pillars holds up the splendid dark **Halles**, or covered market, at the centre of **Châtillon-sur-Chalaronne**, a remarkable village full of the finest timber-frame and brick houses, many smothered with flowers. The covered market, dating back to the 15th century, measures a staggering 80m in length, and still hosts a great Saturday morning market. As to the central **church** with its steep roof, it looks as if it has been transported straight down here from flat medieval Flanders. Organ concerts take place regularly inside. At the far end of its Gothic interior, the stained glass added in the 19th century recalls a major Catholic Reformation figure of the 17th century, St Vincent de Paul. Although he stayed here for a mere five months in 1617, as a high-profile Catholic he used the time to found his first religious Confrérie de la Charité, a model for a whole series of foundations across France.

In the streets around the fabulous Halles, a series of craftspeople have set up studios in some of the prettiest shops. Back on the main square itself, the **Musée du Train Miniature** appeals not just to aficionados with its model trains and substantial displays across a whole kilometre of miniature track.

Pay a visit to the historic **hospital** just across the Chalaronne, signalled by a statue of St Vincent de Paul on the square in front. Its **apothecary** contains a well-preserved array of pharmaceutical

**Musée Traditions et Vie**

*t 04 74 55 15 70; open July–Aug Tues–Sun 10–12 and 2–7; April–June and Sept Tues–Sun 10–12 and 2–6; Oct–mid-Nov Sat and Sun 10–12 and 2–6; adm*

pots made in nearby Meillonnas (*see* p.242), while the emotionally draining, superb triptych of Christ's death and resurrection was commissioned by a rich tanner from Châtillon. A path then leads up past a former salt house held on wooden pillars to the modern **Musée Traditions et Vie** , presenting scenes of local rural life at the start of the 20th century. A hop and a skip further up the hill, you come to the remaining walls of the **castle**, built originally for local squires, but then for several centuries one of Savoie's main Saône frontier fortifications guarding against France.

# Along the Dombes' Saône Frontier

**Musée Vivant de la Plante Aquatique**

*t 04 74 04 03 09, www. lesjardinsaquatiques.fr; open Tues–Sat 9.30–12 and 2–6.30, Sun and public hols 2–6; adm*

**Château de Fléchères**

*t 04 74 67 86 59; open July–Aug 10–12 and 2.30–6; April–June and Sept–mid-Nov Sat and Sun 10–12 and 2.30–6.30; adm*

Delving in detail into the plant and animal life in the waters around this area, the **Musée Vivant de la Plante Aquatique** was set up, along with an aquatic plants shop, beside the Chalaronne's confluence with the Saône at **St-Didier-sur-Chalaronne**.

Given the kiss of life by the dynamic and determined Marc Simonet-Lenglart and his partner Pierre-Albert Almendros, the 17th-century **Château de Fléchères** lies a comfortable distance back from the Saône above **Fareins**. Built for a leading Lyon merchant, Jean de Sève, this 17th-century country mansion suffered a period of sad neglect, but has now made a fine recovery. Most excitingly, the new owners discovered whole expanses of original Italianate murals hidden under whitewash; Pietro Ricci of Lucca, a pupil of Guido Reni, spent the year 1632 decorating the interiors. The action-packed works include depictions of a fantasy hunt, but the most engrossing cycle portrays the labours of Hercules. Even if the classical hero looks a bit brutish, he is shown carrying out his mythological tasks with immense gusto.

To be declared patron saint of all the Catholic parish priests in the world – no, sorry, the universe! – is no mean feat for a humble country boy from the Saône valley, but that's what happened to the late Jean-Marie Vianney in 1929. A model of 19th-century peasant piety, he went from his birthplace at Dardilly (across the other side of the Saône – *see* p.122) to train for the priesthood in Lyon. There he was widely considered the most ignorant seminary student in the city, but his marked devoutness enabled him to become a parish priest. In 1818, he was sent to serve in **Ars-sur-Formans**, leading an exemplary life, serving the community with devotion, taking confession extremely seriously, railing against drinking and dancing. He may have survived mainly on a diet of potatoes, but he cooked up quite a stew of superstition, notably around the dubious vestiges of a supposed early Roman martyr St Philomena...and poltergeists – one of the latter supposedly set fire to his bed on one occasion. Despite his protests at the 'carnival' created around him, others couldn't stop promoting Vianney, and a celebrity cult grew up around him from 1830: special tours were organized from Lyon, and the number of his admirers reached huge figures by the time of his death in 1859.

The Curé d'Ars was then adopted for an overblown advertising campaign by the French Church, which ordered a grandiose new **church** in his honour, creating one of the most popular pilgrimage sites in France. Some half a million people still visit it each year. Its architect, Pierre Bossan, credited with Lyon's showy Notre-Dame de Fourvière (*see* pp.72–3), lent ostentatious Oriental touches to the new edifice here, although the plain brick tower of the old church was kept in place, sticking out like a sore thumb. Vianney's body has been preserved inside, his face coated in wax, while a more idealized statue of him stands in a niche surrounded by indecorous gilded *putti*. Once you've visited Ars, you won't be able to help noticing the Curé d'Ars' kind fox of a face in statues in countless churches around France.

Vianney's **house** has supposedly been preserved in the simplicity in which he kept it, plus cloying religious images. The hagiography gets carried away, with such signs as 'a cassock that the priest ironed himself'. For pilgrims who aren't sated, there's also the

**Historial du Saint Curé d'Ars**, a waxworks museum. A monument on the slope above the village recalls Vianney meeting a shepherd boy who helped him find his way when he first arrived. The priest supposedly declared, 'You have shown me the way to Ars; I will show you the way to heaven.' It's all rather too much for non-believers, but the place offers a flavour of fervent popular French Catholicism, and the fine views over to Beaujolais are there for all to enjoy.

Slope-side **Trévoux** surveys a wide bend in the Saône north of Lyon, a dangerous spot on the river, but an obvious point at which to extract tolls in medieval times. Now the place has the odd riverside restaurant serving river fish and frogs' legs and a popular port. Close to the water, in an historic building attached to the tourist office, the **Exposition sur la Filière en Diamant** displays the curious specialized local craft, developed by a Jewish community here, of stretching metal thread, especially gold. This was just one element that helped make the town rich in contrast to most of the rest of the Dombes, of which it was the tiny independent capital from the start of the 16th century to the eve of the Revolution.

During Trévoux's Ancien Régime golden age, it was ruled by a branch of the royal family and was granted its own Parlement, or regional law courts, lasting from 1676 to 1771. The place also became an important Catholic publishing centre. Grand houses stand along the steep roads up to the plain *Parlement*, now a more ordinary court, but daubed inside with pompous *trompe l'œil* and figures representing peace and justice.

**Historial du Saint Curé d'Ars**
*t 04 74 00 07 22, www.musee-ars.org; open July–Aug Tues–Sun 10–12 and 2–6, Mon 2–6; April–June and Sept–Oct Tues–Sun 10–12 and 2–6; Mar Tues–Sun 2–6; Nov–Feb Sat, Sun and hols 2–5; adm*

**Exposition sur la Filière en Diamant**
*open Mon–Sat 9.30–12 and 2–5, plus Sun and public hols in summer 2–5; adm*

**Trévoux Parlement**
*open Mon–Fri, except if court in session, 9–12 and 2–5; adm*

(i) **Dombes**
*www.ladombes.free.fr*

(i) **Châtillon-sur-Chalaronne >>**
*Place du Champ de Foire, 01400 Châtillon-sur-Chalaronne, t 04 74 55 02 27, www.ladombes.free.fr*

(★) **Clos de la Tour >>**

(i) **Villars-les-Dombes**
*3 Place de l'Hôtel de Ville, 01330 Villars-les-Dombes, t 04 74 98 06 29, www.villars-les-dombes.com*

(i) **Trévoux**
*Place du Pont, B.P.108, 01601 Trévoux, t 04 74 00 36 32, www.mairie-trevoux.fr*

(i) **Pérouges >**
*Entrée de la Cité, B.P.23, 01800 Pérouges, t 04 74 61 01 14, www.perouges.org*

(★) **Ostellerie du Vieux Pérouges >**

(★) **Alain Chapel >>**

## Market Days in the Dombes

**Châtillon-sur-Chalaronne**: Sat am.
**Trévoux**: Wed am and Sat am.

## Activities in the Dombes

The **Etang du Moulin** at St-Paul-en-Varax is popular for **anglers**, and has a major **swimming pool**. Several **golf courses** are scattered below Villars-les-Dombes, and there's one 10km from Trévoux.

For **boating** on the Saône around Trévoux, contact **Nautiboat**, t 06 18 31 62 67, *www. nautiboat01.com*. Guided Saône **river cruises** to Trévoux depart from Pont-de-Vaux (*see* pp.102–3) or from Lyon (*see* **Naviginter**, *www. naviginter.fr*, p.71).

## Where to Stay and Eat in the Dombes

### Pérouges ✉ 01800
★★★**Ostellerie du Vieux Pérouges** , Place du Tilleul, t 04 74 61 00 88, *www. ostellerie.com* (€€€€–€€€). Charming rooms spread out in several splendid buildings off the central square. Some rooms are rated four stars. The beautiful restaurant (€€€) is on the square itself. *Closed second half Feb.*

### Bélignieux ✉ 01360
**La Dépendance B&B**, 155 Chemin de la Grange, t 06 76 79 68 03, *http://*

*perso.wanadoo.fr/ladependance* (€). An appealing, good-value, calm country stop outside a village just a few kilometres southwest of Pérouges. Good *table d'hôte* regional cuisine (€€). Pool.

### Châtillon-sur-Chalaronne ✉ 01400
★★★**Hôtel de la Tour/Clos de la Tour** , Place de la République, t 04 74 55 05 12, *www.hotel-latour.com* (€€€). Close to the old town, with one part (the Clos) in a lovely restored mill in the local style, plus garden and pool. Restaurant (€€€–€€). *Restaurant closed Sun eve, Mon lunch, and Wed.*

**La Porte de Villars B&B**, t 04 74 55 41 32, *http://portedevillars.free.fr* (€€). Two pleasing, comfortable B&B suites in one of the historic gateways into the old town.

### St-Trivier-sur-Moignans ✉ 01390
**Domaine de Paspierre Pampra B&B**, t 04 74 55 90 29, *paspierre@free.fr* (€). Southwest of Châtillon, with great views and pretty rooms in a lovely restored farm. *Table d'hôte* (€€). There is a pool and tennis court in the shaded grounds.

### Mionnay ✉ 01390
★★★★**Alain Chapel** , RN83 t 04 78 91 82 02, *chapel@relaischateaux.fr* (€€€). Legendary restaurant (€€€€), as well as luxury rooms and a well-tended garden. *Closed Mon and Tues, and Jan; restaurant closed Mon, Tues, and Fri lunch.*

**Trévoux castle**
*open May–Sept daily afternoons; adm*

The remnants of a medieval **castle** in ochre stone stand further up the hillside. From on high, you can appreciate what an excellent viewing post Trévoux was, with its natural balconies overlooking the Saône, but quite hidden from view from nearby Lyon by the heights of the Mont d'Or (*see* p.121). However, you can enjoy a river cruise from central Lyon up the Saône to Trévoux (*see* above).

# Beaujolais

*Sloshing across big curvaceous hills west of the Saône, Beaujolais' vines swamp a swath of countryside between Mâcon, on Burgundy's frontier, and the Mont d'Or, within spitting distance of Lyon. The beautiful, brassy vineyards engulf the Beaujolais' hill villages, although the churches stand out in defiant positions, trying with their pencil-sharp spires to put forward some kind of a moral case in this clearly decadent landscape. Many a hilltop Beaujolais village is also overseen by its retired secular lord, the château, too world-weary to put up a fight against the waves of vigorous vines beating at the walls. Despite recent problems selling all the wine, Beaujolais remains a joyous viticultural area to visit.*

## 09

### Don't miss

*See map overleaf*

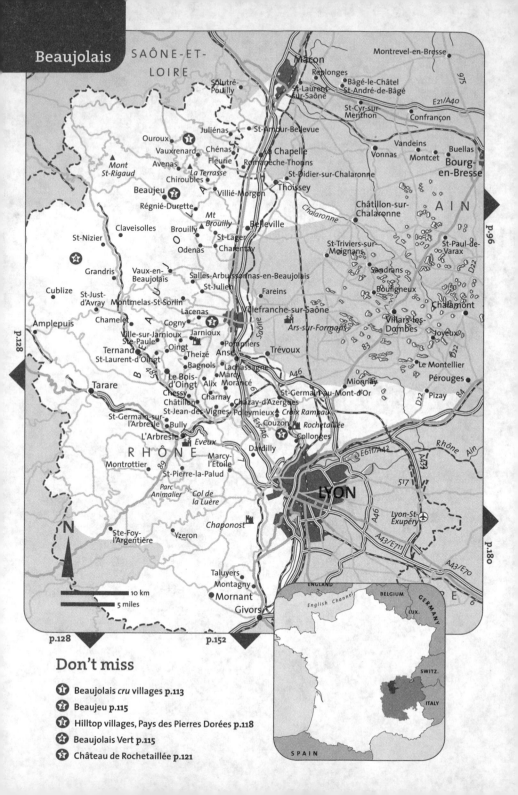

## Getting to and around Beaujolais

**By train**: The nearest TGV **railway stations** are at Mâcon and Lyon. Villefranche- and Belleville-sur-Saône also have useful stations.

**By bus**: For full, up-to-date listings of bus transport around these parts, consult *www.rhone.fr*; look under *transport*, then *les lignes de transport régulières*.

**By taxi**: For specialist tourist taxis, contact **Taxi Rollet**, **t** 04 74 69 63 11.

*Clochemerle*, a deliciously wicked novel of the 1930s (*see* p.42), raises to hilarious mock-epic proportions the petty rivalries that rack one fictional Beaujolais wine village, inhabited by a selection of caricatures from *cette race de vignerons montagnards*, 'this race of mountain winemakers'. They, and the real people of Beaujolais, live in this wonderfully inebriating, rolling Bacchic landscape.

Most of the best Beaujolais wines have traditionally been considered to come from the granite northern half of the area, in the triangle of land between Mâcon, Beaujeu and Villefranche. These include the ten top *crus*. Beaujeu, the historic capital from which the area took its name, has turned into a peaceful backwater, hiding out in the hills beyond the *crus*, but it has one of half a dozen *pôles œnologiques*, museums covering Beaujolais winemaking. The town of Romanèche-Thorins by the Saône also has a major wine museum, while workaday Villefranche, modern capital of Beaujolais, has recently been gifted an extensive collection of regional art, giving it a new cultural focus. South from Villefranche, the wines tend to get lighter, as do the exceptionally beautiful hilltop villages, built in delectable limestone, hence the nickname of the land of *pierres dorées*, 'golden stones'. You won't be able to resist the area's *villages perchés*, such as Oingt, Theizé, Bagnols or Châtillon. You can also unearth winemakers in these parts who have made a considerable effort to make quality produce here.

Press on west beyond the Beaujolais vine line and you leave the **Beaujolais Rouge** for the quiet, pine-forested Haut-Beaujolais, known as the **Beaujolais Vert** because of its greenery. The sober half of Beaujolais, it is an untouristy but beautiful area of logging hills, where small herds munch their way through the sleeply sloping meadows set below dark crests. In the Beaujolais Vert, the one tourist hot spot in summer is the cooling Lac des Sapins; otherwise it's a quiet land of craftspeople and craft producers.

In this chapter we also feature the Mont d'Or and the Monts et Coteaux du Lyonnais. The attractions of the first, the 'golden' mountain separating Beaujolais from the city of Lyon, include a museum in honour of local boy André Ampère, one of the most important collections of cars in France, and one of France's most celebrated restaurants. The Monts et Coteaux du Lyonnais, the continuation south of the sensuous Beaujolais hills, sidle round Lyon's western side; small surprises hide out here, such as

## Beaujolais – The Greatest of Gamay Wines

Beaujolais wine, jokingly referred to as Lyon's third river, along with the Saône and the Rhône, has one of the most widely recognized names in the viticultural world. The Beaujolais rectangle of vines stretching south from the Burgundian frontier measures just 60 by 20 kilometres, but produces almost as much wine as all of Burgundy put together (well, around 1,300,000 hectolitres a year to 1,600,000). While the name of Beaujolais may be very familiar, the variety of its wines proves complex, with 12 *appellations d'origine contrôlée*, not to mention the Beaujolais Nouveau, or *primeur*.

The earliest written record of vines in the Beaujolais dates from 956, although the area's vine-growers claim Roman roots. 'Nasty gamay' was the none-too-complimentary description said to have been used by the mighty 14th-century Duke of Burgundy, Philippe le Hardi, when he tasted some bad Beaujolais. But good gamay has been key to Beaujolais' success. It wasn't until the 17th century that vines became the area's main crop. The story goes that the giant Claude Brosse was responsible for an early marketing coup when he took a cartload of local wine to Versailles in the 1680s. Standing out from the crowd, his wine was tasted and approved by the Sun King.

Beaujolais remained mainly peasant wine-making territory, with few large estates, most of the smallholders bound to the landowners in a system known as *vigneronnage*. *Négociants*, wine merchants, took on the role of selling the produce. The wine was quaffed in vast quantities by the Lyon workers. On a health note, the town of Beaujeu is proud of the fact that its hospital began auctioning its wines for charity from 1797, a full 64 years before Burgundy's Hospices de Beaune followed suit.

In the 19th century, major crises that affected most wine-making areas in France also hit Beaujolais. First came pyralis, a grub more effectively dealt with by boiling water than by prayers to the Virgin of Montmerle, whose chapel lay on the wrong, east bank of the Saône anyway. When mildew attacked, the superstitious called for a Virgin to be planted in the Beaujolais; Notre-Dame du Raisin was erected in 1856 on Mont Brouilly. The credulous believed that Our Lady of the Grape solved the mildew problem; the rational put it down to copper sulphate treatment. In the 1880s, however, nothing could stop the spread of the destructive phylloxera insect, and many *vignerons* were forced into factory work. Local scientist Victor Pulliat became a national hero, halting the epidemic by grafting local vinestock onto resistant American vines, but then overproduction became a problem across the region.

After the crippling disasters of two world wars, the 1945 vintage was a classic, and a good omen. Since then, Beaujolais has enjoyed one of the greatest marketing successes of any French wine area, thanks, in large part, to its ruse, begun in 1951, of dashing out Beaujolais Nouveau each November – the temperature in the wine-making kept low, the fermentation shortened, the wine bottled in its infancy. Although the mad rush each autumn to export its *primeur* encourages widespread celebration, it isn't a recipe for giving Beaujolais a good image among wine connoisseurs. Yet Beaujolais' best-made wines can incite the loyalty of a lover.

Fashion models of the Rhône-Alpes wine scene, with their transparent ruby robes and often heady perfumes, the finest Beaujolais wines are certainly seductive. All Beaujolais red wines – and they are almost exclusively red – are made from gamay. In fact, Beaujolais produces most of the world's gamay wines. Further traditions bind all Beaujolais *vignerons*; even if the pruning and grape yields per hectare vary between the *crus* and the ordinary Beaujolais, all the grapes are harvested by hand. These *vendanges* often start late August, continuing through September.

The best-considered wines of the area, the ten *cru appellations* of Brouilly, Chénas, Chiroubles, Côtes de Brouilly, Fleurie, Juliénas, Moulin à Vent, Morgon, Régnié and St-Amour, only cover a small number of hectares each, but combined they make up roughly a quarter of all the Beaujolais wine produced in a year. They stick firmly to their individual identities and should have far more subtlety and staying power than the basic Beaujolais. They are at their best between three and seven years old. Experts detect raspberries, strawberries or cherries, peppery flavours, even cinammon, licorice and cocoa in mature *crus*. The more green-fingered fantasize about peonies, irises, violets and faded roses.

The territories of Beaujolais-Villages AOC, a cut above ordinary Beaujolais AOC, form a sometimes very thin coating around the 10 *crus* areas, although there are larger pockets around Beaujeu and below Odenas down to the D504, a road that serves as something of a north–south dividing line in Beaujolais wine quality. The 6,000 hectares of Beaujolais-Villages cover 38 parishes, producing roughly a quarter of all Beaujolais wine. A fair amount of Beaujolais-Villages Nouveau is made, too.

The plainer, simpler Beaujolais *appellation* wines come mainly from the vines south of the D504, in the gorgeous Pays des Pierres Dorées, although there's also a strip running down from Mâcon to Villefranche close to the Saône. With 10,000 hectares under vine, it produces about half of all Beaujolais wine, half of which is sold as Beaujolais Nouveau. The area has suffered from a reputation for sloppy vinification by too many winemakers, but through the 1990s efforts were made to buck them up, and some distinguished producers have emerged in these parts too. The new millennium has seen some great vintages, notably from the long, hot summer of 2003, although yields were low then. The excellent 2005 vintage was more generous. The 2004 vintage was a notch up from 2002.

For tastings, or *dégustations*, virtually every village has a general wine-selling cellar. Or pick out individual properties bottling their own production; a select number have been granted the label *Secrets de Terroir*, in recognition of their efforts to receive visitors warmly. The official Beaujolais website (*www.beaujolais.com*) includes details on taking Beaujolais wine courses; the **Ecole Beaujolaise des Vins** (t 04 74 02 22 18, *ecolevins@beaujolais.com*) at Villefranche-sur-Saône can organize them in English. To join in the Beaujolais Nouveau excitement, see *www.beaujolaisnouveautime.com*.).

fragments of Roman aqueducts, a wolf reserve, and a mining town that boasts the dubious honour of having been at the root of the Rhône valley's explosion in industry. Cherry orchards may be more common than vines down in these parts, but the area produces pleasant wines, like Beaujolais, made from the gamay grape.

# Northern Beaujolais

## Cru Territories between St-Amour and Beaujeu

🍷 **Beaujolais *cru* villages**

Let yourselves be lured into Beaujolais' gorgeous vinous hills travelling down the Saône from Burgundy, rather than taking the dull, flat valley routes. The most northerly *cru*, the very romantic-sounding **St-Amour**, is named after a Roman soldier who converted to Christianity. The place unsurprisingly plays on its name to sell the wine from its 310 hectares. **Juliénas** is a more substantial *cru*, its well-formed wines made across 600ha. It puts in a claim to being the place where vines were first planted in the Beaujolais. Above the often lively village centre, a big wine co-operative beckons; in this former church turned into the **Cellier de la Vieille Eglise**, Bacchanalian scenes are painted on the walls. Enjoy the views from the nearby Romanesque **Chapelle de Vâtre**. **Chénas**, smallest of the ten *crus* with just 280ha, produces peppery wines.

**Moulin à Vent Windmill**
*open in season*

A tempting stop, the **Château de Chassignol** contains the wine co-operative. The **Moulin à Vent** *cru* extends down from the village across 650ha to Romanèche-Thorins. It is regarded as the best Beaujolais for ageing, and develops, some say, hints of cocoa. Its name comes from a landmark 15th-century **windmill**.

**Hameau en Beaujolais**
*t 03 85 35 22 22, www. hameauenbeaujolais. com; open April–Oct 9–7; Nov–Dec and Feb–Mar 10–6; closed Jan; adm*

Down at **Romanèche-Thorins**, the most high-profile wine merchant in these parts, Georges Dubœuf, invites you on a major journey through Beaujolais wine at the **Hameau en Beaujolais**, also known as the Hameau du Vin, a plush modern museum bringing life to former railway buildings. The tour is a bit of a marathon, but crams a lot in, including slick films, one featuring a wine-tasting *tastevin* travelling round like a flying saucer. Recover with a tasting in the shopping area. Outside, the **Jardin en Beaujolais** cleverly combines horticultural scents with wine tasting.

Back up the vine-covered slopes, cheerful **Fleurie** benefits from a particularly open position and produces a very elegant Beaujolais from its 869ha; it also has the oldest wine co-operative in the region. The chapel perched high on the slope above was built in the 19th century as part of the superstitious efforts to protect the vines from various diseases. **Chiroubles**, the highest of the *cru* villages, stands in a delightful location too, below a theatre of vines. The wines made from its 370ha have marked floral touches.

*Chemin de vigne*
t 04 74 69 92 20 13;
April–mid-Sept free
guided tour Sat 3pm

**Vauxrenard**, behind Fleurie and Chiroubles towards La Terrasse, is a less well known wine village, but has laid out an educational wine trail, the*Chemin de vigne* , with explanatory panels leading you through its vines. **La Terrasse** offers one of the best viewing platforms over the northern Beaujolais. Pop over the hill to **Avenas**, a hamlet whose Romanesque church breathes the sobering air of a different age and contains a superlative early medieval altar, Christ appearing more like an emperor than a humble man.

**Association
Billebaudez en
Beaujolais Vert**
www.billebaudez.com

Scattered in the countryside around **Ouroux**, north of Avenas, go in search of many of the farms and sites in the**Association Billebaudez en Beaujolais Vert** , which puts traditional crafts to the fore. The **Col de Crie** pass has a **Maison d'Accueil** offering general information on such delights as goat's cheese-making, traditional bread- and jam-making, woodworking and logging. It is also a major starting point for walkers, riders and mountain-bikers. Beyond, **Mont St-Rigaud**, the highest peak of the Beaujolais, reaches just over 1,000m, but is easily reached by car.

Back among the vines, the flavour of rich red fruits is often detected by lovers of the larger Beaujolais *crus* south of Chiroubles. **Morgon**, extending across 1,100ha, often has more than a hint of cherries. At the centre of the quiet village of **Villié-Morgon**, the modest **Château de Fontcrenne** offers a tempting wine-tasting cellar. Down the vine slopes towards the Saône, the splendid towers of the medieval to Renaissance**Château de Corcelles** draw visitors to its highly commercial cellars. You also get to see the inner courtyard, kitchens and prison before the tasting.

**Château de
Corcelles**
t 04 74 66 00 24;
open Mon–Sat 10–12
and 2.30–6.30

The tall towers and rounded end of a grand 19th-century church stand out at **Régnié-Durette**, reminiscent of Notre-Dame de Fourvière in Lyon; the building was in fact designed by the same architect, Pierre Bossan. Several châteaux embellish the surrounding slopes, while the **Grange-Charton** proves an intriguing model wine farm owned by the Hospices de Beaujeu. The makers of Régnié's sharp red-berry-tasting wines fought long and hard to be declared a separate *cru*, achieving *appellation* status in 1988.

## Beaujeu

 **Beaujeu**

**Les Sources
du Beaujolais**
*t 04 74 69 20 56; open
July–Aug daily 10–12.30
and 2–7; Mar–June and
Sept–Dec Wed–Mon
10–12.30 and 2–6;
closed Jan and Feb; adm*

**Musée
Marius Audin**
*t 04 74 69 22 88; open
May–Sept daily 9.30–
12.30 and 2.30–6.30;
Mar–April and Oct–Nov
Wed–Sun 10–12
and 2.30–6; closed
Dec–Feb; adm*

**Huilerie
Beaujolaise**
*t 04 74 69 28 06; tour
by reservation; adm*

**L'Escargot
de Beaujeu**
*t 04 74 04 84 49; tour
by reservation; adm*

Hidden in the hills to the west, outside *cru* territory, Beaujeu became the medieval capital of Beaujolais after the first castle of the Beaujeu family was built on a rock high above the narrow valley here. Today, the little town looks slightly uncomfortably crammed into its tight location, the steep slopes above reserved for vineyards. Attention down below focuses around **St Nicolas' church**, the medieval edifice said to have gone up on the site of a lake where the son of Lord Guichard III of Beaujeu drowned.

On the same square stand two good museums. Behind its timber façade, the lively guided tour round the *pôle œnologique* of **Les Sources du Beaujolais** reveals the history of Beaujeu and Beaujolais using amusing modern techniques. The outstanding stone sculptures on display at the more traditional **Musée Marius Audin** were rescued from Beaujeu's château and church. The other place beyond the Sources for wine-tasting in Beaujeu centre is the **Caveau de Dégustation des Beaujolais-Villages**; or head out to individual properties in the hills.

Apart from sampling wines in town, the nutty aromas emanating from the **Huilerie Beaujolaise** incite visitors to enter this specialist shop near the centre, making highly-prized nut and seed oils the old-fashioned way. On the culinary trail, consider **L'Escargot de Beaujeu**, a snail farm on the Route des Echarmeaux.

# Southern Beaujolais

## Southern Beaujolais Vert

**Beaujolais Vert**

**Ferme de
l'Anneau d'Or**
*t 04 74 02 05 98*

In the hills west of Beaujeu, more members of the Association Billebaudez en Beaujolais Vert may tempt you to explore these pine-crested territories. The Lac des Sapins is the one spot that draws the tourist crowds in this otherwise tranquil rural world.

Getting on for 1,000m, **Mont Tourvéon**'s panoramic view is said to have appealed to 16th-century French star-gazer Nostradamus as a place to read the skies. Douglas pines were planted for logging in the Haut-Beaujolais in the 19th century; some that have survived around **Claveisolles** have been listed as historic monuments, one reaching 55m in height and claimed to be the tallest tree in France.

Cross the deep Azergues valley to explore some of the most beautiful territories of the Beaujolais Vert. The D54 provides a gorgeous rural route south. Outside **St-Nizier**, the **Ferme de l'Anneau d'Or** is a goat and cattle farm run by a handful of cheerful associates making prize-winning cheeses in a whole variety of pleasing forms. The D54 loops round the blissfully bucolic **Château de Pramenoux**, where you can stay (*see* p.125). Continue south for the picturesque villages of **Grandris** and **St-Just-d'Avray**, set on hillocks surrounded by higher, darker heights. Such villages seem to have avoided most of the incursions of the modern age.

Branch west along the D504 for the refreshing **Lac des Sapins** below **Cublize**. Little chalets have sprouted up along the northern end of this large artificial lake, with sandy beaches. Activities take place on and around the waters in holiday time, and country walks to discover the wider area and its food producers are regularly organized. The tourist office even doubles as a local delicatessen.

A quiet little country town, **Amplepuis** makes a song and dance about its links with Barthélemy Thimonnier, claimed as the inventor of the sewing machine, although his creation only used a single thread – it was the rival, two-thread machine created by his American competitor Howe that revolutionized the clothes industry. In a central chapel sweetly converted into the**Musée Thimonnier** , most of the space is devoted to a big collection of machines, but the place also boasts a big range of early bicycles.

**Musée Thimonnier**
*t 04 74 89 08 90; open Mar–Oct daily 2.30–6.30; Nov–Feb daily 2.30–6; adm*

## Brouilly and Southern Beaujolais-Villages

Back in Beaujolais wine territory, you come upon a 'mountain covered in vines', 'the Sinai of the Beaujolais' – a couple of the extravagant descriptions used by local author Gabriel Chevallier to describe totemic **Mont Brouilly**, its conical shape giving away its volcanic origins. The big Virgin-topped **church** was built in the mid-19th century on the summit, a sacred spot since pagan times, with inspiring views. The exclusive 320 hectares of the **Côtes de Brouilly** vineyards form a skirt right round the hill.

The more extensive **Brouilly estates**, making up the largest Beaujolais *cru*, with 1,300 hectares, radiate out in a wider circle lower down around the base of the hill, spreading across several parishes. Experts talk of raspberry flavours in these wines. **St-Lager** may have been given the grandiose title of *Ville Internationale de la Vigne et du Vin*, and claims to be 'capital of Brouilly', but it's really just a pretty village with charming manors nearby.

**Odenas** is signalled by the medieval towers of the otherwise 19th-century **Château de Pierreux**, but the greatest architectural treasure lies hidden in its own separate valley. A magnificently discreet aristocratic property, and also the largest wine estate in the Beaujolais, the **Château de la Chaize** dates from 1676, built up to its magnificent if windowless mansard roofs for François de Lachaise d'Aix, brother of Louis XIV's famed Jesuit confessor, Père Lachaise. Beyond the beautiful terraced gardens with their statues, topiary and white fences, the estate has 100 hectares under vine.

**Charentay**, east on the edge of Brouilly territories, has a charming Romanesque church and old houses. Local legend claims that the super-wealthy bankers of the crusades, the Knights Templars, hid their treasure in the nearby **Château d'Arginy** when they were persecuted by the jealous French king, Philippe le Bel, in the 14th century; at that time, Guichard de Beaujeu was nephew of the Templars' Grand Master, Jacques de Molay. All that remains of the castle is the intriguingly named **Tour d'Alchimie**, in soaring brick.

Leaving the territory of the Beaujolais *crus*, west of the rather misleadingly named town of **Belleville**, the **Pôle Œnologique Capvignes** is set in the restored little **Château de Bel-Air**, at the back of a modern viticultural college, and focuses on the stages of Beaujolais winemaking in entertaining manner. North of town, the **Maison des Beaujolais**, a longer-established *pôle œnologique* and a major Beaujolais wine-tasting centre, was deliberately placed by the busy N6 road at **St-Jean-d'Ardières**. It doubles as a restaurant, offering a moderately priced regional menu with wines thrown in.

A surprisingly grand Ancien Régime hospital, or **Hôtel-Dieu**, stands on Belleville's main street, now breathing a little tourist life into the place. Take the guided tour and you're shown the ornate pharmacy as well as the dormitory and chapel, and treated to descriptions of some of the startling 'medicinal' potions of the past. By the port, the **Maison de la Saône** concentrates on local flora and fauna, with seasonal exhibitions (*see* tourist office).

South of Brouilly, you enter the Beaujolais-Villages wine area. First stop for all has to be **Vaux-en-Beaujolais**, which has a very special place in many a Frenchman's heart, indelibly associated as it is with Gabriel Chevallier's *Clochemerle*, one of the cheekiest books in French literature (*see* p.42), published in 1934, about a battle over a *pissotière*. A huge success, one of the first French international bestsellers of the 20th century, it led several Beaujolais villages to argue over which one of them might have been the inspiration for the fictional, factional Clochemerle. Chevallier visited Vaux one day, and asked his café waiter where he could find Clochemerle, to which the young woman replied emphatically, 'But you're in Clochemerle here!' The author was won over, and Vaux has gone almost as far as rebaptizing itself.

Not one, but two **urinals** have been given special status in the village centre. The community has also just proudly opened a **Pôle Œnotouristique de Clochemerle**, celebrating the great author and his work. The story is condensed in six scenes played out in a little outdoor puppet theatre; inside, the museum shows that Chevallier was more than a one-book man. Born in Lyon in 1895, he was sent out for schooling in the rustic countryside a bit north of Beaujolais, then packed off to the war front. His first major book, *La Peur*, was based on his experiences in the First World War, among the first works to explode the myths of heroic warfare. Some regard it as his greatest novel, but he penned over 20 from his Lyon home. In 1956, he came to inaugurate the renaming in his honour of Vaux's main street, a day he declared to be one of the greatest in his life.

---

**Pôle Œnologique Capvignes**
*t 04 74 66 45 97; open Easter–Nov Wed–Mon 10–12 and 2–6; closed Tues; adm*

**Maison des Beaujolais**
*t 04 74 66 16 46, www. lamaisondesbeaujolais. com; open mid-Jan–mid-Dec daily 9am–10pm, earlier closing Mon and Tues outside July and Aug; adm*

**Belleville Hôtel-Dieu**
*open Mon 3–6, Tues–Fri 10–12 and 2–6, Sat 10–12 and 2–5; guided visits May–Oct Wed–Fri at 10 and 4, Sat at 5, plus July–Sept Sun at 5*

**Pôle Œnotouristique de Clochemerle**
*t 04 74 03 28 82; open Thurs–Tues 10.30–12 and 3–8, Wed 3–8 only; adm*

**09**

**Beaujolais | Southern Beaujolais**

The Beaujolais **tasting cellar** next to the museum is decorated with merry cartoons of scenes from *Clochemerle*. Museum and bar stand beside the attractive terraced village square set above a steep valley, its sides largely carpeted in vines. With the slump in sales of ordinary Beaujolais wine, the parishes around Vaux may be among the worst hit by a planned programme to remove excess plots, but this cheerful new tourist sight may help keep up the spirits of this delightful village so proud of its *pissotières*.

What a dignified contrast at **Salles-Arbuissonnas**. A religious atmosphere still permeates the air here, for this beautiful village centres round the buildings of a former medieval priory that came to serve as a finishing school for noblemen's daughters. **St-Julien**, below, celebrates its famous ancestor, Claude Bernard, the son of a vinegrower who became an eminent scientist in the 19th century, delving into the murky workings of the liver. As *le foie* is a subject of major concern to many a Frenchman, his work, recalled in the village's **Musée Claude Bernard**, is much revered. Defying this medical legacy, the local *chocolatier* makes tempting chocolates flavoured with Beaujolais wine!

**Musée Claude Bernard**
*t 04 74 67 51 44; open April–Feb Wed–Sun 10–12 and 2–5; closed Mon, Tues and Mar; adm*

The descendants of the treasurer to Anne de Beaujeu for whom the original **Château de Montmelas** was built still own this magnificent hilltop property with its many layers of fortifications, although the castle was largely redone in enjoyably extravagant neo-Gothic style in the 19th century. Church towers also stand out in the area, the one at the pretty beige-stoned village of **Montmelas** given colourful patterned tiles. Pilgrims and walkers head up to **Notre-Dame-de-la-Délivrance**, a Romanesque chapel at the summit of the **Signal de St-Bonnet**, with spectacular views.

## The Pays des Pierres Dorées

🛈 **Pays des Pierres Dorées**

Apartment blocks rising from the Saône valley signal Beaujolais' modern capital, **Villefranche-sur-Saône**. It took over in importance from more backward Beaujeu as early as 1514, by order of Anne de Beaujeu, the royal who ruled these parts by marriage at that time; she realized that its location made it more suitable as a regional headquarters. She saw to the restoration of the church of **Notre-Dame des Marais**, its ceiling covered with elaborate tracery and bosses. The town's cultural life has been given a boost with the opening of the stylish **Musée Paul Dini**, a grain exchange transformed to display hundreds of works by artists from Lyon and the Rhône-Alpes region from 1875 to the present, collected by the Dinis.

**Musée Paul Dini**
*t 04 74 68 33 70; open Wed–Fri 11–6.30, Sat and Sun 2–6.30; closed Mon and Tues; adm*

To begin a tour deep into Pierres Dorées territory, meander west from Villefranche along the Morgon river valley to **Lacenas**, its unmissable long 18th-century *cuvage* in typical golden stone used regularly for meetings of the Confrérie des Compagnons du Beaujolais, a fraternity that has fun promoting the area's wines.

**Château de Jarnioux**
*t 04 74 03 80 85; open 1–14 July and 15 Aug–30 Sept Tues and Thurs 9–12, Mon, Wed and Fri 2–6; adm*

South from **Cogny**, a sweet, deep-ochre village, the even more colourful **Jarnioux** cowers below its imposing, many-towered **château**, one of the most striking in the Beaujolais, long a stronghold for important Lyon families. Once past the two sets of fine gateways, you come upon a rather scrappy scene, however, a refined Renaissance wing knocked into by the later main block. A more characterful, older watchtower soars up on the other side to see over the hill. The few rooms you visit are sadly dilapidated, but if you're shown around by the owners their charm makes up for the decorative state. **Ville-sur-Jarnioux** has further gorgeous ochre houses. Its church is medieval, but the murals inside were executed by an Austrian soldier posted here after Napoleon's defeat.

**Château de Rochebonne**
*t 04 74 71 16 10; open May–Oct Wed–Mon 2–6; adm*

**Theizé**, to the south, makes a beautiful picture, overlooked by the imposing **Château de Rochebonne**, a grand classical castle that replaced an earlier one devastated in the Wars of Religion. Now it doubles as a *pôle œnologique*, with cellars devoted to the presentation of Beaujolais wine-making. Also take in the château's Ancien Régime features, including the *trompe-l'œils* in the lord's chamber.

Its round keep rising high above the village houses, **Oingt**, standing out on a hill to the west, competes with Theizé in the stakes for Beaujolais' most dramatic silhouette. The *donjon* offers a 360-degree view, but is all that remains of the medieval castle, destroyed by Protestants in the 16th century. However, the church built to serve the castle contains carved faces said to represent members of the medieval lordly family, a powerful line just one rung down from the lords of Beaujeu who long ruled over the Azergues valley. The lanes carry humorous old names, such as the Rue Trayne-Cul (Drag Arse Street). Craftspeople here include a painter, a potter, a wood turner and a weaver, and delicious smells waft out in the morning from the wood-oven *boulangerie*.

Continue west for **St-Laurent-d'Oingt**, its cemetery and church set apart among the vines, the edifice with a welcoming covered wooden porch known as a *galonnière*. North, **Ste-Paule** lies on a dramatic slope before you reach the Azergues valley, a medieval boundary of the Beaujolais. Perched on a high rock on the opposite bank, **Ternand**'s fortifications were built up for the archbishops of Lyon, major territorial lords in these parts in the early medieval period. Reds, oranges, blues and greens count among the colours of the local stone houses packed tight around the circular cobbled street, 'like grains in a pomegranate', the locals like to say. Enter the church via its charming *galonnière*. The interior has been spruced up, the church treasure now behind glass. Up the Azergues, at **Chamelet**, you can go picnicking with donkeys from the **Ferme de la Vieille Route**.

An old wine press stationed outside a hillside country winery at **Ronzières**, close to Oingt, signals an atmospheric little wine

**L'Histoire du Vigneron en Beaujolais**
*t 04 74 71 35 72; open July–15 Sept Tues–Sat 10–7; 16 Sept–June Sat only 10–7; adm*

museum, **L'Histoire du Vigneron en Beaujolais**, run by the passionate Jean-Jacques Paire. **Le Bois d'Oingt**, nearby, has retained a few remnants of its fortifications, but **Bagnols** boasts one of the best preserved of all the Beaujolais' castles (*see* p.126). Its long stone walls, gateways and drawbridge separate it from the village.

For a quicker trip from Villefranche-sur-Saône through the eastern Pays des Pierres Dorées, head down via Limas or **Pommiers**, with its ruddy stones and a church carved with entertaining country animals. **Anse**, by the Saône, once served as a Gallo-Roman garrison on the route north from Lugdunum. In medieval times, it became a strategic post for the archbishops of Lyon, as witnessed by its **Château des Tours**, holding a modest museum.

**Château des Tours museum**
*t 04 74 60 26 16; open Sat for tour at 3.30; adm*

**Tour Chappe**
*open mid-Mar–Nov Sun 2.30–6*

The D70 up above offers a wonderful route south. Kilometres of stone walls separate the sloping vineyards of the 19th-century **Château de Lachassagne** from its charming village. On the way down to the open village of **Marcy**, square **Tour Chappe** standing on its rise recalls the days before electric telegraphs when, in the first half of the 19th century, a network of 500 such towers was built around France to signal messages round the country.

Pressing south, **Charnay** can claim the grandest village hall in the Beaujolais, occupying part of the big castle in the centre, ordered once again for the archbishops of Lyon. The post office comes with machicolations too, and the castle roof glows with coloured tiles in the Burgundian style. The medieval church is dedicated to the patron saint of travellers, the helpful giant Christopher.

**Espace Pierres Folles**
*t 04 78 43 69 20, www.espace-pierres-folles.asso.fr; open Mar–Nov Tues and Thurs–Fri 9–12.30 and 2–6, Mon, Wed and Sun 2–6; adm*

Reaching the lower Azergues valley, beside the modest slopeside village of **St-Jean-des-Vignes**, the **Espace Pierres Folles**, the most southerly of the Beaujolais' *pôles œnologiques*, takes you back to the region's geological roots, extraordinarily rich in fossils. Surprisingly, the modern building housing the displays wasn't made out of the warm local stone, but from reasonably subtle cement. The reason for such architecture? It was sponsored by the giant cement manufacturer Lafarge, which owns many quarries in the region. Outside, a stretch of old quarry has been transformed into an interesting regional **botanical trail**.

The village of **Chazay-d'Azergues** has kept vestiges of its fortifications, one gateway overseen by the startling statue of a naked, muscular Roman soldier, long lance erect. The historic streets bear many other attractive little details. West along the Azergues, **Châtillon** looks particularly dramatic, its castle towers silhouetted above the river. Although the château is in private hands, you can visit the Romanesque chapel. At **Chessy-les-Mines** the wealthy village houses below the hilltop castle and church are explained by the long, lucrative tradition of copper-mining here.

On a height to the south, the **Carrières de Glay** were open quarries once exploited by local families to extract the golden stone. Abandoned, these left a big ochre gash in the countryside. You are free to wander round the site, with its explanatory panels.

Cherry trees start to pop up among the vines around these parts, presaging the Monts du Lyonnais. However, **Bully**, on the southern frontier of Beaujolais wine-producing territory, boasts the largest of all Beaujolais co-operatives, producing widely exported wines.

## Mont d'Or and the Monts et Coteaux du Lyonnais

Whereas a big flat plain extends east from Lyon, to the west, large, sensuous hills wrap themselves around the city.

### Mont d'Or

The Mont d'Or, a plump, golden-stoned mountain, separates Beaujolais from Lyon. The summit has been largely occupied by the French military, while the A6 and A46 motorways constrict it on either side. But, coming down from Beaujolais via Anse, you can pass under the mountain without taking the *autoroutes* by following the Saône-side roads, a delightful way to approach Lyon, under densely wooded slopes. This stretch of river is favoured by swans and has long been popular with Lyonnais wishing to escape the bustle of the city for some riverside family fun, with bathing areas and restaurants. Suburbia has now stretched out comfortably along the Saône too, although the odd village like **Couzon-au-Mont-d'Or** has retained a pretty old church in golden stone.

The main tourist attraction stands out on the steep east bank, the splendid-looking **Château de Rochetaillée** drawing attention to itself with its Burgundian-style coloured roof tiles. A medieval fort was originally built on the spot as a riverside post for the lords of the Dombes to exact tolls and guard this frontier between the Holy Roman Empire and France. In the 12th century the mighty Lyon religious authorities took over the lucrative property. Destroyed in the Wars of Religion, the castle was rebuilt in the 17th century, and later given its showy neo-Gothic makeover.

It has now become a startling retirement home for old automobiles, the **Musée de l'Automobile Henri Malartre**, with some of the most aristocratic and eccentric characters of the first generation of cars resting quietly in front of upmarket fireplaces. Up until the First World War, a period when France was the world's biggest car producer, Lyon could boast of being the second most important centre of production after Paris; the first Lyonnais car-making company was started up possibly by Marius Berliet.

Ironically, it was a car breaker, Henri Malartre, who from the early 1930s began gathering what is now one of the most important

⭐ **Château de Rochetaillée and Musée de l'Automobile Henri Malartre**
*t 04 78 22 18 80; open winter Tues–Sun 9–6; summer Tues–Sun 10–7; adm*

collections of original and old automobiles in the world. Celebrity numbers include a Lumière brothers Renault, General de Gaulle's Hispano Suiza used after the Liberation, and, most darkly, one of Hitler's armoured Mercedes. On a brighter note, view Edith Piaf's 1950s Pacard, and the Popemobile Renault Espace used by Pope John Paul II on his visit to France in 1986, which included Lyon.

Back down on the west bank of the Saône, **Collonges-au-Mont-d'Or** is home to Paul Bocuse's restaurant, famed across France (*see* p.126). To explore the more traditional Mont d'Or above, take the steep country roads up from Curis or Couzon to the unspoilt, golden-stoned village of **Poleymieux**, where you'll find the **Musée Ampère**, in the country retreat of the Lyonnais silk merchant whose son, André-Marie Ampère, became a household name across the world – it's in his honour that the standard unit of electric current is familiarly known as the 'amp'. He spent much of his childhood here, a precocious student, developing his exceptional aptitude for maths. The tragedies of losing his father to the Revolutionary guillotine and his first wife to illness caused him to leave for Paris, where he became a renowned scientist. The museum remains deliberately old-fashioned, with a very pleasant old-school feel and clear notices in English and French explaining Ampère's achievements. It also has very early examples of interactive displays.

**Musée Ampère**
*t 04 78 91 90 77, http:// musee-ampere.univ-lyon1.fr; open Wed–Mon 10–12 and 2–6; closed Tues; adm*

North above Poleymieux, the **Croix Rampau** is one of the four little peaks of the Mont d'Or, on clear days offering huge views east and west; but most of the Mont d'Or's heights are out of bounds, observation posts signalling the military's presence.

## The Coteaux du Lyonnais

The other side of the A6 motorway from the Mont d'Or, the slopes of the Coteaux du Lyonnais look over their shoulder towards Lyon, the traditional villages in this gently rolling territory, planted with Roman aqueducts, Romanesque chapels and vines, now expanding to make room for city commuters.

**Dardilly** was the childhood home of Jean-Marie Vianney, who went on to become revered as the very model of a parish priest (*see* 'Ars', p.106). The modest family house where he gave charity to the poor has been turned into a museum. The **Domaine de Lacroix-Laval** offers a grand contrast close by, near **Marcy-l'Etoile**. In recent years, this Ancien Régime château has become an increasingly important cultural outpost for the Lyonnais; the **doll museum**, once the main attraction, is now a sideshow, with huts where children can watch films. The **landscaped grounds** include a deer park and woods. Many events take place here, including garden shows and outdoor film screenings. The orangery now contains a smart restaurant. A golf course stands nearby, plus the swanky **Charbonnières casino and spa** and its glitzy **La Rotonde** restaurant.

**Domaine de Lacroix-Laval**
*t 04 78 87 87 00, www.lacroix-laval.com; exhibition open Tues–Sun 10–5; park open 6am–10pm; adm exc Thurs*

The engineering-mad Romans drew on the resources of the Lyonnais hills to provide Lugdunum with plenty of water, building an impressive network of **aqueducts** across the Coteaux du Lyonnais. Large sections were dug just under the ground, but the most substantial portion left standing above ground is at **Chaponost**, the impressive row of crumbling arches within view of the big city below. A trail marks out smaller fragments.

Small patches of vines also lie scattered around the Coteaux du Lyonnais' slopes, between L'Arbresle, touching on Beaujolais territory, and Givors, Rhône-side Côte Rôtie country. The **Coteaux du Lyonnais wines** gained their own AOC in 1984, the vineyards covering over 300ha. As in Beaujolais, the reds come from gamay grapes. A little rosé is also produced, and a little white. Cherry trees compete with the vines, and late-ripening blood-peach trees sometimes grow among the rows. In the south, some interesting Coteaux du Lyonnais estates lie around **Taluyers**, its former priory buildings resembling fragments of a castle. The **Domaine du Clos St-Marc** is one of the best to visit and, with 25ha under vine, one of the largest. **Mornant**, a sweet medieval village with a fine Gothic church, has preserved a painterly rustic fragment of aqueduct below its hillock, while there are fine views above **Montagny**.

## The Monts du Lyonnais

The Monts du Lyonnais line up behind the Coteaux du Lyonnais, forming a tall barrier between Lyon's Rhône valley and the upper Loire valley. The pretty little centre of **L'Arbresle** lies down in the valley dividing the Beaujolais from the Monts du Lyonnais. Three towers rise above the old centre, although an army of modern blocks has taken over the slopes above. The dilapidated 11th-century keep is eclipsed by a rejuvenated Gothic church containing lavish 15th-century stained glass. The third tower dates from the Renaissance. In the compact streets below, the grand houses boast coats of arms in stone. The **Train Touristique des Monts du Lyonnais** follows the tight river valley up to **Ste-Foy-l'Argentière**.

A monastery built on concrete stilts rises on the wooded heights above **Eveux**, L'Arbresle's neighbour. This **Couvent de la Tourette** is a concrete classic by the celebrated architect Le Corbusier; a bell tower precariously perched above the most severe and windowless of churches provides the first obvious sign of playfulness in the at first stark-seeming structure. (For more on Le Corbusier, *see* p.140.)

West of L'Arbresle, explore the cheerful cherry-orchard hills around **Montrottier**, a likeable hilltop town with tall houses curving round the outside, doubling as ramparts, and a huge covered market dating back to Louis XIV's time. South of L'Arbresle, it comes as a shock to discover that this bucolic area is partly responsible for turning the Rhône valley into such an intensely

*Train Touristique des Monts du Lyonnais*
*http://cftb.free.fr; open late June–late Sept Sun only; adm*

*Couvent de la Tourette*
*t 04 74 26 79 70; may be closed for restoration*

**09** Beaujolais | Mont d'Or and the Monts et Coteaux du Lyonnais

industrial zone. **St-Pierre-la-Palud** was a copper-mining town in medieval times, but in 1842 the Perret brothers bought the mines and worked out how to extract sulphur from the pyrite that ran in a thick seam under the town. Sulphur went on to become one of the main ingredients for the Rhône valley chemical industries, and by the early 1900s over 1,000 miners worked here. The **Musée de la Mine** covers its harrowing history and, on a brighter note, displays a huge collection of colourful minerals from around the world.

Continuing south through the Monts du Lyonnais, you can get lost in surprisingly rustic, steep country hills, quickly feeling transported away from any signs of the industrial valleys not far off. Hidden in its own deeply wooded, secretive valley, the **Parc Animalier de Courzieu** is largely devoted to wolves, the message being that they have been much maligned by man. Certainly the pack penned in here seems an apathetic bunch, the hassle of hunting removed for them. On afternoons when there are displays of falconry, the birds of prey have to work harder for their dinner.

Twisting hill roads lead up to the high village of **Yzeron**, where the **Maison de l'Araire** takes you back to rural life and the Monts du Lyonnais' Roman aqueducts.

Wending your way further south, beautiful wide views open out from the hillsides, but the deeply industrial Gier valley lurks down below. Descending towards it, the slopeside **Espace Zoologique de St-Martin-de-la-Plaine** draws large crowds. This substantial, well-run zoo was created in the early 1970s by a local man, Pierre Thivillon, who started by taking an interest in injured local wildlife. He and his wife then agreed to take on an orphaned baby gorilla. One thing leading to another, they rapidly expanded their zoo, inspired by British experts Gerald Durrell and John Aspinall; one gorilla has been as good as adopted by the Thivillons since being sickly and abandoned by her mother as a baby, and now goes home with them in the evening. The story has recently featured in a television documentary, *Un Gorille dans la famille!*

**Musée de la Mine**
*t 04 74 70 39 66; open Mar–Nov Sat, Sun and public hols 2–6; adm*

**Parc Animalier de Courzieu**
*t 04 74 70 96 10, www.parc-de-courzieu.fr; open Mar–Oct daily 10–7; displays pm; adm*

**Maison de l'Araire**
*t 04 78 81 07 79; open April–Nov Wed–Thurs and Sat–Sun 2–6; adm*

**Espace Zoologique de St-Martin-de-la-Plaine**
*t 04 77 75 18 68, www. espace-zoologique.com; open April–Sept daily 9–6; Oct–Nov and Feb–Mar daily 10–5; Dec–Jan check; adm*

(i) **Beaujolais**
*www.beaujolais.com*

(i) **Monts and Coteaux du Lyonnais**
*www. monts-du-lyonnais.org and www.coteaux-lyonnais.com*

## Market Days in Beaujolais

**Juliénas:** Mon am.
**Fleurie:** Sat am.
**Villié-Morgon:** Thurs am.
**Régnié-Durette:** Thurs pm.
**Beaujeu:** Wed am.
**Villefranche-sur-Saône:** Every am exc Tues and Thurs.
**Anse:** Fri am.
**Oingt:** Fri am.
**Le Bois d'Oingt:** Tues am.

**Bagnols:** Fri pm.
**Chessy-les-Mines:** Fri am.
**Châtillon:** Sat am.
**Taluyers:** Wed and Fri am.
**L'Arbresle:** Fri am.

## Festivals and Events in Beaujolais

Beaujolais's main wine festivals include *La Fête des Crus*, 1st weekend May, held in one of the *cru* villages, and *Le Marché aux Vins de Fleurie*, set over 3 days early Nov, with 40 leading *crus* producers gathering together. Beaujeu has the biggest and best Beaujolais Nouveau festival, including a **candlelit procession**, 3rd Thurs of Nov. The **Mont-Brouilly pilgrimage** takes place 8 Sept. The Domaine de Lacroix-Laval puts on a wide programme of events. Montrottier hosts a huge annual Easter egg hunt.

# Where to Stay and Eat in Beaujolais

## Juliénas ✉ 69840

**\*\*Chez La Rose**, t 04 74 04 41 20, *www.chez-la-rose.fr* (€€€–€€). Appealing traditional hotel on the square, with comfy rooms and cheerful restaurant (€€€–€€) or terrace. *Closed mid-Dec.*

## Chénas ✉ 69840

⭐ Château Lambert >

**Château Lambert B&B**, t 04 74 06 77 74, *www.chateau-lambert.com* (€€€–€€). A splendid 17th-century wine property with some spectacular vineyard views. The rooms are extremely smart, the atmosphere very cheerful. *Table d'hôte* (€€). *Closed Jan.*

**Les Platanes de Chénas**, at Deschamps, 2km north along D68, t 03 85 36 79 80 (€€€–€€). Merry, barn-like restaurant, its bright yellow walls hung with brash paintings. Plane-shaded terrace with vineyard views. *July–Aug open daily; closed Tues and Wed April–June and Sept–Nov; rest of year eves by reservation only.*

ⓘ Beaujeu >>
*Square de Grandhan, 69430 Beaujeu, t 04 74 69 22 88, www.beaujeu.com*

## Romanèche-Thorins ✉ 71570

**\*\*\*Les Maritonnes**, Route de Fleurie, t 03 85 35 51 70, *www.maritonnes.com* (€€). Charming house, rooms and garden with pool and tennis court. Good country restaurant (€€€) with more moderate *bistrot* menu.

## Fleurie ✉ 69820

**\*\*\*Hôtel des Grands Vins**, La Chapelle des Bois, 1km south by D119E, t 04 74 69 81 43, *www.hoteldesgrandsvins.com* (€€). A modern block amidst the vines, with decent rooms, plus wines for sale. Pool. *Closed Dec and Jan.*

**Le Cep**, Place de l'Eglise, t 04 74 04 10 77 (€€€). One of the best restaurants in the Beaujolais, but not pretentious, using fresh farm produce.

ⓘ Lac des Sapins/Cublize >>
*Lac des Sapins, 69550 Cublize, t 04 74 89 58 03, www.lacdessapins.fr*

*Booking essential. Closed Sun and Mon, plus Dec and Jan.*

## Chiroubles ✉ 69115

**La Terrasse du Beaujolais**, t 04 74 69 90 79 (€€€–€€). Tremendous views from a wonderfully located restaurant. *Closed Mon, and eves outside July and Aug, plus early Dec–Feb.*

## Avenas

**L'Auberge du Fût d'Avenas**, t 04 74 69 90 76 (€). Pleasing country cooking plus local woodwork displays. *Closed Mon; out of season closed Mon–Fri.*

## Villié-Morgon ✉ 69910

**\*\*Le Villon**, t 04 74 69 16 16, *le-villon@ libertysurf.fr* (€). Simple rooms with vineyard views from this big block of a building above the village château. Regional cuisine (€€€–€€), plus pool and tennis court. *Restaurant closed Sun pm and Mon out of season.*

**Le Clachet B&B**, t 04 74 04 24 97 (€€). East below Villié, one wing of this substantial farm set around a courtyard offers handsome rooms in sober contemporary style. This being an excellent Beaujolais wine-making property, stock up on Foillard vintages. *Closed Xmas–Feb.*

## Beaujeu ✉ 69430

**\*\*Anne de Beaujeu**, 28 Rue de la République, t 04 74 04 87 58 (€). Old-fashioned, comfortable provincial rooms in appealing central 19th-century townhouse with a courtyard. Grandiose dining room (€€€–€€) plus garden. *Closed Sun pm, Mon, and Tues lunch, and most of Feb.*

## Lamure-sur-Azergues ✉ 69870

⭐ Château de Pramenoux >>

**Château de Pramenoux B&B**, t 04 74 03 16 43, *www.chateau-de-pramenoux. com* (€€€–€€; *reductions for more than one-night stays*). Enchanting rustic castle at the end of a deep valley west of Lamure, with beautiful views east from its lordly chambers and terrace, where *table d'hôte* (€€) is served in summer. Occasional concerts.

## Cublize ✉ 69550

**La Voisinée**, t 04 74 89 52 60 (€€). Big, converted stone farm at the heart of the action down at the Lac des Sapins'

⭐ Château de
Bagnols >>

ⓘ Anse/
Beaujolais des
Pierres Dorées
Place du 8 Mai 1945,
69480 Anse, t 04 74 60
26 16, www.tourisme
pierresdorees.com

ⓘ Belleville/
Beaujolais-
Val de Saône
68 Rue de la
République, 69823
Belleville, t 04 74 66
44 67, www.ot-
beaujolaisvaldesaone.fr

ⓘ L'Ouest
Lyonnais
Domaine de Lacroix-
Laval, t 04 78 87 05 21,
69280 Marcy-l'Etoile,
ot.ouestlyonnais@
wanadoo.fr

ⓘ Villefranche-
sur-Saône >
96 Rue de la Sous-
Préfecture, 69400
Villefranche-sur-Saône,
t 04 74 07 27 40,
www.villefranche.net

⭐ Paul Bocuse
Auberge du Pont de
Collonges >>

ⓘ L'Arbresle
18 Place Sapéon,
69210 L'Arbresle,
t 04 74 01 48 87,
ot.paysdelarbresle@
wanadoo.fr

edge, serving hearty local fare. *Open mid-June–Aug daily lunch and dinner; then just weekends and public hols March–mid-June and Sept–mid-Dec.*

### Vaux-en-Beaujolais ✉ 69460
**\*\*Auberge de Clochemerle**, Rue Gabriel Chevallier, t 04 74 03 20 16, *www.georgeslagarde.com* (€). Rooms in a modern annexe, but traditional restaurant (€€€–€€) beside an old house with lovely terrace. *Closed half Aug; restaurant closed Tues and Wed.*

### Pizay/St-Jean-d'Ardières ✉ 69220
**\*\*\*\*Château de Pizay**, t 04 74 66 51 41, *www.chateau-pizay.com* (€€€€–€€€). Grand hotel on the vine slopes north of Belleville; smarter rooms in a wing of the 17th-century castle, modern ones in newer buildings. Restaurant plus courtyard for summer dining (€€€). Formal French gardens, pool, tennis court. With 62ha, this is one of the biggest Beaujolais wine properties, hence the wine shop.

### Denicé ✉ 69640
**Domaine Pouilly le Châtel B&B**, t 04 74 67 41 01, www.pouillylechatel. com (€€). The very welcoming Chevalier wine-making family run this charming property in vineyards a bit west of Villefranche, towards Montmelas, with excellent rooms and *table d'hôte* (€€). Pool.

### Villefranche-sur-Saône ✉ 69400
**La Grande**, 322 Rue de Belleville, t 04 74 60 65 81 (€€). Bright dining room and secluded courtyard off busy road; a lively spot to eat. *Closed Sat–Mon.*

### Theizé ✉ 69620
**La Ferme du Saint B&B**, Le Sens, t 04 74 71 15 48 (€€). Fortified farm with very nice old-style rooms. Pool and mountain bikes for hire.

### Oingt ✉ 69620
**Le Donjon**, t 04 74 71 20 24 (€€€–€€). Great views from the smart dining rooms, even better from the terrace, to accompany creative cuisine. *Closed Tues and Wed, and early Jan.*

### Bagnols-en-Beaujolais ✉ 69620
**\*\*\*\*Château de Bagnols**, t 04 74 71 40 00, www.bagnols.com (€€€€€). One of the most luxurious hotels in southeast France. Protected from village and vineyards behind beautiful walls, the medieval castle was fabulously restored for Lady Hamlyn. It is now run by Rocco Forte Hotels. Some rooms are adorned with historic murals. An ornate stone fireplace oversees the excellent restaurant (€€€€; *lunch is for hotel guests only*). Gorgeous terrace. Pool. Concert programme. *Closed Jan–mid-Mar.*

### Alix ✉ 69380
**Le Vieux Moulin**, t 04 78 43 91 66 (€€€– €€). Old stone mill converted into a tranquil waterside country restaurant with shaded terrace. *Closed Mon, Tues, and mid-Aug–mid-Sept.*

### Marcy-sur-Anse ✉ 69480
**Le Télégraphe**, t 04 74 60 24 73 (€€). Popular traditional village restaurant offering copious food. *Closed Sun, Mon, and Wed eve.*

### Morancé ✉ 69480
**Château du Pin B&B**, 600 Chemin de la Ronze, t 04 37 46 10 10, www. chateaupin.com (€€€€). Enchantingly restored fortified medieval manor overlooking vineyards and the Saône valley. Very smart rooms. *Table d'hôte* (€€€). Pool.

### Collonges-au-Mont d'Or ✉ 69660
**Paul Bocuse Auberge du Pont de Collonges**, t 04 72 42 90 90, www. bocuse.fr (€€€€€). Legendary French address run by the Lyonnais' most famous chef, his fabled, inventive cuisine served in a colourful restaurant just a road away from the Saône.

### Poleymieux ✉ 69250
**L'Auberge de Poleymieux**, t 04 78 91 90 16 (€). Delightful bargain village restaurant a short walk from the Ampère museum, serving traditional French menus, with pretty terrace. Reserve for evenings. *Closed certain school hols.*

# The Loire to its Source

*The upper reaches of the Loire offer one of the most wonderfully secretive yet dramatic retreats in rural France, hidden from view to east and west by ancient volcanic heights and beautiful small, blue-ridged ranges. There are broad, bucolic plains to cross, narrow gorges to slip through, and then the hill ridges to discover, strewn with medieval castle ruins and unspoilt villages. The architectural highlight is pilgrimage Le Puy-en-Velay, although the smaller towns have their own charm, while even industrial St-Etienne conceals cultural surprises.*

*Around the source of the Loire at the Mont Gerbier-de-Jonc, the area's spiritual dimension derives from nature's vastness. After the long, harsh winters, grazing herds emerge, mere specks on the huge slopes in summer.*

# 10

## Don't miss

⓵ **A burnished gold religious town**
Charlieu p.130

⓶ **Sublime slopes**
Forez hill routes p.140

⓷ **Modern art and modernist architecture**
St-Etienne and Firminy p.138

⓸ **Spectacular pinnacles**
Le Puy-en-Velay p.146

⓹ **Vast, timeless landscapes at the source of the Loire**
Mont Gerbier-de-Jonc and Mont Mézenc p.149

*See map overleaf*

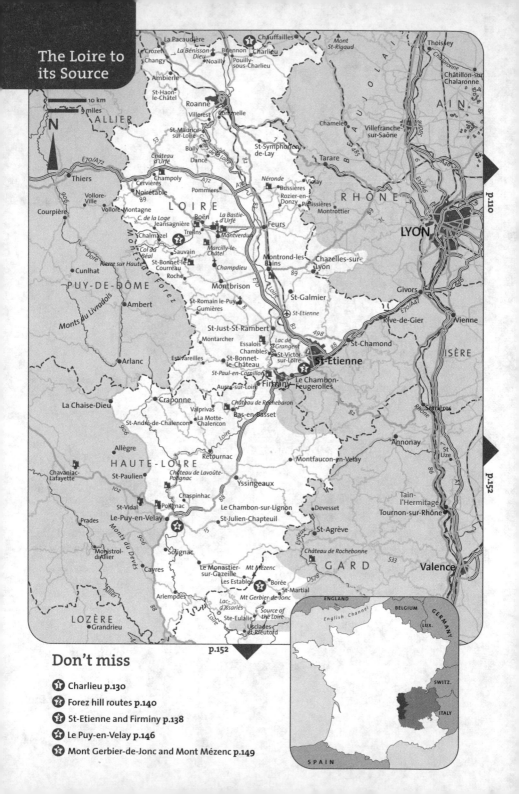

# The Loire to its Source

## Don't miss

⭐1 Charlieu p.130

⭐2 Forez hill routes p.140

⭐3 St-Etienne and Firminy p.138

⭐4 Le Puy-en-Velay p.146

⭐5 Mont Gerbier-de-Jonc and Mont Mézenc p.149

p.110

p.152

p.152

## Getting to and around the Upper Loire Valley

**By train**: Roanne station is useful for the north. St-Etienne has good connections with Lyon, 50mins away, and daily fast TGV train connections with Paris. Regular trains from St-Etienne serve the towns along the Loire valley, such as Feurs, Montrond, St-Galmier and Le Puy-en-Velay.

**By bus**: Bus services radiate out from the main towns. Check full details on *www.loire.fr* down as far as St-Etienne, and *www.cg43.fr* for services further south.

France's longest, most majestic river, the Loire, takes a stately 1,000km to travel from its source in the volcanic Ardèche mountains to the Atlantic, flowing parallel to but in the opposite direction from the Rhône and the Saône for the first stretch of its journey. We take you back along this section from the Roannais on the border with Burgundy, via the Forez and Velay, up to Mont Gerbier de Jonc, the green-bouldered giant from which the great river's first streams trickle. You travel across farming plains where horses and white Charolais cows graze, through tight gorges, past indolent slope-side villages and by more or less bustling towns to reach the volcanic heights, and even the odd volcanic lake, in which you can bathe on warmer days.

The most dramatic city of the upper Loire is Le Puy-en-Velay, churches and religious statues rising crazily from its surreal rocky pinnacles. Montbrison and St-Galmier offer gentler attractions, while former coal-mining St-Etienne has been declared a *Ville d'Art et d'Histoire* for its clutch of fine museums.

From the wide Loire plain, ruined medieval castles look down from the distant heights of the Monts de la Madeleine, Monts du Forez and Montagnes du Matin. Others startle you from much closer quarters as you pass through the Loire's gorges. However, the area's most famous château, the Renaissance Bastie d'Urfé, lies on the flat lake-strewn Forez plain.

Apart from Le Puy, other religious high points include Ambierle, Charlieu and wizened old St-Romain-le-Puy. At St-Bonnet-le-Château, the church conceals not only delicate murals but also sinister mummies, while nowadays the town is devoted to that all-pervasive French ritual – *boules*.

# The Roannais Loire and Monts de la Madeleine

After the religious vision in burnished golden stone of Charlieu, here we follow the once heavily working Loire upstream through Roanne and on to the Roannais gorges. We also venture into the dark hills of the Monts de la Madeleine, barrier in early medieval times between the Roannais, controlled by the counts of Forez, and the territories of the dukes of Bourbon – who eventually took over.

10 | The Loire to its Source | The Roannais Loire and Monts de la Madeleine

# Charlieu

**⓫ Charlieu**

**Centre des Visiteurs**

*t 04 77 60 09 97, www. amisdesartscharlieu. com; open July–Aug daily 10–12 and 1–7; Mar–June and Sept–Oct Tues–Sun 10–12.30 and 2–6.30; Feb and Nov–Dec Tues–Sun 10–12.30 and 2–5.30; closed Jan; adm*

'Monks were masters of the town,' a panel helpfully informs you in the **Centre des Visiteurs**, in case you've wandered through town with your eyes shut to reach this museum and visitor centre housed in a former Benedictine **priory**, the oldest religious establishment in a town once clearly packed with them. This *carus locus* ('beloved spot' in Latin, transformed into 'Charlieu' in French) developed one of the most glorious-looking collections of monasteries in southeast France, and a significant merchant community that thrived on the back of them.

The priory, founded in the 9th century, was rebuilt several times from the 10th onwards. It was terribly vandalized during the Revolution, large parts of it destroyed. However, its entrance, or narthex, has retained some of France's most memorable Romanesque carvings. Look out for the dumb, fleecy Paschal Lamb peering down from a patterned band so finely carved it resembles cloth, Christ appearing with more dignity in person below it. Elsewhere the wedding at Cana and the Transfiguration feature. Via the Centre, you can visit the priory's cloister, the chapter house and the priors' chapel, plus a small surviving section of the 11th-century church, with its own tympanum of the Apocalpyse, and an enchanting carving of the sun and the moon, the latter represented childlike, covering its eyes with its hands. The Centre also presents an overview of the various religious orders established in Charlieu down the centuries, and of monastic daily life in them.

In the streets nearby, fine stone and timber-frame buildings have been turned into tempting shops, such as the *chocolatier* Pralus in the ornate **Maison des Anglais**, English headquarters during the Hundred Years War. On Charlieu's main square, the 13th-century church of **St-Philibert**, its attractive tympana heavily restored, survived the Revolution better than the priory. It contains remarkable decorations, notably late Gothic stalls depicting beautifully robed, banner-carrying saints.

**Musée de la Soierie**

*t 04 77 60 28 84; open July–Aug daily 10–1 and 2–7; Feb–June and Sept–Dec Tues–Sun 2–6; closed Jan; adm*

Charlieu has a long history of weaving. In the 1820s, silk-making was established here: the workers in Lyon were kicking up a fuss, so more amenable rural labour was sought. The story is recalled at the **Musée de la Soierie**, housed in an 18th-century hospital. *Haute couture* dresses made in town and displayed here include an Yves St-Laurent leopard-print silk number created for Catherine Deneuve. Small pieces of silk are sold. Also in town, the **Musée Hospitalier** presents a somewhat sanitized version of hospital history, its rooms scented with medicinal herbs.

**Musée Hospitalier**

*as Musée de la Soierie*

**Couvent des Cordeliers**

*t 04 77 60 07 42; open July–Aug daily 10–1 and 2–7, April–June and Sept–Oct Tues–Sun 10–12.30 and 2–6, Feb–Mar and Nov–Dec Tues–Sun 2–5; adm*

Out in Charlieu's western outskirts is the 14th-century **Couvent des Cordeliers**. The church is typically Franciscan, big and plain, but contains fragments of Gothic paintings, while one side of the cloisters is enlivened by comical stone carvings of cautionary tales.

# The Loire through the Roannais

**Dhus barge**
*t 04 77 60 75 79; open June–Aug daily 10–12 and 1.30–7; April–May and Sept–Oct 1.30–7; closed Nov–Mar; adm*

**Les Marins d'Eau Douce**
*t 04 77 69 92 92, www.elphicom.com/ lesmarinsdeaudouces*

**La Bénisson Dieu church**
*t 04 77 66 64 65; open Easter–11 Nov daily 3–7; adm*

**Musée des Beaux-Arts Déchelette**
*t 04 77 23 68 77; open Mon and Wed–Sat 10–12 and 2–6; Sun 2–6; closed Tues; adm*

**Château de la Roche**
*t 04 77 64 97 68; open July–Aug daily 10.30–12 and 2–7; Mar–June and Sept–Oct Thurs–Tues 2–7; most of Nov Tues and Thurs–Sun 2–6; adm*

An old barge rests out of the water at **Briennon**, a port on the canal built parallel to the Loire in the 1830s, linking Roanne and Digoin (in Burgundy). The canal's working days, when Briennon was a big producer of tiles, are over, and most of the factories have disappeared, but you can take a tour inside the *Dhus* barge. The canal is now dedicated to pleasure boats – **Les Marins d'Eau Douce**, with an office close to the water, hires out boats for mini-cruises, but note that you have to set off from Digoin in Burgundy. However, you can book to play with model boats in the inventive **Parc des Canaux**, a water garden by the barge. Les Marins d'Eau Douce's shop sells local produce and has a minor exhibition of local tiles and pottery. Briennon's **church** stands well back, but its steeple stands out, brightened by Burgundian-style varnished tiles.

As for the enormous Cistercian **church** at nearby **La Bénisson Dieu**, topped by its bright tiles, it looks at first like a joyously vulgar Burgundian *pâtisserie*, but the fact that the soaring tower rising to one side was provided with arrow slits hints at less peaceful times. Inside, the worn medieval frescoes include an extraordinary image of Christ, inverted by light and time, his hair turned yellow, his body black. Baroque murals adorn a later chapel.

Formerly a textile town, working-class Loire-side **Roanne**'s trump card is Troisgros, one of France's most famous restaurants (*see* p.133). For the town's history, visit the smart **Musée des Beaux-Arts Déchelette**, in an Ancien Régime mansion. Its finest collections are of Gallo-Roman finds and political Revolutionary pottery.

South, in the Roannais gorges, hire boats at the little ports around the 30km-long **Lac de Villerest** created by the **Barrage de Villerest**, completed in 1982. Engineering enthusiasts visit the dam; the more frivolous play in pedalos. Along the west bank, the whole village of **St-Jean-St-Maurice-sur-Loire** seems ready to slip into the waters for a swim. It has a new port, but has retained a few picturesque medieval fortifications. The medieval figure painted on the outside of the church indicates that this lay on a pilgrimage route; inside, the Roman martyr Maurice is shown run through with a sword. The statue of St Nicholas recalls that he is the patron saint of the Loire mariners. **Bully** has another pleasure port, while **Le Pêt d'Ane**, a calm meander near **Dancé**, is a lovely spot.

A Romanesque church stands proudly above the vegetable plots in rustic **Pommiers**, part of a once-fortified priory, some of whose defences survive. The church was built in colourful stone, while the dark interior conceals Gothic wall paintings of Christ's life.

Following the Loire's east bank from Roanne, the road hugs the river to the spectacular neo-Gothic **Château de la Roche**, which stands in the midst of the waters, accessible by a low walkway. The interior includes exhibitions on river trading and the Villerest dam.

**Château de
St-Marcel-de-
Félines**
*t 04 77 63 23 08; open
July–Aug Sun and Mon
2–6; Easter–June and
Sept–Oct Sun and
public hols 2–6; adm*

**Musée du Tissage**
*t 04 77 27 33 95; open
July–Aug daily 3–6;
Mar–June and Sept–Oct
Wed–Sun 3–6; adm*

**Musée de
la Cravate**
*t 04 77 28 77 86; open
1st Sun in month
2.30–6; adm*

The gentle hills to the east, known as the **Montagnes du Matin**, separate this stretch of the Loire from the Beaujolais' hills. Entering the **Château de St-Marcel-de-Félines**, not just lions but sphinxes too greet you in the eccentric little courtyard. Dating back to early medieval times, the castle knew its heyday in the Ancien Régime, when the Talaru family from Chalmazel (*see* p.141) moved here. In the delightful *salons*, charming wood panelling features Italianate landscapes, *natures mortes* (including a still life with hamster!) and bouquets. In one corner, a menacing Joan of Arc looks ready to stab any passing Englishman. For wider views, head to the wood-porched chapel of **Notre-Dame** above the village of **Néronde**, or east beyond **Violay** for the **Tour de Matagrin**.

Local craft traditions are recalled at **Bussières**, with its modern **Musée du Tissage** featuring textiles, and at **Panissières**, with a **Musée de la Cravate** – you can also visit a tie-maker here. The blushing remains of Benedictine priory buildings at **Pouilly-lès-Feurs** draw attention with the beauty of their pink-tinged granite.

## The Monts de la Madeleine and Côte Roannaise

As an alternative to following the Loire plain, west of Briennon, head for the **Monts de la Madeleine** to join delightful hillside roads that take you through one fortified village after another. These hardly feel menacing now, more like doddering old war veterans reminiscing about past glories. Above **La Pacaudière**, church and medieval watchtower keep company on **Le Crozet**'s hilltop. The compact village below retains its old gateways and fine old houses made of Charlieu stone; one contains a **local history museum**.

**Le Crozet local
history museum**
*t 04 77 64 31 57*

The east-facing **Côte Roannaise vineyards** start from **Changy** below Le Crozet, their thin 160-hectare line stretching along the lower slopes of the Monts de la Madeleine to **St-Jean-St-Maurice**. Round here, gamay goes by the pseudonym St-Romain and produces fresh AOC reds and rosés in Beaujolais style.

Vines climb the slopes to proud **Ambierle**. Its brightly roofed Gothic church, built in the 15th century, became the centrepiece of a Benedictine **priory** dating back to the end of the Dark Ages. The church entrance is carved with twisting vines. Inside, the local nobility displayed their vanity – heraldry decorates the column capitals and ceiling bosses, while below the lovely stained glass in the choir, a very fine 15th-century Flemish altarpiece shows donors in magnificent attire. American visitors might be surprised to stumble upon the tomb of Monseigneur Jean-Marie Odin, from Ambierle, first bishop of Galveston, Texas, in 1840, then bishop of New Orleans. To appreciate an engrossing, extensive, old-fashioned display of traditional local craft ways, walk over to the **Musée Alice Taverne**, set in a former school. Among the most amusing displays are details on peasant remedies, which include cow pats for burns,

**Musée Alice
Taverne**
*t 04 77 65 60 99; open
Feb–Nov daily 10–12
and 2–6; adm*

or, for sore eyes, alum mixed with the white of an egg laid on a Thursday and washed with urine! Neither the museum nor we would wish to recommend you try these suggestions yourselves!

Seventeen towers once protected **St-Haon-le-Châtel**. See how many you can count the remains of on a stroll round the picturesquely run-down ramparts of this sweet village. The church, a solid 12th-century edifice, has restored murals. Below, seek out the secretive **Jardin du Moyen-Age** garden, run by a passionate local.

## Market Days in the Roannais Loire

**Charlieu**: Wed and Sat am.
**Roanne**: Tues, Wed, Fri, Sat, Sun am.
**Ambierle**: Thurs am.

## Where to Stay and Eat in the Roannais Loire

### Charlieu ✉ 42190

**\*\*Relais de l'Abbaye, t 04 77 60 00 88, www.hotel-relaisdelabbaye-charlieu.fr** (€). Big, plain rooms in dull modern architecture, but just a meadow away from the splendid town centre. Decent restaurant (€€) with terrace. *Closed Jan and end Aug; restaurant closed Sun eve and Mon lunch.*

### Pouilly-sous-Charlieu ✉ 42720

**La Loire**, Rue de la Berge, t 04 77 60 81 36 (€€€–€€). By a bridge over the river, with a charming conservatory. Refined cuisine. *Closed Sun eve and Mon, plus Tues out of season.*

### Noailly ✉ 42640

**Château de la Motte B&B, t 04 77 66 64 60, www.chateaudelamotte.net** (€€). Cheerful little white castle near La Bénisson Dieu, with six stylish rooms overlooking the park. *Table d'hôte* (€€). Pool. Gym. They also run occasional cookery courses.

### Roanne ✉ 42300

**\*\*\*\*Troisgros**, Place de la Gare, t 04 77 71 66 97, www.troisgros.fr (€€€€€–€€€€). France's most famous railway station restaurant (€€€€€), serving up the most refined food in the country, plus sleek contemporary bedrooms and suites. *Closed certain school hols; restaurant closed Tues and Wed.*

**Le Central, t 04 77 67 72 72** (€€). The neighbouring, far cheaper Troisgros *bistrot*, plus shop. *Closed Sun and Mon.*

### Villerest ✉ 42300

**Domaine de Champlong**, 12 Route de Champlong, t 04 77 69 78 78 (€€). A peaceful modern hotel beside an expanding golf course; rooms with terrace. Pool and tennis. *Closed Feb.*

**Château de Champlong**, 100 Chemin de la Chapelle, t 04 77 69 69 69 (€€€–€€). Close by, an elegant Ancien Régime house holds this elegant restaurant. *Closed Sun eve, Mon and Tues, and most Feb.*

### Commelle-Vernay ✉ 42120

**Château de Chassignol B&B, t 04 77 23 06 57, www.chateau-chassignol.com** (€). Bargain rooms in this rustic corner-towered country house by the east bank of Villerest Lake. Pool.

### St-Maurice-sur-Loire ✉ 42155

**L'Echauguette B&B**, Rue Guy de la Mure, t 04 77 63 15 89, www. echauguette-alex.com (€€–€). Run by an enchanting couple, with very tasteful village rooms perched just above the Loire gorges. *Table d'hôte* (€€).

### Ambierle ✉ 42820

**Le Prieuré, t 04 77 65 63 24** (€€€–€€). Tempting, stylish central restaurant. *Closed Tues and Wed.*

### Villemontais ✉ 42155

**Domaine du Fontenay B&B, t 04 77 63 12 22, domainedufontenay.com** (€). Amidst the Côte Roannaise vines, charming rooms run by a Franco-British couple devoted to making local wine using traditional methods.

### St-Haon-le-Châtel ✉ 42370

**Château de St-Haon B&B, t 04 77 62 14 63, www.chateau-de-st-haon.com**

(€€€–€€). Splendid new rooms in this smart welcoming bourgeois home in the historic village. *Table d'hôte* (€€).

**Au Natur'elles, t** 04 77 62 12 01 (€€–€). Nice village inn with terrace. *Closed Mon Easter–Oct, plus Wed rest of year*.

# The Loire Valley across the Forez

Magically bucolic, the Forez is the old county stretching across the Loire valley between the Roannais and St-Etienne. The views are sublime from the hill roads up in the Monts du Forez, the range that separates the Rhône-Alpes from the Auvergne. The rather sleepy villages you encounter along the slopes are a joy, while a couple of extraordinary volcanic hillocks crowned by churches emerge from the flat Forez plain below.

## Surprising Sights on the Edge of the Forez Plain

**La Bastie d'Urfé**
*t* 04 77 97 54 68,
www.ladiana.com; open
July–Aug daily 10–12
and 1–6; April–June and
Sept–Oct daily 10–12
and 2.30–5.30;
Nov–Mar Wed and
Fri–Sun 2–5; adm

The early medieval d'Urfé lords lived high in the Forez mountains, but in the 13th century the family acquired lands on the Loire plain and came down to settle at their manor of **La Bastie d'Urfé**. Claude d'Urfé (1501–58) fought beside King François I in the monarch's wars in Italy and represented him at the first round of the crucial Council of Trent in 1546, helping to reinforce the doctrine of the Catholic Church against Protestantism. He became French ambassador to the Vatican under François' successor, Henri II, before serving as tutor to the royal heir.

Enamoured with Italy, Claude rebuilt the family manor in the Renaissance style. Neglected after the Revolution, it has now been restored. A fashionable sphinx, a symbol of wisdom, greets visitors to the curious perspectival Renaissance gallery. The sand-and-shell-plastered grotto in one corner is crammed with saucy delights, including a mischievous Pan lurking against one pillar – in the past, it wasn't just the fake stalactites that shot out water... The chapel above sent out a rather more elevated Catholic message, emphasizing the Holy Trinity and the Eucharist in a stunning decorative ensemble executed by highly accomplished artists. Further rooms are well furnished, hung with tapestries illustrating the literary masterpiece and European bestseller *L'Astrée*, written by Claude's great-nephew Honoré d'Urfé (1567–1625), brought up here.

### *L'Astrée*, an Ancien Régime Bestseller

*L' Astrée* was a pastoral epic that did much to encourage the rage among Ancien Régime aristocrats for dressing up as peasants. But the intertwining stories are really about the dreadful complexities of love, Amour turning its authority into tragic tyranny in this idyllic country. The local riverbanks serve as the backdrop to the drama from the start, the shepherdess Astrée accusing the good shepherd Céladon of disloyalty. Spurned, he throws himself into the Lignon. Instead of rushing to help, Astrée faints. The story swiftly moves into the realms of higher fantasy as nymphs garlanded with pearls find Céladon on the river bank and carry him to Galathée's castle. The love complications then multiply in this mammoth mythological romp that had the likes of Marie Antoinette and Rousseau gripped. Abridged versions mercifully exist today.

## Montverdun priory

*t 04 77 97 53 33;*
*www.montverdun.com;*
*open April–Oct*
*Mon–Sat 2–6, Sun*
*3–7; Nov–Mar*
*Tues–Sat 2–6; adm*

## Château de la Vigne

*t 04 77 24 08 12;*
*www.boen.fr; open*
*Mar–Nov Tues–Sun*
*2.30–6.30; adm*

## Cave des Vignerons Foréziens

*t 04 77 24 00 12; open*
*April–Aug Tues–Sat 9–12*
*and 2–6.30, Sun from*
*10; Feb–Mar and Sept–*
*Dec Wed–Fri 10–12 and*
*2–6, Tues and Sun 2–6*

## Forteresse de Couzan

*t 04 77 96 01 10;*
*www.ladiana.com;*
*open July–Aug daily*
*2.30–6.30; adm*

## Volerie du Forez

*t 04 77 97 59 14; open*
*mid-Mar–Oct; displays*
*July–Aug daily at 3 and*
*4.30; mid-Mar–June*
*Wed at 3, Sat, Sun and*
*public hols at 3 and*
*4.30; Sept–Oct Sat and*
*Sun at 3; adm*

## Champdieu priory

*t 04 77 97 17 29; guided*
*tours mid-May–mid-*
*Sept Mon–Fri 10–12 and*
*2–6; adm*

## Château de Vaugirard

*t 04 77 58 33 88; open*
*June–Sept Sun–Thurs*
*2.30–6; adm*

## Salle La Diana

*t 04 77 96 01 10; www.*
*ladiana.com; open Tues*
*2–5, Wed and Sat 9–12*
*and 2–5; adm*

The jet-black fortified **priory of Montverdun** stands darkly atop one of the unmissable volcanic hillocks standing up out of the Forez plain nearby. It looks so striking because it was made from the local basalt rock. Inside, the alarming statue of St Porchaire is explained: he had his eyes gouged out by marauding Saracens.

The **Côtes du Forez vineyards** are a mere 10 hectares larger than those of the Côte Roannaise, covering 170 in all; since the year 2000, the wines have won the same right to *appellation d'origine contrôlée* (AOC) status. The mainly gamay vineyards lie scattered on the slopes between Boën-sur-Lignon and Montbrison.

In the little town of **Boën-sur-Lignon**, the **Château de la Vigne** is set in a sober-looking Ancien Régime castle, but inside, this surprisingly well-presented wine museum uses the best of traditional and contemporary techniques to reveal the history of wine-making in the Forez. Also take in the Italianate features of the château's architecture. At times you can follow an expert's tasting here, but carry on to the **Cave des Vignerons Foréziens** in nearby **Trelins** for more regular *dégustations*. A large amount of Côtes du Forez wine is made and sold here.

Staring arrogantly out from a spectacular height just a bit to the west, above the village of **Sail-sous-Couzan**, the tremendous ruined ramparts of the hilltop **Forteresse de Couzan** dominate the meeting point of several wooded valleys. This castle was built for the Damas family, bitter rivals of the counts of Forez. Even though the fortress remains closed much of the year, it's worth visiting to appreciate the awesome sight, reflecting medieval power politics.

Continuing along the lower Forez slopes, the crenellated ruins of the **Château Ste-Anne** stand out by **Marcilly**. Close by, the **Volerie du Forez** offers regular displays of falconry.

**Champdieu**'s **priory** was fortified in the Hundred Years War; its refectory holds some entertaining medieval murals. The 17th-century **Château de Vaugirard** below the village contains a couple of merry chambers illustrating later courtly life.

Capital of the medieval counts of Forez, **Montbrison** boasted their main castle and their main church. Guy IV, one of the most important in the lordly line, a man of culture as well as of war, commissioned the biggest Gothic church in the Forez, **Notre-Dame de l'Espérance**. Begun in 1224, due to wars and financial problems it took 250 years to complete – without enough money to pay for statues on the façade. The lofty interior holds the tomb of Guy IV, however, shown wearing the bonnet of a Sorbonne professor, a sign of his erudition. Given that the **Salle La Diana** behind the church was constructed so hurriedly in 1296 to celebrate the marriage of his grandson, Count Jean I of Forez, to Alise de Viennois, it has survived quite well. But there wasn't time to employ noble materials. Making up for this, the count had the hall ceiling covered with heraldic devices, 1,700 painted squares drumming home the aristocratic connections of the two families. A couple of rooms off the hall form the Montbrison **archaeological museum**. Elsewhere in town, the **Musée d'Allard** presents minerals, carved stones and stuffed birds in its scientific sections, while the highlight of its children's collections is the **Musée de la Poupée**, with some 600 dolls, including *poupées Gégé*, made in Montbrison until 1980. Modern artists are also given a stall here.

Almost nothing remains of the counts' castle in Montbrison, but smart historic houses line the town's main streets, while flowers deck out the sides of the central Vizezy stream – the Saturday market stretches along here for a staggering full mile.

Standing out on its volcanic rock like the Mont-St-Michel of the sea-flat Forez plain, south of town, **St-Romain-le-Puy**'s amazing **priory church** exercises a magnetic effect on travellers. Close up, it looks crooked and ancient – not surprisingly, as it dates back in part to the 10th century. On the blotched stone around the outside of the apse, a frieze of worn animals and symbols spells out a message to the initiated: that man's spiritual journey is a struggle, given the burden of original sin. The interior is covered with a patchwork of faded frescoes. Some murals represent St Romain having his tongue cut off for preaching Christianity, then being imprisoned and murdered; others include semi-vanished figures thought to represent early Christian martyrs of Lyon, St Pothin and St Irénée (or Irenaeus). Intertwining capitals decorate the church, while the crypt contains memorable carvings, for example of a peacock carrying a rainbow on its back, a symbol of hope. The rare viognier white wine made here sells as Vin d'Aldebertus, named after one of the most important figures in the priory's history.

## The Loire from Feurs to St-Etienne

The name of the Forez derives from that of **Feurs**, the main Gallo-Roman centre along this stretch of the Loire, a history recalled in fragments at the sleepy **Musée d'Archéologie** just outside the pleasant grid-plan centre of this low-key town. The museum also focuses on local equine history; the Forez plain is major horse-racing territory, and Feurs stages popular trotter races.

The largest ornithological reserve in the Rhône-Alpes hides out on the flats by the Loire. Rarely will you come across a more joyously presented wildlife centre than the **Ecopôle du Forez**, a wooden ark on stilts set up in the late 1980s, when big new lakes were created across 400 hectares previously ravaged by gravel-quarrying. Birds flock here, and beavers have been introduced.

Built for the counts of Forez to guard a ford across the Loire, the ruined **Château de Montrond-les-Bains** still presents an impressive silhouette at the riverside. Built in the 12th century, embellished in

---

**Musée d'Allard**
*t 04 77 58 83 34; open Wed–Mon 2–6; closed Tues; adm*

**St-Romain-le-Puy priory church**
*t 04 77 76 92 10; open April–Oct 2.30–6; adm*

**Musée d'Archéologie**
*t 04 77 26 24 48; open daily Sun–Fri 2–6; closed Sat; adm*

**Ecopôle du Forez**
*t 04 77 27 86 40; www.frapna.org; open daily 2–6; adm*

**Château de Montrond-les-Bains**
*t 04 77 06 91 91; open July–Aug Wed–Mon 10.30–12.30 and 1.30–7; April–June and Sept–Oct Wed–Sun 10–12.30 and 1.30–5.30; adm*

the 16th, largely destroyed at the Revolution, its restored remains contain a rather wooden **local history museum**. As the name indicates, **Montrond-les-Bains** has a thermal establishment. Set up to treat medical conditions, this **Station Thermale** now welcomes tourists for pamperings, with a new pool and treatment facilities.

**St-Galmier** stands out very attractively on its hilltop above St-Etienne airport (located well outside the city sprawl). In medieval times, the counts of Forez had a castle built up here, plus two sets of ramparts further down. This well-defended 'Balcony on the Forez' became one of the family's favoured residences.

A few vestiges of the ramparts remain, but the castle precinct has disappeared, except for the major Gothic **church**. The towering belfry was added in the 19th century, along with the neo-Gothic decoration inside, notably the startlingly bright stained glass, by the local Mauvernay workshops. But a couple of exceptionally refined Gothic Virgins also stand out. In the lanes descending steeply from here, admire some fine 15th- and 16th-century houses and track down the tiny, modest chapel of **Notre-Dame des Pauvres**. In contrast, the slope-side **casino** is a showy affair, set above the lovely public gardens, and with a very enticing outdoor pool attached. A **glass-blower** draws in tourists with his afternoon displays and studio shop a little further down the slope.

St-Galmier's **lower town** is where that most internationally imbibed of natural sparkling water, Badoit, is produced. Augustin Badoit is honoured here with a statue. He began marketing the local waters successfully in the mid-19th century, although the Romans had, of course, already found and exploited them much earlier. Visitors can pay to visit the original **Badoit extraction chamber**; the massive natural water reserves below town now fill one million bottles a day. St-Galmier also offers regular horse races.

Up in the hills beyond, the misleadingly named **Chazelles-sur-Lyon** has no connection with the metropolis the other side of the Beaujolais. It's the sleepiest kind of provincial French town, but with a lively hat museum, the **Musée du Chapeau**, although some of the explanations on the use of rabbit fur go into a bit too much detail for the squeamish.

Back in the busier valley, the Loire splits **St-Just-St-Rambert** in two. As to its **Musée des Civilisations**, it too is divided, into sections on local history, world cultures and amusing caricatures. The defensive old church is guarded by a fortified bell tower.

The Loire **gorges** twisting and turning west of St-Etienne provide high natural drama just out of sight of the sprawling city and its suburbs. This area has become a retreat for the Stéphanois, as the building of the **Barrage de Grangent**, a hydroelectric dam from the 1960s, created another major Loire lake, the **Lac de Grangent**, with opportunities for swimming and water sports on the east bank.

---

**Station Thermale de Montrond-les-Bains**
*t 04 77 94 67 61*

**Musée du Chapeau**
*t 04 77 94 23 29, www.museeduchapeau. com; open July–Aug daily 2–6; Sept–June Wed–Mon 2–6; adm*

**Musée des Civilisations**
*t 04 77 52 03 11; open Wed–Mon 2–6; closed Tues; adm*

**10**

**The Loire to its Source | The Loire Valley across the Forez**

**Château d'Essalois**
*open daily 10–7; free*

Because of towering cliffs, you can't get close to the river along the west bank, but from the high villages of **Essalois** and **Chambles** you do get sensational views down on it. For the most breathtaking panorama, clamber round the crumbling remains of Essalois' **castle**, or climb the more solid tower at Chambles. Both look down on the waterside village of **St-Victor-sur-Loire**, its adorable marina tucked into an inlet, and on the tempting destination of the **Château de Grangent**, a picturesque ruined castle on the island of Grangent right in the midst of the waters. South, the **Château de St-Paul-en-Cornillon** occupies another dramatic height, a couple of the chambers in this lordly nest occasionally open to visitors. The gated villas of rich Stéphanois who've settled around here are kept even more tightly shut.

## St-Etienne and Firminy

⭐ **St-Etienne and Firminy**

St-Etienne is familiar to the British because of its periodically very successful football team. But it's not the most obvious tourist stop, even if, like Rome, it boasts of being built on seven hills. In fact, this city of 300,000 sprawls over far more hills, grassed-over slag heaps adding to its confusing geography. History isn't St-Etienne's strong point either, but manufacturing has been. From the Middle Ages, the locals specialized in making arms. Coal-mining took off too. Trade in weapons boomed so much that during the Revolution the

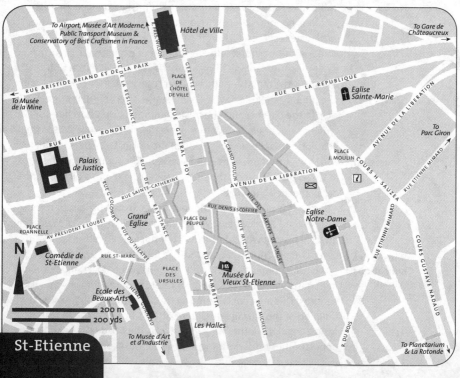

St-Etienne

town briefly changed name to Armeville! Activities diversified in the 19th century, the French associating St-Etienne with the joy of bicycle-making as well as with put-upon miners.

Its friendly people have experienced some upheavals as these industries collapsed, but the town has seen new life in recent times thanks to the retail giant Casino, the arrival of prestigious educational establishments and lots of budding small businesses. It has established itself as a centre of pioneering design, putting on an international Biennale (next in 2008 and 2010) covering innovation in areas from fashion to architecture. In addition, the city hosts music *biennales* celebrating its most famous composers, the 19th-century Massenet and the challenging Pierre Boulez, recognized as one of the greatest composers and conductors of our times. In fact, St-Etienne boasts one of the most highly regarded opera houses in France, so the city is by no means a cultural desert.

It is quite surprising to some, though, that the town has been declared a *Ville d'Art et d'Histoire*. Its main strength all year is an array of major museums. The modest **Musée du Vieux St-Etienne** isn't among the most ambitious, but stands in the small historic quarter, near Place du Peuple. Trendy bars and restaurants radiate out from the appealing little triangular intersection of Place Neuve. Keen church visitors could pay their respects at the **Grand'Eglise** on Place Boivin, dedicated to the town's patron, Stephen; its 15th-century façade appears to have melted like candle wax into intriguing, Gaudiesque forms.

Head north into the central shopping streets, too tightly packed to be entirely comfortable, though a few large squares let you breathe more easily. **Place Jean Jaurès** forms the green hub of central St-Etienne. Although overseen by a dull town hall and greyer cathedral, cheerful restaurants and cafés congregate along its sides. One culinary address that's a must for chocolate-lovers is the renowned **Chocolat Weiss** on 8 Rue du Plateau des Glières.

You will need to head out of town for the main museums. The substantial **Musée de la Mine**, set in a disused mine just to the west, looks dismal on the outside, but is in part run by enthusiastic former miners. To the south, the **Musée d'Art et d'Industrie** has moved into one of the most splendid buildings in town, and explains the city's craft traditions with great panache. Here, the fruits of industry really are transformed into art.

Broad, winding, tree-lined Cours Fauriel makes a grand exit south from town, lined by smart buildings, taking you up to the **Astronef Planétarium** close to the restaurant Chantecler, a Stéphanois institution, opposite the Massenet *conservatoire*.

North of the centre, clearly visible from the A72 motorway which doubles as St-Etienne's ringroad, don't mistake the **Musée d'Art Moderne** for an enormous bathroom showroom. This is a serious,

**Musée du Vieux St-Etienne**
*t 04 77 74 57 79, www.vieux-saint-etienne.com; open Tues–Sat 2.30–6; adm*

**Musée de la Mine**
*t 04 77 43 83 23; open Wed–Mon, guided tours weekdays 10.30 and 3.30, weekends 2.15; closed Tues; adm*

**Musée d'Art et d'Industrie**
*t 04 77 49 73 00; open Wed–Mon 10–6; closed Tues; adm*

**Astronef Planétarium**
*t 04 77 33 43 01, www.astronef.fr; shows Wed, Sat, Sun and school hols at 3.30 and 4.45, plus 2.15 in peak periods; adm*

**Musée d'Art Moderne**
*t 04 77 79 52 52; open Wed–Mon 10–6; adm*

10

The Loire to its Source | The Loire Valley across the Forez: St-Etienne and Firminy

challenging gallery with massive modern art collections. Most aptly for this industrial city, Fernand Léger's industrialized figures stand out, the central woman in his *Trois Femmes* with hair curving like a sheet of black metal. There are further shocking images of women by the likes of Picasso, Dubuffet and Warhol. But one of the museum's most provocative collections is of Surrealists' favourite Victor Brauner, whose liberated subconscious couldn't keep phalluses out of the picture.

West of St-Etienne, the satellite industrial town of **Firminy** closer to the Loire has recently made a great effort to put its exceptional array of Le Corbusier buildings to the fore. The much-admired, much-maligned Modernist architect was called upon, some time after the war, to help develop a whole new quarter, **Firminy Vert**, with bright, airy social housing and advanced social provisions. The ambitious project led to one of the biggest concentrations of Le Corbusier works in France, even if all the plans weren't completed, in part because the famed architect died in 1965. The fascinating, long guided tours, led by devoted guides, generally depart from the **Espace Le Corbusier** on Rue de St-Just Malmont, a cultural centre that doubles as a stadium. For those who mistakenly equate Le Corbusier with unrelenting straight-lined functional efficiency, the jaunty curve of its concrete roof comes as a first surprise. The cultural centre's function rooms are tucked in below the terraces. The arts centre is the best preserved, while the library's seats mimic the stadium rows outside, and act as a reminder that Le Corbusier admired the classical ideal of exercising both body and soul. You can also visit a model apartment, or signature *unité d'habitation*, its wonderful practicality and sense of light shining through, in his characteristic block of flats up the slope, benefiting from uplifting views. The joyous primary school up top, with colourful windows, only closed in 1998.

**Espace Le Corbusier**
*t 04 77 10 07 77, espace.le.corbusier@ wanadoo.fr; guided tours July–mid-Sept daily at 2.30 (exc Sun mid-July–mid-Aug); mid-April–June and mid-Sept–Oct Sat 2.30; adm*

Firminy recently took the bold decision to have the funky church of **St-Pierre** built to Le Corbusier's designs, but almost from scratch, as just the base had been laid much earlier. The intriguing concrete form that has emerged evokes a volcano, or a funnel; on one side, the outer wall is pierced with openings copying the shape of the constellation of Orion, dotting the interior with light.

## The Monts du Forez

 **Forez hill routes**

Across the other side of the Loire, the forested mountain roads leading south from the A72 motorway (Exit 4) are a delight, many offering staggering views down across the Loire's Forez plain. Above **Champoly**, walk to the secluded remains of the medieval **Château d'Urfé** for a start.

**Château d'Urfé**
*adm free*

Simple Gothic arches lead into the fortified hilltop village of **Cervières**, prettily run-down by time. A truncated church survives,

**Maison des Grenadières**
t 04 77 24 98 71, www.grenadieres.com; open April–Oct Wed–Mon 2.30–6, closed Tues; Nov Sat and Sun 2.30–6; closed Dec–Mar; adm

a plump-cheeked peasant Mary standing out inside. Opposite, the fine granite **Maison des Grenadières** attractively presents the local tradition of embroidering gold emblems for the French forces, megalomaniac leaders and top fashion houses. Beyond the scruffy but sporty valley town of **Noirétable**, seek Christian elevation at the high-perched convent of **Notre-Dame de l'Hermitage** (although the religious shop proves deeply tacky).

Around the **Col de la Loge**, you get a rare glimpse of the Auvergne region. Sights across the *département* of the Loire, plus a few in neighbouring Auvergne, have been reproduced in scale models curiously placed among the clumps of heather at the **Parc de la Droséra**; the walk through moorland, spotting the works hidden among the heather, proves quite entertaining. There's a restaurant and *gîtes* up here, plus basic inns in the nearest village.

**Parc de la Droséra**
t 04 77 24 81 44, www.parc-de-la-drosera.fr; open Mar–mid-Nov daily 10–7; adm

The imposing, full-scale medieval **Château de Chalmazel** stands guard at one end of the valley village of **Chalmazel**. The family who have undertaken the castle's restoration show you round just a few rooms with serious enthusiasm. You can also stay here (*see* p.144). Chalmazel lies at the bottom of a straight ski slope coming down from beside **Pierre sur Haute**, at 1,634m the highest point in the Forez range. Up on the heights, you encounter one of the Rhône-Alpes region's most endearingly small-scale ski resorts; although the snow isn't always that predictable, the Chalmazel **ski station** has now invested in numerous snow cannons.

**Château de Chalmazel**
t 04 77 24 88 09, www.chateaudechalmazel.com; open July–Aug daily 2–6, mid-May–June and most of Sept Sat and Sun 2–6; adm

**Chalmazel ski station**
www.loire-chalmazel.fr

Chalmazel castle was built for the local Talaru lords. They were guardians in medieval times of the **Col du Béal**, the exposed, barren pass at around 1,390m in altitude leading into the Auvergne. It's elating to go walking along the Forez crest in these parts, with vast views east over the Rhône-Alpes region, west over the Auvergne. The geological phenomenon here means that the Auvergne side receives a lot of rain, whereas the Rhône-Alpes side remains relatively dry. To learn more about the flora and fauna of these typical high-altitude moors known as the **Hautes Chaumes**, visit the sweet contemporary **Observatoire du Col du Béal**. Despite its slightly confusing name, it's really a visitor centre, with playful displays to try and capture your imagination. The adjoining modern *auberge* serves a blueberry tart typical of these parts. You could also join a guided walking tour with a specialist, or hire a guide – contact **BioSphère Environnement**. *Jasseries*, the traditional stone farm buildings up high that were only used in summer, are dotted across the great slopes. In times past, women and children came to live up in these in summer, guarding their herds, making cheese. Now the *jasseries* have mainly been converted into second homes, but ask at the Observatoire about ones you can visit.

**Observatoire du Col du Béal**
t 04 73 95 56 49; open July–Aug daily 10–12 and 2–6; Sept–June sometimes open during school hols; adm

**BioSphère Environnement**
t/f 04 77 97 94 62, www.biosphere-environnement.com

Cheese pervades the air in the *fromage* capital of the Forez, the cheese-obsessed village of **Sauvain**, still high on the Forez slopes,

**Maison Sauvagnarde**
*t 04 77 76 85 21; open July–Aug Tues–Sun 2.30–6.30; June and Sept–Oct Sun 2.30–6.30; closed Nov–May; adm*

**Fromagerie Forez Fourme**
*t 04 77 76 81 80, www.forez-fourme.com; open daily 9–12*

**Fromagerie du Pont de la Pierre**
*t 04 77 76 82 86; open daily 9–12*

**Moulin des Massons**
*t 04 77 76 86 45, www. moulindesmassons. com; open French school hols Wed–Sun 2–6; rest of period Feb–Nov Sat, Sun and public hols 2–6; adm*

**Musée d'Histoire du 20ème Siècle**
*t 04 77 50 29 20; open daily 2–6; adm*

**Ecomusée des Monts du Forez**
*t 04 77 50 67 97, www.usson-en-forez.fr; open daily 2–6; adm*

with superb views across the Loire. The simple Gothic **church** is protected by a circle of old houses. Just beyond, you can visit craft cheese shops and the **Maison Sauvagnarde**, dedicated to local traditions, cheese-making included. Homage is also paid to Louis Lépine, a dynamic figure from the region who became head of the Paris police force at the turn of the 19th to the 20th century, then governor general of Algeria, and founder of the Lépine competition for innovations. This charming rustic museum, run with enthusiasm by friendly locals, was his former summer home.

The **Maison de la Fourme** indicates cheese-making properties to visit nearby, the main one being the **Fromagerie Forez Fourme**. You can learn here about the variety of cheeses made in the Forez.

Follow the twisting high Forez road south through further peaceful hillside villages like **St-Bonnet-le-Courreau**. The views east down onto the Loire plain are spectacular. Close by, the **Fromagerie du Pont de la Pierre** produces Fourme de Montbrison, the award-winning local blue cheese, given *appellation d'origine contrôlée* status in 2002. Learn here about the various stages in its making.

At **Fraisse** to the south, the ruins of a village and chapel stand on an enchanting pine-covered hilltop with yet more fabulous views. Hidden away in the Vizezy valley below, the old stone buildings of the **Moulin des Massons**, dating back to the Middle Ages, have been very prettily restored. The mill and sawmill closed in the 1960s, but an association has recently brought the place back to life and runs the guided tours. Oils such as rapeseed and walnut made here are on sale in the shop.

**Roche** and **Gumières** are further villages where the views don't disappoint. Then there's a choice of routes to reach St-Bonnet-le-Château. Passing via picturesque **Marols**, you come upon a medieval village built for defence. The tall Gothic tower added on to its Romanesque church looks more military than religious. Taking the alternative route, tiny hilltop **Montarcher** is hard to beat for cuteness and panoramas, with the most exquisite views from its church, which seems to grow out of the rock.

Coming back down to earth, **Estivareilles'** Musée d'Histoire du 20ème Siècle makes a valiant if over-ambitious attempt to cover recent European history, but the **Ecomusée des Monts du Forez** at the more attractive if equally sleepy neighbouring village of **Usson-en-Forez** has more appeal, as it sticks to what it knows best, local life, traditions and legends, all quite imaginatively covered.

Our high Forez trail ends with a real cliff-hanger, **St-Bonnet-le-Château**. *Boules*-lovers from far and wide visit this historic hillside town, self-styled *Capitale Mondiale de la Boule*, no mean claim in a country where so many people adore this leisurely sport, with some 10 million reckoned to practise it on a casual basis, and half a million registered as regular practitioners.

**Musée International Pétanque et Boules**
*t 04 77 50 15 33; open June–Sept Mon 1.30–6, Tues–Fri 8.30–12 and 1.30–6.30, Sat 10–12.30 and 2–6; Oct–May Mon 1.30–5.30; Tues–Fri 8.30–12 and 1.30–5.30; Sat 1.30–5; closed Sun; adm*

**St-Bonnet-le-Château church**
*t 04 77 50 11 15; you must book a tour via St-Bonnet's tourist office (see p.144) to see the mummies and murals; adm*

St-Bonnet-le-Château has gained pre-eminence in this sphere as home to one of France's major metallic *boules*-makers, Obut, and its Musée International Pétanque et Boules. This appealing centre offers up all sorts of information on the sport, from antiquity to the present day, passing via the major schism between *boules* and *pétanque*. You also learn about its stars, and the abject, comical humiliation reserved for total losers, the 'kissing of Fanny's bottom', explained with gravitas. To avoid such public ignominy, there's no substitute for practice, and you can invest in some fine *boules*.

On a more elevated note, make for the church beyond the slightly jaded old squares and streets lined by tall mansions, signalling how this little merchants' town once prospered from its metal-working trade. The Gothic edifice stands aloof on its cliffside terrace, and the views from the church rear are breathtaking.

The interior offers a lesson in sober Gothic style at first sight. But the place has skeletons in the cupboard, almost literally. On the guided tour you are taken down to a chamber whose walls are hung with scary brown **mummies**, not from antiquity, but thought to date from a few centuries back; some claim they were killed in the Wars of Religion. It seems their bodies were buried in ground containing alum and arsenic, natural chemicals that preserved them in this leathery state, with horrifying grimaces. In heavenly contrast, the tour also takes you round to a lower chapel hiding some of the most uplifting Gothic **frescoes** in southeast France, probably commissioned for Anne, Duchess of Bourbon and Countess of Forez. In the *Annunciation* scene, the Virgin appears blonde, but turns brunette for the sumptuous arrival of the three kings. The musical angels on the ceiling play an array of medieval instruments, although many of them wear pained expressions.

After such a fantastic Forez finale, we rejoin the Loire valley below St-Etienne.

---

(i) **Montbrison**
*Cloître des Cordeliers, 42600 Montbrison, t 04 77 96 08 69, www.loireforez.com*

(i) **Feurs**
*Place du Forum, 42110 Feurs, t 04 77 26 05 27, www.officedutourisme defeurs.org*

(i) **Montrond-les-Bains >>**
*Av des Sources, 42210 Montrond-les-Bains, t 04 77 94 64 74, www.montrond-les-bains.com*

## Market Days in the Loire Valley across the Forez

**Montbrison**: Sat am.
**Feurs**: Tues and Fri am.
**Montrond-les-Bains**: Thurs am.
**St-Galmier**: Mon am, Fri pm.
**Chazelles-sur-Lyon**: Tues and Fri am.
**St-Just-St-Rambert**: Thurs, Sat and Sun am.
**St-Etienne**: Every am.
**St-Bonnet-le-Château**: Fri am.

## Where to Stay and Eat in the Loire Valley across the Forez

**Magneux-Hauterive** ⊠ **42600**
**Château de Magneux B&B**, t 04 77 76 10 64 (€). Pleasant, simple rooms to the side of this charming Ancien Régime château, set in nice grounds.

**Montrond-les-Bains** ⊠ **42210**
***Hostellerie La Poularde, t 04 77 54 40 06, *www.la-poularde.com* (€€). An artistic restaurant (€€€€–€€€) run by Gilles Etéocle. The stylish suites are well soundproofed. Snazzy modern

### (i) St-Galmier >

*Bd du Sud, 42330
St-Galmier, t 04 77 54 06
08, www.ot-stgalmier.fr*

### (i) Chalmazel >>

*Place de l'Eglise, 42920
Chalmazel, t 04 77 24
84 92, www.perso.
wanadoo.fr/
otsi.chalmazel*

### (i) Chazelles-sur-Lyon

*9 Place Galland, 42140
Chazelles-sur-Lyon,
t 04 77 54 98 86, ot.
chazelles@wanadoo.fr*

### (i) St-Just-St-Rambert >

*Place de la Paix, 42170
St-Just-St-Rambert,
t 04 77 52 05 14,
www.tourisme-
forez-sud.com*

### (i) St-Etienne >

*16 Av de la Libération,
42000 St Etienne,
t 04 77 49 39 00,
www.tourisme-st-
etienne.com*

### (★) Le Logis de Nantas >

### (i) St-Bonnet-le-Château >>

*Place de la République,
42940 St-Bonnet-le-
Château, t 04 77 50
52 48, www.cc-pays-st-
bonnet-le-chateau.fr*

rooms overlook the small pool. *Closed most Jan and mid-Aug; restaurant closed Mon, and Tues lunch.*

## St-Galmier ✉ 42330

***La Charpinière**, t 04 77 52 75 00, www.lacharpiniere.com (€€). In shaded grounds below town, a pleasing manor that has grown into a spacious hotel with comfortable rooms, some air-conditioned, plus decent **Closerie de la Tour** restaurant (€€) with terrace. Pool, tennis court, sauna.

**Le Bougainvillier**, Pré Château, t 04 77 54 03 31 (€€€–€€). Pleasing restaurant in smart house up in the old town. *Closed Sun eve, Mon, and Wed eve, plus most school hols.*

**Chez Jacotte et Elia B&B**, Le Plat, t 04 77 54 08 27, http://jacotte.elia.free.fr (€€). Up in the countryside outside town, cheerful rooms in a typical old fortified farm.

## St-Just-St-Rambert ✉ 42170

**Le Neuvième Art**, Place du 19 Mars 1962, t 04 77 55 87 15 (€€€). Christophe Roure cooks up a storm in the former railway station.

## St-Victor-sur-Loire ✉ 42230

**Joseph B&B**, Boulain, t 04 77 90 36 90 (€). Just west of St-Etienne, but a world away, beside the Loire, simple rooms in a typical local house.

## St-Etienne ✉ 42000

**Nouvelle**, 28 Rue St-Jean, t 04 77 32 32 60 (€€€€–€€). For the most inventive cuisine, try this stylish central restaurant. *Closed Sun eve and Mon.*

## St-Jean-Bonnefonds ✉ 42650

**Le Logis de Nantas B&B**, t 04 77 95 15 47, www.logisdenantas.com (€€€€). It's not easy to find a special place to stay in central St-Etienne, but this big-boned house built on the ruins of a former château just northeast of town has four splendid contemporary, air-conditioned suites.

## St-Georges-en-Couzan ✉ 42990

**Ferme-Auberge Le Mazet**, t 04 77 24 80 95. Big stone farm with six rooms. Also serves fine farm fare. *Closed Dec and Jan; restaurant closed Sun.*

**Auberge La Sarrazine**, t 04 77 24 53 59 (€). Hidden below the castle ruins, farm turned atmospheric restaurant, with a terrace and a dark, brooding dining room to accompany local *charcuterie.* Open July–Aug daily, weekends April, June and Sept.

## Chalmazel ✉ 42920

**Château de Chalmazel B&B**, t 04 77 24 88 09, www.chateaudechalmazel.com (€€€). Splendid rooms in various historic styles, with modern comforts, in a big, sober castle. *Table d'hôte* (€€).

**Rue de la Cîme**, t 04 77 24 01 78 (€€). A restaurant serving good regional cuisine, which doubles as a tea room and sells local specialities. *Open school hols daily; otherwise Wed–Sun.*

## St-Bonnet-le-Courreau ✉ 42940

**Jasserie Garnier**, t 04 77 76 83 86 (€€). Favourite for Monts du Forez walkers. Hearty local dishes served in basic traditional farm set far on the heights, reached by long track. Book. *Open July–Aug daily, Feb–June and Sept–Nov weekends only.*

## Marols ✉ 42560

**L'Ecusson B&B**, t 04 77 76 70 38 (€). In a fine stone historic village house, some steps sloping with age, simple traditional rooms. Run by a feisty woman full of Forez information and wit. *Table d'hôte* (€€). *Closed Dec–April.*

## La Chapelle-en-Lafaye ✉ 42380

**Auberge du Marais**, t 04 77 50 00 40 (€€). Just below Montarcher, popular country restaurant serving tasty regional dishes either in the beamed dining room, or on the cheerful terrace. *Closed Mon eve and Tues, plus late Jan–late Feb.*

## St-Bonnet-le-Château ✉ 42380

****Le Béfranc**, 7 Route d'Augel, t 04 77 50 54 54, www.hotel-lebefranc.com (€). Sober rooms in former *gendarmerie.* Nice dining room (€€). *Closed Jan.*

**La Calèche**, 2 Place Marey, t 04 77 50 15 58 (€€). Inventive cuisine in typical old central town house. *Closed Sun eve, Tues eve and Wed, and school half-terms.*

# To the Loire's Source via Le Puy-en-Velay

Increasingly dark-stoned castles line the way up to the source of the Loire, reflecting these old volcanic territories. Le Puy-en-Velay has put the vestiges of its explosive geological past to stunning Christian use. The very early stages of the river cut through gorges lined by curious rock formations, as at elephantine Arlempdes, while the even more curious round lake of Issarlès is explained by its formation in a volcanic crater. You reach the source of the Loire at the mighty pyramid of the Mont Gerbier-de-Jonc, though the peak is outdone in majesty by neighbouring Mont Mézenc.

## The Loire from St-Etienne to Le Puy

**Château de Rochebaron**
*for restoration volunteers,* **t** *04 71 61 80 44, www. rochebaron.org*

Pressing south of St-Etienne via **Aurec-sur-Loire**, high above **Bas-en-Basset** you can only reach the **Château de Rochebaron** by a steep hillside walk. But it's interesting to see how this massive medieval castle is being brought back to life by a dedicated association, and you can even join them in their work. **Retournac**, down by the Loire, has recently revived its lace-making traditions, and opened a lace museum, the **Musée des Manufactures de Dentelles**. A detour west takes you past the sweet village of **St-André-de-Chalencon** to the exceptional hamlet of **Chalencon** with its chequered church lost in a deep wooded valley.

**Musée des Manufactures de Dentelles**
*www.ville-retournac. fr/musee; adm*

**Château de Lavoûte-Polignac**
*open July–Sept daily 10–12.30 and 2–6.30; June daily 2–5; Easter hols daily 2.30–5; May Sat, Sun and hols 2–5; adm*

Continuing down the Loire, the darkly picturesque **Château de Lavoûte-Polignac** stands guard over a meander in the river, one of the many impressive homes of the powerful Auvergnat Polignac family, one of the most hated aristocratic clans in France by the time of the Revolution, when it suffered the consequences. Abandoned during that period, this castle was restored in the late 19th century. It now looks rather sorry for itself inside, although the guided tour can offer an absorbing insight into the family.

**Château de Polignac**
*open June–Sept daily 10–7; Easter–May and Oct 2–6; adm*

In an even more ruined state, but an even more dramatic location, atop a volcanic platform, the same family's medieval **Château de Polignac** still elicits awe. This tremendous medieval stage-set was the lordly base for centuries, gradually built up from around 960. On the interesting guided tour, you learn of the centuries-long battle between the often ruthless Polignac nobles and the bishops of Le Puy-en-Velay. In fact, from the fortifications you get truly spectacular views not just of the volcano tops all around, but also down on the cathedral of Le Puy. Recently, the Countess of Polignac has been breathing life back into the castle: the soaring keep at the heart of the fortifications has been made safe enough for visitors to climb to the top, and there's also a programme of events. In the village of **Polignac** below, be tempted inside the church with its seductive glazed roof tiles. The medieval murals include an enchanting Nativity scene. Otherwise, the Polignac family shares the attention with Christ, several important lords depicted in the stained-glass windows.

**Château de St-Vidal**
*open July–Aug daily 2–6.30; adm*

West, the well-preserved **Château de St-Vidal** looks like a children's picture-book image of a medieval fort with its square shape and round corner towers, all built in forbidding black rock.

## Le Puy-en-Velay

 **Le Puy-en-Velay**

The thin pinnacles of volcanic rock protruding so dramatically skywards make the silhouette of Le Puy-en-Velay unforgettable. From distant times, these natural curiosities inspired religious veneration. A slab known as the **Feverish Stone**, possibly part of an earlier Neolithic dolmen, became a significant place of worship in Gallo-Roman times. With the coming of Christianity, Le Puy early embraced the cult of the Virgin Mary, the first church dedicated to her probably being built in the 5th century.

Now, each of Le Puy's pinnacles is topped by a startling Christian church or sculpture. A huge statue of the Virgin, and another of St Joseph, both 19th-century, stand high on two of them. On another rises one of the most eccentric churches in France, perhaps built for Bishop Gothescalk. Tradition has it that he set out in 950 on the first major pilgrimage from Le Puy to Santiago de Compostela in northern Spain. During the Middle Ages, the place developed into one of the four most important meeting points in France for this popular spiritual journey. The craft of lace-making, probably established in the 15th century, became a second source of renown for the city; many women were still employed producing hand-made *dentelle* until the First World War.

One of the most memorable streets in France, steep, many-stepped, deep-purple-stoned **Rue des Tables**, leads up to the **cathedral**. Its huge black porch gapes wide open, like the mouth of a biblical leviathan ready to gobble you up. The alternating stones and columns of the sheer wall above provide a virtuoso display of Romanesque decoration. Rising to the left of the cathedral façade stand the imposing **Hôtel Dieu**, or hospital, and a castle-like building surrounding the cathedral cloister. The whole complex looks like a well-defended holy citadel.

The cathedral is very generous in its opening hours, though, receiving early visitors from 6.30am; a special mass is held daily at 7am for pilgrims setting out from here to Santiago. Enter via the massive **porch**, the size of a decent church, and a piece of extra-ordinarily bold architecture, an extension built out from the hilltop. Once your eyes get accustomed to the darkness, you can make out faded frescoes above you. Pilgrims in centuries past would have climbed up the porch steps to pop straight out of the floor in the centre of the nave; you now often have to take the side stairs.

The interior was restored with a heavy hand in the 19th and 20th centuries. Beyond the glitzy contemporary cross hanging over the crossing, devout pilgrims still venerate the curious Black Virgin. The original is said to have been brought back from the Orient by a medieval French king – it is now thought she may have been a representation of the ancient Egyptian goddess Isis, rather than Mary. Either way, she was destroyed at the Revolution; the copy shows Jesus popping his head out of his mother's clothing like a baby kangaroo. Grandiose Ancien Régime paintings stand out in the aisles, one showing a remarkable ceremony thanking the Black Virgin for supposedly saving Le Puy from an outbreak of plague. The ancient Feverish Stone can be seen in one apse, and the sacristy houses a mixed bag of other religious curiosities.

A labyrinth of further religious buildings surrounds the cathedral. The **Chapelle du St-Sacrement** once served as the library of the cathedral school, one wall decorated in the 16th century with depictions of the liberal arts as enthroned women in period attire. The freestanding **bell tower** is decorated on the outside with intriguing medieval carvings, and contains grand tombs.

**Cloisters museum**
*open July–Aug 9–6.30; mid-May–June and most Sept 9–12 and 2–6.30; rest of year 9–12 and 2–5; adm*

Beyond, the over-restored **cloisters** and the rooms around it house a **museum of religious art**. Its most striking elements include the medieval *Crucifixion* wall painting in the chapterhouse and a 16th-century embroidered coat made for the Black Virgin, featuring a splendid *Tree of Jesse* depicting Christ's lineage.

**Notre-Dame de France**
*open mid-Mar–Sept 9–7; Oct–Feb 10–5; adm*

Gather your energies to walk up to the enormous sickly pink **Notre-Dame de France**, stuck on top of the nearby Rocher Corneille in the 19th century. So striking from a distance, this Virgin turns out to be a bit of a monstrosity close up. Designed by Jean-Marie Bonnassieux, she was built from cannon captured at Sebastopol in the Crimean War. She measures over 50ft in height and weighs in at over 100 tons. You can actually climb up inside her graffiti-covered innards to get even more head-spinning views of the city.

**Centre d'Enseignement de la Dentelle au Fuseau**
*open mid-June– mid-Sept Mon–Fri 9–12 and 1.30–5.30, Sat 9.30–4.30; Oct–mid-June Mon–Fri 10–12 and 2–5; adm*

Back down at Place des Tables, take Rue Raphaël for the **Centre d'Enseignement de la Dentelle au Fuseau**. This presents a video on lace-making in Le Puy-en-Velay, and small exhibitions. Sweet little restaurants take over at least half the cobbled street outside in summer, serving local lentil dishes and verbena-flavoured desserts.

Adjoining Place du Clauzel and Place du Martouret form the heart of the old secular town. The neoclassical **Hôtel de Ville** was completed in 1766, in time to witness the guillotining of over 40 people, including 18 priests, and the burning in 1794 of the original Black Virgin. The other side of the town hall, imposing Rue Pannessac curves from Place du Plot to the stocky gateway of the **Tour Pannessac**, a remnant of medieval defences.

A grand quarter developed on the flat area to the south in the 19th century. It stretches from Place du Breuil via the shaded

**Musée Crozatier**
*open mid-June–mid-Sept daily 10–12 and 2–6; May–mid-June and late Sept Wed–Mon 10–12 and 2–6, closed Tues; mid-Sept–April Mon and Wed–Sat 10–12 and 2–4, Sun 2–4, closed Tues; adm*

*boules*-players' **Vinay Gardens** to the substantial **Musée Crozatier**, crammed with a confusion of artefacts, regional arts and lace. To the west, the church of **St-Laurent** stands close to the Borne river. St Dominic, founder in Toulouse of the Inquisition, came to visit in the 13th century and a Dominican **monastery** was set up, of which the church formed a part. In the Hundred Years War, fearsome French leader Bertrand du Guesclin died besieging Châteauneuf-de-Randon not far south, explaining why his entrails ended up here, along with his tomb effigy.

Isolated high above another atmospheric corner of town, 260 steps lead up another staggering pinnacle to the crooked little **Chapelle St-Michel d'Aiguilhe**. Before the climb, say a quick prayer at the gorgeous **Oratoire St-Grégoire** in patterned stone below. And visit the **Espace St-Michel**, which briefly explains the geology of the area as well as the cult of St Michael. The story goes that Bishop Gothescalk had the extraordinary chapel built in the bellicose archangel's honour on his return from his pilgrimage to Santiago; the architecture certainly appears to contain Spanish to Moorish touches. In the fabulous cave-like interior, nooks and crannies display intriguing religious items.

**Chapelle St-Michel d'Aiguilhe**
*open May–Sept 9–6.30; mid-Mar–April and Oct–mid-Nov 9.30–12 and 2–5.30; Feb–mid-Mar plus Christmas hols 2–7; adm*

If you are captivated by the pinnacles of Le Puy, head out to **Espaly** to acquaint yourself with the enormous **statue of Joseph**, surrounded by more sickly 19th-century religious confections. As with Notre-Dame de France, you can climb up inside.

**Statue of Joseph**
*open July–Aug 2–7; adm*

## The Last Leg of the Loire to its Source

A string of more or less ruined medieval forts marks the banks of the Loire south from Le Puy. Head a little east to marvel at the dark purples, blacks and oranges of **Le Monastier-sur-Gazeille**'s exceptional church, a remnant of the most important abbey of the Velay region in medieval times. The stocky castle behind is less colourful, but with its black volcanic sides and crinkled, red-tiled roofs has plenty of character too. Inside, the **Musée Municipal** is just a modest affair. It cursorily recalls that Robert Louis Stevenson stayed for a month here in 1878, observing the villagers' antics before heading off on his travels with a donkey through the Cévennes. West of the river, the **Lac du Bouchet** is one in a series of circular lakes set in old volcano tops in these parts.

**Le Monastier-sur-Gazelle Musée Municipal**
*open July–Aug Tues–Sun 10.30–12 and 2–6; June and Sept–Oct Tues–Sun 2–5; adm*

Back beside the Loire, you hit upon dark gorges before reaching **Arlempdes**, a village standing in a wonderfully dramatic location, the remnants of its fort clinging to the back of a monster of a rock. Here, the Loire makes an important turn.

The almost perfectly round **Lac d'Issarlès** is a natural wonder created by water collecting in an old volcanic crater, although tourism has now made its mark, and visitors fight for space on the thin pebble beach in high summer. You can take a shaded walk round the lake. Compare Issarlès with the **Lac de Coucouron** just a little to the west, also popular in summer, but with steeper, more exposed banks.

Lost in the countryside a bit southeast of these two, some way outside **St-Cirgues-en-Montagne**, the **Parc du Chien Nordique** makes a surprisingly interesting visit in summer as well as winter, with over 50 Nordic sleigh-dogs to see, many taken in from owners who couldn't cope with their pets. At an altitude of 1,200 metres, the snowy conditions here can be harsh in winter, but the dogs are perfectly adapted, while in summer they certainly seem to enjoy their hotter outings. If you are fit you might try organizing an outing with the dogs, either with wheels, on foot, or even canyoning. Otherwise simply enjoy the guided tour with the passionate staff, who take you into the pack enclosures.

**Parc du Chien Nordique**
*t 04 75 38 91 41; open July–Aug daily 3–7; Sept–June by reservation; adm*

Up towards the beginnings of the Loire, *sucs*, huge majestic, round-topped volcanic mountains, seem to protect the source of the great river. The landscapes look ancient – it would scarcely come as a surprise to see a dinosaur or two wandering around. The villages can look grey and exposed between the winter and summer seasons, and spring comes late, but *ski de fond* signs indicate that people enjoy cross-country skiing here in snowy weather. In summer, beautiful herds of cows and cart horses are left to graze the slopes, reduced to toy size in these vast landscapes, while carpets of flowers emerge in parts. To appreciate traditional life, visit the welcoming, atmospheric farms around **Ste-Eulalie** – ask for opening times at the tourist office (overleaf).

 **Mont Gerbier-de-Jonc**

**Mont Gerbier-de-Jonc**, birthplace of the Loire, for the French a near deity of a river to this day, looks almost man-made, seemingly built up of a great mound of boulders, snow-covered or stained with green lichens. The first waters of the Loire dribble rather inconspicuously down the side of the pyramid. But this rather remote place is firmly on the French tourist map – learning about the Loire and its source has long formed an essential part of early geography lessons in France. Regional stalls line the road below Mont Gerbier in high season, selling local cheese, *charcuterie*, *confiture* and souvenirs, while crowds pay to crawl up the mountainside along marked tracks, created in an attempt to preserve the sight a little better than in the past.

**Mont Mézenc**

Mont Gerbier-de-Jonc's still more impressive brother, **Mont Mézenc**, rises just a bit to the north. Between the two, on warm days you might go for a refreshing dip down at the very pretty mirror of a lake, the **Lac de St-Martial**, enviously overseen by the cemetery tombs and village backed by pine-clad hills.

Also stop to admire the shimmering stone roofs of **Borée**. As for the village church here, it owes its amazingly colourful facade to the local geology. Frivolous animal sculptures add a touch of

## Market Days around the Loire's Source

**Le Puy-en-Velay**: Sat am.
**Le Monastier-sur-Gazeille**: Tues am.

## Where to Stay and Eat around the Loire's Source

(i) **Ste-Eulalie** >>
*Le Village,*
*07510 Ste-Eulalie,*
*t 04 75 38 89 78*

(i) **Le Puy-en-Velay** >
*Place du Breuil,*
*43000 Le Puy-en-Velay,*
*t 04 71 09 38 41,*
*www.ot-lepuyenvelay.fr*

(★) **Ferme de la Besse** >>

(i) **Le Monastier-sur-Gazeille**
*32 Rue St-Pierre,*
*t 04 71 08 37 76,*
*oti.paysdumezenc@*
*wanadoo.fr*

### St-André-de-Chalencon
✉ 43130
**\*\*Relais des Seigneurs**, Place de l'Eglise, **t** 04 71 58 41 41 (€). Caringly renovated little hotel by the church. *Only open mid-July–mid-Sept.*

### Le Puy-en-Velay ✉ 43000
**\*\*\*Régina**, 34 Bd Maréchal Fayolle, **t** 04 71 09 14 71, *www.hotelrestregina.com* (€). Modernized rooms on the boulevards, with delicious menus (€€).
**Tournayre**, 12 Rue Chênebouterie, **t** 04 71 09 58 94 (€€€–€€). Swish restaurant with vaulted dining room for Auvergnat specialities. *Closed Sun eve, Mon, Wed eve, Jan and early Sept.*
**François Gagnaire**, 4 Av Charbonnier, **t** 04 71 02 75 55 (€€€). On the west side of the Vinay garden, a modern restaurant reputed for regional cuisine, where you'll find Puy lentils, for example, served in most imaginative ways. *Closed Sun eve and Mon.*

### Chaspinhac ✉ 43700
**La Paravent B&B**, **t** 04 71 03 54 75, *michel-jourde@wanadoo.fr* (€).

Pleasant, spacious, simple rooms in a village house northeast of town. Run by a couple who work in creative lace design, and who also prepare organic regional cuisine for the *table d'hôte* (€).

### Arlempdes ✉ 43490
**\*Hôtel du Manoir**, **t** 04 71 57 17 14 (€). Appealing old stone hotel with very simple rooms below the castle. Restaurant (€€) with fine view. *Closed Nov–early Mar.*

### Ste-Eulalie ✉ 07510
**\*\*Hôtel du Nord**, **t** 04 75 38 80 09, *www.ardeche.tourisme.com/hotel/du-nord* (€). Unexciting modern building, but in the local style, run by a fisherman who organizes outings. Country cooking (€€). *Closed mid-Nov–late Feb; restaurant closed Tues pm and Wed.*

### Usclades-et-Rieutord ✉ 07510
**Ferme de la Besse**, **t** 04 75 38 80 64 (€€). A splendidly rustic dark vaulted dining room in an ancient country farm run by a passionate family producing its own *charcuterie*, serving very tasty, hearty regional cuisine. *Must book. Closed Dec–early April.*

### Condas/St-Martial ✉ 07310
**Le Hameau Gourmand B&B**, **t** 04 75 29 28 44, *condas@free.fr* (€). Lovingly restored by the Quinons. Madame uses local plants for her *table d'hôte* (€€), and even organizes stays on a plant theme.

humour to this mountainside village. Mont Mézenc dominates the surrounding area, its 1,754m peak offering timeless views all round. Sporty types enjoy paragliding into the air, but the pamorama is breathtaking even if you prefer to stay firmly glued to the ground.

These two brooding mountains, Mézenc and Gerbier-de-Jonc, form part of France's surprisingly easterly *division des eaux*, the line separating the river waters flowing to the Atlantic from those heading for the Mediterranean. On clear days, it feels as if you can see not just across the Ardèche from here, but almost across the whole of the Rhône-Alpes region, to some of the highest Alpine peaks.

# West of the Rhône: Down the Ardèche

*There's scarcely a single straight road in the tortuous département of the Ardèche once you've left behind the west bank of the Rhône, and scarcely a road that isn't beautiful. Although demanding, almost all the winding ways through the densely chestnut-wooded valleys, the gorges crossed by old stone bridges and the more savage mountains out west prove a delight. The villages across these parts are gorgeous, nowhere more sensational than along the middle stretch of the short, dramatic Ardèche river itself; its valley ends with the most spectacular of caves and gorges.*

# 11

## Don't miss

⭐ **A startling mountain retreat**
Mont Pilat **p.154**

⭐ **Chestnut terraces producing** *marrons glacés*
Around Privas **p.160**

⭐ **Life on the edge**
Hill villages around Les Vans **p.168**

⭐ **Fairytale riverside stops**
Ardèche-side villages from Vals to Vallon **p.172**

⭐ **Natural high drama**
Southern Ardèche gorges and caves **p.173**

*See map overleaf*

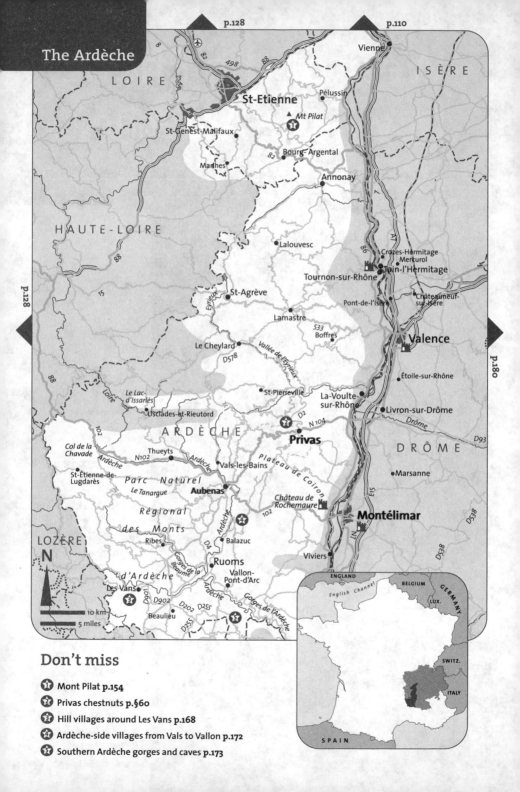

# The Ardèche

ISÈRE

LOIRE

p.128

Vienne

St-Etienne

Pélussin

St-Genest-Malifaux

Mt Pilat

Marlhes

Bourg-Argental

HAUTE-LOIRE

Annonay

Lalouvesc

Crozes-Hermitage
Merturol
Tain-l'Hermitage

Tournon-sur-Rhône

St-Agrève

Évrieux

Châteauneuf-sur-Isère

Lamastre

Pont-de-l'Isère

Boffres

Le Cheylard

Valence

D578

Vallée de l'Eyrieux

St-Pierreville

Étoile-sur-Rhône

Le Lac-d'Issarlès

La-Voulte-sur-Rhône

Livron-sur-Drôme

Usclades-et-Rieutord

Loire

ARDÈCHE

Privas

Drôme

D93

Col de la Chavade

Thueyts

N102

Ardèche

Vals-les-Bains

Plateau de Coiron

DRÔME

Marsanne

St-Étienne-de-Lugdarès

Parc Naturel

Le Tanargue

Aubenas

Château de Rochemaure

Régional

Montélimar

des Monts

Ribes

Balazuc

LOZÈRE

N

d'Ardèche

Ruoms

Viviers

Les Vans

Vallon-Pont-d'Arc

Gorges de la Beaume

Beaulieu

D902

D202

D255

Gorges de l'Ardèche

10 km
5 miles

p.180

## Don't miss

The mountainous Ardèche area (also known as the Vivarais, after its ancient little southern town of Viviers – *see* p.198) dips dramatically down from the Massif Central to the Rhône. The rocks and old stone houses across the *département* tend towards the dark and moody because of the area's volcanic past. Rivers hurtle down from the old craters through twisting Ardéchois valleys – sensational, but hardly conducive to agriculture. In the south, the Vivarais and Cévennes mountains touch.

Although enjoying tourist success now, this has not always been an easy place in which to live; farmers down the centuries painstakingly built up layers of terracing on these difficult lands. The mainstay of the year was chestnuts, not turned into delicious *marrons glacés* as they are today, but made into flour, for human and animal use alike – this was not the territory of wealthy men. Protestantism was quickly adopted from the 16th century in these poor regions, which went on to share a tragic history of religious persecution, although Protestantism stuck in many parts.

The influence of Lyon's silk-makers radiated far and wide, and silk farms and textile factories were established across the Ardèche. These traditions gradually died out, leaving derelict *filatures* – some have now been converted into silk museums and trendy hotels. Fruit flourishes in the more generous valleys towards the Rhône, and small-scale wine-making survived the 19th-century crises. In recent decades the quality of Ardéchois wines has been rising. (For information on the well-established northern Côtes du Rhône wines produced in these parts, *see* pp.187–8.)

With the Rhône passing down one side of the *département* and the Loire beginning on the other side, the Ardèche river itself cuts a jagged path across the southern half of the Vivarais. Its source lies close to that of the Loire, but, while the latter sets off on its leisurely 1,000km journey to the Atlantic, the Ardèche does something of a 100km sprint to reach the Rhône. Starting at breakneck speed, it then slows a bit, its curious rocky banks lined with enchanting villages in a *département* packed with them.

Beyond Vallon-Pont-d'Arc you come to the major Gorges de l'Ardèche, a head-spinning canyon beloved of canoeists, climbers and potholers. Amazing cool caves hide out around here. A sensational one only discovered in the mid-1990s conceals one of the greatest caches of prehistoric art ever found in the world; this Grotte Chauvet will never be opened to the public, but the building of its replica is planned.

These are the heavily touristy parts of the *département*. But in the north, and out west, where large swaths come under the protection of the Parc Naturel Régional des Monts d'Ardèche, it remains largely unspoilt; many of the centuries-old terraces were abandoned, its villages left to fall partly into ruin. A large number

## Getting to and around the Ardèche

Lyon **airport** isn't far north of the northerly half of this chapter; Nîmes airport isn't too far south of the southern half. Valence has an excellent **TGV** station, easily reached from London via Lille, and Avignon TGV station, close to southern Ardèche, offers a weekly summer Eurostar service direct from London.

While you can take **trains** to St-Etienne or the Rhône valley stations such as Vienne, Valence, Montélimar or Pont-St-Esprit, to explore these rugged parts using public transport you have to use **buses**. For Pilat bus services, consult *www.loire.fr*. For the Ardèche, see the full, updated timetables on *www.ardeche.fr*, under *horaires des transports*.

of Brits as well as Belgians, and even some northern European Protestants whose ancestors fled into exile from here, have been helping to restore the ruins. This chapter also includes the secretive little Mont Pilat range, connected to northern Ardèche.

# Mont Pilat and the Northern Ardèche

## Mont Pilat

**⓫ Mont Pilat**

Short, precipitous routes lead into the Pilat heights from the Rhône or Gier, abruptly whisking you away from the industry in the valleys below into a world of rustic high plateaux and forests stretching below rocky peaks. Although the Pilat's villages are now quiet, those within the range's valleys do have an industrial past, recalled in a scattering of museums.

Mont Pilat was made into a regional nature park in 1974. Its name derives from a far-fetched story claiming that a Roman emperor called for the body of Pontius Pilate to be brought to Gaul via the Rhône; at the city of Vienne, locals stole the corpse and disposed of it in the mountains to the west, causing the peaks to become barren, Pilate haunting the range. Several of the Pilat's summits are topped by tortured piles of rocks known as *chirats*, but boring old geologists say these date from the end of the last Ice Age.

The most extraordinary village in the Pilat, a member of the association *Les Plus Beaux Villages de France*, **Ste-Croix-en-Jarez** is in fact a former fortified medieval monastery that was simply divided up by locals at the Revolution to create new homes. Going back in time, the legend here says the monastery was originally founded in the 1280s after a pious woman, Béatrix de Roussillon, had a vision of a silver cross pointing to the spot. For five centuries Carthusian monks prayed and worked here, developing the economy of the Pilat. The last monks were thrown out during the Revolution. Families from nearby Pavezin thought it a good idea to convert the cells into unusual terraced houses, rather than going to all the bother of destroying the place and carting off its stone.

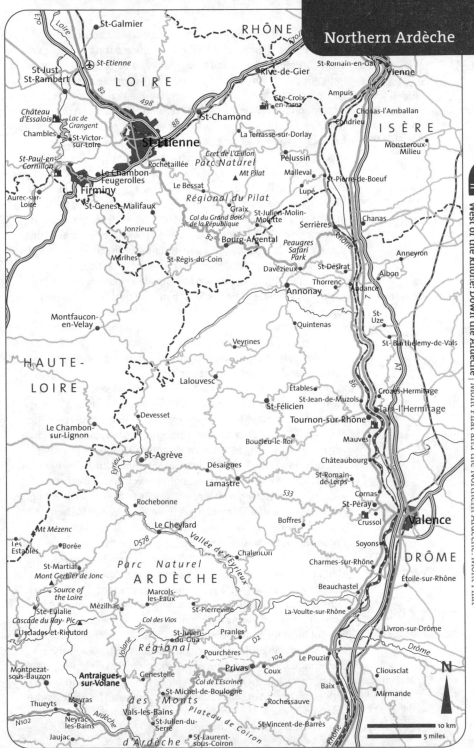

RHÔNE

St-Galmier

St-Etienne

St-Romain-en-Gal

Vienne

St-Just
St-Rambert

Rive-de-Gier

Ampuis

Chonas-l'Amballan

ISÈRE

Château
d'Essalois

Lac de
Grangent

St-Chamond

Condrieu

Monsteroux-
Milieu

Chambles

St-Victor-
sur-Loire

LOIRE

La Terrasse-sur-Dorlay

St-Paul-en-
Cornillon

St-Etienne

Rochetaillée

Cret de L'Œillon

Pélussin

Parc Naturel

Malleval

Aurec-sur-
Loire

Le Chambon-
Feugerolles

Firminy

Mt Pilat

St-Pierre-de-Boeuf

St-Genest-Malifaux

Le Bessat

Régional du Pilat

Lupé

Chanas

Jonzieux

Graix

Col du Grand Bois/
de la République

St-Julien-Molin-
Molette

Serrières

Marlhes

St-Régis-du-Coin

Bourg-Argental

Peaugres
Safari
Park

Anneyron

Davézieux

St-Désirat

Albon

Montfaucon-
en-Velay

Thorrenc

Abdance

St-
Uze

Annonay

HAUTE-

LOIRE

Quintenas

St-Barthélemy-de-Vals

Veyrines

Étables

Crozes-Hermitage

Lalouvesc

St-Jean-de-Muzols

St-Félicien

Tain-l'Hermitage

Le Chambon-
sur-Lignon

Devesset

Tournon-sur-Rhône

Mauves

Boucieu-le-Roi

St-Agrève

Châteaubourg

Désaignes

St-Romain-
de-Lerps

Lamastre

Cornas

Rochebonne

St-Péray

Mt Mézenc

Le Cheylard

Vallée de l'Eyrieux

Boffres

Crussol

Valence

Les
Estables

Borée

Chalencon

Soyons

DRÔME

St-Martial
Mont Gerbier de Jonc

Parc Naturel

Charmes-sur-Rhône

Étoile-sur-Rhône

Source of
the Loire

ARDÈCHE

Beauchastel

Ste-Eulalie

Mézilhac

Marcols-
les-Eaux

St-Pierreville

La-Voulte-sur-Rhône

Cascade du Ray-Pic

Usclades-et-Rieutord

Col des Vios

St-Julien-
du-Gua

Pranles

Livron-sur-Drôme

Montpezat-
sous-Bauzon

Antraigues-
sur-Volane

Régional

Pourchères

Privas

Le Pouzin

Cliousclat

Genestelle

Coux

Baix

Mirmande

Thueyts

Meyras

des Monts

St-Michel-de-Boulogne

Rochessauve

Vals-les-Bains

St-Julien-du-
Serre

Plateau de Coiron

St-Vincent-de-Barrès

Neyrac-
les-Bains

Jaujac

d'Ardèche

St-Laurent-
sous-Coiron

N

10 km

5 miles

So the village is centred around the two monastic courtyards divided by the church. This substantial edifice, dating from the 17th century, preserves its carved wood stalls and paintings of three imploring saints. You can only see the earlier, medieval chapter house, and sacristy with fine medieval murals, on a guided tour.

**Ste-Croix-en-Jarre guided tours**
*ask at gateway*

**Maison des Tresses et Lacets**
*t 04 77 20 91 06; open Feb–Dec Wed–Fri and Sun 2.30–6; also open Sat in July and Aug; closed Jan; adm*

Attention turns to industry near the village of **La Terrasse-sur-Dorlay**, where the Maison des Tresses et Lacets recalls how the local waters were used to power machines to make braid. The machinery swings into action on the guided tours.

**Pélussin** stands in a delightfully airy, open location looking east. The prettily laid-out Maison du Parc offers a helpful introduction to the Pilat regional nature park. The Pélussin area is known for the high quality of its fruit, especially apples, and a delightful orchard-lined road heads for Malleval (*see* p.189). The nearby village of **Lupé** has a restored medieval château and a pretty church.

**Maison du Parc**
*open Easter hols–11 Nov daily 9.30–12.30 and 2–6; rest of year Mon–Wed and Fri 10–12.30 and 2–6, Thurs 2–6, Sat 10–12.30*

Forests surround the highest peaks of the Pilat where, from the 18th century, pines were planted to provide wooden posts for the coalmines around St-Etienne. But there was pastureland up high too, and herds are now being reintroduced to stop the forest encroaching too much. The **Crêt de l'Œillon**, at 1,362m, boasts better views than the highest point of the Pilat range, the **Crêt de la Perdrix** (1,432m). Both are topped by curious piles of *chirats*. The bases for Pilat skiing, **Le Bessat** and **Graix**, stand a bit west along the D8 road. This leads northwestwards to St-Etienne, but, before the dramatic drop down into its valley, an eagle's eyrie of a village, **Rochetaillée**, is made to look even more alarming by the knife-edge of rock on which its ruined castle and church are balanced.

To enjoy the southwestern Pilat heights at their best, take the easy moorland walk to the cross on **Mont Chaussitre**. From here, spectacular views open out west onto the volcano-tops of the Velay. South a little, a duckboard path leads to the **Gimel peat bog**. Lovely, solid traditional farms mark the ways down west from Mont Chaussitre, a few selling local produce.

**Maison de la Passementerie**
*t 04 77 39 93 38; open May–mid-Oct Sun 2.30–6.30; adm*

At **Jonzieux**, the tradition of producing ornate trimmings for textiles is occasionally revived at the Maison de la Passementerie. **Marlhes** is strongly marked by Catholicism, its village church practically the size of a cathedral. Although the Ardèche to the south and the Velay to the west became Protestant strongholds, the Pilat remained strongly Catholic, and the Marlhes edifice sent a forceful message from the Church. Traditionally, in these isolated parts, laywomen could, however, take on pastoral roles for their communities. They were known as *béates* – the last retired in 1930.

**Maison de la Béate**
*t 04 77 51 24 70; open mid-July–Sept Sun and public hols 2.30–6.30*

Find out about them at the old-style Maison de la Béate in the hamlet of **L'Allier**. Sticking to earthly matters, head for **St-Régis-du-Coin** to visit one of the most interesting traditional Pilat country properties, **La Ferme des Champs**.

## Market Days around Mont Pilat

Pélussin: Sat am.
St-Genest-Malifaux: Thurs and Sun am.
Bourg-Argental: Thurs and Sun am.

## Activities on Mont Pilat

For the wide range of sporting activities in the Pilat, from cross-country skiing to summer mountain biking or *devalkarting* (going down a mountain in go-karts), consult *www.parc-naturel-pilat.fr.*

## Where to Stay and Eat around Mont Pilat

### Ste-Croix-en-Jarez ✉ 42800

*Le Prieuré, t 04 77 20 20 09 (€). Four simple rooms in the gateway. Rustic restaurant (€€). *Closed Jan–mid-Feb; restaurant closed Mon.*

### Pélussin ✉ 42410

Auberge de la Rossagny, Route Champailler, t 04 74 87 67 34 (€). Two simple B&B rooms, and hearty country cooking (€). *Closed Jan–Feb; restaurant closed Tues and Wed.*

### St-Genest-Malifaux ✉ 42660

Auberge de la Diligence Ferme-Auberge, Le Château du Bois, t 04 77 39 04 99 (€). Fortified pink-stone farm close to Mont Chaussitre attached to an agricultural school, with basic *gîte d'étape* group accommodation and restaurant using local produce (€€–€). *Closed Mon–Thurs exc July and Aug, when it is open daily.*

### St-Sauveur-en-Rue ✉ 42220

Auberge du Château de Bobigneux, t 04 77 39 24 33 (€). Adorable little 17th-century manor of a château, with six bargain rooms. A wood-panelled restaurant (€€–€) makes the most of family produce from the family farm next door. *Hotel closed Nov–Mar; restaurant closed Wed, and Jan–Feb.*

### St-Julien-Molin-Molette ✉ 42220

La Rivoire B&B, t 04 77 39 65 44, *www.larivoire.net* (€). Serious, solid farm with a round tower above the N82 south of Bourg-Argental. Neat rooms. Farm produce as *table d'hôte* (€€).

### ⓘ St-Genest-Malifaux >>

*1 Rue de Feuillage, 42660 St-Genest-Malifaux, t 04 77 51 23 84, ot.haut-pilat@wanadoo.fr*

### ⓘ Parc Naturel Régional du Pilat

*www.parc-naturel-pilat.fr*

### ⓘ Bourg-Argental

*18 Place de la Liberté, 42220 Bourg-Argental, t 04 77 39 63 49, otbourgargental@aol.com*

### ⓘ Pélussin >

*Moulin de Virieu, 42410 Pélussin, t 04 74 87 52 00*

### Maison du Châtelet

*t 04 77 39 63 49; open mid-June–late Sept daily 9.30–12.30 and 2.30–6.30; May–mid-June Mon and Fri 2–6, Tues–Thurs 9–12, Sat and Sun 9–12 and 2–6; late Sept–April Mon and Fri 2–6, Tues–Thurs and Sat 9–12; adm*

Down in the Déôme valley, the small town of **Bourg-Argental** has retained fragments of historic charm. Racy Romanesque carvings saved from an earlier structure enliven the doorway to the otherwise much later church, events in Jesus' childhood featuring below a surprisingly friendly *Christ of the Apocalypse*. The **Maison du Châtelet**, a sturdy 16th-century townhouse, has been turned in part into a centre presenting the Parc du Pilat, and in part into a local museum, with a heart-warming film on the textile-making tradition here. Just north, the disused factories at **St-Julien-Molin-Molette** are a reminder that this village used to supply textiles and arms to St-Etienne. Now, craftspeople, notably woodworkers, have set up studios, while clever pieces of art are displayed out in the open, bringing a touch of invention to the surrounds.

# The Northern Ardèche

Drunken-looking roads swerve down through the northern half of the *département de l'Ardèche*. Conflict between Protestantism and Catholicism was vicious in these parts, leaving behind a bitter legacy. Below St-Agrève, we venture into the northern half of the Parc Naturel Régional des Monts d'Ardèche.

Big towns aren't exactly the *département* of the Ardèche's strong point, and **Annonay**, the largest, is a worn-out industrial centre encircled by mountains, as though caught at the bottom of a deep bowl. It hardly makes an obvious tourist stop. The ingenious Montgolfier brothers (*see* p.41) escaped from here into the skies by inventing the hot-air balloon towards the close of the 18th century. Find out about them at the gritty black-stoned **Musée Vivarois César Filhol**, which also has little sections on local history and artists. The Montgolfiers aren't the only technical whizz-kids from Annonay: their great-nephew, the engineer Marc Seguin, designed the first French suspension bridges, put up over the Rhône, and, in 1826, one of the earliest French railway lines, linking Lyon and St-Etienne. A statue of the Montgolfier brothers stands on one square; Seguin presides over another.

By the river in Annonay's suburb of **Davézieux**, at the birthplace of the Montgolfier brothers, the **Musée des Papeteries Canson & Montgolfier** concentrates on paper-making rather than ballooning, old machines creaking into action on the tour. The popular **Peaugres safari park** nearby has two well-marked trails, one to be followed in a firmly sealed car, one on foot.

South from Annonay, you enter rural religious territory. **St-Pierre-aux-Liens** at **Quintenas** is a fortified church; southwest, pilgrims head for **Notre-Dame d'Ay**, perched above the valley, to venerate its Black Virgin. West of **Satillieu**, the Romanesque priory of **Veyrine** hides in a gentle hamlet.

The Ay valley continues up to **Lalouvesc**, a more showy religious stop set among dark pine forests. The imposing 19th-century neo-Byzantine church was built by Pierre Bossan (designer of Lyon's showy Fourvière church) and dedicated to St Régis, a 17th-century Jesuit missionary priest sent to the remoter parts of the Vivarais and the Velay to try and proselytize locals away from Protestantism. He features in much of the visual propaganda.

Surrounded by mountain pastures with goats producing little *caillé doux* cheeses, **St-Félicien** makes an open, airy slope-side stop east of Lalouvesc. The place goes mad once a year over one of the biggest (non-competitive) cycling events in Europe, the *Ardéchoise*, which starts from here one day at the end of June. Isolated on its height above the Doux valley, little **Boucieu-le-Roi** was in fact, through the Gothic period, seat of the royal representative in the Haut Vivarais, until Annonay usurped its role. It has retained some fine stone houses. The former château was taken over by the religious order of the Holy Sacrament, a small museum, the **Maison Pierre Vigne**, recalling its zealous Catholic missionary founder.

Pine-forested ways lead to the lively country-crossroads town of **Lamastre**, at a junction of mountain rivers, overseen by the ruins of the **Château de Pécheylard**. In the town's old upper quarter of

---

**Musée Vivarois César Filhol**
*t 04 75 67 67 93; www. mairie-annonay.fr; open July–Aug daily; Sept–June Wed, Sat and Sun 2.30–6; adm*

**Musée des Papeteries Canson & Montgolfier**
*t 04 75 69 88 00; open July–Aug daily; Sept–June Wed and Sun 2.30–6; adm*

**Peaugres safari park**
*t 04 75 33 00 32; www. safari-peaugres.com; open July–Aug daily 9.30–6, April–June daily 9.30–5; Sept–Mar daily 10–4; adm*

**Maison Pierre Vigne**
*t 04 75 06 76 74; open Tues–Sun 2.30–5.30*

**Macheville**, the much-transformed Romanesque church has kept its period carved capitals. The Doux is the main waterway passing through Lamastre, and the century-old Chemin de Fer du Vivarais steam train swerves down the valley to Tournon-sur-Rhône (*see* p.191). Further upstream, a local bathing spot is watched over by the overgrown ruins of the **Château de Retourtour**. Battered by the Wars of Religion, when it was one of the largest towns in the Ardèche, **Désaignes** just a fraction further up the Doux has managed to keep several of its medieval gateways; its quiet streets lead to the rough medieval château, with displays on local history.

Standing exposed at over 1,000m on a high plateau to the west, below the cone of Mont Chiniac, the small town of **St-Agrève** revolves around one simple high street. A stop has existed here between Le Puy-en-Velay and the Rhône since pre-Roman times. The martyr after whom the place is named was a 7th-century bishop of Le Puy who came to a sticky end on the local mountain. Nothing medieval remains in town because this Huguenot stronghold was decimated in the Wars of Religion. The **Galerie du Besset** has opened St-Agrève's horizons to contemporary art, including British artists. Climb **Mont Chiniac** to appreciate the ancient landscapes, or take the old-style Train de la Galoche into the Velay area in the Auvergne. The **Lac de Devesset** north of town is surrounded by woods and a popular base for watersports.

**Château de Désaignes**
*t 04 75 06 63 81; open July–mid-Sept Tues–Sun 2–6; April–June and Oct Sat and Sun 2–6; adm*

## River Valleys to Privas and Vals-les-Bains

Here we head into the wild northerly valleys of the **Parc Naturel Régional des Monts d'Ardèche**. The steep, winding roads can be exhilarating, but at times also difficult and desolate, with very few houses around. The Eyrieux river, starting up by St-Agrève, twists below the deceptive ruins of the medieval **Château de Rochebonne**, semi-camouflaged by the granite from which they rise. This stronghold was destroyed during the Wars of Religion. The vertiginous views from up top reach well beyond the Eyrieux valley.

The town of **Le Cheylard** lies where the Dorne river meets the Eyrieux. Above town stands the medieval **Château de la Chèze**, which survived the strife of centuries until the Germans torched it in the Second World War; now in the midst of a campsite, it's slowly being restored. Below, Le Cheylard proves a still highly industrious industrial town. Despite lying some distance away from main transport routes, the place's surprisingly successful entrepreneurs, including leaders in specialist textiles, bottling and jewellery, export from here across the world. Now they are also trying to put Le Cheylard on the tourist map. There is a *quartier* of narrow old streets to explore by the river, and on the large main square the remarkable Riou *chocolaterie* is one of the most seductive shops. Over in smartly converted premises beside the

**Château de la Chèze**
*t 04 75 29 45 93; tour mid-July–mid-Aug Mon–Fri at 4; mid-April–mid-July and mid-Aug–Oct Wed at 4*

**L'Arche des Métiers**
*t 04 75 20 24 56, www.
arche-des-metiers.com;
open July–Aug Tues–Fri
10–12 and 2–6.30, Sat
and Sun 2–6.30;
mid-April–June and
Sept–Oct Tues–Sun
2–6.30; mid-Feb–mid-
April and Nov–Xmas
Tues–Sat 2–6.30; adm*

Dorne, **L'Arche des Métiers** acts as a contemporary museum-cum-showcase, telling Le Cheylard's working history and putting its entrepreneurial dynamism to the fore. The presentations are slick, if a bit hit and miss. You do leave this startling place with the distinct feeling that Le Cheylard's ambitious business community wants to turn all its children into entrepreneurs, and a good number of visitors too, if possible! Walk out along the river to another popular shopping stop, the **Bijoux GL**, its incongruously glamorous jeweller's factory shop selling items that attract fashion houses such as Christian Lacroix, but at knock-down prices.

If you follow the lower Eyrieux valley to Privas, you might detour to **Chalencon**, a fortified village that became staunchly Protestant and was consequently largely destroyed by order of Richelieu. The Protestant church contains a portable altar that hints at those hard times of secrecy and persecution.

**Miellerie de Boissy**
*t 04 75 29 30 66;
open mid-June–mid-
Sept Mon–Sat 9–7;
adm for guided tours
at 3 and 5.30*

**Maison du Châtaignier**
*t 04 75 66 64 33,
www.chataignier.fr;
open July–Aug daily
11–12.30 and 2.30–6.30;
April–June and
Sept–Nov Fri–Sun and
public hols 2–6; adm*

Back at Le Cheylard, you can branch off south along the D578 following the Dorne valley. Up on the steep slopes above the picturesque castle at **Accons**, the **Miellerie de Boissy** produces honey not just from hives here, but also from others around south-eastern France. A nature trail introduces you to the local flora.

Reaching the high pastures of **Mézilhac**, look for the turning to **Marcols-les-Eaux** and **St-Pierreville**. The gorgeous road to them, east along the **Glueyre valley**, counts among the most beautiful terraced chestnut routes in the whole *département*. St-Pierreville, set in a tremendous location, pays its respects to the venerable provider of centuries past (*see* box) with its **Maison du Châtaignier**, while the **Musée Vivant de la Laine et du Mouton** devotes itself to the sheep that traditionally grazed beneath the chestnut trees; this is as much a woollen clothes shop as a museum, but the tours on wool-making are instructive. The marked **Route du Châtaignier** entices you with further stops among the chestnut trees, for example local farms offering produce and teas.

**② Chestnuts**

**Musée Vivant de la Laine et du Mouton**
*t 04 75 66 66 11,
www.ardelaine.fr; open
July–Aug daily for tours
11, 3, 3.30, 4, 4.30 and 5;
Feb–June and Dec Wed,
Sun and hols 3; adm*

**Musée du Vivarais Protestant**
*t 04 75 64 22 74; open
mid-June–mid-Sept
Tues–Sat 10–12 and 2–6,
Sun 2–6; April–mid-
June and mid-Sept–Oct
Tues–Sat 2.30–6; adm*

From St-Pierreville, you have the choice of several contorted routes to take you down to Privas. Try a western loop going via **St-Julien-du-Gua**, the **Col de la Fayolle** and the perched village of **Pourchères**. Or take an eastern loop, briefly rejoining the Eyrieux valley before taking the D2 south. Branch off for the rural hamlet of **Le Bouschet** near Pranles, where the long and painful story of Vivarais Protestantism is recalled in the old house holding the **Musée du Vivarais Protestant**, focusing on two extraordinary Protestants, Pierre Durand and his sister Marie, born here in the early 18th century. The diminutive Romanesque church of **Pranles** on its separate hillock contains remarkable carved capitals. A track nearby leads you down by foot to the Mandy mill.

For such an unassuming, sweet old country town, it comes as a surprise to learn that **Privas** is administrative capital of the whole

## Chestnuts: From Paupers' Nosh to Posh *Marrons Glacés*

In the past, local pigs and people alike depended on chestnuts for much of the year; the chestnut harvest was roasted, smoked, and also made into flour. Known therefore as *l'arbre à pain*, 'the bread tree', the chestnut is among the latest-flowering in France, blossoming in June. There are many varieties, including 60 traditional ones; the long-established Comballe gives a fine fruit, but Bouche Rouge are used for *marrons glacés*. Crosses of US-Japanese varieties were also brought in, giving bigger, fuller fruits, if less tasty ones, but they proved more susceptible to disease and the groves were decimated in the 1960s. Communities such as St-Pierreville were hard hit. A vaccine discovered in the 1970s saved the remaining trees. For harvesting, the Ardéchois invented savage-looking implements to knock down and shell the chestnuts, notably vicious shoes with sharp points on the sole. Now they are shaken on to nets, the shells or burs (*bogues*) removed by machine. The shells open, the distinction emerges between an ordinary *châtaigne*, a chestnut divided into several separate sections, and a *marron*, a whole, undivided chestnut. When candied, the latter become *marrons glacés*.

The two main Ardèche producers are Faugier of Privas (out on the road to Montélimar) and Sabaton, outside Aubenas. Imbert, also in Aubenas' outskirts, is more exclusive, uniquely making all its produce from freshly picked *marrons*, and consequently more expensive. *Crème de marrons* and other sweet chestnut spreads are less refined but in many people's view equally delicious. In 2006, Ardèche chestnuts received coveted *appellation d'origine contrôlée* status.

11 West of the Rhône: Down the Ardèche | The Northern Ardèche

*département de l'Ardèche*. It's perhaps better known as capital of *crème de marrons* and *marrons glacés*. Beyond the modern concrete eyesore of the town hall's tower, appealing old squares climb up to the solid stone penitentiary. Privas suffered badly after espousing Protestantism in the Wars of Religion, but became one of the main Huguenot strongholds to be officially accepted at the end of that bloody 16th-century conflict. However, when in 1629 the populace defied the regional governor, attacking the castle because a Catholic had been appointed lord, Richelieu and Louis XIII came to camp outside town along with thousands of troops. Matters got out of hand: although the Cardinal tried to stop the carnage, many Privas Protestants were massacred. One local girl who escaped was adopted by Richelieu, and became known as *La Fortunée de Privas*. To improve relations, the royalists built the bridge over the Ouvèze.

**Coux**, a forward defensive post for Privas in times past, has managed to keep its well-armoured head above the urban sprawl east of town. South from Privas, twisting country roads lead across the **Plateau du Colron**. The N104 main road heads west via the **Col de l'Escrinet**, a big pass into the southern half of the *département*.

Back north at **Mézilhac**'s country crossroads, to the west of its pass, several rivers hurtle down from close to Mont Gerbier-de-Jonc (*see* p.149), travelling along parallel valleys to join the Ardèche river. Along the **Bourges valley**'s white-water-driving experience of a road, don't miss the **Cascade du Ray-Pic**, a spectacular volcanic waterfall in most seasons, 30mins' walk from the car park. The intrepid might try the roads along the parallel **Bézorgues valley**.

The **Volane valley** route just a tad east is slightly better known. The village of **Antraigues-sur-Volane** sits isolated atop its volcanic hill, surrounded by higher, green-lichen-covered slopes. It became a significant centre of the Maquis in the Second World War, and, given its remoteness, you can see why. The open main square, renamed Place de la Résistance, has some appealing café terraces, and is popular for *boules*. A metal *boulomane* in fact counts among many sculptures dotted around the village, made by locals, helped by the numerous craftspeople here. Amusing carved heads have even been incorporated into the sides of the old church.

The contorted roads east of Antraigues offer beautiful country routes. Make for hillside **Genestelle**, where you feel you're on top of the world. The ruins of the **Château du Crau** stand out on the border of a volcanic crater, a tempting walking destination through typical chestnut woods. A ridiculously convoluted but pretty route can lead you round the Oize valley to the dramatic ruins of the **Château de Boulogne**, close to **St-Michel-de-Boulogne**, although they're more easily reached off the N304 main road between Privas and Aubenas. Perched above two ravines, the castle's surprisingly glamorous Renaissance twists, such as the stunning gateway, were added to the medieval structure in the 16th century, although the place was in good part demolished in the 19th century.

ⓘ **Annonay**
*Place des Cordeliers,
07100 Annonay,
t 04 75 33 24 51, www.
ardeche-verte.com*

ⓘ **Lalouvesc**
*Rue St-Régis, 07520
Lalouvesc, t 04 76 67 84
20, lalouvesc@fnotsi.net*

ⓘ **St-Félicien**
*Place de l'Hôtel de Ville,
07410 St-Félicien,
t 04 75 06 06 12*

⭐ **Auberge et
Clos des Cimes >>**

ⓘ **Désaignes**
*Porte du Bourg-de-
l'Homme, 07570
Désaignes, t 04 75 06 61 19*

ⓘ **Lamastre >>**
*Place Montgolfier,
07270 Lamastre, t 04 75
06 48 99, www.
valleedudoux.com*

ⓘ **St-Agrève >>**
*Hôtel de Ville, 07320 St-
Agrève, t 04 75 30 15 06,
www.saintagreve.com*

## Market Days in Northern Ardèche

**Annonay**: Wed and Sat am.
**Lamastre**: Tues and Sat am.
**St-Agrève**: Mon am.
**Le Cheylard**: Wed am.
**Privas**: Wed and Sat am.

## Activities in Northern Ardèche

Annonay is renowned for **hot-air balloning**; see *www.mairie-annonay.fr*. The annual Annonay balloning festival takes place in early June. The **Golf St-Clair** lies outside Annonay. **Cycling** and **mountainbiking** are big in this terrain. The best port of call for all sporting and nature activities in the Ardèche is *www.ardeche-guide.com*; click on *Loisirs Nature* to download.

## Where to Stay and Eat in Northern Ardèche

**St-Marcel-les-Annonay**
✉ **07100**
***Auberge du Lac**, Le Ternay, t 04 75 67 12 03, *www.aubergedulac.com*

(€€€–€€). This bright country hotel lies in a great setting beside the big cedar and sequoia-surrounded Lac de Ternay northwest of Annonay. The dozen rooms are decorated on floral themes and have excellent views. You can sample the cuisine (€€€–€€) on a lovely terrace. *Restaurant closed Sun eve, some Mons, and all Jan.*

**St-Bonnet-le-Froid** ✉ **43290**
****Auberge et Clos des Cimes** , t 04 71 59 93 72, *contact@regismarcon.fr* (€€€€). Pinnacle of fabulous regional cuisine (€€€€) just on the Auvergne side of the border, west of Lalouvesc. Very stylish contemporary rooms. *Closed mid-Dec–mid-Mar; restaurant closed Tues and Wed, plus Mon eve out of season.*

**Lamastre** ✉ **07270**
***Le Midi Barattéro-Perrier**, Place Seignobos, t 04 75 06 41 50 (€€). Old-fashioned central hotel with comfortable rooms and splendid menus (€€€) in classic French provincial style. *Closed late-Dec–mid-Feb; restaurant closed Fri eve, Sun eve and Mon.*

**St-Agrève** ✉ **07320**
***Domaine de Rilhac**, t 04 75 30 20 20, *hotel_rilhac@yahoo.fr* (€€). Old stone converted farm 2km south of

(i) **Parc Naturel Régional des Monts d'Ardèche**
*www.parc-monts ardeche.fr*

(i) **Le Cheylard**
*Rue du 5 Juilllet 1944, 07160 Le Cheylard, t 04 75 29 18 71, www.otlecheylard-ardeche.com*

(i) **Privas >>**
*3 Pl du Général de Gaulle, 07000 Privas, t 04 75 64 33 35, www.paysdeprivas.com*

(i) **St-Pierreville >**
*Place du Clos, 07190 St-Pierreville, t 04 75 66 64 64*

(★) **Château de Rochessauve >>**

town. Very tasty cuisine (€€€–€€). *Closed Jan–Feb; restaurant closed Tues eve, Wed, and Thurs lunch.*

### St-Martin-de-Valamas
✉ **07310**
**La Croix St-Pierre B&B, t** 04 75 30 29 25 (€€–€). Spacious, well-presented, good-value rooms in this substantial house just in the countryside up above the village. Hearty *table d'hôte* (€€). Run by the Rious, Monsieur the impassioned *chocolatier* with shops in Le Cheylard and Arcens.

### Boffres ✉ **07440**
**Domaine de Reiller B&B, t** 04 75 58 15 14, *www.reiller.com* (€). Traditional stone architecture set among chestnut woods, with a pool and pleasant views. *Table d'hôte* (€€).

### St-Pierreville ✉ **07190**
**\*\*Hôtel des Voyageurs, t** 04 75 66 60 08 (€). Traditional option, with fishing expertise to hand. Restaurant. Pool. *Closed Dec–Feb.*

### Antraigues ✉ **07530**
**La Manufacture, t** 04 75 38 77 35, *www.art-de-vie-lamanufacture.com* (€€€; but €€ if 2 nights plus). Exciting contemporary mill conversion with big, calm rooms. Spa and relaxation

spaces, plus pool and court. Restaurant (€ barbecue, *eves only*).
**La Remise**, Pont de l'Huile, **t** 04 75 38 70 74 (€€). Passionate chef serving fresh regional cuisine in a converted barn. *Closed Fri and Sun eve out of season, plus late June, early Sept and mid-Dec–early Jan.*

### St-Julien-du-Serre ✉ **07200**
**Mas de Bourlenc B&B, t** 04 75 37 69 95 (€). The hosts are charming in this property lost in the hills a few km above Aubenas, with splendid views. *Table d'hôte* (€€).

### Privas ✉ **07000**
**\*\*\*La Chaumette Portes des Suds**, Av du Vanel, **t** 04 75 64 30 66, *www. hotelchaumette.fr* (€€). Modern, pretty rooms in the centre. There is also a refined restaurant (€€). Pool. *Restaurant closed Sat lunch.*

### Rochessauve ✉ **07210**
**Château de Rochessauve B&B, t** 04 75 65 07 06, *www.chateau-de-rochessauve.com* (€€€). Sensational cliff-edge rustic property with a charming courtyard. The antiques-dealing owners also run courses on furniture care. Tasteful rooms, delightful garden, pool with view, plus hearty *table d'hôte* (€€€).

# The Southern Ardèche
## The Upper Ardèche River and Savage Southwest

Vals-les-Bains, tucked into its deep valley, and Aubenas, standing proud on its high ridge, sit close together at the northeast corner of the triangle of land in this section. This territory extends across the southwest corner of the *département* of the Ardèche between the N102, following the ravine of the upper Ardèche river, and the D104, which leads down to some of the most cheerful small Ardéchois towns. The wild, mountainous areas of the Tanargue and the Vivarais Cévenol fan out between these two roads.

### Vals-les-Bains and Aubenas

Every six hours, a geyser spurts into life at **Vals-les-Bains**, an amusing symbol for this cheery old spa town straddling the Volane. In the 17th century, the springs acquired a medical reputation, and Mme de Sévigné (*see* p.224) and Jean-Jacques Rousseau (*see* pp.259 and 280) counted among its illustrious visitors. Grand hotels went up in the Belle Epoque. Vals' water was also bottled and became popular across France long before many of its younger rivals. During the First World War, some American soldiers were sent to recuperate in this calm spot. Recently, tourists have been coming to receive a pampering at the renovated spa.

On the east bank of the Volane, opposite temptingly unhealthy food shops, this smoked-glass modern **spa** offers free tastings of the local waters in its snazzy reception area, with bookings desk and boutique. The various springs around Vals are reputed to hold many different restorative properties. Relaxation and slimming breaks are very much on the cards these days, after a 2005 revamp: as well as medical treatments you can simply visit for a half-day, to enjoy the indoor pool, or for spa and beauty treatments.

The geyser in the public garden outside performs better in hotter weather. A leisurely stroll in the shade leads to the 1920s **Pavillon**

**Vals springs**
*open to all May–Sept*

**St-Jean** close to Pont St-Jean, a good place to taste from three of the local**springs**. Nearby, the early 20th-century Vals water-bottling factory is still going strong. Numerous bridges span the Volane in town, and pretty gardens extend along a stretch of the west bank. There's also an Olympic-size **outdoor swimming pool**

**Maison
Champanhet**
*t 04 75 37 81 60; open
mid-July–mid-Aug daily
10–12.30 and 3.30–8;
mid-June–mid-July and
mid-Aug–mid-Sept
Tues–Sun 10–12 and
2–6; mid-Mar–mid-June
and mid-Sept–mid-Oct
Tues, Thurs and Fri
10–12 and 2–6, Sat and
Sun 10–12; adm*

this side. Off the main shopping street with its hotels and restaurants is the entrance to the**Maison Champanhet**, a grand town house converted into the local museum, telling the history of Vals as well as that of the family who once owned the house.

Nearby, historic **Aubenas** makes quite an impression high on its ridge above the Ardèche valley, its turreted castle and domed chapel dramatically silhouetted against the sky. Modern developments have sprawled somewhat messily down the slopes. Once you've scaled the old town's defensive flanks, it's a pleasure to stroll around its scruffily merry old streets and squares.

**Château d'Aubenas**
*t 04 75 87 81 11; open
July–Aug daily 11–3;
June and Sept Tues–Sat
tours at 10.30 and 2.30;
Oct–MayTues, Thurs, Fri
and Sat at 2; adm*

While both the soaring keep and the Gothic towers at the front of the massive**château** were built for the medieval Montlaurs, the brightly coloured roofs date from the 17th century, when the Burgundian d'Ornanos took control. Enter the château via one of the twin main doors, each with its own staircase. Through the sober inner courtyard, the grand Ancien Régime staircase was added for the de Vogüés (*see* p.172), an up-and-coming family from central Ardèche who moved in in the late 1730s. Pillaged at the Revolution, at least the panelling survived in some of the château's Ancien Régime rooms. A few chambers are devoted to regional artists. Climb the keep for a medieval guard's view of the region.

Originally part of a Benedictine convent, the many-sided **Dôme St-Benoît** also bears the stamp of the d'Ornanos' decorative changes. Converted into a grain market at the Revolution, inside it

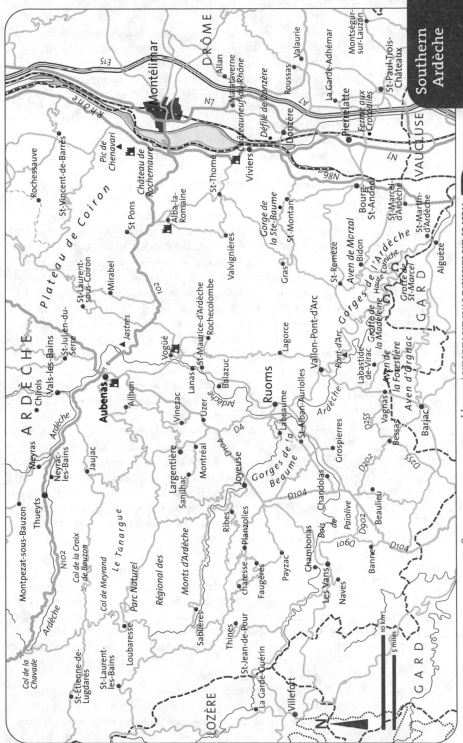

holds the d'Ornanos family mausoleum, but also presents other religious artefacts. Aubenas became a Protestant stronghold in the Wars of Religion, the central medieval church of **St-Laurent** devastated, two Jesuit priests murdered. Afterwards, the Jesuits reimposed strict Catholicism. St-Laurent was rebuilt in uninspiring style, but inside it contains startlingly dynamic Baroque wood-carvings, a legacy from the town's Jesuit college.

For those in search of a moment of chestnut ecstasy, producers **Imbert** and **Sabaton** have outlets on the outskirts of town.

## Up to the Source of the Ardèche

Heading up the steep Ardèche river valley from Vals or Aubenas, traces of volcanic lava flows still mark the way. By the village of **Jaujac**, set to become home to the Maison du Parc Naturel Régional des Monts d'Ardèche, you can walk inside a volcano crater.

**Château de Ventadour**
*t 04 75 38 00 92; open July–mid-Oct Mon–Fri 9–12 and 2–7; also Easter and Whitsun weeks; donations appreciated*

The 12th-century **Château de Ventadour** cuts a sensational silhouette high above the Ardèche river, a ruin that has been rising from its ashes since 1969. That year, the dedicated M. Potiers, with the aid of many volunteers, began restoring the shell of a château left over from a pummelling in the Hundred Years War, followed by plundering at the Revolution, when it became a quarry.

**Ecomusée du Moulinage**
*t 04 75 94 54 07; open June–Sept Wed–Mon 2–7; closed Tues; adm*

The roads beyond take you into rough country to the north. At **Chirols**, the **Ecomusée du Moulinage** recalls the local silk industry. Press on north for **Montpezat-sous-Bauzon**, backed by a series of volcanic tops. Below, the Romanesque church of **Notre-Dame-de-Prévenchère** displays solid character.

Back beside the Ardèche, **Meyras** has feisty historic feel, with its old houses and its church fronted by an intimidating volcanic stone entrance. It became a thermal stop in Roman times, but now conceals one of the most private, peaceful spas in France, **Neyrac-les-Bains'**Thermes de Neyrac, tucked away in woods the other side of the N102 from the old village. If you're looking for a really quiet break and pampering, this place might well fit the bill.

**Thermes de Neyrac**
*t 04 75 36 46 00*

**Musée Ardèche Autrefois**
*t 04 75 36 46 27; open July–Aug daily 9–12 and 2–6; April–June and Sept–Oct Thurs–Tues 9–12 and 2–6; closed Nov–Mar; adm*

By **Thueyts**, built on a terrace above a solidified lava flow, you feel you've left modern civilization behind. The simple **Musée Ardèche Autrefois** recalls old peasant traditions. Rewarding walks lead from here: one to the **Château de Blou**, only open for exhibitions but set in pleasant grounds, another to the **Pont du Diable**, a Roman rather than a devil's bridge, where people bathe. Walk down the **Chaussée des Géants**, a stairway cut into the lava. The N102 climbs relentlessly, following the Ardèche almost to its source at **La Chavade**.

## Savage Southwest Ardèche

Daunting lines of mountains descend from the Massif Central in the territory between the N102 and D104, presenting a tough adventure even by car. The reward is the savage scenery. Once the snows clear, the mountaintops are covered in green lichen, giving them an alien look before the purple heather flowers.

The most northerly mountain line in this area, the **Massif du Tanargue**, isn't for the lily-livered. Out in the *département*'s Far West, Christian civilization makes a grandiose statement at **St-Etienne-de-Lugdarès** with a huge church built in bands of volcanic stone. To the south, in the 19th century, Trappist Benedictines set up at the isolated, now-modernized **Notre-Dame des Neiges**. The most famous monk to have spent time here, Charles de Foucauld, left for adventures far afield, becoming a renowned explorer in North Africa, and Robert Louis Stevenson (of the same generation) stopped here on his journey recorded in *Travels with a Donkey in the Cévennes*. The abbey shop sells the fruits of the monks' labour. Nestled into the huge mountainside just east, the remote little spa town of **St-Laurent-les-Bains** offers hot natural springs and treatments at the **Centre Thermal de St-Laurent**. To journey into dark, lost terrain, join the **upper Drobie valley** for **Le Mas**, its solid houses built to combat winter cold, and for **Sablières**, where even the roofs are of stone against the harsh elements.

For an alternative route through the Tanargue mountains, you can travel up via the **Col de la Croix de Bauzon** and the **Col de Meyrand**, snowy territory in winter. Twig-thin branches planted to mark the edges of the roads indicate that this is not sophisticated ski territory as on the eastern side of the Rhône-Alpes region!

The **Beaume river** sets out on its dramatic journey to join the Ardèche from **Loubaresse**, with massive views down the valley. You then plunge into very pretty, if narrow, gorges to Joyeuse (*see* p.168). By **Ribes**, not far from that town, you reach civilization in the form of terraced vines that almost encircle this airy hilltop village.

Before Ribes, a turning leads into the boulder-strewn **western valley of the Drobie** – a sunbather's secret paradise in summer. A hair-raising detour along difficult narrow roads takes you up high via lost hamlets to the **Ron des Fades** at **Pourcharesse**, where an eccentric local builder has recreated local sights in miniature, as well as sculpting outsized carved chestnuts – a local obsession!

## From Aubenas to Les Vans

The easier route skirting the edge of the *département*'s savage southwest, and running parallel to the middle section of the Ardèche river, takes you along the D104. You might actually start by taking a back road from Aubenas to the dead-end delight of **Ailhon**, with its scattering of hamlets, its main Romanesque church, and its arboretum. The lovingly restored village of **Vinezac**, with its castle and rampart ruins, makes a good next port of call, set among its vines. Gargoyles hang out from the medieval church. Prehistoric men probably worshipped at the nearby menhirs.

**Centre Thermal de St-Laurent**
*t 04 66 69 72 72,
www.st-laurent-les-bains.com; open April–Nov*

**Ron des Fades**
*t 04 75 36 96 08, www.ron-des-fades.com, open May–Nov 10–sunset; donations appreciated*

As the name suggests, silver (*argent*) was discovered long ago around the dramatic hill town of **Largentière**. In medieval times, the bishops of Viviers controlled its mining, and minted coins; silver-mining continued on a small scale right up to 1980. The castle, built for the bishops, stamps its military authority over the historic centre, rising above the tall spire of the restored Gothic church, although a messy modern hospital now besieges the castle walls. Appealing streets and vaulted passageways run down the hill to the **Porte des Recollets**, the gateway that still stands guard by the Ligne river. On the opposite bank stands a melodramatic **law court** resembling a classical temple.

**Château de Largentière**
*rarely open; check at tourist office*

The hilltop village of **Montréal** has a splendid **château** mirroring Largentière's. In season, the **Roseraie de Berty** 6km away attracts garden lovers with the scent of its 600 rose varieties.

**Château de Montréal**
*t 04 75 89 91 81; open July–Aug Sun–Fri 10–12.30 and 3–7; mid-Feb–June and Sept–Dec Sat and Sun 2–6; adm*

The little hillside town of **Joyeuse** lives up to its name – 'happy' in French – although many traces of stern fortifications remain here. At the top of the hill, the castle has been transformed into the town hall. Nearby, the amusingly provocative **Maison de la Caricature** features small exhibitions by cutting-edge artists in one of the nicest old houses up by the sharp-spired church on its charming square. By the entrance to the church, the more traditional **Musée de la Châtaigneraie** has taken over the premises of a former monastery, treating Ardèche chestnuts and chestnut trees with all the seriousness the Ardéchois know they deserve (*see* p.161). Some eccentric pieces of rural chestnut furniture add a lighter note. The main old street along the crest of the hill has the odd interesting shop and restaurant. To reach the more ordinary main shopping drag, pass down through steep dark passageways under the ramparts.

**Roseraie de Berty**
*t 04 75 88 30 56, www.roseraie-de-berty.fr.st; open late May–late June Mon–Sat 10–12.30 and 2–6; adm*

**Maison de la Caricature**
*t 04 75 39 30 14; open July–Aug daily 10–12.30 and 3–7.30; April–June Tues–Sat 10–12.30 and 3–7.30, Sun 2–7.30; adm*

**Musée de la Châtaigneraie**
*t 04 75 39 90 66, musee-chataigneraie@ paysbeaumedrobie.com; open July–Aug Tues–Sat 10–12.30 and 3–7, Sun and Mon 3–7; mid-Mar–June and Sept–Nov Tues–Sat 9–12 and 2–6, Sun and Mon 2–6; closed mid-Nov–mid-Mar; adm*

Southwest of Joyeuse, on the first slopes before the wild mountains further west, you encounter villages surrounded by fertile terracing, those at **Planzolles** given over to vines. **Faugères** has for centuries huddled around its priory. **Payzac** grows olives as well as grapes, producing an excellent oil.

Reaching the laid-back town of **Les Vans**, it sprawls across a wide basin of land surrounded by layered hills that look as if they've had their tops decapitated. The area around is major olive country, **L'Olivier de Vincent** an irresistible shop in the centre devoted to olive products in all their forms. The passionate man who runs it has his own mill, but there are several others that can be visited nearby (contact the tourist office). An unmissable statue in Les Vans' main square honours Léopold Ollier, a 19th-century pioneer in skin-grafts, but most of the attention focuses on the many cafés.

Churches and chapels occupy some precarious positions on the heights around Les Vans, good objectives for outings. So too are the **villages set on high**. A picturesque château with corner towers

**ℹ️ Hill villages around Les Vans**

oversees **Chambonas**, reached via the largest Gothic bridge in the region. The castle is private, but look in at the images of the Romanesque church. In a beautiful barn at the hamlet of **Sièlves**, visit the pig-mad **Musée Vivant du Cochon**. Just west of Les Vans, little **Naves** stands perched precariously on the side of a circus of stratified rocks. Beyond the cobbled, arched lanes with the odd craft shop, the church stands in a near-suicidal position.

**Musée Vivant du Cochon**
*open April– Sept Wed–Sun 11–7; Oct, and Christmas hols–Mar, Wed, Sat and Sun 2–6; adm*

Further west up the Chassezac valley, you will find the track for **Thines**, hidden on densely wooded slopes. As dead ends go, the one up to this remote hamlet is rather enchanting: there are no car parks or pavements, just sliced rocks to walk on. The roofs are of stone as well. Slashed, one-eyed statues of saints stare madly from the church doorway. A monument recalls the *maquisards*, the Resistance fighters who hid out in these obscure parts, and a crooked old shop sells local produce.

South from Les Vans, the amazingly shaped boulders look as though they've been strewn by giants around the cork oak **Païolive forest**, providing a magical setting in which to go walking, the weird rocky shapes stirring the imagination. **Banne**'s twin villages stand higher up just to the south, the defensive medieval castle camouflaged like a bunker, the upper village pressed against it. Dreamy, open country roads, the D901, D202, then D255, cut through gently undulating fertile lands east from here to the more barren scrubland but deep drama of the southern Ardèche gorges.

*11 West of the Rhône: Down the Ardèche | The Upper Ardèche River and Savage Southwest*

## Market Days in the Southwest Ardèche

**Vals-les-Bains**: Sun am; in summer, evening markets Wed and Thurs.
**Aubenas**: Sat am extravaganza.
**Largentière**: Tues am. July and Aug, Fri evening market.
**Joyeuse**: Wed am. In July and Aug, look out for evening markets.
**Les Vans**: Sat am; mid-June–mid-Aug evening markets on Tues.

## Where to Stay and Eat in Southwest Ardèche

### Vals-les-Bains ✉ 07600

**Château Clément B&B**, La Châtaigne-raie, t 04 75 87 40 13, *www.chateau clement.com* (€€€€). This sumptuous, amusingly turreted home built for a Vals water magnate has been beautifully restored. It stands above town, in wonderful grounds with great views.

Even the elaborate staircase to the fabulous rooms is a joy. The *table d'hôte* (€€€) meals are exceptional; and owner-chef Eric organizes half-day cookery courses. Pool.

**\*\*\*Le Vivarais**, Rue Claude Expilly, t 04 75 94 65 85 (€€€–€). Belle Epoque, with a wide range of pleasant old-fashioned rooms looking onto the river. Well-regarded regional cuisine (€€€). Pool. *Closed Feb*.

**\*\*\*Grand Hôtel des Bains**, Montée des Bains, t 04 75 37 42 13, *www.hotel-des-bains.com* (€€). 19th-century extravaganza behind the spa. Good rooms and stylish, lively restaurant (€€€). Pool and garden. *Closed Nov–Mar*.

### Neyrac-les-Bains ✉ 07380

**\*\*\*Hôtel du Levant**, t 04 75 36 41 07, *hotellevant@wanadoo.fr* (€). Relaxing spa hotel with traditional rooms. Restaurant (€€€– €€) offering elaborate cuisine and great shaded terrace. *Closed 11 Nov–mid-Jan; restaurant closed Sun eve*.

ⓘ **Vals-les-Bains >**
*116 Rue Jean Jaurès, 07600 Vals-les-Bains, t 04 75 37 49 27, www.vals-les-bains.com*

★ **Château Clément >**

**ⓘ Aubenas ›**
*4 Bd Gambetta, B.P.208,
07204 Aubenas,
t 04 75 89 02 03,
www.aubenas-
tourisme.com*

**ⓘ Les Vans ››**
*Place Ollier, 07140 Les
Vans, t 04 75 37 24 48,
www.les-vans.com*

**★ Château
d'Uzer ›**

**ⓘ Largentière ›**
*41 Av de la République,
07110 Largentière,
t 04 75 39 14 28,
www.largentiere.net*

**ⓘ Joyeuse**
*Montée de la
Chastellane, 07260
Joyeuse, t 04 75 39 56
76, joyeuse@fnotsi.net*

## Aubenas ✉ 07200

**Le Fournil**, 34 Rue du 4 Septembre, t 04 75 93 58 68 (€€). Vaulted dining room plus courtyard, serving fine regional cuisine. *Closed Sun and Mon.*
**L'Entracte**, 2 Bd Gambetta, t 04 75 35 90 68 (€€). Fantastic views and good value for simple local menus at this large-windowed restaurant. *Closed Mon and late-June–early July.*

## Vinezac ✉ 07110

**★★La Bastide du Soleil**, Le Bourg, t 04 75 36 91 66, *bastidesoleil@chateaux hotels.com* (€€€). A wonderful stone building in the centre of the village, with a few simple elegant rooms. The restaurant (€€–€€€) turns towards Provence in its cuisine and spreads outside on warm days. *Restaurant closed Tues and Wed.*

## Uzer ✉ 07110

**Château d'Uzer B&B**, t 04 75 36 89 21, *www.chateau-uzer.com* (€€€–€€). Magical restored castle and keep, with most stylish, airy rooms. *Table d'hôte* (€€). Pool and exotic garden.

## Largentière ✉ 07110

**★★★Domaine de l'Eau Vive**, Le Roubreau, t 04 75 89 20 53, *www. domaineeauvive.com* (€€). Recent conversion of a 19th-century riverside mill; the poshest rooms have luxury bathrooms. Excellent restaurant (€€). *Closed Jan; restaurant open daily in July–Aug, weekends only in Sept–Dec and mid-Mar–June, by reservation.*

## Sanilhac ✉ 07110

**★★La Tour de Brison**, t 04 75 39 29 00, *www.belinbrison.com* (€€). West of Montréal, nicely modernized rooms in typical old hillside house with spectacular views, shared by the terrace of the fine restaurant (€€; *must book*). Great pool. Tennis. *Closed Nov–Mar.*

## Vernon ✉ 007260

**Le Mas de la Cigale**, La Croix, t 04 75 39 68 69, *www.masdelacigale.com* (€€). Calm, neat white rooms in this handsome square mid-slope stone house in the country north of Joyeuse. Excellent *table d'hôte* (€€). Pool.

## Les Vans ✉ 07140

**★★Le Carmel**, 7 Montée du Carmel, t 04 75 94 99 60, *www.le-carmel.com* (€€). Delightful rambling converted convent above the centre. The vaulted restaurant (€€€–€€) is of a high standard. *Mainly closed mid-Nov–Mar.*
**Le Grangousier**, Place de L'Eglise, t 04 75 94 90 86 (€€). Regional fare in fabulous historic house. *Closed Wed in high season, Tues and Wed in low season, and mid-Nov–mid-Mar.*
**★★Mas de l'Espaïre**, Bois de Païolive, t 04 75 94 95 01, *www.hotel-espaire.fr* (€€–€). Spacious rooms in tranquil silk farm 6km south of town, meals for guests only, served on the splendid shaded terrace by the pool. *Closed mid-Nov–mid-Mar.*

## Ribes ✉ 07260

**Auberge du Côquou**, Le Haut-Grand-Val, t 04 75 39 44 39 (€€). Lost up in the wooded hills, locals love making the stomach-churning journey up here to savour the dedicated chef's rustic local delights (*book, as only open Fri pm and weekends*).

## Beaulieu ✉ 07460

**★★★Hôtel de la Santoline**, t 04 75 39 01 91, *www.lasantoline.com* (€€). Lovely sprawling rustic stone hunting lodge lost in the deeply picturesque *garrigue* southeast of Les Vans. Colourful bedrooms, fresh cuisine (€€), beautiful terrace and pool. *Note half-board compulsory. Closed Oct–April.*

# The Middle Ardèche River and Southern Gorges de l'Ardèche

A string of stunning villages lines the middle stretch of the Ardèche between Aubenas and Ruoms. Lumpy, elephantine rock formations oversee the bright pebbly riverside beaches where canoeists take to the waters in droves. Then, between Vallon-Pont-d'Arc and St-Martin, the Ardèche has, down the millennia, cut a massive trench through the high limestone plateau. Several hundred feet deep, the Gorges de l'Ardèche counts among the most famous natural phenomena in France, making for one of the country's most sensational stretches of river. Signs point to fabulous caves hidden here and there along the cliffs.

So many remarkable competing attractions make the middle and southern stretches of the Ardèche river heavily touristy. Head just a little away from the main action, and quieter delights await around yet more enchanting but less crowded villages, often surrounded by vines or even lavender.

### The Middle Ardèche River: Vogüé to Vallon-Pont-d'Arc

Before heading down the Ardèche river from Aubenas, do consider an elating detour east for two spectacularly located villages, **St-Laurent-sous-Coiron** and **Mirabel**, hanging startlingly on the black bottom lip of the **Plateau de Coiron**. From their cliff-edge positions, you get vertiginous views south. Above the volcanic village of Mirabel, its church sometimes serving for art exhibitions, you can climb the black medieval tower that stands lone guard.

Down below, the N102 main road leads east from Aubenas to Alba-la-Romaine via **Lavilledieu**, a spot that became one of Europe's main centres for silk production in the 19th century, only to be threatened by total destruction by disease, according to the tale told in Italian writer Alessandro Baricco's recent success of a short story, *Soie* (*Silk*). The protagonist heads off to Japan to try to save the region's industry, and is entranced by that mysterious country and its silken seductions.

Although *alba* usually means 'white' in Latin languages, a black castle dramatically rises above the village of **Alba-la-Romaine**. Or more precisely, a black and white castle stands above Alba-the-medieval. It's all a bit confusing. Truth is, through the Roman centuries, a sizeable town existed down the slope. The major feature remaining, built in light limestone, is the discreet ruins of an ancient **theatre**, with an **archaeological site** alongside. The theatre seated 3,000, signalling how important this outpost once was. But it would lose its position as an early Christian bishopric to Viviers (*see* pp.198–9) and Roman Alba was abandoned.

In medieval times, a castle was built higher up, protecting a tight-packed village, the architecture mixing the black basalt of the hilltop with the white limestone already quarried below. A **Salle d'Exposition** tucked away in a corner of the village displays Gallo-Roman objects, from an exquisite if headless naked divinity to a superb mosaic of colourful fish. The robust **château**, heavily restored in 19th-century style, has long welcomed contemporary art for its regular exhibitions.

**Alba-la-Romaine theatre and archaeological site**
*t 04 75 52 45 15; open all year; theatre free, adm for site*

**Château d'Alba-la-Romaine**
*t 04 75 52 42 90; open late June–mid-Sept daily 10–12 and 3–7; April–June and mid-Sept–Nov 2–6; adm*

Vineyards proliferate around Alba and the Escoutay valley. Seek out well-named **Valvignières**, south among the vines, its wines lauded since Roman times. The sleepy shell of a village has preserved portions of medieval ramparts and a church with an impressive spire, while the **wine co-operative** sells a range of good-value single variety wines. East, the village of **St-Thomé** stands aloof and neglected by time up on its thin crest of rock, while south, **Gras**, another fine medieval village with a fortified church, has been left in peace by the tourist world.

Back west on the **Ardèche river**, it is often tourist madness. The magnificently picturesque **Château de Vogüé** was built against a curving rockface in the valley side. Flanked by rounded towers, it stands slightly aloof above the other village houses, although its Roman-tiled roofs match those below. Its history is closely linked with the aristocratic de Vogüés for whom the castle was first built. Dispossessed for a time during the Hundred Years War, then at the Revolution, after the castle had been largely remodelled in the 17th century a de Vogüé descendant bought it back and restored it. From the terraced garden, you get a lovely view of the Ardèche's waters, as you do also from the riverbank row of houses with canoeing centres and cafés. Take in the whole ensemble from the other side, and you're presented with a real, living picture postcard – not surprisingly, Vogüé is a member of the association of *Les Plus Beaux Villages de France*.

Next along the river, pretty **Lanas** is more low-key, with a couple of simple hotels by the bridge. Delightful **Rochecolombe** stands back from the rush of the Ardèche, dramatic castle ruins running along a crest above this sloping hillside village.

**Balazuc**, by contrast, tumbles right down to the Ardèche. Above the village, a 19th-century church with its tall tower stands firm. But then come some shaky rampart ruins, and the remnants of an early medieval castle. *The Stones of Balazuc* by John Merriman takes you on a fascinating journey through a thousand years of the place's history; in particular, Balazuc remained a Catholic island as Protestantism spread like a wave across the Ardèche during the Wars of Religion. You have to negotiate a warren of dark, narrow streets on foot to reach the water; along the way, a few craft shops hide out, while the arches of the medieval church's **bell tower** rise above the houses. At the foot of the village, you emerge into a wonderful rocky riverside landscape, curious-shaped cliffs lining up along the Ardèche. In summer, bathers and canoeists jostle for space on the pebble beach.

A long but rewarding walk south along the river takes you to the **Ferme Ecovillage du Viel-Audon**, a farm renowned not just for producing excellent goat's cheese, herbs and cordials, and even for weaving its own silk, but also for recycling everything. A bit further

---

**Valvignières wine co-operative**
t 04 75 52 60 60; open Mon–Sat 8–12 and 1.30–5.30

⭐ **Ardèche-side villages**

**Château de Vogüé**
t 04 75 37 01 95, www.chateaudevogue.net; open July–mid-Sept daily 10.30–6; April–June Thurs–Sun 2–6; mid-Sept–Oct Sat and Sun 2–6; tours; adm

**Ferme Ecovillage du Viel-Audon**
t 04 75 37 73 80

south below **Chauzon**, the **Cirque de Gens'** walls of rock follow, in a spectacular natural meander in the Ardèche; rock-climbers love this challenging spot.

**Ruoms**, a stop on a slightly larger scale, and on the flat, is a major tourist halt, with lots of boutiques selling the tools necessary for enjoying a typical family holiday along the Ardèche river. The pale local stone is so beautiful that it's been quarried and exported around southeast France, going into the building of such famous structures as the Pont d'Avignon, on the Rhône just beyond this region. Some locals assert that the base of New York's Statue of Liberty (a gift from the French nation to the USA) comes from here, although there's no evidence for this claim.

**Vinimage**
*t 04 75 93 85 00, www.vinimage.tm.fr; open April–Oct Tues–Sun 10–12.30 and 2–6.30; adm*

Ruoms' wine museum,**Vinimage**, has taken over an old tannery on the church square. You're given a *tastevin* on the tour; at the end you get to put it to use in the *dégustation*. Four wine-touring circuits lie within easy reach of town, inciting you to go in search of individual properties. A short way east of Ruoms, in sleepy hillside

**Ma Magnanerie**
*t 04 75 88 01 27; open July–Aug daily 10–12 and 2.30–6.30; May–June and Sept daily 2.30–6.30; adm*

**Lagorce**,**Ma Magnanerie** is a simple museum on silk-making, with silk scarves for sale in the shop.

Cross the Ardèche river by Ruoms for further extraordinary riverside sights. You could take the D4 north along the dramatic limestone side of the **Défilé de Ruoms**. Best of all, branch off for **Labeaume**, a fairytale village, its castle (private and impossibly inaccessible) perched on a needle of rock. The old houses standing along the smooth-stoned lanes below have been beautifully restored, with improbable corner gardens tucked into various nooks and crannies. The church porch stands on two huge columns like outsized stilts. Enormous plane trees create even more impressive columns in front of the Beaume river (a tributary of the Ardèche) forming a dark roof of leaves in the hot season under which the cafés can sprawl. Most enchanting of all is the riverside itself. Huge rocks line up like a row of stone elephants, their trunks dipping down to drink from the pebbly waters. In summer, you can swim in this gorgeous spot.

**Mas de la Vignasse**
*t 04 75 39 65 07, www. musee.daudet.free.fr; open July–Aug daily visits at 11 and 12, and on the hour 2–6; April–June and first half Sept daily visits on the hour 2–5; adm*

The**Mas de la Vignasse** is a traditional farm in which fifteen generations of the Reynaud family lived in virtual independence, with their own bread oven and milling wheels. Adeline Reynaud was the mother of Alphonse Daudet, one of southern France's favourite 19th-century writers, hence the reverently presented memorabilia on this much-loved figure. Continue to **St-Alban-Auriolles** and **Chandolas**, sitting in the midst of fragrant *garrigue* scrubland concealing Neolithic dolmens.

## The Southern Ardèche River Gorges and Caves

Southern Ardèche Gorges and Caves

Now for the major natural drama of the Gorges de l'Ardèche. Two big tourist events have occurred since the war to totally transform

## Sorting Your *Grottes* from your *Avens*

*Grottes* and *avens* are a major feature of the southern Ardèche. Most of these sensational caves were dug into the limestone by underground rivers gradually eating away at the rock, or were caused by the collapse of fragile strata. The waters changed course hundreds of thousands of years ago, finding other paths through the limestone at lower levels. In the vacated, dripping caverns, stalactites and stalagmites (*'les stalactites tombent, les stalagmites montent'* is the manner in which the French remember which grow downwards, which upwards; in English it is 'mites grow up, tites fall down') built up over the millennia from an accumulation of limestone deposits from individual droplets. Other concretions formed, like drapery, or vast cauliflowers. A concentration of oxydized minerals brought vivid colours to some caves. As animals and mankind evolved, they took refuge in certain caverns, or were accidentally trapped and died in them, enabling archaeologists to recover prehistoric material. In recent centuries, locals, notably shepherds, sheltered in the caves, while in times of conflict such as the Wars of Religion or the Second World War, oppressed Protestants and *maquisards* hid in them.

The Ardèche caves divide into two types: *grottes* tend to be more horizontal, following the course of ancient rivers; *avens*, or swallow holes, are vertical, natural wells. Cave systems are still being discovered in the Ardèche, and in the mid-1990s, sensational prehistoric art was found in the Grotte Chauvet (*see* below).

the town of **Vallon-Pont-d'Arc**, located just before the high thrills. First, the new tourist era took off with an explosion in canoeing. Rock-climbing and potholing attracted further enthusiasts. All this sporting activity turned this appealing place with its stocky squares and jovial café terraces into a honeypot, and it is now crammed with touristy shops.

Second, in the mid-1990s came the discovery, a short way east of town, of one of the most exciting prehistoric finds in the world. In 1994 three dedicated local potholers squeezed themselves into a fabulous cavern filled with arguably the greatest variety of prehistoric cave paintings ever found. The walls were covered with an even wider array of animals than at the celebrated Lascaux cave in the Dordogne.

Lascaux's paintings were ruined by uncontrolled tourism, so, learning from this mistake, the **Grotte Chauvet** will never be opened to the public. The building of a replica is planned; in the meantime, the **Exposition Grotte Chauvet-Pont-d'Arc** offers amazing glimpses of these treasures. An excellent half-hour film shows the cave paintings in all their beauty. Such is their finesse, it's hard to believe that they were executed some 30,000 years ago, making them virtually the earliest cave art ever discovered. As well as the deer, horses and mammoths, the prides of prehistoric lions and gatherings of prehistoric bears, the unforgettable parade of prehistoric rhinos takes your breath away. One figure is thought to represent a hyena, another a leopard – if so, figures unique in cave art discovered to date.

Close by, at the heart of the tourist action, the **Hôtel de Ville** or town hall, a grand 17th-century building (also known as the château) constructed for the local Counts of Vallon, holds

**Exposition Grotte Chauvet-Pont-d'Arc**
*t 04 75 37 17 68; open June–Aug Tues–Sun 10–1 and 3–8; mid-Mar–May and Sept–mid-Nov Tues–Sun 10–12 and 2–5.30; closed Mon, and mid-Nov–mid-Mar; adm*

**Hôtel de Ville**
*t 04 75 88 02 06; open Mon–Fri 8–12 and 1.30–5; adm*

remarkable Aubusson tapestries illustrating in heroic fantasies the exploits of the ruthless crusader Godefroy de Bouillon.

In the countryside away from the gorge, quaint villages lie like lizards immobile on rocks in the sun. Head south from Vallon via Salavas for **Labastide-de-Virac**. The little lanes all lead up to the friendliest-looking of village castles. Crowning the hill, the **Château des Roure** proves atmospherically rustic inside, the pleasant self-guided tour revolving around the silk-worm farming trade that once employed so much of the community. But there are more sinister tales retold along the way too. The peaceful-seeming hamlet of **Les Crottes** hiding out on the flat near Labastide remembers its inhabitants martyred by Germans in 1944, in revenge for a successful Resistance attack on a convoy near here.

**Château des Roure**
*t 04 75 38 61 13, www. chateaudesroure.com; open July–Aug daily 10–7; April–June and Sept Thurs–Tues 2–6, closed Wed; adm*

Set among scrubland and vineyards, the most famous swallow hole in the Ardèche, and one of the largest in Europe, the **Aven d'Orgnac** lies 135m underground. You are taken down by lift to be shown just a few caves out of a whole network. The main swallow hole is enormous, a curious cool house for weird stalagmites forming a bizarre cartoon copse of tree trunks in stone. The collection includes the largest stalagmite in France, rocketing up 24m.

**Aven d'Orgnac/ Musée Régional de la Préhistoire**
*t 04 75 38 65 10, www.orgnac.com; open July–Aug daily 9.30–6.30; April–June and Sept daily 9.30– 5.30; Oct–Nov daily 9.30–12 and 2–5.15; Christmas hols and Jan–Mar daily 10.30–12 and 2–4.45; adm*

Prehistoric finds of major significance have been made in the area, and are displayed in the **Musée Régional de la Préhistoire** by the *aven*. This is a serious educational museum, to reflect an area declared a *Grand Site de France*. The place concentrates on the 350,000 or so years that *Homo erectus* has lived around the southern gorges of the Ardèche, from the early Palaeolithic era, when he busied himself preparing flint tools, to the great leap forward in sophistication of Cro-Magnon man, some 40,000 years ago. The story goes as far as the more developed Bronze and Iron Ages, with a superb bronze dagger from the 2nd millennium BC among the most remarkable objects on display.

**Aven de la Forestière**
*t 04 75 38 63 08; open July–Aug daily 10–7; April–June and Sept 10–6; adm*

The caves are much smaller at the nearby **Aven de la Forestière**, but refined. With only 60 steps, access is much easier than to most of the Ardèche's other subterranean sites. The deep red stains come from iron oxide rather than blood left by the hairy rhinoceros, which is among the prehistoric remains found down here.

Half of France seems to have canoed down the spectacular **Gorges de l'Ardèche** at some time or other, starting just south of Vallon-Pont-d'Arc. In fact, half of France may appear to be doing so if you visit in high summer, with the queues of canoes in the waters almost matching the queues of cars on the road far above. The full **canoe trip** down the gorges from Vallon covers some 30km. Be aware that sections of the river can be somewhat difficult to negotiate because of boulders, and that in the height of summer the waters can dwindle considerably, causing you to have to scrape your canoe across shallow rocky patches. As for hardy hikers, they can take the roadless national GR path along the south side of the river.

By road, before reaching the *corniche*, you pass a couple of small caves. Still wet (and slippery), a sign that its formations are still growing, the entrance to the **Grotte des Tunnels** was, until quite recently, a blacksmith's workshop and goat pen – disappearing goats in fact gave a big clue as to the cave concealed beyond. The **Grotte des Huguenots** hid Protestants during the Wars of Religion; the exhibition inside explains cave formations generally.

**Grotte des Tunnels**
*t 04 75 88 03 73;
open April–Sept daily
9am–9.30pm; adm*

**Grotte des Huguenots**
*t 04 75 88 06 71;
open mid-June–Aug
daily 10–7; adm*

Then you come upon one of the most stunning natural phenomena in France. Nature occasionally carves out bridges of stone; rarely do they come more picturesque than the **Pont d'Arc**, spanning the Ardèche river across 66m, the arch a full 30m high. Canoes pass beneath like shoals of exotic fish. In summer, bathers venture into the bright emerald waters below it.

The *corniche* road then rises rapidly onto the high plateau, a scrubby wilderness broken only by the vast canyon of the Ardèche valley. Space is limited at the various car parks along the way; peer down sheer apricot-coloured limestone walls towards the black snake of a river heading towards the Rhône. The entrance to the **Grotte de la Madeleine** stands beside one of the most breathtaking views down on the gorges. The tour takes you on a rollercoaster kilometre-long walk to two vast caverns in particular, the most grandiose in the Ardèche.

**Grotte de la Madeleine**
*t 04 75 04 22 20, www.
grottemadeleine.com;
open July–Aug daily
9–7; April–June and
Sept daily 10–6; Oct
daily 10–5; adm*

Several attractions are gathered together at the **Aven de Marzal**. Large dinosaur models lurk along the twisting *garrigue* paths of the quite amusing and informative so-called **prehistoric zoo**. The small **Musée du Monde Souterrain** pays homage to pioneering potholers who came up with such finds as the impressively fanged skull of a sabre-toothed tiger. The *aven* itself is somewhat sinister, and not at all recommended for vertigo sufferers, with hundreds of steep steps down. The hole turns out to be named after a man killed by an angry shepherd, who pushed him and his dog down the terrifying abyss. At the bottom, there are impressive concretions, although the name of the Salle des Diamants, covered with calcite crystals, rather exaggerates the effect.

**Aven de Marzal**
*t 04 75 04 38 07; open
April–Sept daily 10.30–
6; Mar and Oct–Nov
Sun 10.30–6; adm*

For a more restful visit, head to picturesque **St-Remèze**. Nearby, you'll find the fresh, laboratory-white **Musée de la Lavande**, set amidst lavender fields, with lavender-making film, exhibition and demonstrations, as well as a gift shop full of lavender products.

**Musée de la Lavande**
*t 04 75 04 37 26, www.
ardechelavandes.com;
open May–Sept daily
10–7; April and Oct
daily 10–5; adm*

To the south, **Bidon** has an interesting small geological museum, the **Musée de la Vie**, run by a passionate archaeologist. Monsieur may allow you to feel a piece of mammoth hair if you're lucky, and you can often have a go at chipping away at your own piece of fossil.

**Musée de la Vie**
*t 04 75 04 08 79;
open April–mid-Nov
daily 10–6; adm*

**Grotte de St-Marcel**

*t 04 75 04 38 07; open July–Aug daily 10–7; mid-Mar–June and Sept daily 10–6; Oct–mid-Nov daily 10–5; adm*

The **Grotte de St-Marcel** isn't at the gently touristy village of **St-Marcel-d'Ardèche** at all, but 12km southwest, beside the Gorges de l'Ardèche. A relatively easy ramp of steps leads down to the first massive cave, known as the Galerie des Peintres because of its naturally colourful walls. Other impressive caves include the Cascade des Gours, boasting an extraordinary natural cascade of rock pools like giant oyster shells. Ravel's *Boléro* plays when you enter the largest of the caves, the vast Salle de la Cathédrale, reaching up to 60m in height; here, the stalagmites really do resemble organ tubes.

By **St-Martin-d'Ardèche**, you've descended back down to the riverside, the place where many of the canoe trips end. The village feels lively and cheerful in season, loads of snack bars catering to the tired adventurers at the end of their gorgeous voyage. A neo-Gothic bridge connects St-Martin to aloof **Aiguèze**, perched dramatically on the opposite bank, its crenellated ramparts merging with the cliff, guardedly surveying the southern frontier of the Ardèche from the Languedoc frontier.

ⓘ **Vogüé**
*t 04 75 37 01 17, voque@fnotsi.net*

ⓘ **Ruoms**
*t 04 75 93 91 90, ruoms@fnotsi.net*

★ **Château de Balazuc >>**

## Market Days in the Gorges de l'Ardèche

Vogüé: July–Aug, Mon am.

Ruoms: Fri am.

Vallon-Pont-d'Arc: Thurs am; July–Aug, also Tues am.

St-Martin-d'Ardèche: mid-June–mid-Sept, Wed am and Sun am.

## Sports and Activities in the Gorges de l'Ardèche

Canoeing, rock-climbing and potholing are wildly popular in these parts. There's plenty for walkers too. Start by consulting the *département* website, *www.ardeche-guide.com*, under *Loisirs Nature*, or contact the tourist offices for precise information.

## Where to Stay and Eat in the Gorges de l'Ardèche

### St-Pons ✉ 07580

**\*\*\*La Mère Biquette**, Les Allignols, t 04 75 36 72 61, *merebiquette@wanadoo.fr* (€€). At the end of a quiet valley north of Alba-la-Romaine, with goats all around, a very calm country retreat, plus a pleasant restaurant (€€). Pool and court. *Closed mid-Nov–mid-Feb. Restaurant closed Mon eve, Wed lunch and Sun eve.*

### St-Maurice d'Ardèche ✉ 07200

**\*\*Domaine du Cros d'Auzon**, t 04 75 37 75 86, *www.hotel-cros-auzon.com* (€). Very good location right close to the river between Vogüé and Balazuc. Nice stone architecture and reasonable rooms. Restaurant. Pool. Court. *Closed Oct–Mar.*

### Balazuc ✉ 07120

**Château de Balazuc B&B**, t 04 75 88 52 67, *www.chateaudebalazuc.com* (€€€). An eagle's eyrie in the restored sections of the ruined castle. Plunging views down on the village and the Ardèche from the very stylish contemporary bedrooms. Lovely terrace or chic dining room for tasty *table d'hôte*. They have even fitted a narrow pool up here.

### St-Alban-Auriolles ✉ 07120

**La Villa St-Patrice B&B**, t 04 75 39 37 78, *www.villastpatrice.com* (€€€–€€). Spacious village house with splendid rooms. Fantastic pool.

### Grospierres ✉ 07120

**\*\*\*La Ferme de Bournet**, t 04 75 39 08 35, *www.fermedebournet.com* (€€).

ⓘ **Vallon-Pont-d'Arc/Gorges de l'Ardèche >**
*Place de l'Ancienne Gare, 07150 Vallon-Pont-d'Arc, t 04 75 88 04 01, www.vallon-pont-darc.com*

ⓘ **St-Martin-d'Ardèche**
*Place de l'Eglise, 07700 St-Martin-d'Ardèche, t 04 75 98 70 91, www.ot-stmartin-ardeche.com*

Exclusive address with handful of rooms in a farm built out of an old fortified manor, in Bournet. It has a big restaurant, **La Bergerie** (€€), with vaulted dining room and terrace. Pool. *Restaurant closed Mon.*

### Vallon-Pont-d'Arc ✉ 07150

**\*\*Hôtel du Tourisme et du Pont d'Arc,** t 04 75 88 02 12, *www.hotel-tourisme-pont-darc.com* (€). Practical central town option with modern rooms. Big restaurant with terrace (€€). *Closed Dec–Feb.*

### Labastide-de-Virac ✉ 07150

**Le Mas Rêvé B&B, t** 04 75 38 69 13, *www.lemasreve.com* (€€). Within a

stone's throw of the Ardèche gorges, splendid, spacious 17th-century converted farm. *Table d'hôte* (€€). Pool. *Closed mid-Nov–mid-Mar.*

**La Petite Auberge,** t 04 75 38 61 94 (€€). Lovely stylish terrace on the edge of the village, a sweet address at which to try traditional cuisine. *Closed Oct–Mar.*

### Vagnas ✉ 07150

**Le Mas d'Alzon B&B, t** 04 75 38 67 33, *www.masdalzon.com* (€€). Lovingly restored farm close to Labastide. Pool and garden.

# Down the Rhône

The narrow band of the Rhône valley between Lyon and the Provence border is notoriously busy, and marred by industry and quarries along certain stretches. But halt in the right spots and you can enjoy some fabulous surprises: great Roman remains, perched medieval castles, bountiful orchards, and vineyards that produce some of France's finest wines. There are top-notch restaurants and hotels to savour too, not to mention some very sweet culinary specialities. The towns, like Montélimar, Valence and Vienne, are full of new tourist promise, the rejuvenated ports on the Rhône very appealing, and the restored hillside villages exquisite.

# 12

## Don't miss

⭐ **Roman finds**
Vienne p.182

⭐ **Wine towns linked across the Rhône**
Tain-l'Hermitage and Tournon p.190

⭐ **A revived Rhône-side city plus dramatic ruins**
Valence and the Château de Crussol p.192

⭐ **Nougatville**
Montélimar p.196

⭐ **Competing cathedral towns**
Viviers and St-Paul-Trois-Châteaux p.198/p.201

*See map overleaf*

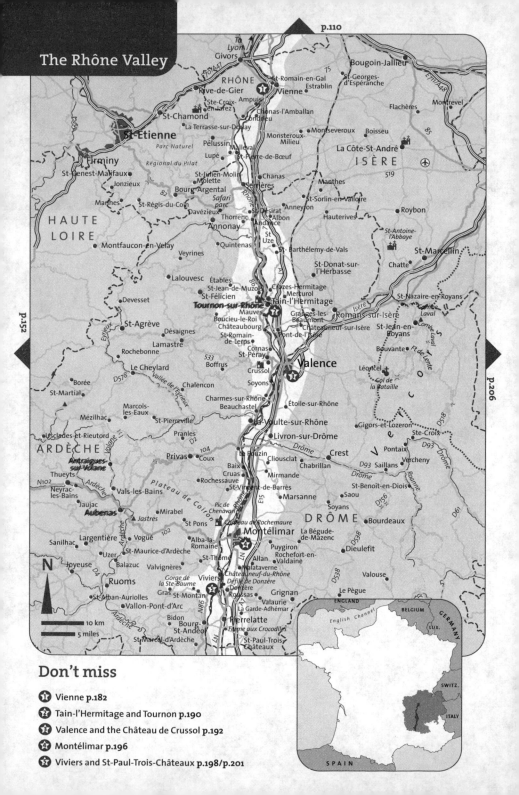

The Rhône Valley

## Don't miss

⭐1 Vienne **p.182**

⭐2 Tain-l'Hermitage and Tournon **p.190**

⭐3 Valence and the Château de Crussol **p.192**

⭐4 Montélimar **p.196**

⭐5 Viviers and St-Paul-Trois-Châteaux **p.198/p.201**

For those readers who have the misfortune of having to rush straight down the Rhône from Lyon without getting off the main valley roads, here we concentrate on the highlights along the very narrow strip of land these roads take up – one that has given the vast and varied region of Rhône-Alpes such a misleading tourist image. Millions rush as fast as possible along the three extremely busy major arteries: the A7 motorway, and the N7 and N86 main roads just east and west of the Rhône. There are fine attractions right by these routes or just a ridge away, and we will tempt you with those, but first let's get the negatives out of the way.

True, this industrial band has been dubbed France's 'chemical corridor', and it contains some of the most intense concentration of industrial plant in France. Cement quarries scar the valley banks, while many of the factories, as well as the nuclear installations, have been built to exploit the Rhône's energy. These large-scale enterprises have generated wealth for the region, but have spoilt the undoubted natural beauty of this ribbon of land. Electricity pylons seem as much a feature of the landscape as woods or vines.

On top of that, it's scarcely a secret that the Rhône valley here has a terrible wind problem. South of Valence, the notorious mistral makes its regular violent escape. It is, however, a blessing as well as a curse, clearing the air, chasing away clouds and making way for those intense blue skies that presage Provence. From the confluence of the Drôme and the Rhône, the weather turns markedly more Mediterranean.

Starting to feel more positive? Then see how, below Lyon, sensationally steep vineyards cling pluckily to the valley cliffs. These northern Côtes du Rhône vines produce some of the greatest wines in southern France. Dense fruit orchards planted in more generous patches yield not just superb crops, but also liqueurs. As for Montélimar, it has long been reputed for its nougat, while superlative Valrhôna (look at the name) chocolate is made in Tain. So there are sweet culinary reasons to stop. And cultural ones too: many a dramatic castle ruin looks down on the valley roads, along with hilltop villages, the artistically minded Cliousclat, Mirmande and La Garde-Adhémar among the finest. But the most surprisingly arresting places are the towns, if you take the trouble to penetrate their dusty commercial outskirts. Vienne offers one of the most staggering Roman legacies in France; Tournon and Tain-l'Hermitage face each other in the most beautiful, vine-covered locations along this stretch; and Valence, where Napoleon enjoyed his cherry-picking days, is spied on across the Rhône by the ruins of the medieval Château de Crussol. As to historic Montélimar, it hides its many charms behind thick layers of plane trees.

We end with all-too-often bypassed little gems. Viviers west of the Rhône and St-Paul-Trois-Châteaux to the east each have a

## Getting to and around the Rhône South of Lyon

**By train:** Vienne is just 20mins from Lyon-Part-Dieu by train. Valence's TGV station stands 10km east of town (to which it's connected by shuttle bus) with rapid links across France – Paris is 2hrs 30mins away, and Lille with its Eurostar links to London not much longer. Avignon TGV station, with a direct weekly summer Eurostar link with London, lies just south of the Ardèche and the Drôme. Tain-l'Hermitage, Montélimar and Pierrelatte have useful train stations too.

**By bus:** Buses link the valley towns; for detailed timetables west of the Rhône, consult *www.ardeche.fr*; east of the Rhône, see *www.transisere.fr* and *www.ladrome.fr*.

**By boat:** River cruises are listed in the text.

---

striking cathedral. In addition, Viviers boasts a marina, St-Paul a Maison de la Truffe, revealing that it lies in the most important truffle-producing area in France. Bourg-St-Andéol's historic treasures go from former silk merchants' mansions on the Rhône to remains from Roman times. These places alone should leave you with a definite desire to press further east and west into the Ardèche, Isère and Drôme (*see* Chapters 11 and 13).

# Lyon to Vienne

From Lyon, three major Rhône valley roads rush south through industrial quarters. A cluster of routes forms knots around **Givors**. Its new **Halte Fluviale** (a little port) attracts yachting tourists using the Rhône as a short cut from the Mediterranean to the Channel, avoiding Atlantic storms. In the past, sailors used oars and sails, or had their vessels pulled from the bank; now northward-heading yachtsmen resort to engines. By Givors' riverside, spot the statue paying homage to the mighty Rhône river god and see if you can visit the **Maison du Rhône**, undergoing renovation, but reopening one of these days to present the river between Lyon and Provence with the respect it deserves. The town is also proud of its funky **Etoile** contemporary housing project by Jean Renaudie; it's star-shaped, as its French name makes clear. For the Mont Pilat park a short, steep world away, *see* p.154.

Climb the slopes east of the Rhône towards Vienne, and around **Seyssuel** the first northern **Côtes du Rhône vineyards** (*see* pp.187–8) come into view at one of the narrowest points in the whole Rhône valley. A team of dynamic regional winemakers has been investing here to produce some exciting new wines from the vines growing on the extremely steep slopes; taste their sotanum syrah and taburnum viognier creations at their wine-making premises on top of the slope, **Les Vins de Vienne**, at **Bas Seyssuel**.

**Les Vins de Vienne**
*t 04 74 85 04 52,*
*www.vinsdevienne.com*

### St-Romain-en-Gal and Vienne

 **Vienne**

Amazing secrets from the very glamorous past life of Vienne and its sibling St-Romain across the river have been unearthed in recent times. These places may look scruffy at first, but take the time to acquaint yourselves with them – especially lovable, slightly tatty old Vienne. It's an exceptional grandee, steadily dribbling antiquities, although it has been revived and spruced up to look more presentable in recent times.

Vienne proves to have many a tale to tell. Main settlement of the powerful Celtic Allobroges tribe from the 3rd century BC, it was taken over by the Romans after they conquered these territories at the northern limit of their beloved Provence. This became a very important place in Gallo-Roman and early Christian times: it enjoyed a period of immense trading prosperity from the 1st century AD to the 3rd, as did **St-Romain-en-Gal**. Head there first, perhaps via the footbridge from Vienne, to appreciate the area's

**St-Romain-en-Gal
Musée et Site
Archéologique**
*t 04 74 53 74 01,
www.musees-gallo-
romains.com; open
Mar–Oct Tues–Sun
10–6; Nov–Feb Tues–
Sun 10–5; closed Mon;
adm, but free Thurs*

magnificent ancient legacy at the superlative modern **Musée et Site Archéologique** , presenting fabulous finds in a slightly suffering contemporary glass block by the Rhône. The traders ordered sumptuous dwellings; over 250 mosaic floors have been uncovered either side of the river, making this one of the most prolific areas for such art in the Roman world. Some tell mythological stories; others, with their divinities, masks and animals, reveal some of the main concerns of the civilization. The greatest mosaic, forming a huge carpet in its own separate room, tells the legend of Lycurgues, seen battling naked through a forest of vines, fighting the evils of alcohol. There are also outstanding Gallo-Roman mural paintings, models of Vienne and St-Romain-en-Gal in ancient times, and all the other archaeological finds typically associated with Roman towns – amphorae, pottery, tools – creating a highly evocative picture of Vienne's Gallo-Roman life. Don't miss the luxurious latrines rescued for posterity, either! Outside lies an extensive archaeological site, with its network of streets and partially reconstructed villas.

Wandering along St-Romain-en-Gal's riverfront, it's hard to miss the brutish **Tour des Valois**, recalling the medieval centuries when the Rhône was the frontier between France and the Holy Roman Empire; nor, in the summer holidays, the joyous screams coming from the large outdoor public **swimming pool**. On the Rhône, rowing boats count among the vessels that ply these waters.

**Vienne** itself seems overwhelmed by the sheer weight of its intense cultural legacy. At the top of the slopes above the Rhône, the ruined medieval bishops' castle peers wearily down on the town; the 19th-century church with its massive statue of the Virgin stands out more confidently; but most obvious of all is the modern hospital, a slightly unfortunate symbol of Vienne's decrepitude. Fear not: the historic town centre really has a feisty old heart. If you plan on visiting several of Vienne's museums, invest in the cheap all-in-one ticket, valid for 48hrs, from the tourist office (see p.202).

**Roman theatre**
*t 04 74 85 39 23;*
*open April–Aug daily*
*9.30–1 and 2–6;*
*Sept–Oct Tues–Sun*
*9.30–1 and 2–6;*
*Nov–Mar Tues–Sat*
*9.30–12.30 and 2–5,*
*Sun 2–5.30; adm*

Vienne's **Roman theatre** lies snugly embedded in the hillside, yet with over 40 tiers of seats counts among the largest built in Gaul. Today the place hosts the prestigious Vienne summer jazz festival, as is made clear in colourful style in a big recent outdoor mural illustrating Vienne's history on the back of the **town theatre** – this building, its 1930s front concealing an Italianate interior, offers an elegant covered venue beside the Roman theatre. The impressive ancient corner arches in the nearby archaeological **Jardin de Cybèle** may have formed one angle of Vienne's extensive forum, although the name comes from a time when researchers thought this was part of a former temple to the Roman nature goddess.

**Musée des Beaux-Arts et d'Archéologie**
*t 04 74 85 50 42;*
*open April–Oct*
*Tues–Sun 9.30–1 and*
*2–6; Nov–Mar Tues–Sat*
*9.30–12.30 and 2–5,*
*Sun 2–5.30; adm*

Sitting squarely in the middle of Place de Miremont, the grand 1820s granary was long ago transformed into what is now the distinctly old-fashioned yet still interesting **Musée des Beaux-Arts et d'Archéologie**. A mammoth's tusk and Neolithic tomb signal inhabitants in these parts before the Allobroges, from whose times just the odd metallic object remains. Buried Gallo-Roman treasure discovered in the 1980s is a highlight; possibly hidden from the invading barbarian hordes, the exceptional banqueting pieces include two exquisite silver platters, one decorated with exotic animals and men at work, the other with recumbent women. The collections of ornate Ancien Régime and 19th-century paintings and ceramics seem fussy by comparison.

**St-Pierre**
*t 04 74 85 20 35;*
*open April–Oct*
*Tues–Sun 9.30–1 and*
*2–6; Nov–Mar Tues–Sat*
*9.30–12.30 and 2–5,*
*Sun 2–5.30; adm*

Skirting round the massive medieval cathedral, perhaps via the tree- and café-lined Cours Romestang, then Place de la République, you arrive at the battered church of **St-Pierre**, with some of the oldest Christian roots in Vienne. But since the 19th century this has been used as a chaotic storehouse for all sorts of truly extra-ordinary Gallo-Roman fragments taken from around town – archaeological pornography of the highest order. A beautiful, monumental classical face greets you at the entrance; more unusual figures follow, including dancers disporting themselves in distinctly Indian style. Also root out the remnants of remarkable early Christian tombs. The one engraved with peacocks pecking at grapes may have been made for Léonien, an abbot of prime importance when a monastery was founded on this spot in the 6th century. The grey, neglected church is essentially Romanesque.

The rest of the monastery has vanished, but in 1349 it witnessed the first meeting on the sale of the Dauphiné region to the French crown (*see* pp.189 and 191). However, it would take until 1450 for Dauphin Louis II (later King Louis XI of France) to take away control of Vienne from its archbishops. Nearby, the town has revived its riverside with a new **port** in front of the tourist office and public gardens. You can embark on a short **cruise** on the Rhône from here.

Before focusing on the cathedral, just to the north of it, Vienne's most exceptional Roman monument still stands out proudly in the

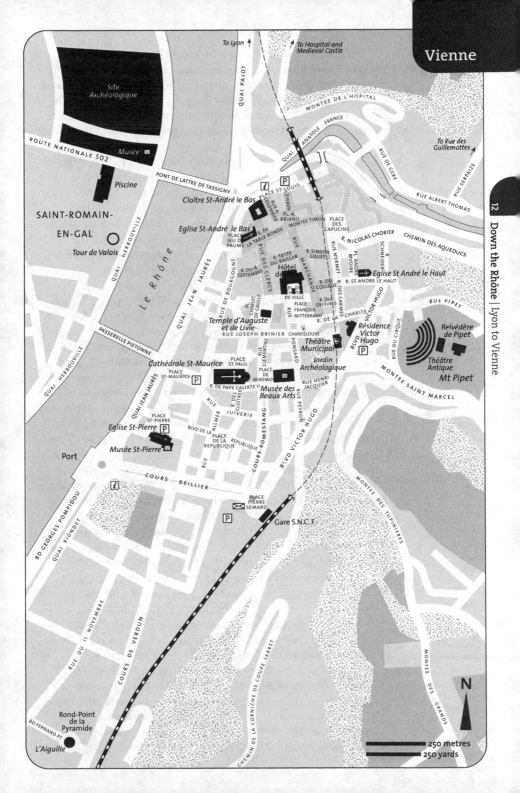

To Lyon ↑

To Hospital and
Medieval Castle

QUAI PAJOT

MONTEE DE L'HÔPITAL

Site
Archéologique

QUAI ANATOLE FRANCE

RUE DE GÈRE

RUE SERPAIZE

To Rue des
Guillemottes ↗

ROUTE NATIONALE 502

Musée ℹ

RUE ALBERT THOMAS

PONT DE LATTRE DE TASSIGNY

PLACE ST-LOUIS

L'EPERON

PL. A.
BRIAND

MONTEE TIMON

PLACE DES
CAPUCINS

R. NICOLAS CHORIER

CHEMIN DES AQUEDUCS

Piscine

SAINT-ROMAIN-

EN-GAL

Tour de Valois

QUAI HERBOUVILLE

Le Rhône

QUAI JEAN JAURÈS

Cloître St-André le Bas

Eglise St-André le Bas

PLACE
JEU DE
PAUME

RUE DE COLOMBIER

LA TABLE RONDE

RUE MARCHAND

R. SIMEON
GOUET

RUE MERMET

R.
SCHNEIDER

PL. ANDRE
RIVOIRE

RUE DE BOURGOGNE

R. TESTE
DU BAILLER

RUE DU 4
SEPTEMBRE

RUE DE DES CLERCS

Hôtel
de

R. DU
COLLÈGE

R. DES CARMES

R. ST ANDRE LE HAUT

Eglise St André le Haut

PLACE
CHARLES
DE GAULLE

PL. DE
L'HÔTEL
DE VILLE

PLACE
FRANÇOIS
MITTERRAND

R. DES
ORFÈVRES

RUE DE LA CHARITÉ

RUE PIPET

Belvédère
de Pipet

Temple d'Auguste
et de Livie

RUE JOSEPH BRINIER

RUE
CHANTELOUVE

PONSARD

Théâtre
Municipal

BLVD VICTOR HUGO

Résidence
Victor Hugo

RUE DU CIRQUE

Théâtre
Antique

Mt Pipet

PASSERELLE PIETONNE

QUAI HERBOUVILLE

Cathédrale St-Maurice

PLACE
ST PAUL

PLACE
ST-MAURICE

RUE CLEMENTINE

PLACE
DE
MIREMONT

Jardin
Archéologique

RUE HENRI
JACQUIER

MONTEE SAINT MARCEL

R. DE PAPE CALIXTE II

Musée des
Beaux Arts

RUE
DES
CLOÎTRES

RUE PEYRON

QUAI JEAN JAURÈS

PLACE
ST-PIERRE

Eglise St-Pierre

RUE
ALLMER

JUIVERIE

BLVD DE LA

PLACE
DE LA
REPUBLIQUE

COURS ROMESTANG

BLVD VICTOR HUGO

Musée St-Pierre

Port

COURS BRILLIER

PLACE
PIERRE
SEMARD

BD GEORGES POMPIDOU

QUAI RIONDET

Gare S.N.C.F.

MONTEE DES TUPINIÈRES

RUE DU 11 NOVEMBRE

COURS DE VERDUN

CHEMIN DE LA CORNICHE DE COUPE JARRET

MONTEE DES GRANDS

N

Rond-Point
de la
Pyramide

BD FERNAND PT.

L'Aiguille

250 metres
250 yards

very heart of town, the **Temple of Augustus and Livia** on Place Charles de Gaulle. Its columns may look chipped, and the building may have undergone major surgery in the 19th century, but this temple stamps Roman imperial authority on the centre to this day. Well-placed cafés allow you to pay homage from a comfortable seat, while the tower of the **law courts** peers down on proceedings from one side.

Vienne's many medieval churches, which would have been highly visible to travellers along the Rhône in centuries past, help recall what an extremely important Christian centre this was too. From the front, the **Cathédrale St-Maurice** resembles the muscular cathedral of Lyon. Various structures succeeded each other on the site from perhaps as early as the 3rd century. In the 8th, the establishment came by the supposed head of the 3rd-century Roman military convert Maurice, martyred with his men in Switzerland. After King Boson of Burgundy had established a base here in the 9th century, donations followed from that line of rulers, for whom the cathedral became a final resting place.

The present cathedral is a mix of Romanesque and Gothic. Among the delightful decorations in the three battered late Gothic entrance portals, look out for the adorable musical angels. You'll need to strain your neck to make out the sixty Romanesque capitals that survive high up inside the nave, with their amusing carved decorations. A series of Ancien Régime tapestries in the choir illustrates the story of martyr Maurice. Leave by the north door to admire further wonderful stone carving, some taken from much earlier Gallo-Roman architecture.

Continue strolling north either from the Roman temple or from spacious **Place François Mitterrand**, hosting the daily market, with the impressively arcaded **town hall** standing to one side. You then enter Vienne's most interesting network of historic streets. The towers sticking out high above the lively shopping drags were originally built to provide wealthy inhabitants with fresher air and more light. **Rue des Clercs**, lined by the arcades of 15th-century shops, became home to popular 19th-century Lyon puppeteer Laurent Mourguet (see 'Vieux Lyon', p.76). **Rue des Orfèvres** boasts some of the finest towers, continuing into Rue Marchande.

You then arrive at Vienne's second most important historic religious establishment, **St-André-le-Bas**. Its big church contains just a few mighty capitals, a couple Roman, a couple with Romanesque interpretations of biblical stories. But the main interest is in the separate **Cloître St-André-le-Bas**, its greying Romanesque cloister held up on elegant columns with small-scale animal decorations. The mass of epitaphs on the walls behind stretch from the 5th to the 18th century, making an exceptional collage, clearly indicating the age of Vienne's Christian past.

**Cloître St-André-le-Bas**
*t 04 74 85 18 49; open April–Oct Tues–Sun 9.30–1 and 2–6; Nov–Mar Tues–Sat 9.30–12.30 and 2–5, Sun 2–5.30; adm*

Contemporary art exhibitions provide a contrast in rooms off the cloisters. Down closer to the river, the free **Salle du Patrimoine** gives clear, brief introductions to the main stages in Vienne's history.

South of the centre, seek out one last Gallo-Roman remain, the **Aiguille**, claimed, in one of the more far-fetched Christian legends, to be the tomb of Pontius Pilate (*see* 'Mont Pilat', p.154). In fact the imposing arch, topped by a soaring obelisk, probably formed the centrepiece of a Roman circus. Also, east of the centre, consider climbing **Mont Pipet**, with the Roman theatre at your feet, to enjoy views almost as good as the Black Virgin atop the church up there. The vistas prove magnificent, and surprisingly unspoilt.

## Vienne to Valence

Heading down the west bank of the Rhône, immediately below St-Romain-en-Gal you enter **Côte Rôtie** country, although the vines fight it out with the factories. For keen cyclists, a track has been laid through the vineyards to **Ampuis**, part of the much greater project to create an uninterrupted cycle route along the Rhône from Geneva to the Mediterranean. Ampuis itself looks a bit scruffy, despite some of the richest Côtes du Rhône family wine companies having bases here, notably the very upmarket Guigal. An oasis along this heavily industrial stretch, the small **Centre d'Observation de la Nature de l'Ile de Beurre** introduces the natural life of this protected Rhône island which attracts many birds.

**Condrieu** has long been a mariners' village as well as a winemakers' one. One of Condrieu's finest houses, the **Maison de la Gabelle**, where salt was taxed, serves as a reminder that this was another of the most precious commodities transported along the Rhône down the millennia, brought up from the salt pans beside the Mediterranean. Georges Vernay, one of the most acclaimed believers in the region's viognier wines, has a welcoming **cellar**.

**Centre d'Observation de la Nature de l'Ile de Beurre**
*t 04 74 56 62 62;*
*open Mon–Sat 8–12 and 1–5, Sun and public hols 2–5; adm*

**Vernay cellar**
*open Mon–Sat; tasting charge if you don't buy*

### Northern Côtes du Rhône Wine Exclusives

The famous northern Côtes du Rhône vineyards stretch between Vienne and Valence. What a contrast with the wines of Beaujolais just a little way north of Lyon (*see* pp.112–13). Here, not far south of that city, instead of those light 'feminine' numbers, your palate is confronted by big, beefy wines, the finest, brooding ones remaining quite impenetrable for the first few years. Even the whites have muscle in these parts, the finest giving the great reds a run for their money in ageing potential, which is a rarity. And rare many of these wines are.

Wine experts agree that some of the very finest vintages in the world, both red and white, are made along this narrow stretch of the Rhône valley. You pay not just for the high quality and rarity, but also for the difficult working conditions – some of the steepest patches of vines can only be reached by ladder. All told, these are extremely exclusive, somewhat awkward wines. Many estates produce only small quantities and sell via merchant families and companies (the *négociants*), who also tend their own vines. They market internationally rather than locally, despite their manic tendency to plaster their names on every section of vineyard wall belonging to them.

There is the odd high-quality co-operative, merchant's shop and property happy to receive visitors, but this is not the easiest area to visit wineries unannounced. The Côtes du Rhône's official body, the **Interprofession des Vins AOC Côtes du Rhône** (*www.rhone-wines.com*) offers introductory information on the many *appellations* involved. Get hold if you can of the latest slim *Route des Vins* brochures, with details on properties open for visits. There are official wine trails you can follow; the Saffron Route covers the northern Côtes du Rhône from Vienne to Valence.

Most of the viticultural action takes place on the west bank of the Rhône, although the dramatic hills of Hermitage and Crozes-Hermitage rise above the east bank. In the reds, the syrah grape reigns supreme – you probably know it better as shiraz; they're the same thing. These wines wear deep purple robes, in such contrast to the light red chiffon of Beaujolais. Barrels are often used for their ageing. For the whites, viognier gives the intensely mature fruit flavours of Condrieu. Marsanne and roussane mix power with fragrance in the other whites.

Immediately below St-Romain-en-Gal, the first almost legendary *cru*, or fine wine, is **Côte Rôtie**, the 'Burnt Slope', a world-class ambassador for the northern Côtes du Rhône. Its mature reds typify the serious side of the area, smoky and meaty, with plenty of blackcurrant accompaniment. Condrieu and Château-Grillet then produce some of the finest whites in France. The **Condrieu** vineyards only extend over some 250 hectares; **Château-Grillet** is a single-property *cru* covering under ten. Sweet scents of peaches and apricots emerge intensely, yet in taste these are sober, dry numbers, with complex layers of flavours.

Next come the vineyards of the less exclusive **St-Joseph** *appellation*. The quality of this west bank wine varies, the 1,700 hectares stretching from Chavanay to Guilherand (opposite Valence). For tourists, these can, though, be particularly attractive, easier to find, costing much less than the wines above, and producing delicious surprises. The syrah seems to soften rapidly in these parts. The whites, from marsanne and roussane, tend to be more middle-of-the-road.

Two separate small *crus* stand out just before the St-Joseph *appellation* comes to an end. **Cornas** wines, produced from 220 hectares of syrah, are so impenetrable that they can look as if they've been dragged up from the bottom of the Rhône. They are considered among the greatest 'peasant-style' wines in France. In total contrast, **St-Péray** produces light whites and frothy sparkling wines from 160 hectares of marsanne and roussane, quaffable and improving fast.

Sober-sounding **Hermitage** is the exceptionally high-quality red *appellation* on the east bank, covering some 320 hectares. Its stupendously powerful wines start out bursting with tangy ripeness, pepperiness mixed with the blackcurrants, but they also have a tarry tinge, as in a great Bordeaux. Spicy tastes emerge with age. While the odd great **Crozes-Hermitage** is made, most are a rung or two down from the Hermitages. The Crozes-Hermitage vines spread over more than 2,550 hectares of beautiful hillsides well worth touring round. Wine experts talk of herbal flavours in the reds, which dominate, taking up around 90 per cent of the *appellation*.

Across the northern Côtes du Rhône area, 1997, 1998 and 1999 were classic years. The year 2000 reds turned out rich and ripe, although not a match for the exceptional depth of the 1999s, one of the finest of all post-war vintages. The whites of 2000 were truly exceptional, however. 2001 continued a long good run, although 2002 was mediocre by comparison. The sun-baked tiny yields of 2003 were packed with powerful flavours. The recent vintages, 2004, 2005 and 2006, all hold great promise. Experts recommend keeping the finest Côte Rôtie, Cornas and Hermitage reds at least five years before opening, and they can develop for a good quarter century. Best drink the easier reds like Crozes-Hermitage and St-Joseph between three and six years of age.

**Lake watersports**
*t 04 74 56 52 22,
www.canoed.fr*

Across the Rhône from Condrieu, **Les Roches-de-Condrieu** boasts a splendidly picturesque marina looking over to a row of vine-covered hills, backed by the black-wooded heights of the Pilat mountain range beyond. The place is doubling in capacity to make it into one of the largest ports on the Rhône. Nearby, there's a **lake** for bathing and more exhilarating watersports. Back on the

Rhône's west bank, climb the very steep lanes above Condrieu to tour the dramatic vineyards spreading up towards the Pilat. For the white-water sports possibilities down below at **St-Pierre-de-Bœuf**, *see* 'Activities', p.202.

Tucked out of sight from the Rhône, the very name of **Malleval** (Evil Vale) sounds menacing, and the old hilltop village with its dark stone buildings is somewhat shunned, but in fact it proves a quite adorable place. Its secretive location is so well protected by higher hills that cacti as well as vines thrive on its slopes.

At **Arcoules**, you enter the Rhône-side territories of the *département* of the Ardèche, getting off to a very fruity start, thick ranks of orchards challenging the power station installations. With its broad flat riverbank, **Serrières** was an obvious spot to site a useful port. Although local fishermen appreciate the place, the vacuous riverside could be made more enticing for tourists beyond the times when entertaining water-jousting tournaments are held here. However, the church of **St-Sornin** holds the newly cleaned up **Musée des Mariniers**. Mariners' colourful processional crosses brighten the interior, along with restored medieval murals. For the popular Peaugres safari park nearby, *see* p.158.

While factories hug the river around **St-Désirat**, the **Cave St-Désirat** stands out in a sea of fruit. The excellent big shop stocks Condrieu and St-Joseph and much simpler, cheaper *vins de pays*, made by grape variety. The divine aromas of a big selection of fruit liqueurs fill the air at the nearby **Musée de l'Alambic** and **Gauthier fruit liqueur shop**. A collection of copper stills is displayed at the heart of the distillery in stilted set pieces with life-size automata.

The fortunes of the inhabitants of riverside **Andance** were tied for centuries to the Rhône. It has the oldest-serving suspension bridge on the formidable river, built in 1827. The place has recently tidied up its spacious quay to encourage the huge *bateaux-hôtels* that cruise up the Rhône to stop.

For a little detour transporting you rapidly away from the Rhône into the savage atmosphere typical of northern Ardèche, head for **Thorrenc**, the cowering hamlet and defensive castle (not open) caught in a time-trap in their densely wooded gorge.

Past an industrial stretch of riverside, close to Tournon, at **St-Jean-de-Muzols**, turn onto the D238 to discover the **Maison Delas**, a reputable family wine business taken over by a Champagne house.

Taking the east bank of the Rhône from Vienne, steering clear of St-Alban-St-Maurice's nuclear power station, at **St-Rambert-d'Albon** you enter the *département* of the Drôme. The Albon area was once the base of the family of counts who won power over the substantial province of the Dauphiné in medieval times, their territories spreading east from the Rhône to the frontier with rival Savoie. Up on its height, the **Tour d'Albon** signals the site of what

**Musée des Mariniers**
*t 04 75 34 00 46; open 2nd week June–3rd week Sept Tues–Sun; adm*

**Cave St-Désirat**
*t 04 75 34 22 05, www.cave-saint-desirat.com*

**Musée de l'Alambic**
*t 04 75 34 23 11, www. jeangauthier.com; open July–Aug weekdays 8am–7pm, weekends 10–7; rest of year weekdays 8–12 and 2–6.30, weekends 10–12 and 2–6.30; adm*

**Maison Delas**
*open daily*

12

Down the Rhône | Vienne to Valence

**Lafuma
factory store**
*open Mon–Sat*

**Maison de la
Céramique**
*t 04 75 03 98 01,
www.territoire-
ceramique.com; open
mid-Jan–mid-Oct
Wed–Sun 2–7; adm*

was once the lordly headquarters, a sorry remnant, but with fine views. Northeast, at **Anneyron**, the **Lafuma factory store** sells high-quality outdoor wear and accessories; **Jars** sells stylish pottery.

Winding wooded gorges lead from the Rhône to **St-Uze**, devoted to porcelain since the early 19th-century, thanks to the discovery of the all-important ingredient, kaolin, nearby. Learn more at the old-fashioned **Maison de la Céramique** and pick up traditional pieces at the factory store. As much a natural as a Neolithic curiosity, seek out the cromlechs (stone circles) at nearby **St-Barthélemy-de-Vals**.

## Tain-l'Hermitage and Tournon

**✪ Tain
l'Hermitage
and Tournon**

One of the best ways of taking in the twin towns of Tain-l'Hermitage and Tournon, which face each other across the Rhône, is to walk out to the centre of the pedestrian bridge connecting the two. The two sides were first linked in 1825, by the earliest suspension bridge in continental Europe, designed by the great local engineer Marc Seguin (*see* 'Annonay', p.158). Sadly, this was destroyed in 1965 to make way for larger ships plying the Rhône. However, the slightly later footbridge is a crossing often full of cheerful bustle. The views onto both sloping banks are wonderful: the towers and ramparts of Tournon make an impression to the west, while the vine-baldened hills behind Tain form a grand backdrop to the east, their pates protruding high above the river.

**Musée de Tain-
l'Hermitage**
*t 04 75 07 15 54, www.
tain-tourisme.com;
open April–Oct Sat and
Sun 3–6; adm*

The centre of **Tain-l'Hermitage** is spoilt by the busy N7 road cutting mercilessly through town, but stop here and you can find plenty of attractions. For a start, enjoy a leisurely walk beside the Rhône. Unlike in Tournon, the riverside road is mercifully quiet, the views magnificent; a sleek modern cruise liner of a building adds a note of glamour to the more traditional riverside architecture. Set in a stylish former river merchant's house, do seek out the **Musée de Tain-l'Hermitage**, an art museum run with passion.

**Valrhôna
chocolate shop**
*t 04 75 07 90 62*

**Ecole du
Grand Chocolat**
*t 04 75 07 90 95;
ecole@valrhona.fr;
English speakers catered
for, but book well in
advance*

Then there are Tain's viticultural and culinary delights to sample. South along the N7 itself, the cramped **Valrhôna chocolate shop** attracts chocoholics like bees to the hive; the staff offer generous tastings of the exceptionally high-quality chocolate made here, recently winning out in a comparative chocolate tasting on the prestigious BBC Radio 4 *Food Programme*. Valrhôna also runs short chocolate cookery courses under the banner of its irresistibly named **Ecole du Grand Chocolat**.

**Michel Chapoutier**
*www.chapoutier.com;
tasting room open
daily, closed lunchtimes*

**Tain-l'Hermitage
wine co-operative**
*open daily, closed
lunchtimes*

The most famous wine-maker and merchant in these parts is the irrepressible Michel Chapoutier, champion of organic methods as well as the highest quality, one of the great names in modern French wine-making. His company has a modern **tasting room** at 18 Avenue du Dr. Paul Durand towards the railway station. The big **Tain-l'Hermitage wine co-operative** lies beyond, on a calm vine-covered slope, and has a very spacious, well-presented shop.

Best of all, go for a wander in the bacchic hills above Tain, where vines have colonized almost every inch of ground. Follow the **Route des Belvédères** and walk along the ridges to the **Chapelle de l'Hermitage** to appreciate some of the most dreamy views along the whole of the Rhône, the river cutting a romantic ribbon across the plain to Valence, mountains rising to east and west.

Away from the river, try some friendly wine-making addresses among the hilly vineyards of **Mercurol**, in Crozes-Hermitage territory. Southeast at **Châteauneuf-sur-Isère**, **Vinéum** , the smart new emporium of the renowned Jaboulet wine company, is rival to Chapoutier in northern Côtes du Rhône supremacy.

**Vinéum**
*t 04 75 47 35 55; open Tues–Sat 10–12 and 2–6; tastings free; cellar tours (adm) for groups of 10 or more only*

Its château rising straight out of the riverside rock, historic **Tournon** imposes a stop for anyone coming down the Rhône's west bank – partly because traffic jams so frequently clog the place up, but more importantly because it's delightful. Up the hill, the odd isolated tower marks the line of the town's former outer **ramparts**, although small cohorts of vines have scaled the walls, viticulture winning over military culture. Down by the river, rows of huge planes shade the car parks in front of the small **port**. Major buildings near the water include the **Lycée Faure**, originally a religious school founded in the mid-16th century by the raging Catholic Cardinal François de Tournon. Head into the old town via appealing shopping streets, venturing into the shadowy Gothic church of **St-Julien** for sobering murals tracing Christ's life: Jesus' donkey is sniffed at by a dog as he arrives in Jerusalem, where he is brought before Pontius Pilate, seemingly wearing cardinal's robes.

**Château de Tournon**
*t 04 75 08 10 31; open June–Aug daily 2–6; late Mar–May and Sept–Oct Thurs–Tues 2–6; closed Nov–Feb; adm*

Tournon's **château** , aloof on its rock, was built in stages from the 10th to the 16th centuries. This strategic seat served as the headquarters for French royal negotiations to buy the independent province of the Dauphiné across the Rhône in the 14th century. Tournon lords held posts at the French court in the 15th and 16th centuries. Just de Tournon was killed fighting alongside François I at the disastrous Battle of Pavia of 1525, at which the sovereign was captured. François de Tournon, Just's brother, negotiated with the Holy Roman Emperor Charles V for the king's release.

A demoralizing royal tragedy took place in town in 1536: the young heir to the French throne, also called François, died here in agonizing sickness. As for Hélène de Tournon, daughter of Just II, some claim her crazed love story made her the model for Ophelia in Shakespeare's *Hamlet*. The family line came to an end in the 17th century, the castle then long serving as a prison, before turning in part into a museum. Beyond the tremendous nail-covered door by which you enter, the contents today take into consideration mariners on the Rhône, as well as the aristocratic Tournons. The surprising perched chapel boasts a stunning triptych, Christ rising to heaven in a flaming ball, an extraordinary falling skeleton contrasting with his ascent. This complex work includes a superb portrait of the donor, Cardinal François, with his dog.

Keen walkers could tackle Tournon's old ramparts by following the **Sentier des Tours**. For a less strenuous way to explore the area, book a **cruise up the Rhône**, allowing you to take in the vineyards and castle at a leisurely pace; or head up into the rugged, scarcely populated Ardèche hills by old train on the **Chemin de Fer du Vivarais**, taking you up the dramatically twisting Doux valley. Alternatively, follow the locals to **Douce-Plage** (about 5km along the Lamastre road) for a refreshing summer dip.

While Tournon is often described as the cradle of St-Joseph wine, around **Mauves** you enter the area of the largest St-Joseph producers. Above the village, follow the dramatic **Corniche du Rhône**, or Route Panoramique, for spectacular views from the heights of St-Romain-de-Lerps. Back by the Rhône, you pass defensive **Châteaubourg**, the village subservient below its fast-shut castle. Then comes **Cornas**' secretive theatre of vines.

**Chemin de Fer du Vivarais**
*t 04 75 08 20 30; runs July–Aug daily; May–June and Sept Tues–Sun; April and Oct Wed, Sun and public hols; adm*

## Crussol and Valence

Opposite Valence, the spectacular bone-white ruins of the medieval castle of **Crussol** lie like a huge battered snail's shell baked bone-dry on the extremely steep Rhône west bank. Back in the 12th century, Bastet de Crussol decided to have a **castle** built on this ridiculously difficult spot 230m above the Valence plain. Later members of the family presumably had had enough of the hair-raising route home and headed off, to play greater roles on the national stage. In the 17th century, the castle was partly destroyed. But what remains is, with Rochemaure (*see* p.195), by far the most sensational castle ruin along the Rhône.

**Valence and Crussol**

**Château de Crussol**
*free, but take extreme care climbing the ruins*

Halfway up the slope, below the ruins, you'll find a shop selling regional produce and an outdoor green theatre with staggering views way over Valence to the Vercors. The reward if you make it up the treacherously slippery paths (take great care) to the ruins themselves is still more amazing views. As the sun descends, the castle casts a huge shadow across the Valence plain. Far down below, the vineyards of **St-Péray** surround the sweet little village of the same name, producing the surprise of a rather enjoyable sparkling white, although a bit of a frivolous wine compared with the much more serious ones we've covered so far.

In history, **Valence** started out as a military stop along the Rhône back in Roman times, a role it served for many centuries. It also became a religious and mercantile town of note, control of the salt trade along the Rhône forming a particularly important source of revenue. The young Napoleon is said to have appreciated some of the lighter things in life during his stay in Valence as a young army officer in the late 18th century. Arriving by boat in November 1785, he apparently enjoyed flirting with the daughters of the local *bourgeoisie*, cherry-picking, reading voraciously, and even penning a passionate military novel. The story goes, however, that he almost died on the perilous climb to the top of Crussol castle – how different European history might have been! As it was, Napoleon left in August 1786 to help put down a silk-workers' riot in Lyon, briefly returning to the same élite regiment in 1791. Pope Pius VI didn't have as good a time in Valence as Bonaparte, ignominiously dragged from Rome as far as here once the imperious *petit caporal* was setting about his brief European domination. The sickly pontiff died here in 1799. His body was eventually returned to Italy, the Rhône-side city receiving a bust by way of thanks.

In recent times, the city has become much more welcoming, turning its attentions more and more to tourism. Although in a central location, however, the **Cathédrale St-Apollinaire** turns its back on the jolliness of Valence's main historic square. Much reconstructed in the 17th century, the edifice retains the form and certain fragments of the Romanesque original. Inside, the bust of Pope Pius VI stands out in the colonnaded ambulatory. Occupying the plain 18th-century bishop's palace, the town's **Musée des Beaux-Arts** is undergoing a major restoration programme over the coming years, when its dramatic mosaics, drawings of classical sights and portraits of important figures in Valentinois history will be shown in a new light. In the last category, the youthful Jean-Etienne Championnet, one of Napoleon's brilliant boy-generals, is a character whose name pops up several times around town.

*Musée des Beaux-Arts*
*t 04 75 79 20 80,*
*www.musee-valence.org; adm*

The end of the cathedral protrudes unapologetically into **Place des Clercs**, now the lively centre of the old town, and along with Place de l'Université hub of the spectacular Saturday morning market. The main old shopping streets lead off these squares, including the stylish **Grande Rue**, which boasts the liveliest façade in town, the well-named 16th-century **Maison des Têtes**, containing a small, free permanent exhibition on Valence's history. But the main interest is on the exterior, its opulence and erudite classical references reflecting the 15th–16th-century golden period when fairs and a university brought prosperity to Valence – this façade was commissioned by a leading town councillor and professor of law. Classical allusions feature large, from the heads on high representing the winds, via Fortune and Time gadding about naked on the first floor, to nine philosophers presiding over the ground floor.

*Maison des Têtes*
*t 04 75 79 20 86;*
*open July–Aug daily*
*9.30–12.30 and 2–6;*
*Sept–June Mon–Sat*
*9.30–12.30 and 2–5.30,*
*Sun 2–5.30*

On the town's guided tours, you are shown the elaborate courtyard behind, and that of the **Maison Dupré-Latour** on parallel Rue Perrolerie. At the bottom of that street, the perfect little 16th-century classical funerary monument of **Le Pendentif** stands in a quiet corner, while at the other end, appealing restaurant terraces spread out on confidential **Place de la Pierre**.

Just up Rue St-James, the **Temple**, or Protestant church, occupies the former Catholic St Rufus priory, where pilgrims used to stop on their way down the Rhône. An aside in English Church history, in the 12th century, one Nicholas Breakspear made quite an impression when he joined the order here; he went on to become the only ever English pope, Adrian IV. In the 18th century the church interior was decorated with fine stucco, while Napoleon later ordered the ornate obelisk honouring Championnet.

Reaching grandiose **Place de la Liberté**, the 19th-century **Hôtel de Ville** and **theatre** vie for attention with their massive egos. Continue to **Place St-Jean**, embellished with a light covered market, looked down upon by the **Eglise St-Jean-Baptiste**.

**Centre Arménien**
*t 04 75 80 13 00, www. patrimoinearmenien. org; open Jan–mid-Aug and Sept–Christmas Tues–Sun 2.30–6.30; adm*

Do also visit the new **Centre Arménien**, which tells the harrowing story of why so many Armenians fled to France from 1915, as the Turkish authorities began carrying out what is now widely seen as the first major genocide of the 20th century. Many estimates put the total who died at around 1.5 million. Many Armenian refugees travelled to Marseille at the mouth of the Rhône, to be kept there for some time in miserable camps. Liberated, they were allowed to settle across France, and many established themselves in towns up the Rhône, building businesses. Valence has an exceptionally large percentage of inhabitants of Armenian descent. Here, you gain an understanding of their families' past sufferings, but also of their triumphs, their successful integration, and the importance of their culture and traditions. Once in the know, wandering along Valence's streets you'll notice the distinctive Armenian names of quite a number of the shops.

Wide boulevards encircle Valence's historic centre, following the course of the former ramparts. Just to the south lies the enormous **Champ de Mars**, the biggest terrace in town; the statue once again stars Championnet. Behind, a further array of bright shopping streets lines up, but the view westwards may tempt you down into the shaded **Parc Jouvet**, with its magical ring of towering planes under which the *boules*-players gather. The gates at the end prevent anyone from running out onto the thundering roads cutting the Valentinois off from their river in the centre of town.

On the watery theme, however, Valence does offer several possibilities. The most curious is a special tourist office guided tour of the city's **underground canals**, which date back to Roman times. More significantly, quite some distance south of the centre is the largest **marina** along the Rhône, in fact the largest river pleasure boat harbour in France. Valence's port proves surprisingly glamorous, with views across the water to spectacular jagged hills among which the ruins of the Château de Crussol merge. Come down here and you may feel more like you're on the Côte d'Azur. For a trip out on the river, contact **Bateaux Taxi Valentinois**.

**Bateaux Taxi Valentinois**
*t 06 85 08 44 26*

# Valence to Montélimar

Following the west bank of the Rhône, **Soyons** appears to have been the place to head in prehistoric times for butchering woolly mammoths along the river: a hoard of bones was unearthed here in the 1980s. This mysterious story counts among the most compelling told in the modest but interesting **Musée Archéologique**. The evidence reveals human habitation here going back 150,000 years, while the separate archaeological site of **La Brégoule** uncovers a comparatively short 10,000 years of civilization.

**Soyons Musée Archéologique**
*t 04 75 60 88 86; under restoration; check times*

Pretty old villages with castle ruins follow at **Charmes-sur-Rhône** and at **Beauchastel**. Leave civilization totally behind to walk to the craggy ruins of the **Château de Pierre-Gourde** above **St-Laurent-du-Pape**, just rising out of the dense greenery surrounding it, a dozen melting layers of hills disappearing to the west.

**Château de La Voulte-sur-Rhône**
*t 04 75 62 44 36; open mid-June–Aug Wed only at 10.30; adm*

A black **castle** dominates **La Voulte-sur-Rhône**, its Gothic to Renaissance forms at one time hosting the estates general of the whole Languedoc region, which stretched further north in previous times. Among the dark arcaded streets, the church of **St-Vincent** treasures its beautifully carved 16th-century marble altarpiece.

One of the worst victims of the Rhône valley's massive industrialization, dusty **Cruas** does still boast one of the most splendid religious edifices along the river. Pope Urban II consecrated the

**Cruas abbey church**
*t 04 75 49 59 20, www.cruas.com; open April–Sept Mon–Sat for visits at 11, 3 and 5, Sun at 3.30 and 5.30; Oct–Mar Mon, Tues, Thurs and Fri for visits at 2.30 and 4.30, Sat at 10; adm*

**abbey church** in the late 11th century. The abbey of which it was a part became a powerful establishment, ruling over extensive territories, while up to 100 monks were based here. They held on doggedly through the Wars of Religion, defending themselves up in the compact fort on the hillside, now in ruins. A bishop of Viviers it was who rang the death knell for the abbey, closing it in the 18th century. Just the church remains. Inside, it presents a confusing number of layers. Admire the finely carved capitals. The intriguing mosaic formed part of the original 11th-century symbolic decorations. Later medieval murals illustrate exemplary martyrdoms. Down in the Carolingian crypt, the motifs look far more primitive, one little figure depicted in wildly uplifting prayer.

For a divine little country detour avoiding Cruas, branch off the N86 north of Baix onto the D22, then join the D2 going south, offering a cheerful, peaceful route, a world away from the Rhône-side industry. Pay a visit to **St-Vincent-de-Barrès**, a hill village marked out by crumbling towers.

Back by the Rhône, balanced on top of a startling volcanic pinnacle, the **Château de Rochemaure** counts among the most sensational sights along the great river. The medieval fort was for a time the stronghold of one of the branches of the Adhémar family from Montélimar. Restored in the 19th century, the ramparts extend further along the high ridge, protecting an upper village.

Several of the houses huddled in the sweet village far below display little religious statues. For another amazing view, head west to the **Pic de Chenavari**, reached by foot.

On the east bank of the Rhône below Valence, the A7 and N7 get involved in a slightly twisted race to Montélimar. Protected from them by remnants of its ramparts, **Etoile-sur-Rhône** has kept its historic atmosphere. Closer to the Rhône, a tiny number of vineyards around **Livron** produce the rare Brézème, a much sought-after, if elusive Côtes du Rhône wine.

South from **Loriol**, take to the slopes for two enchanting neighbouring artistic old villages. **Cliousclat** keeps very tightly in its shell, protecting itself from modern encroachments. This is a potters' village, where the houses really are as tightly packed as pieces in a kiln. Visit the many galleries, and the old-style **Musée Histoire de**

**Musée Histoire de Poteries**
*t 04 75 63 15 60; open July–Aug daily 10–1 and 2–7; April– June and Sept–Nov Tues–Sun 2–6; adm*

**Poteries**, still operating the old-fashioned way. **Mirmande** faces the Rhône valley with more open defiance, built in layers up a pudding-shaped hill. Early in the 20th century, many locals abandoned their houses for the valley. But Mirmande then welcomed an artists' colony when Cubist painter André Lhote fell in love with the place in the 1920s. Stylishly restored, it remains a favourite with an intellectual and artistic crowd, a couple of galleries standing on the way up to the church, itself something of a cultural centre.

A beautiful forest road leads to **Marsanne**, once Mirmande's rival, set in a panoramic spot above the Roubion plain leading to Montélimar, contorted peaks rising to the east. The ruins of a castle tumble down the hillside. Clamber up to what remains of medieval **St-Félix**. Below, the 19th-century stamps its mark confidently: Marsanne was the birthplace in 1838 of France's first so-called 'peasant president', Emile Loubet (read about his attachment to nougat in the box opposite).

🏆 **Montélimar**

Travelling down to **Montélimar**, it's hard to wipe the vast chimneys of the Cruas nuclear power station from the corner of your eye, one of them quite cynically daubed with a huge image of a child playing innocently on a beach. Its compact historic kernel caught between major nuclear installations along the Rhône, the name of Montélimar does, though, conjure up very sweet images for French children. Before the A7 motorway was opened in the late 1960s, legions of families would stop in town to buy a bag or two of nougat...in part, one suspects, to keep the children quiet on the journey, by almost literally glueing their teeth together. To see how nougat is made, visit one of the 15 or so producers in town in the morning. Just north of the main boulevards, the central **Nougaterie Chaudron d'Or** is one of the smallest and friendliest, run by the delightfully enthusiastic Hervé Contaux. The maker with the biggest reputation has moved his premises to a new commercial zone off the main southern road out of the centre, but despite the

## Nougat de Montélimar

The almonds, pistachios and honey mixed with whites of egg to make nougat make you think of a Moorish dessert, and legend has it that this was one of the delights brought over to France by way of the Arabs. One story claims the recipe arrived with the 8th-century Moorish incursions into southern France; another that it was via an Adhémar lord who came back from crusade with a native cook in tow. It's only in the 16th century that there's clear evidence of almond trees being planted here.

One highly placed ambassador for Montélimar's confectionery at the start of the 20th century was long-time mayor Emile Loubet, who made it to top post of president of France. A staunch Republican, as well as seeing to the pardoning of the framed Jewish soldier Alfred Dreyfus, the quintessential Republican separation of French Church and State and the signing of the Entente Cordiale with Britain, he apparently spoilt all his guests with Montélimar's sticky sweets!

dull surroundings, Arnaud Soubeyran, tireless modern-day ambassador for nougat, has created a swanky shop, with a corner turned into a **Musée du Nougat**. The nougat is divine, putting to shame the stuff you find in those chocolate selection boxes, but for any dentist no doubt Montélimar is regarded as tooth hell.

**Musée du Nougat**
t 04 75 51 01 35, www.
nougatsoubeyran.com;
open Mon–Sat 8.30–7,
Sun 10–12 and
2.30–6.30

In the last few years, central Montélimar has really brightened up, and great effort has been put into creating enticing events to encourage tourists to stop; these range from the potters' fair in April to the Christmas market, via the very colourful lavender festival around mid-July. The tourist office also organizes guided tours to a Drôme lavender property in summer. In fact, Montélimar now acts as something of a showcase for the wonderful *produits du terroir* to be found in the Ardèche and Drôme countryside to either side of it. Approaching the old town, though, be patient driving through the relentless commercial zones, although many a nougat shop still lines the way. The latest addition to the confectionery attractions on the outskirts is the grandiose-sounding, heavily commercial **Musée International des Sucreries** at the Palais des Bonbons et du Nougat north of the centre. You can learn about sugary confections here, but nougat is just treated with a film.

**Musée International des Sucreries**
t 04 75 50 62 66, www.
palais-bonbons.com;
open July–Aug daily
10–7, late Jan–June and
Sept–Dec Tues–Sat
10–12 and 2–7,
Mon 2–7; adm

Traffic dashes incessantly round the boulevards that encircle the historic kernel. But the wonderful shade of the layers of plane trees, up to six rows deep, of the **Allées Provençales** should tempt you to stop. Many of the historic streets in the heart of town are reserved for pedestrians. From a few, you get fleeting glimpses of the medieval castle on the hill, a short but steep climb away. Around the 11th century, the Adhémar family took up home here on Monteil hill, which became the Mont-Adhémar, hence the name Montélimar. Although you don't feel the presence of the Rhône in Montélimar, their solid keep surveyed its valley down to the Donzère straits, where tough little mountains tighten their grip around the river's throat. The Adhémar family subsequently split into several competing hilltop factions, one branch taking you to La Garde-Adhémar (*see* p.201), another to Rochemaure (*see* p.195), a third to Grignan (*see* p.224). As for the merchants of Monteil, they

**Château des Adhémar**
t 04 75 00 62 30; open April–Oct daily 9.30–12 and 2–6; Nov–Mar Wed–Mon 9.30–12 and 2–6; adm

**Musée de la Miniature**
t 04 75 53 79 24; open July–Aug daily 10–6; Sept–June Wed–Sun 2–6; adm

**Musée Européen de l'Avion de Chasse**
t 04 75 53 79 49, www. meacmtl.com; open Mon–Fri 9–12 and 1.30–5.30, Sat and Sun 2–6; adm

**Golf de la Valdaine**
t 04 75 00 71 33

were granted franchises from taxes early on. The acquisitive popes of Avignon, not far south, ensured that many monasteries were built in the town when they gained control in the 14th century, but the place suffered terribly in the Wars of Religion. Calmer times followed with the planting of mulberries for silk-making and almonds for nougat.

Montélimar's semi-ruined feudal **Château des Adhémar** looks slightly Moorish. It has been given a new lease of life as a **Centre d'Art Contemporain**, holding retrospectives on major international artists, and inviting newer talents to fill the empty medieval chambers with bold works for a season.

Montélimar's ramparts were brought down in the 19th century, but one Ancien Régime **gateway** survives at the northern end of the main street, **Rue Pierre Julien**. Explore the maze of unfussy to scruffy lanes and squares off this main artery. There's a varied and tempting selection of shops in the centre. Many façades have been painted in cheerful powder-puff colours, one of the brightest, a former religious building, converted into the curious but stylish **Musée de la Miniature** dedicated to miniature works of art.

On the outskirts of Montélimar, fans of military aviation shoot off to the **Musée Européen de l'Avion de Chasse**, which has been recently spruced up. Golfers head for the 18-hole **Golf de la Valdaine** east at **Montboucher-sur-Jabron**.

# From Montélimar down the West Bank of the Rhône to Languedoc

🔟 Viviers

Continuing along the west bank of the Rhône below Montélimar, a tiara in stone crowns the fine cathedral of **Viviers**, a startling if neglected town on its hilltop above the river. Its Gallo-Roman name, Vivarium, is probably linked to *viviers*, fishponds, established by the river, perhaps supplying the once more important city of Alba-la-Romaine (*see* p.171) to the west. Then Bishop Ausonne made the big move from Alba to here in the 5th century. Viviers grew to such importance that it gave its name to a whole mountainous area west of the river, the Vivarais, roughly equivalent to the present-day *département* of Ardèche. Despite feeling semi-abandoned now, the tiny city still has a bishop. Large episcopal buildings stand out in the lower town.

It's a steep climb to the hilltop **cathedral**, protected within a precinct of tall white stone walls. The windowless, aisleless nave is of staggering proportions, an awesome religious cave, in some way rivalling the celebrated natural grottoes of the Ardèche gorges close by (*see* pp.173–7). Consecrated by Pope Calixtus II in 1119, the place still feels strongly Romanesque, although apparently largely redone in the 18th century. Seven splendid Gothic windows in the choir signal clearly how that end was rebuilt in the late 15th century. A major cycle of 18th-century Gobelin tapestries below illustrates episodes in Christ's life. They've kept their fresh colours, but also the sickly-sweet tone favoured in Ancien Régime story-telling. The cathedral's separate **campanile** towers 40m into the air, doubling as a huge defensive post, but from the terrace beyond the views are marred by industry.

The liveliest thing in the sadly dying streets below is the façade of the grand **Maison Noël Albert**, a striking carving showing victorious knights on horseback, their vigour seeming somewhat ironic today. From the lower town, a splendid avenue of squat plane trees leads to the picturesque Rhône-side **port**.

Below Viviers, the Rhône valley narrows into the extremely tight **Défilé de Donzère**, its cliffs closing dramatically in on the river. **St-Montan**, named after a 5th-century religious man who sought refuge from the world here, today offers a refreshing haven away from the roar of the main Rhône valley roads. Streams congregate at the bottom of the village, whose lovingly restored roofs you can appreciate by climbing beyond the main church and the cobbled maze of steep lanes up to the substantial crenallated remnants of a castle. It squats on top of a pyramidal hill, guarding the entrance to the unspoilt rocky terrain of the **Gorge de la Ste-Baume**, wild parts appreciated by rockclimbers and potholers.

**Bourg-St-Andéol** makes a last, and surprisingly rich historic stop on the Ardèche side of the Rhône. Its quays may now be quiet, but the major merchants' houses behind them still stand, recalling the centuries when this was a major river-trading town. The place carries the name of a 2nd-century Christian martyr savagely put to death by order of Emperor Septimus Severus, enraged at witnessing his success in converting the locals. Andéol's dismembered body was thrown in the Rhône. Christianity was never an innocent cult, however; in their early days in Gaul, Christians smashed rival religions like Mithraism. This military cult reserved for men, introduced to the Roman Empire from Persia, featured a young saviour killing a bull, symbol of evil. A Mithraic carving has miraculously survived below the terraces of a rustic public garden near the centre; although it's badly defaced, you can make out the caped young hero stabbing the bull. Hope springs from his act, corn sprouting from the beast's tail. Sun and moon oversee proceedings, the former wearing rays like an early Statue of Liberty.

Old Christian buildings triumph above the quays. A powerful octagonal tower rises from the imposing if heavily restored **Romanesque church**. It contains the highly decorated Roman sarcophagus of a child, later transformed into the tomb of saint Andéol; a Latin inscription retells his martyrdom. It was that great author Victor Hugo who rediscovered this exceptional reliquary when he stopped at Bourg-St-Andéol and read the Latin.

**Palais des Evêques**
t 04 75 54 41 76;
open June–Sept Wed,
Thurs, Sat and Sun
3.30–7.30; adm

Nearby, the substantial **Palais des Evêques** long served as the residence of the bishops of Viviers. Battered by the centuries, and only just being revived, certain Gothic features still stand out on the outside of this hulking building, and massive fireplaces within. Under the 17th-century Monseigneur de la Baume de Suze, made bishop of Viviers at just 17, some of its chambers were embellished with painted ceilings, as you can see on a tour inside. Cultural events are now staged in this sprawling edifice.

**Musée de la
Dentelle**
t 04 75 54 00 73; call
between 10am and
8pm for appointment

**Musée Lena-
Vandrey**
t 04 75 54 51 49;
guided visits by appt
only; adm

Another grand building above the Rhône, the **Hôtel Doize**, houses the **Musée de la Dentelle**, a private lace museum run by a British woman passionate about her craft, on which she organizes courses. In stark contrast, in a further splendid bourgeois house above the river, the **Musée Lena-Vandrey** displays daring contemporary art in a host of media – drawings, collages, cut-outs, sculptures, paintings – by this accomplished German artist. You will come face to face with many raw interpretations of the female form as you wander from one room to the next.

For one of the most stunning views over the Rhône, taking in much of the gorgeous *département* of the Drôme, climb the D4 from Bourg towards Vallon. There are also Côtes du Rhône wine estates with views to visit closer to Bourg-St-Andéol, while above historic **St-Marcel-d'Ardèche**, tucked away on its hillside, almonds and fruit trees thrive. Below **St-Just**, truffle oaks and peach orchards have been planted close to the Rhône.

Reaching the border with the *département* of the Gard in the Languedoc region, one last, lovely sandy beach stretches along the Ardèche riverbank beside a romantically ruined bridge, making a popular summer bathing spot. For the Ardèche gorges a little west, *see* Chapter 11.

# From Montélimar down the East Bank of the Rhône to Provence

Heading south from Montélimar along the Rhône's east bank, keeping close to the river, **Châteauneuf-sur-Rhône**, with its old line of ramparts running down the hill, still looks like a feisty medieval military village, but the place really is embattled by industry. Set some way back from the Rhône, the old village of **Allan** on its ridge was totally abandoned long ago, leaving an impressive array of ruins stretching along the hillside like a mighty, vanished fort.

A back road leads to better-preserved **Roussas** on its dramatic ridge, churches vying for attention along with the restored ruins of its castle. Nearby, the steep narrow lanes of **Valaurie** protect a couple of art galleries in a hilltop village known for attracting a close-knit intellectual crowd. For gorgeous Grignan to the east, *see* p.224.

Standing defiantly on its high terrace above the Rhône, **La Garde-Adhémar** has to contend with noisy Rhône valley traffic below. But, enchantingly restored, this splendid village has the character to deal with the situation. Its serene Romanesque church confidently overlooks the valley, inside offering a calm, dark, womb-like refuge, and the comfort of a solid peasant Virgin and child in front of which to pray. Below the church, explore the very pretty little formal **herb gardens**, colour-coded according to their medicinal properties. The rest of the village turns its back on the Rhône, with plenty of resources to draw on, including delightful houses, craft shops and cafés.

To the south, a **tower** rises from the rock-top hamlet of **Clansayes**, a landmark visible from afar, topped by a big Virgin who looks quite dismayed at the nuclear power station visible down in the Rhône valley. French people do go in their hundreds of thousands to visit the **Tricastin nuclear installations** beside **Pierrelatte** every year, while the bizarre **Ferme aux Crocodiles** also attracts huge numbers. Its waters are heated by the warmth generated by the power station, providing a suitable habitat for a whole range of crocodile species, living in exotic surroundings.

**Ferme aux Crocodiles**
*t 04 75 04 33 73, www. lafermeauxcrocodiles. com; open Mar–Sept daily 9.30–7; Oct–Feb daily 9.30–5; adm*

We end the chapter with a forgotten joy hidden just out of sight of the Rhône, an ancient little city still surrounded in good part by medieval walls: adorable **St-Paul-Trois-Châteaux**. Those of you hoping from the name to discover three castles here will be sorely disappointed, as there is none – the name derives from a mis-translation of the one-time Celtic tribe here, the Tricastani. But the Romanesque **cathedral** helps make up for any initial disappointment, a remarkable edifice that incorporates fragments of previous Roman buildings. In fact, the place is named after a Bishop Paul who served here in the late Roman period; and this tiny spot would remain a bishopric up until the Revolution.

 **St-Paul-Trois-Châteaux**

The cathedral's almost total lack of windows clearly indicates its pre-Gothic roots. It was built mainly in the 11th and 12th centuries. Intriguing features to seek out include the noble stone-carved heads squashed in above the main door, itself an accomplished piece of carving in wood. Wander round the exterior looking out for intriguing stonemasons' marks and even a few tiny rough carvings of warriors. In the dauntingly tall interior, a mosaic in the apse depicts a naïve Jerusalem. Elsewhere, carved details and patches of medieval murals add to the intrigue.

**Maison de la Truffe et du Tricastin**
*t 04 75 96 61 29, www. truffle-and-truffe.com; ring to check times, but normally summer daily 9–12 and 2–6; winter Tues–Sat 9–12 and 2–6, Mon 2–6; adm*

The lands east of here are the most prolific truffle-producing territories in France, hence the **Maison de la Truffe et du Tricastin** in the shadow of the cathedral. The explanations on truffle-growing get a little overtechnical for the uninitiated – take the tour CD for assistance. You can buy samples of the massively priced 'black diamonds' here.

Vines proliferate in the lands to the east too, producing excellent-value Coteaux du Tricastin and Côtes du Rhône wines, while at nearby Suze-la-Rousse, the old castle has been converted into a university of wine. Read the next chapter for more on this, but at the Maison they can offer you tastings of all the Tricastin wine producers. Make sure you also explore the enchanting maze of squares away from the cathedral area. If you head further down the Rhône from here, you enter Provence, although why you should need to venture south is a mystery to us here, when the rest of the Ardèche and Drôme, so staggeringly beautiful, lie so temptingly to east and west, and in the chapters either side of this one.

ⓘ **Givors**
*Maison du Rhône,
1 Place Liberté, 69700
Givors,* **t** *04 78 07 41 38,
office.tourisme.fleuve@
wanadoo.fr*

ⓘ **Vienne >>**
*Cours Brillier,
38200 Vienne,* **t** *04 74
53 80 30, www.vienne-
tourisme.com*

⭐ **La Pyramide >>**

## Market Days along the Rhône South of Lyon

**Givors:** Wed, Fri and Sun am.
**Vienne:** Every am; Sat extravaganza.
**Tournon-sur-Rhône:** Sat am.
**Tain-l'Hermitage:** Sat am.
**St-Péray:** Wed am.
**Valence:** Sat am.
**La Voulte-sur-Rhône:** Fri am.
**Montélimar:** Wed am and Sat am.
**Viviers:** Tues am.
**Bourg-St-Andéol:** Wed am.
**St-Paul-Trois-Châteaux:** Tues am; truffle market Nov–Mar Sun am.

## Festivals along the Rhône South of Lyon

Many of the Rhône-side towns and villages put on **summer festivals** by and on the river, with races, jousting and even waterskiing. **Vienne Jazz Festival**, the first fortnight in July, is one of the most important jazz events in France. Look out for local wine festivals, too.

## Activities along the Rhône South of Lyon

At St-Pierre-de-Bœuf, some of the Rhône's waters have been diverted to feed the **Rivière Artificielle**, a man-made white-water rafting course run by **Espace Eau Vive, t** 04 74 87 16 09,

*www.espaceeauvive.com*. There is a lake for swimming nearby, and another one across at Les Roches-de-Condrieu. The **Golf Club d'Albon**, **t** 04 75 03 03 90, has one of the Drôme's three 18-hole golf courses.

## Where to Stay and Eat along the Rhône South of Lyon

### Vienne ✉ 38200

****La Pyramide** , 14 Bd Fernand Point, **t** 04 74 53 01 96, *www.lapyramide.com* (€€€€). Bright, modern Provençal chic in the splendid rooms, but known above all as a temple of *haute cuisine* (€€€€) – the street is named after Fernand Point, the legendary chef who made its name, the first ever to be awarded three Michelin stars. The cooking is still sublime. *Closed Feb; restaurant closed Sun and Mon.*

***Grand Hôtel de la Poste**, 47 Cours Romestang, **t** 04 74 85 02 04, *www.hotel-vienne.fr* (€). Not grand, but a bargain, well positioned close to the station and the centre, with brightened-up rooms and plans for air-conditioning.

**Le Cloître**, 2 Rue des Cloîtres, **t** 04 74 31 93 57 (€€€–€€). Romantic restaurant by the cathedral; refined cuisine. *Closed Sat and Sun.*

**Le Restique**, 16 Rue Boson, **t** 04 74 85 48 65 (€). Both a simple, appealing restaurant for tasty local dishes and

### ⓘ Tain-l'Hermitage
*70 Av Jean Jaurès, 26600 Tain-l'Hermitage, t 04 75 08 06 81, www.tain.tourisme.com*

⍟ **La Gabetière >**

⍟ **Michel Chabran >>**

⍟ **Domaine/ Jardins de Clairefontaine >**

### ⓘ Valence >>
*Parvis de la Gare, 26000 Valence, t 04 75 44 90 40, www.tourisme-valence.com*

⍟ **Maison Pic >>**

### ⓘ Condrieu >
*Place du Séquoia, 69420 Condrieu, t 04 74 56 62 83*

### ⓘ La Voulte-sur-Rhône
*Place Etienne Jarjeat, 07800 La Voulte-sur-Rhône, t 04 75 62 44 36, www.ardecheplein coeur.com*

### ⓘ Albon >
*Maison de la Valloire, RN7, 26140 Albon, t 04 75 03 17 05, www.lavalloire.com*

### ⓘ Tournon-sur-Rhône >
*Hôtel de la Tourette, 07300 Tournon-sur-Rhône, t 04 75 08 10 23, www.valleedudoux.com*

a tempting delicatessen. *Closed Sat lunch, Sun, and Wed eve.*

## Estrablin ✉ 38780
**\*\*\*La Gabetière**, 7km east of Vienne on D502, t 04 74 58 01 31, *www.la-gabetiere.com* (€). Utterly charming 16th-century manor, and a bargain, with spacious *salons*, tasteful rooms hung with art, plus pool in shaded grounds. *Closed Christmas–mid-Jan.*

## Chonas-l'Amballan ✉ 38121
**\*\*Domaine de Clairefontaine**, Chemin des Fontanettes, t 04 74 58 81 52, *www.domaine-de-clairefontaine.fr* (€€–€). Set back in large gardens on the Rhône's east bank, an excellent traditional French family-owned hotel with a reputed restaurant, **Les Jardins de Clairefontaine** (€€€€–€€€). Tennis. *Restaurant closed out of season; also closed Sun eve, Mon, and Tues lunch, plus mid-Aug, and mid-Dec–mid-Jan.*

## Condrieu ✉ 69420
**\*\*\*\*Beau-Rivage**, 2 Rue du Beau Rivage, t 04 74 56 82 82, *www.hotel-beaurivage.com* (€€€). By the Rhône, below vine-covered slopes, a large modern building with smart air-conditioned rooms, many with terraces with a river view. Fine traditional restaurant (€€€€– €€€), dining possible right by the Rhône.

## Serrières ✉ 07340
**\*\*\*Hôtel Schaeffer**, 34 Quai Jules Roche, t 04 75 34 00 07, *www.hotel-schaeffer.com* (€). Standing out among the simpler cafés by the bridge is this well-located traditional riverside hotel. Good restaurant (€€€) with river views and mural. *Closed Jan; restaurant closed Tues in high summer, otherwise Sat lunch, Sun eve and Mon.*

## Albon ✉ 26140
**Domaine des Buis**, by golf course, t 04 75 03 14 14, *www.domaine-des-buis.com* (€€€– €€). Exclusive 18th-century house built with the pebbles of the area. Spacious rooms with luxurious bathrooms. Pool in a lovely leafy garden. *Closed Dec–Feb.*

## Tournon-sur-Rhône ✉ 07300
Le Chaudron, 7 Rue St-Antoine, t 04 75 08 17 90 (€€). On a pedestrian street, a

restaurant reputed for its Ardèche specialities and excellent wines. *Closed Thurs eve, plus Sun Christmas–mid-Jan.*

## Pont de l'Isère ✉ 26600
**\*\*\*Michel Chabran**, 29 Av du 45ème Parallèle, t 04 75 84 60 09, *www.michelchabran.fr* (€€€€–€€€). Delicious cuisine at the smart restaurant (€€€€–€€€) of this establishment, with superb local wine list and sunny patio, plus a dozen reasonable rooms. *Restaurant closed Wed lunch and Thurs lunch in April–Sept; all of Wed, Thurs lunch and Sun eve in Oct–Mar.*

## Valence ✉ 26000
**\*\*\*\*Maison Pic**, 285 Av Victor Hugo, t 04 75 44 15 32, *www.pic-valence.com* (€€€€€–€€€€). Long established as one of the great family-run stops down the Rhône. On an uninspiring road south of the centre, but a fabulous oasis within. Delightful contemporary rooms and décor, and a bastion of superlative cuisine (€€€€–€€€). The young Sophie Pic has just won her third Michelin star for her daring inventions, the only female chef with this accolade at present. *Restaurant closed Sun eve, Mon and Tues lunch out of season.* Try less elaborate Pic dishes at adjoining **Brasserie 7**, t 04 75 44 53 86 (€€). *Closed Wed out of season.*

**\*\*Hôtel de France**, 16 Bd de Gaulle, t 04 75 43 00 87, *www.hotel-valence.com* (€€). A renovated option close to the historic heart.

**Bistrot des Clercs**, 48 Grande Rue, t 04 75 55 55 15 (€€). In the central house where Napoleon stayed, really well-priced food from the Chabran stable (*see* Pont de l'Isère above). *Closed Sun lunch in summer, Sun eve rest of year.*

## Soyons ✉ 07130
**\*\*\*\*/\*\*\*Domaine de Soyons**, N86, t 04 75 60 83 55, *www.ledomainede soyons.com* (€€€€–€€€). Plusher rooms in the handsome main 19th-century block, more rustic Provençal ones in the outbuildings. Smart restaurant (€€€) with veranda. Pool and tennis court. *Closed Nov–Feb; restaurant closed Jan, and Mon out of season.*

⭐ **Autour d'une Fontaine >**

ⓘ **Bourg-St-Andéol >>**
*Place du Champ de Mars, 07700 Bourg-St-Andéol, t 04 75 54 54 20, bourg-st-andeol@fnotsi.net*

⭐ **Digoine >>**

⭐ **La Cardinale et sa Résidence >**

ⓘ **Viviers**
*5 Place Riquet, 07220 Viviers, t 04 75 52 77 00, viviers@fnotsi.net*

⭐ **Le Moulin de Valaurie >>**

ⓘ **La Garde-Adhémar >>**
*Rue Marquis de la Baume, 26700 La Garde-Adhémar, t 04 75 04 40 10, www.la.garde-adhemar.com*

ⓘ **St-Paul-Trois-Châteaux >>**
*Place Chausy, 26130 St-Paul-Trois-Châteaux, t 04 75 96 59 60, www.st-paul-3-chateaux-tourisme.com*

ⓘ **Montélimar >**
*Allées Provençales, 26200 Montélimar, t 04 75 01 00 20, www.montelimar-tourisme.com*

## Charmes-sur-Rhône ✉ 07800

***Autour d'une Fontaine**, Rue Paul Bertois, t 04 75 60 80 10, *www.autourdunefontaine.com* (€€). Delightful bright rooms in this stylish little hotel. Striking restaurant (€€€–€€) and relaxing terrace. *Restaurant closed Sun pm and Mon.*

## Le Pouzin ✉ 07250

***La Cardinale et sa Résidence**, Quai du Rhône, t 04 75 85 80 40 (€€€€€). A farm converted into a splendid smart, bright hotel, with pool in large grounds; 3km away at Baix, the main restaurant (€€€), set in a grand old house, has lovely views of the Rhône.

## Cliousclat ✉ 26270

***La Treille Muscate**, t 04 75 63 13 10, *www.latreillemuscate.com* (€€€–€€). Adorable, in the heart of the village, with fine pottery plates among the decorations. Pleasing Provençal-style cuisine (€€). *Closed Dec–Feb; restaurant closed Wed.*

## Mirmande ✉ 26270

***La Capitelle**, Rue du Rempart, t 04 75 63 02 72, *www.lacapitelle.com* (€€€–€€). Tasteful rooms in this fine village house, plus a vaulted restaurant (€€) serving good regional cuisine. *Closed Dec–Feb.*

**Hôtel de Mirmande**, t 04 75 63 13 18, *www.hoteldrome.com* (€€€–€€). Recently opened by the same people who run La Treille Muscate above, a renovated 18th-century village house offering elegant, spacious rooms.

**Goriou B&B**, t 04 75 63 01 15, *www.maisondemarinette.com* (€). Joyously artistic touches all around this lovely property at the foot of the village. Run with charm. *Closed Jan–mid-Feb.*

## Montélimar ✉ 26200

**Aux Gourmands**, 8 Place du Marché, t 04 75 01 16 21 (€€). A friendly restaurant that doubles as a delicatessen at which to try or buy regional produce, with an excellent *menu du terroir. Closed Sun and Mon.*

**Le Chalet du Parc**, Allées Provençales, t 04 75 51 16 42 (€€). Contemporary glass-sided dining room with terraces tacked on to an old villa in the public gardens. Refreshing for a Provençal meal, opposite the café-lined Allées Provençales. *Closed Mon eve and Tues.*

## Bourg-St-Andéol ✉ 07700

**Digoine B&B**, Quai de Madier de Montjau, t 04 75 54 61 07, *www.digoine.com* (€€). In a fine Ancien Régime mansion looking on to the Rhône, built for a silk merchant; extravagantly colourful-to-eccentric, spacious rooms on the theme of the Silk Route. *Table d'hôte* (€€).

## Malataverne ✉ 26780

***Le Domaine du Colombier**, Route de Donzère, t 04 75 90 86 86, *www.domaine-colombier.com* (€€€–€€). An oasis close to Montélimar and motorway exit 18, a converted medieval religious establishment with bright rooms and excellent restaurant taken over by a budding young team (€€€–€€). Pool. *Restaurant closed Sun.*

## Valaurie ✉ 26230

***Le Moulin de Valaurie**, Le Foulon, t 04 75 97 21 90, *www.lemoulinde valaurie.com* (€€€€–€€€). Set quietly away from the village, a beautifully restored mill with lovely rooms, good, bright restaurant (€€€), pool, and a lily pond to make Monet green with envy. *Closed Sun eve and Mon.*

## La Garde-Adhémar ✉ 26700

***Le Logis de l'Escalin**, Les Martines, t 04 75 04 41 32, *www.lescalin.com* (€€). Charming, outside the village. Enchanting terraced restaurant (€€€–€€) serving truly wonderful meals. Good rooms too. Pool. *Restaurant closed Sun eve and Mon.*

## St-Paul-Trois-Châteaux ✉ 26130

***Hôtel L'Esplan**, 15 Place de l'Esplan, t 04 75 96 64 64, *www.esplan-provence.com* (€€). Quite stylish behind its 16th-century front on a central square, even if the modern modifications look a bit chaotic. Air-conditioned rooms, enclosed patio, smart dining room (€€€–€€). *Closed mid-Dec–mid-Jan; restaurant closed Sat lunch, plus Sun eve out of season.*

# East of the Rhône:
## From the Isère into the Drôme

With the jagged Chartreuse and Vercors mountains forming the dramatic backdrop, the rolling hills and exceptionally fertile valleys of the lower Isère and Drôme can't fail to enchant you. In the cooler northern half, splendid walnut orchards, steep Dauphiné roofs and pebble walls predominate. From the Drôme valley, the look turns much more southern: you enter a pre-Provençal paradise, lavender, olives, vines and fruit orchards all thriving. The pleasing little towns hold memorable markets, while the hill villages look dreamy, often topped by a château. The one at Suze-la-Rousse is now even home to a wine university – perhaps a spur to higher studies?

# 13

## Don't miss

**1** Polished pebble surprises
Hauterives **p.216**

**2** A tasty cheese and nut tour
Lower Isère **p.212**

**3** A lavender trail among sparkling wines
Drôme valley vines and lavender route **p.221**

**4** Sublime olives and orchards
The Route du Goût south from Nyons **p.229**

**5** The archetypal Drôme craft village
Grignan **p.224**

*See map overleaf*

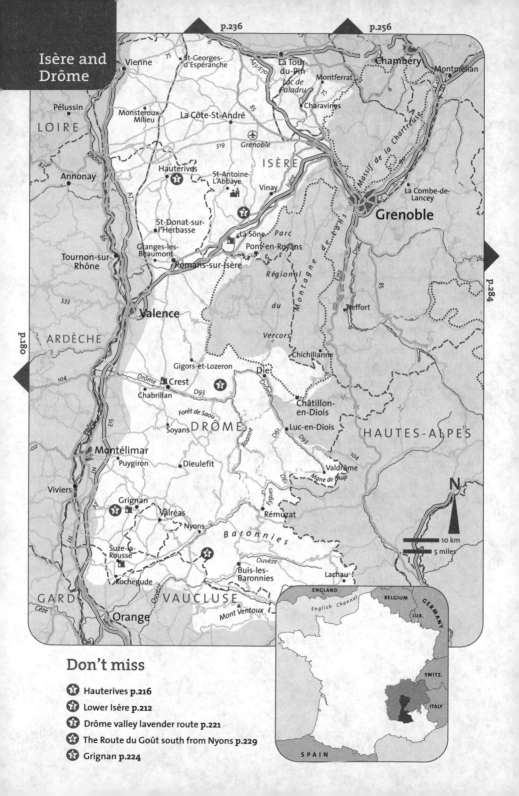

# Isère and Drôme

Vienne
St-Georges-d'Espéranche
La Tour-du-Pin
Chambéry
Montmélian
Pélussin
LOIRE
Montferrat
Lac de Paladru
Montseroux-Milieu
La Côte-St-André
Charavines
Annonay
Hauterives
Grenoble
ISÈRE
St-Antoine-L'Abbaye
Vinay
Massif de la Chartreuse
La Combe-de-Lancey
St-Donat-sur-l'Herbasse
La Sône
Pont-en-Royans
Grenoble
Granges-les-Beaumont
Tournon-sur-Rhône
Romans-sur-Isère
Parc
Régional
du
Montagne de Lans
Treffort
Valence
ARDÈCHE
Vercors
Chichilianne
Gigors-et-Lozeron
Die
Crest
Chabrillan
Châtillon-en-Diois
Forêt de Saou
DRÔME
Luc-en-Diois
HAUTES-ALPES
Soyans
Roanne
Montélimar
Puygiron
Dieulefit
Valdrôme
Mgne de Aup
Viviers
Grignan
Valréas
Rémuzat
Nyons
Baronnies
Suze-la-Rousse
Ouvèze
Lachau
Buis-les-Baronnies
GARD
Rochegude
VAUCLUSE
Orange
Mont Ventoux

N

10 km
5 miles

ENGLAND
BELGIUM
GERMANY
English Channel
LUX.
SWITZ.
ITALY
SPAIN

## Don't miss

1 Hauterives **p.216**
2 Lower Isère **p.212**
3 Drôme valley lavender route **p.221**
4 The Route du Goût south from Nyons **p.229**
5 Grignan **p.224**

With the sharp wolves' ears of pre-alpine ranges rising menacingly in the background, the lands we look on so fondly here roll playfully down to the Rhône. The Isère and the Drôme are the main rivers that trip west to join their master through the area we cover in this chapter, consisting of the western, less elevated halves of the two *départements* named after these rivers. Historically, these territories fell within the province of the Dauphiné, joined to the French crown in the 14th century. In contrast with the tortuous Ardèche on the other side of the Rhône, these are generous, open lands; instead of eking a living from meagre terraces and narrow valleys, the farmers here benefited from exceptionally fertile soil. These undulating hills are sprinkled with cheerful little towns and seductive villages built in light stone.

In the northern half, the round glacial stones of the valleys have long been put to decorative effect in the traditional architecture. A 19th-century postman got rather carried away by these polished pebbles, and created one of the most famous follies in France, the Palais Idéal du Facteur Cheval, Architecture Naïve at Hauterives. You can admire further pebble architecture in places such as La Côte-St-André, bourgeois birthplace of that most passionate figure of 19th-century high culture, Berlioz, or at the beautiful religious halt of St-Antoine-l'Abbaye, headquarters of medically minded medieval monks. Further east, around the pleasingly low-key Lac de Paladru, the traditional, steeply curving Dauphiné roofs with their fish-scale tiles serve as a reminder that the winters get harsher nearer the mountains. The dignified walnut orchards lining the Isère banks below the forbidding Vercors range also signal fresher climes, but refreshment is the order of the day at Pont-en-Royans, with a joyous museum dedicated to water.

South of the shoe-addicts' dream town of Romans-sur-Isère, sunnier orchards of peaches, nectarines and cherries prevail. Down in the very south, you come to the positively paradisiac Drôme Provençale, the southern slice of the Drôme *département*, where not just fruit orchards and vines proliferate, but also lavender and olive trees. As if that weren't bountiful enough, 'black diamonds' are unearthed under the oak trees – this is the largest truffle-yielding area in France. The centre of this closely guarded crop is the former Knights' Templar village of Richerenches, set in a curious, long-independent little enclave of papal territory.

Major castles occupy high points in the southern half of the Drôme, such as Crest, with the tallest keep in France; Grignan, intimately associated with that most refined of Ancien Régime correspondents, Madame de Sévigné; or Suze-la-Rousse, now home to the wicked-sounding Université du Vin. Many students have no doubt dreamt of following such serious studies – you might make the fantasy a reality, as the place can organize courses in English.

## Getting to and around Western Isère and Western Drôme

**By air:** Lyon airport lies just north of this area, Avignon and Nîmes airports not far south.

**By train:** There are great choices coming by train from London: take the Eurostar to Lille, then simply change platform there for rapid TGVs to Lyon or Valence TGV station; the latter lies between Valence and Romans-sur-Isère. Romans-sur-Isère and St-Marcellin have railway stations on the line from Valence to Grenoble. Crest and Die lie on the rail line from Valence to Gap. Montélimar has the nearest station for the Drôme Provençale and Baronnies.

**By bus:** For bus services in Western Isère, see *www.transisere.fr*. For full Drôme bus services, consult *www.ladrome.fr*.

We avoid the vicious pre-alpine heights of the Chartreuse and Vercors here (*see* Chapter 16), but we do venture into the friendlier, more southerly Diois and Baronnies *montagnettes*, where you encounter an extraordinary, quieter landscape, huge, bald cowboys-and-Indians mountaintops rising skywards. But below, the land remains fertile, producing divine apricots, among other things, while goats graze on the mid-slopes, and majestic birds of prey survey the gorgeous territories, circling high above.

# Western Isère and Northern Drôme

## From a Pebbly Land to Lac de Paladru

### Bourgoin-Jallieu to Berlioz

We start here at that ancient geographical dividing line between territories, the A43 motorway between Lyon and Chambéry! For those interested in contemporary architecture, **L'Isle d'Abeau** has plenty to show, a new town that has sprung up since the 1970s, a spacious modern satellite for the overspill from Lyon.

Neighbouring **Bourgoin-Jallieu**, by contrast, has long-established working class credentials, which in these parts means that much of the populace was involved in clothes-making. The town's pompous claim to have been French capital of *l'ennoblissement textile* since the 17th century really signifies that the speciality here was printing on cloth. The tradition has lost out to cheaper international labour and computers, but, even at the end of the last millennium, one or two specialist local companies were still working the old-fashioned way for leading fashion houses. In the bustling commercial centre, the **Musée de Bourgoin-Jallieu** traces in style the path of this now dying industry. In addition, the place serves as a smart local art museum, and the sumptuous scarves on sale come at knockdown prices.

**Musée de Bourgoin-Jallieu**
*t 04 74 28 19 74,
www.bourgoinjallieu.fr;
open Tues–Sun 10–12
and 2–6; adm*

**La Tour-du-Pin** may have been the centre of the last branch of independent medieval lords of the Dauphiné, but the place continued to thrive after they lost power, to judge by the Renaissance houses. In the church hangs a remarkably sensitive

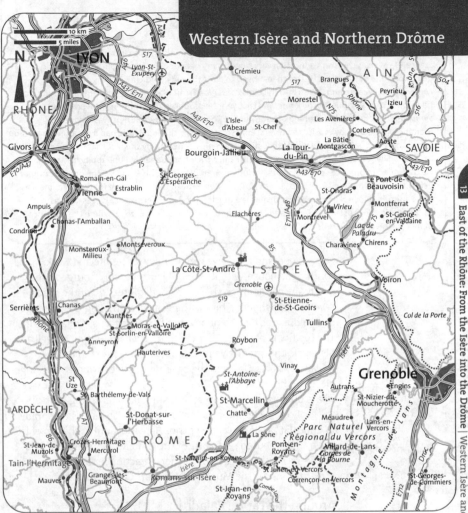

16th-century triptych by Georg Pencz, a pupil of Dürer; he donated it in thanks for the care he received when sick at the local hospital.

Head south for the stunningly flat former glacial **Plaine de la Bièvre**, the view onto the unbroken patchwork of fields like a natural masterpiece of abstract art. Mountains fill the backdrops east and west. Its Romanesque church signalled by a brick and pebble tower, its old covered market held up on an impressive six rows of wooden pillars, the slope-side town of **La Côte-St-André** above the plain has many appealing aspects. But the main attraction is the renovated **Musée Hector Berlioz**, honouring the composer of such ecstatic pieces as *Les Nuits d'été*. This excellent museum, situated in the substantial townhouse where the great composer was born, introduces Berlioz in the context of early 19th-century political upheaval and the Romantic movement it

**Musée Hector Berlioz**
*t 04 74 20 24 88, www.musee-hector-berlioz.fr; open June–Sept Wed–Mon 10–7; Oct–May Wed–Mon 10–6; closed Tues; adm*

## Berlioz, the Brilliant Romantic Composer

The composer's father was a forward-looking doctor, among the first to introduce acupuncture into France. He oversaw his son's education very closely: 'my master of languages, literature, history, geography and even music'. Hector then moved to Paris to study medicine, but his passion for composing overcame him. Taken into the Paris *conservatoire* in 1826, by 1830, the brilliant young man had won the prestigious *Prix de Rome*, and that year he produced one of his best-loved pieces, the *Symphonie fantastique*. Something of a tormented Romantic dreamer, Berlioz was inspired by literature as much as by music, and several English authors, including Byron, had a profound impact on him. But it was Shakespeare's words that stirred him most – helped by the fact that he met and married a Shakespearean actress, Harriet Smithson, with whom he settled unhappily in Montmartre. He continued to produce splendid works, including *Harold en Italie*, his *Requiem*, the opera *Benvenuto Cellini* and the symphony *Roméo et Juliette*, but his style proved too innovative for French audiences, and Berlioz had to make a career principally as a music critic. However, further pieces such as *La Damnation de Faust*, his *Te Deum* and *Les Troyens* were fêted across Europe, where the brilliance of his musical achievements was recognized.

encouraged, and then gives an overview of his life and work. Touring the house, with its strongly 19th-century bourgeois feel and many mementoes, you get a good impression of the man, several busts showing him with his hair resembling the plumage of a wild, exotic bird, somehow befitting such a passionate figure. The top floor concentrates on Berlioz's brilliant writing as well as his music, the interactive posts allowing you to listen to short musical extracts. Down in the basement, you can appreciate longer pieces in the small auditorium.

**Paradis du Chocolat**
*t 04 74 20 35 89, www.paradis-chocolat.com; open Sat, Sun and public and school hols 2–6; adm*

Passionate chocolate-lovers may sniff out a tempting shop on the lively main shopping street. The owner also directs the**Paradis du Chocolat** , a slightly earnest chocolate museum at the top of the town, in the abused remnants of the château, now resembling a factory as much as a castle. Another attraction in town for the sweet-toothed is the **Musée des Liqueurs Cherry Rocher**.

## Around the Lac de Paladru

The three parallel diagonal valleys of the Bourbre, Bièvre and Ainan form a splendidly undulating area known as the **Pays des Trois Vallées** east of the A48 motorway, and south of the A43. This patch on the borders of the Dauphiné and Savoie was long ruled over by the lords of Clermont.

**Château de Virieu**
*t 04 74 88 27 32, www.chateau-de-virieu.com; open July–Aug Tues–Sun 2–6; Easter–June and Sept–Oct Sat, Sun and public hols 2–6; adm*

The intimidating**Château de Virieu** stands arrogantly high above the little town of **Virieu** with its lovely old covered market. The castle's roofs are covered with distinctive Dauphiné tiles resembling brown fish-scales. Although a medieval stronghold of the Clermonts, it was for a leading Grenoblois that the towers went up. The formidable place has never been disturbed by wars. The entrance looks so forbidding that you can understand why – you enter the courtyard via a door covered with over 1,000 sharp nails, to be greeted by five cannons, a gift from Louis XIII when he visited in 1622. The military theme continues through the handful of chambers you're shown inside.

Close by, the **Lac de Paladru** may be a poor relation of the more glamorous great lakes of Savoie not far to the east (*see* Chapter 15), but as the fifth-largest natural lake in France, formed with the melting of the last Ice Age, it makes a relaxing introduction to the Rhône-Alpes' lakelands. Good-value little family resorts lie around its emerald-to-blue waters, with thin pebbly beaches and clusters of boats. One of the advantages of Paladru is that motorboats are not allowed, just quieter activities like pedalos, rowing and sailing. The waters are rich in fish, so angling is much practised.

**Musée du Lac de Paladru**
*t 04 76 55 77 47, www.
museelacdepaladru.
com; open July–Aug
Tues–Sun 3–7; June and
Sept Tues–Sun 2–6;
May Sat, Sun and public
hols 2–6; adm*

Paladru turns out to have preserved an exceptional pre-tourist prehistory, explained at the **Musée du Lac de Paladru** at **Charavines**. In the lake's shallow waters, remains have been discovered, not just of medieval settlements from around the year 1000, but also of Neolithic ones dating back 5,000 years. The lake's chalky bottom (giving Paladru a particularly light colour in parts) has preserved the vestiges very well, providing archaeologists with plenty of material; check on the possibilities of visiting the site itself at the tourist office. Modern Charavines has a gentle family holiday feel, with the most appealing of lthe lakes' beaches; a horse and trap can transport you gently up into the hills.

**Grange Dimière de la Silve Bénite**
*t 04 76 06 60 31;
generally open
April–Sept Sat, Sun and
public hols 3–7; adm*

Pressing into these hills, the older villages boast houses topped with superb wide-brimmed Dauphiné roofs. A bit west of Paladru, the **Grange Dimière de la Silve Bénite**, the tithe barn of the abbey of the Chartreuse de la Silve-Bénite, recalls the importance of this religious establishment. The roofs are of staggering proportions, while the spacious interior offers a striking space for seasonal art exhibitions.

**Prieuré de Chirens**
*t 04 76 35 20 02, www.
prieuredechirens.fr;
open mid-June–Aug
Wed–Mon 10–12 and
3–7; Easter–mid-June
and Sept–Oct check
times; adm*

East of Charavines, the **Grange Louisias** sports a huge thatched hat over its earthen walls. The pretty **Vergers de Louisas** farm beside it produces excellent fruit jams and cordials. The rounded forms of the medieval **priory of Chirens** show its Romanesque roots; inside, you can watch a video about the Cistercian monks based up in the high Alps at Tamié (*see* p.270), although Chirens was in fact built by a Benedictine community. Naïve Baroque wall paintings were added later. In modern times, as the place had been abandoned, an artist turned the church into his home for a time, and parts of his conversion, as well as his geometric works, are still visible. There are also interesting displays of pottery. Chirens is best known now for hosting a fine range of chamber music concerts.

**Château de Longpra**
*t 04 76 07 63 48,
www.longpra.com;
open May–Oct daily
2–6; adm*

A hop and a skip further east, beside **St-Geoire-en-Valdaine**, the **Château de Longpra** stands behind its moat, presenting a refined image of Dauphinois good living, kitted out with superb wood-work by the reputed Hache family in the 18th century.

# The Culinary Isère Valley

**Lower Isère**

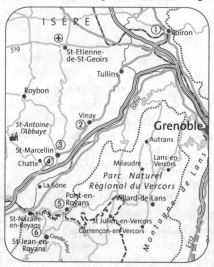

ISÈRE
519
St-Etienne-de-St-Geoirs
Tullins
Roybon
Voiron ①
Isère
Vinay
St-Antoine-l'Abbaye ②
Grenoble
Autrans
St-Marcellin ③
Chatte ④
Méaudre
Lans-en-Vercors
Parc Naturel
Régional du Vercors
Montagne de Lans
La Sône
Pont-en-Royans ⑤
Villard-de-Lans
St-Nazaire-en-Royans
St-Julien-en-Vercors
Corrençon-en-Vercors
St-Jean-en-Royans ⑥
Combe Laval
E712

The Isère river emerges from its staggering mountain journey (*see* Chapter 18) via a narrow gap between the Chartreuse and Vercors ranges north of Grenoble. Then, below the town of Voiron, three busy roads accompany it on its last leg to join the Rhône, running below the sheer, spectacular wall of the Vercors range. The beautiful hilly area immediately around this stretch of the river is known as the **Pays du Sud Grésivaudan**. Don't let the tricky name put you off; get off those main road to explore these remarkably bucolic and fertile parts, an astonishing valley of exceptional culinary delights.

## Voiron and its Potions

With such daunting pre-alpine slopes for a backdrop, **Voiron** responded to the natural drama in the 19th century by commissioning a grand church from that wildly enthusiastic Gothic revivalist Viollet-le-Duc. He answered the peaks with the soaring twin spires and colourful roofs of the **Eglise St-Bruno**. The town's older, less showy church of **St Peter** is of interest too. The ruins of the medieval **Barral tower** recall how strategic Voiron served as a forward post of Savoie until the mid-14th century.

The Chartreuse range immediately behind town is indissociably linked with the monks of its famous charterhouse (*see* p.290), the Carthusians. Founded up in those heights, the Order encouraged rigorous contemplation. But it valued hard work, pine-logging and mining counting among its activities. It also inherited a recipe in the 17th century for a medicinal brew made from scores of plants, which it has gone on to commercialize on a massive scale. The violently coloured green and yellow **Chartreuse liqueurs** used to be made up in the mountains, but after a destructive landslide a factory was installed down in Voiron. The Carthusians do however still retain overall control of this multinational business.

On the interesting tour of the immense underground **Caves de la Grande Chartreuse** ① you'll learn about the Order, as well as the

**Caves de la Grande Chartreuse**
*t 04 76 05 81 77,
www.chartreuse.fr;
open April–Oct daily
9–6.30; Nov–Mar daily
9–11.30 and 2–5.30*

process of making the liqueurs, but the herbal recipe remains a firmly guarded secret. It would take a miracle for you to work out its very complex blend of ingredients. In the vast cellars, huge ageing barrels ooze sticky liquid, filling the air with a heady scent. In the extensive shop, sample the range of concoctions the company now makes. On the subject of naughty treats, chocolate-lovers should pay a visit to the **Bonnat** shop ①, run by one of the best *maître-chocolatiers* in France.

Vibrant liqueurs aren't Voiron's only special beverage. At

**Les Secrets d'Antésite**
*t 04 76 05 85 65,*
*www.antesite.com;*
*open shop hours daily*
*exc Sun am and Mon*

**Les Secrets d'Antésite**, at **Coblevie** along the N75 main road, you can learn about the making of *Antésite*. In contrast to the heady Chartreuse liqueurs, this interesting non-alcoholic drink flavoured with licorice and aniseed was heavily promoted to the French First World War troops as a substitute for *pastis* and the like, to wean them off the comforts of alcohol. *Antésite* has been making a comeback as a healthy thirst-quencher.

## South from Voiron

For an uplifting start to the journey south along the Isère from Voiron, start with a little pilgrimage up to the priory of **Notre-Dame-de-Parménie**, in a superb spot above **Tullins**. Then wend your way through the hills to the small town of **Vinay**, capital of walnuts, although its name recalls earlier times when vines were king here. Outside town, the new **Grand Séchoir** ② presents the

**Le Grand Séchoir**
*t 04 76 36 36 10,*
*www.legrandsechoir.fr;*
*open April–Oct*
*Tues–Sun 10–6; Nov–*
*Dec Tues–Sun 2–6;*
*Jan–Mar Sat, Sun and*
*public hols 2–6; adm*

history of walnuts in these parts. Although the stories of the community and crop are interesting, the presentation, if attractive and contemporary, proves a bit dry. You learn how modern techniques have triumphed in walnut production, but the *mondée* is one old tradition maintained to some degree: the locals gathering for evenings of chat and song while cracking open walnuts. The centre displays a few nice pieces of furniture in walnut wood, and sells walnut products.

---

### Culinary Delights of the Lower Isère

Splendid orchards of walnut trees line large stretches of the lower Isère valley. In summer, the glossy green leaves shimmer in the sunshine. In winter, the black forks of the trees mark the countryside. The walnut harvest takes place from October into November. To protect these superb orchards and their delicious produce, they were early given *appellation d'origine contrôlée* status, the designated area stretching from Montmélian to Romans-sur-Isère. Historically though, it's surprising to learn that the predominance of walnuts along this portion of the Isère only dates from the late 19th century. Before that, vines proliferated, along with mulberry trees for rearing silk worms. Bugs decimated those plantations, so farmers turned to *noix*, for eating or for oil.

Walnuts aren't the only local culinary speciality. On the hillsides, white cattle graze in lush pastures beside wide-brimmed farms, their milk making melting St-Marcellin cheese, one of the Rhône-Alpes' best *fromages*, gooey and intense in flavour. As to *ravioles de Royans*, these tiny ravioli, named after an area within the Sud Grésivaudan, are the most delicate you can imagine, stuffed with goat's cheese and herbs, almost translucent when cooked, a divine fast food on menus across the Dauphiné.

The little town of **St-Marcellin** ③ has given its name to the delicious cheese produced in the hills round and about. Just west at **Chatte**, Clermont castle may not be open to the public, but in August you can see walnut oil being made at the **Moulin à Huile de Léon** ④. Also at Chatte is the popular **Jardin Ferroviaire** or Railway Garden, a remarkable miniature world created by Christian Abric, one of the best outdoor networks of model trains in Europe.

For gorgeous St-Antoine-l'Abbaye a little west, see p.215. Sticking to the Isère valley, the village of **La Sône** lies quietly on the river's north bank. It wasn't so peaceful in times past. For centuries, this spot had one of the few bridges over the Isère, hence the castle guarding the spot. The power of the waters was later used to power factories. These have closed, but this place now offers several tourist attractions. The **Château de la Sône**, perched on a dramatic ledge above the village, and immediately above the Isère's waters, has been watching over this strategic point since the Middle Ages. Its fine silhouette dominated by its main tower, it makes a lovely picture. Left to fall into disrepair in the 20th century, it has been restored by the Pons family since the 1970s; for example they have redone the roofs with colourful patterned tiles. On the gentle guided tour you'll learn about the place's history, the odd royal visit, and the occasional literary connection, with Stendhal, the greatest author from the Dauphiné (see p.293), and with Françoise Sagan, who became friends with the previous family here when her father ran a local factory. You can also wander round the shaded grounds.

A more touristy garden, the **Jardin des Fontaines Pétrifiantes**, lies immediately below, set between river and cliff. Nature has provided the dramatic centrepiece: a waterfall that doesn't cease even in the driest summers. The well-protected garden proves remarkably exotic, delicate and colourful flowers flourishing here. In a grotto below the cascade, the heavily limestone-rich waters are exploited to cover objects with a glittery coating. Outside, they power ingenious musical instruments made from wood.

Close to this garden you'll find the jetty to board the paddle boat *Royans-Vercors*, which takes you on an enjoyable river journey down to St-Nazaire-en-Royans, with a commentary filling you in on the history of the Isère, which flows some 300km from its source in the Alps above Val d'Isère to the Rhône. Navigation went on for some 2,000 years, boats starting from as high up as Albertville, but the travelling season only lasted around 150 days a year. Railways and roads put paid to most of the river traffic. Then dams were built in the 20th century; six now block the river's course between Grenoble and the Rhône. That means the Isère's steely grey or chalky blue waters are calm now. However, because it was so long prone to flooding, there are virtually no constructions along its

---

**Moulin à Huile de Léon**
*t 04 76 64 59 65; open Aug daily 4–7; adm*

**Jardin Ferroviaire**
*t 04 76 38 54 55, www. jardin-ferroviaire.com; open July–Aug daily 10–8; April–June daily 10–7; Sept Mon–Fri 2–4; Mar and Oct Sat,Sun, public hols and school hols 10–7; Feb, Nov and Dec Sat, Sun, public and school hols 2–4; adm*

**Château de la Sône**
*t 04 76 64 41 70, www. chateaudelasone.com; open late June– mid-Sept Wed–Mon 10–12 and 3–6.30; April–June and Oct 2nd weekend of month; adm*

**Jardin des Fontaines Pétrifiantes**
*t 04 76 64 43 42, www.jardin-des-fontaines.com; open May–mid-Oct; adm*

**Royans-Vercors boat**
*t 04 76 64 43 42, www. bateau-a-roue.com; June–mid-Sept daily one tour am, two tours pm; April–May and mid-Sept–Oct Sun and public hols one tour am, one pm; adm*

banks until you reach St-Nazaire, and birds reign among the reedy banks. However, plastic bottles and detritus often feature large.

On the south side of the Isère around here, the pocket of country known as the Royans sits tucked under the sensational vertical sides of the Vercors range. Set right below a huge wooded wall of rock, at **Pont-en-Royans**, the old riverside houses look as if they're about to jump into the clear waters of the Bourne rushing down from the heights. Lots of youngsters do splash about in the river in the summertime. Up to one side, jets of water freshen the air at the playful **Musée de l'Eau**, a brilliantly designed museum that offers a great introduction to waterpower and ecology, especially in the Vercors. At the end, taste the amazing selection of $H_2O$ vintages from around the world at the **water bar** ⑤.

The traditional little wood-working town of **St-Jean-en-Royans** specialized in tableware, hence the term *tabletterie* around the place. The Ancien Régime church with its stocky stone tower contains beautiful carved stalls rescued from the former monastic Chartreuse du Val Ste-Marie. For walnut oil and walnut products, try **Cave Noisel** ⑥, in a restored mill. At **Les Cuillères du Royans** on the Route de Lente you can see wooden spoons being made.

**St-Nazaire-en-Royans** lies close to the confluence of the Bourne and the Isère, the Vercors still providing the spectacular backdrop. The **aqueduct** adds greatly to the immediate drama. The structure dates from 1876, built to bring water down from the Vercors to irrigate the crops on the often parched Valence plain. Get up onto it by taking the lift. Just below, the **Grotte de Thaïs** boasts colourful walls, plus surprising concretions and nooks. This cave is well known for its prehistoric finds. Among the tools and weapons, a bone with notches counts among the earliest pieces of evidence of a human numerical system. For details on the boat *Royans-Vercors*, see p.214. For Romans-sur-Isère, go to p.217.

No amount of water could soothe the burning pains and dreadful convulsions suffered by the patients in the religious foundation of **St-Antoine-l'Abbaye** west of St-Marcellin. In medieval times, ergotism, a terrible wheat borne fungal disease, ravaged communities, although the cause long remained a mystery. However, a religious order called the Antonins developed here in the 13th century to look after those afflicted by the agonizing illness, which became known as 'St Anthony's Fire'. The place contained supposed relics of St Anthony, one of the greatest figures of the early Christian centuries, who experienced torment of a different nature during his days as a hermit in the desert, but who was adopted as patron saint of this Order.

Work began on a great Gothic **church** in the 13th century, but it wasn't completed until the 15th. This was the most successful period in the abbey's history; from the 16th it fell into decline.

**Musée de l'Eau**
*t 04 76 36 15 53, www. musee-eau.com; open July Aug daily 10–6.30; Sept–June Tues–Sun outside school hols 10–12 and 2–5.30; adm*

**Cave Noisel**
*t 04 75 47 56 54, www. ferme-du-vercors.com; open April–Sept daily 10–12 and 3–7; Oct–Mar Mon–Sat 10–12 and 3–7, Sun 10–12*

**Les Cuillères du Royans**
*t 04 75 48 64 56; open early April–mid-Dec Mon–Sat 9–12 and 2–6, Sun 3–6*

**St-Nazaire aqueduct**
*t 04 75 48 49 80; open July–Aug daily 10–12 and 1–7; June and Sept Tues–Sun 2–6; April–May and Oct Sun and public hols 10–12 and 2–6; adm*

**Grotte de Thaïs**
*t 04 75 48 45 76, www. grotte-de-thais.com; open July–Aug daily 10.30–7; May–June and Sept–Oct Mon–Fri 2–6, Sun and public hols 10.30–7; April Sun and public hols 10.30–6; adm*

13

East of the Rhône: From the Isère into the Drôme | Western Isère and Northern Drôme

Much of its glorious architecture has survived, however, and is being restored. The church contains many riches, including wall paintings. In the choir, the finest Aubusson tapestries depict scenes in the life of Joseph. The **Musée Le Noviciat** in adjoining buildings houses a permanent collection on the Antonins and presents contemporary art exhibitions.

**Musée Le Noviciat**
*t 04 76 36 40 68; open July–Aug daily 11–12.30 and 1.30–6; Sept–June Wed–Mon 2–6; adm*

**Roybon,** in the midst of the high, wooded Chambaran plateau, boasts the distinction of one of three miniature copies made of Bartholdi's *Statue of Liberty*, plus a church decorated with pebbles in typical local herringbone patterns. Nearby, there's a big lake for swimming, while the **Parc Naturel du Chambaran** reserves 300 hectares for wild animals, notably deer, to wander round.

# The Pebbly Northern Drôme to Romans

⭐ **Hauterives**

At **Hauterives,** a local postman, Ferdinand Cheval, fell, almost literally, in love with the pebbles of the area. Having tripped over one in 1879, he picked it up, took it home, and embarked on a crazy building programme that lasted 34 years, creating the **Palais Idéal du Facteur Cheval**, *architecture naïve*. All this in the back garden of a quiet Drômois village house where you'd really just expect to find a well-tended vegetable plot.

**Palais Idéal du Facteur Cheval**
*t 04 75 68 81 19, www. facteurcheval.com; open July–Aug daily 9–12.30 and 1.30–7.30; April–June and Sept daily 9.30–12.30 and 1.30–6.30; Feb–Mar and Oct–Nov daily 9.30– 12.30 and 1.30–5.30; Dec–mid-Jan daily 9.30–12.30 and 1.30–4.30; closed mid–late Jan; adm*

After the grottoes came a tomb for the family, in Egyptian-Christian form. A Hindu-style temple followed, guarded by giants. And so on, the various constructions all cemented together, topped by concrete vegetation. '*Monument original*', reads one of the most understated quotes among many more vacuous, arrogant ones written across the architecture by its maker. Actually, Cheval's vision isn't wholly original. A thwarted traveller, unable to afford trips to the exotic locations he might read about in the magazines of the time, he plundered visual ideas and vague notions of foreign cultures to create his own fantasy world in his back yard. Models of great buildings from around the globe were stuck on here and there. The whole clutter of the so-called Palais Idéal is at one and the same time admirable, entertaining, laughable and lamentable. The building's title is definitely to be taken with a strong pinch of salt, but the enterprise is fascinating.

**L'Art en Marche**
*t 04 75 68 95 40, www. art-en-marche.com; open Mon–Sat 10–12 and 1.30–5.30, Sun 1.30–5.30; adm*

From *architecture naïve* to *art brut* – more disturbing, disturbed, grotesque, hilarious anti-establishment works hang out in **L'Art en Marche**. While you feel the naïveté in Postman Cheval's work, though, many of the artists here are clearly more knowing.

**Les Labyrinthes Végétaux**
*t 04 75 68 86 82; open May–Aug daily 11–7; Sept Sat and Sun only 11–7; adm*

Ferdinand's fans walk out to the village **cemetery** to view the moving family mausoleum he created in similar style to his main work. One further eccentric village attraction, **Les Labyrinthes Végétaux**, entangles you in four hectares of shrubs and lavender, although the main lavender territories of the Drôme lie south.

**Palais Délphinal**
*t 04 75 45 15 32;*
*guided tours July–Aug*
*2.30–6; adm*

Part of the priory buildings sitting pretty at the top of the village of **St-Donat-sur-l'Herbasse** have been given the grandiose title of **Palais Délphinal** (Palace of the Dauphiné). Reaching the medieval religious buildings via steep streets, you'll see how the place was savaged in the Wars of Religion. Just a Gothic end stands behind the 20th-century church. One side of the cloister survived too, decorated with entertaining carvings. The 'palace' hosts exhibitions, the church concerts thanks to its exceptional organ.

Shoe-addicts hotfoot it south for riverside **Romans-sur-Isère**, a bustling town where several of France's top shoe designers are based, including Robert Clergerie, Stéphane Kélian and Charles Jourdan. The place has a long tradition of tanning, which explains why it became a major centre of shoe manufacturing from the mid-19th century. The utterly startling **Musée International de la Chaussure** offers a voyage into the sole of civilization... It has very successfully set up shop in an immense Italianate convent to present, via its visual and explanatory history of footwear, truly surprising insights into the customs of past centuries and cultures. Famous shoes are treated like relics, safe behind glass. The big chapel serves for extraordinary exhibitions of footwear.

**Musée International de la Chaussure**
*t 04 75 05 51 81, www.ville-romans.com; open July–Aug Mon–Sat 10–6, Sun 2.30–6; Sept–June Tues–Sat 10–5, Sun 2.30–6; adm*

On the trail of the modern shoe, Romans has attracted all manner of brands. Look along the **Côte des Cordeliers**. Another interesting street of more varied shops, **Côte Jacquemart** slopes down from the medieval **Tour Jacquemart**, which, despite its butch looks, has a high-pitched voice when its bells ring out.

At the riverside church of **St-Barnard**, battered Romanesque sculptures greet you at the spot where Bishop Barnard of Vienne created an abbey in the 9th century. The structure was enlarged in Gothic times. Some murals have survived from the redecoration. The rare 16th-century embroideries of the *Mystery of the Passion* are kept under lock and key in the **Chapelle du Saint-Sacrement**

**Chapelle du Saint-Sacrement**
*open for guided tours only, mid-June–mid-Sept Mon–Fri 11.30–12.30 and 2–5.30, Sun 2–5.30; adm*

While on the 16th century, a truly remarkable, painstaking and revealing piece of historical research on Romans in that period was carried out by the brilliant contemporary French micro-historian Emmanuel Le Roy Ladurie. His *Le Carnaval de Romans*, exposing the intricate fractures in the community that led to a terrible outbreak of violence, proves an even more fascinating book for the general reader than his much more widely known *Montaillou* (about the Cathars), although harder to find in English.

Back with contemporary consumer culture, up beyond **Place Jean Jaurès**, Romans' main, vast rectangular square stretching out from the Tour Jacquemart, **Marques Avenue** lies along Avenue Gambetta. Setting up hard on the heels of the shoe shops, this brand outlet village has stylishly transformed a policemen's training college into a retail heaven.

13 East of the Rhône: From the Isère into the Drôme | Western Isère and Northern Drôme

## ⓘ Voiron

*58 Cours Becquart-Castelbon, 38500 Voiron, t 04 76 05 00 38, www. paysvoironnais.info*

## ⓘ Pont-en-Royans

*38680 Pont-en-Royans, t 04 76 36 09 10, www. ot-pont-en-royans.com*

## ⓘ St-Jean-en-Royans

*13 Place de l'Eglise, 26190 St-Jean-en-Royans, t 04 75 48 61 39, www.royans.com*

## ⓘ St-Antoine-l'Abbaye >>

*Place Gilibert, 38160 St-Antoine-l'Abbaye, t 04 76 36 44 46*

## ★ Le Mas du Vernay >>

## ⓘ Hauterives >>

*Rue du Palais Idéal, 26390 Hauterives, t 04 75 68 86 82, ot.hauterives@ wanadoo.fr*

## ⓘ La Côte-St-André >

*Place Berlioz, 38260 La Côte-St-André, t 04 74 20 61 43, www.cc-bievre-liers.fr*

## ⓘ Charavines/ Lac de Paladru >

*Rue des Bains, 38850 Charavines, t 04 76 06 60 31, www. paysvoironnais.info*

## ⓘ Romans-sur-Isère >>

*Place Jean Jaurès, 26100 Romans-sur-Isère, t 04 75 02 28 72, romanstourisme@ wanadoo.fr*

# Market Days in Western Isère and Northern Drôme

**La Côte-St-André**: Thurs am.

**Charavines**: Sun am.

**St-Jean-en-Royans**: Sat pm.

**Hauterives**: Tues am.

**Romans-sur-Isère**: Tues, Wed, Fri, Sat and Sun.

# Where to Stay and Eat in Western Isère and Northern Drôme

## Césarges ✉ 38300

**Château de Césarges B&B, t** 04 74 93 20 42, *www.chateau-cesarges.com* (€). Bargain characterful rooms in this big block of a building below Bourgoin. *Closed Dec–Mar.*

## St-Georges-d'Espéranche ✉ 38790

**Castel d'Espéranche, t** 04 74 59 18 45, *www.castel-esperance.com.* Atmospheric village restaurant (€€€–€€) set in a 13th-century guards' tower, plus *gîtes* in little modern cottages around the garden with its modern pool. *Closed Mon–Wed, plus Mar and Nov.*

## La Côte-St-André ✉ 38260

**\*\*Hôtel de France**, Place St-André, **t** 04 74 20 25 99 (€). Welcoming rooms in an old building by the church, with a superb traditional country restaurant (€€€€–€€€). *Restaurant closed Sun eve and Mon.*

## Charavines ✉ 38850

**\*\*Beau Rivage**, 115 Rue Principale, **t** 04 76 06 61 08, *www.hotel-restaurant-beaurivage.com* (€). Big hotel and restaurant (€€) making the most of its lakeside setting. *Closed Christmas–Jan; restaurant closed Sun eve, plus Mon, and Tues eve out of season.*

**Hôtel des Bains**, 365 Rue Principale, **t** 04 76 06 60 20 (€€–€). Actually no longer a hotel, just a delightful restaurant, for fish fry-ups or tasty regional cuisine, on fine days served outside under a great parasol of plane trees.

## Montferrat ✉ 38620

**Auberge Féfête**, Le Vernay, **t** 04 76 32 40 46 (€€). Refined cuisine at this intimate family restaurant on the north end of Paladru lake. *Closed Mon eve and Tues, and short school hols.*

## St-Ondras ✉ 38490

**Le Pas de l'Ane B&B, t** 04 76 32 01 78, *www.lepasdelane.com* (€). Spacious Dauphiné property up from Virieu. *Table d'hôte* (€€).

## St-Antoine-l'Abbaye ✉ 38160

**Auberge de l'Abbaye, t** 04 76 36 42 83 (€€€–€€). Lovely food in wonderful location on the gorgeous square to the side of the abbey. *Closed Jan, plus Mon eve and Tues out of season.*

**L'Antonin B&B, t** 04 76 36 41 53 (€). Sweet old village house in which to stay for a bargain. *Table d'hôte* (€).

## St-Bonnet-de-Chavagne ✉ 38840

**Le Mas du Vernay B&B**, Les Terras, **t** 04 76 38 07 87, *www.masduvernay. com* (€). Lost in rolling countryside south of St-Antoine-l'Abbaye, west of La Sône, a very calm, good-value country retreat. Stylish contemporary rooms in a specially converted farm building. Pool. *Table d'hôte* (€€).

## Hauterives ✉ 26390

**\*\*Le Relais, t** 04 75 68 81 12 (€). In typical pebble architecture, with reasonable rooms and decent cuisine (€€). *Closed mid-Jan–Feb; restaurant closed Sun eve in winter, and Mon.*

**Les Beaumes de Tersanne B&B**, Le Malfas, **t** 04 75 68 90 56, *www. lesbaumes.com* (€). Nice, neatly restored traditional pebble-built farm outside the village, with *gîtes* as well as B&B rooms. *Table d'hôte* (€€).

## Romans-sur-Isère ✉ 26100

**\*\*\*L'Orée du Parc**, 6 Avenue Gambetta, **t** 04 75 70 26 12, *www .hotel-oreeparc.com* (€€). Smart villa with pool, all in the town centre not far from Marques Avenue.

**La Charrette**, 15 Place de l'Horloge, **t** 04 75 02 04 25 (€). Lovely terrace at the foot of the Tour Jacquemart, offering local ravioli or dish of the day. *Closed Sun.*

Les Cèdres >

### Granges-lès-Beaumont
✉ **26600**

**Les Cèdres, t** 04 75 71 50 67 (€€€€).
Immaculate, refined décor reflecting
the splendid cuisine at this very
special village restaurant west of

Romans run by the Bertrand family.
Chef Jacques Bertrand concentrates
on the finest seasonal produce from
the Drôme, cooked to perfection.
*Closed Mon and Tues, plus early Jan
and late Aug.*

## Southern Drôme

### Up the Drôme River into the Diois

Travelling east up the Drôme valley from its confluence with the
Rhône, you gradually leave behind the industrial activity and, once
past the imposing tower guarding Crest, enter increasingly
dramatic countryside, embellished by patches of lavender and
vines producing Clairette de Die, named after the tiny, rustic
cathedral city cowering beneath the vast walls of the Vercors.

**Chabrillan** makes a first potential stop, with its ruined castle and
the remains of its ramparts still partially protecting it. It's one of
many Drômois villages to have started displays around a specific
botanical theme, here peonies.

**Tour de Crest**

*t 04 75 25 32 53, www.
mairie-crest.fr/tour;
open May–mid-Sept
daily 10–7; Feb–April
and mid-Sept–Oct daily
2–6; Nov–Jan Sat and
Sun 2–6; adm; sign on
for abseiling July–Aug
Sat pm*

Adventurous tourists abseil down the **Tour de Crest**, the massive
medieval *donjon* rising far above the town of **Crest**. You need a
strong head for heights, as it claims to be the tallest keep in France,
with over 50m of sheer walls. The building stands firmly astride
the narrow ridge of rock after which the town is named. A truly
awesome piece of military architecture, it consists of three towers
incorporated one into the other, all backed by the highest wall of
all, the *mur bouclier*.

The bishops of Die originally owned this castle; the local nobility,
the Comtes de Valentinois, made do with a *château inférieur*, that
is, one further down the slope. From the 13th century, the two were
in conflict. The counts took full control in the 14th century, joining
the two castles with further walls, and became powerful enough
to mint coins in the tower. But their line died out in 1419. The
French crown, the new owner, passed the place on to various
absentee nobles. Crest became a Catholic stronghold during the
Wars of Religion, the castle resisting a major Protestant attack in
1577 and serving as a prison. Although Louis XIII ordered the
destruction of all the fortifications, local protests saved the tower.
It then went on to receive persecuted Protestant inmates, who
started the unusual art collection, of protest graffiti. The place saw
its last prisoners, who added scrawled political slogans, after an
1850s uprising against the future Emperor Napoleon III.

Climbing inside the impressive interior, take in not just the
graffiti, but also the ingenious medieval provisions incorporated

against sieges. Also admire the amazing ideal city carved in wood on a door rescued from Crest's church. The medieval nobles lived on the third floor, with fireplaces and latrines. From the top of the tower, you get fabulous views along the Drôme valley.

You also enjoy a view down on the theatre of Roman tiles formed by the roofs of the **old town**. The main shopping street, with Provençal pottery and gifts on offer, passes below the white pillars of the temple-like 19th-century **church** set on the narrow market square. Either side of the church, explore the *calades*, the dilapidated cobbled lanes, in search of pretty covered wash-houses.

East around **Aouste**, the vineyards producing sparkling Clairette de Die (*see* below) begin. Continuing east, the Drôme valley becomes increasingly rural and beautiful, overseen by the well-named **Trois Becs**, a trio of peaks resembling young birds greedily poking their beaks up to be fed. Down below, you arrive in lavender-growing territory. The **Route de la Lavande association** spanning the Rhône-Alpes region and Provence, has created itineraries for drivers, cyclists and walkers. While the lavender fields this far north aren't as extensive as in the Drôme Provençale, they can flower into August, offering a later season than further south.

One lavender trail takes you towards the Vercors via **Beaufort-sur-Gervanne**, a lovely old fortified village, a few towers still standing. At **Gigors-et-Lozeron**, a village with splendid views down on the Gervanne valley from its perch, try the excellent herbal products shop at the **Domaine des Arômes Sanoflore** with its herbal garden.

Or take a delicious detour south from Crest for **Saou**, an enchanting village at the entrance to the magical, secretive **Forêt de Saou**, sloping up to catch the Trois Becs unawares from behind. At **Soyans**, climb to the eccentric **Musée International de l'Œuf** at the top of the village, and enjoy the medieval surroundings as well as the owner's extensive, eccentric egg collections. Rough remnants of fortifications stick out above laid-back **Bourdeaux**. Follow the D156 road round the Trois Becs via the **Col de la Chaudière** for amazing distant views to the highest Alpine peaks.

Back down by the Drôme river, the wrinkly old village of **Saillans** has preserved its character, with its hunched, narrow streets and arches, its fountains and old houses. The church clings on to its Romanesque details. Saillans' vines produce Clairette, but the place also once lived off silk-making, recalled at **La Magnanerie** At the end of the tour you see how silk is unwoven from its cocoon.

Branching off the D93, head up the Roanne valley for attractive **St-Benoît-en-Diois**. Explore refreshing bathing spots in the waters of the Roanne, and further villages perched up the winding roads to the south, like **Rimon-et-Savel**, **Pennes-le-Sec** or **Aucelon**.

**⓭ Route de la Lavande association**
www.routes-lavande.com

**Domaine des Arômes Sanoflore**
t 04 75 76 46 60, www.sanoflore.net; open July–Aug daily 10–12 and 2–7; May–June and Sept Sat, Sun and public hols 2–7

**Musée International de l'Œuf**
t 04 75 76 00 15, www.lemuseedeloeuf.com; open June–Sept Wed–Mon 3.30–7; closed Tues; adm

**La Magnanerie at Saillans**
t 04 75 21 56 60; open May–Sept daily 10–7; adm

**13 East of the Rhône: From the Isère into the Drôme | Southern Drôme**

## Sparkling Clairette de Die

Today the main centre selling sparkling Clairette de Die is the modern wine co-operative **Jaillance** (t 04 75 22 30 15, www.jaillance.com; open July–Aug daily 9–7; Sept–June daily 9–12.30 and 2–6.30; adm), outside Die, representing some 90 per cent of growers and roughly three quarters of total production. This highly perfumed wine gained the right to its *appellation d'origine contrôlée* in 1942, but it has much, much older credentials, as you gather in the somewhat over-poetic tour through the co-operative cellars. The local Gallo-Roman tribe had apparently already found a way of making its wine sparkle naturally as early as the 1st century, by keeping their *amphorae* in the cool river waters. Pliny the Elder sang the praises of the results.

These are high altitude vineyards for wine-making, the 1,300ha planted up to 700m above sea level, extending from Aouste-sur-Sye to Luc-en-Diois. But the south-facing slopes receive large quantities of southern sunshine. Despite the name, the main grape in Clairette de Die is in fact muscat blanc. It gives much of the perfume and sweetness. Clairette only represents around 10 per cent of the mix.

**Musée de la Clairette**
*t 04 75 21 73 77;
www.caves-carod.com;
open Mon–Fri 8–12 and
2–6, Sat, Sun and public
hols 9.30–12 and 2–6*

**Musée d'Histoire**
*t 04 75 22 40 05;
open July–Aug Mon–Sat
3–6; April–June and
Sept–Oct Wed–Sat
2–5; adm*

**Chapel of the bishops of Die**
*contact the tourist
office for visits*

**Abbaye de Valcroissant**
*t 04 75 22 12 70;
tours July–Aug Mon,
Wed and Fri at 5, June
and Sept Wed at 5;
May Fri at 5; adm*

Back close to the D93, the **Musée de la Clairette** at **Vercheny** is attached to a wine producer, offering re-creations of wine-making scenes from the start of the last century. **Pontaix** looks in danger of toppling into the Drôme; swimmers take to the muddy waters here in summer. The next dramatic village close to the river is **Ste-Croix**.

Dwarfed by the sheer, massive 2,000m yellow limestone wall of the **Montagne de Glandasse**, southern rampart of the Vercors range, it seems unbelievable that such a tiny, remote town as **Die** served for very many centuries as a cathedral city. The town is still bound by its medieval walls, but the place has more ancient roots. Roman traces remain, such as the St-Marcel arch. Further vestiges are displayed in the **Musée d'Histoire** on the main shopping drag, an appealing line cutting through Die's compact centre. The museum also covers the area's prehistory, and the painful 16th-century religious division, when Die suffered as a Protestant centre.

With cafés and plane trees to one side, the **cathedral** stands out in the centre. Originally built in the Romanesque period in its pale stone blocks, it was ransacked by Protestants in the 16th century and rebuilt in the 17th century. A few Romanesque carved capitals still embellish the entrance tower. Elaborate paintings in the spacious, aisleless interior recall the 17th-century Catholic revival.

A splendid mosaic lies in the quite separate private **chapel of the bishops of Die**. Covering the floor like a carpet, this sumptuous, rare piece isn't Roman, as you might think, but 12th-century. From the pointed star in the centre, 12 lines branch out, possibly symbolizing the months, or the 12 tribes of Israel. Four faces spit out water, thought to represent the four great biblical rivers. The walls teem with big-breasted grotesques, snails and butterflies on wallpaper ordered by an extravagant 18th-century bishop.

One of the most sensational hairpin roads in France winds north from Die, past lavender fields, way up high to the **Col de Rousset**. It's a head-spinning route up into the Vercors mountain range (*see* Chapter 16). Continuing along the Drôme, the remains of the **abbey of Valcroissant**, now a farm, hide in an enchanting corner.

Branching up the Bèz valley to **Châtillon-en-Diois**, lovely stone huts for the vineyard-workers sit among the vines. This area produces whites, reds, rosés and sparkling wines. Occasional patches of lavender also survive up here. Follow the botanical trail leading through Châtillon-en-Diois' quiet, charming lanes, looking out for the remains of its ramparts and three church bell towers. Some claim Hannibal and his elephants came this way on their journey through the Alps to Rome (*see* p.28). It takes a major effort of the imagination to think of Châtillon being disturbed by such an extraordinary army on the march.

Walnut orchards line the upper stretches of the Drôme valley. Above Luc, the D61 leads south to fabulous lost villages, **Chalancon** the most dramatic, pressed against a curving mountainside. Open, friendly **Luc-en-Diois** attracts sports people for rock-climbing and hang-gliding. A chaos of grey boulders tumbles down the steep valley at the **Saut de la Drôme**, and, just above, you come upon restful roadside pools of turquoise waters. A peaceful flat stretch of valley road follows. The D306 continues past the hamlet of **Valdrôme**, past the sources of the Drôme, to arguably France's most discreet ski resort. Here, the *département* of the Drôme comes to a natural end with the barrage of the **Montagne de l'Aup**.

## Into the Drôme Provençale

In the mesmerizing countryside east of Montélimar, elegant pyramidal mountains slope down to olive groves and cherry and apricot orchards. The flats are carpeted with vines and lavender, and oaks are planted in rows to encourage truffles to grow. Crafts and the culinary arts thrive in the sculptural villages and little towns – Grignan, almost crushed by its castle, being the archetype. Dieulefit is dedicated to ceramics, Nyons to olives, and Buis-les-Baronnies to *tilleul*, linden tree blossom transformed into *tisane*. These places are very relaxing, until market day. East, the Baronnies range offers deep calm. Its rivers occasionally run through narrow gorges, but they also linger in fertile bowls of land. Bald-topped Mont Ventoux and the Montagne de Lure, guardians of northwest Provence, loom over these parts – the Baronnies mark the historic boundary between Dauphiné and Provence.

### To Dieulefit and Grignan

Take the D540 road from Montélimar along the **Jabron valley**. The village of **Puygiron** makes a sweet first stop with its intriguing private château. Moving on to **Rochefort-en-Valdaine**, **castle ruins** don't come much more uplifting and tranquil than these, running along a ridge offering views to north and south. The **Monastère de la Trappe d'Aiguebelle** tucked away in its own valley dates back to the 12th century, but has been heavily restored. There's a well-stocked store selling produce from monasteries across France, including liqueurs and fruit cordials under the Aiguebelle label, plus a craft exhibition space. The church offers space for quiet contemplation.

Further along the Jabron valley, branch off for the *vieux village* of **Le Poët-Laval**, a member of the association of *Les Plus Beaux Villages de France*. Beautiful it is, if semi-ruined on its steep hillside, its main church just a shell. Its small **Musée du Protestantisme Dauphinois** preserves a rare historic Protestant chapel, one of the few to have survived in the Rhône-Alpes, and recalls the sufferings experienced by the people in these parts for defying the Catholic

**Rochefort-en-Valdaine castle ruins**
*t 04 75 46 62 16; open mid-July–Aug daily 3–7; mid-Mar–mid-July Sun and public hols 2–6*

**Monastère de la Trappe d'Aiguebelle**
*t 04 75 98 64 70, www.abbaye-aiguebelle.com; open Tues–Sat 10–11.45 and 2.30–5; Sun and Mon 2.30–5*

**Musée du Protestantisme Dauphinois**
*t 04 75 46 46 33, www.museeduprotestantisme dauphinois.org; open Easter–Sept Mon–Thurs and Sat 11–12 and 3–6.30, Fri 3–6.30; adm*

**Château des Hospitaliers**
*t 04 75 46 44 12; open July–mid-Sept Tues–Sun 11–12.30 and 3–7; adm*

**Centre d'Art Raymond du Puy**
*t 04 75 46 49 38, www.centre-art-drome.com; open April–mid-Sept daily 11–12.30 and 3–7; adm*

**Maison de la Terre**
*t 04 75 90 61 80, www.maisondelaterre.org; check on opening times; adm*

⚙ **Grignan**

**Château de Grignan**
*t 04 75 91 83 55; open April–Oct daily 9.30–12 and 2–6; Nov–Mar Wed–Mon 9.30–12 and 2–6; adm*

**Musée de la Typographie et du Livre**
*t 04 75 46 57 16; open July–Aug Mon–Sat 10–7 and Sun 11–6; Sept–June Tues–Sat 10–12.30 and 2–6.30, Sun 11–6; adm*

**Terres d'Ecritures**
*t 04 75 46 01 32, www.terres-ecritures.asso.fr; open July–Aug Tues–Sun 11–1 and 3–7; Easter–June and Sept–Dec Thurs–Sun 10.30–12.30 and 3–6.30*

Church. Courageous wartime Resistance is also recalled. In recent decades, the devoted Morin family have given the village a boost, opening an enchanting hotel, redoing the hilltop **Château des Hospitaliers**, once home to a branch of the knightly order of St John of Jerusalem, and putting on intriguing art exhibitions at the **Centre d'Art Raymond du Puy**, featuring rare works by leading 20th-century artists. Also look up the atmospheric café-cum-bookshop, **La Bouquinerie**.

**Dieulefit**, 'God made it', has made it rich through modelling clay of its own. The cramped streets of this hippy-chic town are filled with potters. The traditional style is of simple glazes in blue, green, yellow or caramel – typically Provençal – but a clutch of more experimental-to-wacky artists have also set up shop. As for the **Maison de la Terre**, it holds splendid pottery exhibitions.

A stunning mountain route leads east from Dieulefit, the D130 road narrowing into tight gorges, patches of lavender clinging to the slopes towards the **Défilé des Trente Pas**. The easier, but equally irresistible D538 **lavender route** leads south to **Grignan**.

The haughty, aristocratic **Château de Grignan** sits dramatically aloof on its rock above the village houses clustered so subserviently below, although this substantial French Renaissance castle lost its head at the Revolution. However, its fascinating Ancien Régime connections are brought to the fore on the guided tours. Mme de Sévigné, the court socialite and prolific letter-writer of Louis XIV's day, spent three long periods here thanks to her daughter, recording her impressions in her correspondence. She loved the good days, but the mistral wind almost drove her crazy... and she eventually died here towards the close of the 17th century. Her daughter, Françoise-Marguerite, also quite a character and a fine catch, was regarded as one of the greatest beauties of her day. In 1669 she had married François, Comte de Grignan, who spent vast sums on lavish entertainment. The couple's daughter, Pauline, was forced to sell the family castle in 1732 to pay off his debts. On the tour around some 20 modestly furnished rooms, the lives of the castle's other significant owners are also explained. Afterwards, step out onto one of the most decadent terraces in southern France, gloriously located on the roof of the substantial church.

In this intensely artistic village, beautiful old roses perfume the air in season. Run with passion, the appealing **Musée de la Typographie et du Livre** celebrates the art of making books, the dedicated team printing its own charming works. This place also fits in a courtyard café and a bookshop specializing in famous correspondence, including that of Mme de Sévigné, who is buried in the vast Gothic cave of a **church** against the hillside.

On the writing theme, **Terres d'Ecritures** not only has displays and exhibitions on writing implements; it also organizes

## Coteaux du Tricastin and Truffles

Essentially Rhône valley vineyards, the Coteaux du Tricastin cover around 2,600 hectares in a triangle of land between Montélimar, Grignan and St-Paul-Trois-Châteaux. They are named after the Celtic tribe that was based in these parts before the Romans arrived, but evidence has been unearthed of one of the largest Roman wine estates ever found across the Empire having existed here. Touching on better-known Côtes du Rhône wine territory, bargains are to be had in the Coteaux du Tricastin, as the name is not as well known. However, its vintages reliably share similar traits. The Grignan Caveau and St-Paul-Trois-Châteaux's Maison de la Truffe et du Tricastin (*see* p.201) are good places to start discovering this *appellation*, as they represent the bulk of the producers, both co-operatives and individual properties. After tasting, the Caveau employees can organize a visit to the properties.

Look carefully around the Coteaux du Tricastin, and you'll see that in certain areas oak trees have been planted in neat rows, like the vines. These are to encourage the growing of truffles, as this area has proved to be most propitious for the ultimate in luxury tubers. Read more about these 'black diamonds' under St-Paul-Trois-Châteaux.

**Caveau des Vignerons du Tricastin**
*open April–Dec daily 9.30–7*

**Village Provençal Miniature**
*t 04 75 46 91 68; open July–Aug daily 10–7; spring and rest of summer daily 10.30–12 and 2–7; winter Mon and Wed–Fri 2–6, Sat and Sun 10.30–12 and 2–6; adm*

calligraphy courses. Among other crafts shops in the upper village, the five artisans who've clubbed together to form **Roue Libre** produce particularly joyous pieces in a variety of media.

Down below, the remarkable round, colonnaded village wash-house looks like a temple to laundering. Beside the town hall, a statue shows a young Mme de Sévigné concentrating on her writing, quill in hand. The **Caveau des Vignerons du Tricastin** in a courtyard nearby, however, encourages you to take up a glass of wine, introducing visitors to this curiosity of an *appellation* where the vines share the land with lavender and truffle oaks.

East of Grignan, the **Village Provençal Miniature** provides amusement with its wide array of Provençal figures made by *santonniers*, local traditional specialist craftspeople.

## South of Grignan into Papal Territory

**Tour de Chamaret**
*t 04 75 46 55 85; check for opening hours; adm*

Just south of Grignan, the emaciated **Tour de Chamaret**, the very tall remnants of a medieval keep, towers over a pretty village and overlooks a curious historical anomaly to the east, a Provençal **papal enclave**. Centred around **Valréas**, it was acquired by the papacy when it moved to Avignon, just to the south, in the 14th century. The story goes that when the sickly Pope John XXII was elected in 1316, few thought he would survive long, but his particular liking for the wines around Valréas supposedly sustained him for 18 years as pontiff. Encircled by the Drôme, the enclave has been administered by the *département* of the Vaucluse in Provence most of the time since the Revolution. Valréas is a pleasing little historic town, proud of its premier position in the world of carton-making, a subject covered, along with printing, by its **museum**.

The lands around Grignan are the most prolific truffle-producing territories in France. **Richerenches** in the papal enclave holds the biggest truffle market in France, every Sunday in midwinter. Truffles bring money now, but the name of this little place, and its mighty defences, indicate that it was wealthy long before. While most of the historic villages in these parts were built on defensive slopes, this one is on the flat, presenting an almost perfect square of fortifications. Panels along the streets help visitors build up a picture of the Knights Templars for whom this *commanderie* was founded in 1130. The mighty chivalric order became hugely wealthy, controlling much of the finances raised for the Crusades, buying vast territories overseen by such *commanderies*. But the order was viciously destroyed in the early 14th century by a jealous King Philippe le Bel of France, who pressurized Pope Clement V in Avignon into excommunicating them and then had them tried on trumped-up charges including idolatry and sodomy. A rival knightly order, the Hospitallers of St John of Jerusalem, took over many of their properties, including this one.

**Château de Suze-la-Rousse**
*t 04 75 04 81 44; open April–Sept daily 9.30–12 and 2–6; Oct–Mar Wed–Mon 9.30–12 and 2–6; adm*

Back in the Drôme, at Grignan, the ruddy-hued medieval **Château de Suze-la-Rousse** sits snobbishly on its pedestal of rock above the village grovelling at its feet. Standing out so imposingly from afar, close up, the crenellated, round-towered château looks severe. But note the caricature of a lion sticking its tongue out at you, above the coat of arms as you arrive at the moat. The inner courtyard proves ornate, embellished in elaborate classical style as a wedding gift for powerful owner Comte François de la Baume. A fierce Catholic, in the Wars of Religion he served as governor of Provence. The carved coats of arms and symbols signal the family's proud military history, while the bishop's hat recalls that the gift was made by François' episcopal uncle. A later family bishop ordered the magnificent double staircase inside, redone after the Revolution. The family line only died out in 1958. You can tour the elegant wood-panelled chambers on one floor, sadly empty when not hosting exhibitions, although a couple of intriguing murals stand out. One may represent the battle for Montélimar in 1587 at which François de la Baume was mortally wounded.

**Université du Vin**
*t 04 75 97 21 30, www. universite-du-vin.com*

Much of the rest of the castle is occupied by the **Université du Vin**, installed in these sumptuous surroundings in 1978. The name

## Not So Sober Côtes du Rhône Wines

From the castle windows of Suze-la-Rousse, you look down on a sea of Côtes du Rhône vines (*www.rhone-wines.com*) stretching out across the wide Eygues valley. Follow the exceptionally picturesque wine route east to Nyons, the ends of the rows marked by blood-red roses (planted to spot mildew more than for aesthetic reasons). The Baronnies hills and the Mont Ventoux make a perfect photographic backdrop. A huge wine co-operative stands on the outskirts of each village, that of the **Cellier des Dauphins** on the edge of Tulette the most enormous, the others on a more human scale. But be tempted into trying individual properties, too. This area produces excellent, powerful wines, generally extremely reliable and reasonable value. Each of the villages has a Provençal feel, with plane-tree-shaded squares and trickling fountains. A couple of the parishes have earned the distinction of labelling their wine Côtes du Rhône-Villages. Contrary to expectation, the hilarious-sounding (and delectable) wine village of Vinsobres is said to take its name from the Latin for 'above the vines', rather than from any *vignerons'* humour.

proves slightly misleading, as anyone can enrol on a wine course here, but the place is mainly geared to professionals. Short courses can be run for English-speaking tourists. The installations for studying oenology range from the superb to the outrageous, with a former chapel converted into one tasting room!

Another well-located rock top castle stands out from the centre of the charming village of **Rochegude**, marking the Rhône-Alpes' frontier with Provence, on which it turns its back. This castle has been transformed into a splendid luxury hotel (*see* p.233).

## From Grignan to the Olive Groves of Nyons

A further stunning wine route leads east from Grignan to Nyons, taking you under the mountaintops of the **Lance** and the **Vaux**, ranged like huge, neat pyramids in a row. The historic villages below huddle in tight circles. At **Taulignan**, the outer houses form a defensive ring with towers, but now only the fountains disturb the peace. Beyond the walls, an elegant former school with an arcaded front has been converted into the **Atelier-Musée de la Soie**, charting the history of silk-making both in the region and around this village, where young girls lacking family support were sent to work to build up their dowries. All is presented in spick-and-span fashion, while the shop sells Lyon silk scarves and ties.

Quiet, withdrawn **Le Pègue** contains a surprisingly interesting **Musée Archéologique**, run with enthusiasm. A pre-Roman Celtic settlement of importance surveyed the edge of the very wide plain from up on its height, the views stretching over to northern Provence, and to the Cévennes the other side of the Rhône.

**Rousset-les-Vignes** looks down from mid-slope onto a sea of vines, in the most northerly area of Côtes du Rhône-Villages, local properties offering wines. The chapel of **Notre-Dame de Beauvoir** remains aloof, the only construction on the pyramidal hills above. Most picturesque and defensive of all the villages, **Venterol** hides like a snail in its shell, surrounded by orchards and vines.

Olives are the main crop associated with **Nyons**, a pleasing market town basking in its sunny corner against the Baronnies mountains. The place is practically synonymous with its golden oil, sold at near-golden prices, although vineyards and orchards also abound around town. The exclusive gourmet Tanche olive here has been granted the distinction of its own *appellation d'origine contrôlée*. The town hosts the **Institut du Monde de l'Olivier** near the tourist office, with exhibitions on olive-related subjects and interesting introductory comparative tastings of French olive oils on certain days. Nearby, the renovated central **Place des Arcades** provides a lovely setting for cafés, boutiques, and magnificent markets. Dark covered alleyways lead up from here to the exotic neo-Gothic calvary of the **Tour Randonne** crowning the old town.

---

**Atelier-Musée de la Soie**
*t 04 75 53 12 96, www. musee-soie.fr; open July–Aug daily 10–6; Feb–June and Sept–Nov Mon–Fri 10–12.30 and 1.30–5.30, Sat and Sun 10–6; adm*

**Le Pègue Musée Archéologique**
*t 04 75 53 68 21; www. museearcheolepegue. com; open June–Sept daily exc Mon, Tues, and Sun am, 9–12.30 and 2.30–6; rest of year Sat 10–12 and 2–5, plus 1st Sun of month 2–5; adm*

**Institut du Monde de l'Olivier**
*t 04 75 26 90 90, www. monde-olivier.com; open Mon–Fri 8.30–12.30 and 1.30–5.30; adm – sign on for tastings Thurs June–Sept at 3*

**13** **East of the Rhône: From the Isère into the Drôme | Southern Drôme**

A spectacular single-arched medieval **bridge** spans the turquoise waters of the Eygues at Nyons. By the 14th century, when it was built, the town's merchants were already entitled by charter to sell and transport their olive oil. Beside the bridge, along with shops selling olive products, visit a couple of atmospheric old oil-making mills hidden under the houses at the **Vieux Moulins à Huile**. Beyond its culinary pleasures, and its use in lamps, olive oil was employed in the making of soap, and an old soap-making chamber has also been unearthed here; it dates from the 18th century, although it looks like an ancient archaeological site. Upstream, the **Scourtinerie** provides another odd visit related to olives – *scourtins* were the traditional round mats through which the oil was filtered, the natural fibres often coming from far afield, and curious sources. The manufacturing of *scourtins* flourished until the disastrous frost of 1956, when many Nyonsais olive trees died. But the Fret family decided to branch out, using the Catherine-wheel-like looms to make circular pieces from table mats to carpets.

Strolling west along the Eygues, the **Distillerie Bleu Provence** often scents the riverside with a heady lavender perfume. You can see the old-fashioned process in action in summer, while the shop sells a range of lavender products. Next comes a popular new indoor-and-outdoor pool complex. Close by stands a discreet small riverside herb garden. A little way north, Nyons' **Musée de l'Olivier** may be terribly old-fashioned, a messy single-room display covering olive history, legends and traditions, but a chat with the guide can prove more illuminating, while the neighbouring modern co-operative sells all manner of olive products, fine local produce and wine, including by the pump. For further culinary stops around town, ask at the tourist office. A lovely book, *La Charrette bleue*, by René Barjavel, recalls his family's life running a *boulangerie* in Nyons, revealing all sorts of details on traditional life in these parts, from the deep-rooted division between Catholics and Protestants to the tricks of the local wind, the *pontias*.

**Vieux Moulins à Huile**
*t 04 75 26 11 00, http:// vieuxmoulins.free.fr; open July–Aug Mon– Sat, visits at 11.30, 3 and 4; Feb–June and Sept–Dec Tues–Sat, visits at 11 and 3; adm*

**Scourtinerie**
*t 04 75 26 33 52; open daily 9.30–12 and 2.30–5*

**Distillerie Bleu Provence**
*t 04 75 26 10 42, www. distillerie-bleu-provence. com; shop open all year; guided tour July–Aug Mon–Sat 5, April–June Thurs and Sat at 5; adm*

**Musée de l'Olivier**
*t 04 75 26 12 12, www.guideweb.com/ musee/olivier; open daily 10–11.30 and 2.30–5.30; adm*

## Into the Baronnies Range

From the Tour Randonne, Nyons looks like a stopper wedged into the narrow entrance to the gorgeous Baronnies, named after the little local lords. Olive and cherry trees, vines and lavender find patches in which to thrive between the heights. The symbol of this range, though, is the apricot; it produces the most divine variety, plump, deep orange and bursting with juice, a completely different fruit from the pale, insipid things you find in shops back home. Crumbling, semi-abandoned, semi-restored villages cling to the hillsides. In summer you may encounter a goatherd guarding his, or her, flock; these parts produce excellent goat's cheese, *picodons*.

Two stupendously beautiful routes lead from Nyons to Buis-les-Baronnies, one looping north round the western mountains, the other looping south of them. Both are included on the **Route de l'Olivier** – this whole area is classified as a *Site Remarquable du Goût*, recognizing its exceptional agricultural landscapes.

## Routes from Nyons to Buis-les-Baronnies

The northern way first winds along the Eygues river gorges, the different strata reading like thick pages in the book of geology. Before turning off along the languorous **Ennuye valley**, explore the villages hiding up in the limestone rocks above the Eygues, **Villeperdrix** hidden from the road, **St-May**'s beautiful necklace of houses set on the wrinkliest of old skin of rocks. Climb up to its tiny triangular clifftop cemetery to see the high spiny dinosaur mountains peering hungrily down on it.

Beyond the meagre ruins of the **Abbaye de Bodon** above St-May, follow the signs for '*Vautours*' where, in the morning, you should be able to see vultures swirling across the valley. These birds, with wing-spans up to three metres, are awesome. The indigenous population of the southern Alps was destroyed in the 19th century by improved husbandry hygiene, by poisoned carcasses left out to get rid of wolves, and by hunters. The birds have been reintroduced here, from Spain, since 1996. Learn more on this large colony down in **Rémuzat** far below its Table Mountain, at the charmingly run **Maison des Vautours** Book here for specialist nature walks.

**Maison des Vautours**
*t 04 75 27 85 71, www. remuzat.com; open July–Aug Tues, Wed and Fri–Sun 10–12 and 3– 6.30, Mon 10–12, Thurs 3–6.30; April–June, Sept and other school hols Tues, Wed and Fri–Sun 10–12 and 2–5*

🎯 Route du Goût

Back on the way to Buis, **Ste-Jalle**, with its diminished castle and two churches, signals the entrance to an exceptionally beautiful, tranquil, fruitful bowl of land totally encircled by *montagnettes*. The thick shade of the village's wide plane alley is beloved of *boules*-players. Perched dramatically to the north, **Le Poët-Sigillat**'s silhouette is marked by its open-gated belltower. To the south, paragliders often circle like colourful dragonflies above the **Col d'Ey**, the high pass leading down to Buis.

The **southern route from Nyons to Buis**takes you through vine and olive country via **Mirabel-aux-Baronnies** to join the **Ouvèze valley**. Up in the village of **Piégon**, wine seems to have turned the head of a modern sculptor, who made the enormous outdoor piece in homage to the vine. Nipping across to the Ouvèze just above Vaison-la-Romaine in Provence, you come to **Mollans-sur-Ouvèze**, its natural fortification a massive lump of a rock, topped by an impressive medieval keep. Down below, the **Moulin à Huile Chauvet**still turns the old-fashioned way. By the river, the cutest, least assuming chapel stands one side of the water, an enchanting colonnaded wash-house the other.

**Moulin à Huile Chauvet**
*t 04 75 28 90 12; open July–Sept daily 10–12.30 and 2.30–7, April–June weekends and public hols, same times; adm*

At **Pierrelongue**, a 19th-century church perches startlingly on a thinner ridge of rock, inciting walkers and pilgrims alike to take on the almost irresistible challenge of climbing up to it. Fittingly, the place holds a **Musée d'Art Religieux**.

*Tilleuls*, linden (or lime) trees, beautify the routes to Buis-les-Baronnies, their plump forms yielding blossoms for one of France's most popular infusions. In early summer, you may see wooden ladders propped against many a tree for the traditional harvest.

The lost little town of **Buis-les-Baronnies** is backed by a bony dinosaur dorsal of a mountain. In ancient times, Hannibal and his elephants may possibly have sneaked through here on their epic journey to take on Rome. But until archaeological elephant droppings are unearthed, it remains pure speculation as to whether the Carthaginian's extraordinary warhorses drank at the fountains. Buis and its environs certainly attracted a hippy crowd from the 1960s, as did many of the semi-ruined villages of the southern Drôme and Ardèche, even if the slightly harsher than expected winters made many of them run back to home comforts. A few remained here, however, topped up in season by young followers.

Between ancient and modern times, the medieval barons had a solid little town built in their little mountains. Arcades of plane trees bring shade to the cafés along the main boulevard encircling the compact old centre. Within, the enchanting, eccentric arcades lining **Place du Marché** were apparently built by Swiss settlers in the 15th century, each plump arch adopting a slightly different pose. Among the narrow lanes beyond, look out for the lovely, simple cloister of the converted Dominican **monastery** before the sturdy restored **church**, as well as the odd new oil and herbal shop popping up amidst the array of old butchers' shops.

**Maison des
Plantes
Arômatiques et
Médicinales**
*t 04 75 28 04 59, www. maisondesplantes.com; open July–Aug Mon–Sat 9–12 and 3–7, Sun and public hols 10–12 and 3–6; April–June and Sept Mon–Sat 9–12 and 2–6, Sun and public hols 10–12 and 3–6; Oct–Mar Mon–Sat 9–12 and 2–5, plus Sun up to mid-Nov and from mid-Feb, plus public hols 10–12 and 3–6; adm*

It's not just linden trees that thrive in the fragrant Baronnies; aromatic herbs generally proliferate, as explained at Buis' **Maison des Plantes Arômatiques et Médicinales** above the tourist office, although the panels and videos concentrate on linden and lavender in particular. The presentation proves a tad dry, though, as can the herb garden outside.

**Musée des Arts
et Traditions**
*t 04 75 28 01 42; open on request*

To breathe in the scents of the Baronnies at first hand, take the **Menon valley** east of Buis, olive groves thriving on one steep side, apricot orchards on the other. **La Roche-sur-le-Buis** sits among a cascade of big boulders, the remains of a castle desperately clinging to the highest one. The gravestones in the tiny cemetery are almost choked by dense planting around them, with a miniature **Musée des Arts et Traditions** next door focusing on old ways.

## The Baronnies beyond Buis

Pressing east, a gorgeous, unspoilt country route takes you up to the **source of the Ouvèze**. As well as having apricot orchards and lavender fields, this tranquil corner is marked by wrinkled ridges of rock dragged up from the ocean in a distant era. According to a plaque in the most peaceful hilltop village of **St-Auban-sur-l'Ouvèze**, America recognizes the important role that François d'Albert, Comte de Rions, who died here in 1802, played in its War of Independence against Britain. Continue up to the **Col de Perty** for startling views of some of the Alps' eternally snow-capped peaks.

A still more dramatic route follows the southern frontier of the Drôme from Buis-les-Baronnies in the black shadow of the **Mont Ventoux**. Clinging defiantly to its slope, facing the forested north flank of Provence's great 'Windy One', **Brantes** is a charming isolated fortified village that lies in the neighbouring region, but should really be claimed by the *département* of the Drôme.

A ruined French Renaissance **château** gives the finishing touch to the fine silhouette of **Montbrun-les-Bains**, a substantial old village climbing its hillside via a series of stone terraces. It's a member of the association of *Les Plus Beaux Villages de France*, but not over-prettified. Through the gateways, the medieval church contains surprisingly ornate Ancien Régime decorations. The *châtelain* most remembered in these parts, Charles Dupuy-Montbrun, became one of the most feared Protestant campaigners in the Wars of Religion, said to have gone to war with a sword in one hand, and a Bible in the other. After terrorizing Catholic communities around the Rhône valley, he suffered a blow when his castle was destroyed; but it was he who ordered the fine Renaissance one whose remains you now see. He eventually got his come-uppance, condemned to death for stealing Polish treasure from King Henri III.

**Thermes de Montbrun**
*t 04 75 28 80 75, www.valvital.fr*

It's a shame that modern houses have been so insensitively dotted around the valley below. The eggy smell sometimes emanating from here signals the posh **Thermes de Montbrun** Its main building, with classical style colonnade apparently partly modelled on Baden-Baden in Germany, was set up to receive the sickly in search of cures for respiratory problems and rheumatism. But a stylish new structure in wood has gone up recently to enable this thermal establishment to offer relaxation treatments as well.

**Château d'Aulan**
*t 04 75 28 80 00; open July–Aug daily 10–12 and 2–6.30; June and Sept Sat, Sun and public hols by reservation only; adm*

Lost in a narrow valley to the north, the gathering of towers overseen by the imposing square keep of the **Château d'Aulan** comes as a big surprise along the unoccupied **Gorges de Toulourenc**. You wonder what the medieval lords might have been trying to protect in this barren landscape, but this was once a strategic gateway to Provence, on a salt-trading route. Although a stone keep was built here perhaps as early as the 12th century, the one you see now is a 19th-century reconstruction. All told, the place has a slightly scruffy neo-Gothic look. Restored in engagingly amateurish manner since the war, when it served as a refuge for Resistance fighters, it is now cluttered with family memorabilia and bric-a-brac; much of the pleasure of the tour comes from the anecdotes the objects provoke on the adventurous past of the Suarez-d'Aulan family.

East of Montbrun, the countryside remains magnificently unspoilt. The village of **Barret-de-Lioure**, marked out by three wooden crosses perched on a rock in the midst of its high, deep valley, enjoys spectacular views back to the Mont Ventoux. A war monument recalls three local Resistance fighters caught out in this tight spot. Around **Ferrassières** you reach the most southerly frontier of the Rhône-Alpes region, the expansive lavender-covered slopes descending gently into Provence. Old stone huts known as *bories* scattered in the fields around the open village add to the photogenic surrounds. The **Château de la Gabelle** has a lovely lavender boutique.

Heading back round the forbidding **Montagne d'Albion**, follow the Méouges river. The village of **Séderon** lies protected in a narrow valley. On the southeastern limits of the *département de la Drôme*, **Lachau**, with its castle and fountained squares, has the charms you'll have come to expect from Drômois villages. The Méouges runs on into Provence, through bright gorges leading to the huge natural sliding doors of rock making fortified Sisteron one of the most impressive gateways into that region.

## Market Days in the Southern Drôme

**Crest**: Tues and Sat am.
**Saillans**: Sun am.
**Die**: Wed and Sat am.
**Châtillon-en-Diois**: Fri am.
**Luc-en-Diois**: Fri am.
**Dieulefit**: Fri am.
**Grignan**: Tues am.
**Suze-la-Rousse**: Fri am.
**Nyons**: Thurs am, plus Sun am, June–Sept.
**Buis-les-Baronnies**: Wed and Sat am.
**Montbrun-les-Bains**: Sat am.

## Festivals in the Southern Drôme

Interesting musical events include the **Château de Grignan** season (*Feb–April*), the **Le Poët-Laval** cycle (*May–Sept*), the acclaimed **Saou Mozart festival** (*July*), the **Crest jazz festival** (*Aug*) and the **Grignan jazz festival** (*Nov*). Grignan also hosts a **festival of correspondence** (*July*) and summer-evening **theatre** in the castle (*July–Aug*).

**Wine festivals** can pop up throughout the year.

## Activities in the Southern Drôme

**Canoeing** is popular on the Drôme: at Aouste-sur-Sye, with **Cap Plein Air**, t 04 75 40 60 60, *www.cappleinair. com*; at Saillans, with **Eaux Vives Aventures**, t 04 75 21 55 71, *www.eaux vivesaventure.com*, or with **Lido Location**, t 04 75 21 54 20, *www.canoe-france.com/drome*, the latter even offering canoeing by moonlight; at Vercheny from the **Camping Les Acacias**, t 04 75 21 72 51, *www.camping lesacacias.com*; at Pontaix, with **Aloa'venture**, t 04 75 21 13 63.

## Where to Stay and Eat in the Southern Drôme

### Saou ✉ 26400

**L'Oiseau sur sa Branche**, t 04 75 76 02 03. Both a *bistrot* (€; *open all year, but closed Mon–Tues in winter*) and an enchanting restaurant (€€; *open Feb–Nov daily exc Wed and Sat*) in this village mad about local goats' cheese. **L'Auberge de l'Etang**, t 04 75 76 05 70 (€). Country inn with simple menus in a beautiful setting under limestone walls. *Closed in winter.*

ⓘ **Crest**
*Place du Dr Maurice Rozier, 26400 Crest,* t 04 75 25 11 38, *www. vallee-drome.com/ot-crest*

ⓘ **Saillans**
*Montée Soubeyranne, 26340 Saillans,* t 04 75 21 51 05, *ot.saillans@ wanadoo.fr*

ⓘ **Grignan >>**
*Grande Rue, 26230
Grignan, t 04 75 46
56 75, www.guideweb.
com/grignan*

ⓘ **Die >**
*Quartier St-Pierre, 26150
Die, t 04 75 22 03 03,
www.diois-
tourisme.com*

ⓘ **Châtillon-en-
Diois >**
*Square Jean Giono,
26410 Châtillon-en-
Diois, t 04 75 21 10 07*

⭐ **Au Clair de la
Plume >>**

**Luc-en-Diois**
*Place de la Croix,
26310 Luc-en-Diois,
t 04 75 21 34 14*

ⓘ **Dieulefit >**
*1 Pl Abbé Magnet, 26220
Dieulefit, t 04 75 46
42 49, www.tourisme-
paysdieulefit.com*

**Suze-la-Rousse >>**
*Av des Côtes du Rhône,
26790 Suze-la-Rousse,
t 04 75 04 81 41, http://
perso.wanadoo.fr/
ot.suze-la-rousse*

⭐ **Les
Hospitaliers >**

⭐ **Château de
Rochegude >>**

⭐ **Le Mas des
Alibeaux >**

## La Chaudière ✉ 26340

**L'Arche des 3 Becs B&B**, Ferme
Couteau, t 04 75 21 59 32, *www.3becs.
com* (€). Simple, welcoming country
stop in beautiful spot with views, a
few holiday chalets sharing the slope.
Covered pool. *Table d'hôte* (€).

## Die ✉ 26150

**\*\*Le St-Domingue**, t 04 75 22 03 08
(€). Central hotel with basic bargain
rooms and friendly old-style
restaurant (€€–€). Tiny pool.
*Restaurant closed Sun pm and Mon.*

## Châtillon-en-Diois ✉ 26410

**\*\*Le Mont Barral**, Les Nonières,
Treschenu-Crayers, t 04 75 21 12 21,
*www.hotelmontbarral-vercors.com* (€).
Towards the Col de Menée, simple
French country hotel with pleasant
rooms and solid country cooking
(€€–€). Covered pool. Court. *Closed
mid-Nov–mid-Feb; restaurant closed
Tues eve and Wed.*

## Pontaix ✉ 26150

**Moulin de Pontaix B&B**, t 04 75 21 20
31, *http://moulindepontaix.tibone.com*
(€). Plain, practical recently done
rooms in a village house perched just
above the Drôme's waters. Run by a
knowledgeable, gentle local couple.
M. Chevillon, a former *vigneron*, cooks
good *table d'hôte* (€).

## Dieulefit ✉ 26220

**Domaine de la Fayence B&B**, t 04 75
46 35 10, *www.domainedelafayence.
com* (€€– €). Classic converted farm.
*Table d'hôte* (€€). Pool. Court.

**Auberge des Brises**, Route de Nyons,
t 04 75 46 41 49 (€€). Nice country
cooking under linden trees 1.5km
outside town. *Closed Tues in July and
Aug, Mon eve, Tues and Wed out of
season, and Feb.*

## Le Poët-Laval ✉ 26160

**\*\*\*Les Hospitaliers**, t 04 75 46 22 32,
*www.hotel-les-hospitaliers.com*
(€€€–€€). Divine little hotel up in the
semi-ruined hillside village. Delicious
cuisine on small menu (€€€). Pool.
*Closed mid-Nov–mid-Dec and
Jan–mid-Mar; restaurant closed low
season Mon and Tues.*

**Le Mas des Alibeaux B&B**, t 04 75 46
35 59, *www.masdesalibeaux.com* (€).

Lovingly restored farm looking over to
the historic hilltop village, with
gorgeous rooms set round a courtyard.*Table d'hôte* (€€). Shady grounds.

## Grignan ✉ 26230

**\*\*\*\*Manoir de la Roseraie**, Route de
Valréas, t 04 75 46 58 15, *www.manoir
delaroseraie.com* (€€€€). Exclusive
19th-century walled property below
the village with pool and tennis.
Stylish restaurant (€€€). *Closed half of
Dec and early Jan–mid-Feb; restaurant
closed Tues, Wed out of season.*

**\*\*\* Au Clair de la Plume**, Place du Mail,
t 04 75 91 81 30, *www.chateauxhotels.
com/clairplume* (€€€). Very romantic
hotel in the village, mixing classic and
contemporary décor in air-conditioned
rooms, overlooking a delightful
garden where non-residents can enjoy
the café. *Closed late Jan–Feb.*

**Le Poème**, t 04 75 91 10 90, Place du
Jeu de Ballon (€€). Charming
restaurant serving elegant regional
cuisine. *Closed Mon lunch, Wed, and
Thurs lunch.*

## Montségur-sur-Lauzon
✉ 26130

**\*\*Auberge des Tarraïettes**, t 04 75 98
13 24, *www.auberge-des-tarraiettes.
com* (€). Set back in its scruffily
appealing courtyard-garden off the
village roundabout, welcoming old
inn with nice restaurant (€€).
*Restaurant closed Sun eve and Mon.*

## Suze-la-Rousse ✉ 26790

**Les Aiguières B&B**, t 04 75 98 40 80,
*www.les-aiguieres.com* (€€). Good
rooms, plus pool with view of
château. *Table d'hôte* (€€) – Madame
does thematic dinners around
regional wines.

## Rochegude ✉ 26790

**\*\*\*\*Château de Rochegude**, t 04 75
97 21 10, *www.chateauderochegude.
com* (€€€€€–€€€€). Amazing
converted hilltop castle offering lordly
luxury. Fine courtyard as well as
dining room for meals (€€€€–€€€).
Pool and court. *Closed most of Nov.*

**Café du Cours**, Cours de l'Apparent,
t 04 75 98 24 83 (€). At the other end
of the scale, a charming village café.
*Closed Tues eve in season, Mon eve,
Tues eve and Wed eve out of season.*

(i) **Buis-les-Baronnies >>**
*Bd Eysserie, 26170
Buis-les-Baronnies,
t 04 75 28 04 59, www.
buislesbaronnies.com*

(i) **Nyons >**
*Place de la Libération,
26110 Nyons, t 04 75 26
10 35, www.
nyonstourisme.com*

(★) **Hôtel
La Badiane >>**

(i) **Rémuzat**
*Place du Champ de
Mars, 26510 Rémuzat,
t 04 75 27 85 71,
www.remuzat.com*

(i) **Montbrun-les-Bains**
*26570 Montbrun-les-Bains, t 04 75 28 82 49,
www.guideweb.com/
montbrun*

## Vinsobres ✉ 26110

**Auberge du Petit Bistrot, t** 04 75 27 61 90 (€€–€). *Enchanting village restaurant by the fountain. Closed mid-Dec–Jan, plus Wed; also phone to check weekday eves out of season.*

## Nyons ✉ 26110

**La Bastide des Monges**, Route d'Orange, **t** 04 75 26 99 69, *www. bastidedesmonges.com* (€€€–€€). *Among the vines west of town, smartly restored roadside farmhouse with views to Mont Ventoux. Pool. Closed mid-Oct–Easter.*

**\*\*\*Le Colombet**, Place de la Libération, **t** 04 75 26 03 66, *www.hotelcolombet. com* (€€). *Traditional French provincial hotel with restaurant at the heart of the action. Closed late Nov–late Jan.*

## Aubres ✉ 26110

**Auberge du Vieux Village, t** 04 75 26 12 89, *auberge.aubres@wanadoo.fr* (€€€–€€). *On the castle ruins of a hilltop village east of Nyons, many rooms with terraces with great views, as there are from the restaurant (€€) terrace. Pool. Restaurant closed Wed.*

## Les Pilles/Condorcet ✉ 26110

**La Charrette Bleue**, Route de Gap, **t** 04 75 27 72 33 (€€). *Cheerful roadside restaurant serving consistently excellent Provençal cuisine. Closed Wed high season, Tues, Wed and Sun eve low season, plus mid-Dec–Jan.*

## Valouse ✉ 26110

**\*\*\*Le Hameau de Valouse, t** 04 75 27 72 05, *www.hameau-de-valouse.com* (€€). *Delightful huddle of old stone cottages set in a peaceful valley along the D130, the mountainous route between Dieulefit and Nyons, turned in part into gîtes, in part into hotel rooms. Pleasant simple restaurant (€€) with terrace. Pool. Closed Nov–Feb; restaurant closed Mon and Tues.*

## Mollans-sur-Ouvèze ✉ 26170

**\*\*Le St-Marc**, Av de l'Ancienne Gare, **t** 04 75 28 70 01, *www.saintmarc.com* (€€–€). *Charming village hotel with welcoming garden, colourful rooms and nice restaurant (€€). Pool and court. Closed Nov–Mar; restaurant closed lunch.*

## Buis-les-Baronnies ✉ 26170

**L'Ancienne Cure B&B, t** 04 75 28 22 08, *www.ancienne-cure.com* (€€). *Enchanting rooms in a centrally located house by the church, with Jacuzzi in the enclosed garden. Table d'hôte (€€).*

## Plaisians ✉ 26170

**Auberge de la Clue**, Place de l'Eglise, **t** 04 75 28 01 17 (€€). *Old-style generosity at this delightful inn. Closed Feb and late Oct; April–mid-Oct closed Mon, rest of year closed Sun eve and weekdays.*

## St-Auban-sur-l'Ouvèze ✉ 26170

**La Clavelière, t** 04 75 28 61 07, *www.laclaveliere@wanadoo.fr* (€). *Appealingly simple traditional village inn along the ramparts. There's a handful of rooms and an unpretentious restaurant (€€–€). Pool. Closed mid-Sept–Easter; , restaurant closed Nov–Feb, and Sat.*

## Montauban-sur-l'Ouvèze ✉ 26170

**Hôtel La Badiane**, Hameau de Ruissas, **t** 04 75 27 17 74, *www.la-badiane-sejours.com* (€€€–€€). *Gorgeous, tranquil new hotel in converted old sheepfarm set in lavender fields. Just seven rooms, each with its own terrace and the odd oriental touch. Heated pool. Massage available. Pool and sauna. Dinner (€€). Closed Dec–Mar.*

## Ferrassières ✉ 26570

**Château de la Gabelle B&B, t** 04 75 28 80 54, *www.chateau-la-gabelle.com* (€€). *With its towers rising out of the lavender fields, surprising property in this deeply peaceful corner of the Drôme. Run by a woman devoted to lavender. Simple rooms. Table d'hôte (€€).*

## Eygalayes ✉ 26560

**Les Forges Ste-Marie, t** 04 75 28 42 77, *Isabelle.muse@wanadoo.fr* (€). *For tranquillity lost in the southeast Drôme. Lavender spa tub. Table d'hôte (€€).*

# The Rhône from Lyon to Lac Léman

The Rhône between Lyon and Geneva may not be well known to tourists, but it's sensational, surely the most beautiful stretch of the great river. The great number of swans shows how much they appreciate it. Its banks are much quieter and generally less scarred by industry than the length between Lyon and Provence.

Near Lyon, the Isle Crémieu peninsula has preserved its lovely towns, villages and sights. Next comes the Bugey, magical mountainous terrain lined by vines and Rhône-side ports. Beyond the hidden Valserine valley, we finally reach the Gex, dramatically overlooking Lac Léman (Lake Geneva) and the Alps, from the Jura side – in this chapter, we explore the southernmost reaches of that range.

# 14

## Don't miss

**1** Two cultured little towns
Crémieu and Morestel pp.238/240

**2** A dreamy slope-side route
The Revermont p.242

**3** A devastating war museum
Maison Mémorial, Izieu p.247

**4** Idyllic wine stops
Bugey villages below the Grand Colombier p.250

**5** Traditional Jura charms
The Valserine valley p.252

*See map overleaf*

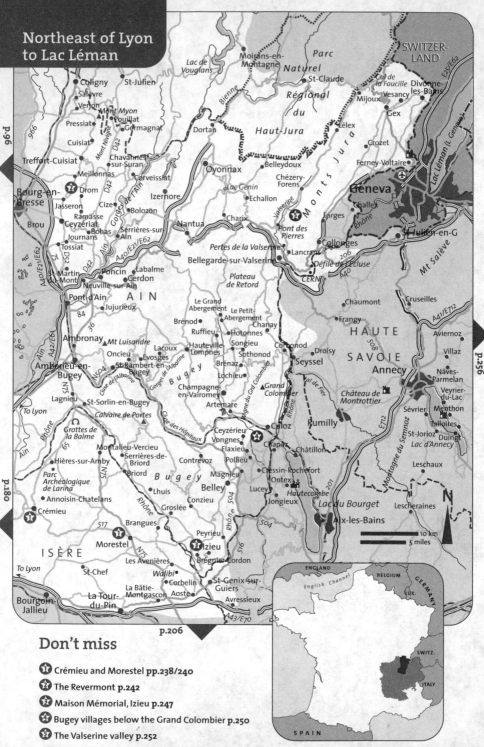

p.96

SWITZER-LAND

Parc
Naturel

Régional

du

Haut-Jura

Monts Jura

Lac de
Vouglans

Moirans-en-Montagne

St-Claude

Col de
la Faucille
Vesancy

Divonne-les-Bains

Mijoux

Gex

Bienne

Coligny
Salavre
Verjon
Mont Myon
Pouillat
Pressiat
Germagnat
Cuisiat

St-Julien

Dortan

Lélex

Crozet

Ferney-Voltaire

Treffort-Cuisiat
Meillonnas
Chavannes-sur-Suran
Corveissiat

Belleydoux

Oyonnax

Chézery-Forens

GENEVA

Bourg-en-Bresse
Drom
Jasseron
Cize
Ramasse
Ceyzériat
Bohas
Journans
Tossiat

Izernore
Bolozon
Serrières-sur-Ain

Lac Genin
Echallon

Challex

Brou

Nantua

Charix

Valserine

Farges

St-Julien-en-G

Pont des
Pierres

Collonges

Pertes de la Valserine

Lancrans

St-Martin-du-Mont
Poncin
Labalme
Cerdon
Neuville-sur-Ain

Bellegarde-sur-Valserine

Défilé de l'Ecluse

Mt Salève

Pont-d'Ain
AIN
Jujurieux

Plateau
de Retord

CERN

Rhône

Le Grand
Abergement
Brénod
Ruffieu
Le Petit
Abergement
Hotonnes
Chanay

Chaumont

Cruseilles

Ambronay
Mt Luisandre
Lacoux
Oncieu
Evosges
St-Rambert-en-Bugey
Hauteville-Lompnes
Songieu
Sothonod
Brénaz
Lochieu

Corbonod
Droisy
Seyssel

Frangy

HAUTE

Aviernoz

Villaz

SAVOIE

Annecy

Amberieu-en-Bugey

Bugey

Lagnieu
St-Sorlin-en-Bugey
Calvaire de Portes

Champagne-en-Valromey
Artemare

Grand
Colombier

Château de
Montrottier

Naves-Parmelan

Veyrier-du-Lac

Sévrier
Menthon

To Lyon

Rhône

Grottes de
la Balme
Montalieu-Vercieu
Serrières-de-Briord
Hières-sur-Amby
Briord

Ceyzérieu
Vongnes
Flaxieu
Contrevoz
Pollieu
Magnieu

Culoz

Chapaz
Châtillon

Rumilly

Talloites
St-Jorioz
Duingt
Lac d'Annecy

Leschaux

Parc
Archéologique
de Larina
Annoisin-Chatelans
Crémieu

Lhuis
Belley
Conzieu
Groslée

Cressin-Rochefort
Ontex
Lucey
Jongieux

Hautecombe

Lac du Bourget

Lescheraines

Brangues

Peyrieu

Morestel
Les Avenières

Izieu
Brégnier-Cordon

Aix-les-Bains

10 km
5 miles

p.180

To Lyon

St-Chef

Walibi

Corbelin

St-Genix-sur-Guiers

La Bâtie-Montgascon
Aoste

Bourgoin-
Jallieu

La Tour-
du-Pin

ISÈRE

Avressieux

A43/E70

p.206

p.256

ENGLAND

English Channel

BELGIUM

GERMANY

LUX.

SWITZ.

ITALY

SPAIN

This splendid if little-known section of the Rhône stretches from the gently rolling lands east beyond Lyon airport, via the Bugey and Gex, spectacular southern spines of the Jura range, to the doorstep of Geneva to the northeast. Along with the Bresse, this batch of territories stretching from the Saône to the border with the feisty Swiss enclave came firmly under the French royal thumb when King Henri IV put down the troublesome expansionist Duke Charles-Emmanuel I of Savoie in 1601.

We stay mainly north of the Rhône in this chapter, although we start with l'Isle Crémieu just to the south. This is not an island, as its name might have you believe, but a limestone plateau that forms a triangle of land jutting out into the river.

There follow delightful asides a little to the north. The restful ridges of the Revermont, outer lines of the Jura range, end with dreamy views down on the Bresse. We also cover a stretch of the river Ain, almost as spectacularly dammed as the Rhône.

Then comes the Bugey, a big, barbed arrowhead of territory pointing south into the Rhône. Although difficult to penetrate, this is a fabulous mountainous land. It extends roughly from the A40 motorway between Ambronay and Bellegarde in the north to its sharp point below Izieu in the south, and offers an unspoilt, natural rollercoaster ride up across flower-filled, panoramic plateaus, down along straight dark diagonal gorges known as *cluses*.

In the east you bump into the exceptionally broad-shouldered Grand Colombier, the Bugey's most impressive bodybuilder of a mountain. Way below its muscular frame lie the most beautiful flat marshes and enchanting vine-covered slopes. This convivial countryside produced the most famous French writer on good living, Brillat-Savarin, from the cathedral town of Belley. But the Bugey's history is by no means all joyous, Nantua and Izieu retelling Second World War tragedies. However, with the major damming of the Rhône after the war, lovely little ports and watersports centres have been created along the now calm river.

Finally, we head over to the Gex above Bellegarde. In these parts bordering on the Franche-Comté region, where the bulk of the French Jura mountains rise, the similarities with that old province become clear in the architecture, especially the characteristic church towers topped by little domes resembling military hats, as well as in the Comté cheese-making and the pine-forested, wood-working surrounds.

The Gex's horn of territory forms part of the wider Parc Naturel Régional du Haut-Jura. This rises up the long wooded flank of the highest of all the French Jura ridges, known as the Monts Jura. The Valserine valley to the west seems lost in time, continuing the old Comtois traditions, but the great curving slope to the east has been transformed by its proximity to Geneva, peering over the city

## Getting to and around the Isle Crémieu, Bugey and Gex

**By air**: Lyon airport lies just west of the Isle Crémieu, Geneva airport just east of the Pays de Gex.

**By train**: The closest train station for L'Isle Crémieu is Bourgoin-Jallieu, reached from Lyon. Culoz and Bellegarde are on the fast line from Paris to Geneva.

**By bus**: For detailed bus information in the Isle Crémieu, consult *www.transisere.fr*; for the Bugey, Valserine and Gex, see *www.ain.fr*.

to Lac Léman. Political stirrer Voltaire sought refuge from the angered French monarchy in this frontier territory at the end of the Ancien Régime; now it is home to one of the earliest successful European co-operative ventures in science and technology, CERN.

# L'Isle Crémieu

⭐ **Crémieu**

Start a tour of the Isle Crémieu with the old fortified town of **Crémieu** itself, at the entrance to the plateau east of Lyon-St-Exupéry. Once a feisty defensive outpost, this gorgeous little historic town now makes a delightful first or last stop if using that airport, or a great place to pause if you're skirting east round the big city. The remnants of the medieval **Château Délphinal** look down from one hill, the ruins of an impressively guarded Benedictine **priory** from another; from the latter, you get plunging views down on the town, and wide vistas out west.

Massive ramparts protect the old town on the flat, entered via huge medieval gateways to rival those of any Italian city state. The clever church builders adapted one defensive rampart tower to serve as the base for a soaring spire. Beside the **church**, enjoy a tranquil moment in the gorgeous restored cloisters next to very prettily renovated Place de la Nation, with its café terraces. Wandering along the grid of streets for a little appetizer of the Renaissance mansions that make up Vieux Lyon, you'll also encounter interesting craft boutiques. In the heart of town, attention centres on the splendid covered market, many simple restaurants looking on to it, the odd one even making the most of the shade under the great timberframe structure to protect diners from the elements. The local limestone provided blocks for building, but also thin slices for its roofing, in what is called *lauze*. A short way northeast, at **Annoisin-Chatelans**, you can admire the effects of the local *lauze* in the houses, and discover more about the techniques of preparing this stone at the **Musée de la Lauze**.

**Musée de la Lauze**
*t 04 74 83 11 28; open late Jan–Dec Wed–Mon 9–5; closed Tues; adm*

To the north, the **Plateau de Larina** provided an important look-out post above the Rhône down the civilizations. Archaeological traces have been unearthed, ranging from Neolithic huts and a Roman temple to Carolingian remains. The **archaeological site** is free; the **historical trail** here is explained more fully at the

**Maison du Patrimoine de Hières-sur-Amby**
t 04 74 95 19 10, www.
mairie-hieres-sur-amby.
com; open Mar–Oct
daily 2–6; Nov–Feb
Mon–Fri 2–5; adm

**Grottes de la Balme**
t 04 74 90 63 76, www.
grotteslabalme.com;
open May–Aug daily
10–6; Sept daily 10–12
and 2–6; Feb–April and
Oct–mid-Dec Sat and
Sun 2–6; closed mid-
Dec–Jan; adm

**Lac de la Vallée Bleue**
open July–Aug daily;
May–June and Sept Sat,
Sun and public hols

**Le Moulin de l'Arche**
t 04 74 88 61 61;
generally only open
summer Fri–Sun; adm

**Maison du Patrimoine de Hières-sur-Amby.** Today, however, the area around here is marked by the nuclear power station across the Rhône at **St-Vulbas**.

Well hidden from this are the spectacular **Grottes de la Balme**. A chapel was fitted into the huge gaping mouth at the entrance to these extraordinary caves. The tour takes you into vast caverns, past beautiful pools, and through tight labyrinths. King François I admired these caves on a visit in the 16th century, an event recalled by a well-preserved wall painting, while the shenanigans of Louis Mandrin, the notorious 18th-century smuggler on the borders of Savoie, now provide entertaining anecdotes, although some of the modern lighting effects get a bit carried away.

Turning L'Isle Crémieu's northern point, you come to the glorious little village of **Vertrieu**. Although it's quiet today, its lords clearly cared a great deal about guarding this strategic Rhône-side spot. The **keep** in black stone on the hillside recalls the medieval masters here. A stunning Ancien Régime **château** (*private*) was then placed down beside the river, its Jura-style roofs making a lovely picture, the Bugey mountains rising the other side of the broad river. Local anglers find tranquil places to fish in this enchanting setting.

Things get more lively just south. White-water rafting is possible on the Rhône from the **Isle Serre** by **Sault-Brénaz**. As to the Rhône's **Lac de la Vallée Bleue** at **Montalieu**, it has grown into an extensive watersports centre very popular with the Lyonnais. There are rows of speed- and sail-boats here, and jet-skiing is a major speciality, but there are also all manner of other entertainments on offer, such as trips in amphibious vehicles. The heated pool, boutiques and basic restaurants add to the buzz of city people at play. Unfortunately, the beauty of the natural scenery is rather spoilt by a huge cement works to one side.

You just have to head away from the river to find yourself back amidst the Isle Crémieu's rural charms. Seek out the picturesque old-fashioned flour mill, **Le Moulin de l'Arche**, still grinding flour, and making bread the old-fashioned way.

Continuing along the Rhône's west bank, past the disused Creys nuclear power station, the quietly attractive ridge village of **Brangues** witnessed one of France's most notorious 19th-century crimes of passion. During a church service in 1827, Antoine Berthet, a local trainee priest consumed with love and jealousy, tried to shoot dead Madame Michoud de la Tour, the local bigwig's wife. Stendhal (*see p.293*) twisted the tale into *Le Rouge et le Noir* (*Scarlet and Black*), one of the most powerful of all French novels, cruelly exposing the shock of a young man's loss of innocence.

Stendhal was loathed by one of France's most famous 20th-century writers, pious Catholic playwright and poet Paul Claudel, who settled at Brangues castle and was buried here in 1955. These

**Espace d'Exposition Claudel et Stendhal**

*t 04 74 80 32 14; open July–Aug Wed–Mon 10–12 and 3–7; May–June Sat, Sun and public hols 10–12 and 3–7; April and Sept–Nov Sun 2–6; adm*

⭐ **Morestel**

**Maison du Pays des Couleurs**

*t 04 74 80 39 30; open early Feb–mid-Dec Tues–Fri 10–12 and 2.30–5.30, Sun 2.30–5.30*

**Maison Ravier**

*t 04 74 80 06 80, www.maisonravier.com; open Mar–Oct Wed–Mon 2.30–6.30; closed Tues; adm*

**Carmin gallery**

*t 06 14 56 04 13, www.carmin-gallery.eu*

**St-Chef abbey church and Musée Maison du Patrimoine**

*t 04 74 92 59 92; open July–Aug daily 10–12 and 2.30–6.30; April–June and Sept–Oct daily 2.30–6.30; adm*

**Parc Walibi**

*t 04 74 33 71 80, www. sixflagseurope.com; open July–Aug daily 10–9; June daily 10–5; May and Sept–Oct Sat, Sun and public hols 10–5; adm*

strongly contrasting literary figures are recalled in the **Espace d'Exposition Claudel et Stendhal**. Following the terrible incident in the church, it was rebuilt, and given the distinctive Franche-Comté-style tower that now stands out.

The extremely pretty little historic centre of **Morestel** has long attracted painters. It has continued to encourage the tradition in recent times, and now proudly declares itself a *Cité des Peintres*. It is also rather proud of its four-star award for the flower displays liberally strewn around town. The historic quarter stands perched on a rock above the N75. The traffic on this busy road passes right by a pretty, long-legged timber-frame *séchoir*, a typical old building for drying tobacco – in times past, L'Isle Crémieu was a big tobacco-producing area and a few farmers still cultivate the crop. Beside the *séchoir*, the **Maison du Pays des Couleurs** fills visitors in on the area's varied cultural aspects, holding three exhibitions a year.

Climb past the **Picture'Halles** contemporary art gallery into the streets of the upper town and you soon get away from the traffic. The beautiful Gothic **church** offers one peaceful, interesting stop. In the 19th century, landscape painters led by Auguste Ravier were attracted to Morestel; his spacious, beautifully located town house, the **Maison Ravier**, pays homage to him, showing some of his atmospherically charged landscapes, while a whole separate floor is dedicated to contemporary artists and temporary exhibitions, that in 2007 featured a dozen or more Turner pieces, showing how the great English artist inspired Ravier. Still on an artistic note, the painter Carola Minssieux, a specialist in poppy paintings who runs the **Carmin gallery** in town, also organizes afternoons where she takes people out to paint in the locations that inspired Ravier. Continue up to the prettily restored medieval **keep** crowning the old town, where more artists are given a space to display their works in season; here is the best viewing platform in Morestel, looking east across the Rhône as far as the Mont du Chat, its sharp tooth signalling the Lac du Bourget beyond (*see* p.272).

Discover major medieval art works at the **abbey church** dominating quiet **St-Chef**, a village west of Morestel. The building may look plain on the outside, but one of its chapels conceals one of the most splendid, colourful displays of religious wall paintings in the Rhône-Alpes, dating back to the 12th century. The most arresting images depict scenes from the fiery Apocalypse. You can gain admission via the **Musée Maison du Patrimoine**, which also covers the history of the abbey more generally.

Back towards the Rhône, the **Parc Walibi** amusement park attracts families from far and wide with all manner of funfair rides behind its palisaded park at Les Avenières. By complete contrast, at **La Bâtie-Montgascon** there is a museum that focuses on traditional working-class weaving, offering good demonstrations;

## Market Days in L'Isle Crémieu

Crémieu: Wed.
Morestel: Sun.

## Where to Stay and Eat in L'Isle Crémieu

### Crémieu ✉ 38460

**Le Castor Gourmand**, Rue Porchaire, t 04 74 90 02 49 (€). There are lots of simple eateries around the splendid covered market, but seek out this restaurant not far away for more exciting cuisine. *Closed late April–early May.*

**La Bicyclette Fleurie B&B**, Moirieu, t 04 74 90 06 55, *la-bicyclette-fleurie@club.fr* (€). In a hamlet immediately west of Crémieu, a cheerful and cheap place to stay.

**Soleil et Cacao B&B**, St-Julien, Siccieu, t 04 74 83 68 01, *www.soleiletcacao.fr* (€). A renovated farmhouse a few kilometres east of Crémieu, on the slope above the hamlet of St-Julien, facing its splendid château, with simple, nicely renovated rooms. *Table d'hôte* (€€).

### Bouvesse-Quirieu ✉ 38390

**Moulin d'Arche**, t 04 74 88 61 61 (€€). Beside the 16th-century mill known for its organic bread, a simple restaurant with a copious country menu on summer weekends. *Open Fri eve–Sun eve; closed late Sept–mid-May.*

### Morestel ✉ 38510

**\*\*\*Hotel de France**, 319 Grande Rue, t 04 74 80 04 77, *www.hoteldefrance-morestel.com* (€). Pre-Revolution roadside inn rejuvenated just a tad, with traditional restaurant serving tasty Savoie-inspired cuisine (€€). *Restaurant closed Sun eve and Mon.*

**Les Franciscaines B&B**, 205 Rue Ravier, t 04 74 80 56 82, *soeurs-francis@wanadoo.fr* (€). A rare chance to stay in a nunnery, in a lovely building beside the church. Rooms are plain and pleasant, with fabulous views, although the road below can be noisy.

### Vignieu ✉ 38890

**\*\*\*Château de Chapeau Cornu**, t 04 74 27 79 00, *www.chateau-chapeau-cornu.fr* (€€€–€€). A magical little many-towered medieval castle with a range of smart rooms. Vaulted restaurant (€€€). Pool beside which barbecues (€) are served on summer weekends.

---

**ⓘ Morestel >>**
*100 Place des Halles, 38510 Morestel, t 04 74 80 19 59, www.morestel.com*

**ⓘ Crémieu >**
*5 Place de la Nation, 38460 Crémieu, t 04 74 90 45 13, www.ville-cremieu.fr*

**★ Château de Chapeau Cornu >>**

---

**Musée du Tisserand Dauphinois**
*t 04 74 83 08 99, www.batie-montgascon.com; open May–Oct Wed–Sun 2–6; adm*

**Musée Gallo-Romain**
*t 04 76 32 58 27, www.musee-archeologique-aoste.com; open Jan–Nov Mon and Wed–Fri 10–12 and 2–6, Sat and Sun 2–6; adm*

a section of this **Musée du Tisserand Dauphinois** is also devoted to bicycle history.

Head a little way south, and back in time. **St-Didier** has a very pretty medieval church. **Aoste** takes you back to the Roman era with its very neat, attractive **Musée Gallo-Romain**. The area's cooking pots apparently became known across the Roman Empire. To the east lies the Guiers river (*see* p.282), frontier between France and Savoie until the latter joined France in 1860. For the Avant-Pays Savoyard immediately to the east, *see* Chapter 15.

# The Revermont, Ain and Northern Bugey

Before exploring the heart of the Bugey, in this section we cover the areas to the northwest of it, in a triangle of land between Ambérieu-en-Bugey, Coligny and Nantua, roughly bound by the A39 and A40 motorways. Here, you're exploring the southwestern corner of the Jura range.

14

The Rhône from Lyon to Lac Léman | The Revermont, Ain and Northern Bugey

## The Revermont

The Revermont forms the dreamy backdrop to the Bresse (*see* Chapter 08) to the west and offers a gentle introduction to the mountainous Jura terrain to the east. There's a wonderful hiking trail, the GR59, along the Revermont heights. To appreciate the stone villages resting sleepily along the Revermont's western slope, join the D52 above Pont-d'Ain; this road forms the dividing line between the flat *poulet de Bresse* plain and the green, wooded, vertical world that leads to Lac Léman (Lake Geneva).

The well-exposed ridge was wine-producing territory in times past, although only Pétillant de Gravelles, a perfumed sparkling wine, is now made. Religion still marks the way. **St-Martin-du-Mont**'s church was built for a venerated 16th-century *Pietà*. A 16th-century cross stands before the Gothic church at **Tossiat**, which contains remnants of murals. At **Journans**, a gilded St Vincent, patron saint of wine-makers, counts among the church treasures. **Ceyzériat**'s steeple draws attention with its twisted spire; inside the church boasts 15th-century stained glass. **Jasseron**'s church conceals carved delights from various epochs.

Since the Ancien Régime, **Meillonnas** has retained its reputation for pottery, with *ateliers* signalled around the neatly kept village, whose very street signs are made in ceramics. Flowers feature among the motifs on the traditional ware, and the lanes are well provided with real blooms. Having served as the main centre of production in the 18th century, the castle may one day be devoted to Meillonnas pottery again, with plans for a new museum.

A stylish dome stands out on **Treffort**'s hillock, the odd fountain splashing along this village's steep streets, the houses provided with handy wine cellars. The Gothic church retains wooden stalls representing the life of regional monastic hero St Bruno (*see* p.290), works rescued from the charterhouse of **Sélignat** further east. Just one or two vestiges of a medieval castle stand out to one side.

At cute **Cuisiat** the old school has been turned into the charming **Musée du Revermont**, which recalls the area's vanished wine-making traditions, as well as local pottery. The sweet gardens put forgotten fruit and veg to the fore.

You then reach the tallest, pyramidal tops of the Revermont slopes, their highest point, at 768m, along **Mont Nivigne**. As for **Mont Myon**, it's a favourite spot for hang-gliding; French champion Jean-Marc Caron often displays his skills here. A *sentier mémorial*, a steep track lined with contemporary sculptures, leads walkers down to **Pressiat**, a village partially destroyed by German soldiers towards the close of the war, although the Gothic church survived with its 15th-century murals. Beyond **Verjon**, a village with a pretty bridge, and **Salavre**, tucked in its valley, **Vergongeat**'s hosts of daffodils draw crowds in March.

**Musée du Revermont**
*t 04 74 51 32 42; open early April–Oct Sun and public hols 10–6, Mon and Thurs–Sat 2–6; adm*

**Coligny** brings you back to the busy modern world, although a gorgeous Roman statue of Apollo and a Gaulish calendar count among treasures unearthed here, with copies on show in the *mairie* of this once lordly town on the Franche-Comté border.

Over the first Revermont ridge, the D42 and D59 follow the route of the Suran, the river flowing through the midst of the range. You might join the valley at **Pouillat**, with its isolated Gothic church. On the other side, **Germagnat** in its delightful location has a medieval church containing a gilded Baroque altarpiece. Press further up for the castle ruins. **Chavannes-sur-Suran**'s church protects Ancien Régime works rescued from the nearby **Chartreuse de Sélignat**, reoccupied by monks since the 1920s, and onto which you can get a fabulous view by climbing a track between Arnans and Corveissiat. Vestiges of castles line the routes south, the ruins of the **Château de Bohas** the result of German destruction in 1944. Also seek out the dramatic silhouette of the **Donjon de Buenc** and the vestiges of the **Château de Beaurepaire**. The Suran then joins the Ain.

## The Middle Ain Valley

Compared with the tranquil Revermont, the Ain valley has been much more visibly marked by human intervention, with not just factories to the south, but also a large number of dams further north. The wooded banks and unnaturally bright waters of the middle section we cover here provide a pleasing riverside journey.

Starting with **Pont-d'Ain**, this strategic river crossing stands in a corner where Bresse, Dombes and Bugey meet. The remnants of the castle recall that Louise de Savoie, mother of one of France's most ambitious kings, François I, came into the world here, though the 19th-century hillside church now draws more attention.

The beautiful form of **Ambronay**'s hillside **abbey** beckons seductively across the wide expanse of the Ain valley in these parts. This very well-located monastery was founded in 800 for Barnard, a former officer to Emperor Charlemagne. Just a few signs remain of the Carolingian building, but the church and cloisters are largely in uplifting Gothic style. One doorway is graced by an engrossing Resurrection scene. The cool Gothic interior contains tender period murals and stained glass, soberly carved wooden stalls and a remarkable stone *Pietà*, Christ rigid in death on the knees of his shocked mother. A door leads into the beautiful Gothic cloisters. An important **cultural centre** has been set up here, and the abbey hosts a prestigious programme of Baroque music concerts.

Imposing châteaux line up along the wooded slope at **Jujurieux**, also dramatically visible from far across the Ain valley. This place long lived from silk-making, a large factory still standing out in the centre, built from the 1830s for Claude Bonnet, a local who became one of Lyon's biggest silk merchants. The company's working girls led a cloistered life here up to the Second World War. The factory specialized in high-quality work for leading fashion houses until around the year 2000; it has now been turned into a **silk museum**

West back by the Ain, arcaded **Poncin** has kept something of a medieval fortified air. At **Neuville-sur-Ain** with its sturdy stone bridge, the picturesque riverside houses offer one reason to stop, and the old oil mill still at work another. Heading up the Ain, the Allement dam has helped create a river lake with water sports by **Merpuis**. Climb east to the **Col de Berthiand** for dramatic views.

**Jujurieux silk museum**
*t 04 74 37 23 14;
open mid-June–mid-
Sept Mon and
Wed–Fri 10–12.30 and
2.30–6, Sat and Sun
2.30–6; adm*

Continuing up the Ain's meanders, between **Bolozon** and **Cize**, marvel at the bold late 19th-century double **viaduct** crossing the waters on huge arches. Restored after its destruction in 1944, the lower level serves for cars, the upper one for trains. The *corniche* road along the west bank of the river provides the more dramatic route to the border with Franche-Comté. For the best view of the medieval **Château de Conflans** marking the regional frontier, carry on up to **St-Maurice-d'Echazeaux**.

The **Oignin valley** parallel to the Ain conceals the odd surprise, such as small fragments of a Roman temple at **Izernore**, but the heavily industrial **Ange valley** and area around **Oyonnax** has long been nicknamed Plastics Valley after traditional craft-making skills (especially of elaborate comb-making in wood and horn) were superseded. However, the well-groomed **Musée du Peigne et de la Plasturgie**covers the history of the comb and of plastics in a surprisingly attractive manner. During the Second World War, the feisty town of Oyonnax famously witnessed an extraordinarily defiant march by Resistance members on 11 November 1943, paying their respects to the Allied dead of the First World War.

**Musée du Peigne et de la Plasturgie**
*open July–Sept
Mon–Sat 2–6; Feb–June
and Oct–Dec Tues–Sat
2–6; adm*

Nearby, Gothic masons showed off their carving skills in saucy sculptures at the church of **Arbent**. To the north, **Dortan** was destroyed in the Second World War, but it still defends its long-held position as one of the world's major chessboard producers.

In the heights east of Oyonnax, locals appreciate **Lac Genin**, a gem of a round lake. Fishermen love the magical spot, surrounded by woods. People swim across the waters in summer, but ice-skate on them in winter. The Nazis chased Resistance fighters up here during the war. Past **Echallon**, a pyramidal **war monument** lost in the prairies recalls Allied parachute drops to the Resistance groups.

## The Northern Bugey

Steep vineyards crop up most surprisingly in unlikely corners of the mountainous eastern half of the Rhône-Alpes region, but perhaps nowhere more dramatically than around the sprawling village of **Cerdon**, set at the bottom of a deep bowl of land sur-rounded by limestone-topped heights a short way east of Poncin on the Ain. The vineyards seem to be trying desperately to climb up and out over the rim. Far below, in the tight village streets, as well as sampling the extraordinarily perfumed local wines, visit the **Cuivrerie**, an old copper-making factory still using old machinery to produce vats, cups, medals and the like. The church perched above the village has a cemetery happily surrounded by vines, while a solid white Virgin oversees proceedings from an even higher rock; every evening, two villagers walk up to light her with candles.

**Cerdon Cuivrerie**
*t 04 74 39 96 44;*
*shop open daily all year;*
*guided tours May–Sept*
*am and pm; Oct–April*
*pm only, and depending*
*on sufficient numbers;*
*adm*

Along the high main N84 road east, the **Monument aux Morts du Val d'Enfer**, with its naked-breasted female figure flying from the stone, recalls the Resistance fighters from the Ain and Bugey who died in the Second World War. Further along, at the **Grotte de Labalme**, visitors can take a train into a series of caves with weirdly shaped geological formations, where local cheesemakers used to age their *fromages*.

**Grotte de Labalme**
*t 04 74 37 36 79;*
*open July–Aug daily*
*10–6; Easter–June and*
*Sept–Oct Sat and*
*Sun; adm*

The main road continues on to the shockingly bright **Lac de Nantua**, created at the end of the last Ice Age. Although the busy road limits possibilities for stopping on the northern side of the lake, overseen by its sheer limestone cliffs, the open eastern end offers plenty of opportunities for swimming and messing around in boats, or even for setting off sailing or windsurfing. However, wandering round to the lake's southeast corner, you can't miss a chilling, large **war memorial**. In revenge for strong local Resistance activity, and as the Germans couldn't manage to unearth the Maquisards, they rounded up many of the menfolk of Nantua between 18 and 40 years of age and sent them to concentration camps. Some 1,000 were deported; over 600 never returned.

Bereft of many of its old shops, the old town of **Nantua** looks rather grey and depressed today, but the former prison has been turned into an interesting if harrowing war museum, the **Musée de l'Histoire de la Résistance et de la Déportation**. The cells have been put to very effective use: in them, you learn about stories of Second World War martyrdom in the Ain and Haut-Jura. Many successful operations are also charted, including the help given by the Allies – the first American DC3 Dakota to land in France did so around here. Among the most extraordinary objects on display is a wedding dress made from material recovered from parachutes used in the Allied drops.

**Musée de l'Histoire de la Résistance et de la Déportation**
*t 04 74 75 07 50;*
*open May–Sept*
*Tues–Sun 9–1 and*
*2–6; adm*

Nantua originally grew up around an abbey founded in the Dark Ages by Amand, said to have converted the henchmen sent to assassinate him into the new monastery's first monks. The atmospheric medieval church of **St Michael** had most of the Romanesque decorations round the doorway hammered off in later violence, but the *Last Supper*'s table remains set. In the Gothic interior, the pillars curve disconcertingly under the pressure. The striking painting by Delacroix depicts an alarmingly foreshortened *St Sebastian*, a strangely beautiful symbol of martyrdom.

ⓘ **Pont-d'Ain**
*Carrefour des 4 Vents,
01160 Pont d'Ain,
t 04 74 39 05 84*

ⓘ **Cerdon**
*Place Allombert, 01450
Cerdon, t 04 74 39
93 02, perso@
wanadoo.fr/si.cerdon*

ⓘ **Nantua**
*Place de la Déportation,
01130 Nantua,
t 04 74 75 00 05,
www.ville-nantua.com*

## Market Days in the Revermont, Ain and Northern Bugey

**Treffort-Cuisiat:** Fri.
**Jujurieux:** Tues.
**Pont-d'Ain:** Sat.
**Cerdon:** Fri.
**Nantua:** Sat.

## Events in the Revermont, Ain and Northern Bugey

The programme of **Baroque concerts** at Ambronay runs mid-Sept–mid-Oct, t 04 74 38 74 00, *www.ambronay.org*.

## Activities in the Revermont, Ain and Northern Bugey

**Rev'airMont Parapente,** t 04 74 51 58 67, *www.revairmont-parapente.com*. For **paragliding** on Mont Myon.

## Where to Stay and Eat in the Revermont, Ain and Northern Bugey

**Jasseron** ✉ 01250
**Auberge de la Terrasse,** t 04 74 25 05 77 (€€). Unpretentious lively village inn, local cuisine nicely done. *Closed Sun eve and Mon, plus 2nd half Aug and most of Jan.*

**Meillonnas** ✉ 01370
**Auberge au Vieux Meillonnas,** t 04 74 51 34 46 (€€). Stone and cobs and *soigné* cuisine. *Closed Tues eve and Wed.*

**Charrix** ✉ 01130
**Auberge du Lac Genin,** t 04 74 75 52 50, *http://lacgenin.free.fr* (€). A well-positioned lakeside inn beside a campsite. Built after the war by a local family whose farm had been torched by the Germans, the place has just a few, beautifully modernized rooms. Simple hearty cooking and barbecues are served in the restaurant (€€–€). *Closed mid-Oct–Nov.*

# The Heart of the Bugey

Now we strike into the heart of the Bugey, that magnificent mountainous southern arrowhead of the Jura, its edges tipped not with poison, but with wine. The Bugey has a character all of its own, its gorgeous village houses marked by characteristic stepped gables, originally designed to help maintain the reed-thatched roofs that have now vanished. The countryside is inebriating in these parts, and the local wines aren't bad either.

## The Western Edge of the Bugey

The stretch of the Rhône from industrial Lagnieu to country Izieu forms the western edge of the Bugey's arrowhead. **St-Sorlin-en-Bugey** has kept its centuries-old charm, its church visible from afar, crowned by a sharp spire. One house boasts a remarkable old painted front showing the giant St Christopher crossing a river, the child Jesus on his shoulders. Roses cling to the village houses, patches of vines to the slopes beyond. Climb to the **Col des Portes** for a winding route up and over into the central Bugey.

Back down along the Rhône, vineyards beautify the riverbank. At **Serrières-de-Briord**, the **Point Vert lake** overseen by the flanks of the **Molard de Don** provides a big expanse of water for fishing, swimming or boating, catering to the crowds, reflecting the facilities of the **Lac de la Vallée Bleue** on the opposite bank.

Just south, climb the steep mountainside to reach **Montagnieu**, a sweet village known for producing a typical fragrant Bugey sparkling wine from the roussette grape. The views from up here extend far to the west, although they do reveal unsightly patches of industrialization along the Rhône.

**Briord** has a little pleasure port down by the river. South from here, you enter further delightful vineyard territory. The pretty Rhône-side road is marred by the Creys nuclear power station. However, the mid-slope route via **Lhuis** is a joy, old stone huts scattered among the steep vineyards. Signs for wine properties, for example in the village of **Pont-Bancet**, incite you to stop to try the local chardonnay or gamay, but also the rarer mondeuse and manicle, some estates producing really flavoursome mountain wines. Below Pont-Bancet, **Groslée** makes a wonderful picture, with a ruined château standing out to one side of the beautiful village.

The Rhône's banks around **Le Port-en-Groslée** incite people to stop for a walk, a picnic, or a meal at the local inn. Further down, a dramatic waterfall attracts attention beside **Glandieu**. At **Brégnier-Cordon**, the **Maison des Isles du Rhône** focuses on the islands and their flora and fauna at this major river turning point, but is geared towards groups; a new museum should open soon on the subject.

**Maison des Isles du Rhône**
*t 04 79 87 26 62*

The village of **Izieu** looks idyllic at first sight, with its array of traditional gabled houses, set on high, overlooking the southern tip of the Bugey and the mountains beyond. But this place was the setting for a horrific event in the Second World War, recalled in the extremely harrowing **Maison Mémorial**, in a large isolated farm on the hillside. This place became a secret refuge for Jewish children rescued from persecuted families, many from Eastern Europe. But the hideaway was uncovered, and on 6 April 1944 the Gestapo came and took away 44 of them, along with their teachers; 47 would die in Auschwitz; three others would be shot in Estonia; and just one, Léa Feldblum, survived to reveal the horror. Klaus Barbie, the Gestapo head in Lyon, at his trial in 1987 denied that he gave the order for the Izieu raid, but it seems unlikely that he didn't know about it. After the traumatic case, this spot was turned into this exceptionally important museum, with the support of Sabine Zlatin, director of the clandestine school (who was by chance away the day of the tragedy) and that of the local civil servant, Pierre-Marcel Wiltzer, who had found the farm where the children could be hidden in the first place. The beauty of the site just adds to the agony of the story. Seeing the children's happy photos and lovely drawings and letters is absolutely heartrending.

⭐ **Izieu Maison Mémorial**
*t 04 79 87 21 05, www.izieu.alma.fr; open mid-June–mid-Sept daily 10–6.30; Feb–mid-June and mid-Sept–Nov Mon–Fri 9–5, Sat 2–6, Sun 10–6; Dec and Jan Mon–Fri 9–5; adm*

The museum, in a big barn down from the house, confronts the terrible ghosts of France's as well as Germany's anti-Semitic

*14* **The Rhône from Lyon to Lac Léman | The Heart of the Bugey**

wartime past. The anti-Jewish laws of Pétain's Vichy government following the Nazi example are unflinchingly exposed. In all, some 76,000 Jews were deported from France, around a quarter of the country's entire Jewish population in 1939. Around 43,000 were gassed in concentration camps. Just 2,500 survived. The 63,000 French Resistance figures and political objectors deported are also remembered. 37,000 of these returned alive.

## Into the Heart of the Bugey

For sensational paths into the heart of the Bugey, back west you could start from **Ambérieu-en-Bugey**, the remnants of towers around this rail and aviation town indicating how in medieval times it was a major stronghold close to the Dauphiné and Savoie frontier. Up in the hills, the pure medieval defensive forms of the **Château des Allymes** went up for the Dauphiné side, while the Savoyards sat on the height of Mont Luisandre. Les Allymes preserves the memory of the 1601 treaty negotiated by local lord René de Lucinge by which the duke of Savoie gave up his rights to Bresse, Bugey and Gex to the French king.

The N504 road leads along the **Albarine valley**, this section marked by the textile industry. **St-Rambert-en-Bugey** is overseen by further defensive towers; its **Ecomusée des Traditions Bugistes**, however, concentrates on traditional crafts from 1850 to 1940.

The long, tight **Cluse des Hôpitaux** gorge leads directly to Belley, but first tackle the dramatic terrain to the north to discover some of the most enchanting parts of the Bugey. Climb to the village of **Oncieu** for a magnificent little detour, and continue round via **Evosges**. The village of **Lacoux** lies hidden up in its own dramatic, boulder-strewn gorge. It lost its school some time ago, but this has been converted into an energetic **Centre d'Art Contemporain**, regularly shocking visitors with its cutting-edge exhibitions.

Attracting a curious mix of the ultra-sporty and the extremely sickly, **Hauteville-Lompnes** further up the Albarine is appreciated by both for its pure air. The skies are so clear around here that an **observatory** has been set up at the **Col de Lèbe**, encouraging an interest in astronomy among the general public. If your French is up to it, book in advance for a night course here; during the day, you can follow an easier introductory trail.

Try a delightful country loop around the high plateau north from Hauteville to join Ruffieu, going via **Champdor**, with its remarkable Ancien Régime castle, on to **Brénod**, with its cheese-making *fruitière*, then round to the butch sister country villages of **Le Petit Abergement** and **Le Grand Abergement**, their well-built traditional farms marked by distinctive big rounded gates. All this high terrain turns into cross-country skiing territory when it snows. From Le Grand Abergement, roads head north up across the almost wholly

**Château des Allymes**
*t 04 74 38 06 07; open May–Sept daily 10–12 and 2–6; Mar–April and Oct–Nov Wed–Mon 2–6; Dec–Feb Sat and Sun 2–5; adm*

**Ecomusée des Traditions Bugistes**
*t 04 74 36 32 86; open June–Oct Tues–Sat 9–12 and 2–6, Sun 2.30–5.30; Nov–May Tues–Sat 9–12 and 2–5; adm*

**Lacoux Centre d'Art Contemporain**
*t 04 74 35 25 61, www. cac-lacoux.com; check on spring, summer and autumn exhibitions*

**Col de Lèbe Observatory**
*t 04 79 87 67 31, www.astroval.free.fr; open daily 2–6; adm*

houseless **Plateau de Retord**, renowned for its spring daffodils as well as its summer flowers, given attention in a little museum at **Les Plans d'Hotonnes**. To the north, walkers head for the isolated **Chapelle de Retord**, a 19th-century sanctuary on a spot consecrated by the great 17th-century Catholic Reformation figure of Savoie, St François de Sales (*see* pp.33 and 259). It has now gained a certain comical reputation for the annual August ceremony to bless cars. On the eastern edge of the plateau, big views open out to the Alps.

Back with rustic **Ruffieu**, or neighbouring **Hotonnes**, enchanting views southwards will tempt you down into the **Valromey**, the romantic wide valley of the Seran river that cuts through the centre of the Bugey. Famous writers sought inspiration in this rustic paradise in the first half of the 20th century, including the avant-garde American Gertrude Stein. The villages have a wonderful unspoilt feel to this day, their old communal bread ovens still in place, and sometimes even the *travail*, where horses were shoed.

A western route goes via **Ruffieu**, lovingly restored and utterly tranquil. Then potter through the quiet villages around the D31. The church at **Champagne-en-Valromey** conceals the remnants of a beautiful 16th-century triptych. By **Cerveyrieu**, you can admire the waterfall of the Seran before the pleasant stop of **Artemare**.

An eastern route takes you from Hotonnes under the mighty wooded flank of Le Grand Colombier. The **Grotte du Pic** by Songieu was favoured by Neolithic men, while **Songieu** itself served for centuries as medieval capital of the Valromey. It has kept vestiges of its period castle.

The next villages have retained signs of their connection with the **Abbey of Arvières**, founded in the 12th century way up on the wooded heights of Le Grand Colombier, but in ruins; now a **Jardin Ethnobotanique** occupies the site, cultivating plants from the Neolithic to the discovery of the New World. The château at **Sothonod** belonged to the Artaud family, whose St Arthaud created the abbey. **Brénaz**'s church contains an altar rescued from the religious establishment.

**Lochieu**'s church holds relics of St Arthaud. The wider traditions and culture of the Valromey are beautifully presented in its **Musée du Bugey-Valromey**, spread around a fine Renaissance house. As well as the more typical historical displays, one section is devoted to outstanding contemporary woodwork.

Distinctly alarming mountain routes climb up into the dense woods of **Le Grand Colombier** from Lochieu and **Virieu-le-Petit**, not roads for the faint-hearted. The reward for reaching the top of the Bugey's giant is fantastic views over Lac du Bourget to the Alps. Then tremendously precipitous ways twist down to the stretch of the Rhône marking not just the eastern side of the Bugey's arrowhead, but also a historic divide between France and Savoie.

**Jardin Ethnobotanique**
*t 04 79 87 02 06,
www.multimania.com/
arvieres; open
mid-May–mid-Oct
Wed–Sun; adm for tour*

**Musée du Bugey-Valromey**
*t 04 79 87 52 23; open
April–Oct Sun and
public hols 10–6,
Mon and Thurs–Sat
2–6; adm*

## The Eastern Edge of the Bugey

Starting back down at the Bugey's southern tip, enjoy the rural Rhône marina at **Murs-et-Gélignieux**. Heading north, you get wonderful views over to the Avant-Pays Savoyard and the line of mountains concealing the Lac du Bourget. At **Peyrieu**, it was thanks to the generosity of Grace Whitney-Hoff, an American who loved the Bugey, that the village became the first in France to put up a monument to its dead from the First World War, as early as 1919.

The beautiful views across the Rhône valley continue unabated to the Bugey's main town, **Belley**. Centrepiece of this little capital, the Gothic **cathedral** has an impressive chancel almost as long as the nave. The latter was redone in the 19th century, when a grand organ was also added. The extravagant decoration inside includes double rows of stained glass in the choir, plus side chapels draped with fake cloth, and an ornate reliquary contains remnants of the city's important 12th-century bishop, Anthelme.

Belley's elegant curving main street with its substantial houses was the address of Brillat-Savarin, Belley's most famous son and its one-time mayor, a peculiarly French concoction, a figure who represented the region's Third Estate at the 1789 Revolution, but who also wrote the Bible on French good living, *La Physiologie du goût* (1826), a philosophical culinary classic. Press west of Belley for a glimpse of good country living, and to explore more of the typical villages like **Conzieu**, with its medieval church and its lakes. East of Belley, below **Magnieu**, lies the river stop serving the town.

Continuing north along the Rhône, beside **Cressin-Rochefort**, its old houses sitting below a medieval castle, a large artificial lake offers all manner of water sports by the canal running parallel to the Rhône. Nearby, the quite wild **Lac de Barterand** has a strip of beach, and the surprise of a giant sculpted figure of Gargantua.

⭐ **Bugey villages**

Then a gorgeous string of **villages** basks along the wine route of the eastern Bugey below the magnificent Grand Colombier. Start out with such delightful places as **Flaxieu** and **Pollieu**, but don't miss **Vongnes**, whose reds not only employ gamay and pinot noir, but also the rarer manicle and mondeuse. The place has a jolly wine museum, the **Caveau Bugiste**, part of a wine property. The

**Caveau Bugiste**

*t 04 79 87 92 32; open daily 9–12 and 2–7; free*

family that manages this place maintains some 40 hectares of vines, but also buys in grapes from smaller holdings, producing around 400,000 bottles a year. They are very generous with their tastings, but try to keep some room to follow a *dégustation* or two in other properties. Virtually all the villages around here have kept their traditional features, for example **Avrissieu** and **Ceyzerieu**.

Below the Grand Colombier's southern flank you come upon a magical flat marsh, the **Marais de Lavours**, created around the Séran's confluence with the Rhône, now a protected nature reserve. Take a splendid lesson on the marsh habitat by making for the unspoilt village of **Aignoz**, its lovely houses provided with intricately divided barn doors. There you'll find the wonderful **Maison du Marais de Lavours**, revealing the frog-eat-frog world of this beautiful marsh in most engaging style. There are lashings of gory film footage to grip even the surliest adolescent, for example. Then go walking into the marsh on what is billed as the longest boardwalk on stilts in Europe, 2.4km in length.

Above the marsh, **Culoz** keeps its feet dry clinging to the Grand Colombier's lower slopes. A road then slips under the mountain's eastern flank. Closely overseen by vast walls of mountains on both sides of the Rhône, the riverside town of **Seyssel** was an important port for Rhône mariners down the centuries. In truth, despite sharing the same name, there are two distinct settlements (*see also* p.267), one each side of the river, each provided with its own church and other social amenities. On the Bugey side, modern artists put on regular shows at the **Ateliers de la Poudrière**.

Seyssel is well known for its wines. Although the AOC vineyards only cover some 90 hectares, they do embellish both banks. Stay on the Bugey side to find wine estates to visit. The results can taste delicious, the whites tinged with sweet flavours of apples, goose-berries and lychees. Seek them out around enchanting villages like **Corbonod** or **Chanay**. Continuing via such idyllic rustic spots as **Lhôpital**, you can see as far as the straits between tall tops where the Rhône emerges beyond Geneva and Lac Léman.

## Sidebar (left column)

**Maison du Marais de Lavours**
t 04 79 87 90 39; open June–Aug daily 10–7; April–May and Sept 2–6.30; Feb–Mar and Oct–Nov Sat and Sun 2–6; adm

ⓘ **Ambérieu-en-Bugey**
Place Robert Marcelpoil, 01500 Ambérieu-en-Bugey, t 04 74 38 18 17, www.ville-amberieuenbugey.fr

ⓘ **St-Rambert-en-Bugey**
7 Av de l'Europe, 01230 St-Rambert-en-Bugey, t 04 74 36 32 86, www.tourisme-albarine.com

ⓘ **Hauteville-Lompnes**
15 Rue Nationale, 01110 Hauteveille-Lompnes, t 04 74 35 39 73, www.plateau-hauteville.com

ⓘ **Champagne-en-Valromey**
Maison de Pays, 01260 Champagne-en-Valromey, t 04 79 87 51 04, www.valromeyretord.com

## Market Days in the Heart of the Bugey

**Lagnieu:** Mon.
**Ambérieu-en-Bugey:** Wed, Fri and Sat.
**St-Rambert-en-Bugey:** Thurs.
**Hauteville-Lompnes:** Thurs and Sat.
**Champagne-en-Valromey:** Thurs.
**Culoz:** Wed.
**Belley:** Sat.
**Seyssel:** Sat.

## Where to Stay and Eat in the Heart of the Bugey

### Les Granges-de-Montagnieu ✉ 01470

**\*\*Hôtel Rolland, t 04 74 36 73 45 (€).** Down below Montagnieu's vine slopes, this roadside village inn looks plain on the outside, but the rooms have been beautifully designed with the aid of a local furniture-making company. Rabelaisian portions are served at the merry country restaurant (€€–€). *Closed mid-Sept–early Oct; restaurant closed Fri eve and Sun eve.*

### Port-de-Groslée ✉ 01680

**Chez Penelle, t 04 74 39 71 01 (€€).** Rhône-side restaurant in a traditional building with terrace beside the water, specializing in local dishes, including frogs' legs, and Bugey wines.

### Ruffieu ✉ 01260

**Le Relais St-Didier, t 04 79 87 71 60,** relaisstdidier@wanadoo.fr (€€–€). Cute village inn for fresh cuisine. *Closed Sun pm, most of Jan, plus late Nov.*

### Châtillon-en-Michaille ✉ 01200

**\*Auberge Le Catray, Plateau de Retord t 04 50 56 56 25 (€).** A breathtaking location, on the edge of the high plateau west of Bellegarde. Basic rooms. Lovely terrace for dining (€€) on mountain products or more elaborate cuisine. *Closed 2wks Sept and 2wks Nov; restaurant closed Mon and Tues.*

(★) **Auberge de Contrevoz** >

(★) **Le Pressoir et la Forge** >>

(i) **Belley**
*34 Grande Rue, 01300 Belley, t 04 79 81 29 06, ot_belley@club-internet.fr*

(i) **Seyssel** >>
*2 Chemin de la Fontaine, 74910 Seyssel, t 04 50 59 26 56, www.usses-et-bornes74.com*

(★) **La Métairie Davis** >

**Contrevoz** ✉ 01300
**Auberge de Contrevoz** La Plumardière, t 04 79 81 82 54 (€€). Delightful, stylish country restaurant with terrace, 8km northwest of Belley on the D32. *Closed Sun eve, Mon and Thurs, Xmas–Jan.*

**Artemare** ✉ 01510
**\*\*Hôtel Michallet**, Rue de la Poste, t 04 79 87 39 33 (€). Friendly country town hotel with spacious rooms. Restaurant (€€), with shaded terrace. *Closed early Sept and early Jan; restaurant closed Sun eve and Mon.*

**Ceyzérieu** ✉ 01350
**La Métairie Davis B&B** Hameau de Chavoley, t 04 79 42 52 14, *www.metairiedavis.com* (€€–€). Lovingly converted old stone house with charming rooms, in a big garden close to the Lac de Chavoley. *Minimum 2-night stay.*

**Relais du Marais**, t 04 79 87 01 61, *relaisdumarais@wanadoo.fr* (€). Simple but appealing village hotel. Basic rooms, nice Bugey menus (€€), superb pool. *Restaurant closed Mon.*

**Avrissieu** ✉ 01350
**Le Pressoir et la Forge B&B** t 04 79 87 92 56 (€). Crammed with Bugey character, with a wine press for company in one apartment – the rooms have kitchenettes. *Closed Nov–Mar.*

**Seyssel** ✉ 01420
**\*\*Hôtel du Rhône**, Quai Charles de Gaulle, t 04 50 59 20 30, *www.hotel durhone-seyssel.com* (€). In a delightful location beside the Rhône, an old-style hotel run by a couple passionate about theatre, hence the theatrical dinners in summer. The rooms are very simple and old-fashioned, the cuisine (€€) more elaborate.

# The Valserine and Pays de Gex

At the confluence of the Valserine and the Rhône, industrial **Bellegarde**, the first French town on the Rhône after Geneva, marks a crossroads between different areas. North of Bellegarde, the Valserine's waters are constricted into a tight gulley by **Lancrans** known as *Les Pertes de la Valserine*, to be discovered on foot.

Climbing to the villages around **Pont-des-Pierres**, the views open out. Beyond, though, you enter the highly secretive **Valserine valley**.

 **Valserine valley**

While France acquired most of the lands around these parts at the start of the 17th century, the Spanish Holy Roman Emperors held on to this valley route, enabling their armies to travel between their immense southern and northern territories bypassing France. Untroubled now, the Valserine is reputed for its tranquillity, its streams much appreciated by fishermen.

Overlooked by an imposing natural theatre of rock, at **Chézery-Forens** the valley widens out to offer high pastures. The cow's milk goes into making Bleu de Gex cheese and Comté at the modern *fromagerie*. Passers-by through the year stock up on sausages at the traditional butcher's in **Lélex**. When the snows come, the place offers cross-country and downhill skiing along with its neighbour, **Mijoux**. Mijoux provides plenty of amusement at any time, in fact: in the series of modern **murals** illustrating traditional trades on the outside of the village houses; in the jewellery on sale at the major shop doubling as the **Musée des Pierres Fines et Précieuses**; and, just across the regional frontier river close to the church, in the vegetable plot protected by a fence made entirely of colourful skis.

**Musée des Pierres Fines et Précieuses**
*t 04 50 41 31 72, www.vuillermoz.fr; open Tues–Sun 10–12 and 2–6.30; free*

Reaching the **Col de la Faucille**, the staggering views across Lac Léman and the Alps come as a breathtaking shock. From the pass, walkers follow the GR9, a splendid path along the highest crest of the French Jura, confusingly known as the Monts Jura.

Plunging down towards Geneva, you enter the **Pays de Gex**, controlled through the early Middle Ages by the counts of that city. In the 13th century one branch set up an independent barony in the steep town of **Gex** itself, with its sloping squares. But in the mid-14th century the house of Savoie gained control. For a taste of the traditional rural Pays de Gex, visit the village of **Vesancy** with its castle tower, church and rustic houses still surrounded by orchards.

In the suburban sprawl below, particularly in the border town of **Divonne-les-Bains**, you see the influence of booming Geneva; indeed, the locals asked to join Switzerland in the 19th century, but only the lakeside communities were admitted. However, with the creation of the *Zone Franche du Pays de Gex*, the rest of the area has benefited since 1815 from exceptional tax breaks, while Divonne has long attracted Swiss wealth with both its **spa** and its showtime **casino** – although the Helvetian authorities have recently loosened their own gambling laws, diminishing Divonne's popularity. One passionate Divonne inhabitant runs regular guided tours around the natural **springs** in town. Many people who suffered so traumatically in Nazi concentration camps were sent to Divonne's cold-water spa after the war to try to help them recover. Now the place caters both to depressives and to those in need of relaxation. Plus there's a splendid **golf course** next door.

This border territory appealed to that provocative campaigning Enlightenment iconoclast, Voltaire, who sought safety from the enraged French royal authorities at **Ferney** from 1754 to the end of his life. He hardly slummed it. In fact, he had the **Château de Ferney** rebuilt in classical style for himself and his niece-cum-mistress, Marie Louise Denis. From 1760, this became his favourite residence. As well as entertaining lavishly at Ferney and encouraging local enterprise, from here he mounted his famously successful defence of the Protestant Calas, wrongly accused of the murder of his Catholic son, while the Caprony mill at Divonne provided the paper on which the first editions of his brilliant satire *Candide* was printed. Today the château tries to follow in Voltaire's footsteps with its cultural programme as well as the intelligent tour.

For an even more intellectually challenging visit, book a tour of **CERN**, the European Centre for Nuclear Particle Research. The massive facilities spread across both Swiss and French sides of the border, but the visitor entrance lies beyond **St-Genis-Pouilly**, just after the Swiss border. One of the earliest co-operative Western European ventures after the war, CERN was set up in 1954, to become a world leader in atomic particle research. Although such

**Château de Ferney**
*t 04 50 28 09 16,
www.visitvoltaire.com;
open May–late-Sept
Tues–Sun 10–1 and 2–6;
tours on the hour until
5pm; adm*

**CERN**
*t 00 41 227 67 61 11,
http://public.web.cern.
ch; open Mon–Sat for
visits at 9 or 2, but NB,
reservation obligatory
well in advance; free*

14

The Rhône from Lyon to Lac Léman | The Valserine and Pays de Gex

highbrow physics may bring to mind frightening thoughts of the nuclear age, the projects here aim to further much more benign technologies, and are playing a significant part in the great quest to get to the root of the creation of the universe, and the minuscule particles from which it is formed. Put your thinking caps on if you wish to follow the demanding three-hour visit. Famously, this is also the place where British researcher Tim Berners-Lee invented the World Wide Web.

The less taxing option is to head a bit up the Monts Jura slopes to enjoy a natural curve of exceptionally pleasing proportions. Explore the relatively peaceful villages along the way, although suburbia has been creeping up into these parts.

You come out at the **Défilé de l'Ecluse** (just east of Bellegarde), the most alarming strategic post along the gully of the Rhône valley separating Jura and Alps, a spot where France, Switzerland and Savoie met in times past. The dauntingly defensive **Fort l'Ecluse** was built as an awesome frontier fortress. Prepare for the more than 1,100 steps of the underground staircase leading up from the Ancien Régime parts to the 19th-century fortified terraces far above, offering superb plunging views on the gorge. Down below, displays and screenings help tell the history of this awesome strategic military site. To follow the Rhône right up to Geneva, you have to enter Swiss territory.

**Fort l'Ecluse**
*t 04 50 59 68 45, www.fortlecluse.fr; open mid-June–mid-Sept Mon–Sat 2–7, Sun 1–7; adm*

ⓘ **Gex/ La Faucille >>**
*Square Jean Clerc, 01174 Gex, t 04 50 41 53 85, www.pays-de-gex.org*

ⓘ **Divonne-les-Bains >>**
*Rue des Bains, 01220 Divonne-les-Bains, t 04 50 20 01 22, www. divonnelesbains.com*

★ **Château de Divonne >>**

ⓘ **Ferney-Voltaire**
*26 Grand'Rue, 01210 Ferney-Voltaire, t 04 50 28 09 16, www.ferney-voltaire.net*

 ⓘ **Lélex-Mijoux >**
*t 04 50 20 91 43, www. monts-jura.com*

## Market Days in the Valserine and Gex

**Gex**: Sat.
**Divonne-les-Bains**: Fri and Sun.
**Ferney-Voltaire**: Wed and Sat.

## Activities and Events in the Valserine and Gex

Divonne, as well as having a **golf course** and **spa**, also sees major international singers perform at its Grand Hôtel, which holds a **casino** too. The Château de Ferney-Voltaire runs a **cultural programme**.

## Where to Stay and Eat in the Valserine and Gex

### Mijoux ✉ 01410

**\*\*Le Soleil**, Rue Royale, t 04 50 41 31 04, *www.hotellesoleilmijoux.com* (€). Good traditional central village hotel. Copious food (€). *Closed Nov.*

### Gex/Col de la Faucille ✉ 01170

**\*\*\*La Mainaz**, Col de la Faucille, t 04 50 41 31 10, *www.la-mainaz.com* (€€). Wonderful views on to Lac Léman and the Alps from this wood-built mountain hotel beside the pass. The darkly furnished rooms have balconies. Fantastic vistas too from the dining room (€€€). *Closed Nov–early Dec; restaurant closed Sun eve and Mon.*

### Divonne-les-Bains ✉ 01220

**\*\*\*\* Château de Divonne**, 115 Rue des Bains, t 04 50 20 00 32, *www.grandes etapes.fr/chateau-divonne* (€€€€€–€€€€). Divonne has several swanky hotels, the four-star wedding cake **Grand Hôtel** marking the centre with its luxury rooms, many restaurants, casino and crooners, the state-of-the-art modern block of the **Villa du Lac** the latest addition But this extravagant 19th-century home is on a more intimate scale, and boasts fabulous views. It has splendid bedrooms, reception rooms, restaurant (€€€€€) and terrace, large grounds and a pool.

# Savoie's Great Lakes

As the massive glaciers of the last Ice Age melted, a trio of gorgeous lakes, Lac d'Annecy, Lac du Bourget and Lac d'Aiguebelette, settled themselves comfortably into splendid locations in the pre-alpine ranges, below their larger cousin Lac Léman, and bounded to the west by what is now an amazing, vine-sprinkled stretch of the Rhône. Ravishing castles, churches and villages went up on the lakes' wooded slopes. Today, smart little ports offer all manner of possibilities for getting out on their magical waters.

The towns are spectacular too: arcaded Annecy is one of the most exquisite cities in France, Aix-les-Bains a venerable old spa town on the move, while Chambéry, historic capital of Savoie, proves a vibrant place. The last lies a stone's throw from dreamy vineyards spreading beneath the gaze of the beautiful, forested Bauges, a deeply wooded, hidden-away range.

# 15

## Don't miss

**①** A diamond of a city by crystal-clear waters
Annecy and its lake **p.258**

**②** Stunning Rhône-side vineyards
The Chautagne and Marestel **pp.267/268**

**③** Lake ports and belvedere views
Lac du Bourget **p.272**

**④** Savoie's historic capital
Chambéry **p.277**

**⑤** A magical secret of a lake
Lac d'Aiguebelette **p.281**

*See map overleaf*

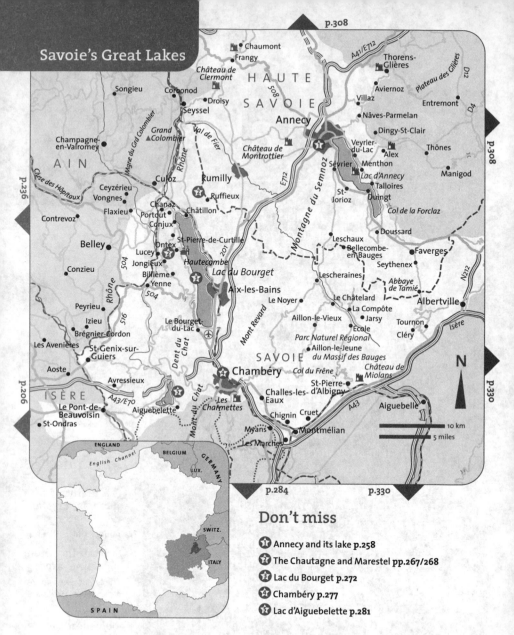

p.308

Chaumont
Frangy
Château de Clermont

HAUTE

Thorens-Glières

SAVOIE

Aviernoz
Villaz

Songieu
Corbonod

Plateau des Glières

Droisy
Seyssel

Annecy

Nâves-Parmelan

Entremont

p.308

Champagne-en-Valromey

Grand Colombier

Château de Montrottier

Dingy-St-Clair

AIN

Veyrier-du-Lac
Sévrier

Alex
Menthon

Thônes

Manigod

Culoz

Rumilly

St-Jorioz

Lac d'Annecy
Talloires
Duingt

Ceyzérieu
Vongnes

Ruffieux

Contrevoz

Chanaz
Portout
Conjux

Châtillon

Flaxieu

Col de la Forclaz

Belley

St-Pierre-de-Curtille

Leschaux
Bellecombe-en-Bauges

Doussard

Faverges

Conzieu

Ontex
Lucey
Jongieux

Hautecombe

Lescheraines

Seythenex

Billième
Yenne

Lac du Bourget

Abbaye de Tamié

Aix-les-Bains

Peyrieu

Le Noyer

Le Châtelard

Albertville

Izieu

Aillon-le-Vieux

La Compôte

Tournon

Brégnier-Cordon

Le Bourget-du-Lac

Jarsy
Ecole

Cléry

Les Avenières

Parc Naturel Régional

Aillon-le-Jeune
du Massif des Bauges

Aoste

St-Genix-sur-Guiers

SAVOIE

Chambéry

Col du Frêne

Château de Miolans

Avressieux

St-Pierre-d'Albigny

ISÈRE

Le Pont-de-Beauvoisin

Aiguebelette

Challes-les-Eaux

Aiguebelle

St-Ondras

Les Charmettes

Chignin

Cruet

Myans

Montmélian

Les Marches

10 km
5 miles

p.236

p.206

p.330

p.284

p.330

N

ENGLAND
BELGIUM
GERMANY
LUX.
English Channel
SWITZ.
ITALY
SPAIN

## Don't miss

Here you have the first of our touring chapters focusing on Savoie. Long an independent European state, it expanded and shrank through the centuries according to the ambitions or failures of its counts, and later its dukes, who gained the nickname of 'gatekeepers of the Alps', as they controlled such important passes linking northern Europe and Italy. Rivalries and ties with France and Switzerland were strong, as were the Italian influences, but Savoie was, historically, French-speaking.

# Getting to and around Savoie's Great Lakes

**By air**: Several low-cost airlines offer direct links from a variety of UK destinations to Chambéry/Aix-les-Bains airport – *see* **Planning Your Trip**, pp.56–7.

**By train**: There are rapid TGV trains to the big towns. Regular trains from Paris-Gare de Lyon serve Annecy, Aix-les-Bains and Chambéry. Vions-Chanaz and Chindrieux have local stations north of Lac du Bourget. For the Avant-Pays Savoyard and Aiguebelette, there's a reasonable selection of local railway stations, at Le Pont de Beauvoisin, Lépin-le-Lac and Aiguebelette-le-Lac.

**By bus**: **Eurolines** runs buses from London to Chambéry, the journey lasting *c.* 16½ hours. For detailed information on bus transport within the region, see *www.cg74.fr* (under *infos pratiques*, then *transports*; or go to *http://infotransports.cg74.fr*) and *www.cg73.fr* (under *routes et transports*).

A political stitch-up organized by Emperor Napoleon III and Camillo Cavour saw Savoie joined to France in 1860, the treaty ratified by overwhelming popular vote – but the electorate wasn't given a choice of joining Switzerland or a newly unified Italy, let alone of its own independence. The region was then divided into two *départements*, Haute (Upper) Savoie in the north, plain Savoie to the south. Its flag, like the Swiss, consists of a white cross on a red background; you can tell them apart by the fact that the arms of Savoie's cross reach right to the flag's edge. The region has its own little independence movement in the *Ligue Savoisienne*, which polls very poorly in elections but plasters signs here and there for a *Savoie Libre*. Founded in 1998, the non-politically partisan association of *La Région Savoie, j'y crois!* has gained more popular support by calling for a separate French region of Savoie, with devolved regional government. Less controversially, in tourism terms, the two *départements* have just teamed up to promote their delights, summer as well winter, under the banner of Savoie-Mont-Blanc (*www.savoie-mont-blanc.com*).

In this chapter, we concentrate on Savoie's fabulous pre-alpine scenery. Surely the most romantic lake in France, Lac d'Annecy attracts a glamorous crowd. It's surrounded by stylish resorts, and by glorious mountains reflected in the clear waters' depths. Annecy itself is one of the most picturesque towns in France. Macho castles survey the lake, those of Menthon and Duingt looking unashamedly down; the one at Annecy is more discreet but once was an important feudal centre, long home to the counts of the Genevois (the area below Geneva). The beautiful arcaded streets below stretch out beside the canals around the Thiou river.

Further fascinating castles lie within easy reach of Lac d'Annecy – Arenthon, converted into a startling contemporary art centre; Montrottier, above the tortured Gorges du Fier, crammed with art and artefacts; Chaumont, in ruins but still atmospheric; and Clermont, now a thriving Renaissance cultural centre. Beyond Clermont, vineyards lead down the Rhône to Lac du Bourget via the Chautagne.

The alternative route between Lac d'Annecy and Lac du Bourget takes you up into a peaceful, self-contained mountain range quite detached from the cosmopolitan, noisy lakes; in the shaggily forested mountains of Les Bauges, old ways have been preserved in the traditional villages, old crafts continuing at gentle pace – although there are major hang-gliding centres, too. Vines grip the slopes below the nature reserve of the eastern heights.

To appreciate the natural grandeur of Lac du Bourget at its best, explore the northern end, with its adorable string of tiny harbours and stunning viewing points, including the promontory abbey of Hautecombe, the last resting place of the dukes of Savoie and kings of Italy. Towns cluster round the southern end, Le Bourget, after which the lake is named, eclipsed by the old spa town-cum-youthful port of Aix-les-Bains, and by proud Chambéry, home for a while – before it was moved to Turin for greater safety from the French – to one of Christianity's most revered and disputed relics, a shroud said to have covered Christ's body at his death.

Little-known, much smaller Lac d'Aiguebelette takes you away from the frenzy to a calmer pre-alpine lake where motorboats are forbidden and fishermen and ducks rule the roost, putting up with the odd hearty rowing team. The Avant-Pays Savoyard beyond looks dreamily down over the neighbouring historic province of the Dauphiné, although the Guiers river was once a much fought-over frontier.

## Annecy and Lac d'Annecy

### Annecy

**① Annecy and its lake**

The canal-criss-crossed, chocolate-box-pretty city of Annecy hides somewhat coyly by the northwest corner of its lake. In tourist terms, though, this is no shy, retiring violet. Annecy knows just how well it has preserved its extraordinary beauty, often reflected in its mirror-like, crystal-clear waters. Comparisons with Venice are bound to disappoint, but the glorious historic centre has a character all of its own, and opens out onto one of Europe's most beautiful, mountain-surrounded lakes. The lake waters are now among the clearest on the Continent, winning many prizes; and as for national flower awards, the story goes that Annecy won so irritatingly often that it was banned from taking part!

#### History

Modern Annecy has sprawled right across the lake's north shore. However, this is in fact where the oldest traces of settlement have been unearthed, submerged remnants going back to Neolithic times. The medieval town grew up around the 12th-century castle to the west, built by the counts of Geneva as one of their main bases, and serving as something of a capital to them for a time. After the death of Robert of Geneva, Annecy was purchased in 1401 by Amédée VIII of Savoie, and from the mid-15th to mid-17th centuries its lordship was reserved for junior members of the house of Savoie; as a result, merchants and trade prospered.

With the splits caused by the Reformation in the 16th century, Annecy acquired wider religious importance. Geneva had become the stronghold of the Protestants, the city's Catholic monastic communities expelled. Many moved to Annecy, which became the seat of a new bishopric for the Genevois area. The most famous of its bishops was the charismatic **François de Sales**, who devoted his life to the gentle but persuasive preaching of a virtuous Catholic life (*see also* p.33, plus Thonon, p.313). In 1610, de Sales established the charitable Order of the Visitation at Annecy with Jeanne de Chantal (grandmother of that superlative socialite at the Sun King's court, Madame de Sévigné – *see* Grignan, p.224). He was also a founder member here of the Académie Florimontane, a high-minded cultural institution set up to encourage good writing and good morals in the literary arts, a model for Cardinal Richelieu's slightly later Académie Française. François de Sales was buried in Annecy, canonized in 1665, and proclaimed patron saint of writers and journalists in 1923, when the Basilica of the Visitation was being built above town – it now stands out more visibly than the castle from afar, along with a few unfortunate modern apartment blocks.

In 1728, the young **Jean-Jacques Rousseau** arrived in town, fleeing misery as an engraver's apprentice in Geneva. At the Convent of the Visitation, he met a somewhat older Swiss in exile, the eccentric, kind-hearted, potion-concocting divorcee and Catholic convert, Madame de Warens. It was *sympathie* if not love at first sight with the woman he would call his *maman*, his real mother having died giving birth to him. Madame de Warens supported the impetuous young Rousseau enormously; *see also* Chambéry, p.280.

## Sights in the Town

Heading into the tourist-packed, arcaded canalside streets, start on **Pont Perrière**, from where the town's most celebrated building, the **Palais de l'Isle**, resembles a stone vessel anchored in the midst of the river. It dates back to the 12th century, and has served as residence, prison, mint and law courts. It now contains the **Musée de l'Histoire d'Annecy**, offering a light introduction to local history. The basic-looking **Café des Arts** also on the island puts on Savoyard events. Looking in the other direction from the Pont Perrière, the grand scrolled front of the church of **St-François de Sales** signals

**Musée de l'Histoire d'Annecy**
*t 04 50 33 87 30; open June–Sept daily 10.30–6; Oct–May Wed–Mon 10–12 and 2–5; adm*

## Annecy

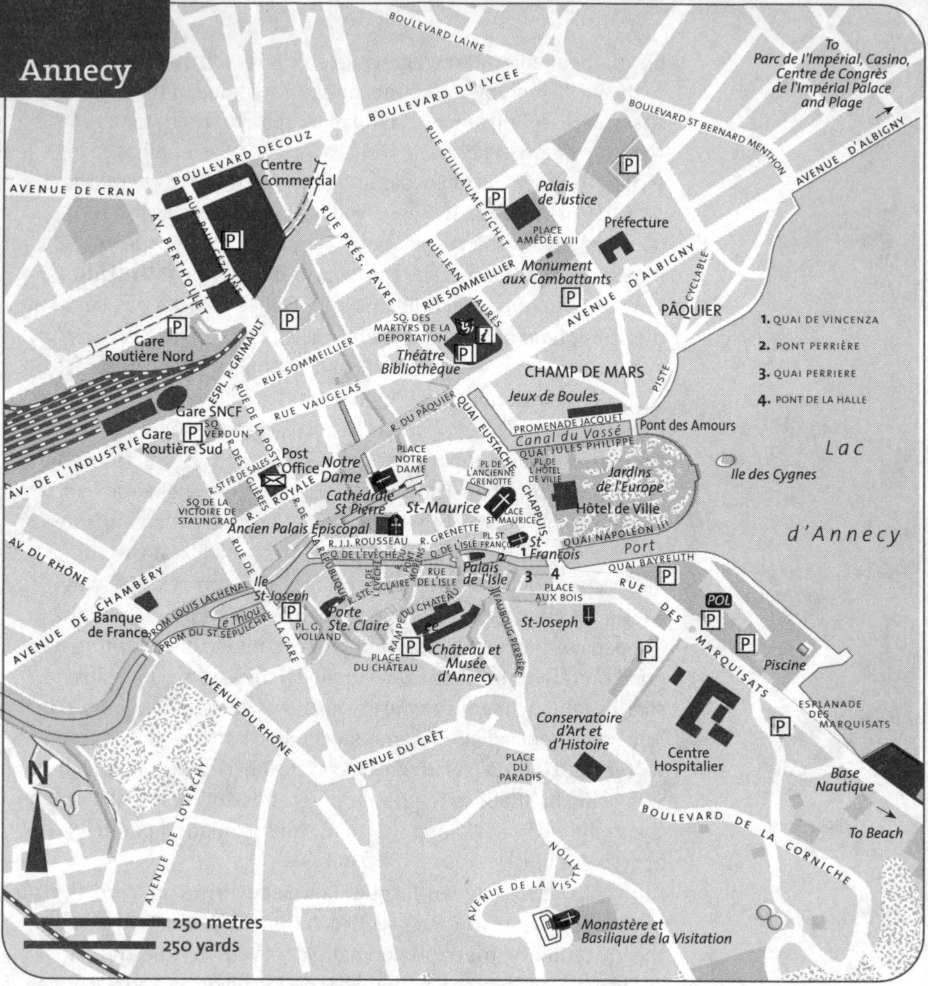
Boulevard Laine
Boulevard du Lycee
Boulevard Decouz
Avenue de Cran
To Parc de l'Impérial, Casino, Centre de Congrès de l'Impérial Palace and Plage
Boulevard St Bernard Menthon
Avenue d'Albigny
Centre Commercial
Av. Berthollet
Rue Paul Cézanne
Rue Prés. Favre
Rue Guillaume Fichet
Palais de Justice
Place Amédée VIII
Préfecture
Rue Jean Jaurès
Rue Sommeillier
Monument aux Combattants
Cyclable
Pâquier
Sq. des Martyrs de la Déportation
Théâtre Bibliothèque
Gare Routière Nord
Espl. P. Grimault
Rue de la Poste
Rue Vaugelas
R. du Pâquier
Quai Eustache Chapuis
Champ de Mars
Jeux de Boules
Piste
1. Quai de Vincenza
2. Pont Perrière
3. Quai Perrière
4. Pont de la Halle
Gare SNCF
Sq. Verdun
Gare Routière Sud
Av. de l'Industrie
Promenade Jacquet
Canal du Vassé
Quai Jules Philippe
Pont des Amours
Lac d'Annecy
Ile des Cygnes
Post Office
Notre Dame
Place Notre Dame
Pl. de l'Ancienne Grenotte
Pl. de l'Hôtel de Ville
Jardins de l'Europe
Hôtel de Ville
R. St Fr. de Sales
R. des Glières
R. Royale
Sq. de la Victoire de Stalingrad
Cathédrale St Pierre
St-Maurice
Place St Maurice
Ancien Palais Episcopal
R. J.J. Rousseau
R. Grenette
Q. de l'Evêché
Q. de l'Isle
Pl. St François
St-François
Quai Napoléon III
Port
Quai Bayreuth
Av. du Rhône
Rue de la République
Rue de l'Isle
Palais de l'Isle
Place aux Bois
Rue des Marquisats
POL
Avenue de Chambéry
Banque de France
Prom. Louis Lachenal
Ile St-Joseph
Le Thiou
Prom. du St Sépulchre
Rue de la Gare
Pl. G. Volland
Porte Ste. Claire
Rampe du Château
St-Joseph
Faubourg Perrière
Place du Château
Château et Musée d'Annecy
Piscine
Esplanade des Marquisats
Avenue du Rhône
Avenue du Crêt
Conservatoire d'Art et d'Histoire
Place du Paradis
Centre Hospitalier
Base Nautique
To Beach
Boulevard de la Corniche
Avenue de Loverchy
Avenue de la Visitation
Monastère et Basilique de la Visitation
N
250 metres
250 yards

the location of the first monastery of the Order of the Visitation. Now restored, the church was badly damaged during the Revolution and the tombs of François de Sales and Jeanne de Chantal demolished. A short way north, the Dominican Gothic barn of **St-Maurice** is the oldest church left in Annecy, but only dates from 1422. Look out for the creepy funeral picture of Philibert de Monthouz and the *Deposition* by Pourbus the Elder.

Walk along the gorgeous colourful quays or almost equally lovely parallel Rue Grenette and Rue Jean-Jacques Rousseau to reach the **Cathedrale St-Pierre**, with its striking façade. Built for the Franciscans in 1535, it was converted into the bishops' seat with the move from Geneva. Dramatic *chiaroscuro* paintings stand out inside, including another *Deposition*, this one attributed to Caravaggio. The **Bishops' Palace** now houses a school of music and the Académie Florimontane.

The tempting shops of Rue Filaterie lead you up to further enchanting quays before the fourth central church of note, imposing **Notre-Dame-de-Liesse**, signalled by its tall, leaning bell tower rising above a bright square. This very striking place was rebuilt after the Revolution, its classical front topped by a gilded statue of the *Virgin and Child*. Murals brighten the dull classicism inside, although the figures' faces aren't well executed. An English church hides in the extremely elegant house next door.

Among other arcaded streets, don't miss **Rue du Pâquier** with the **Hôtel de Sales**, a mansion bearing figures of the seasons. Its continuation, Rue Royale, is a major but more mundane shopping artery. Further modern shopping quarters lie to the north.

Crossing south of the Thiou via one of Annecy's many photogenic bridges, arcaded **Rue Ste-Claire** curves irresistibly around the base of the castle's rock, the main thoroughfare of medieval Annecy, now lively night and day, the boutiques of the excellent competing local ice-cream-makers often causing queues. The **Château d'Annecy** stands aloof above the tourist bustle, a short, steep walk up the hill. The enormous 13th-century **Tour de la Reine** forms the oldest part of this massive ensemble. The 14th–15th-century Gothic **Logis Vieux** and the 16th-century, Renaissance **Logis Nemours** contain a **regional museum** filled with religious statues and all-too-pretty paintings of Annecy. The **Observatoire Régional des Lacs Alpins**, set apart in the **Logis Perrière**, delves in more contemporary fashion into the formation of the region's lakes and their ecology.

The **Conservatoire d'Art et d'Histoire**, further out, occupies a plain seminary building where, until 1970, trainee priests were still educated. It now contains a mixed bag of art, including exotic faces sculpted by Evariste Jonchère on his early 20th-century world travels, and contemporary works from the Lyon School. An engrossing new interactive section devoted to pre-cinema experiments in moving images occupies the former chapel.

Up on its height, the showy white **Church of the Visitation**, consecrated in 1949, holds relics of François de Sales and Jeanne de Chantal. Pilgrims go to venerate them in large numbers.

Immediately east of the historic centre, the Thiou widens out, forming Annecy's **port**, where big cruise boats line up when awaiting the tourist hordes. A trip out on the lake is a must. A popular alternative to booking a mini-cruise is to take a pedalo on the waters to create your own little magical voyage of discovery; a host of companies hire out pedalos from the edge of the **Jardins de l'Europe**. These well-shaded gardens were laid out behind Annecy's smart **Hôtel de Ville** in the Belle Epoque, and are now embellished with mature trees. The patronizing statue of Berthollet you may encounter recalls a celebrated 19th-century scientist from Lac d'Annecy. Opposite, the name of the diminutive **Ile des Cygnes**

**Château d'Annecy**
*t 04 50 33 87 30; open June–Sept daily 10.30–6; Oct–May Wed–Mon 10–12 and 2–5; adm*

**Conservatoire d'Art et d'Histoire**
*t 04 50 51 02 33; open Mon–Fri, exc bank hols, 10–12 and 2–6; free*

evokes the swans so closely associated with Annecy, although these have been mysteriously dwindling in number recently. Panels by the water explain the great diversity of fowl and fish found in the crystal-clear waters.

South of the port, down the lake, you'll find a popular narrow paying **beach** and **open-air pools**. Continue north along the shore to reach the refreshingly plane-shaded, boat-filled **Canal du Vassé**, crossed by the well-named **Pont des Amours**. Along the north shore, the extensive waterside lawns beyond the smart buildings and apartment blocks look rather vacuous, but wander along here for some of the most memorable views of all onto Lac d'Annecy, opening up to the south. You arrive at the unmissable wedding-cake **Impérial hotel**, in front of which you'll find another paying beach with sporting facilities, and romantic rose gardens, to be enjoyed free of charge by all.

## Lac d'Annecy

Beautiful hotels fight for space at the waterside just like the visitors to the summer beaches. Castles peer down from the wooded slopes above. Layers of peaks recede into the distance beyond the huge showy molar-shaped mountains in the middle distance. Lac d'Annecy is so glorious, it's impossible not to fall under its spell.

While Annecy became capital of the *département de la Haute Savoie* when Savoie became French, its lake grew increasingly polluted as industry developed in 19th and 20th centuries. After the war, the city's dynamic mayor, Charles Bosson, set about reviving it, and the waters are now among the clearest and healthiest in Europe, winning prizes and plaudits, although the hordes of visitors can be hard to regulate. Although this may be one of the largest lakes in the country, the single road around it often gets annoyingly crowded. Patience is a virtue driving round these parts in full holiday season.

Of course, the best way of appreciating Lac d'Annecy is to get out onto the water or into it – each parish has at least one free beach, but the ones that charge will have better facilities. For boat trips, Annecy's port may be the most obvious point of departure, but you can hire boats and pedalos from many spots, the local tourist offices keeping lists of hire companies. One benefit of taking a guided boat tour is that the commentaries fill you in on the interesting geological, historical and cultural features, as well as bombarding you with a host of lacustrine facts and figures.

Staying on dry land, do seriously consider following the lake's west bank from Annecy by bicycle, given the excellent, broad, 30km-long cycle path avoiding the car-choked road. Along this shore, even if the feel tends to be more built-up and suburban, it is more family-friendly than the other side, the beaches sloping very gently down into the waters. Plus the views east are phenomenal.

**Sévrier beach**
*adm in summer*

**Musée du Costume Savoyard**
*t 04 50 52 41 05,
www. echo-de-nos-montagnes.com; open mid-June–mid-Sept Mon–Fri 10–12 and 2.30–6.30, Sun 10–12; May–mid-June and late Sept Sun–Fri 2–6; adm*

At **Sévrier**, with its spectacular views of the toothy mountains opposite, the **beach** and **marina** attract the most attention. Up by the smart neo-Gothic **church**, Savoyard traditions are recalled in the enthusiastically run **Musée du Costume Savoyard**. Along the main road, the Paccard foundry, celebrated at the company's **Musée de la Cloche**, has been making bells the old-fashioned way for eight generations. Numerous copies of the Philadelphia Liberty Bell have been cast by Paccard.

**Musée de la Cloche**
*t 04 50 52 47 11,
www.paccard.fr; open July–Aug Mon–Sat 10–12.30 and 2–6.30, Sun 2–6.30; Sept–June Mon–Sat 10–12 and 2.30–5.30; adm*

Charming lakeside **St-Jorioz** has a good expanse of beach, while a sensational private château once owned by the de Sales family sticks out from the peninsula of **Duingt**. Nature-lovers explore the marshy reedbeds at the southern end of the lake by **Doussard**, which also benefits from a good beach. This place carries the nickname of 'the source of the lake', as most of the waters that feed Lac d'Annecy enter here.

Lac d'Annecy's east bank can claim to have some of the most beautiful and extraordinary waterside resorts in France. Bathing is slightly trickier on this rockier, more abrupt shore, but there are plenty of magical beaches and places to hire boats.

**Veyrier-du-Lac** boasts one of the poshest hotels in the country, but it does also have two public beaches. Delightful **Menthon-St-Bernard** with its beach is overseen by the spectacular **Château de Menthon**, its magical many-towered silhouette thought possibly to have been a source of inspiration for Walt Disney. Its real history makes an extraordinary story.

**Château de Menthon**
*t 04 50 60 12 05,
www.chateau-de-menthon.com; open July–Aug daily 12–6; May–June and Sept Fri–Sun and public hols 2–6; adm*

The castle dates back to the 12th century, but its exceptionally important lordly family may have settled up here still earlier. They have never left. The château is claimed as the birthplace of St Bernard, an Alpine hero (*see* p.41), in 1008. While Bernard flew off to do his charitable work, the medieval lords who stayed served as some of the most powerful figures under the counts of Geneva, guarding a strategic mountain route.

Three major towers went up: the **Tour du Lac**, the **keep**, and the **Tour des Armes**. The local populace would seek refuge in the courtyard in times of trouble. Made more comfortable at the Renaissance, the castle was modified in the 18th century, with a new façade overlooking the lake. In the late 19th century, René de Menthon ordered decorative additions, including turrets, to give the place a more Romantic air. On the tour, you see half a dozen grand rooms, with many images of St Bernard on display, but also other fine family portraits and pieces of furniture. The library holds a magnificent collection of works. You may be told the extraordinary story of François de Menthon, father of the present owner, one of the founding figures of the French Résistance (*see* p.90), afterwards a Minister of Justice for Charles de Gaulle and French prosecutor at the Nuremberg military tribunal.

Another château worth taking on lies in the mountains just a little east towards Thônes. The **Château d'Arenthon** above the pretty village of **Alex** wears a defiant air, standing opposite a massive wall of limestone. Inside, it has been given a radical make-over, the Salomon family, renowned in the Alps for making its fortune through ski manufacturing, having turned it into a cutting-edge centre for contemporary art exhibitions. The gardens are planted with more discreet contemporary sculptures and the café is distinctly funky.

Back at Lac d'Annecy, lakeside resorts don't come more chic than **Talloires**. This is one of the most glamorous waterside haunts in France, with its swanky port, its golf course, and its fabulous array of waterside hotels and restaurants. At times, you feel there are more staff than tourists racing round the place. The setting is simply sublime. Nearby, the **Roc de Chère** promontory is so rich in flora that it has been turned into a nature reserve. The Compagnie des Bateaux du Lac d'Annecy (*see* box, below) organizes special cruises with guided tours to this reserve.

Take one of the rather hairy roads up to the **Col de la Forclaz** for arguably the finest of all views over the whole of Lac d'Annecy. The sight will take your breath away, even if you don't take to the air paragliding: this is one of the most famous spots on the continent for practising the sport. Admire the fearlessness or folly of the winged people taking off from the comfort of wonderfully located restaurant and café tables.

**Château d'Arenthon**
• t 04 50 02 87 52,
www.fondation-
salomon.com; open
July–Oct Wed–Sun 2–7;
Mar–June Thurs–Sun
2–7; adm

## Market Days around Lac d'Annecy

**Annecy**: Tues, Fri and Sun am.

## Festivals and Events around Lac d'Annecy

Annecy puts on a large number of cultural events, including a March *carnaval*, international **film festivals**, **boat shows**, musical programmes, plus fabulous 14th July **fireworks** displays and a major *Fête du Lac* in early August.

See *www.lac-annecy.com*.

The **Château de Menthon** puts on a *son-et-lumière* three evenings in July and Aug.

## Sports and Activities around Lac d'Annecy

For the huge choice of activities on and around Lac d'Annecy, including canoeing, diving, paragliding, rock-climbing, sailing, windsurfing and more, see *www.lac-annecy.com*, or get the annual Annecy brochure guide for the Agglomération d'Annecy/Lac d'Annecy. Also consult *www.leventdularge.com* for special offers.

For **boat trips** on Lac d'Annecy, the main operators include: **Compagnie des Bateaux du Lac d'Annecy, t** 04 50 51 08 40, *www.annecy-croisieres.com*; **Groupement des Loueurs de Bateaux de Haute-Savoie, t** 04 50 66 01 75; and **Bateaux Dupraz, t** 04 50 52 42 99, *www.bateauxdupraz.com*. You can also hire boats from the specialist companies listed on the website and in the brochure.

The Col de la Forclaz above the southern end of Lac d'Annecy is one of the most famous spots in France for **paragliding**. Some dozen operators offer introductory jumps; once more see the Lac d'Annecy website or brochure. There are summer **toboggan courses** on the Semnoz and at La Sambuy. Look out for Lac d'Annecy marathons and triathlons.

There are two fine 18-hole **golf courses** around Lac d'Annecy, at Talloires (*www.golf-lacannecy.com*), and al Giez (*www.golfdegiez.com*).

# Where to Stay and Eat around Lac d'Annecy

## Annecy ✉ 74000

**★★★★L'Impérial Palace**, Allée de l'Impérial, t 04 50 09 30 00, *www.hotel-imperial-palace.com* (€€€€€). Huge, swanky extravaganza with fabulous lake views from the north shore, a bit away from the centre. Bag a room with a view, clearly. **La Voile** (€€€) is the main restaurant. There is also a flash casino.

**★★★Les Trésoms**, 3 Bd de la Corniche, t 04 50 51 43 84, *www.lestresoms.com* (€€€€–€€€). Colourful big house with Art Deco touches on its slope south of the centre, many of the rooms with lake views. Panoramic restaurant, **La Rotonde** (€€€€–€€€), plus a cheaper traditional restaurant. Pool, garden.

**★★★Palais de l'Isle**, 13 Rue Perrière, t 04 50 45 86 87, *www.hoteldupalaisdelisle.com* (€€€–€€). Wonderfully located right in the historic centre, in a fine house on the main (sometimes noisy) canal. Modern rooms, some smallish.

**★★★Les Marquisats**, 6 Chemin de Colmyr, t 04 50 51 52 34, *www.marquisats.com* (€€). Stylishly decorated rooms in this appealing home also on the slope south of town, half a dozen rooms with some view of the lake.

**★★Alpes**, 12 Rue de la Poste, t 04 50 45 04 56, *www.hotelannecy.com* (€). Close to the station, with some charm and nicely renovated rooms.

**★Central**, 6 Rue Royale, t 04 50 45 05 37, *www.hotelcentralannecy.com* (€). Central and calm.

**Auberge de Savoie**, 1 Place St-François de Sales, t 04 50 45 03 05 (€€€–€€). Annecy's canal-sides are packed with touristy restaurants; sample lake fish at this excellent address at the heart of the action. *Closed Tues and Wed, plus early Jan and 2nd half Nov.*

**Ciboulette**, Cour du Pré Carré, 10 Rue Vaugelas, t 04 50 45 74 57 (€€€). Gastronomic address in courtyard off one of the main arcaded streets lined with more basic options. *Closed Sun and Mon, and most of July.*

**L'Etage**, 13 Rue Pâquier, t 04 50 51 03 28 (€€). Good for Savoyard specialities such as fondue, in a beamed historic building.

## Talloires ✉ 74290

**★★★★Auberge du Père Bise**, t 04 50 60 72 01, *reception@perebise.com* (€€€€€). A truly exceptional villa, with private, shaded lakeside garden, the lake serving as a pool. Sumptuous rooms with views. Lake fish is dressed up in the first-rate restaurant (€€€€€–€€€€). *Closed Christmas– mid-Mar, restaurant closed Tues lunch and Fri lunch in season, Tues and Wed out of season.* The same family runs the splendid lakeside **★★★★Hôtel Cottage Bise**, t 04 50 60 71 10 (€€€€), one rung down the luxury ladder, but with a fine restaurant and pool.

**★★★★L'Abbaye**, Chemin des Moines, t 04 50 60 77 33, *abbaye@alp-link.com* (€€€€€–€€€€). Former Benedictine abbey, now with piano bar, solarium, and private beach. Rooms around a graceful 17th-century cloister. Good restaurant (€€€€–€€€). *Closed late Dec and most of Jan.*

## Veyrier-du-Lac ✉ 74290

**★★★★La Maison de Marc Veyrat**, 13 Vieille Route des Pensières, t 04 50 60 24 00, *contact@marcveyrat.fr* (€€€€€). Fabulous, fabulously expensive, blue lakeside villa-hotel with own lakeside terraces and jetty. Luxurious rooms with views, many with balconies. Owner Marc Veyrat is one of the country's star chefs, a flamboyant figure blending herbs in stunning ways, but prices are astronomical. *Closed Nov–mid-May; restaurant closed weekday lunch, Mon pm, and Tues pm.*

# Via the Rhône to Lac du Bourget

Skirting west of Lac d'Annecy and Lac du Bourget, this section of the great Rhône valley long formed a dramatic piece of the frontier between Savoie and France, the Savoie side sometimes referred to as Le Petit Bugey in contrast to Le Grand Bugey opposite (for which, *see* Chapter 14). Some fascinating châteaux stand out in these parts; the Clermont family were the major lordly family in former times. There are also secretive patches of vines to seek out.

**Château de Montrottier**

*t 04 50 46 23 02, www. chateaudemontrottier. com; open June–Aug daily 2–7; mid-Mar–May and Sept–mid-Oct Wed–Mon 2–6; adm*

The easiest castle to reach from Annecy, medieval **Château de Montrottier** boasts especially grand views from its soaring 15th-century keep, the finest of its many formidable towers. Inside are the collections of Léon Marès, bequeathed to the Académie Florimontane. Among jaded weapons, tapestries and Napoleonic artefacts, the finest works are the Vischers' supreme Renaissance bronzes of the Battle of the Centaurs, commissioned by the super-rich Fuggers of Augsburg, but rejected because they featured too many naked buttocks. Nearby, the narrow path you can take along the precipitous **Gorges du Fier** reveals how the rocks were drilled dramatically down by the power of the waters many moons ago.

**Gorges du Fier**

*t 04 50 46 23 07, www.gorgesdufier.com; open mid-June–mid-Sept daily 9–7; mid-Mar–mid-June and mid-Sept–mid-Oct daily 9–12 and 2–6; adm*

At the hamlet of **Lagnat** by Vaulx, the Moumen family has created a host of intriguing gardens and wooden structures in their **Jardins Secrets**. West along the Fier, **Rumilly**, little capital of this little area known as the Albanais, was once a more important town, but it has retained some fine arcaded houses. The former tobacco factory now holds the old-fashioned clutter of the **Musée de l'Albanais**.

**Jardins Secrets**

*t 04 50 60 53 18, www. jardins-secrets.com; open mid-June–Aug daily 1.30–7; early April–mid-June Sat, Sun and public hols 1.30–7; Sept–Oct Sun 1.30–6; adm*

The **Château de Clermont** stands in a wonderfully confident location on its hilltop. It was transformed in the 16th century from a sturdy Savoyard home into a more graceful residence of the Renaissance, a period to which the place remains devoted, with a fine collection of furniture. In summer, cultural exhibitions and events add life to the place, the balustraded arcades in the big courtyard serving as backdrop to the performances. The dignified hillside church is listed as well.

**Musée de l'Albanais**

*open July–Aug Wed–Mon 10–12 and 3–7; June and Sept Wed–Mon 9–11 and 2–6; closed Tues*

North of Clermont, vines ski down the steep slopes to **Frangy**, a quiet town on the trout-teeming Usses river, and on the route of pilgrims walking from Geneva to Santiago in Spain. The local AOC Roussette de Savoie is a respectable sweet white wine.

**Château de Clermont**

*t 04 50 69 63 15; open May–Sept daily 2–6; adm*

A few kilometres away, make for the pretty little hill village of **Chaumont**, where you can scramble up to the atmospheric, battered white ruins of the **Château de Chaumont** to appreciate commanding views. Chaumont stands on the protruding southern rump of the **Montagne de Vuache**, which stretches up to the Rhône at the Défilé de l'Ecluse on the French frontier with Switzerland. The mountain's lower slopes are still covered with

**Château de Chaumont**

*free access; take care*

orchards, while a hiking path follows its ridge, the views sometimes giving onto Geneva.

To reach the stretch of the Rhône immediately west of Clermont,
climb across the Montagne des Princes via the peaceable village of
**Droisy**, in its wonderful open location. Take a last longing look back
east, right across to Mont Blanc, before stepping on the brakes for
the extremely steep slope down to Rhône-side **Seyssel**.

Twins separated by the cruel Rhône, there are in fact two Seyssels
(*see* also p.251), defying the river that once regularly tore into them.
On each bank, a completely separate town developed, Savoie-side
Seyssel venerating its stone Virgin, the west side its black Virgin. In
both, important communities of mariners carried out their river
trade, their special barges known as *seysselannes*, as recalled at the
modest **Maison du Rhône**. A big Virgin stands watch atop the
suspension bridge that has linked the two sides since the 1840s;
the Rhône swept earlier crossings away. Now, a dam has tamed the
river passing through this narrow, wildly beautiful section. For a
note on Seyssel's delightful wines, *see* p.251 again.

The huge dark flanks of the Montagne du Gros Foug and the
Grand Colombier lie like primordial sleeping monsters on either
side of the narrow stretch of the lovely, vine-covered Rhône-side
stretch known as the **Chautagne**. On the flat, below **Châteaufort**, al
the confluence of the Fier and the Rhône, the **Espace Nature** lies in
a romantic spot, allowing you to appreciate the Rhône at close
quarters, as well as providing lots of sporting facilities.

The gorgeous **Chautagne vineyards** stretch south from **Motz**,
with its Baroque church on high. **Ruffieux** boasts a huge wine
co-operative. Surprisingly, red production outdoes the white here.
The village looks over a vast, intriguing poplar plantation, one of
the largest in Europe, which you can cycle round.

Stick to the Rhône for attractive **Vions** and for **Chanaz**, the latter
an especially delightful historic village, linked to Lac du Bourget
by the **Canal de Savière**, its waterfront lined with cafés and
restaurants. In the pretty lanes behind, seek out specialist craft
shops, including a stained-glass maker, and, up the slope, a mill
making walnut oil. A short walk west takes you to Chanaz's port, to
embark on a boat trip on the Rhône, or across the canal to Lac du
Bourget. Frogs give impressive summer evening concerts, while
special night-time cruises allow you to observe families of beavers.

Around Chanaz, the Rhône splits into two quite separate
branches. A stunning further **wine route** continues south along
the steep slopes above the eastern arm of the river; here, you enter
the northern half of the **Avant-Pays Savoyard**, a historic frontier
outpost of Savoie. **Mont de la Charvaz** separates the great curve of
the Rhône's east bank from Lac du Bourget. A dramatic château
selling Vins de Savoie stands above **Lucey**, with its onion-bulb

**Maison du Rhône**
*t 04 50 56 77 04; open
mid-June–mid-Sept
Wed–Mon 9–12.30 and
1.30–5, closed Tues;
April–mid-June and
mid-Sept–Nov Wed and
Fri–Sun 9–12.30 and
1.30–5; adm*

**Espace Nature**
*most sections free*

 **Chautagne
vineyards**

15 Savoie's Great Lakes | Via the Rhône to Lac du Bourget

**Marestel vineyards**

church. **Jongieux**'s exquisite scattering of hamlets lies amidst very steep **Marestel vineyards**. **Billième** is backed by a stunning semicircle of mountains. **La Chapelle St-Romain** stands out on a hillock amid the vines. This wine route is so magical, the landscapes look as if they've been lifted from the backdrop of a splendid Gothic painting; stop not just to take in the views, but also for some of the wine estates that produce rare wines, much appreciated by the dukes of Savoie. Up at the **Mont du Chat** there's the most uplifting of viewpoints; down below, beside **St-Jean-de-Chevelu**, the jolly little lakes here attract merry summer bathers.

The town of **Yenne**, its ancestor by the Rhône founded in Roman times, retains some of its medieval character and arcaded houses. The church conceals intriguing Romanesque and Gothic elements. The place has culinary traditions too, being known for its feather-light *gâteau de Savoie* sponge cake, while its cheese co-operative just outside town, the largest in Savoie, has been specializing in organic produce for some time. Nearby, you can go canoeing on the eastern branch of the Rhône.

The **Défilé de Pierre Châtel** leads down to the main river, the spectacularly perched **Chartreuse of Pierre Châtel**, built on the site of a fortress of the counts of Savoie, now in private hands, but to be spied from the GR9 hiking path.

ⓘ **Ruffieux/ La Chautagne >>**
*Maison de Chautagne,
73310 Ruffieux,
t 04 79 54 54 72,
www.chautagne.com*

★ **Château des Avenières >**

ⓘ **Yenne**
*Route de Lucey, 73170
Yenne, t 04 79 36 71 54,
yenne.tourisme@
wanadoo.fr*

## Market Days along the Rhône

**Yenne**: Thurs am.

## Where to Stay and Eat along the Rhône

### Cruseilles ✉ 74350

★★★★**Château des Avenières**, Route du Salève, **t** 04 50 44 02 23, *www.chateau-des-avenieres.com* (€€€€€–€€€€). On slopes north of Cruseilles, 25km north of Annecy, a many-balconied mansion with fabulous views, built at the start of the 20th century for the daughter of an American industrialist. Sumptuous rooms with imaginative décor. Extravagant restaurant (€€€€) for a memorable meal. Pool. Large grounds.

### Motz ✉ 73310

**Auberge de Motz**, **t** 06 76 60 93 12 (€). Model of a new bargain village inn in a cleanly restored old building, with neat, plain rooms. Restaurant (€€).

### Ruffieux ✉ 73310

**Lachat B&B**, Chez M. et Mme Baltz, **t** 04 79 54 20 18, *baltzgite@yahoo.fr* (€). Sweet, bargain room in fantastic location among high vineyards looking down on the Rhône.

### Chanaz ✉ 73310

**Auberge de Savières**, **t** 04 79 54 56 16 (€€). For its wonderful terraces by the canal and for local fish dishes. *Closed most weekday eves out of season, plus Jan–early Mar.*

### Jongieux ✉ 73170

**Auberge Les Morainières**, Coteau Marestel, **t** 04 79 44 09 39 (€€€). Refined cuisine in a dining room in cellars in the heart of the Marestel vineyards, or on the terrace with melting views. There's a slightly cheaper lunchtime menu. *Closed Sun eve, Mon, and much of Jan.*

### St Jean de Chevelu ✉ 73170

★★**La Source**, Route du Col du Chat, **t** 04 79 36 8016, *www.hotel-lasource.com* (€). Very decent, with great views, renovated rooms, tasty cuisine (€€).

# Les Bauges

Although rising between ever-so-popular Lac d'Annecy and Lac du Bourget, the heavily wooded pre-alpine range of Les Bauges feels lost in time and far removed from the lakes' tourist hordes. Huge limestone walls rise around it, protecting its secretive heart. The range was declared a regional nature park in 1995, helping to retain to some degree its old crafts. Woodworking used to be a major activity, *argenterie des Bauges* an ironic name for its once-common tableware, made from wood rather than silver. In cheese terms, Tome des Bauges differentiates itself from the rest of this type of Savoyard *fromage*, spelling itself with just one 'm', and gaining its own AOC for its exceptional quality. On Les Bauges' eastern side, sloping down to the stretch of the Isère valley known as the Combe de Savoie, vineyards embellish the mountainous scene, producing intriguing Savoie wines. The summits above are a protected reserve where ibex and rare flora hide out.

For the straight route from Lac d'Annecy into the centre of the Bauges, head over the dramatic **Montagne du Semnoz**, with splendid views back to Lac du Bourget. Beyond the **Col de Leschaux**, branch off for **Bellecombe-en-Bauges**, with its traditional big farms and the specialist thrill of its 19th-century saw, operated by water power. South, you can walk to the daunting crevasse leap of the Pont du Diable (Devil's Bridge).

**Lescheraines** lies at an open crossroads practically at the centre of the range, by the fish-rich Chéran river. It has one lake for anglers, another for swimmers. **Le Châtelard** nearby, tiny 'capital' of Les Bauges, has preserved its old shop fronts along its narrow main street, with craftspeople and an art gallery established here. The 19th-century church proudly presents its own set of murals.

Delightful little barns stand out in the fields as you arrive at airier **La Compôte**, where hang-gliding is a major pull. At **Ecole**, the **Maison Faune et Flore** presents the natural world of Les Bauges in modern but mellow style. The **chocolate-maker** at **Jarsy** may tempt you there. Up the exceptionally narrow **Vallon de Bellevaux**, a short forest walk leads you to **Notre-Dame de Bellevaux**, a 19th-century chapel on the site of another former medieval monastery.

Starting back at Lescheraines, an alternative wooded route takes you southwest to pretty **Le Noyer**, home to more craftspeople and artists, including one address by the delightful name of the *Sanglier Philosophe* (Philosophical Boar). The road continues into the cross-country ski domains of **La Féclaz**. A walk leads from here to the **Croix du Nivolet**, a landmark of a cross way above Chambéry. Or climb by car to **Mont Revard** for great views over Lac du Bourget.

Back in the heart of the Bauges, the delectable **Aillon valley** cuts north–south through the southern half of the range, lined by

**Maison Faune et Flore**

*t 04 79 52 22 56, www.
pnr-massif-bauges.fr;
open late June–mid-
Sept Tues–Sat 10.30–
12.30 and 1.30–7,
May–late June and
mid-Sept–Oct Sat and
Sun 1.30–6 ; adm*

**Jarsy chocolate-maker**

*open Tues–Sun
afternoons*

sugarloaf mountains; again you can set out to explore this valley from Lescheraines. A *Sentier Botanique* at **Aillon-le-Jeune** leads you on a wild orchid trail (best mid-May–mid-July). See how the reputed Tome des Bauges is made in the old village's neat **Fruitière-Espace Découverte du Val d'Aillon**. East through the chalet-strewn slopes of Aillon's little ski resort, **La Correrie** with its chapel and ruined façade recalls the location of one more of the major medieval monasteries in Les Bauges. A cultural centre is planned.

Alternatively, from the southern tip of Lac d'Annecy you can skirt round the eastern side of the range via Faverges and Albertville to follow the **Combe de Savoie** to Chambéry. **Faverges** lies in the funnel of mountains south of the lake. The castle on the town's hill looks impressive, but proves curiously low-beat up close, its keep netted for safety, the bulk of the place residential, but with a **butterfly collection** for persistent visitors. There's also a little **archaeological museum** in a church down in a dull residential quarter on the outskirts. For Albertville, *see* Chapter 18.

Do try the dramatic mountain 'shortcut' up from Faverges onto the western slopes of the Combe de Savoie, passing via the **Col de Tamié**. Before Seythenex, at the **Grottes de Seythenex** you can climb to see an impressive double waterfall and go underground into the less exciting, cramped underground caverns. **Seythenex**, the village, has retained its old-fashioned Alpine look. Far above stands the one-chalet ski resort of **Le Sambuy**, with just the one ski lift, but they keep it going in summer, allowing you to take sensational walks up high in Les Bauges.

A little lower down, the **abbey of Tamié**, set in its own spectacular location, acts as the most powerful reminder that medieval monks largely oversaw the development of Les Bauges. A shop sells the abbey's cheese as well as religious books and fairtrade items, a video presenting the life of the Trappist order here. The **Fort de Tamié**, opposite, was a major piece of French 19th-century frontier-building, now taken over by local enthusiasts bringing cultural life to this dramatic defensive spot above the Isère. They lend you torches on the visit inside the fort. Outside, don't miss the head-spinning views down on the Combe de Savoie.

You pass through pretty slopeside orchards to join the western flank of the Combe, a steep mid-slope road then leading you through surprising vineyards. Past **Cléry**, with its well-located Romanesque church, follow the D201. **Grésy**'s **Ecomusée**, in the main area of vineyards, preserves the memory of many local crafts.

The medieval **Château de Miolans** looks forbiddingly down on the confluence of the Isère and Arc rivers. The lords who occupied this powerful location were close allies to the house of Savoie, who inherited it in the 16th century, turning the gift into a prison. The Marquis de Sade was incarcerated here in 1772, but escaped. The

**Fruitière-Espace Découverte du Val d'Aillon**
t 04 79 54 60 28; open daily 9–12 and 3–7.30

**Grottes de Seythenex**
t 04 50 44 55 97, www.cascade.fr; open May–mid-Sept 10–5.30; adm

**Abbey of Tamié**
t 04 79 31 15 50, www.abbaye-tamie.com; open daily 10–12 and 2.30–6

**Fort de Tamié**
t 04 79 31 37 50; open daily 10–7; adm

**Ecomusée**
t 04 79 37 94 36, www.perso.orange.fr/lescoteauxdusalin; open all year; adm

**Château de Miolans**
t 04 79 28 57 04; open July–Aug daily 10–7; adm

slopeside town of **St-Pierre d'Albigny** has kept its quaint old wooden shop fronts, a wine route signalling wineries nearby, while the dead end of **Montlambert** attracts paragliders.

The impressive **Château de la Rive** by **Cruet** has yielded its rare medieval frescoes of knightly tales to Chambéry (*see* pp.278–9). **Arbin** has long been associated with a nice, light red wine, produced from the mondeuse grape, which developed here.

**Montmélian** lies in a dramatic riverside location below the shapely Roche du Guet. This strategically located town was once thoroughly fortified. Although its defences were torn down under Louis XIV, it has retained grand houses and is now proud home of the **Musée Régional de la Vigne et du Vin** covering a couple of millennia of wine-making in Savoie with some style.

The wine trail continues along the **Cluse de Chambéry**, a magnificent, broad valley left over by a former glacier. The vineyards, spreading out between the heights of the Bauges and the Chartreuse ranges, are of a rare beauty. The molar tooth of **Mont Granier** towering above this area marks the northern end of the Chartreuse (*see* p.289). A huge chunk fell off it in a diluvian rainstorm in 1248. Communities were destroyed, most horrifically St-André. Today, the hamlets around St-André are gloriously beautiful and peaceful. Consider pausing or picnicking beside the exquisitely located **Lac St-André**. In the village of **St-André** itself, there's a pleasingly dark, musty, old-fashioned and charmingly run little **Musée du Vigneron** part ot the Caveau du Lac St-André J.-C. Perret, offering a good selection of local wines. Lost amidst the vines nearby, discover how paper used traditionally to be made on an interesting tour at the **Moulin de la Tourne**.

**Myans**, below St-André, survived the medieval Mont Granier disaster, so the superstitious claimed, thanks to the protection of its Black Virgin. Its church still attracts pilgrims. While the black figure is protected inside, a gilded 19th-century Virgin stands triumphantly outside. The boulders of the Abymes de Myans still act as reminder of the trauma that rocked the area so many centuries back. Big boulders sit immovably among the vineyards towards **Apremont**, another village synonymous with a distinctive Savoie wine, a white made from the jacquère grape.

The other side of the valley, around **Chignin**, the equally beautiful vineyards are surveyed by ruined medieval towers. The wineries here produce the most reputed local white wines under the appellations Chignin and Chignin Bergeron. **St-Jeoire-Prieuré** has a sober church, sole remnant of its priory. **Challes-les-Eaux** became a major medicinal spa centre in the 19th century, along with the usual diversionary accoutrements like its plush casino, and the place is still just about keeping up. You are now practically on the outskirts of Chambéry (*see* p.277).

---

**Musée Régional de la Vigne et du Vin**
*t 04 79 84 42 23; open July–Sept Tues–Sat 9.30–12 and 2–6; Sun and Mon 2–6; adm*

**Musée du Vigneron**
*t 04 79 28 13 32; open mid-July–Sept daily 2–7; April–mid-July and Oct–Christmas Sat and Sun 2–7; adm*

**Moulin de la Tourne**
*t 04 79 28 13 31; open May–Sept daily tours at 3 and 4; mid-Jan–April and Oct–mid-Dec, tour Mon, Wed, Sat and Sun at 4; adm*

(i) **Le Châtelard/
Les Bauges**
*Place Grenette,
73630 Le Châtelard,
t 04 79 54 84 28,
www.lesbauges.com;
also see www.pnr-
massif-bauges.fr*

(★) **Château de la
Tour du Puits >>**

(★) **Le Clos de la
Tourne >>**

(★) **La Tour du
Pacoret >**

(★) **Château des
Allues >**

## Market Days around Les Bauges

**Le Châtelard:** summer only, Fri am.

## Sports and Activities around Les Bauges

For **paragliding:** *www. parapente-bauges.com,* t 04 79 54 88 63.

## Where to Stay and Eat around Les Bauges

**Aillon-le-Jeune** ✉ 73340
**La Grangerie B&B,** t 04 79 54 64 71, *www.lagrangerie.com* (€). Basic rooms in old farm above the ski resort in the centre of Les Bauges. Copious *table d'hôte* (€).

**Montailleur** ✉ 73460
***La Tour du Pacoret,** t 04 79 37 91 59, *www.chateauxhotels.com/pacoret* (€€). Atmospheric hotel in part-13th-century building, rooms in medieval tower overlooking the Isère valley. Restaurant (€€€–€€) in new wing with terrace; try the local wines. Pool. *Closed mid-Oct–April; restaurant closed Tues, plus Wed lunch outside July–Aug.*

**St-Pierre-d'Albigny** ✉ 73250
**Château des Allues B&B,** t 06 75 38 61 56, *www.chateaudesallues.com* (€€€). Tough-looking manor on the

outside, concealing very elegant rooms with extravagant beds. Set in grounds beside local vineyards. Smart *table d'hôte* (€€€) cuisine using the kitchen garden.

**Coise-St-Jean-Pied-Gauthier** ✉ 73800
****Château de la Tour du Puits,** Le Puits, t 04 79 28 88 00, *www. chateaudelatourdupuits.fr* (€€€€). This stocky 18th-century manor has divinely decorated rooms inside and large gardens outside from which to appreciate the Combe de Savoie. Its restaurant, **La Table du Baron** (€€€), serves refined cuisine. Pool. *Closed mid-Oct–Nov; restaurant closed Mon, and Tues lunch.*

**St-André-les-Marches** ✉ 73800
**Le Clos de la Tourne B&B,** Lachat, t 04 79 28 05 34, *www.closdelatourne.com* (€). Amidst the vines, in an adorable, peaceful location beside the Moulin de la Tourne, run with passion by the same family, offering sweet, simple, bargain rooms. *Table d'hôte.* Pool.

**Challes-les-Eaux** ✉ 73190
****Château des Comtes de Challes,** 247 Montée du Château, t 04 79 72 72 72, *www.chateaudescomtesdechalles. com* (€€€–€€). Variety of rooms, some magnificent, in a fortified medieval manor and its outbuildings (hence price differences), with fine views. Pleasing restaurant (€€€–€€). Pool.

# Lac du Bourget

(★) **Lac du Bourget**

The Lac du Bourget, Lac d'Annecy's closest rival for the title of France's finest lake, beats it in size. In fact it's the largest natural lake wholly located in France, 18km in length. It's sensationally beautiful, surrounded by mountains, with quite a number of ports dotted around its shores. The southern end may be marked by urban sprawl, but then Aix-les-Bains and Le Bourget can offer big marinas and lots of tourist facilities. It's not as posh as Lac d'Annecy; also, don't expect the clear waters of that lake here, as du Bourget has a muddy bottom. But the views from the glorious belvederes are pretty much as spectacular, as are sights like the abbey of Hautecombe, thrusting its chest out over the waters.

For by far the most charming little ports on Lac du Bourget, explore the havens at its northern end. **Châtillon**'s marina hides in an enchanting little bay below a picturesque **castle**, the latter set on a pimple of a hill above the port. In early medieval times, this château held the key to the lake, which was in fact known as the Lac de Châtillon up to the 13th century – the lordly family then moved to Le Bourget, hence the lake's change in name. The place also has the best beach on the north end of the lake. **Portout** boasts a sweet new **marina** tucked out of sight from the lake, plus Gallo-Roman pots from its **archaeological site**, displayed in the

**Musée des Potiers**
t 04 79 52 11 84; open
July–Aug daily 2.30–
6.30; mid-April–June
and Sept–mid-Oct
Fri–Mon 2.30–5.30; adm

**Musée des Potiers. Conjux**, in a more open position beside the lake, has a beach, and a clutch of professional fishermen still working.

The western side of Lac du Bourget has remained wilder than the eastern side, woods often obscuring views of the lake from this shore. But head up via peaceful, pastoral **St-Pierre-de-Curtille**, with its curiosity of a circular church, for an unforgettable view onto Lac du Bourget from the belvedere at **Ontex**.

**Abbaye de
Hautecombe**
t 04 79 54 26 12,
www.chemin-neuf.org/
hautecombe; open
Wed–Mon 10–11.15 and
2–5; closed Tues

Make sure you then make it down to the majestic **Abbaye de Hautecombe**, looking like a mighty stone vessel about to launch into the waters from its promontory. A Cistercian foundation dating back to 1135, it became one of the religious powerhouses of Savoie, sending missions to the crusades, while two of its abbots became pope in the 13th century, Celestine IV – for just 17 days – and Nicholas III, for slightly longer. In its highly prosperous 14th century, a chapel was constructed here to house the tombs of the counts (and later, dukes) of Savoie. Over 40 members of the family would be buried inside, up until the start of the 16th century, when the abbey fell into dire decline. The ruins became a favoured destination for tormented Romantics, most harrowingly the poet Lamartine and his fated love Julie Charles (see p.275). Charles-Félix of Savoie had the place sumptuously restored in 19th-century neo-Gothic style by Ernesto Melano, northern Italian artists adding a super-abundance of sculptures and decorative flourishes, while a religious community was reinstalled. Crammed with Romantic statues and paintings, the **church** looks more like a celebration of revivalism than a quiet resting place, troubadour style triumphing.

The descendants of the house of Savoie became kings of Italy for a brief period, with Hautecombe as their final resting place. In fact, the last king of Italy, Umberto II, was buried here as recently as 1983, although he had been deposed after just 33 days of rule in 1946, when a referendum saw the abolition of the Italian monarchy by a narrow margin, forcing Umberto into exile. The abbey is now home to the religious Communauté du Chemin Neuf. As well as visiting it, go down to the lake to admire the medieval **barn** built to receive the riches of the abbey's estates by water.

Southwest, climb to the most distinctive peak overlooking Lac du Bourget, the sharp **Dent du Chat**, or Cat's Tooth. A very silly legend says the name derives from the story of a dishonest fisherman in these parts. Desperate at not hooking any fish, he vowed to throw back the first creature he did catch, for luck. But when he landed a big fat pike, he forgot his promise. The next rapid catch surprised him, of a sweet kitten, which he also pocketed – but it grew into a monster that began devouring people who crossed its path. It was only killed by a brave soldier who got wise to the pattern of its behaviour. For the best views of all, walk to the nearby **Molard Noir**.

Below, the sturdy private **Château de Bourdeau**, occupying a great location above a sweet little port, has survived since the medieval period rather better than the centre of **Le Bourget-du-Lac**, but this town's privileged medieval **priory** still stands out here, its muddy-green *molasse*-stone church built on the remains of a Roman temple. It contains a colourful, action-packed and amusing 13th-century carved frieze, Christ riding into Jerusalem on a donkey resembling a rabbit. The priory buildings were converted into a home for an American woman early in the 20th century. The grounds with their irreligious statues of naked ladies are now a public garden. Count Thomas II of Savoie had an important **castle** closer to the lake, its ruins being restored to create a cultural centre focusing on Savoie's old forts. Le Bourget's lakeside **beaches** and **port** prove full of life, action and activities, if somewhat suburban.

Following the east bank of Lac du Bourget, for one of the most breathtaking views over its whole expanse, brave the scary road from **Chaudieu** behind Châtillon to **La Chambotte**'s belvedere, a sight to be enjoyed with calming tea and scones, a tradition maintained here since Queen Victoria's day. Far below, the main lakeside road hugs the lake down to Aix-les-Bains.

**Le Bourget priory**
*t 04 79 25 01 99; open July–Aug for guided tours via tourist office; adm*

**Le Bourget castle**
*t 04 79 25 01 99 for guided tours July–Aug; adm*

## Aix-les-Bains

Aix-les-Bains is a town of two halves, the historic, rather dignified spa town some way up the slope from Lac du Bourget, while, down below, the brash contemporary **port area** has been growing at a rate of knots right beside the lake. However pleasing all the developments may be for investors, the look is distinctly suburban, at odds with the unspoilt natural beauty on the opposite bank. However, the harbours are impressively full, the marinas offering over 1,500 berths. Lots of sailing and watersports events take place down here; in fact, the town has been awarded the coveted label of *Station Nautique* because of its exceptional facilities, the first French harbour away from the sea to receive the distinction. Towards the north, there are one or two appealing shaded terraces behind the older marina, plus the odd boutique on board a quirky boat. Walking south, the marinas are quite smart but can feel lacking in atmosphere. Further down, you come to a long beach and popular watersports centre.

Up the slope, the more genteel old **thermal spa resort** has been somewhat affected by the developers too. But this place has a long, distinguished history that is still clearly visible. The hot sulphurous waters here were celebrated by the Celtic Allobroges, then the Romans built splendid baths, important vestiges still standing. Forgotten for a vast period, in the early 1600s Henri IV brought a spark of life back to the place, while in the 18th century grand new spa buildings began to go up. Napoleon's family liked taking the waters here, but the best-remembered French visitor is the sickly young Romantic poet Lamartine, who came in October 1816 and met Julie Charles, a young married woman suffering from tuberculosis. They fell in love and promised to meet again the following season. Tragically, Julie was too ill to make it back, dying before the end of 1817; the forlorn Lamartine immortalized her in his poetry, notably 'Le Lac', under the name of Elvire.

Another famous visitor to Aix-les-Bains went by the subtle pseudonym of Countess of Balmoral. She was none other than Queen Victoria, and a whole British colony followed in her wake. The Anglo-Saxons didn't mix with the locals, but marked the place with their eccentricities. Lavish villas and hotels were built for the mega-wealthy 19th-century visitors. The First World War killed the trend for fashionable spa resorts; the generous French health service has kept the place going, but spa Aix is now working hard to promote more tempting pampering breaks for tourists.

The old town is something of an architectural jumble, but retains quite some style, and that curious spa mixture of sickness and celebration. Opposite the grand if mistreated Art Deco façade of the Thermes Nationaux stand the remnants of two major Roman monuments, the **Arch of Campanus** and the **Temple of Diana**, with a **Musée Archéologique** On guided tours of the town you're taken into the rather grim interior of the **Thermes Nationaux** to peer at the dark remnants of the Roman baths beneath.

Even if you detest gambling, peek inside the outrageous **Casino Grand Cercle** nearby, opened by King Victor Emmanuel II in 1850. Some of the original mosaics by Salviati and the stained glass are still in place above the fruit machines and their addicts in this extravaganza. Its theatre was the first place in France to stage Wagner's *Tristan and Isolde*, in 1897, and still puts on events.

Close by, the elegant **public gardens** exude a genteel air. The statue of Lamartine recalls his tragic connection. Followers of British royalty can pay homage to the severe statue of Victoria on a nearby square, and might seek out the modest **English church** beyond. Also discover **Place Carnot**, one of Aix's prettiest squares.

The majestic former hotels still mark the slopes with their fine silhouettes. However, there's a discreet but swanky new addition up in these parts, the contemporary **Thermes Chevalley**, once again

---

**Musée Archéologique**
*tours via tourist office; adm*

**Thermes Nationaux**
*t 08 10 44 33 32; specializes in treating rheumatism, but now caters to the general public too*

**Casino Grand Cercle**
*www.casinogrand cercle.com*

**Thermes Chevalley**
*t 08 10 44 33 32*

---

**Musée Faure**
*t 04 79 61 05 57; open
6 Jan–19 Dec Wed–
Mon 10–12 and 1.30–6;
closed Tues and public
hols; adm*

treating rheumatism, but also catering now in part for those in search of luxury treatments, with superb pools. The **Musée Faure**, set in a grand hillside villa, adds a delightful dash of culture, containing unusual Impressionist works. Up top, you'll find a room of contorted Rodin sculptures looking across to the vicious Dent du Chat, as well as some rather miserable memorabilia of Lamartine.

At the southern end of the lake, industry has long triumphed on the flat plain leading to Chambéry, added to by business and research parks. But one corner of the lakeside has recently been spruced up with the landscaped **Site des Mottets** and its **Port des Quatre Chemins**. There are little beaches and facilities for the sports-mad Savoyards on offer, but also explanations on the lake's ecology and its reed beds, which, as part of a concerted effort to clean up the Lac du Bourget, have been expanding again.

ⓘ **Aix-les-Bains >>**
*Place Maurice Mollard,
73100 Aix-les-Bains,
t 04 79 88 68 00,
www.aixlesbains.com*

ⓘ **Le Bourget-
du-Lac**
*Place Général Sevez,
73371 Le Bourget-du-
Lac, t 04 79 25 01 99,
www.bourgetdulac.com*

## Market Days around Lac du Bourget and Aix

**Le Bourget-du-Lac**: Thurs am.
**Aix-les-Bains**: Wed all day and Sat am.

## Events in Aix-les-Bains

Main events in Aix include the early summer **romantic nights** concert programme, and *Aquascénie*, a show on Savoie history including music, dance and fireworks. The port hosts many events, including the major gathering of *Navig'Aix* in August.

## Activities around Lac du Bourget and Aix

For **boat trips** on Lac du Bourget, try Aix-les-Bains tourist office, or, from Chanaz, **Compagnie des Bateaux du Lac du Bourget et du Haut-Rhône**, t 04 79 63 45 00, *www.gwel.com*, or **Bateaux de Chanaz**, t 04 79 54 29 13.

There are several spots from which to take to the skies **hang-gliding** or **paragliding** around Lac du Bourget; they include the Mont Revard, the Dent du Chat and La Chambotte.

Aix-les-Bains, as well as offering **spa** pamperings and **watersports** galore, has a reputed **golf course**, t 04 79 61 23 35, *www.golf-aixlesbains.com*. It also has the only **racecourse** in Savoie, the **Hippodrome de Marlioz**, *http:// aix.marlioz.free.fr*.

## Where to Stay and Eat in Aix-les-Bains

**Aix-les-Bains** ✉ **73100**

★★★**Le Manoir**, 37 Rue Georges 1er, t 04 79 61 44 00, *www.hotel-lemanoir.com* (€€€). Smart, calm address up close to the new Thermes, but with a stylish indoor pool and sauna of its own. Restaurant (€€€–€€) and garden with panoramic views. *Closed mid-Dec.*

★★★**Astoria**, 7 Place des Thermes, t 04 79 35 12 28, *www.hotelastoria.com* (€€). In the heart of the spa town, stylish rooms beyond the Art Deco entrance, and traditional restaurant (€€). *Closed early Dec.*

★★★**Adelphia**, La Marina, 215 Bd Robert Barrier, t 04 79 88 72 72, *www. adelphia-hotel.com* (€€€). Big, modern, comfortable block of a spa hotel just set back from the modern marina. Bright rooms with balconies, views either to lake or mountains. Indoor pool, spa pamperings, shaded garden. Restaurant (€€€–€€).

★★**Au Petit Vatel**, 11 Rue du Temple, t 04 79 35 04 80, *www.petit-vatel.com* (€). Old-style charm and simple rooms, by the Anglican church. Traditional regional cuisine (€€). *Closed Jan.*

★★**Davat**, 21 Chemin des Bateliers, Le Grand Port, t 04 79 63 40 40, *www.davat.fr* (€). Pleasant traditional hotel just behind the port. Garden where meals (€€) can be served. *Closed Jan and Feb; restaurant closed Sun eve and Mon.*

# Chambéry

⭐ **Chambéry**

In this cultured, culinary city, historic capital of Savoie, set amidst mountain ranges, regional symbols stand out prominently, notably the Savoyard flag, and a bellicose heraldic black lion, another proud symbol of the house of Savoie. The place acquired its political importance in the 13th century, when it was suddenly elevated to regional capital. The line of Savoie lords saw to the development of their headquarters. In 1453 the then duke came by a fabulous shroud said to have covered Christ's dead body; displayed here, it drew large numbers of pilgrims. But the expansionist French monarchy was pressing at the gates, briefly taking the city. The dukes moved to Turin for safety, taking their precious shroud, although Chambéry remained an important administrative centre, with senate and ducal treasury. French troops continued to harass the place. Then, after the 1730s, in which Jean-Jacques Rousseau famously lived here, in the 1740s a Spanish army wrought devastation. Victor-Amédée III had much of the castle rebuilt in grand style. The French returned at the Revolution, making Chambéry capital of the large if short-lived *département du Mont-Blanc*. After Napoleon's defeat, the Savoyards regained control until unification with France. Adventurer General Benoît de Boigne avoided the European upheaval altogether, fighting in India and making a fortune there, which he ploughed back into civic provisions for his home town, as you'll be reminded by Chambéry's most famous and curious monument, featuring elephants.

Grandiose buildings went up around Chambéry in the 19th century: the huge Napoleonic barracks, now opened up as the Carré Curial; the theatre, another gift from de Boigne, although reconstructed in Italianate style after a fire; and the law courts.

Occupied by Italians, then Germans, in the Second World War, Chambéry in May 1944 saw bombardment by the Allies, causing the destruction of one fifth of the city. But many of the historic quarters survived and have since been spruced up, pedestrianized, and bedecked with Savoyard banners. And in recent decades, this expanding university town has commissioned an array of striking contemporary buildings.

**Château de Chambéry**

*t 04 79 33 42 47; tours organized via tourist office; open July and Aug Mon–Fri for tours at 10.30, 2.30, 3.30 and 4.30; other school hols, plus May–June and 1st half Sept weekday tour at 2.30 only; adm*

The pleasingly compact historic kernel is encased in broad, busy boulevards. If you land in town on the right day, start with a tour of the huge **castle** of the dukes of Savoie, still an administrative city within the city, with a vast Ancien Régime front behind imposing machicolated medieval towers, one of these containing a chamber that can serve as a schoolroom for the guides to give you a lesson in Savoie history. The castle's aloof-looking **Sainte Chapelle** is where the 'Turin' shroud once lay. Despite a damaging fire, the chapel preserves fine 16th-century stained glass, even if Christ curiously changes face several times in his story. On certain Saturdays you're allowed up to the **bell-organ loft** perched way on high; every first and third Saturday in the month, at 5.30, the extraordinary musician here presses the 70 bells into riotous tune. The town authorities have also opened up the castle to the people in recent times for a whole programme of exciting, free summer evening concerts, *Les Estivales du Château*, in the great courtyard.

**Place du Château** below is overseen by grand mansions and an arresting statue of the de Maistre brothers, passionate Savoyard writers. **Rue Basse du Château**, curving away from here, has retained some of the features of its medieval shop fronts, while picturesque, stocky **Rue Juiverie** offers a tempting parallel route, with some nice present-day addresses.

But the main shopping artery leading from the château is **Rue de Boigne**, a major arcaded avenue of pink fronts, taking you straight as an arrow to Chambéry's most famous monument, topped by a statue of Benoît de Boigne. Certain shops may distract you along the way: chocoholics should pay homage **Au Fidèle Berger**, now a tea room, but the place where, in 1828, *chocolatier* Antoine Dufour invented the chocolate truffle. He soon went on to international success, opening a shop in London's Piccadilly Arcade.

Off to one side of Rue de Boigne, don't miss **Place St-Léger**, the most vibrant square in the centre, with its pinkish cobbles and fountains overseen by façades whose wooden shutters bring to mind Alpine chalets. It's a great place to stop at a café terrace. Explore the maze of alleyways off the square; here and there you'll stumble across *trompe l'œil* decoration, a Chambéry speciality.

One end of Place St-Léger, **Rue Croix d'Or**, lined with substantial houses, has a fine selection of shops. Among culinary specialities to look out for, Chambéry has companies producing their own pasta, vermouth and fruit cordials, while the vineyards just outside town supply the city's boutiques as well as its restaurants. Beyond the fancy 19th-century **theatre**, nicknamed 'the little La Scala' by the locals, and flatteringly lit up at night, like much of central Chambéry, you'll find further interesting shops along **Rue d'Italie**.

Tucked away from the shopping and in its own square between Place St-Léger and Rue Croix d'Or stands the well-concealed **cathedral**. It originally formed part of a medieval Franciscan abbey, but changed in status in 1779, when Chambéry became a bishopric. It was built in sober style, apart from the Flamboyant Gothic door. But brace yourselves for the dizzying *trompe-l'œil* tracery splashed all over the interior, like the wildest neo-Gothic wallpaper, the 19th-century work of Vicario. Fragments of older wall paintings survive, while the treasury displays beautiful items.

The big regional museum, the **Musée Savoisien**, sprawls across the rest of the former monastery, containing displays going back to

**Musée Savoisien**
*t 04 79 33 44 48; open Wed–Mon 10–12 and 2–6; closed Tues and public hols; adm, but free 1st Sun in month*

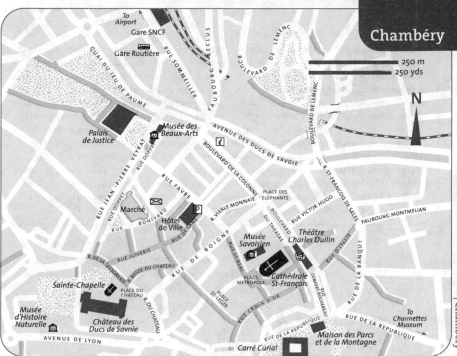

250 m
250 yds

N

To
Airport

Gare SNCF

Gare Routière

QUAI DU JEU DE PAUME

RUE SOMMEILLER

FAUBOURG RECLUS

RUE SOMMEILLER

BOULEVARD DE LEMENC

BOULEVARD DE LÉMENC

Palais
de Justice

Musée des
Beaux-Arts

AVENUE DES DUCS DE SAVOIE

BOULEVARD DE LA COLONNE

RUE JEAN - PIERRE VEYRAT

RUE DOPPET

RUE DOPPET

RUE FAVRE

RUE BONIVARD

Marché

Hôtel
de Ville

P

RUE DE LANS

R. VIEILLE MONNAIE

PLACE DES
ELEPHANTS

BOULEVARD DU THÉÂTRE

RUE VICTOR HUGO

R. ST-FRANÇOIS DE SALES

FAUBOURG MONTMELIAN

RUE JUIVERIE

R. DE LA TRÉSORERIE

RUE BASSE DU CHATEAU

RUE DE BOIGNE

RUE ST-RÉAL

Musée
Savoisien

Théâtre
Charles Dullin

RUE D'ITALIE

RUE DE LA BANQUE

RUE DERRIÈRE BOCHEREAU

Sainte-Chapelle

PLACE DU
CHATEAU

R. DU CHATEAU

PLACE
MÉTROPOLE

PLACE
ST-LÉGER

Cathédrale
St-François

RUE CROIX D'OR

Musée
d'Histoire
Naturelle

Château des
Ducs de Savoie

AVENUE DE LYON

Carré Curial

RUE DE LA REPUBLIQUE

RUE DE LA REPUBLIQUE

Maison des Parcs
et de la Montagne

To
Charmettes
Museum

the prehistoric communities that settled along Lac du Bourget 3,000 years ago. The Gallo-Roman section includes intriguing little finds. One level is devoted to paintings, many connected with the region, the explanations filling in pieces in the jigsaw puzzle of Savoyard history. One room even displays 13th-century murals ripped from the Château de la Rive – its illustrations of non-religious life, including an attack on a castle, are rare in medieval art. Further sections focus on Savoie rural life and the war.

Wide Boulevard du Théâtre leads to the **de Boigne column** and **Fontaine des Eléphants**, with its serene pachyderms unconcerned that they've lost their posteriors. Boulevard de la Colonne takes you on to further grandiose buildings on **Place du Palais de Justice**. You probably won't want an invitation into the law courts, despite their very grand look, but do visit the **Musée des Beaux-Arts** Its Italian collections are particularly rich, and a few well-known Flemish and French artists also get a look in.

In the opposite direction from the de Boigne column, the burly arcaded Napoleonic barracks of the **Carré Curial**, built around a very large central courtyard, have been given a modern makeover. As well as the odd boutique and restaurant under its arcades, the **Galerie Eurêka** covers scientific advances, with a special space devoted to the mountain environment. The striking, striped curves of the contemporary **Espace Malraux** next to the Carré Curial were designed by architect Mario Botta for theatre and major shows.

**Musée des Beaux-Arts**

*t 04 79 33 75 03; open Wed–Mon 10–12 and 2–6; closed Tues and public hols; free, exc temporary exhibitions*

### Rousseau in Chambéry

A deeply confused young Rousseau arrived in Chambéry from Annecy (*see* p.259) with Madame de Warens, his most important mentor. She found him a job in smelly offices working on the duke of Savoie's map to establish a more equitable tax system, but Rousseau resigned to follow his passion for sweeter music, which he taught in town. He and Madame de Warens then spent some of their happiest times renting Les Charmettes. Although he suffered a terrible and mysterious physical attack here, Rousseau loved the place, and, through his voracious studies, developed his '*magasin d'idées*', a store of ideas from which sprang his radical thinking on equality, education, nature, and society's general will, opposed to individual freedom. Study his world-changing works such as *La Nouvelle Héloïse*, *Emile* or *Du Contrat Social* to understand the mind credited with bringing the world the concept of the rights of man, and damned for creating the creed of the vilest totalitarian regimes. Or try his autobiography, *Les Confessions*, a spanking good read, with many details on Annecy and Chambéry. Rousseau has also gone down as a champion of the Alps, seeing in them a reflection of awesome divine power, foreshadowing the Romantics.

The latest addition around here for tourists is the **Maison des Parcs et de la Montagne**, introducing the region's ranges with films, photos, quizzes and temporary exhibitions; you'll spot mountains at the end of many a street in town.

**Maison des Charmettes**
*t 04 79 33 39 44; open April–Sept Wed–Mon 10–12 and 2–6; Oct–Mar Wed–Mon 10–12 and 2–4.30; closed Tues and public hols; free; evening performances July–Aug Wed and Fri; adm*

A steep two-mile route uphill beyond the Carré Curial leads you into almost unspoilt countryside and the **Maison des Charmettes**, briefly home to Chambéry's most famous 18th-century resident, Jean-Jacques Rousseau (*see* box, above), and still surrounded by sloping orchards with lovely views to the Bauges mountains. Les Charmettes' simple, faded interiors have retained a period charm. A few of Rousseau's brilliant quotes are presented, but, if you understand French, the most delightful way of appreciating his time in Chambéry is to attend one of the atmospheric evening performance-tours put on here, in costume, with music, followed by light refreshments with the affable cast.

## Market Days and Festivals in Chambéry

**Chambéry**: Tues and Sat am.

Chambéry organizes cultural events through the summer, including the free *Estivales du Château* from June to August, and classical and jazz festivals in September.

## Where to Stay and Eat

**Chambéry** ✉ **73000**

****Château de Candie**, Rue du Bois de Candie, t 04 79 96 63 00, *www. chateaudecandie.com* (€€€€–€€€). Beautifully furnished rooms in a 14th-century Savoyard fortress above town. The restaurant (€€€€–€€€) serves up *trompe-l'œil* decorations with refined

cuisine. Pool. *Restaurant closed Mon, Tues lunch, and Sat lunch June–July, plus Sun pm rest of year. Weekend deals of two nights for the price of one.*

***Les Princes**, 4 Rue de Boigne, t 04 79 33 45 36, *www.interhoteldesprinces. com* (€€). Sober, central, the décor rather dark, but with comfortable air-conditioned rooms, some themed. *Weekend deals of two nights for the price of one.*

**Les Pervenches**, Chemin des Charmettes, t 04 79 33 34 26, *www. pervenches.net* (€). In a delightful spot close to Rousseau's house 2km above town. Nice neat rooms; traditional bright restaurant (€€). *Restaurant closed Sun pm and Mon.*

La Ferme du Petit Bonheur B&B, 538 Chemin Jean-Jacques, t 04 79 85 26 17, *www.chambresdhotes-chambery.net*,

ⓘ **Chambéry** >
*24 Bd de la Colonne, 73000 Chambéry, t 04 79 33 42 47, www.chambery-tourisme.com*

★ **Château de Candie** >

(€€). Also up the slope towards Rousseau's house, this lovely renovated farm has four smart rooms and a large terraced garden. **Le Saint Réal**, 86 Rue St-Réal, **t** 04 79 70 09 33 (€€€€–€€€). Classic smart restaurant in historic central house. *Closed Sun, and 1st half Aug.* **L'Hypoténuse**, Carré Curial, **t** 04 79 85 80 15 (€€). Imaginative cuisine and modern décor. *Closed Sun and Mon, plus spring hols and mid-July–mid-Aug.* **La Maniguette**, 99 Rue Juiverie, **t** 04 79 62 25 26 (€€). Fashionable, serving an interesting single menu. *Closed Sun, Mon, and Tues eve.* **Le Z**, 12 Avenue des Ducs de Savoie, **t** 04 79 85 96 87 (€€). Big, trendy new central brasserie.

## Lac d'Aiguebelette and the Avant-Pays Savoyard

☆ **Lac d'Aiguebelette**

Moving to more tranquil waters via the dramatic Col de l'Epine pass, charming **Lac d'Aiguebelette** lies discreetly west of Chambéry, but still in a fabulous mountainous setting. It actually counts among the largest lakes in France, yet it makes for a wonderfully secretive discovery. The waters are an amazing colour, often an intense emerald-green; little boathouses line the lake's reedy sides, and fishermen make the most of the exceptional catches. Boats with engines are banned, but rowing teams from around the world come to train and compete here. In summer, Aiguebelette has the warmest waters of all the big lakes, recorded going up to 28°C, though you have to pay for the seven beaches. Consider cycling the relatively unstrenuous 17km round the whole lake; for example, beside the Nances motorway exit, hire bikes at **Vertes Sensations**.

**Vertes Sensations**
*t 04 79 28 77 08 or t 06 15 20 81 87, www.vertes-sensations. com; also organizes canoeing, via ferrata and paragliding; for more paragliding, also contact www.aiguebelette parapente.com*

The east bank road sticks to the lake, unlike the western one, but from there you look across to the spectacular **Montagne de l'Epine** – walk to this summit along the GR9A trail. Down below the **Château de Chambost**, beautiful, restful restaurant terraces cluster on the southern waterside, looking out to the two lake islands. Opposite, at **St-Alban-de-Montbel**, you'll find the biggest beach, **Le Sougey**, with glorious views and imported sand.

Beyond Lac d'Aiguebelette, the beautiful border land of the southern **Avant-Pays Savoyard**, once disputed territory, now proves most calming, with far more cows than people, producing mountains of Emmental and Tomme de Savoie cheese. Stop at the **Col de la Crusille** for mesmerizing views down on the Dauphiné, the ruins of the **Château de Montbel** a tempting destination for walkers. The nearby ruined **Château de Rochefort** retains memories of one of the most notorious smugglers in this frontier zone, the 18th-century Louis Mandrin. To confound the authorities, he even shoed his horses back-to-front! He was caught at this castle, and sent to be executed in Valence. Close to the Col du Banchet, the **Grottes de Dullin** were caves where Mandrin hid merchandise and arms. The listed church at **Dullin** conceals its own enticing features.

Savoie's Great Lakes | Lac d'Aiguebelette and the Avant-Pays Savoyard

**Château de Montfleury**

*t 04 76 32 92 71; open July–Aug daily 1–6; May–June and Sept Sat, Sun and public hols 2–6; adm*

**Radio Musée Galletti**

*t 04 76 31 76 38; open July–Aug Mon, Thurs, Sat and Sun 3–6; May–June and Sept Sun 3–6; adm*

**Attignat-Oncin Tanner**

*t 04 79 36 00 26; open July–Aug for tours Wed at 4, Sat at 3; adm*

ⓘ **Avant-Pays Savoyard**

*Bouvent, 73470 Novalaise, t 04 79 36 09 29, www.avant-pays-savoyard.com*

ⓘ **St-Genix-sur-Guiers**

*Rue du Faubourg, 73240 St-Genix-sur-Guiers, t 04 76 31 63 16, www.valguiers.com*

ⓘ **Lépin-le-Lac/Aiguebelette**

*Place de la Gare, 73610 Lépin-le-Lac, t 04 79 36 00 02, www.lac-aiguebelette.com*

ⓘ **Le Pont-de-Beauvoisin**

*Rue Gambetta, 38480 Le Pont-de-Beauvoisin, t 04 76 32 70 74*

★ **La Chesneraie >**

Down on the flats, seek out the **Château de Montfleury**, somewhat neglected by time, its 13th-century tower and Ancien Régime wings having served some 30 years as a holiday home. It was then taken over by a painter-cum-collector who has crammed it with his brash works and a massive display of objects, most impressive of which are the weapons and armour. To the north, the hamlet of **St-Maurice-de-Rotherens** lies below **Mont Tournier**, high point of the frontier **Pays de Guiers**. Climb to the ruined medieval castle for majestic views. The cute little **Radio Musée Galletti** tells the story of a pioneering 20th-century engineer.

The fish-rich frontier **Guiers river** now offers great canoeing possibilities. Its waters join the Rhône close to the quiet town of **St-Genix-sur-Guiers**, just one gateway remaining from its medieval defences. The place's name is linked to a slightly sickly cake with lumps of praline, *brioche de St-Genix*, deliberately breast-shaped, in honour of the 3rd-century Sicilian martyr Agatha. Legend has it she had her breasts cut off by cruel Romans for her faith...but that they grew back. This religious figure became popular in Savoie once the dukes had also become kings of Sardinia.

South, **Le Pont-de-Beauvoisin** consists of two competitive, colourful towns mirroring each other either side of the Guiers, known for *chocolatiers* and furniture makers. The D921 via **Attignat-Oncin**, with its rare traditional **tanner**, leads south towards the daunting but stunning walls of the Chartreuse range.

## Market Days in Aiguebelette and Avant-Pays Savoyard

**Novalaise**: Wed and Sun am.
**St-Genix-sur-Guiers**: Wed am.
**Le Pont-de-Beauvoisin**: Mon am.

## Where to Stay and Eat in Aiguebelette and Avant-Pays Savoyard

### Aiguebelette Port ✉ 73610

**Les Belles Rives**, t 04 79 36 05 03, *www.bellesrives-berthet.com* (€€). Enchanting waterside address with great terraces and views, serving lake specialities. *Closed Dec–Feb.*

### St-Alban-de-Montbel ✉ 73610

**La Chesneraie B&B**, t 04 79 36 04 33, *www.lachesneraie.com* (€€€). Wonderful lakeside home, built for an opera singer at the start of the early 20th century, in an operatic setting. Extremely well furnished, beautiful rooms with dramatic views. Great for peace, or fishing.

### Novalaise-Lac ✉ 73470

**\*\*Novalaise-Plage**, t 04 79 36 02 19, *www.novalaiseplage.com* (€€–€). A big white house by the water, with its own beach. Imaginative cuisine (€€€–€€), thanks to the welcoming new chef-owner who cooked with the fabled Troisgros. *Closed Jan; restaurant closed Tues and Wed in winter.*

### Champagneux ✉ 73240

**\*\*Les Bergeronnettes**, Hameau de l'Eglise, t 04 76 31 81 01, *www.silencehotel.com* (€€). Spectacular views on the Rhône and Bugey from the mid-slope location in the shadow of the church, and neat, bargain modern rooms. Big restaurant (€€–€) with several terraces. Small indoor pool with views.

# Chartreuse,
# Grenoble and Vercors

South of Savoie's great lakes, the pre-alpine drama continues with the formidable, jagged natural fortifications of the Dauphiné's Chartreuse and Vercors ranges, divided by the deep trench of the Isère valley, in which dynamic Grenoble stands guard. That highly scientific city is always buzzing, but the mountains immediately above offer beautiful, peaceful retreats. The Chartreuse has been doing so for centuries, home as it is to the headquarters of the austere Carthusian monks, also makers of violently coloured herbal Chartreuse liqueurs. The Vercors is more edgy, with alarming roads up to it, dark caverns to visit, and martyred villages recalling Second World War atrocities, though today its high plateaux are geared mainly to pleasure. East below the Vercors, and encircled by natural drama, the Trièves and Maythesine stretch out calmly to upper Provence.

# 16

## Don't miss

🌟 **The Chartreuse's huge teeth**
Mont Granier and the Dent de Crolles pp.289/291

② **A scientific city with lashings of history**
Grenoble p.292

③ **A Revolutionary castle**
Château de Vizille p.300

④ **The Trièves' totem**
Mont Aiguille p.302

⑤ **The spine-chilling Vercors**
Les Grands Goulets, the Choranche caves and war museums pp.304/305

*See map overleaf*

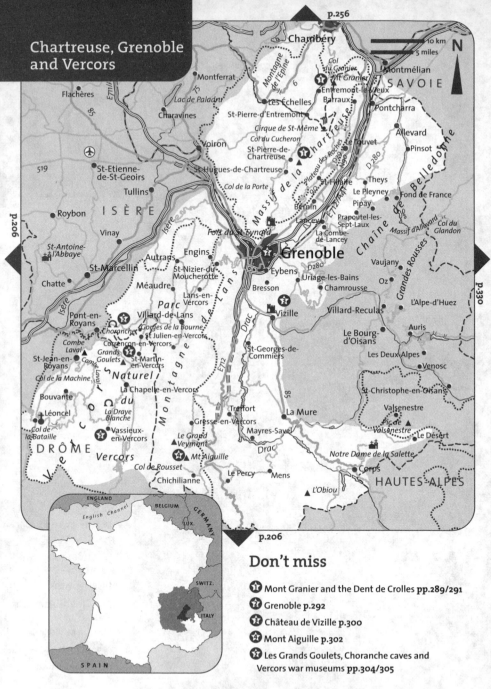

Chartreuse, Grenoble and Vercors

p.206

## Don't miss

⬩ Mont Granier and the Dent de Crolles **pp.289/291**

⬩ Grenoble **p.292**

⬩ Château de Vizille **p.300**

⬩ Mont Aiguille **p.302**

⬩ Les Grands Goulets, Choranche caves and Vercors war museums **pp.304/305**

The sensational Chartreuse and Vercors ranges make up the mountainous, forested, eastern half of the Dauphiné. Sandwiched between them, the historic capital of that former province, ever-expanding Grenoble, has squeezed out all over the big, flat

# Getting to and around Chartreuse, Grenoble and Vercors

**By air**: Chambéry/Aix airport lies just north of the Chartreuse. Note that Grenoble airport lies *c.* 40km northwest of the city, by St-Erienne-de-St-Geoirs.

**By train**: Grenoble, hub of public transport for this chapter, is just under 3hrs from Paris-Gare de Lyon. Ordinary trains between Grenoble and Lyon take *c.* 2hrs.

**By bus**: For detailed bus services, *see www.transisere.fr.*

crossroads of the Isère and Drac valleys. Not just the Chartreuse and Vercors oversee the city – the Belledonne forms a massive snowy barrier to the east. Grenoble's location is stunning, but so are all the territories covered here...even if the roads up into all these mountains count among the most daunting in France.

The Belledonne's western slopes (for the eastern side, *see* p.344) now offer small ski *domaines* in winter, and a narrow balcony of a tourist route in summer, with splendid walks to remarkable high-altitude lakes. While the Belledonne is topped by traditional triangular Alpine peaks, amazing molar-shaped mountains mark the ranges across the Isère. Either end of the Chartreuse, the Mont Granier and Dent de Crolles match each other in haggish grandeur. The name of Chartreuse may conjure up images of potent monkish brews in poisonous green and yellow, but the most important historical fact is that the Chartreuse (Carthusian) order of monks was created here in the 11th century by St Bruno, a medieval model for an uncompromising life of work and prayer.

Grenoble, host of the Winter Olympics in 1968, may have the image of an ultra-modern city, but it also turns out to have a fantastic historic legacy. Drink in the past, and the studenty present, in its café- and restaurant-lined streets and squares. The place is peppered with excellent museums. South, the Château de Vizille, built for the Dauphiné's great Ancien Régime Protestant leader, Lesdiguières, is now home to an engrossing museum tracing the French Revolution through art – significant early revolutionary rumblings were heard in these parts. Vizille also lies along the Route Napoléon, recalling the *petit caporal*'s final desperate bid to reclaim power in Paris, coming over from his exile on Elba in 1815 on a last wave of popular support. This road cuts through the Matheysine, on the east bank of the Drac, beautiful former mining land. The other side of the Drac, the calmly gorgeous, agricultural Trièves has as backdrop the Mont Aiguille, perhaps the most photogenic of all France's pre-alpine toothy tops.

Mont Aiguille is just one of the many extremely challenging peaks of the Vercors. From whichever side you approach this formidable natural fort, the roads up to it are hair-raising. On high, you reach gentle plateaux dotted with small, open resorts, the pastures carpeted with the densest flora from late spring. But in these parts many villages preserve terrible memories of the

Second World War, when the Germans mounted a full-scale offensive to root out the Resistance fighters here. Some hid in the Vercors' huge caves, but not in the most spectacular, the Grottes de Choranche. The Vercors ends in the south with head-spinning drops into the Drôme valley.

# The Isère Valley and Belledonne

Overseen by the Chartreuse's massive teeth to the west and the Belledonne's almost eternally snow-tipped peaks to the east, the stretch of the Isère from Pontcharra to Grenoble offers a remarkably flat route through these tortured mountainous parts. It's known as the **Grésivaudan** – roughly speaking, the valley of Grenoble. In 1960, the river was canalized to put a stop to its impetuous mood swings, allowing cereals to grow on the flats. On the safer first slopes, walnuts, fruit trees, vines and cattle have long shared the meagre space. But industry took root early too.

## The Western Belledonne

**Pontcharra**, in border territory with Savoie, was the birthplace of Pierre III Terrail, lord of Bayard, long a hero in the French history books. The **Musée Bayard** relating his story is located in the **Château Bayard** above town, the place where he was born in 1476. Portrayed in old-fashioned French history as the ideal knight, sans peur et sans reproche ('beyond fear or reproach'), he was first sent to be a pageboy for the duke of Savoy, but went on to serve three French kings in a row, Charles VIII, Louis XII and François I. Best known for his valiant, even foolhardy bravery in the Italian campaigns of the megalomaniac François, after one remarkable act of courage he was even given the honour of knighting the king himself, but finally ended up mortally wounded in Italy.

Close to Pontcharra and the village of **St-Maximin**, the soaring landmark **Tour d'Avalon**, although 19th-century, recalls earlier history, because of its association with the 12th-century Carthusian Hugues d'Avalon, who became Bishop of Lincoln under Henry II of England. Up the Bens river lay an outpost of the Grande Chartreuse monastery (see pp.290–91), the **Chartreuse de St-Hugon**. Virtually nothing remains, but the setting is awesome. The Buddhist retreat now established here received the Dalai Lama in 1997.

Pressing into the Belledonne range, **Allevard** grew into a curious mix of industrial iron and steel town and spa town, its mining past recalled at the **Musée Jadis Allevard**, while the spa life and casino cling on. In its 19th-century heyday the place received many celebrities; its waters were used to treat voice complaints, hence its popularity with theatrical types...and politicians!

**Musée Bayard**
*t 04 76 97 68 08,
www.ville-pontcharra.fr;
open late May–late
Sept Wed–Mon 2–6;
closed Tues; adm*

**Musée Jadis
Allevard**
*t 04 76 45 16 40,
www.musee-jadis-
allevard.fr; open
July–Aug Sun–Thurs
10–12 and 3–6; check
tims rest of year; adm*

One mountain route up from the town takes you via the **Collet d'Avellard**, where you can take a ski-lift to an exceptional signed hiking trail, the **Sentier 2000**, its name indicating the altitude. Allevard is also the gateway up into the beautiful, hidden **Bréda valley**, reaching deep into the Belledonne. The villages here have preserved their old character, **Pinsot** holding on to its metal and milling traditions with the **Musée des Forges et Moulins** The countryside teems with wild orchids in season.

The name of **Fond-de-France** acts as a reminder that this was once frontier territory with Savoie. With the valley above sealed off by the Gleyzin glacier, it's a great place to start out on summer walks through the **Massif d'Allevard**, below some of the Belledonne's highest peaks, which reach almost to 3,000m. Thousands of sheep congregate at the **Combe Madame** for summer grazing. The valley road turns up to the little ski station of **Le Pleyney**, one of three making up the Belledonne ski terrain of **Les Sept-Laux** (*see* p.394) – a series of high-altitude lakes are strung out to the south, hence the name.

Snaking along the mid slopes above the Isère between Allevard and Uriage, the D280 road is known as the Belledonne's **Route des Balcons**, twisting and turning through steep orchards, the odd vineyard below, sharp peaks above. The village of **Theys** has preserved its traditional architecture. Branch off for **Pipay** or **Prapoutel**, Les Sept-Laux's two other resorts. Beyond, the most uplifting way to appreciate the Belledonne is to walk the GR549, a looping path taking you through the heart of the range. A daring engineer, Aristide Bergès, found a way of raising the **Lac du Crozet** higher in the 19th century, all the better to exploit it for *houille blanche*, 'white coal', or hydroelectric power. This was a major technological advance, turning the Alps' water power into electricity. Bergès is honoured at the **Musée de la Houille Blanche** at **Lancey** down by the Isère.

Above, still on the Route des Balcons, the diminutive **Musée Rural d'Arts et Traditions Populaires** at **La Combe-de-Lancey** offers an insight into peasant life in the Belledonne range alongside the village castle, its gardens accessible via the museum, offering particularly fine views across the valley. Also visit the very sweet **Miellerie de Montgoutoux**, its exhibition on mountain honey-making set in an 18th-century barn.

The D280 draws squiggles around the slopes east of Grenoble to land up at the still elegant old valley spa resort of **Uriage**, a green haven. From the Belle Epoque onwards, it has attracted glamorous literati such as André Gide and Colette, the latter one of several authors to feature the town in her writing, under a thin literary disguise. The palatial **Grand Hôtel** with its thermal spa still dominates the scene.

**Musée des Forges et Moulins**
*t 04 76 13 53 59, perso.orange.fr/forges-moulins; open July–Aug Wed–Sun for tours at 10.30, 2, 3.30 and 5; May–June and Sept Wed–Sun for tours at 3 and 4.30; adm*

**Musée de la Houille Blanche**
*under renovation*

**Musée Rural d'Arts et Traditions Populaires**
*t 04 76 90 50 25; open all year, by appt only; adm*

16 | Chartreuse, Grenoble and Vercors | The Isère Valley and Belledonne

The awe-inspiring looping D111 road then takes you far above to **Chamrousse**, among the very earliest ski resorts in France. On the way, pass through **Prémol forest**, and by the **Luitel lake and peatbog**, the exceptional flora explained on panels. From Chamrousse itself (*see* **Winter Sports**, p.394), take the cable car (July–Aug) to the **Croix de Chamrousse** for fabulous views across to many other Alpine ranges. Up here you can join the GR549 hiking trail once again, and enjoy the southern Belledonne's high-altitude lakes, for example the lovely **Lac d'Achard**.

## Along the Chartreuse's Eastern Flank

Following the west bank of the Isère through the Grésivaudan, the N90 paralleling the motorway is industrial and commercial. Climb to the lower eastern slopes of the Chartreuse to appreciate a calmer route and splendid vistas onto the Belledonne.

**Barraux fort**
*t 04 76 85 16 15 for details of tours*

By **Barraux**, just west of Pontcharra, the star-shaped **fort** has an interesting history, but also conserves terrible more recent memories as an internment camp during the world wars. **Ste-Marie-d'Alloix** is dedicated to the happier production of decent white wine, and **La Flachère** to pottery. The **Château du Touvet**, a proud, family-owned manor in the Dauphiné style, boasts the most elegant formal French gardens set around water features, all in a sensational setting. The rich interiors include Empire touches, and a dining room lined with Cordoba leather.

**Château du Touvet**
*t 04 76 08 42 27, www.touvet.com; open July–Aug Mon–Sat 2–6; April–June and Sept–Oct Sun 2–6; adm*

Extremely steep routes lead up onto the otherworldly mid-slope **Plateau des Petites Roches**, an uplifting spot for walkers, set under the spectacular **Dent de Crolles**. The views east are stunning, reaching as far as Mont Blanc. The plateau is a favourite spot for hang-gliders and paragliders. Almost as exhilarating is the cable car from **Montfort** (runs April–late Nov) whisking you up 800m, passing above the **Oule waterfall**.

(i) **Pontcharra**
*21 Rue Laurent Gayet, 38530 Pontcharra, t 04 76 97 68 08*

(i) **Allevard**
*Place de la Résistance, 38580 Allevard, t 04 76 45 10 11, www.allevard-les-bains.com*

(i) **St-Hilaire-du-Touvet >>**
*102 Route des 3 Villages, 38660 St-Hilaire-du-Touvet, t 04 76 08 33 99, st-hilairedutouvet@ wanadoo.fr*

(i) **Uriage >>**
*5 Av des Thermes, 38410 Uriage-les-Bains, t 04 76 89 10 27, www.uriage-les-bains.com*

 **Grand Hôtel >>**

## Market Days in the Isère Valley and Belledonne

**Allevard**: Thurs am.

## Activities in the Isère Valley and Belledonne

For **paragliding** from St-Hilaire-du-Touvet, contact **Prévol Parapente**, *www.prevol.com*.

## Where to Stay and Eat in the Isère Valley and Belledonne

**Le Touvet** ✉ 38660

**Fontrier B&B**, 81 Rue de la Charrière, Le Pré Carré, t 04 76 08 42 30 (€). Pretty old-stone 18th-century farm with charming rooms.

**Uriage** ✉ 38410

****Grand Hôtel**, Place Déesse Hygie, t 04 76 89 10 80, www.grand-hotel-uriage.com (€€€€–€€€). Very grand, restored 19th-century hotel, luxurious modern hydrotherapy centre and fabulous restaurant, **Les Terrasses**

## Sidebar

(i) **Les Sept-Laux**
*Les Curtillets, 38190 les Sept-Laux, t 04 76 08 17 86, www.les7laux.com*

 **Les Mésanges >**

(i) **Chartreuse**
*Association de Développement Touristique de Chartreuse, t 04 76 88 64 00, www.chartreuse-tourisme.com*

*Maison du Parc, 38380 St-Pierre-de-Chartreuse, t 04 76 88 75 20, www.parc-chartreuse.net*

⭐ **Mont Granier**

**Musée de l'Ours**
*t 04 79 26 29 87, www.musee-ours-cavernes.com; open July–Aug daily 10–12.30 and 2.30–6.30; June and Sept daily 2.30–6.30; May Mon–Fri 2.30–6.30, Sat and Sun 10–12.30 and 2.30–6.30; Feb–April and Oct Sat and Sun 2.30–6.30; Jan Sun 2.30–6.30; closed Nov–Dec; adm*

**Cirque de St-Même**
*May–early Sept parking charge and restricted numbers*

**Grottes des Echelles**
*t 04 79 36 65 95; open mid-June–mid-Sept daily 10–6; Easter–mid-June and mid-Sept–Oct Sat and Sun 10–6; adm*

## Top column text

(€€€€). *Restaurant closed Mon, and Tues lunch, in July–Aug; rest of year closed Sun, Mon, and Tues–Thurs lunchtimes, plus late Aug.*
**\*\*Les Mésanges**, St-Martin d'Uriage, **t** 04 76 89 70 69, *www.hotel-les-mesanges.com* (€). A really bright, bargain family-run hotel 1km up from Uriage, with fabulous views over the valley. Good practical rooms, some with balconies. Lovely restaurant (€€€–€€) with divine terrace views. Large grounds and pool. *Closed late-Oct–Jan; restaurant closed Mon lunch and Tues in May–Oct, as well as Sun eve and Mon eve in Feb–April.*

# The Chartreuse Range

This fabulous fortress of tormented mountains rises between Grenoble and Chambéry. In fact, the northern Chartreuse lies in Savoie today. As its name indicates, the **Entremont** ('Between the Mountains') **valley** cuts through the middle of the range; climb the formidable mountain road from Chambéry to the **Col du Granier**, with wonderful glimpses back down onto Lac du Bourget.

The awesome molar of **Mont Granier** towers over these parts. A vast **cave** below the summit was only discovered as recently as 1988, its entrance long obstructed. Inside, explorers encountered a huge cache of bones – bears' bones, dated from 45,000 BC to 24,000 BC. The reasons for this high spot of ursine hibernation are explained at the contemporary **Musée de l'Ours** in **Entremont-le-Vieux**. A **cheese co-operative** stands temptingly close by.

For keen hikers, the most sensational Chartreuse walking path, the GR9, links the Mont Granier in the north to the Dent de Crolles in the south. But, continuing along the road into the heart of the range, **St-Pierre-d'Entremont** is the tourist nub, overseen by the ruins of the medieval **Château de Montbel**. The Chartreuse was declared a regional nature park in 1995; St-Pierre's tourist office doubles as a **Relais du Parc**, presenting its aims and highlights, and has a good craft shop, with local herbs also on sale.

East, the **Cirque de St-Même** ends with a theatrical dead end of mountains named after a hermit who hid out here. Walkers head for the spectacular waterfalls, sources of the Guiers-Vif river.

On the Chartreuse's western edge, you can reach the **Grottes des Echelles** via the **Gorges du Guiers Vif**. To get to the two long, narrow caves, you then need to walk down a small canyon of a stone path dating back to Roman times. The folk hero recalled here, the smuggler Mandrin, has gone down in legend as a kind of Ancien Régime Robin Hood. The concretions in the second cave include some surprising natural phallic forms. You emerge even more alarmingly in the midst of a cliff-face, albeit with painterly views of the Avant-Pays Savoyard (*see* p.281).

Head for the southern half of the Chartreuse range via the **Col du Cucheron**. **St-Pierre-de-Chartreuse** consists of a scattering of charming hamlets on steep slopes, including a little ski resort. The village of **St-Hugues-de-Chartreuse** lies contentedly in a more open valley. Its church, converted into an Isère **Musée Départemental d'Art Sacré Contemporain** contains an intriguing cycle of paintings and decorations, the work of the artist Arcabas, inspired to grand designs here on three separate occasions, in 1952, 1973 and 1985. The display ends with the superb drama of his *Last Supper*.

On an even more elevated religious note, the Chartreuse (or Carthusian) monastic order was founded in a splendidly isolated mountain spot west of St-Pierre. The monks didn't live in abject conditions; you can visit a typical double-levelled Carthusian cell at the **Musée de la Grande Chartreuse** at **La Correrie**, former monastic buildings constructed for lay brothers on the roadside two kilometres from the Grande Chartreuse itself, now converted into a beautiful museum giving an excellent picture of the order's history and punishing monastic life. The **Couvent de la Grande Chartreuse**, to be admired in photos here, took on its magnificent architectural forms, with a fine array of steep slate roofs worthy of a palace, when it was rebuilt after a fire in 1676. Banished at the Revolution, the Carthusians only returned to France and the Chartreuse range in 1940. Today, there are 19 Carthusian monasteries worldwide.

Do walk up to behold the Grande Chartreuse itself, hidden away in its own circle of mountains, in a *zone de silence* encouraging you to follow the order's example for a short time. The magical spot exudes a spiritual air, and has shown its power to move visitors' souls down the centuries. Two of the most significant Englishmen to put the Alps on the map for the British, the poets Thomas Gray and William Wordsworth, declared this place to be the most moving they saw in the whole Alps. Gray described the Grande Chartreuse as 'one of the most solemn, the most romantic, and the most astonishing scenes I ever beheld.' But he could not go inside the monastery and neither can you, the monks still famously devoted to isolated work, study and prayer.

**Musée Départemental d'Art Sacré Contemporain**
*t 04 76 88 65 01, www.arcabas.com; open Wed–Mon 10–6; closed Tues; adm*

**Musée de la Grande Chartreuse**
*t 04 76 88 60 45, www.musee-grande-chartreuse.fr and www.chartreux.org; open June–Sept daily 9.30–6.30; April–May and Oct–early Nov daily 10–12 and 2–6.30; adm*

## Seven Stars for Seven Brothers

The Carthusian story begins with saintly Bruno of Cologne. His religious education led him to the highly reputed theological school of Reims, where he became a renowned teacher. But Bruno was dismayed by the corruption he encountered. Unable to change it, he left in his fifties to devote himself to a life of solitude, gathering six followers along the way. The story goes that Hugues, bishop of Grenoble at that time, had a vision of seven stars in a dream. When Bruno and his men came to him in 1084 to ask for a place to found a hermitage, he led them up to this spot. After just a few years, Bruno was called away to serve the papacy, and would die in Italy.

But the Carthusian establishment grew. Guigues, the fifth prior, wrote down its statutes in 1127. He oversaw the construction of the first solid buildings, although these were destroyed by an avalanche that killed seven monks. By 1140, the Carthusian order was, however, officially recognized. While the monks were devoted to an extremely strict life of study and meditation, the lay brothers busied themselves with hard labour and mastered many crafts, including iron-working. They also developed and made the heady herbal Chartreuse liqueurs; find out more about those on pp.212–213.

However, a fascinating recent film, *Into Great Silence*, gives a very good picture of the monks' highly ordered daily routine, centred around the chapel. Surely the true antidote to a Hollywood action movie, the film encouraged contemplation, repeating Christ's main messages, including the giving up of worldly goods. The monks are also shown on their weekly walk, the only time when they can chat, but the few times they are heard proves disappointing, as they discuss petty rules or utter platitudes on God's benevolence, without addressing all the evil that exists outside their enclosed world.

Not far off, for a challenging walk reflecting the high drama of the Chartreuse, try the exhilarating way to the **Belvédère des Sangles**. It's not such a difficult path up through meadows to **Charmant Som**, one of the best viewing platforms in the range.

Southeast of St-Pierre-de-Chartreuse, a small road leads to the most distinctive southern tooth of the Chartreuse, the well-named **Dent de Crolles**. You can walk right to the top. Explorers have discovered that the mountain is hollow beneath its solid-looking exterior. In fact, the whole of the Chartreuse is a potholers' delight.

🟉 **Dent de Crolles**

Heading out of the heart of the range towards Grenoble via the **Col de la Porte**, the distinctive tower of the church of **Le Sappey** is regarded as one of the symbols of the Chartreuse for the Grenoblois far below. This pretty village has a place in French skiing history, having hosted some of the country's earliest ski competitions. It lies below the Chartreuse's heighest height, **Chamechaude**, reaching 2,082m. As the giant mountain's name implies, the fields below it receive plenty of warm sunshine.

Reaching the southern edges of the Chartreuse, the **Fort du St-Eynard**, one of a rash of dramatic 19th-century defences built around Grenoble, stands in near-suicidal position on a cliff edge. The sheer view down on to the valley-bottom city from 1,338m induces vertigo. Recover your senses at the fort's café.

ⓘ **Les Echelles**
*Rue Stendhal, 73360 Les Echelles, t 04 79 36 56 24, www.chartreuse-tourisme.com*

ⓘ **St-Pierre-d'Entremont >**
*73670 St-Pierre-d'Entremont, t 04 79 65 81 90, ot.entremonts@wanadoo.fr*

ⓘ **St-Pierre-de-Chartreuse >>**
*38380 St-Pierre-de-Chartreuse, t 04 76 88 62 08, www.st-pierre-chartreuse.com*

## Where to Stay and Eat in the Chartreuse

### St-Pierre-d'Entremont
✉ **73670**

**\*\*Hôtel Château de Montbel, t** 04 79 65 81 65 (€). Old-fashioned central village inn serving excellent regional food (€€). *Closed Easter and late Oct–mid-Dec; restaurant closed Sun eve and Mon.*

**\*\*Chalet du Cirque de St-Même, t** 04 79 65 89 28, *www.chalet-hotel.com* (€). In excellent peaceful country location close to this superb natural sight; a modern building, but in local style. Plain, simple rooms, and restaurant (€) serving decent regional food.

### St-Pierre-de-Chartreuse
✉ **38380**

**\*\*\*Beau Site, t** 04 76 88 61 34, *www.hotelbeausite.com* (€€). Good option in a village with a number of pretty hotels. Restaurant (€€). Pool. *Closed April–early May and mid-Oct–mid-Dec; restaurant closed Sun pm, Mon and Tues.*

**Pirraud B&B,** Pré Montagnat, **t** 04 76 88 65 44 (€). Stylish new chalet, but in traditional style. *Table d'hôte* (€).

**Le Sappey 38700**

**Le Chant de l'Eau B&B, t** 04 76 88
83 16. A lovely Chartreuse address.

**La Grignotte**, Les Charmettes, t 04 76
88 83 36. A restaurant in a splendid
chalet with fabulous terrace views,
serving mountain specialities.

# Grenoble

⚡ Grenoble    Encircled by sensational jagged mountain ranges, Grenoble lies
totally on the flat, a rare thing in the Alps, and at the junction of
several valleys, a great advantage in such rugged terrain, enabling
trade to develop. Unfairly burdened with a reputation for being
uncompromisingly modern and industrial, it turns out to be a
cosmopolitan place, with wonderful squares and fine museums
recalling a fascinating history.

## History

Grenoble's Gallo-Roman predecessor, Gratianopolis, was insignificant compared to magnificent Vienne on the Rhône (*see* pp.182–7),
under whose authority it lay, but by the 3rd century AD it was
surrounded by substantial walls, perhaps to keep out the tempes-
tuous river waters as well as invaders. Christianity got an early
footing here, as you can still see in two extraordinary subterranean
fragments of ancient churches.

In medieval times, the bishops battled with the local lords for
power over the city. They shared it for some time, until the mighty
counts of Albon took control. One of them, Guigues IV, was given
the name of Dauphin (Dolphin), adopted by his descendants, the
region they ruled then becoming known as the Dauphiné.

The well-guarded city took on the role of commercial and
political capital of the Dauphiné. Dauphin Humbert II established
his council and treasury here. He even created a university, but
disastrously overstretched himself and was forced to sell – the
whole region. So French king Philippe V bought the Dauphiné in
1349, giving it to his eldest son. From that time on, the heir to the
French throne would be known as the Dauphin. Only one, the
future Louis XI, truly ruled the region before becoming king; he
created the Dauphiné *Parlement* or law courts in Grenoble in 1453.

The 16th-century Wars of Religion caused bitter fighting in the
region, the fanatical Baron des Adrets wreaking devastation. But
the leading Protestant Lesdiguières put his stamp firmly on
Grenoble, securing it in 1590 on behalf of King Henri IV, extending
the ramparts, and also defending the Dauphiné from the dukes of
Savoie. The Catholic Church hit back in the 17th century by building
religious communities around town. This remained a military city,
however, with further fortifications sprouting up through the
Ancien Régime; and in this period the city's merchants, and its
libertines, also prospered. The production of gloves, a symbol of

status, became one of Grenoble's major industries, using skins supplied by the goats on the slopes far above.

Despite its image of aristocratic elegance, as the Ancien Régime cracked up, Grenoble flared up. The Journée des Tuiles in June 1788 was named after a riot caused by the monarchy's attempt to close France's regional *Parlements*; protesters threw tiles from the roof-tops at the royal troops. Some historians have seen this as a significant first anti-royalist tremor before the Revolution. The three Estates of the Dauphiné gathered to call for a national meeting of the French Estates. Local boy Henri Beyle, better known by his pseudonym Stendhal, recorded his impressions of the Revolution in Grenoble before maturing into one of France's greatest 19th-century novelists.

## Grenoble's Grudge towards its Greatest Literary Genius

Grenoble has long sulked about Stendhal, the greatest author the city ever produced, and one of France's very finest. The town didn't celebrate this fiery literary figure, because he wrote about his profound feelings of misery here. He had good reason not to be cheerful: his mother's death when he was a boy led to a deeply unhappy childhood in the dark shadow of Chérbuin, his far from cherubic father, a distant, conservative Catholic lawyer. The town used to keep open two dingy museums grudgingly recalling Stendhal, but these have shut. There are plans to create a more fitting museum.

Stendhal was in fact born Henri Beyle in 1783. He recalled his early days in Grenoble in his *Vie de Henry Brulard* (he never could stick to the one name). It seems his liberal views and desire to escape the constraints of bourgeois life were greatly shaped by his opposition to his father. Leaving stifling Grenoble, he was disillusioned by his first taste of Paris. Under Napoleonic rule, a well-placed cousin found him a job first in the war ministry, then a posting with the dragoons. This took him to Italy with the army of occupation. He fell in love with that country, spending two long stints there.

However, Stendhal's first great novel, *Le Rouge et le Noir*, published in 1830, focuses on Restoration France after Napoleon, both in the provinces (in the Franche-Comté just north of the Rhône-Alpes) and in Paris. The outrageously ambitious, impetuous Julien Sorel, son of an illiterate lumberjack, almost manages to climb the greasy pole to the heights of French society, but mad notions of romance bring about his downfall, mirroring a tragic real-life event that took place in Brangues by the Rhône (*see* p.239). Stendhal's other classic novel, *La Chartreuse de Parme*, follows similar themes, but takes readers into Italy, albeit only after the young Fabrice del Dongo fails to find the field of action at Waterloo in a farcical scene ridiculing notions of the glory of war.

Both novels brilliantly combine the study of personal ambition with the politics of the times. Both crush the illusions of youth and vanity of power, ironically rubbishing Romanticism. As to Stendhal himself, although the popular image is of a Don Juan notching up innumerable conquests, he was defeated by the quest for real love.

Despite once writing of Grenoble's being 'the very incarnation...of nausea', his views on the city and his family were more nuanced than might appear in quick summary. For example, he was close to one of his sisters, and influenced by a dandy of an uncle who introduced him to the theatre in Grenoble. While awaiting the new museum here, fans of the firebrand author can now follow a special theatrical guided tour through the city, the *Mystérieuse Affaire Stendhal* (*mid-June–Aug on Fri evenings*).

Stendhal seemingly missed out on the steamier side of Grenoble high society that is said to have provided one of the main sources of inspiration for that most sensationally scandalous of Ancien Régime novels, *Les Liaisons dangereuses*. Its author, the tongue-twistingly titled Choderlos de Laclos, apparently fed off the cynical shenanigans of high-society figures he met while serving as an officer in the army here to create his appallingly exploitative and cynical characters. Whichever way you look at it, it seems Grenoble was not a place to foster innocence.

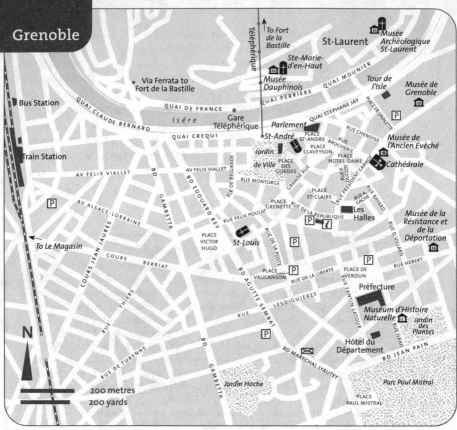

In truth, the Revolutionary period passed off relatively peacefully in town, with just two people guillotined compared with a couple of thousand executed in Lyon. Napoleon then caused a major stir with his unexpected arrival via the Drac valley in 1815 on his brief last attempt to regain power. Early in the century, Napoleon's army in Egypt had unearthed the Rosetta Stone, with its three parallel texts, holding the key to the lost language of hieroglyphics. Although it was handed over by treaty to the British, and Thomas Young struggled to decipher it there, it would take another genius educated in Grenoble, Champollion, though working in Paris, to solve the clues, thanks to his understanding of Coptic Egyptian; his work on the Stone opened up the study of Ancient Eygpt.

In the 19th century, the city was massively fortified, notably with the building of the Fort de la Bastille high above the Isère. The conquest of *houille blanche*, or hydroelectric power from mountain rivers, led to rapid industrialization in the late 19th century. Working-class struggles accompanied these developments. But the Grenoblois bourgeoisie had built themselves a solid base. In the centre, they ordered extravagantly decorated apartment blocks, in the Vinay company's ground-breaking moulded cement. By way of entertainment, the first attempts at recreational and competitive skiing in France took place at Chamrousse east above town.

Grenoble was a major centre for arms production in the First World War, and its chemical industries developed greatly in the 20th century. A first wave of Italian workers arrived in the 1920s. But in the course of the Second World War, the city, as with much of the French Alps, would be occupied by Italian soldiers. Although Pétain and Vichy notables were warmly greeted when they visited, the town became the main centre of Resistance in the Alps, and was awarded the Croix de la Libération after the conflict.

A second wave of Italian immigrants then settled in the 1950s. You'll notice the Italian influence around the place today, and the North African one that has also developed, but with three universities, it's the 60,000 students who make their presence most felt. Industry having expanded ever more along its valleys, the wider city has grown to around half a million inhabitants. It has also gained a world reputation in technology; the big scientific excitement in 2006 was the opening of Minatec, a leading new European centre for micro- and nano-technologies.

Despite the highbrow laboratories, despite the appalling rush-hour jams, when this bowl in the mountains gets too hot, cooling outdoor pleasures are never far away. The city hosted the Winter Olympics in 1968. Now, it's one of the major gateways to the Alpine resorts, summer as well as winter, with all manner of exhilarating sporting challenges on offer; you can even try *via ferrata* climbing in the very centre of the city. And when the 2006 football World Cup final pitted France against Italy, with the victory of the team from across the Alps, there were still major celebrations in the streets. In fact, Grenoble is a very cosmopolitan city these days. It may look scruffy in parts, but it feels vibrant, and bit by bit it's cleaning up its act.

## Sightseeing in Town

On a tour of Grenoble, head first for the grand **Place Notre-Dame**, in the quarter where the bishops of Grenoble held sway in medieval times. The **cathedral** looks as if it has had to fight to stay on the square, with town houses shouldering in beside it. The stocky front is topped by a mighty, square brick 13th-century **bell tower**. The interior proves very plain apart from the showy tall *ciborium* (to store the eucharistic bread and wine) in the choir. From inside the edifice you can visit the adjoining church of **St-Hugues**, another grim early-Gothic building.

While a new tramway was being prepared around here in the 1980s, the vestiges were unearthed of earlier episcopal buildings, including a rare 5th-century baptistry, plus Gallo-Roman walls, all

**Musée de l'Ancien Evêché**
*t 04 76 03 15 25,*
*www.ancien-eveche-*
*isere.com; open*
*Wed–Mon 9–6,*
*Tues 1.30–6*

now well contained within the splendidly presented **Musée de l'Ancien Evêché**. The section on the Dark Ages boasts the magificent rare Vézeronce helmet. You can then follow the history of the medieval lords of the Dauphiné, and the foundation here of three religious orders in early medieval times – not just the Chartreuse or Carthusian, but also the Antonine (*see* p.215) and the Chalais (absorbed by the Cistercian). The story then moves on to and beyond the city's aristocrats in the Ancien Régime, shown in rather more sober portraits than those drawn by Laclos.

**Musée de Grenoble**
*t 04 76 63 44 44,*
*www.museede*
*grenoble.fr; open*
*Wed–Mon 10–6.30;*
*closed Tues; adm*

The even swisher modern **Musée de Grenoble** is the city's fine arts museum. It stands on the eastern edge of the historic centre, near the river. Among the highlights are Perugino's *St Sebastian*, Giuseppe Cesari's *Portrait of an Architect*, Rubens' *Pope Gregory Surrounded by Saints*, an extraordinary series of New Testament scenes by Zurbarán, and French works by Philippe de Champaigne, Vouet and Claude Lorrain. David's 1780 *Tête de femme* looks like a precursor of Lucien Freud. Henri Fantin-Latour, an accomplished 19th-century artist from Grenoble, has his own space. The museum also boasts one of the finest modern art collections in France outside Paris: there are good Fauvist and Cubist pieces, several Matisses, and canvases by the likes of Léger and Modigliani. Major sculptures stand scattered in the garden leading to the Isère.

West of the Musée de Grenoble lie the city's liveliest, most atmospheric historic streets. Sumptuous residences built for members of the *Parlement* stand along **Rue Chenoise** and **Rue Brocherie**. Rue Chenoise is now lined with North African shops, as well as the odd Italian and Indian one. To one side of Rue Brocherie, **Place aux Herbes** hosts a sweet food market under its lightly constructed **Halles**; the locals joke that the imperceptible rise of the ground here represents the highest point in Grenoble!

The substantial, extremely picturesque **Place St-André** is overseen by the church of **St-André** and the former *Parlement* building. Thirteenth-century St-André became the resting place of the medieval Dauphiné lords, although their tombs were savagely treated by the Baron des Adrets' fanatics during the Wars of Religion. The statue in the centre of the square pays homage to a more respected military figure from earlier in the 16th century, the Seigneur de Bayard (*see* p.286). The *Parlement*, or historic Dauphiné law court, dates from his times, boasting a fabulous Flamboyant Gothic façade, with some Renaissance features. You might pause to watch the world go by from the **Café de la Table Ronde**, which claims to be the second-oldest café in France.

Almost adjoining, Place des Gordes leads to the **Jardin de Ville**, a leafy garden created for Lesdiguières, now a lively public park, with formal French flowerbeds and balustrades, and a recently reinstated statue of Hercules. The views north look onto the Fort de la Bastille (*see* overleaf); the **Gare Téléphérique** with its bubble cars whisking visitors up there stands at the northern end of the garden, close to the Isère's quays.

Just south, the grandiose Ancien Régime church of **St-Louis** dominates one side of the major **Place Grenette**. Among the cafés and shops, look out for the boutique **La Noix de Grenoble**, selling all manner of regional walnut products (*see* p.213).

Take the major shopping artery of **Rue de la République** east, leading to the tourist office in its slightly scrappy architectural setting. One side of it stands the **Maison de la Montagne**, a good place to book guides for sporting activities in the area. Just east again, across the wide boulevard used by the trams, the covered market of the **Halles Ste-Claire** makes a tempting stop for foodies. Press on to Rue Bayard for **La Laiterie Bayard**, a reputed cheese shop in a quarter where you'll also find antiques dealers.

South of the historic core, a whole grand city went up from the mid-19th century, mimicking Parisian Haussmann style, but with many of the façades built in groundbreaking moulded cement. The most impressive set piece in the grid is the immense **Place de Verdun**, overseen by imposing civic and army buildings in a variety of pastiche styles, although the departure of Napoleon's statue, which once stood in the middle, left an empty feeling. Not far off, the **Musée de la Résistance** is a very sobering, serious Second World War museum, with excellent explanatory modern presentations.

South, beyond the ambitious **Muséum d'Histoire Naturelle** covering the Alps' natural history, the spacious, elegant **Jardin des Plantes** holds splendid greenhouses. In adjoining Parc Paul Mistral, the **Tour Perret**, a pioneering cement skyscraper, went up for a 1925 international exhibition on *houille blanche*. Memories of the Winter Olympics also stand out, including the **Olympic bowl**.

North across the Isère's steely grey waters, Grenoble's oldest church has been converted into the maze of the **Musée Archéologique St-Laurent**. So many layers of Christian buildings have been discovered one on top of another here that the architecture looks deeply confusing. In the 4th century, a Christian necropolis was established on the spot, just outside the city, protected from the floods of the Isère. At the end of the 5th century, a rectangular chapel went up. A rare little funerary church in the shape of a cross, with trefoil ends to each arm, was then built here in the 6th century. This was transformed in the 8th and 9th centuries, with a whole new church built on top. Following all this, in the 11th and 12th centuries the church was transformed as part of a Benedictine priory!

Confused? Through the church's now floorless nave, amid a jumble of gaping tombs, you can set about trying to identify the different periods. It makes a quite fascinating archaeological and

**Musée de la Résistance**
*t 04 76 42 38 53,*
*www.resistance-en-isere.com; open*
*July–Aug Wed–Mon*
*10–7, Tues 1.30–6;*
*Sept–June Wed–Mon*
*9–6, Tues 1.30–6*

**Muséum d'Histoire Naturelle**
*t 04 76 44 05 35, www.museum-grenoble.fr;*
*open Mon–Fri 9.30–12*
*and 1.30–5.30, Sat and*
*Sun 2–6; adm*

**Musée Archéologique St-Laurent**
*t 04 76 44 78 68, www.musee-archeologique-grenoble.com; closed for renovation – should reopen soon; adm*

architectural puzzle. Above, alarming swastikas feature among the early 20th century decorations on the ceiling; when they were innocently painted on in 1910 they were merely regarded as ancient solar symbols. Venturing into the labyrinth below, don't miss the **crypt of St-Oyand**, wolfish monsters and birds featuring among the foliage of its beautiful Carolingian carved capitals.

Outside, the narrow **St-Laurent quarter**, with its massive 14th-century gateway, its 19th-century fortified terraces and its ethnic restaurants, has a more laid-back, alternative feel than central Grenoble. The quayside is lined with a suspiciously large number of pizzerias, a reminder of the strong Italian links with the city.

**Musée Dauphinois**

*t 04 76 85 19 01, www.
musee-dauphinois.fr;
open June–Sept
Wed–Mon 10–7; rest of
year Wed–Mon 10–6;
closed Tues*

A steep track up the hill takes you to the Musée Dauphinoiş, set in a huge former convent, **Ste-Marie-d'en-Haut**, built in its prominent site during the Counter-Reformation by François de Sales' and Jeanne de Chantal's Order of the Visitation. Its nuns came from wealthy families, and the architecture has a spacious air, although the interiors have been much transformed, having served since the Revolution as prison, school, barracks and housing centre before being turned into a museum. However, the Baroque chapel has survived intact, covered head to toe with paintings depicting the life of François de Sales (*see* p.33). The outrageous gilded retable with twisted columns is topped by a figure of God looking like a wild-eyed preacher. The museum has two interesting permanent collections, one on Alpine village life, the other devoted to the history of skiing, while temporary exhibitions on aspects of the Dauphiné are mounted in the other spaces.

**Bubble cars**

*www.bastille-
grenoble.com; adm*

The cute bubble carstaking you high over the metallic grey-green waters of the Isère have become a symbol of Grenoble, and provide much the best way to reach the **Fort de la Bastille**, guarding the city to the north. Works have been carried out to smarten up its once very scruffy fortified terraces. From way on high, you'll see how dramatically Grenoble is surrounded by peaks, and how far Grenoble has sprawled along the valleys below. The amazing straight main artery heading south down the Drac valley is said to be the longest unbroken boulevard in Europe.

**Musée des
Automates**

*t 04 76 43 33 33, www.
automatesanciens.com;
open daily 2–6.30; adm*

Down on the flat towards the railway station, the Musée des Automatespays homage to one of the major French makers of automated puppets, Vaucanson of Grenoble; this place is run by a man passionate about his craft.

## Outside the Centre

**Le Magasin, Centre
National d'Art
Contemporain**

*t 04 76 21 95 84,
www.magasin-cnac.org*

A short way out west, close to the Drac, Le Magasin, Centre National d'Art Contemporain(take the tramway towards Fontaine) is Grenoble's answer to London's Tate Modern, only this major industrial building was designed by Gustave Eiffel, and converted well before the British gallery. However, it only holds temporary exhibitions of contemporary art. Be prepared to be shocked, not just by the brash works, but also by the space – it's staggering, huge, and beautifully lit by skylights. There is a boutique and café.

A more conventional, smart artistic address to seek out northeast of the centre, in the wealthy suburb of **La Tronche**, the **Musée Hébert** stands in elegant surrounds. It occupies an Ancien Régime villa with views of the Belledonne peaks. As it was being restored, bold, rough *trompe-l'œil* scenes were discovered in its rooms. But the museum is dedicated to a 19th-century artist, son of a wealthy Grenoble lawyer. Although Hébert spent much of his life in Paris and Italy, his family left many of his works to the city. They include gorgeous male and female figures, somewhat in pre-Raphaelite style, including the most sensual of Joan of Arcs. While none of Hébert's major works depicted his native land, his watercolours did.

The colourful caves of the **Cuves de Sassenage** in Grenoble's western suburbs were carved into curious shapes by water erosion millions of years ago. Alongside their geological interest and prettiness, they offer a cooling spot in the hot season.

**Musée Hébert**
*t 04 76 42 97 35, www.patrimoine-en-isere.com; open Wed–Mon 10–6; closed Tues; adm*

**Cuves de Sassenage**
*t 04 76 27 55 37, www.sassenage.fr; open July–Aug daily 10–6; June and Sept Tues–Sun 1.30–6; April–May and Oct Sat and Sun 1.30–6; closed Nov–Mar; adm*

(i) **Grenoble >>**
*14 Rue de la République, 38019 Grenoble, t 04 76 42 41 41, www.grenoble-isere.info*

(★) **Park Hôtel >>**

## Market Days in Grenoble

**Grenoble:** Tues–Sun.

## Festivals and Events in Grenoble

Grenoble has a great cultural buzz, as well as a technological one. The main summer event, *Cabaret Frappé*, t 04 76 00 76 85, www.cabaret-frappe.com, in the second half of July, consists of a wonderful mix of free concerts in a wide variety of genres, set in the central gardens, and paying ones under a marquee.

## Sports and Activities in Grenoble

Try *via ferrata* climbing in the very centre, at the western end of Quai de France – contact the Maison de la Montagne opposite the tourist office. It can also organize hiking, cycling, paragliding and the like in the surrounding mountains.

There are three competing **golf courses** on the outskirts of Grenoble.

## Where to Stay and Eat around Grenoble

**Grenoble** ✉ **38000**

**\*\*\*\*Park Hôtel**, 10 Place Paul Mistral, t 04 76 85 81 23, www.park-hotel-grenoble.fr (€€€€€– €€€€). Looking on to a picturesque park, a luxury, quite central option. Refined restaurant (€€€–€€). *Closed most of Aug; restaurant closed weekend lunch.*

**\*\*\*Angleterre**, 5 Place Victor Hugo, t 04 76 87 37 21, www.hotel-angleterre-grenoble.com (€€€). Businesslike, opposite a busy garden square. Some of the smart, soundproofed, air-conditioned rooms have spa baths. Weekends 2 nights for price of 1 with *bon week-end en ville* promotion.

**\*\*L'Europe**, 22 Place Grenette, t 04 76 46 16 94, www.hoteleurope.fr (€). Good-value, central location, in an old-style apartment block with wrought-iron decorations, but modern rooms. Weekends 2 nights for price of 1 with *bon week-end en ville* promotion.

**Auberge Napoléon**, 7 Rue Montorge, t 04 76 87 53 64 (€€€€–€€€). Very posh little restaurant, in historic house where the Emperor stayed on his way back from Elba, by the central garden. Sumptuous menus based around truffles, *foie gras* and champagne. *Closed Sun and Mon–Fri lunch, early Jan, early May and late Aug–early Sept.*

**L'Escalier**, 6 Place Lavalette, **t** 04 76 54 66 16 (€€€). Excellent restaurant in characterful house close to the art museum; classic French cuisine. *Closed Sat lunch, Sun, and Mon lunch.*

**Le Jardin de Ville**, Rue Berlioz, **t** 04 76 01 15 15 (€€). Above the central sunken flower garden, trendy restaurant and bar with wonderful terrace with views, a great outdoor salon for people-watching. Also a club with DJ. *Closed Sun and Mon.*

**Le Téléphérique**, **t** 04 76 51 11 11 (€€). Stunning views down on Grenoble from this restaurant perched on the cliff edge beside the top exit of the bubble car – free return ticket up and down if you reserve. The breathtaking view is more interesting than the cuisine. Not for vertigo sufferers.

**Le 5**, Place Lavalette, **t** 04 76 63 22 12 (€€). Trendy spot for light lunch in the fine arts museum. *Closed Tues.*

**La Glycine**, 168 Cours Berriat, **t** 04 76 21 95 33. A lovely, quite refined but reasonably priced restaurant on the square outside the huge Magasin art gallery. Fabulous old wisteria giving great shade to the front terrace. *Closed Sun and Mon.*

### Eybens ✉ 38320

**\*\*\*Château de la Commanderie**, 17 Av d'Echirolles, **t** 04 76 25 34 58, *www. commanderie.fr* (€€€). Little castle in lovely grounds just south of Grenoble. Smart rooms and restaurant (€€€; weekday lunch menu €€) plus terrace for summer dining. Pool. *Closed late Dec–early Jan; restaurant closed Sat lunch, Sun pm and Mon.*

### Bresson ✉ 38320

**\*\*\*\*Chavant**, Rue de la Mairie, **t** 04 76 25 25 38, *www.chateauxhotels.com/ chavant* (€€€). Reputable family hotel in sweet village south of town. Great restaurant (€€€€–€€€), garden, pool. *Closed one week Aug; restaurant closed Sat lunch, Sun pm and Mon.*

# The Drac, Matheysine and Trièves

## Down the Drac

East below the formidable Vercors lies the quietly dramatic **Drac valley**. We take our section of the Route Napoléon (now the N85) the opposite direction to *le petit caporal*, from Grenoble into the **Matheysine**, above the Drac's east bank.

Head first to take on the brutally massive **Château de Vizille**, set in splendid **grounds**. This intimidating castle was built from 1600 to 1619 for Lesdiguières, but now houses an engrossing **Museum of the French Revolution**. On 21 July 1788 it hosted the celebrated meeting of the representatives of the Dauphiné's three Estates in a ground-breaking act of independent co-operation between nobles, Church and bourgeoisie. The entrance hall contains a useful time chart, while throughout, grand paintings, sculptures and models are fused with text to illustrate the complex stages of the Revolution. It makes a fascinating way of following the events, and British reactions, particularly against the Revolution, emerge as you go along. Recover a sense of calm in the utterly glorious park, the formal part set around a beautiful stretch of water.

Continuing south for La Mure, the upheaval of Napoleonic times is recalled at **La Prairie de la Rencontre** above the Lacs de Laffrey. The equestrian statue of the power-crazed Corsican stood for a while in

**Château de Vizille grounds**
*open June–Aug daily 9am–10pm; Mar–May and Sept–Oct Wed–Mon 9–7; Nov–Feb Wed–Mon 10–5; closed Tues; free*

**Museum of the French Revolution**
*t 04 76 68 07 35, www. musee-revolution-francaise.fr; open April–Oct Wed–Mon 10–12.30 and 1.30–6; Nov–Mar Wed–Mon 10–12.30 and 1.30–5, closed public hols; free*

the centre of Grenoble, before being moved to this apparent backwater, although it is a place of some significance – Napoleon's battalion had regrouped on his surprise arrival back from exile on Elba, but here encountered royalist troops supposedly loyal to Louis XVIII. It's said the *petit caporal* had merely to flash open his coat like a military Jesus, and the cry went up of '*Vive l'Empereur!*'; the monarchists changed sides on witnessing this apparition.

Observing the determined figure of Napoleon riding on against the backdrop of the huge flanks of the Oisans, you may hear joyous cries rising from the valley below today; that's because the expansive **Lacs de Laffrey**, dating back to the melting of the last Ice Age, have become popular destinations for summer watersports.

As an alternative to the N85, hug the steep east bank of the Drac. The once formidable river, compared in legend to a wild *drac*, or dragon, has in parts been exploited by industry and tamed by dams, the latter allowing people to practise watersports along sections of its violently bright waters. One of the earliest electrified rail lines in France winds along an astonishing route like a mule track far above. Built to transport coal from the Matheysine, the **Chemin de Fer de La Mure** now serves as a popular tourist train linking St-Georges-de-Commiers and La Mure.

This surprising mining history is recalled in the local museums, the underground **Mine Image** at **La Motte-d'Aveillans**, and the **Musée Matheysin**, the latter at the busy sloping town of **La Mure**, and covering other local craft traditions with style.

Further south down the Drac at **Mayres-Savel**, board *La Mira* to appreciate the valley's drama by boat (meal possible). The river here has been dammed, creating the long, narrow, beautiful deep-green **Lac de Monteynard**. For greater elation, bungee-jumpers experience a heady 100m drop from the **Pont de Ponsonnas** a bit south of La Mure, billing itself as the number one site in Europe for the crazy sport.

Continuing down the Drac, **Corps** makes a pleasant last stop on the border with Provence, set beside the **Lac du Sautet**, created by another dam on the river, and offering another major expanse for water sports. A quite hairy mountain road leads up from Corps to **Notre-Dame-de-la-Salette**, a major Catholic shrine located at 1,800m in a stage-set of mountains, and an extraordinarily celebrated place of Catholic pilgrimage in France, the second most popular after Lourdes. The reason why this pilgrimage spot is perched so high is that two young shepherds, Maximin and Mélanie, claimed to have witnessed a vision of the Virgin Mary up here in 1846. The 19th-century Church seizing on such opportunities, a whole new religious centre arose in the dramatic location.

To enjoy unspoilt reflection on nature's majesty, head via **Valbonnais** into the **Ecrins National Park**; hiking trails lead into the

**Chemin de Fer de La Mure**
t 08 92 39 14 26,
www.trainlamure.com;
runs April–Oct; adm

**Mine Image**
t 04 76 30 68 74, www.
mine-image.com; open
June–mid-Sept daily for
tours 10–5, May and late
Sept daily 2.30–4.30;
April and Oct Wed, Sat
and Sun 2.30–4.30;
other months Sat and
Sun 2.30–4.30; adm

**Musée Matheysin**
t 04 76 30 98 15; open
May–Oct Wed–Mon
1–6.30; closed Tues; adm

**La Mira**
t 04 76 34 14 56, bateau.
lamira@wanadoo.fr;
operates daily mid-
May–Oct; adm

**Pont de Ponsonnas**
t 04 76 47 42 80
to book, www.vertige-
aventures.com; open
July–Aug daily; May–
June and Sept–Nov Sat
and Sun; adm

**Notre-Dame-de-
la-Salette**
t 04 76 30 00 11,
www.nd-la-salette.org;
closed Nov

splendid mountains from the dead-end villages of **Valsenestre** and **Le Désert**.

## The Trièves

Following the west bank of the Drac from Grenoble, you pass under the gaze of the Vercors' highest heights. The N75 route is stunning, but busy. **Treffort** has another landing stage for cruising on *La Mira* (*see* p.301). Branch west from **Vif** to get up away from the traffic onto the gorgeous slopes around the **Gresse valley**. Head up to **Gresse-en-Vercors** for the walking trail to the top of that range's highest peak, **Le Grand Veymont** (2,342m). From up there, you can see as far as Mont Blanc.

Using your imagination, you might think you can spot perhaps the most isolated pasture in France, on top of the bald **Mont Aiguille** (2,086m). This is the totemic symbol of the Trièves, the beautiful rumpled cereal lands between Vercors and Drac. Though called 'the Needle' in French, the unmissable Aiguille sticks out much more like a vast exposed, isolated tooth. At the close of the 15th century, King Charles VIII passed this way on his Italian campaigning. In a mood to conquer all he saw, he ordered Lord Antoine de Ville to organize the ascent of the inaccessible-looking summit. But the exploit was achieved, with the elaborate use of ladders. This event is often claimed to be the first example of French mountaineering; it still offers a great challenge (*see* right).

The village of **Chichilianne** sits in an exceptional location below Mont Aiguille. Its **Relais d'Information du Parc Naturel Régional du Vercors**, in a characterful house, introduces Vercors and Trièves.

The writer Jean Giono, well-known in France for his deeply evocative novels on traditional rural life, set several of his books in the Trièves, hence the little **Espace Jean Giono** at **Lalley**. The passes to the west lead over the southern end of the Vercors.

Pleasantly laid-back **Mens** a bit to the east has an understated charm, a long-Protestant market town that hasn't spruced itself up yet. Stroll around to take in its little fountains, its covered market, its churches, and the delightful Belle Epoque **Café des Arts**, whose walls are covered with murals of the local landscapes. Local history and traditions are covered at the **Musée du Trièves**.

**Terre Vivante**, hidden in the countryside out of town, proves a well-run ecological park encouraging environmentally friendly practices with exceptional good sense. The aims include showing visitors how to garden and eat organically, and how to make your home ecologically friendly. There are guided tours and a shop. The organic lunchtime restaurant is set in a lovely spot.

East of the N75, lose yourself in beautiful mountainous dead ends on the frontier with the Hautes-Alpes of northern Provence, marked by the majestic **Obiou** (2,790m).

### ⭐ Mont Aiguille

**Relais d'Information du Parc Naturel Régional du Vercors**
*t 04 76 34 44 95, relais.parc.mont.aiguille @club-internet.fr; open July–Aug Tues–Sat 10.30–12 and 4–6, Mon 10.30–12, Sun 4–6; April–June and Sept–Nov Tues, Fri and Sat 10.30–12, Thurs–Mon 4–6; free*

**Espace Jean Giono**
*t 04 76 34 78 23; open summer Tues, Thurs, Sat and Sun 4–7; winter Fri and Sat 4–6; adm*

**Musée du Trièves**
*t 04 76 34 88 28, www. musee-trieves.com; open May–Sept Tues–Sun 3–7; Oct–April school hols 2–7; adm*

**Terre Vivante**
*t 04 76 34 80 80, www. terrevivante.org; open late April–late Oct daily 10–6; boutique and restaurant open July–Aug daily, rest of opening season Sat and Sun; adm*

## Market Days in the Drac, Matheysine and Trièves

La Mure: Mon am.

Mens: Sat am, plus summer Wed am.

## Activities in the Drac, Matheysine and Trièves

**Pont de Pontsonnas** is a major European **bungee jumping** site.

In the Trièves, if you feel the urge to conquer Mont Aiguille, contact the **Bureau des Guides du Mont Aiguille**, t 04 76 34 13 19; *www.guidesmont aiguille.com*, based at St-Michel-des-Portes, who also offer other climbing and sporting challenges in the area.

## Where to Stay and Eat in the Drac, Matheysine and Trièves

### Vizille ✉ 38220

**\*\*\*Château de Cornage**, Chemin des Peupliers, t 04 76 68 28 00, *http://* *chateaudecornage.com* (€€). Elegant hillside bourgeois house, plus decent cuisine (€€). Pool. *Restaurant closed Sun eve.*

### Le Percy ✉ 38930

**Les Volets Bleus B&B**, Hameau des Blancs, t 04 76 34 43 07 (€). Intense Trièves pleasures at this former farming property. Vaulted room for *table d'hôte* (€€). *Closed Nov–Easter.*

### Chichilianne ✉ 38930

**\*\* Château de Passières**, t 04 76 34 45 48 (€). Enchanting medieval castle with relaxed style and interesting art. A real find. Restaurant (€€). Pool. *Closed Oct; restaurant closed Sun eve and Mon out of season.*

**Sauze B&B**, Ruthières, t 04 76 34 45 98 (€). Spacious rooms in a traditional farm in a hamlet 3km from main village. *Table d'hôte* in old barn (€).

### Mens ✉ 38710

**L'Engrangeou B&B**, Place de la Halle, t 04 76 34 85 63 (€). Tasteful rooms above an art gallery by the market. *Table d'hôte* (€).

---

ⓘ **La Mure**
43 Rue de Breuil, 38350
La Mure, t 04 76 81 05
71, *tourisme.lamure@*
*wanadoo.fr*

 **Château de Passières >>**

ⓘ **Mens >>**
Rue du Breuil, 38710
Mens, t 04 76 34 84 25,
*www.alpes-trieves.com*

ⓘ **Vizille >**
Place du Château, 38220
Vizille, t 04 76 68 15 16,
*info@ot-vizille.com*

ⓘ **Vercors**
Association pour le
Développement
Touristique du Vercors,
t 04 76 95 15 99,
*www.adt-vercors.com*

---

# The Vercors Range

Menacing peaks rising on all sides, the natural fort of the Vercors range rises between Grenoble to the north and Die to the south. It's only reachable by very disturbing roads from whichever way you approach. But once you've scaled the near-sheer walls, the high plateaux prove much easier to travel round. The villages up top long remained cut off from the outside world; this hidden territory, offering caves for further protection, became a hide-out for Resistance fighters in the Second World War, leading to terrible Nazi attacks and bitter memories. Gradually developing its tourism, helped by a role in the 1968 Winter Olympics, in 1970 the Vercors became one of the earliest regional nature parks in France.

Typically alarmingly steep roads lead up from the suburbs of Grenoble to the Vercors. Heading past the **Tour sans Venin**, a meagre remnant of medieval defence, make for **St-Nizier-du-Moucherotte**, a balcony of a village on the northern end of the range, with staggering views down on Grenoble, up the Isère valley and as far as Mont Blanc. Overseen by three peaks known as the **Trois Pucelles** (Three Virgins), much of the village was destroyed in Nazi attacks, the **Nécropole**, in its beautiful location well below the houses, dedicated to the memory of those killed by the Germans.

The highest, eastern line of Vercors mountains reach over 2,000m. The only way to get close to their summits is via the GR91 hiking trail, part of the **Grande Traversée du Vercors** network which you can join by St-Nizier. The route is accessible for mountain bikes and donkeys as well. An alternative route up from Grenoble into the Vercors takes you along the **Furan valley**, past **Engins**, a village with an 11th-century church. The Vercors draws potholers with challenges such as the nearby **Gouffre Berger**, its underground drop of more than 1,000m hidden to the west. Walkers are guided more easily by instructive signs to the fresh **Gorges du Bruyant**.

Making for **Lans-en-Vercors**, you enter the gentle, quiet pasturelands of the northern Vercors, the scattered villages settled peacefully below the long wooded spines stretching to east and west. They still proudly recall the parts they played in the 1968 Winter Olympics. In summer, the pure air and flowery meadows make this a good place to breathe easy. However, regardless of when you visit **La Magie des Automates** on the edge of Lans, you're not allowed to forget the snowy season and Christmas: a mad collector of automata has created a plethora of cutesy scenes.

A loop to the west takes you to typical open Vercors villages. **Autrans** has kept its lovely old-style feel, especially around the central square, despite having become a major centre of cross-country skiing. A *fromagerie* keeps Vercors cow's cheese traditions going. See if you can visit the **Musée La Ferme de Martine et François**, a traditional farm on the outskirts.

**Méaudre** has a nice feel with its scattered hamlets, although modern constructions are spreading. Lively **Villard-de-Lans**, amid its meadows, is a sporty resort all year round, signalled by its central ice-rink and outdoor wave pool. **Ludi Parc** (*see* p.306) offers the further attractions of a treetop assault course, archery and summer bobsleighing on a section of the 1968 Winter Olympics track. **Corrençon-en-Vercors** at the end of the road is known for its beautiful, tranquil golf course. In stark, chilling contrast, just a bit west, the hamlet of **Valchevrière** was wiped out by the Nazis, ghostly ruins recalling this devastated Resistance hideout.

The main D531 road west from Villard plunges through the **Gorges de la Bourne**. The sensational entrance to the **Grottes de Choranche** hangs on a lip of rock sticking out from a massive, sheer face of forested mountainside here. These sensational caves were only discovered in 1875; their main wonders are their delicate stalactites, *fistuleuses*, like spaghetti glued to the ceiling.

Terrifying roads lead into the southern half of the Vercors from the **Bourne valley**, as frightening as any rollercoaster ride. The most notorious takes you along the side of the **Vernaison gulley** via the **Petits** and **Grands Goulets**, head-spinning distances all-too-visible above and below. The rival route forces you to cling to the side of

**Grande Traversée du Vercors**
*www.vercors-gtv.com*

**La Magie des Automates**
*t 04 76 95 40 14, www.magiedesautomates.com; open Jan–Sept and Nov–Dec daily 10–6; closed Oct; adm*

**Musée La Ferme de Martine et François**
*t 04 76 95 73 63; open by appt only; adm*

✪ **Grottes de Choranche**
*t 04 76 36 09 88, www.grottes-de-choranche.com; open July–Aug daily 10–6; May–June and Sept daily 10–12 and 1.30–6; April daily 10–12 and 1.30–5.30; Nov–Mar Mon–Sat 1.30–4.30, Sun 10.30–4.30; adm*

✪ **Grands Goulets**

**Monastère St-Antoine**

*t 04 75 47 72 02; open daily 11 30–12.30 and 2–5; adm*

⭐ **Musée de la Résistance**

*t 04 75 48 28 46; open mid-July–mid-Aug daily 10–7; April–mid-July and mid-Aug–Oct daily 10–12 and 2–6; Feb–Mar and Nov–Dec Wed–Sun 2–5; adm*

**Nécropole**

*open July–Aug daily 10–12 and 2–6; May–June and Sept Thurs–Sun 10–12 and 2–6*

⭐ **Mémorial de la Résistance**

*t 04 75 48 26 00, www. memorial-vercors.fr; open May–Sept daily; 2nd half April and Oct–mid-Nov, plus Xmas hols 10–5; adm*

**Grotte de la Luire**

*t 04 75 48 25 83; open July–Aug daily 10.30–7; May–June and Sept–Oct Mon–Fri 2–6, Sun and hols 10.30–7; April Sun and hols 10.30–6; adm*

**Grotte de la Draye Blanche**

*t 04 75 48 24 96, www. drayeblanche.com; open May–Aug daily 10–6; Feb–April, Sept–mid-Nov and Xmas hols 10–12 and 2–5; adm*

**Musée de la Préhistoire**

*t 04 75 48 27 81, www. prehistoire-vercors.fr; closed till 2008*

**Col du Rousset Télésiège**

*open summer hols only, daily 10–5.45; adm*

the **Combe Laval**, with further terrifying canyon views. Tucked away in a sensational location, the small Russian Orthodox community at the **Monastère St-Antoine** explains to visitors the rich iconography of the masterful recent murals decorating its church.

Up on the main plateau of the southern Vercors, a moving memorial and plaques at **La Chapelle-en-Vercors** tell how this was one of the range's main villages to be martyred by the Nazis from July 1944 as they wiped out the Resistance groups up here. On a happier note, there's a cheerful outdoor pool right in the centre.

**Vassieux-en-Vercors** was another terrible victim of the Nazis. Some 600 Resistance fighters, along with around 200 villagers, were assassinated by SS soldiers who flew in silently in gliders. The horror is retold both at the old-fashioned **Musée de la Résistance** in the reconstructed village, at the **Nécropole**, a cemetery with a memorial room showing a video on the war campaign, and up at the new-fangled **Mémorial de la Résistance**, snaking down the ridge from the Col de Lachau. Seeking refuge in the dark **Forêt de Lente** spreading west beyond the Mémorial are deer, chamois and mouflons; but the Grenoblois and others decamp in summer to picnic in large numbers in these shaded woods.

You'll hear further horrific war tales on a visit into the bowels of the Vercors range at the **Grotte de la Luire** east of **Vassieux**. North of the village, the massive **Grotte de la Draye Blanche** has revealed a lot about animal prehistory with all the remains unearthed here. But the most immediate excitement comes from the colour of the natural concretions and what's aptly nicknamed a cascade in stone. For another long view of civilization in the Vercors, seek out the **Musée de la Préhistoire**, going back a quarter of a million years, but concentrating on Neolithic finds on the spot.

The southeast heights of the Vercors are protected by their status as the **Réserve Naturelle des Hauts Plateaux du Vercors**, the largest nature reserve in France, jam-packed with alpine flora. The huge fanning dorsal mountain of the **Grand Veymont**, the highest peak in the Vercors at 2,341m, oversees this secretive land. You can't reach this area by car, but even on the lower Vercors plateaux, from late spring you can enjoy the dense carpets of mountain flowers.

Out west, the stoical church of the **abbey of Léoncel** offers a calm halt before the sensational twisting roads down from the range. By whichever dramatic road you leave the southern Vercors, it comes as a shock going from the chilly, chilling clifftops to the warm, dry lavender fields and vineyards of the southern *département de la Drôme* (see p.219). The most sensational way down is via the **Col de Rousset** to **Die**. Before the tunnel to the great drop, you'll find the little resort of the same name, offering mountain biking as well as hiking in summer. The *télésiège*, or chairlift, gets you up to the magnificent heights of the Hauts Plateaux du Vercors.

ⓘ **Lans-en-Vercors**
*Place de la Mairie,*
*38250 Lans-en-Vercors,*
*t 04 76 95 42 62, www.*
*ot-lans-en-vercors.fr*

ⓘ **Autrans**
*Route de Méaudre,*
*38880 Autrans, t 04 76*
*95 30 70, www.ot-*
*autrans.fr*

ⓘ **Vassieux-en-Vercors ››**
*Av du Mémorial, 26420*
*Vassieux-en-Vercors,*
*t 04 75 48 27 40, ot.*
*vassieux@wanadoo.fr*

ⓘ **Villard-de-Lans ›**
*101 Place Mure Ravaud,*
*38250 Villard-de-Lans,*
*t 04 76 95 10 38, www.*
*ot-villard-de-lans.fr*

ⓘ **Méaudre**
*38112 Méaudre,*
*t 04 76 95 20 68,*
*www.meaudre.com*

ⓘ **Corrençon-en-Vercors ›**
*Place du Village, 38250*
*Corrençon-en-Vercors,*
*t 04 76 95 81 75,*
*www.ot-correncon.fr*

ⓘ **La Chapelle-en-Vercors ›**
*Place Piétri, 26420*
*La Chapelle-en-Vercors,*
*t 04 75 48 22 54,*
*www.vercors.com*

## Market Days in the Vercors

**Autrans:** Wed am.
**Méaudre:** Tues am.
**La Chapelle-en-Vercors:** Thurs am, plus Sat am in summer.

## Activities in the Vercors

To learn about crossing the Vercors on foot via the **Grande Traversée du Vercors**, see *www.vercors-gtv.com*. The Vercors is a major area for *spéléologie* (potholing): contact the **Maison de l'Aventure, t** 04 75 48 22 38, *www.maison-aventure.com.*

For **Ludi Parc**'s attractions, including summer bobsleighing, contact **t** 04 76 95 06 95, *www.ludi-parc.com.*

## Where to Stay and Eat in the Vercors

### Villard-de-Lans ✉ 38250
**\*\*\*Le Christiania**, Av Prof Nobecourt, t 04 76 95 12 51, *www.hotel-le-christiania.fr* (€€€–€€). Big modern family-run chalet with well-furnished rooms, many with private balconies. Gastronomic cuisine (€€). Covered pool. *Closed mid-April–mid-May and late Sept–mid-Dec; restaurant closed weekday lunch out of season.*

**\*\*Villa Primerose**, 147 Av des Bains, t 04 76 95 13 17, *www.hotel-villa-primerose.com* (€). Charming bargain hotel. Former restaurant kitchen at your disposal. *Closed Nov–mid-Dec.*

### Corrençon-en-Vercors ✉ 38250
**\*\*\*Hôtel du Golf, t** 04 76 95 84 84, *www.hotel-du-golf-vercors.fr* (€€€). Really good three-star beside the golf course in meadows at the end of the village. Smart rooms. Restaurant. Pool. *Closed April–early May and mid-Oct–mid-Dec; restaurant closed Sun eve and Mon outside main hols, plus lunch Mon–Thurs in low season.*

### La Chapelle-en-Vercors ✉ 26420
**\*\*Bellier**, Av de Provence, t 04 75 48 20 03, *http://hotel-bellier.com* (€).

Chalet with spacious rooms with balconies. Alpine-style restaurant (€€). *Closed Nov–April; restaurant closed Tues eve and Wed out of season.*

**\*\*Hôtel des Sports**, Av des Grands Goulets, t 04 75 48 20 39, *www.hotel-des-sports.com* (€). Nice and simple, with a pleasant restaurant (€€). *Closed late Nov–Jan; restaurant closed Sun eve and Mon.*

### St-Agnan-en-Vercors ✉ 26420
**\*Auberge Le Veymont**, Place du Village, t 04 75 48 20 19, *leveymont@wanadoo.fr* (€). Nice mountain feel to the simple rooms and restaurant (€€–€). *Closed mid-Mar–late April and late Sept–Christmas.*

### Vassieux-en-Vercors ✉ 26420
**\*\*Auberge du Tetras Lyre**, Rue Abbé Gagnol, t 04 75 48 28 04, *www.tetraslyre.com* (€). Welcoming simple village chalet, rooms with balconies. Restaurant (€€–€) putting an accent on local cuisine. *Closed mid-Nov–mid-Dec.*

### Lente ✉ 26190
**\*\*Hôtel de la Forêt, t** 04 75 48 26 32, *www.hotel-de-la-foret.com* (€). Lost in the countryside. Very simple rooms, a warm welcome and themed weekends. Good dishes (€€). *Closed most Jan and Dec; restaurant closed Mon eve and Tues out of season.*

### Col de la Machine ✉ 26190
**\*\*Hôtel du Col de la Machine**, at the pass, t 04 75 48 26 36, *www.hotel-coldelamachine.com* (€). Appealing family hotel. Excellent regional cooking (€€). Pool. *Closed mid-Nov–mid-Dec; restaurant closed Tues eve and Wed in low season.*

### Bouvante ✉ 26190
**\*Auberge du Pionnier**, Col du Pionnier, t 04 75 48 57 12, *www.lepionnier.com* (€). A rustic retreat in forest clearing, with a warm chalet feel inside. Tasty country cooking in the restaurant (€€). The owner organizes accompanied nature outings in summer as well as winter. *Closed mid-Nov–mid-Dec; best to reserve for restaurant mid-week.*

# Haute Savoie:
## Lac Léman to Mont Blanc

Haute Savoie really has an enormous amount to boast about, including Western Europe's highest peak, Mont Blanc, and a major stake in its biggest lake, Lac Léman. Haute Savoie is also world-renowned for its ski resorts – Chamonix and Megève among the glamorous names – which remain surprisingly busy in summer, full of hikers and extreme sports fans.

But there is much more to discover: villages and churches in locations that might seem more appropriate for mountain goats, walking trails taking you up and away from civilization, or deeply relaxing spa resorts like Thonon and Evian. Whichever way you turn, the views will be glorious.

# 17

## Don't miss

⭐ **The cutest, chicest lakeside ports**
Nernier/Yvoire **pp.311/312**

⭐ **Taking to the waters**
A cruise on Lac Léman from Evian **p.315**

⭐ **The grandest dead end in France**
The Cirque du Fer à Cheval via Samoëns **p.319**

⭐ **A gap-toothed mountain tour**
The Aravis range from La Clusaz to Megève **p.323**

⭐ **Sheer exhilaration**
Up Mont Blanc from Chamonix **p.325**

*See map overleaf*

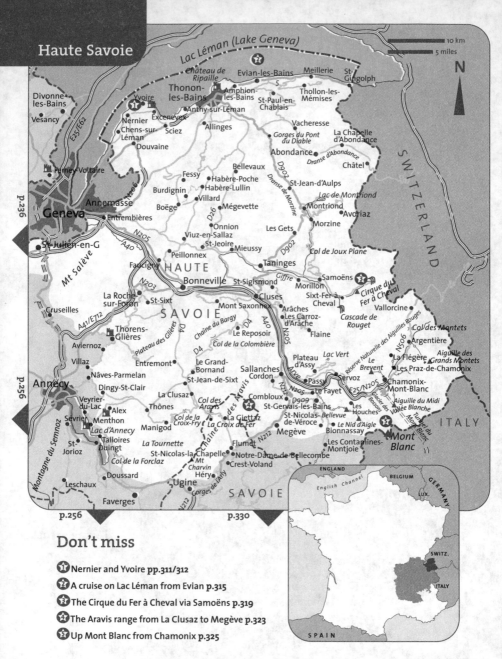

## Don't miss

⭐ Nernier and Yvoire **pp.311/312**

⭐ A cruise on Lac Léman from Evian **p.315**

⭐ The Cirque du Fer à Cheval via Samoëns **p.319**

⭐ The Aravis range from La Clusaz to Megève **p.323**

⭐ Up Mont Blanc from Chamonix **p.325**

What exceptional luck, being so intimately associated with two of Europe's largest, most spectacular natural wonders. Breathtaking as these are, Haute Savoie shouldn't crow too selfishly: it shares the Mont Blanc range with Italy and Switzerland, while only the south shore of Lake Geneva, that great blue croissant on the maps, is French. In France, the lake is always referred to as Lac Léman.

## Getting to and around Haute Savoie

**By air**: Geneva airport lies very close by.

**By train**: Reach Thonon and Evian from Geneva, Paris via Bellegarde, or direct on rapid TGV trains in high season winter and summer. The main Arve valley towns have good rail links, but the connection to Chamonix can be slow. Most villages to Vallorcine have a station, too.

**By bus**: For detailed bus timetables, consult *http://infotransports.cg74.fr.*

---

(i) **Savoie**
*www.savoie-mont-blanc.com*

In little corners close to the lake, vines thrive, producing refreshing wines to accompany the lake fish. Swanky Evian is renowned. Neighbouring Thonon may be less well known, but shares many of these attributes, and was more important historically – its vinous Château de Ripaille even became the retirement home of one of Savoie's most remarkable dukes.

In this chapter we also cover the areas of the **Chablais**, Bas and Haut (Lower and Upper), rising high between the great lake and the awesome Arve valley, and the **Faucigny**, stretching along the Arve towards Mont Blanc. Chablais turned Protestant after the invasion of new ideas and armies from Switzerland in the 16th century. The most famous figure in its history, however, is the steadfast Catholic St François de Sales, revered for his sensitive work in restoring regional faith in the Catholic Church in the 17th century. In the elevated Haut Chablais there are plenty of traditional places to visit outside the snowy season. Visiting many of these parts in summer, ringing *clarine* cowbells accompany you through fabulous flower-strewn pastures to gorgeous lakes, and to waterfalls cascading down from stupendous heights. Just don't expect to be alone during the short, intense summer season.

We also introduce you to the **Aravis**. The routes east via this rural range offer more picturesque paths to Chamonix and Mont Blanc than the more industrial **Arve**. Around the Aravis, you can pose in the glamorous resorts summer as well as winter; Megève established itself between the wars as the St-Tropez of the Alps. There are more rustic corners to uncover, both in the Aravis and the Val d'Arly east of it. Closer to Lac d'Annecy, Thônes, Thorens and the Plateau des Glières have important historic tales to tell.

Finally, we come into the presence of **Mont Blanc**. Right below the mighty mountain, Chamonix may look chaotic, but there's always excitement in the air here, as palpable as falling snow, even in the height of summer. The **Aiguilles** (Needles), viciously sharp peaks surrounding the greatest summit, add to the high drama, but Mont Blanc itself rises above the rest like an otherworldly deity, sometimes majestically aloof, at other times mysteriously lost in cloud. To appreciate the Mont Blanc range at its best, climb closer to the summits by foot, cable car or tram. You could even fly over by helicopter. Whichever way you choose, at such high altitude, the experience may literally take your breath away.

# To Lake Geneva, or Lac Léman

We first offer you a choice of several mountain routes round from Geneva to Léman, before concentrating on the great lake itself.

## Routes from the Lower Arve to Lac Léman

The Rhône, coming down from its source in the Swiss Alps to the east, is the main river to supply the immense Lac Léman and the main river to leave it, via Swiss Geneva in the west. The most interesting route bypassing this thorny Swiss enclave is the D41 over **Mont Salève** (or even the GR hiking path along it), ensuring a spectacular arrival in Haute Savoie, dominating Lac Léman, spying on Geneva. The N206 then heads straight for the lake. But a series of enchanting parallel mountain roads lead north off the glorious D907, which follows the course of the **Foron valley**.

One forested route goes up the **Menoge valley**, nicknamed the Vallée Verte, through **Boëge**, with its typical colonnaded covered market, past **Villard** and **Burdignin**, villages that compete with their grand churches, to the hamlets of the **Habères**.

**Fessy Musée d'Art et de Folklore**
*t 04 50 39 46 30; open July–Oct daily 2–6; adm*

Or at Boëge branch west for **Fessy**, with its **Musée d'Art et de Folklore** displaying a huge collection of objects representing traditional Chablais life. The impressive form of the **Château d'Avully** nearby recalls the lordly medieval Chablais, as do the murals inside, while the historical sections cover the some eight centuries of the independent state of Savoie, from 1032 to 1860. The topiary gardens provide light relief.

**Château d'Avully**
*t 04 50 36 11 59, www. chateau-avully.com; open July–Aug daily 2–6; Sept–June Sun 2–6; adm*

Over the passes, the heights offer staggering views north. From the vestiges of the two **Châteaux des Allinges** perched ridiculously close together on their spur, you get wide views onto Lac Léman, but you also see how heavily developed the flat lakeside areas have become. The older of the ruins, **Allinges-le-Vieux**, became a stronghold of the lords of Faucigny in early medieval times, traditionally supporters of the Dauphiné counts. The disgruntled counts of Savoie built right next door to put the wind up the Faucignys, in the 14th century eventually pushing them out. Despite its name, **Allinges-le-Neuf**'s chapel contains a striking Apocalypse *Christ in Majesty* dating back to the 11th century, the oldest painting to survive in Savoie. François de Sales settled here for a time from 1594, as he battled to bring the Chablais back into the Catholic fold through his persuasive rhetoric.

**Allinges-le-Neuf chapel**
*t 04 50 72 01 04, www.allinges.com; open July–Aug, variable times, so check; adm*

**Peillonnex abbey church**
*t 04 50 36 89 18, www. paysalp.asso.fr; open July–Aug Wed–Fri and Sun tours at 2, 3, 4 and 5; rest of year 1st Sun of month, same times; adm*

Back between the Foron and Arve valleys, the sober **abbey church** at **Peillonnex** overlooks proceedings dispassionately from its delightful mid-slope terrace, a splendid ancient yew tree providing company over the centuries. When the Romanesque buildings were rebuilt after Swiss troops had devastated the place in the 16th century, the church was decorated with an extravaganza of

Baroque altarpieces. The theatrical levels of decoration are very well explained in a commentary covering the history of the Baroque movement generally as well as the particular riot of detail here, which includes prophets dangling from the cornices. St François de Sales features, of course, gazing devotedly up to God.

At **Viuz-en-Sallaz**, with its views as far as Mont Blanc, the ultra-modern **Paysalp** presents a vast number of regional craft objects and costumes collected by the Hermanns, defenders of popular culture across the whole arc of Europe's Alps, but those artefacts are now presented in curiously characterless surroundings. The *fruitière*, or cheese-making area, is also ultra-modern. The plainer, separate **Musée Paysan** covers Savoyard rural life and traditions from 1850 to 1950. The *pele* (from the word *poêle*, stove) was the only room lived in in winter, because of its heat, while in summer families decamped up the slopes to their *chalets d'alpage*, moving with their cattle to higher pastures.

The D26 offers a lovely route up from **St-Jeoire** to Thonon. A massive landslide in 1943 caused a huge natural dam to form across the Brevon river, creating the **Lac de Vallon**. Bathing is forbidden in its dangerous waters, but its surroundings make for pretty walking country. Amidst these relatively unspoilt mountains, **Bellevaux** quietly defends its traditions with its minor **Musée de l'Histoire** and **Musée de la Faune**, while a new garden has been laid out below its muscular church.

## Lac Léman

Reaching the huge, beautiful crescent of water of Lac Léman, you may feel more as if you've arrived at the edge of a sea than a lake. The statistics are impressive: it's 73km long, and 14km at its widest. But it's the natural grandeur of the place, and the beauty of its ports, that will captivate you. Virtually all the lake's southern half is French, although the Swiss have grabbed hold of both ends.

Starting in the west, we ignore the enclave of Geneva sticking its defiant Protestant tongue out at France. Between **Douvaine** and the lake, the **Musée Miloutl** is housed in the **Granges de Servette**, typical 17th-century barns where old Chablais crafts are recalled.

Join the French lakeside at **Chens-sur-Léman**. The gorgeous waterside village of **Nernier** then occupies a particularly lovely spot at the end of the so-called 'Petit Lac', the thin, mainly Swiss, western tail of Lac Léman. Despite the swanky marina, Nernier hasn't been over-prettified. Enjoy a wander along the promenade, perhaps after a meal at one of the tempting restaurant terraces just behind, and you may spot a plaque on an old stone wall recalling how Mary Shelley was inspired to write a little of her ground-breaking, spine-chilling novel *Frankenstein* in this tranquil corner (*see* box, overleaf).

---

**Paysalp**
*t 04 50 36 89 18, www.paysalp.asso.fr; open July–Aug daily 2–6; Sept–June Mon–Sat 10–12 and 2–5; adm; cheese-making July–Aug daily al 9.15; Sept–June Sat and Sun 9.15*

**Musée Paysan**
*t 04 50 36 89 18, www.paysalp.asso.fr; open July–Aug daily 2–6; Sept–June 1st Sun of every month 2–5; adm*

**Musée de l'Histoire/Musée de la Faune**
*t 04 50 73 71 53; open school hols at appointed times; check at tourist office; adm*

ⓘ **Lac Léman**
*www.leman-sans-frontiere.com*

**Musée Milouti**
*t 04 50 94 10 55, www.granges-de-servette; open July–Aug daily 3–7; adm*

 **Nernier**

## The Lake That Gave Birth to Frankenstein

The precocious 19-year-old Mary Shelley (née Godwin) spent a rather famous literary holiday on Lac Léman in 1816 with fellow travellers Percy Shelley and Byron. Confined much of the time to their villa near Geneva by 'a wet, ungenial summer' (now thought possibly to have been caused by the Tambora volcano explosion), they began to read each other ghost stories, then set themselves a competition to create their own. Mary's masterpiece of Gothic horror was the result, telling the story of the maddened ambition of a scientist who decides to create an artificial man from body parts. Widely considered the first science fiction novel, but also seen as a criticism of the supposed scientific 'advances' of the industrial revolution, her story was sparked off by a vision she had when she went to bed one night by Lac Léman, of 'the pale student of unhallowed arts kneeling beside the thing he had put together... Frightening must it be; for supremely frightful would be the effect of any human endeavour to mock the stupendous Creator of the world.'

### ⭐ Yvoire

Yvoire is an absurdly cute village that looks as though it's been lifted out of a fairytale. It stands where the views broaden out to take in the much wider, deeper Grand Lac. It's so irresistible that it's often completely overwhelmed by tourists. Its church spire appears wrapped in silver foil, like an elaborate confection, and shines out above the gorgeous old stone houses smothered in flowers in summer. Tourists crawl over the place like an infestation of ants in high season, when boutiques and restaurants seem to take over every house. The spectacular port is lined with delectable cafés, overseen by a magnificent picture-book **castle**. Although you can't see inside, you can visit its enchanting **Jardin des Cinq Sens** for a floral experience appealing to all the senses. This fragrant spot can also sometimes offer a haven of peace away from the hordes.

**Jardin des Cinq Sens, Château d'Yvoire**
*t 04 50 72 88 80, www.jardin5sens.net; open mid-May–mid-Sept daily 10–7; mid-April–mid-May daily 11–6; mid-Sept–mid-Oct daily 1–5; adm*

**Excenevex** just south may not be as smart as the previous lakeside villages, with its campsites and its ranks of pedalos, but it boasts the nicest sandy beach on the whole French side of the lake, with plenty of space for beach games. Looking eastwards from here, the triangular peak of the **Dent d'Oche** forms a brilliant backdrop to Léman's southern shore, soaring to 2,222m.

**Sciez Musée de la Préhistoire**
*t 04 50 72 53 28; open July–Aug Wed 10–12 and 3–6, Sat 10–12; adm*

For those wishing to delve into the prehistoric lakeside communities, try **Sciez's Musée de la Préhistoire**. The more dynamic **Aigles du Léman** offers shows featuring hundreds of animals, ranging well beyond eagles. Back on the water's edge, the village of **Anthy** has a tiny port below its sweet church, plus traditional fish stall and huts, and pebbly waters to dip into from patches of grassy beaches. **Corzent** just to the east has a lovely beach, the Château d'Yvoire just visible from one end, across the Golfe de Coudrée.

**Les Aigles du Léman**
*t 04 50 72 72 26, www.lesaiglesduleman. fr; open mid-April–early Sept daily 10–7; adm*

## Thonon-les-Bains to Amphion

Split in two by its cliff, imposing **Thonon-les-Bains** was historically capital of the Chablais. Down below, it has a good choice of beaches, both supervised and more natural, an impressive marina and a huddle of old fishermen's cottages, some still used, one batch containing a modest fishing museum, the **Ecomusée de la**

**Ecomusée
de la Pêche**

*t 04 50 70 69 49; open
July–Aug daily 10–12
and 2.30–6.30; June
and Sept Wed–Sun
2.30–6; adm*

**Musée du
Chablais**

*t 04 50 70 69 49; open
July–Aug daily 10–12
and 2.30–6; Sept–June
for exhibitions
Wed–Sun 2.30–6; adm*

**Château de
Ripaille**

*t 04 50 26 64 44; www.
ripaille.com; open July–
Aug daily 11–6; April–
June and Sept daily
10.30–12 and 2–6;
Feb–Mar and Oct–Nov
daily 2.45–4.15; adm*

**Arboretum**

*t 04 50 26 28 22;
open May–Sept
Tues–Sun 10–7; Oct–Nov
Tues–Sun 10–4.30*

**Eaux Minérales
d'Evian**

*t 04 50 26 93 23;
www.evian.fr; open
Mon–Fri, by
appointment only*

Pêche. Locals pick up their fresh fish in this quarter. Following the long promenade east along the lake makes for a wonderful walk.

You can scale Thonon's cliff on foot if you're feeling energetic, but the upper town, with historic and shopping quarters, is also connected to the port by cable car. Perched on the edge of the high promontory, the **Musée du Chablais** celebrates regional culture in sober fashion in its grand house. Nearby, the interconnecting churches of **St-François de Sales** and **St-Hippolyte** vie for attention with their over-elaborate decorations. The older, a Gothic structure, had its interior plastered with ornate Baroque additions at a later date; it witnessed François de Sales preaching to the town's recalcitrant Protestants and winning them over. The early 20th-century artist Maurice Denis covered the later church with big bold classical-style biblical scenes, all tinged with his distinctive pinks and mauves. In the shopping streets outside, look out for **Boujon**, a fine Savoyard shop devoted to the art of *affinage*, or ageing cheese.

Surrounded by vineyards on the flats east of town, the impressive **Château de Ripaille** served as a hunting lodge for the lords of Savoie. Duke Amédée VIII enlarged it and retired here with six like-minded gentlemen to devote himself, up to a point, to a pious life, drawing the line at the table; he loved his food, hence, apparently, the origins of the French expression *'faire ripaille'* for enjoying a hearty banquet. However, as the Papal Schism split the Church, Amédée was elected anti-pope Felix V at the Council of Basle of 1439. Resigning nine years later, he helped end the dreadful division. From the 17th century to the Revolution, Carthusian monks settled here. On the tour you see their kitchens and wine press. But the bulk of the interiors were later redecorated in mock Gothic style with an Art Nouveau twist, and are geared to receptions.

The forest behind contains the **Clairière des Justes**, a national memorial in honour of French people who rescued Jews in the Second World War, and an **Arboretum**, still recovering from the storm damage of 1999. The swanky new waterside development of **Port-Ripaille** lies hidden on the wooded end of the peninsula.

## Evian-les-Bains to the Swiss Border

Just west of Evian, **Amphion** makes another popular summer waterside resort, without the chi-chi of Evian itself. But it is the location of the **Eaux Minérales d'Evian** factory where some four million bottles a day are filled. Evian water is apparently the most consumed mineral water in the world (*see* box, overleaf).

Despite the palatial hotels on its slopes, despite the very posh marina and prize-winning floral displays, particularly along its promenade, the town of **Evian** immediately behind the waterside had been looking a bit jaded in recent times. However, the place has been transformed, undergoing a rather successful facelift.

## 1789: A Revolutionary Year for the Waters of Evian

The year 1789 proved doubly revolutionary for Evian – that was when its mineral water was 'discovered', thanks to the sickly Marquis de Lessert, who came to take the waters at Amphion for his kidney stones. To little effect. At Evian, he tried St Catherine's spring, below a certain Monsieur Cachat's garden. That appeared to do the trick. News of the water's miraculous power soon spread, doctors prescribing it, Cachat fencing off the spring to make his fortune. Bottling took off in earnest from 1826, while the first public baths went up in 1827. The Société des Eaux d'Evian, created in 1869, drilled for and bought further springs, financed refreshment pavilions, hotels, a theatre and a casino, and the place grew into a highly fashionable spa resort, attracting the extremely wealthy...as it still does.

The biggest change has been to the vast **Palais Lumière**, given a complete makeover and crowned with a splendid glass dome to serve as Evian's main cultural venue, hosting high-quality art exhibitions, among other events. Its first summer show, in 2007, kicked off in collaboration with St Petersburg, on the theme of water paintings by Russian artists of the 19th and 20th centuries.

The restored Palais Lumière has eclipsed the other flash buildings lined up behind the promenade, including the irreverent **casino**, mocking the shape of a Greek-cross church, only separated from the real church by an elaborate mock-Renaissance villa, now the **town hall**. This spacious house was built for the Lumière family of cinema fame (*see* p.42) – enter during working hours for a free peek at the Belle Epoque decorative extravaganza. The villa was slightly damaged during demonstrations at the G8 summit held in town in 2003, although a police cordon kept most of the protesters on the Swiss side of the lake. Evian, with its very grand hotels, has a history of hosting international conferences as well as well-heeled honeymooners; the Accords d'Evian of 1962 saw the French government officially acknowledge Algeria's independence.

The brand-new addition to the row of major buildings behind the waterfront is the ultra-modern **Hilton Hotel**, containing the first ever **Buddha Bar spa**, a synonym for trendiness and claiming to be one of Europe's largest. Not far off lies the more discreet contemporary, glass-covered **Thermes**, a surprisingly intimate, family-orientated thermal spa, with mother-and-baby packages (*see* p.316).

**Evian Buvette Thermale**

*open mid-June–mid-Sept daily 10.30–12.30 and 3–7; early May–mid-June and late Sept daily 2.30–6.30*

Up on the main pedestrian shopping street, the Art Nouveau **Evian Buvette Thermale** cuts quite a dash. It houses an exhibition on Evian water, with the company's designer bottles, a boutique, and the desk for booking tours of the Amphion factory. On the slope just above the building, people queue to top up on Evian water for free at what is now the elegant Cachat public fountain, with a statue of a naked lady thrown in for good measure.

**Evian cable car**

*free; lowest stops behind the Palais Lumière or beside the Cachat spring*

Evian's **cable car** has been revived in the town's revamp, saving you a very daunting walk further up the steep slope behind the town centre. At the top, you come out beside the intriguing wooden structure of the **Auditorium La Grange au Lac**, a kind of Alpine Globe Theatre, designed by the architect Patrick Bouchain in honour of the celebrated cellist and humanitarian Rostropovich. Set among tall shade-giving trees, it provides an excellent venue for a programme of concerts. On an ordinary day, you could use the cable car to go and take tea in the Royal or the Ermitage hotel.

**㉗ Boat trip on Lac Léman**

Clearly, a **boat trip** is *de rigueur* when in Evian, although the immaculately manicured **promenade** offers a relaxing alternative view from dry land, and a very long, easy walk on the flat. The glamorous crowd go yachting on the lake from Evian's swanky marina. The boats for hoi polloi and crossings to Lausanne (directly opposite Evian on the Swiss side) are run by the monopoly-holding Swiss Compagnie Générale de Navigation sur le Lac Léman.

**Jardins de l'Eau du Pré Curieux**
*reserve via tourist office, May–Sept Wed–Sun 10, 1.45 and 3; adm*

However, there is a lovely shorter boat trip you can take along Evian's western shore, to the **Jardins de l'Eau du Pré Curieux** You're transported along on what is billed as France's first-ever solar-powered boat, designed by Jean Nouvel, best known as a cutting-edge contemporary architect, although this creation is modest and practical. The pink farm you arrive at has been turned into a didactic centre dedicated to wetlands, and to the management of the world's water resources. You learn most about Lac Léman, the improved quality of its waters in recent decades, but also its environmental issues. Outside, the charming small-scale lakeside gardens show aspects of wetland ecosystems, from torrents to

**Musée du Pré Lude**
*open mid-June–Sept Tues–Sun 10.30–12 and 3–7; adm*

marshes. The separate, more traditional **Musée du Pré Lude** on the main road behind covers local crafts in a renovated farm.

Pressing east from Evian, the Chablais mountains descend practically to the water. You can climb swiftly up to **Thollon-les-Mémises**, known as the Balcony of Lac Léman for its views over the waters. The man often regarded as the first ever paraglider, Jean-Claude Bétemps, teaches here (*see* p.316).

**Musée des Barques du Léman**
*t 00 41 24 482 7022, www.st-gingolph.ch/ musee; open mid-June–mid-Sept daily 2–5.30, April–mid-June and mid-Sept–Oct Sat 2–5.30; adm*

Clinging to the lakeside, **Meillerie** has a delightful quay. A rock here is dedicated to Jean-Jacques Rousseau (*see* pp.259 and 280), who set some of the events in his hugely influential, idealistic novel *La Nouvelle Héloïse* in the village. In the book, the protagonists Julie and St-Preux seek refuge here from a storm on the lake...just as Byron and Shelley had to in real life on their celebrated visit. They were staying in Swiss territory, but **St-Gingolph** on the border doesn't know which side it's on. No need to cross customs to visit the **Musée des Barques du Léman**, a pleasant museum on boating on Lake Geneva, set in part of the school-like castle.

*17 Haute Savoie: Lac Léman to Mont Blanc | To Lake Geneva, or Lac Léman*

## Market Days by Lac Léman

**Viuz-en-Sallaz**: Mon am.
**Bellevaux**: Mon am.
**Thonon-les-Bains**: Thurs am.
**Evian-les-Bains**: Tues am.

## Activities by Lac Léman

**Cruises** across Lac Léman from Thonon and Evian are run by **CGN**, **t** 04 50 71 14 71 or **t** 00 41 848 811 848, *www.cgn.ch*. The best Léman **beaches** are at Excenevex, Corzent, Thonon (around Ripaille peninsula) and Evian

(i) **Viuz-en-Sallaz**
*La Gare, 74250 Viuz-en-Sallaz, t 04 50 36 86 24, www.alpesduleman.com*

(i) **Bellevaux**
*74470 Bellevaux, t 04 50 73 71 53, www.bellevaux.com*

(i) **Thonon-les-Bains >>**
*Place du Marché, 74200 Thonon-les-Bains, t 04 50 71 55 55, www.thononlesbains.com*

(i) **Evian-les-Bains >>**
*Place d'Allinges, 74501 Evian, t 04 50 75 04 26, www.eviantourism.com*

(★) **Royal/Ermitage >>**

(i) **Yvoire >**
*Place de la Mairie, 74140 Yvoire, t 04 50 72 80 21, www.presquile-leman.com*

(★) **Hôtel du Port >**

(★) **Château de Coudrée >**

(i) **Thollon-les-Mémises >>**
*74500 Thollon-les-Mémises, t 04 50 70 90 01, www.thollonlesmemises.com*

(with pools by the beach; *open May–Sept; adm*); boat hire, sailing, rowing, diving and water-skiing all possible. Also try Anthy or Amphion.

For **spa** pamperings, Evian has a renowned centre, **Les Thermes Evian**, t 04 50 75 02 30, *www.lesthermes evian.com*. The **Thermes de Thonon**, t 04 50 26 17 22, have been renovated.

**Paragliding** was invented in these parts by Jean-Claude Bétemps, one of the pilots at **Médasports**, t 04 50 70 95 75, *www.medasports.com*, in Thollon-les-Mémises.

## Where to Stay and Eat around Lac Léman

Note that a number of hotels insist on half-board.

### Bonne ✉ 74380

***Hôtel Baud**, t 04 50 39 20 15, *www.hotel-baud.com* (€€€). On the busy main street of an unexciting village east of Annemasse, but with excellent rooms in sleek contemporary style, most giving onto the smart garden. The refined cuisine (€€€) is divine, served on the terrace in summer. *Restaurant closed Sun.*

### Yvoire ✉ 74140

***Hôtel du Port**, t 04 50 72 80 17, *http://hotelrestaurantduport-yvoire. org* (€€€€–€€€). Irresistible, like a chalet about to slip in to the lake for a swim. Enchanting rooms. Spacious popular restaurant (€€€) on several floors, with glorious parasolled terraces. *Closed Nov–mid-Feb; restaurant closed Wed out of season.*

***Le Pré de la Cure**, t 04 50 72 83 58, *www.pre-delacure.com* (€€). Modern, picturesque hotel outside the main village gate. Excellent restaurant (€€). Indoor pool. *Closed mid-Nov–early Mar.*

### Sciez-sur-Léman ✉ 74140

****Château de Coudrée**, Bonnatrait, t 04 50 72 62 33, *www.chateauxhotels. com/coudree* (€€€€–€€€). The 12th-century keep is encased in later wings offering wonderful rooms in this magical lakeside location. Classic refined cuisine (€€€€–€€€). Facilities include beach, pool, court, and cookery lessons. *Closed Nov; restaurant closed Tues and Wed outside July–Aug.*

### Anthy-sur-Léman ✉ 74200

***Auberge d'Anthy**, t 04 50 70 35 00, *www.auberge-anthy.com* (€€). Good value, well-run family inn by village church up from beach. Plain but pleasant light-wood little rooms, and a fine restaurant (€€€–€€). The family can organize bikes, rowing, even a yacht. *Closed most Jan; restaurant closed Sun eve and Mon.*

### Thonon-les-Bains ✉ 74200

****Alpazur**, 8 Av Général Leclerc, t 04 50 71 37 25, *www.hotel-alpazur.fr* (€). Ask for a lake view in this neat 1970s building down by the cute central port. *Closed Nov–mid-Feb.*

**Prieuré**, 68 Grande Rue, t 04 50 71 31 89 (€€€). Venerable restaurant close to the central churches. *Closed Sun eve, Mon, and Tues lunch.*

**Le Scampi**, 1 Av du Léman, t 04 50 71 10 04 (€€). Central, for fish with views. *Closed Mon, early April and mid-Nov.*

### Evian-les-Bains ✉ 74500

Note that a luxurious big new **Hilton** hotel with spa and restaurants opened in 2006 down beside the lake.

*****Royal** and ****Ermitage**, t 04 50 26 85 00, *www.evianroyalresort.com* (€€€€€). Splendid palatial early 20th-century sister establishments of the highest order, the Ermitage higher up the slope, with more fabulous views. Sporting and pampering facilities and a variety of restaurants (€€€€€–€€€) in each, with superb terraces.

****Hôtel des Cygnes**, 8 Av Grande Rive, t 04 50 75 01 01, *www.hotellescygnes. com* (€€). A charming timber-frame villa beside the port with the great advantage of being the only hotel on Evian's very water's edge. As well as nice traditional rooms, it has its own beach and pontoon. There's a good old-fashioned restaurant (€€), plus a tea room. *Closed Jan.*

### Thollon-les-Mémises ✉ 74500

****Bon Séjour**, t 04 50 70 92 65, *www. bon-sejour.com* (€). Sweet old-styled family hotel. Good traditional cuisine (€€). Tennis court. *Closed mid-Oct–mid-Nov and 2 wks April.*

****Hôtel Bellevue**, t 04 50 70 92 79, *www.hotelbellevue.fr.fm*. Right next door, equally good, and has a pool.

# Haut Chablais and the Giffre

*Dranse* is the Savoyard word for a torrent. A trip along the **Gorges de la Dranse** above Thonon, beloved by white-water rafters, plunges you into rocky mountain terrain. This river derives its power from the three separate *dranses* that join together at **Bioge**.

The **Dranse d'Abondance valley** takes you up via the historic town of **Abondance**, overseen by its Augustinian abbey, one of the most important in medieval Savoie, its cloisters decorated with striking remnants of 15th-century frescoes, a mix of Gothic elegance and naivety. Abondance is also a slightly smoky hard cheese, a small version of Beaufort. Thick, creamy Vacherin is produced here too.

From **La Chapelle d'Abondance**, climb up to the GR5 hiking path to admire cows and flowers in the nature reserve of **Vacheresse**. The GR5 is the great walking trail linking Lac Léman with Mont Blanc – you can buy a detailed *Topoguide* to this path, as well as many others. The best way to get close to the traditional chalet-and-pastures life of the whole Haut Chablais area is to go walking out from the resorts and up the valleys, with mountain lakes, waterfalls, or even remote chalet-restaurants providing goals.

The south-facing chalets of **Châtel** by the Swiss border bask in sunshine late into the afternoon. Sports-mad types take the hair-raising *Fantasticâble*, at speeds of up to 100kph down from Plaine Dranse. The twisting D228 road takes you on a startling route to the Lac de Montriond or to Avoriaz and its lake, but the more usual way to these spots from Thonon goes via the **Dranse de Morzine valley**, also known as the **Vallée d'Aulps**, from Thonon. This stretch stands at the start of the famous old 700km French Alpine motoring **Route des Grandes Alpes** from Lac Léman to Menton on the Med, but you can only scale all the highest passes in summer.

A path through splendid, steep towering beech woods takes you down to the **Gorges du Pont du Diable** On the guided tour here, marvel at the tortuous forms carved some 60m down into the marble rocks by the raging waters caused by the big melt at the end of the last Ice Age. The deep green of the waters derives from microscopic mosses. The daredevil-challenging bridge of rock spanning the gorges helped give the name to the sight; it is no longer accessible, but used to be used by locals as a shortcut.

The romantic early Gothic ruins of the **Abbaye d'Aulps** speak calmly of the former importance of this Cistercian religious centre. However, it entered into bitter rivalry with the abbey of Abondance and the charterhouse at Bellevaux. In most unseemly fashion, these communities even sent out peasant raiding parties against each other's territories in the 14th century: wealth and power had gone to the monks' heads. The Reformation caused these places to put their houses back in order. However, the Abbaye d'Aulps fell

---

**Abbaye d'Abondance**
*t 04 50 81 60 54;
open Christmas–Oct
Wed–Mon 10–12 and
2–5; closed Tues; adm*

**Route des Grandes Alpes**
*www.routedes
grandesalpes.com*

**Gorges du Pont du Diable**
*t 04 50 72 10 39,
www.les-gorges-du-
pont-du-diable.com;
open May–Sept daily
9–7; adm*

**Abbaye d'Aulps**
*t 04 50 72 15 15,
www.valleedaulps.com;
Centre d'Interprétation
open mid-June–mid-
Sept daily 10–6.30;
Oct–mid-Dec Wed–Mon
12–12 and 2–6; adm*

## John Berger Gets Your Hands Dirty in Peasant Haute Savoie

For an engrossing insight into the tough old country ways and country people of Haute Savoie, brace yourself before starting *Into Their Labours*, an unflinching trilogy of short stories dedicated to peasant life in these parts, by British artist and Booker Prize-winning novelist John Berger. The trio begins with *Pig Earth*. This portrait of a dying breed of men and women proves a masterpiece of visual writing. From the opening story, which begins with the graphic but unsentimental slaughter of a cow, the peasants working 'like tailors' to skin it, you are gripped, by the throat. Animals play roles almost as important as the humans in these brooding tales. Berger moved to Haute Savoie decades ago, finding a more meaningful life in his adopted mountain community. The trilogy turns out to be an exceptional homage to the farmers of the Alps, and a heartfelt defence of the European peasant tradition.

into terminal decline in the 18th century. Then, when the villagers of **St-Jean-d'Aulps** lost their church to a fire in 1823, they came to take stones from the abbey to build a new one. Still, the ruins look fabulously picturesque; a herb garden lies to one side. On the odd summer evening, enjoy a torchlit visit or outdoor theatre. A surviving barn is being turned into a museum.

One major draw to the abbey down the centuries was the pilgrimage to St Guérin, the establishment's second abbot, seen as protector of cattle. Even as late as the 1950s, crowds attended his saint's day. With the decline in the number of Savoyard farmers, as well as in religious belief, that tradition has waned. However, from here and the hamlets making up **Les Esserts**, take the short routes up the slopes to where the roads run out, and walk into the high pastures in their grandiose settings, the odd old summer *chalet d'alpage* still surviving. One of the most popular places to start out is the **Alpage de Graidon**. Strange local legends haunt these parts, for example of a demonic black cow that terrorized the local herds.

Narrow hairpin bends lead east to the emerald-green **Lac de Montriond**, formed by a landslide that blocked the waters here many centuries ago, or maybe many millennia ago – no one quite remembers. The accidental natural dam was, however, only made fully watertight in 1990. Fishing and canoeing are popular now, as is hiking. In season, tourists mob the traditional village of **Ardent** above. Mountain-bikers swarm over the slopes of the linked **Portes du Soleil** resorts that follow (*see* also p.351), the ski lifts being open to bikes in summer. For keen walkers, the GR5 hiking path continues south via a spectacular route into the Giffre valley.

**Ardoisière des 7 Pieds**
*t 04 50 79 12 21, www. ardoise-morzine.com; open summer tours, Tues and Fri at 10.30 and 5; adm*

The distinctive beige slate roofs of the attractive, roomy valley-bottom chalets of **Morzine** take on silvery tones in the sunshine. Visit a traditional slate worker at the **Ardoisière des 7 Pieds**. Chic boutiques line the main street, but the centre lacks cohesion despite the church with its spiked onion dome. The resort of **Avoriaz** perched far above remains lively year-round with sports fanatics. **Les Gets**, with its array of chalets and quirky **Musée de la Musique Mécanique**, hosted the 2004 mountain-bike world championship. Consider devalkarting: go-karting down a mountain!

**Musée de la Musique Mécanique**
*t 04 50 79 85 75, www. lemuseedesgets.free.fr; open July–Aug daily 10.15–12.15 and 2.15–7.15; Jan–June and Sept–Oct daily 2.15–7.15; adm*

From Les Gets, cross south into the surprisingly generous, fertile **Giffre valley**. Fruit trees and delightful old hamlets lie scattered across its slopes, the traditional chalets often with a smaller *mazot* alongside, in which precious objects were stored separately in case of a chalet fire. Waterfalls cascade down from the heights.

**Taninges** makes a good first stop, for the Gothic ruins of the **Chartreuse de Mélan**, destroyed as recently as the 1960s. What's left acts as an atmospheric setting for summer exhibitions of art. West, the typical village of **Mieussy**, its flash, Flamboyant Gothic church with onion-bulb steeple added on, took its place in the history of extreme sports in 1978 as the place where paragliding was born, or the art of 'armchair flight' as it's been nicknamed!

East of Taninges, the pretty hamlets are all outdone by higgledy-piggledy **Samoëns**, actually reached most dramatically from Morzine via the lofty **Col de Joux Plane**, close to which a visit to the

**Ecomusée Ferme du Clos Parchet**

*t 04 50 34 46 69; tours July–Aug Tues, Thurs and Fri at 3, June and Sept Thurs at 2 30; book at Samoëns tourist office; adm*

18th-century **Ecomusée Ferme du Clos Parchet** proves absorbing. The stonemasons of the Giffre (and of Samoëns in particular), nicknamed the *frahans*, became renowned for their craft across France. Beyond the village's covered market lies the rose-surrounded church, its door guarded by two ancient Chinese-looking lions, a feature adopted from northern Italy. To one side rises a delightful Alpine garden, **La Jaÿsinia**, created by a local girl made good, co-founder of the celebrated Seine-side Samaritaine department store in Paris. The array of plants that thrive in what is in effect a rockery on a grand scale is exceptional.

Neighbouring **Sixt-Fer-à-Cheval**, also a member of the association of *Les Plus Beaux Villages de France*, is surrounded by hamlets, chapels and crosses, signalling the religious influence of its abbey in times past, parts of which remain around the main square. Learn more about its history, and that of the valley and its special natural environment, at the **Maison de la Réserve Naturelle de Sixt**. Just south of Sixt, a splendid section of the GR5 trail takes you up into this **nature reserve**, past the high-altitude, fish-filled **Lac d'Anterne**, at over 2,000m. Here you find yourself in the land of marmots and mountain hares. Continue via the **Col d'Anterne**, at 2,257m, and you can head down through the **Aiguilles Rouges** mountainside to Chamonix, the Mont Blanc range facing you in all its glory.

 **Cirque du Fer à Cheval**

*fee for cars*

East from Sixt along the Giffre, you hit against the huge **Cirque du Fer à Cheval** the most overwhelming dead end in the Alps, where the limestone rocks of the pre-alpine ranges bang into the granite of the mighty Mont Blanc range. Sensational waterfalls drop from the great heights encircling you. Legends of golden-hoofed ibex, their feet powdered with precious metal, led prospectors to the maddest acts of mountaineering folly to find seams. Most notoriously, Mont Blanc's conqueror Jacques Balmat died on the highest peak, the **Ruan**, chancing his luck once too often.

ⓘ **Abondance**
*74360 Abondance,*
*t 04 50 73 02 90,*
*www.abondance.org*

ⓘ **St-Jean-d'Aulps**
*74430 St-Jean-d'Aulps,*
*t 04 50 79 65 09,*
*www.valleedaulps.com*

ⓘ **Morzine >>**
*La Crusaz,*
*74110 Morzine,*
*t 04 50 74 72 72,*
*www.morzine.com*

ⓘ **Les Gets**
*B.P. 27, 74260 Les Gets,*
*t 04 50 75 80 80,*
*www.lesgets.com*

ⓘ **Samoëns >>**
*Place de l'Ancienne*
*Gare, 74340 Samoëns,*
*t 04 50 34 40 28,*
*www.samoens.com*

ⓘ **Sixt-Fer-à-Cheval**
*Pl de la Gare, 74740 Sixt,*
*t 04 50 34 49 36, www.*
*sixtferacheval.com*

**Musée
Départemental de
la Résistance**
*under restoration*

**Musée de
l'Horlogerie**
*t 04 50 89 13 02,*
*www.cluses.com; open*
*July–Aug daily 10–12*
*and 1.30–6; Sept–June*
*Mon–Sat 1.30–6; adm*

## Market Days in the Haut Chablais and Giffre

**Châtel:** Wed am.

**Morzine:** Wed am.

**Les Gets:** Thurs am.

**Samoëns:** Wed am.

**Sixt-Fer-à-Cheval:** (crafts July–Aug) Tues pm.

## Activities in the Haut Chablais and Giffre

For **mountain-biking**, Les Gets and Morzine are renowned, but in summer possibilities are vast.

**White-water rafting** is very popular in the Giffre valley, as are **rock-climbing** and **paragliding** – *see* Sixt, Samoëns or Morzine tourist office websites for addresses.

Les Gets has a **golf course**, t 04 50 75 87 63.

## Where to Stay and Eat in the Haut Chablais and Giffre

For places known mainly as ski resorts, hotel and restaurant listings appear in the **Winter Sports** chapter.

### La Chapelle d'Abondance and Avoriaz

*See* **Winter Sports**, p.353.

### Morzine ✉ 74110

\*\*\***La Bergerie**, Rue du Téléphérique, t 04 50 79 13 69, *www.hotel-bergerie. com* (€€€–€€). In a resort with several chalet-hotels (*see* p.353). Pool. *Closed mid-April–June and mid-Sept–mid-Dec.*

### Samoëns ✉ 74340

\*\***Le Moulin du Bathieu**, Vercland, t 04 50 34 48 07, *www.bathieu.com* (€€). Very picturesque chalet up among meadows (signs for Samoëns 1600). Savoyard cuisine (must reserve; €€). *Closed May and Nov–mid-Dec.*

# To Mont Blanc via Arve or Aravis

## Via the Arve to Mont Blanc

Taking the more obvious, busy **Arve valley** towards Mont Blanc, the main settlements are industrial but do have historic hearts. **La Roche-sur-Foron** oversees the lower Arve. Climb from the medieval town to the tower; for centuries this place was a centre of the counts of Geneva, closely related to Savoie's lords. At **Bonneville**, Duke Charles-Félix of Savoie looks down on the Arve from his 30m column, commemorating the taming of the river. The town boasts grand neoclassical buildings on Place du Marquet. The **castle** is medieval, but holds the **Musée Départemental de la Résistance**.

Avoid the main roads on to Cluses and take the hair-raising route along the **Gorges du Bronze**. From Notre-Dame-de-l'Assomption church at the resort of **Mont-Saxonnex**, the views reach north to the Jura. Up the D4, the **Chartreuse du Reposoir** is a magnificent sight nestling in its valley, but is private, occupied by Carmelites.

Originally a clock-making centre, industrial **Cluses** has specialized in *décolletage* since the 20th century, which has nothing to do with women's fashion, and everything to do with precision machine parts; learn about this, along with the older traditional craft from which it was born, in the **Musée de l'Horlogerie**. For a clock centre that has kept its historic heart beating, head for **Arâches**, also known for rock-climbing and canyoning.

Flaine, an isolated, purpose-built ski resort resembling a vision of a bureaucrats' retirement city lost high in the mountains, does have a summer season. The **Désert de Platé**, reached by its

**Grandes Platières cable car**
t 04 50 90 40 00,
www.grand-massif.com;
open early July–late
Aug Sun–Thurs 9–12.45
and 2–5; adm

**Grandes Platières cable car**, offers an extraordinary, blinding white limestone hiking landscape, with Mont Blanc as backdrop.

By **Sallanches**, you've passed round the barrier of the Aravis chain, and Mont Blanc completely fills the end of the Arve valley. The old town was destroyed by fire in 1840, and a new one was built with arcaded streets typical of 19th-century Savoie. The interior of the Eglise St-Jacques was restored with a riot of decoration. The plain

**Château des Rubins**
t 04 50 58 32 13, www.
rubinsnature-asso.fr;
open July–Aug Mon–Fri
9–6.30, Sat and Sun
2–6.30; Sept–June
Mon–Fri 9–6.30, Sat,
Sun and public hols
2–6; adm

14th-century **Château des Rubins** presents Alpine nature, a good place for interactive learning on a rainy day. **Les Ilettes** offers three lakes at the foot of the Aiguilles Rouges, with lifeguards in summer.

Climb above the valley north of Sallanches for the Parking du Burzier at the **Alpage de Doran**, then take the trail of well over an hour to see *gypaètes*, bearded vultures, recently reintroduced after disappearing at the start of the 20th century.

## Via the Aravis to Mont Blanc

The most direct way from Annecy to the Arve is via the A41 motorway or parallel N203, but the mountain roads through the Aravis are much more intriguing. The picturesque slope road via **Nâves-Parmelan** and **Aviernoz** takes you to the **Château de**

**Château de Thorens**
t 04 50 22 42 02;
open July–Aug daily
2–7; May daily by
appointment; adm

**Thorens**, its array of towers calling for attention, as do its connections with famous Savoyards. It was built by a count of Geneva as a gift for a devoted vassal, but a later count confiscated it from a barbarically misbehaving one. The château was then sold to François de Sales – not the famous religious figure, but his father. However, the future St François (*see* p.33 and p.259) was born in a nearby oratory in 1567. The family had a good eye for art: splendid 16th-century Antwerp tapestries illustrate the story of Tobit; the most remarkable paintings on show include a girlish boy of a *St Stephen* by Marco d'Oggiono and a later Van Dyck representing a duke of Savoie. Of equal interest for Savoyard visitors are the objects that belonged to the local saint including a scissor case said to contain a slice of his heart, and to a distinguished politician-descendant, Camillo Cavour,. Cavour negotiated the ceding of Savoie to France in 1860 in exchange for military help to expel the Austrian army occupying northern Italy; the rooms devoted to him include the table on which the treaty was signed in Turin.

A road leads up to the gentle high pastures of the **Plateau des Glières**. A large **monument** inaugurated in 1973 pays homage to the Second World War Resistance fighters up here, even if it looks at first sight more like an advert for local cheese-makers. Some 500 Maquisards hid out here in the winter of 1944, receiving some of the earliest Allied munitions supplies dropped by parachute. The

Vichy military tried in vain to dislodge them. Then, in March 1944, a huge German force was sent to eradicate them. While a hundred Maquisards died, many more Germans fell. The Nazis took revenge on nearby communities. Below the southern end of Les Glières, on the road from Annecy to Thônes, the **Cimetière des Glières**, trapped in a tight gorge, became the resting place of many of the martyrs; a stirring **Musée de la Résistance** is attached to the cemetery.

**Musée de la Résistance**
*t 04 50 32 18 38; open June–mid-Sept daily 10–12.30 and 2–6.30*

Everyday Savoyard traditions are recalled in and around traditional **Thônes**, its arcaded, rounded main square sitting prettily under the western wall of the Aravis. The onion-bulb church contains the obligatory Baroque altarpiece, but also plaques for the war dead, including from a German bombing. The central **Musée du Pays de Thônes** looks none too exciting, but contains nicely carved wooden objects. On the outskirts of town, you'll find a fine choice of Reblochon *fermier*, plus other regional cheeses and specialities, at **La Coop du Reblochon**, while the *sabotier* in his new wooden chalet may incite you to stop and pick up a pair of clogs.

**Musée du Pays de Thônes**
*t 04 50 02 96 92; open July–Aug 10–12 and 3–7; Jan–June and Sept–Dec Mon–Sat 9–12, plus Mon, Wed and Sat 2–5.30; adm*

**La Coop du Reblochon**
*t 04 50 02 05 60*

The wood theme continues in the **Ecomusée du Bois**, out of town at an old sawmill up the tall, tight **Montremont valley**.

Two routes lead from Thônes to La Clusaz. The chalet-filled valley up to **Manigod** is lovely, pastures cut like windows into the massive wooded slopes. Explore further traditional hamlets to the south. The parallel, equally dramatic road wends its way over via the **Col de la Croix-Fry**, with many chalets to admire on the way.

**Ecomusée du Bois**
*t 04 50 32 18 10; open July–Aug daily exc Wed 10–12 and 2.30–5.30, April–June and Sept–Oct Tues and Thurs tour only at 4, Sun 2.30–5.30; adm*

Far below, modern **La Clusaz** looks most appealing with its big apartment-block polished wooden chalets climbing out of a steep bowl. Hikers might be interested in taking the little **Vallon des Confins** to join the sensational GR96 hiking path, allowing walkers to shadow the highest crests of the Aravis range right to Cluses.

Around La Clusaz and the higher resort of **Le Grand-Bornand** to the north, sniff out traditional farms producing Reblochon *fermier*. Exploring Le Grand-Bo's enchanting if confusing scattering of traditional hamlets, also hunt down picturesque chalets dotted around the slopes. One restored 19th-century farm serves as home to the **Maison du Patrimoine**, presenting traditional Aravis life. If you continue up to the **Col de la Colombière** you'll pass **Le Chinaillon**. This way forms part of the magical car-touring Route des Grandes Alpes, the walkers' GR96 running parallel far above.

**Maison du Patrimoine**
*t 04 50 02 79 18; open July–Aug Tues–Sat 10–12 and 3–5.30, Sun 4–7; mid–late-June and first half Sept Fri 2–6; Christmas–Easter Tues–Sat 3–5.30; adm*

---

## Pull the Udder One: the Story of Reblochon Cheese

A comic tale showing the local Aravis farmers hoodwinking their medieval landlords recounts how Reblochon cheese came into being around Thônes. In the 13th century, renting farmers had to give their masters a return in proportion to the amount of milk their cows produced. But when the landlords came to measure this, the farmers deliberately only did a partial milking to lower the figure. Once the patron had gone, they did a second milking (*reblocher* meaning to pull the udders a second time), producing a rich, fat result, excellent for making cheese. It takes a full nine litres of milk to make a kilo of Reblochon. These soft, early-eating cheeses are ripened for just three or four weeks.

**⚜ Aravis range from La Clusaz to Megève**

Heading **south from La Clusaz by road**, the Route continues up to the **Col des Aravis**, the single, high, tooth-gap pass through the range, where tourist pandemonium can break out as crowds take in the spectacular view of Mont Blanc. Swooping down the steep eastern side of the Aravis chain, the more daring take the **Route de la Soif**, a track leading through exposed pastures, where chamois, mouflons and bearded vultures hang out, to **Chaucisse**, the old hamlet's wooden church roof resembling a dog's shaggy coat.

Taking the more conventional road down, a solid Baroque church marks the centre of **La Giettaz**. It has welcoming saints in its sky-blue altarpiece and fine stained glass. The little house of **A la Rencontre du Passé** invites you in to discover an old-style Savoyard interior. For modern woodwork, cast an eye over André Porret's wooden furniture and sculpture shop below.

**A la Rencontre du Passé**
*t 04 79 32 92 29, www. la-giettaz-patrimoine. org; open July–Aug Tues and Thurs 3–6; Jan–Mar Tues and Thurs 9.30–12 and 3–6; adm*

Traditional **Flumet**, at a crossroads right down in the **Arly valley**, has been making efforts to liven up its defensive historic heart. The medieval church has been restored, and the riverside mill has been undergoing renovation to receive visitors (check at the tourist office). The cheese co-operative and the *charcuteries* are good places to pick up local culinary specialities. The little resorts around the Arly above Flumet make a change from the flash big boys to the north, settled around charming traditional villages. Climb to **St-Nicolas-la-Chapelle**, where gilded Baroque altarpieces and gory paintings fill the big church with its silvery spire. Wooden sculptures by a local electric-saw artist bring fun to the resorts of **Notre-Dame-de-Bellecombe** and **Crest-Voland**, the latter lying in a stunning location on an open promontory backed by wonderful shaded woods. For splendid forest walks, go on to **Le Cohennoz**.

Heading south to Ugine, the narrow **Arly gorges** look forbidding, but take the dramatic, winding route via **Héry** and its waterfall up towards **Mont Charvin** (2,407m), high point of the Aravis chain, for awesome vistas from in front of the sheer cliff. **Ugine** looks clearly industrial down in the valley, known for its stainless steel production, although it does have a historic core. The **Musée du Crest-Cherel** in the restored castle covers non-industrial traditions.

**Musée du Crest-Cherel**
*t 04 79 37 56 33, www.ugine.com; open mid-June–mid-Sept Wed–Mon 2–6; closed Tues; adm*

North up the Arly from Flumet, at materially minded **Megève**, you'll find the Hermès boutique handily close to the church, the latter filled, appropriately enough for this wealthy resort, with gilded Baroque altarpieces. Although the **Musée du Haut Val d'Arly** occupies an old-style chalet absolutely crammed with objects associated with traditional Alpine crafts, Megève was totally rebranded by Noémie de Rothschild in the 1920s, and has since catered to the mega-rich as a kind of St-Tropez of the snows. Megève's mountain **golf course** is a great pull. If you over-indulge here, do penance by taking the popular walk above town along the steep calvary path marked with its little altars.

**Musée du Haut Val d'Arly**
*t 04 50 91 81 00; open Mon–Sat 2.30–6.30; adm*

ⓘ **La Roche-sur-Foron**
*Place Andrevetan,
74800 La Roche-sur-
Foron, t 04 50 03 36 68*

ⓘ **Bonneville**
*Place de l'Hôtel de Ville,
74130 Bonneville,
t 04 50 97 38 37*

ⓘ **Flumet >>**
*Av de Savoie,
73590 Flumet, t 04 79
31 61 08, www.flumet-
montblanc.com*

ⓘ **Cluses**
*100 Place du 11
Novembre, 74300
Cluses, t 04 50 98 31 79,
www.cluses.com*

ⓘ **Sallanches**
*32 Quai de l'Hôtel de
Ville, 74701 Sallanches,
t 04 50 58 04 25,
www.sallanches.com*

ⓘ **Thorens-Glières**
*22 Place de la Mairie,
74570 Thorens-Glières,
t 04 50 22 40 31*

ⓘ **Notre-Dame-de-Bellecombe >>**
*73590 Notre-Dame-de-
Bellecombe, t 04 79 31
61 40, www.notre
damedebellecombe.com*

ⓘ **La Giettaz**
*73590 La Giettaz,
t 04 79 32 91 90,
www.la-giettaz.com*

ⓘ **Crest-Voland >>**
*73590 Crest-Voland,
t 04 79 31 62 57,
www.crestvoland-
cohennoz.com*

ⓘ **Thônes >**
*Pl Avet, 74230 Thônes,
t 04 50 02 00 26, www.
thones-tourisme.com*

Despite so many highly prized attractions, however, Mont Blanc lies tantalizingly out of sight from Megève; to get a view of it, consider the paragliding company based here. Or go to the village of **Praz-sur-Arly** to the south; it's known for its hot-air ballooning companies, allowing you take to the skies for fabulous trips.

## Market Days in Arve and Aravis

**La Roche-sur-Foron**: Thurs am.
**Bonneville**: Tues and Fri am.
**Sallanches**: Sat am.
**Thônes**: Sat am.
**Megève**: Fri am.

## Activities in Arve and Aravis

Flaine has a **golf course**, t 04 50 90 85 44, Megève a more famous one.

**Megève Parapente**, t 06 62 13 27 71, *www.megeve-parapente.com*, specializes in paragliding. Praz-sur-Arly down the road from Megève is known for **hot-air ballooning**, two companies running trips: **Alpes Montgolfière**, t 04 50 55 50 60, *www.alpes-montgolfiere.fr*, and **Les Ballons du Mont Blanc**, t 04 50 58 08 46, *www.alpes-montgolfiere.com*.

## Where to Stay and Eat in Arve and Aravis

For places known mainly as ski resorts, hotel and restaurant listings appear in the **Winter Sports** chapter.

### Aviernoz ✉ 74570
**\*\*Auberge Camelia**, t 04 50 22 44 24, *www.hotelcamelia.com* (€€). Very comfortable village inn northeast of Lac d'Annecy, south of Thorens-Glières, run by a wonderfully enthusiastic British couple. Bar-restaurant serving regional cuisine (€€).

### Manigod-Thônes ✉ 74230
**\*\*\*La Croix-Fry**, t 04 50 44 90 16, *www.hotelchaletcroix-fry.com* (€€€€€–€€€€). High-perched former farm, beamed rooms with wooden furniture. *Table d'hôte* (€€€–€€) for guests. Heated pool. *Closed mid-Sept–mid-Dec and mid-April–mid-June.*

### La Clusaz/Le Grand-Bornand
*See* **Winter Sports**, p.365.

### Flumet ✉ 73590
**La Ferme du Rocher**, Le Pracet, t 04 79 31 80 30 (€€). Just the one menu of Savoyard specialities, but served in the most adorable dining rooms in this lovingly done-up farm north of town along the Arly. *Always book.*

### St-Nicolas-la-Chapelle ✉ 73590
**\*\*L'Eau Vive**, t 04 79 31 60 46, *www.hotel-eauvive.com* (€). An appealing chalet in this sweet village perched high above the Arly. Simple restaurant (€€–€). Lively owners; Monsieur is a mountain guide. *Closed Easter–May and Oct–mid-Dec.*

**La Ferme du Mont Charvin B&B**, Les Passieux, t 04 79 31 62 89 (€ for compulsory half-board). A true farm with basic rooms run by a woman devoted to Reblochon and old ways. Delicious farm produce at the *table d'hôte*. *Open summer May–late Sept.*

### Notre-Dame-de-Bellecombe ✉ 73590
**\*\*Le Tétras**, Les Frasses, t 04 79 31 61 70, *www.hotel-tetras.com* (€). Big chalet with basic rooms, in appealing neat, terraced slope location. Pool.

**Ferme de Victorine**, Le Planay, t 04 79 31 63 46 (€€€–€€). Delightfully restored farm near Les Saisies, for regional cuisine. *Closed mid-June–early July and mid-Nov–mid-Dec.*

### Crest-Voland ✉ 73590
**\*\*Le Mont Charvin**, Le Cernix, t 04 79 31 61 21, *www.hotel-montcharvin.com* (€€ for compulsory half-board). Friendly, all-wood-clad chalet, balconies with views. Restaurant (€€) decorated with teddy bears. *Closed mid-April–June and Sept–mid-Dec.*

### Megève
*See* **Winter Sports**, p.362.

# Coming Face to Face with Mont Blanc

(i) **Mont Blanc**
*www.pays-du-mont-blanc.com; for the specialist ski resorts, see Chapter 19*

Reaching the wonderful twin villages of **Combloux** and **Cordon** high on the open slopes above the Arve river, marvel at some of the most staggering views of Mont Blanc to be had, the monstrously large triangular summit totally blocking the end of the valley. Combloux has big fat farms liberally scattered on its slopes, but is outdone in quaintness by quieter Cordon. Both boast typically colourful Baroque churches.

**Up Mont Blanc (from Chamonix)**

**St-Gervais-les-Bains** is the traditional base for the ascent of Mont Blanc's summit, but you can't see much of Western Europe's ultimate mountain from this cheerful resort. With large Belle Epoque hotels standing across from the Baroque church and its broad main square, it makes a popular stop. Down the valley at **Le Fayet**, a long, lush, shaded public garden leads to the revived thermal spa centre. This may not have extensive facilities, but specializes in one-to-one treatments, including with mud.

Most visitors come to join the mountaineers on the highest train journey in France. Heaving up on to the shoulders of the Mont-Blanc range like a determined little caterpillar, the spectacular

**Tramway du Mont-Blanc**
*t 04 50 53 22 75; runs mid-June–Sept and mid-Dec–mid-April; adm*

**Tramway du Mont-Blanc** from Le Fayet or St-Gervais may be the highest, steepest line in France, but clearly it isn't one of the fastest. With its spectacular pauses for breath, walkers can get on and off at **Montivon**, **Col de Voza** or **Bellevue** before the terminus, the **Nid d'Aigle**, or 'Eagle's Eyrie'. Built before the First World War, the line takes you up to a very heady 2,380m; the original intention was to transport visitors right to the summit of Mont Blanc by rail, but the technical obstacles stopped travellers being offered such an easy option. From the end of the line, the views of the **Bionnassay glacier** will take your breath away.

For a somewhat simpler option to admire Mont Blanc, head up by road from St-Gervais to **St-Nicolas-de-Véroce**, with one of the most captivating churches in the area, its cemetery, surely one of the most uplifting in France, looking across to the summit.

There are further chapels to discover far down below on the way to **Les Contamines-Montjoie**, a rather exclusive ski resort hidden at the end of its own valley. Magical **Bionnassay**, up a side road, puts in a claim to being the closest village to the summit of Mont Blanc.

**Ecomusée de la Vieille Maison**
*t 04 50 93 40 78; open mid-July–late Aug Mon–Fri, two-hour guided tour only at 2.30 and 4.30*

Enter one of the characterful old chalets by visiting the **Ecomusée de la Vieille Maison** run by an enthusiastic local. Walkers in search of a burst of adrenaline-pumping adventure can try the walk to the Nid d'Aigle, taking on glacier territory with fixed ladders.

Back at the Arve, for a relatively peaceful way through these busy parts, head up the north side of the valley from **Sallanches**, offering some of the finest views of Mont Blanc. Thanks to the persuasive Canon Devémy, **Passy**'s church doubles as a modern art gallery, **Notre-Dame de Toute Grâce** bursting with the most colourful Christian pieces by an amazing array of the most famous artists of the first half of the 20th century. Architect Novarina's chalet of a church went up through the war. On the façade, Fernand Léger's fan of bright mosaics replaces more typical flowers or saints. Among the bold, almost garish works inside, the most alarming, Jean Lurçat's tapestry clash between *Apocalyptic Good and Evil*, depicts a combative female statue-of-liberty figure facing up to the seven-headed monster. By contrast below, the bowed, gouged crucifixion *Christ* by Germaine Richier has a simple power. Over the side altars, the economical lines of Matisse's *St Dominic* contrast with the frenzied activity in Bonnard's *St François de Sales*, who appears, unfortunately, to be suffering from a terrible bout of bishop's sunburn. Look out too for the gorgeous array of stained-glass windows and the calm, totemic figures carved on the beams.

The metallic green **Lac Vert**, boulders spaced out over its limpid waters, is overseen to one side by rocks that resemble the funnels of a great stone ocean liner. From chalet-strewn **Servoz**, further spectacular views open out on to Mont Blanc. A well-maintained track allows you to walk along the beautiful **Gorges de la Diosaz**.

Approaching Chamonix, **Les Houches** may be the closest village to Mont Blanc's summit, but it lies trapped in the valley. The **Parc Animalier du Merlet** further up allows you almost to rub noses with shy mountain wildlife such as ibex, chamois and marmots.

**Parc Animalier du Merlet**
*t 04 50 53 47 89. www. parcdemerlet.com; open July–Aug daily 9.30–7.30; May–June daily 10–6; Sept Tues–Sun 10–6; adm*

To appreciate the largest river of ice in Europe, flowing 3,500m down the mountainside, reach the **Chalet du Glacier des Bossons** by foot or by cable car. As well as the stunning views of the ice, of a rare purity, there are chilling displays here on air catastrophes in the Mont Blanc range.

**Chalet du Glacier des Bossons**
*t 04 50 53 03 89; open mid-May–Sept daily*

Torrents of tourists race through the centre of **Chamonix** like the bubbling waters of the Arve. It's not that the place is particularly beautiful – in fact it's developed in a scrappy manner – but it exudes great excitement as the closest town to Mont Blanc. The place is always buzzing. From beside the heavily touristy shopping quarter by the river, the maddened statues of Balmat and Paccard point up to Mont Blanc's summit, which they were the first to conquer, with barometer and brandy, and not many other specialist tools (*see also* **Topics**, p.41).

**Musée Alpin de Chamonix**
*t 04 50 53 25 93; open daily 2–7, plus school hols 10–12; adm*

The **Musée Alpin de Chamonix** stands back a little from the crowds, in one of the huge but dilapidated Belle Epoque hotels scattered around the centre, recalling the resort's glamorous heyday. Displays go into detail on the many major events to have taken place in these parts, from the conquest of Mont Blanc to the first Winter Olympic Games, held here in 1924.

## Rubbing Noses with Mont Blanc: Activities and Trips

The third most visited natural site in the world, the majestic meringue of Mont Blanc (4,808m) proves unforgettable in any close encounter. However, special trips are expensive, and the weather high up is unpredictable – consider staying a few days to see the summit properly...and go to other parts of the Rhône-Alpes to walk alone. However, the high natural drama here is unbeatable in Europe.

For the ultimate experience of **climbing** to Mont Blanc's summit, contact the reputed **Compagnie des Guides de Chamonix (t** 04 50 53 00 24, *www.chamonix-guides.com*). The Massif du Mont Blanc is the most famous range for **hiking** in the Alps; at local tourist offices you can pick up maps of the innumerable, well-signed paths. Always take weather predictions very seriously. The lakes, especially the Lacs Blanc, Noirs and Cornu, high up west of the Arve, make for extremely popular destinations. Seasonal cafés, village inns and Alpine refuges mean that food, drink and comfort are surprisingly well catered for; in the higher spots, provisions are helicoptered in! The lucky among you may spot chamois and ibex, or marmots rushing away as a rare golden eagle circles overhead. For the keenest walkers, the 170km **Tour du Mont-Blanc** takes you round through Switzerland and Italy as well as France.

You might try a magical tour of Mont Blanc by **helicopter** (e.g. with **Mont Blanc Hélicoptère, t** 04 50 92 78 21, *www.mbh.fr/helicopterc.htm*). For even more exhilaration, several companies offer **paragliding** (e.g. **Les Ailes du Mont-Blanc, t** 04 50 53 96 72, *www.lesailesdumontblanc.com*; **Kaïlash Adventure, t** 06 83 29 43 67, *www.kailashadventure.com*; or **Summits Parapente, t** 04 50 53 50 14, *www.summits.fr*), plus other activities. For **hot-air ballooning**, *see* Praz-sur-Arly, p.324.

Easier popular options for less adventurous mortals include several exhilarating **cable-car trips** around Chamonix, many run by the **Compagnie du Mont-Blanc** (*www.compagniedumontblanc.fr*). The **Aiguille du Midi** (reservations **t** 04 50 53 30 80 or **t** 04 50 53 22 75) is the closest most visitors come to the top of Mont Blanc: the first viewing platform isn't of much interest, the second is stupendous, the third even better, at 3,842m (c. 12,000ft) still almost 1,000m below the summit. The climbers seem ant-sized. From level two, the most magical of all cable-car rides whisks you over sparkling glaciers to the **Hellbronner peak** on the Italian border. Many locals say the finest views of Mont Blanc are to be had from the heights west of Chamonix. Take the cable car to **Le Brévent** (reservations **t** 04 50 53 13 18 or **t** 04 50 53 22 75), just over 2,500m, or, from Les Praz, north of town, try the cable car for **La Flégère** (reservations **t** 04 50 53 18 58 or **t** 04 50 53 22 75).

The journey by little red mountain train to the **Mer de Glace glacier** (from Montenvers station behind Chamonix railway station; reservations **t** 04 50 53 12 54 or **t** 04 50 53 22 75) is less spectacular, but a classic, taking you painstakingly up to c. 2,000m. The Mer de Glace is massively impressive, but in summer the glacier can look grubby. It was first properly investigated by two bold Englishmen, William Windham and Richard Pococke, back in 1741. Climbing down now, its main attraction is an ice grotto. Up above it are displays on crystals and fauna, and a café from which to watch parties walking on the glacier; contact the tourist office in advance to join them.

Around Chamonix, **rock-climbing**, **canyoning**, **white-water rafting** and **mountain-biking** are all possible. The **Compagnie des Guides** also puts on a programme of mountaineering activities for youngsters called **Cham Aventure**. Among more leisurely sports, Chamonix has a splendid **golf course** (**t** 04 50 53 06 28, *www.golfdechamonix.com*). For pampering, the **Thermes de St-Gervais** (**t** 04 50 47 54 54, *www.thermes-st-gervais.fr*) are reputed for mud treatments.

Separate temporary exhibitions on Alpine themes are held within the slick modern architecture of the **Espace Tairraz** (named after a family fascinated by the Alps for generations) beyond the offices of the legendary **Compagnie des Guides**. Beside these is the richly gilded interior of the town's Baroque **church**, once the main feature of historic little Chamonix, before it was swamped by tourists and hotels.

Huge glaciers curve menacingly down the mountainsides towards the small centre of **Argentière**, an old settlement as well as a ski resort, its churches nestling close to the source of the Arve. Get up close to the glaciers, even in summer, by taking the **cable car** up to the **Aiguille des Grands Montets**; the magical view up the white valley ends with **Mont Dolent**, its peak marking the point where France, Switzerland and Italy meet.

The atmosphere changes heading for **Vallorcine**, entering the **Réserve Naturelle des Aiguilles Rouges**. At the **Col des Montets**, the official **Chalet** offers slightly old-fashioned displays on the geology, flora and fauna of the valley, strewn with interesting plants growing amidst big boulders that turn green in summer – a world apart from the glacial grandeur of the Arve, but with great walking, and more traditional communities on the way to the Swiss frontier. Until the 19th century, this valley was completely cut off from the world by winter snows, and back in the Middle Ages was apparently almost as populated with bears as with people, hence the name Vallorcine. At the border hamlet, the **Musée Barberine** recalls traditional ways in an old farm. To end with a sensational view over Haute Savoie and the Swiss Alps, why not walk up via the **Bérard waterfall** to **Mont Buet**, its peak, at 3,099m, of a relatively manageable height in these soaring parts.

**Cable car**
*book tickets in advance,*
*t 04 50 54 00 71*

**Réserve Naturelle des Aiguilles Rouges Chalet**
*t 04 50 54 08 06;*
*open June–mid-Sept daily 9.30–12.30 and 2–6.30*

**Musée Barberine**
*t 04 50 54 63 19;*
*open July–Aug 2.30–5.30; adm*

ⓘ **St-Gervais-les-Bains** >>
*115 Av du Mont Paccard, 74170 St-Gervais,*
*t 04 50 47 76 08,*
*www.st-gervais.net*

ⓘ **Vallorcine**
*Maison du Betté, 74660 Vallorcine,*
*t 04 50 54 60 71,*
*www.vallorcine.com*

ⓘ **Combloux** >
*49 Chemin des Passerands, 74920 Combloux,*
*t 04 50 58 60 49,*
*www.combloux.com*

ⓘ **Chamonix-Mont-Blanc** >>
*85 Place du Triangle de l'Amitié, 74400 Chamonix,*
*t 04 50 53 00 24,*
*www.chamonix.com*

## Market Days around Mont Blanc

**Combloux**: Wed am.
**St-Gervais**: Thurs am (plus Sun am July–Aug).
**Chamonix-Mont-Blanc**: Sat am (plus Tues am July–Aug).

## Where to Stay and Eat around Mont Blanc

For places known principally as ski resorts, hotel and restaurant listings appear in the **Winter Sports** chapter.

**Cordon** ✉ **74700**
***Les Roches Fleuries**, t 04 50 58 06 71, *www.rochesfleuries.com* (€€€€–€€€). Stunning Mont Blanc views from the balconied rooms of this enchanting, quiet hotel. Two good restaurants (€€€–€€), one refined, one Savoyard. Pool. *Closed late-Sept–mid-Dec and early April–early May.*

**Combloux** ✉ **74920**
***Au Cœur des Prés**, t 04 50 93 36 55 (€€). Excellent chalet, many rooms with splendid Mont Blanc views. Good restaurant (€€) with views too. *Closed early April–May and Oct–mid-Dec.*

**St-Gervais** ✉ **74170**
***Chalet Hôtel Igloo**, 3120 Route des Crêtes, t 04 50 93 05 84, *www.ligloo.com* (€€€€; compulsory half-board). In fabulous location by Mont Arbois' summit, great views of Mont Blanc and extremely comfortable rooms. Hearty cooking (*à la carte*). Pool. *Closed mid-April–mid-June and mid-Sept–mid-Dec.*

**La Maison Blanche**, 64 Rue du Vieux Pont, t 04 50 47 75 81, *www.chaletlamaisonblanche.com* (€). Just below the church, warm typical hotel with nicely done rooms. Restaurant (€€) serving either Savoyard specialities or one menu. *Restaurant generally closed lunchtimes.*

**Chalet Rémy**, Le Bettex, t 04 50 93 11 85 (€). 18th-century farm packed with old-fashioned atmosphere. Basic little rooms. Copious local cooking (€€; must book). *Closed early Nov–mid-Dec.*

## Chamonix-Mont-Blanc, Les Houches and Argentière
*See **Winter Sports**, p.359.*

# Savoie's Vanoise Valleys and Oisans

*Encircled by the Isère river to the north and the Arc to the south, the second greatest French Alpine range, the Massif de la Vanoise, is separated from Mont Blanc by pastures producing the memorable, delicious Beaufort cheese.*

*The Arc and upper Isère valleys are much better known as the Maurienne and Tarentaise, the latter's upper slopes famed for the biggest range of ski resorts in the world, covered in the Winter Sports chapter; but here we focus on the Vanoise's older cultural riches, its beautifully preserved heart, and its many summer possibilities.*

*We also slip across to the Oisans, the Rhône-Alpes' half of the third most sensational French Alpine range, the deeply dramatic Ecrins. It's all stunning, and at times a little scary.*

# 18

## Don't miss

**1** Idyllic villages
Hauteluce, Boudin and
Conflans p.332/333/334

**2** Conquering
the heart of the
Vanoise
Around Pralognan **p.337**

**3** The Tarentaise
Baroque trail
Moûtiers to Séez
pp.337–8

**4** Maurienne forts
and frescoes
The upper Arc valley
p.342

**5** The uplifting
Ecrins
The Vénéon valley **p.347**

*See map overleaf*

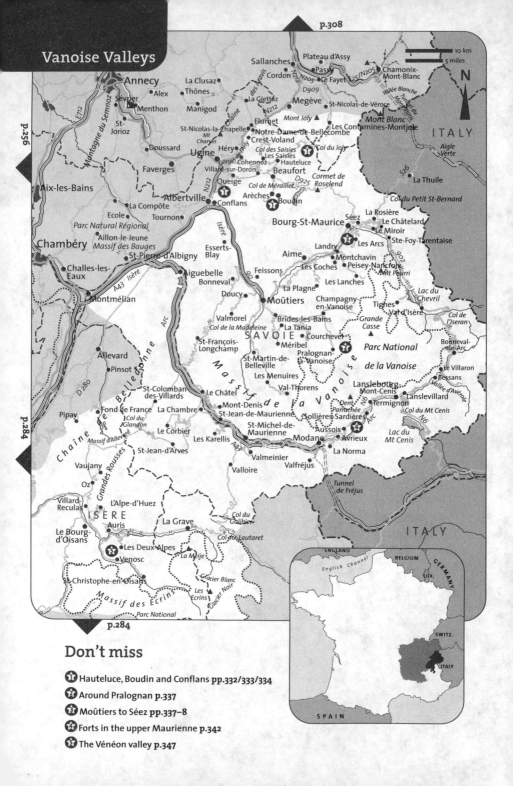

p.308

10 km
5 miles

N

p.256

p.284

p.284

Sallanches
Plateau d'Assy
Passy
Cordon
Le Fayet
Chamonix-
Mont-Blanc
La Clusaz
Annecy
Alex
Thônes
Sévrier
Menthon
Manigod
La Giettaz
Megève
St-Nicolas-de-Véroce
Vallée Blanche
St-Jorioz
St-Nicolas-la-Chapelle
Flumet
Mont Joly
Mont Blanc
ITALY
Doussard
Notre-Dame-de-Bellecombe
Les Contamines-Montjoie
Ugine
Héry
Crest-Voland
Col des Saisies
Col du Joly
Aigle
Verte
Faverges
Villard-sur-Doron
Les Saisies
Hauteluce
La Thuile
Aix-les-Bains
 Queige
Cohennoz
Beaufort
Cormet de
Roselend
Albertville
Col de Méraillet
Arêches
Boudin
Col du Petit St-Bernard
La Compôte
Conflans
La Rosière
Séez
Le Châtelard
Ecole
Tournon
Bourg-St-Maurice
Le Miroir
Ste-Foy-Tarentaise
Parc Natural Régional
Chambéry
Aillon-le-Jeune
Massif des Bauges
St-Pierre-d'Albigny
Esserts-
Blay
Landry
Les Arcs
Challes-les-
Eaux
Aiguebelle
Bonneval
Feissons
Aime
Montchavin
Peisey-Nancroix
Mt Pourri
Lac du
Chevril
Montmélian
Doucy
La Plagne
Champagny-
en-Vanoise
Tighes
Val d'Isère
Moûtiers
Valmorel
Col de la Madeleine
Brides-les-Bains
La Tania
Grande
Casse
Col de
l'Iseran
SAVOIE
Courchevel
Bonneval-
sur-Arc
St-François-
Longchamp
Méribel
Pralognan-
la-Vanoise
Parc National
Le Villaron
Allevard
St-Martin-de-
Belleville
de la Vanoise
Bessans
Pinsot
Les Menuires
Val-Thorens
Vallée d'Avérole
St-Colomban-
des-Villards
Le Châtel
Lanslebourg-
Mont-Cenis
Lanslevillard
Pipay
Fond de France
La Chambre
Mont-Denis
St-Jean-de-Maurienne
Dent
Parrachée
Termignon
Col du Mt Cenis
Le Corbier
St-Michel-de-
Maurienne
Sollières-Sardières
Aussois
N6
Massif d'Allevard
St-Jean-d'Arves
Les Karellis
Modane
Avrieux
Lac du
Mt Cenis
Vaujany
Valmeinier
La Norma
Oz
Valloire
Valfréjus
Villard-
Reculas
L'Alpe-d'Huez
Col du
Galibier
Tunnel
de Fréjus
ISÈRE
Auris
La Grave
Col du Lautaret
ITALY
Le Bourg-
d'Oisans
Les Deux-Alpes
Venosc
La Meije
St-Christophe-en-Oisans
Les
Ecrins
Glacier Blanc
Glacier Noir
Massif des Ecrins
Parc National

ENGLAND
English Channel
BELGIUM
GERMANY
LUX.
SWITZ.
ITALY
SPAIN

## Don't miss

Hauteluce, Boudin and Conflans **pp.332/333/334**

Around Pralognan **p.337**

Moûtiers to Séez **pp.337–8**

Forts in the upper Maurienne **p.342**

The Vénéon valley **p.347**

# Getting to and around the Vanoise Valleys and Oisans

Albertville , Moûtiers, Aime-La Plagne, Bourg-St-Maurice, St-Jean-de-Maurienne and Modane have good
**TGV** links. For **bus** services around the Beaufortain and Vanoise, see *www.cg73.fr*, under *routes et transports*.
For buses in the Oisans, consult *www.transisere.fr*.

ⓘ **Savoie**
*www.savoie-
mont-blanc.com;
for the tourist offices
of the major ski
resorts, see Chapter 19,
Winter Sports*

The heart of the Vanoise offers France's answer to those stunning
Ansel Adams mountain images in North America. With its massive
triangular peaks and its mammoth glaciers, it has been pretty well
preserved from human encroachment, and was declared France's
first national park, back in 1963. Its highest heights reach around
3,800m, aloof above the highest pistes. For the world-renowned ski
resorts out along the sensational slopes of the jagged upper **Isère
valley**, *see* Chapter 19, **Winter Sports**. The equally awesome sides
of the **Arc valley** have smaller resorts (also *see* Chapter 19), but
more formidable forts, recalling the days when this was a jealously
guarded frontier. The Arc developed more industrial muscle.
Although many factories have closed, the locals are going back to
the gym to hone their beautiful brawn to show off to tourists.

These two intimidatingly grand Vanoise valleys are best known
as the **Tarentaise** and **Maurienne** respectively, reflecting historical
territories. The little city of Moûtiers and ancient Aime count
among the most interesting historic stops in the Tarentaise. The
cathedral city of St-Jean-de-Maurienne was the cradle of the lordly
house of Savoie, via Humbert aux Blanches Mains ('White Hands' –
he was reputed for his purity), in the 11th century. The main cultural
surprise the valleys share is a string of extraordinarily decorated
churches, both Gothic and Baroque. The latter swarm with *putti* so
lively you could imagine them flying out after you on your
discoveries of the natural wonders in these parts. For many visitors,
the summer season is devoted to walking, or more daring sports.

It makes good sense to present these two great Vanoise valleys
in a loop, as the last settlements at either end, Val d'Isère and
Bonneval-sur-Arc, are neighbours of a sort. However, be warned
that the road pass linking them via the Col de l'Iseran is, at 2,764m,
the highest in Europe, so not open much outside of summer.

There are enchanting delights beyond this valley loop. Definitely
climb into the centre of the park to visit the areas around
charming Champagny-en-Vanoise and remote Pralognan-en-
Vanoise. Off towards the Col du Petit St-Bernard, La Rosière clings
to the most sensational summer spot along the Isère.

Host of the Winter Olympics in 1992, Albertville, west along that
river, along with snooty Conflans looking down its nose at it, acts
as our entrance point to the Vanoise. But before embarking on our
circuit, we greatly encourage you to stop in the **Beaufortain**,
beautiful link between Mont Blanc and the Vanoise ranges. The
cows, almost up to their necks in flowers and grasses in summer,

produce the finest of cheeses. Nearby Hauteluce can put in a fair claim to being one of the most heavenly villages in the French Alps.

At the end of the chapter, we pole-vault south via the superlative passes of the Col du Galibier and Col du Lautaret to the third great French Alpine range, the **Ecrins**. On the dividing line between the northern and southern French Alps, this route only stays open a few short summer months. We then take you round the **Oisans**, the Rhône-Alpes' portion of the Ecrins, nestling under La Meije. T he Oisans' best valleys branch off from the huge ravine of the Romanche valley leading to Grenoble.

# Into the Beaufortain

The N212 Val d'Arly road from Sallanches to Albertville via Megève is the main road link between the Mont Blanc and Vanoise ranges. Branch off it at Flumet for the **Col des Saisies** and the delicious pasturelands of the Beaufortain.

Up high, the well-planned modern resort of **Les Saisies**, a bit of a one-street cowboy-like ski village, was built for cross-country sport and makes for relatively easy walking territory in summer. During the Second World War, the open terrain up here proved a good dropping point for munitions for the Resistance.

⭐ **Hauteluce**

Gorgeous **Hauteluce**, one of the prettiest villages in Savoie, set high on its slope above the Dorinet river, casts a coquettish sideways glance towards Mont Blanc. Its seductive ornamental steeple draws you to its Baroque church, but the faded skeleton with scythe on the sundial comes as a shock. It isn't there to remind you that you're in a land of meadows so steep that some of them are still cut by hand. Hinting at a happy life after death, inside, the acrobatic Christ balanced on the main beam sports a gilded loincloth, while *putti* heads float at his feet. An **Ecomusée** recalls traditional Savoyard ways, while bars offer superb terrace views. The ruins of the **Châteaux de Beaufort** lie down in the valley. Further up, the chapel in the hamlet of **Belleville** contains medieval murals. From the **Col du Joly**, take in splendid views to Mont Blanc.

**Hauteluce Ecomusée**

*t 04 79 38 80 31; open July–Aug daily 10–12 and 3–7; adm*

**Beaufort**, down at the meeting of Doron and Argentine valleys, is synonymous with one of France's greatest cheeses. It is also a big, burly traditional village with a beefy Baroque church. This edifice is dedicated to St Maxime, credited with converting the Tarentaise to Christianity, but more traditional Fathers of the Church sit enthroned on the remarkable 18th-century pulpit in the clean-lined interior. The cows that graze in the exquisite pastures cut out of the deep dark forests around here produce rich milk, much of it turned into cheese at Beaufort's **Coopérative Laitière**. The sight of thousands upon thousands of rounds of *fromage* in the cellars bowls visitors over. A film, available in English, explains the

**Beaufort Coopérative Laitière**

*t 04 79 38 33 62; open July–Aug daily 8–12.30 and 2–7; Sept–June Mon–Sat 8–12 and 2–6, closed Sun and public hols; adm*

## Beaufort Cheese, Prince of Gruyères

Beaufort cheese, a *fromage* as dense in subtle flavours as *foie gras*, was deemed *'prince des gruyères'* by the great French *bon vivant*, Brillat-Savarin (*see* p.45). It was granted its *appellation d'origine contrôlée* in 1968. The area of production covers large swaths of pastures not just in the Beaufortain, but also in the Maurienne and Tarentaise. Some 800 farmers keep the beloved Tarine cows, and some 40 centres are allowed to make Beaufort cheese. In summer, the farmers send their cattle *en alpage* for around 100 days. They gradually climb the mountain slopes to the highest pastures, then munch their way back down again, this endurance test in alpine eating now regulated by electric fencing. The traditional farmers follow the cattle, staying in the old wooden *fermes d'alpage* only used in summer. It's a gruelling schedule for them, having to work long days in Spartan conditions. The milking done, the milk collected, the Beaufort *fromages* are made in big rounds each weighing 40 to 50 kilos and most distinctive because of their concave sides, derived from the beechwood circles in which they're pressed. But it's the cows' exceptionally rich diet, the painstaking curdling process and the special *morge* bacteria working on the cheese that, combined, give Beaufort such a profound, distinctive taste. The cheeses are aged, often half a year and more, before being sold.

cheese-making process well. Beaufort is also associated in France with the novelist Roger Frison-Roche, a passionate mountaineer who spent his boyhood holidays nearby and used the Alps as the setting for his gripping novels.

South of Beaufort, a tortuously beautiful road leads to the picturesque, protected traditional Alpine chalet villages of **Arèches** and **Boudin**, although once the snows melt, many of the houses are left with rather unsightly corrugated roofs exposed. The wood-surrounded pastures ring with the sound of cowbells in summer.

🔞 Boudin

So do the the big, bare slopes of the **Lac de Roselend**. This very large artificial lake, created by the building of a massive dam in 1961, looks peaceful enough, but generates enormous amounts of hydroelectric power. The Roselend area's name derives from the pink-flowering rhododendrons that thrive around here. According to legend, the distinctive **Pierre Menta** peak marking these parts was kicked over here from the Aravis chain (marked by its tooth-like gap in its middle) by the frustrated giant Gargantua, finding that he had bitten off more than he could chew with Mont Blanc.

Above the lake, an austere, almost treeless, houseless and completely resortless shortcut leads to Bourg-St-Maurice, avoiding the Isère valley's huge meanders by going via the **Col de Méraillet**, with its superlative views of Mont Blanc, and across the eerie **Cormet de Roselend**. The GR5 walking trail cuts across the Cormet.

Back with the road towards Bourg-St-Maurice, for a challenging, at times even chilling route onto the southern end of the Mont Blanc range, branch off via **Les Chapieux**'s rich pastures up to **Ville des Glaciers**. The walk past the ruins of the **Auberge des Mottets** takes you along a section of the famed **Tour du Mont Blanc** hiking route, huge glaciers and spiky peaks forming the sensational backdrop as you reach the **Col de la Seigne**, once an important way into Italy's Aosta valley. From here you get views onto the less familiar, far more daunting Italian face of Monte Bianco.

## Market Days in the Beaufortain

**Beaufort**: Wed.

## Where to Stay and Eat in the Beaufortain

### Les Saisies ✉ 73620

**\*\*\*Le Calgary**, t 04 79 38 98 38, *www.hotelcalgary.com* (€€). High-quality big modern chalet. Spacious rooms. Good restaurant (€€). Pool. *Closed late April–mid-June and early Sept–mid-Dec.*

### Beaufort ✉ 73270

**\*\*Grand Mont**, Place de l'Eglise, t 04 79 38 33 36 (€). Smart and comfortable by the church. Regional cuisine (€€). Half-board compulsory in high season. *Closed late April–mid-May and Oct.*

(i) **Beaufort ›**
*Grande Rue, 73270 Beaufort, t 04 79 38 37 57, www.areches-beaufort.com or www.lebeaufortain.com*

### Arèches ✉ 73270

**\*\*Grand Mont**, Route du Grand Mont, t 04 79 38 10 67, *www.le-grand-mont.fr* (€). Same name, but a separate comfortable option in central Arèches, with restaurant (€€–€). *Restaurant closed Sun out of season.*

**\*\*Poncellamont**, Route de Carroz, t 04 79 38 10 23 (€). A more old-fashioned option in a flowery chalet. Good traditional cuisine (€€). *Closed mid-April–May and Oct–Christmas; restaurant closed Sun eve and Mon out of season.*

### Lac de Roselend ✉ 73270

**La Pierre Menta**, Col du Pré, t 04 79 38 92 45 (€€–€). Eat here while enjoying the great view down onto the lake. *Closed mid-Oct–early May; evenings open by reservation only.*

Alternatively, heading west of Beaufort to Albertville, **Villard-sur-Doron** and **Queige** have churches with interesting interiors, the calm *Pietà* in the latter contrasting with the typical Baroque show. A winding mountain road above Villard brings you to the **Signal de Bisanne** (also reachable from Les Saisies), with remarkable views. Below Queige, make a detour to the hamlet of **Les Pointières**.

# The Upper Isère, or Tarentaise

## From Albertville to Moûtiers

*Maison des Jeux Olympiques d'Hiver*
*t 04 79 37 75 71; open July–Aug Mon–Sat 9.30–7, Sun and public hols 2–7; Sept–June Mon–Sat exc public hols 9.30–12.30 and 2–6; adm*

 **Conflans**

Set on the flats at a big elbow in the Isère, where the Arly river joins it, **Albertville**'s main claim to fame is having hosted the Winter Olympics in 1992, recalled in the flashy sporting facilities in the outskirts, and in the entertaining, central **Maison des Jeux Olympiques d'Hiver**. A fairly modern creation anyway, the town was named after its founder in 1836, Charles-Albert of Savoie. Several grandiose administrative buildings left from that time mark the centre, but they were upstaged by the rebuilding of central **Place de l'Europe** for the Olympics, in somewhat overblown salmon-pink Italianate style. The café terraces help soften the look.

Visible from the terraces, on a nearby rocky outcrop, the much older, atmospheric village of **Conflans** peers down at Albertville. Its ramparts and gateways protected magnificent dwellings built on the proceeds of prosperous trading on the route between the Rhône and northern Italy. The picturesque **Grand-Place** with its cafés and oval fountain looks most Italian, as does the arcaded

Conflans Musée
d'Art et d'Histoire
*t 04 79 37 86 86; open
mid-June–Sept daily
10–7; Feb–mid-June
Wed–Mon 2–6; adm*

**Maison Rouge,** the muscular brick mansion that holds the **Musée
d'Art et d'Histoire,** with quite interesting religious pieces as well as
rooms dedicated to the place's military past – Albertville was the
original home of the élite mountaineering *Chasseurs Alpins.* The
whole village beyond looks almost over-prettified now, the place
laying on thick its 'olde worlde' charms, with competing craft shops
and broad-terraced restaurants. Even the **church** tries to seduce
you with its saints painted on the outside, while the Baroque
attractions within include dynamic pulpit figures. From a broad
esplanade one side of the village, wide views open up of the Isère
valley beyond the 16th-century **castle of Manuel de Locatel**

Along the Isère between Albertville and Moûtiers, stubs of
medieval castles stick out at the start of the slopes, their towers
overwhelmed by the huge wooded expanses above. There are
several parallel, spectacular hiking trails linking the Isère and Arc
valleys along here. And there is just one little-known road connection between the two valleys beyond the formidable, distant
Col de l'Iseran – it's the route branching off here via the Col de la
Madeleine, only completed in 1968. Head up through chestnut
woods to the memorably named village of **Pussy,** its church
containing an ornate Baroque altar. You then enter wild gorges,
**Bonneval** and **Celliers** clinging dramatically to them. At the **Col de
la Madeleine,** among high pastures, enjoy splendid views over both
the Vanoise and Mont Blanc ranges. The way then winds down via
the modern ski resort of **St-François-Longchamp.**

## Moûtiers, and Summer in the Trois Vallées

Continuing to the next big elbow-turn in the Isère, **Moûtiers** was
clear capital of the Tarentaise for centuries, until the ski resorts
took pride of place. Now, most visitors to Savoie ignore the little
city with its workaday outskirts. But the place conceals a pleasing
Italianate heart, the substantial old houses in the centre given
colourful coats of paint. A fine stone bridge spans the bounding
river close to the **cathedral,** a mix of Romanesque and Gothic.
Exquisite small religious objects are displayed in the treasury, while
the *Crucifixion* and *Entombment* are life-size. The bishop's palace
houses a tempting **Musée des Traditions Populaires** Cheese-lovers
should sniff out the **Coopérative Laitière de Moûtiers.**

Moûtiers Musée
des Traditions
Populaires
*t 04 79 24 04 23;
open Mon–Sat 9–12
and 2–6; adm*

On any map, you'll notice how, south of Moûtiers, flailing
tentacular roads lead up a series of valleys, heading to the major
skiing territories of the **Trois Vallées.** Although these valleys come
into full tourist bloom in the winter ski season, there is natural
beauty to explore in summer, plus the usual array of Baroque
churches, hiking trails and mad Alpine summer sports on offer.

The short valley to **Valmorel** turned to skiing later than the rest
and developed with more restraint. Make the detour west to **Doucy**

for its refined church altar, including a remarkably distressing 19th-century painting of the *Crucifixion of St Andrew*.

The much longer **Vallée de Belleville** leading to Val-Thorens has the most character in summer, with its string of chapels and mountain lakes. Above wonderfully located **St-Martin-de-Belleville**, **Notre-Dame de la Vie** up on its rock has been a significant place of worship since medieval times. **Val-Thorens** may not be everyone's cup of tea architecturally, but the scenery is spectacular, as are the sporting possibilities.

Back close to Moûtiers, **Brides-les-Bains** lies in a gentle, deeply wooded section of the **Doron valley** towards Méribel. The name, in English, inevitably brings women to mind, and this thermal spa has in fact played heavily on that clientele, encouraging slimming breaks and treatments...to the point that Brides now bills itself as the number one spot in France for dieting. The thermal springs, already enjoyed by the Romans, are supposed to have beneficial effects on the metabolism and circulation. You can register for a serious slimming week or two, or enjoy day treatments.

Exclusive **Méribel**, its heliport tucked away down its own private wooded valley, is the Isère ski resort with the most style, looking good even in high summer. Mountain-bikers and golfers are among the sporty types attracted here in the warmer season, by stunning facilities. The slope road connecting Méribel and Courchevel passes through that rarity in these parts, a genuine old settlement, **Méribel-Village. Courchevel**, although an upmarket ski resort, looks rather dishevelled in the summer months. It too has a golf course, among many summer sporting possibilities. Below the chaotic cluster of Courchevel's modern resorts, the village of **St-Bon** has held on to its old character. The village church contains a suitably glitzy Baroque retable of the *Assumption of the Virgin*.

## Into the Heart of the Vanoise

Delightful small resorts hide out east of Courchevel, heading for the heart of the Vanoise and its national park. At **Bozel**, the church has all the usual bright Baroque frills. The stocky **Tour Sarrazine** is misleadingly named; it didn't go up at the time of the Saracens, but for the powerful medieval lordly family of these parts. Recently graced with an upbeat modern sundial, it holds exhibitions.

Attractive **Champagny-le-Bas** is a village made up entirely of chalets, with no modern excrescences whatsoever. The orange-hued church crowning the hillock in front of it makes it all the more appealing. Inside, the Baroque retable, surely the silliest in Savoie, looks as if it's being attacked by a swarm of pink doll-like *putti*. A precipitous road hanging on a cliff edge makes for a slightly nerve-racking drive up to **Champagny-d'en-Haut**. But once on high, you reach a delightful flat, generous valley with old hamlets strung along it. The road is one of the most unspoilt of the Vanoise, the sound of the torrent accompanying you along the way. Hiking paths head into the park.

Reached via a separate, tighter, more forested road, and surrounded by breathtaking peaks, **Pralognan-la-Vanoise** lies isolated in a large clearing at 1,400m, making a peaceful base for superb walks to mountain lakes and heights. The GR55 hiking path crosses the Vanoise east of Pralognan, skirting round the park's most striking peaks, including the tallest, the **Pointe de la Grande Casse**, at 3,855m. This summit also carries the nickname of the Pointe Matthews, in memory of a British climber who, along with French companions, carved more than 1,000 steps here in 1860 to help walkers reach the top. Not something the agile *bouquetin*, or ibex, would be fussed about. It was mostly for this endangered species, with its trademark thick, ridged, curving horns, that the Vanoise National Park was originally created, although the park's remit has spread to take in considerate, well-planned tourism, including 600km of marked trails and some 40 mountain refuges.

**22** Pralognan-la-Vanoise

## The Tarentaise from Aime to Bourg-St-Maurice
Back some way to the north, and way down by the Isère, the cheery, open town of **Aime** has a long history for these parts, stones bearing Roman inscriptions on show in the crypt of the severe 11th-century Romanesque church, built in part from pebbles gathered from the riverbed. In the cubic medieval forms of the main church, a few fragments of frescoes remain in place, including one showing a boyish God creating Adam and Eve. But the major scene depicts Herod's *Massacre of the Innocents*. Aime also has a more typical Baroque parish church with two sundials outside, and a plethora of painted details within. To the north, the **Chapelle St Sigismond** has been turned into the Haute Tarentaise's archaeological and ethnographic **Musée Pierre Borrione**, including fragments from Roman Aime as well as rare minerals and fossils. Baroque art also gets a look-in, plus the story of La Plagne's mines.

Musée Pierre Borrione
*t 04 79 55 67 00; open July–Aug daily 10–12.30 and 2–6.30; adm*

South of Aime, modern **La Plagne** consists of a handful of ski resorts in different styles. This, and the massive string of experimental resorts of Les Arcs, have a sporty summer season catering to mass-market holidays. Between the two, more traditional **Landry** has a church with a spiked onion dome and many sundials.

Higher up, **Peisey-Nancroix** claims the highest pointed steeple in the Tarentaise. No fewer than seven **Baroque** retables fight for attention inside. At Peisey, you can wander round an 18th–19th-century silver-bearing mine, **Le Palais de la Mine – Circuit des Monts d'Argent**. The **Sanctuaire Notre-Dame des Vernettes** is a prized goal for pilgrims who go up by foot to this Baroque gem with magnificent views of **Mont Pourri**, the mighty northeastern

 Baroque trail

Le Palais de la Mine – Circuit des Monts d'Argent
*adm free*

marker of the Vanoise at 3,779m. Press on to **Les Lanches**, from which you can join the GR5 walking trail.

The pretty hamlets huddling together on their high perches on the north side of the valley between Aime and Bourg-St-Maurice offer quite a contrast to the south side so marked by the massive modern resorts. Traditional rural ways are kept going by the inhabitants, who've rebaptized their stretch of valley *Le Versant du Soleil* ('The Sunny Side'). At **La Côte d'Aime**, pay a visit to the *fruitière*, explaining the tradition of collective Beaufort cheese-making and presenting local craft objects, while a real-life oldie may take you on a guided visit of a traditional house. From above **Valezan**, the GR5 trail can guide hikers north to Pierre Menta.

**Vulmix** has a chapel hiding a whole colourful 15th-century fresco cycle telling how St Grat found the head of St John the Baptist in the Holy Land and brought it back to the pope; the scene where he presents what looks like the holy man's dentures to the pontiff can't help but raise a smile. (St-Jean-de-Maurienne was to receive other supposed bits of Christ's great cousin – *see* p.343.)

**Bourg-St-Maurice** spreads out down at another of the major elbow turns in the Isère. It may serve as a major gateway to the ski resorts in winter, but in summer canoeists and rafters take to the river here in large numbers; its lively waters have even hosted world canoeing championships. The town also has a sprightly main shopping street and a cheese co-operative. A flood ruined the

**⓲ Baroque trail**

**Fort de la Platte**
*t 04 79 60 59 00*

**⓲ Espace Baroque Tarentaise St-Eloi**
*t 04 79 40 10 38; open July–Aug Mon–Fri 10–12 and 2.30–6.30, Sun 2.30–5.30; 2nd half June and 1st half Sept Mon–Fri 2.30–6; adm*

**Filature Arpin**
*www.sav.org/e/ index.html*

church in the 19th century, but the **Baroque** interiors were restored.

North above town, standing way on high at 2,000m, the **Fort de la Platte** is nowadays transformed from June to November into a local farmers' showcase. On the great slopes just south of Bourg, the major mountain resorts of **Les Arcs** were built to cater to the masses, the big holiday apartment blocks benefiting from splendid views. Summer package holidays are all the rage here, with excellent sporting facilities. Les Arcs 1950 in particular has been developing its mountain-biking network for enthusiasts.

Bourg-St-Maurice's valley-bottom neighbour, the former tanning town of **Séez**, conceals several Baroque attractions. The rich church of **St Peter** contains an outrageous image of Christ on the cross sporting what looks like a gold lamé loincloth more suited to a raunchy disco-dancer – sometimes Baroque artists just didn't hit the tone. The **Espace Baroque Tarentaise St-Eloi** enlightens visitors about the aims of their art in these parts, including demonstrations of the crafts involved. On traditional ways, the **Filature Arpin** keeps alive the production of Bonneval cloth on listed looms.

## The Tarentaise from La Rosière to Val d'Isère

A serpent of a road takes you to **La Rosière**, overlooking perhaps the most spectacular sharp turn in the Isère's course, layer upon layer of mountains visible to south and west. It's a tad surprising to find a golf course here, but this is a great spot at any time of year.

Up above, the **Col du Petit St-Bernard** was once a much more important pass into Italy. The rather grim-looking remnants of the Hospice du Petit-St-Bernard (*see* **Topics**), which offered shelter to travellers through medieval times, but suffered from Second World War bombings, are being restored. The **Chanousia Alpine botanical garden**, created here at over 2,000m by a dedicated abbot at the end of the 19th century, has already been revived. At the pass itself, Mont Blanc suddenly appears startlingly close. The road then leads down to the glamorous Italian resort below it, **Courmayeur**.

**Chanousia Alpine botanical garden**
*t 04 79 41 00 15; open July–mid-Sept daily 9–1 and 2–7; adm*

Heading south towards the source of the Isère, in summer, try the vertiginous route from La Rosière past the whitewashed church of **Le Châtelard**, standing out like an Alpine lighthouse on huge, near-vertical slopes, and the pretty hamlet of **Le Moulin**, to reach the splendid stepped chalets of **Le Miroir**. **Ste-Foy-Tarentaise**, a new, exclusive resort, is worth a look in summer for the high quality of its architecture, even if you may find it a bit dead, but further along the slopes, hamlets like **Le Monal** or **La Gurraz** remain well pickled in the past, very tricky to reach, and best approached discreetly, as you can feel like an intruder in such startling mountain hideaways where farming families continue to live in the old-fashioned way.

Down by the big, artificial **Lac du Chevril** with a vast, unmissable mural covering the side of what is one of the biggest dams in the world, a road leads up to **Tignes**. The **Espace Patrimoine Le Cœur de Tignes** recalls not just the traumatic times in 1952 when the village of Tignes-Les-Boisses was deliberately drowned for the making of the lake, but also centuries of history and the emergence of the high-altitude modern ski resort. Its fortresses of ski apartments were built in a wide open bowl surrounded by sensational snowy peaks and glaciers that offer almost year-round skiing. But there are plenty of other sporting possibilities available here in summer. As at Les Arcs, mountain-biking is big here in the warmer season.

**Espace Patrimoine Le Cœur de Tignes**
*t 04 79 40 04 40; open July–Aug and mid-Dec–April Sun–Fri 4–7; adm*

**Val d'Isère**, the final, exclusive resort set deep at the end of the Isère valley, has more style, and a glamorous reputation, although it looks somewhat bedraggled once out of its white winter furs. The boutiques and hotels remain upmarket. Hardy walkers head out early to spot ibex and chamois, those rare, shy creatures well protected in this high, wild corner of the Vanoise National Park adjoining Italy's Gran Paradiso National Park. Marmots also abound in this area, getting up early to avoid the summer traffic going over the challenging **Col de l'Iseran**, Europe's highest road pass at 2,764m. When this was laid in the 1930s, the **Route des Grandes Alpes** linking Lac Léman with the Mediterranean was complete – the Tarentaise and Maurienne were finally joined together by more than a mule track.

**Route des Grandes Alpes**
*www.routedes grandesalpes.com*

18 | Savoie's Vanoise Valleys and Oisans | The Upper Isère, or Tarentaise

340

Savoie's Vanoise Valleys and Oisans | The Arc Valley, or Maurienne

ⓘ **Bourg-St-Maurice**
*105 Place de la Gare, 73700 Bourg-St-Maurice, t 04 79 07 04 92, www.bourgstmaurice.com*

ⓘ **Champagny-en-Vanoise**
*73350 Champagny-en-Vanoise, t 04 79 55 06 55, www.champagny.com*

ⓘ **Pralognan-la-Vanoise >>**
*73710 Pralognan, t 04 79 08 79 08, www.pralognan.com*

ⓘ **Moûtiers**
*Place St-Pierre, 73600 Moûtiers, t 04 79 24 04 23, www.ot-moutiers.com*

ⓘ **Albertville >**
*Place de l'Europe, 73204 Albertville, t 04 79 32 04 22, www.albertville.com*

★ **Million >**

ⓘ **Aime**
*Av de Tarentaise, 73212 Aime, t 04 79 55 67 00, www.aimesavoie.com*

ⓘ **Séez**
*Rue Fréppaz, 73700 Séez, t 04 79 41 00 15, www.seezsaintbernard.com*

## Tarentaise Market Days

**Albertville:** Wed, Thurs and Sat.
**Moûtiers:** Tues and Fri.
**Champagny-en-Vanoise:** Tues.
**Pralognan-la-Vanoise:** Tues and Fri.
**Aime:** Thurs.
**Bourg-St-Maurice:** Sat.
**Séez:** Thurs.

## Tarentaise Activities

**Méribel golf course,** t 04 79 00 52 67.
**Courchevel golf course,** t 04 79 08 17 00, www.golfdecourchevel.com.
**Tignes golf course,** t 04 79 06 37 42.

## Where to Stay and Eat in the Tarentaise

For places known mainly as ski resorts, hotel and restaurant listings appear in the **Winter Sports** chapter.

### Albertville ✉ 73200
★★★ **Million,** 8 Place de la Liberté, t 04 79 32 25 15, www.hotelmillion.com (€€€€–€€€). Excellent central hotel. Spacious, stylish rooms. Exquisite, smart restaurant (€€€€–€€) hung with art. The owners also run a cookery school here, **La Cuisine de Savoie,** and can cater to English-speakers. *Closed early May; restaurant closed Sat lunch, Sun pm and Mon.*

### Conflans ✉ 73200
**Le Ligismond,** Place de Conflans, t 04 79 37 71 29 (€€). Great terrace on main square, with a vaulted room for traditional cuisine. *Closed July–Aug Sun eve and Wed; Sept–June Sun eve and Mon.*

### Pralognan-la-Vanoise ✉ 73710
★★**Le Grand Bec,** t 04 79 08 71 10, www.hoteldugrandbec.fr (€€). Balconies on all sides, and rooms in regional style, as well as the cuisine (€€). Pool and tennis court. *Closed late April–May and mid-Sept–mid-Dec.*
★★**Les Airelles,** Les Darbelays, t 04 79 08 70 32 (€€). Modern, appealing chalet beside forest c. 1km from the village, its balconied rooms with great mountain views. Decent restaurant (€€). Pool. *Closed late April–May and late Sept–mid-Dec.*

### La Rosière/Val d'Isère/Tignes
*See **Winter Sports,** p.377.*

# The Arc Valley, or Maurienne

Heading down the Arc river with its metallic green and blue tinges, this valley may prove more industrial and more heavily fortified than the upper Isère, but the Arc's upper stretches have remained unspoilt. In these parts, the GR5 hiking trail roughly parallels the main road to Modane. Traditionally, there have been tensions and teasing between the people of the Maurienne and Tarentaise, living so close in distance, but separated by the huge barrier of the Vanoise. In the Maurienne, they may have felt rather jealous of their neighbours since the war, watching them climb so rapidly out of traditional poverty, making a mint from developing huge ski resorts. But in tourist terms the Maurienne's confidence has been growing, the secretive villages and sights coming out of their shells, the natural and cultural attractions obvious.

Orange lichen brightens the beautifully patterned stone roofs of deeply traditional **Bonneval-sur-Arc** in summer, the houses turning into tourist shops. East towards the river's source, make an expedition up to ultra-traditional **L'Ecot**. Walkers climb to the peak of **Les Evettes** for stunning 360° views. The GR5 adopts the other, western bank of the Arc. Along here, the old hamlet of **Le Villaron** is only accessible on foot, making it all the more irresistible. Crossing back the other side of the Arc here, the **Avérole valley**, known for its summer flowers, offers an even calmer walking retreat. Continue up the **Vallon de la Lombarde**; as the name implies, the trail takes you into Italy via the 3,073m-high Col de l'Autaret pass.

Back down in the Arc, it seems incredible that remote **Bessans** should have been largely destroyed during the war, but the duo of church and chapel on their funny hillock mercifully survived, with one of the most elaborate and engrossing ensembles of Savoyard Christian art. Worn frescoes of nobles and exotic beasts, plus traces of a complicated tale involving Christ and a pair of golden sandals, feature on the outside of the **Chapelle St-Antoine**. The interior is covered in vibrant paintings, 40 naïve panels representing episodes in Jesus' life, but the tight-lipped participants sport late Gothic fashions. The main church contains a bright array of saints' statues. However, the major woodworking obsession in the village today is for crude and colourful devils, a tradition started by Etienne Vincendet in the mid-19th century as a snub to the local priest.

**Chapelle St-Antoine**
*small adm*

At **Lanslevillard**, the amazing Gothic-decorated **Chapelle St-Sébastien** is plastered head to toe with splendid naïve frescoes on the lives of Christ and St Sebastian – the arrow-pierced saint was called upon to combat the agonizing plague, and one Sébastien Turbil who survived the dreaded disease commissioned these. The crowds once again show off Gothic fashions.

**Espace Baroque Maurienne**
*t 04 79 05 91 57, www.
hautemaurienne.com;
open late Dec–late April
Mon–Wed 9.30–12,
Thurs and Fri 3.30–7.15;
mid-June–mid-Sept,
Mon–Wed 9.30–12,
Thurs, Fri and Sun
3.30–6.30; adm*

Lanslevillard's larger twin, **Lanslebourg**, has less charm, but its **Espace Baroque Maurienne** in a converted church offers a good general introduction to Baroque art. Here, or at Lanslevillard's town hall, pick up the keys for the **Circuit Chapelles**, encouraging you to follow a kind of treasure hunt to chapels hidden on the nearby mountainsides, each interior devoted to a different local theme.

An important historical, if rather barren-looking route leads up from Lanslebourg to the **Col du Mont-Cenis** and **Susa** in Italy. This was one of the most important passes through the western Alps from classical times. Charlemagne's army came this way, as did Napoleon's; the *petit caporal* saw to the building of one of the major roads through the Alps here. The route remained tricky: the artist Turner got stuck in a storm being carried over by sedan-chair and sleigh. Then a pioneering mountain railway line was built, defying the incline, before the completion of the Fréjus tunnel.

**Musée de la Pyramide**
*t 04 79 05 92 95;
open mid-June–early
Sept daily 10–12
and 2–6; adm*

Beyond the pass, the route comes to **Lac du Mont Cenis**, trebled in size by various dams, drowning a former travellers' hospice and Napoleonic border barracks; the history is explained in the **Musée de la Pyramide** in the curiously shaped contemporary lakeside structure that also serves as a chapel. The lake can look morose in certain seasons, but is made merry by summer sailing. Visit the

**Maison Franco-Italienne**
*t 04 79 05 86 36; open mid-July–Aug daily 9–7; mid-June–mid-July and 1st half Sept Mon–Thurs 10–6 and Fri–Sun 9–6*

**Maison de la Vanoise**
*t 0479 20 51 67; open July–Aug Mon–Sat 9–12 and 3–7, Sun 9–12 and 4.30–7; Sept–June Tues–Sat 9–12 and 3–6; small adm for permanent exhibition*

**Musée d'Archéologie**
*t 04 79 20 59 33; open mid-June–mid-Sept Tues–Sun 3–6.30, Jan–mid-April Sat–Mon 2.30–6; adm*

**🟊 Forts**
*t 04 79 20 30 80, or see www.savoie-patrimoine.com*

**Fort St-Gobain**
*t 04 79 05 84 31, www.fortifications-maurienne.com; open July–Aug daily 10–12 and 2–7; April–June and Sept–Nov Fri–Mon 10–12 and 2–7; Dec–Mar during school hols Mon–Fri 4.30–7; adm*

**Maison Franco-Italienne**, presenting geology, history and traditions from both sides of the frontier. From 1862 to 1947, the Mont-Cenis area lay under Italian rule, its army building a chain of forts, now destinations for walkers, the **Fort de Ronce** the easiest to take on.

West along the Arc, sweet **Termignon's Maison de la Vanoise** is a tourist centre devoted to the national park, with permanent and temporary exhibitions. The cows around Termignon produce a rare but distinctive blue cheese. A branch of the GR5 leads up into the glacial heights of the Vanoise. The other side of the Arc, in the quiet village of **Sollières-Envers**, the **Musée d'Archéologie** is dedicated to the surprising prehistoric finds men made in these parts, notably at the Grotte des Balmes, recreated here, and revealing the earliest traces of human agriculture in the French Alps.

The Arc then turns more industrial, the slopes bristling with **forts**, many open for visits. A handful, known as the **Forts de l'Esseillon**, were built between 1817 and 1834 to defend Savoie from France, the most sensational, the **Barrage de l'Esseillon**, with half a dozen levels of fortifications marching stiffly down the mountainside. As to **Fort St-Gobain**, it was built as part of the unsuccessful 1930s French Maginot line, which extended as far down as the Alps.

The village of **Avrieux** set among these forts boasts an extravagant Baroque **church** dedicated to Thomas à Becket, represented in six naïve carved scenes. The **Chapelle Notre-Dame-des-Neiges** next door is covered with further elaborate decorations, with intriguing grisaille paintings on its tower, executed by the same artistic priest who painted the virtues and vices on the main church.

**Aussois**, a sunny little resort on the plateau above, overseen by the dramatic **Dent Parrachée**, totemic peak in the south of the Vanoise range, faces the summits of the Italian frontier, but head up north via the artificial lakes and you can climb into the heart of the Vanoise from this cheerful old village. In the centre, a hellfire *Last Judgement* greets you sternly at the entrance to the Baroque church, but it's all floating *putti* within. East of Aussois, seek out the **Parc Archéologique des Lozes**, with two trails leading you to prehistoric engravings on the rocks and to staggering towering monoliths popping their heads out above the pines. One of the menhirs reaches almost 100m, but these aren't man-made, rather a remarkable natural curiosity. The **Fort Marie-Christine** nearby, part of the Esseillon defences, now acts, among other things, as an introductory centre to the Vanoise National Park.

Right down in the Arc valley again, **Modane** stands at one end of the stylish but very expensive **Tunnel de Fréjus**. The earlier tunnel here was the first great one to be dug through the Alps, a huge engineering achievement for the times, opened in 1871. Heavy industry has left its mark in the bottom of the Arc valley west from here, but a remarkable trio of mountains, the **Aiguilles d'Arves**, rise way above it all, drawing your attention upwards to their spear-heads. The pioneering American mountaineer Coolidge (*see* also p.347) conquered them in 1878, and memorably described them as 'the most beautiful Trinity in Europe'. Far below, many factories have shut in recent times, leading to economic troubles. But tourism is developing. Discover traditional villages hiding on the slopes, such as **Mont-Denis**, with its crafts and high pastures.

Don't dismiss **St-Jean-de-Maurienne** because of the huge aluminium works down in the valley. Despite suffering from war bombings which left it tattered at the edges, and which explains several postwar squares, the bright historic centre boasts dignified monuments below mountainsides marked by crosses. Beside a soaring keep-cum-bell tower stands the **cathedral**, one of the most intriguing in the whole Rhône-Alpes region, given a classical arcaded front, but mainly dating from medieval times. It was built in part to hold revered relics, three supposed fingers of St John the Baptist, brought back by 6th-century Sainte Thècle – small matter that some 180 fingers of the Baptist have been recorded around the Christian world... Staggering religious decorations adorn the choir, notably a towering *ciborium* (to contain the eucharistic bread and wine), and walnut-wood stalls. These were supremely well carved, probably by German craftsmen, with 300 images, mostly prophets and saints. Via the Gothic **cloister**, an entrance leads down to the **crypt** containing rough Carolingian carvings.

**Musée des Costumes et Traditions Populaires**
*t 04 79 83 51 51; open July–Aug Mon–Sat 10–12 and 2–6; otherwise ask tourist office*

The massive, vibrantly coloured former bishop's palace is home to the **Musée des Costumes et Traditions Populaires**, a rambling collection of local culture and costumes; also admire some ostentatious Ancien Régime chambers. For traditional Savoyard products, look along sloping, pedestrian **Rue St-Antoine**, or stay for the large, lively Saturday market. Close to the centre, the **Musée Opinel** celebrates one of the most famous pocket-knife-makers in France. Although the workshop stopped making *couteaux* in the 1960s, manufacture moving to Chambéry, the family company's story is still celebrated here. The workshop dates back to the 19th century, when the knife-makers practised their craft lying on their stomachs, dogs sitting on their legs to keep them warm in winter!

**Musée Opinel**
*t 04 79 64 04 78, www.opinel-musee. com; open Mon–Sat 9–12 and 2–6*

**Musée du Mont Corbier**
*t 04 79 64 00 24; open July–Aug Mon–Sat 10–12 and 2–7, rest of year Tues–Fri 10–12 and 3–6; adm*

The picking of mountain herbs to make Mont Corbier liqueur sounds slightly easier. The history of making herbal alcohols is traced at the curious **Musée du Mont Corbier**: the local heady concoction was invented by a 19th-century priest who peddled its supposed medicinal qualities in outrageous advertising claims.

While the bishops ruled the roost for some time in town, the local lords observed them from their perch across the Arc valley, at **Le Châtel**, an enchanting mountainside village in an exceptional spot. This eyrie was the birthplace of the mighty house of Savoie, just the ruins of a castle now standing aloof to one side. The ever-so-worthy 11th-century Savoie ruler Humbert aux Blanches-Mains came from these parts, and is considered father of the dynasty.

Above St-Jean, you can follow a head-spinning loop of roads round the eastern side of the **Belledonne range**, old villages and small new ski resorts dug into the steep slopes along the way. Heading up the **Arvan valley**, make a detour up the dead-end to **Jarrier** for its Baroque church. Then **Fontcouverte** boasts another of interest. Making a loop within a loop to the big blocks of the uncompromisingly modern ski stations of **La Toussuire** and **Le Corbier**, you can visit a fine potter at **Les Anselmes**.

The other side of the Arvan, **Albiez-Montrond** proves a cute little ski station by comparison with the more brutish ones around. Summer as well as winter, donkeys provide rides and entertainment, while once the weather warms, hens wander freely around the open village, giving it a delightful rustic air.

Further up, the slopes become harsher. At **St-Sorlin-d'Arves**, the curious decorations hung on the outside of the pretty church look merry from a distance, but close up, prove to be ornate funerary wreaths. Baroque pieces and 19th-century ceiling paintings create a lively interior. The place is dedicated to St Saturnin, patron saint of shepherds and grazing beasts. Down the slope, the Beaufort **cheese co-operative** makes an appealing morning stop.

At the top of our big eastern Belledonne loop, the **Col de la Croix de Fer** and **Col du Glandon** are surrounded by sinister craggy peaks. The natural surroundings look awesome. The massive **Grandes Rousses** dominate to the south, the Belledonne's tallest peaks to the west. Looking right across the Vanoise on clear days, you can enjoy the surprise of Mont Blanc glowing in the distance.

The road through the wooded **Villards valley** races back down to the Arc. Put on the breaks for **St-Colomban-des-Villards**, its cheerful hamlets strewn either side of the narrow valley. At **La Pierre**, the sweet little **Maison du Patrimoine** is run by enthusiastic locals. They recall what a harsh country this used to be, many of the men forced to work winters as door-to-door salesmen, younger ones as chimney sweeps. But the people's best costumes were elaborate and bright, described by the British ethnologist and painter Estella Canziani as looking like bright scarab beetles in the snow.

Rejoining the main Arc roads between St-Jean and the river's confluence with the Isère, this section of the valley looks intimidating, big factories below, huge wooded slopes above. But little country routes offer some relief. Try the D75 to the picturesque ruined château and church at **Epierre**, then visit the delightful **Musée du Félicien** at **Argentine**, depicting life across the seasons.

Across the valley at **St-Georges-des-Hurtières**, modern **Le Grand Filon** takes you deep into the mining history of these parts. Above ground, admire a traditional **glassblower** at work.

**St-Sorlin-d'Arves cheese co-operative**
*t 04 79 59 70 16; tours daily 9–11.30*

**Musée du Félicien**
*t 04 79 44 33 67, www. museedufelicien.com; open July–Aug daily 2–5.30; Feb–June and Sept–Nov Wed–Sun 2–5.30; adm*

**Le Grand Filon**
*t 04 79 36 11 05, www. grand-filon.com; open July–Aug daily 10–7; May–June and Sept–Oct Sun–Fri 2–6; adm*

**Glassblower**
*t 04 79 44 35 39; open Thurs–Fri 5–7*

## Market Days in the Maurienne

**Bessans:** Mon.
**Lanslevillard:** Wed.
**Aussois:** Tues.
**St-Jean-de-Maurienne:** Sat.

## Where to Stay and Eat in the Maurienne

For places known mainly as ski resorts, hotel and restaurant listings appear in the **Winter Sports** chapter.

**Bonneval-sur-Arc** ✉ 73480
**Auberge Le Pré Catin**, t 04 79 05 95 07 (€€). Enchanting. *Closed Sun eve and Mon, and late April–mid-June and late Sept–mid Dec.*

**Bessans** ✉ 73480
**Gîte d'Etape Le Petit Bonheur**, t 04 79 05 06 71 (€). Bargain half-board; simple rooms for four, or dorm, in neat, plain modern chalet. Friendly.

**Lanslevillard** ✉ 73480
**\*\*Nanook**, t 04 79 05 91 24, *www.hotelnanook.com* (€). One of several simple, pleasant options here, run by Franco-British couple. Restaurant (€€). *Open summer mid-June–mid-Sept.*

### Sidebar

(i) **Lanslebourg** »
*Rue du Mont-Cenis, 73480 Lanslebourg, t 04 79 05 91 57, www. hautemaurienne.com*

(i) **Aussois** »
*Rte des Barrages, 73500 Aussois, t 04 79 20 30 80, www.aussois.com*

(i) **St-Jean-de-Maurienne** »
*L'Ancien Evêché, 73300 St-Jean-de-Maurienne, t 04 79 83 51 51, www.saintjeandemaurienne.com*

(i) **Bonneval-sur-Arc** >
*73480 Bonneval-sur-Arc, t 04 79 05 95 95, www.bonneval-sur-arc.com*

(i) **Bessans** >
*73480 Bessans, t 04 79 05 96 52, www.bessans.com*

(i) **Val Cenis/ Lanslevillard** >
*Rue Sous l'Eglise, 73480 Lanslevillard-Valcenis t 04 79 05 23 66, www.valcenis.com*

(i) **Oisans**
*www.tourisme-oisans.com*

**Lanslebourg** ✉ 73480
**\*\*\*Hôtel Club Le Val Cenis**, Sablon, t 04 79 05 80 31, *www.mmv.fr* (€€–€). Good standard big hotel with pool. *In summer, open July–late-Aug.*
**Le Terroir Savoyard**, Montée du Coin, t 04 79 05 82 31 (€€). Lots of regional specialities, served below the church.

**Aussois** ✉ 73500
**\*\*\*Hôtel du Soleil**, 15 Rue de l'Eglise, t 04 79 20 32 42, *www.hotel-du-soleil.com* (€). Cosy central rooms. Restaurant (€€; evenings book). *Closed mid-April–mid-June and mid-Oct–mid-Dec.*

**St-Jean-de-Maurienne** ✉ 73300
**\*\*\*Hôtel St-Georges**, Rue de la République, t 04 79 64 01 06, *www.hotel-saintgeorges.com* (€). Central, with smallish, neat, family-friendly rooms. For dining, try the jolly vaulted restaurant (€€) of the **Hôtel du Nord**, t 04 79 64 02 08. *Restaurant closed Sun eve, Mon, and Tues lunch.*

**Le Châtel** ✉ 73300
**Café-Grange Le Châtel**, t 04 79 64 25 77 (€). Splendid location above St-Jean-de-Maurienne, family village inn with terrace for tasty *charcuterie* and cheeses. *Closed Wed, and Sat lunch, and Jan–Mar.*

# Crossing to the Oisans or Ecrins

The staggering passes linking the northern and southern French Alps take you across from the Vanoise to the Ecrins range, but only in summer; otherwise, you need to pass via Grenoble. The Ecrins, with ravine-like valleys overseen by towering mountains garlanded with showy glaciers, remained practically impenetrable for centuries. It would take outsiders, notably impassioned British mountaineers, to make these mountains better known.

At the Revolution, the Ecrins were split between two *départements* and two regions. The *département de l'Isère* in the Rhône-Alpes oversaw the northwestern portion of the range. In these tourist times, the traditional name Oisans is usually used to refer to this area, comprising the Romanche valley and its handful of tributary valleys. Despite industry exploiting the phenomenal water-power in the area from the 19th century on, and despite two enormous modern ski resorts popping up on the heights, these valleys have remained for the most part in their own little worlds.

**Parc National des Ecrins**
www.les-ecrins-parc-national.fr

Some fall under the guardianship of the **Parc National des Ecrins**, created in 1973. But this is no longer virgin territory; tourists now flock here in summer as well as winter.

Set exclusively in its own valley between the Vanoise and Ecrins ranges, sports-crazy **Valloire** feels curiously like a Far West town of the French Alps, with an air of isolation and mad excitement, trapped in its very own bowl of mountains. Surrounded by steep slopes, extreme sports are often on the agenda. The exuberance continues inside the broad-shouldered Baroque church.

Two of the highest road passes in Europe then lead you across to the southern Alps, but check that they're open before you head off. The **Col du Galibier** (2,646m) offers some of the most magnificent mountain views of any in the Alps: to the north is Mont Blanc; to the south, the vast summits of the Ecrins, in particular La Meije. Leaving the northern, Savoie Alps behind, dropping down to the **Col du Lautaret** (2,058m), a profusion of meadow flowers adds dashes of colour in early summer, while the exposed but flourishing **Jardin Alpin** presents a varied display of mountain plants from across the globe among its open rockeries and streams. These two amazing passes stand roughly at the halfway point of the Route des Grandes Alpes from Lac Léman to the Med, but rather than leading you south into the Alpine ski area of Serre-Chevalier and Briançon, we branch west into the Oisans.

**Jardin Alpin du Lautaret**
www.ac-grenoble.fr/jardin/jardins.htm

First, though, although rising just beyond the Rhône-Alpes region, we can't ignore **La Meije**, the most emblematic of the Ecrins, its white triangular peak unmissable, rising to almost 4,000m. A fabulous cable-car ride takes you up towards it from the traditional village of **La Grave**, down in the Romanche valley.

The Romanche river has to circle around La Meije, coming down from the heart of the Ecrins. Then its **Combe de Malaval** leads west to the two huge modern Oisans resorts, L'Alpe d'Huez and Les Deux-Alpes (*see* **Winter Sports**). These offer mass-market holidays

## How British Mountaineers Inspired Gaspard des Montagnes

La Meije's summit is associated in French Alpine history with a legendary local guide known simply as Gaspard des Montagnes. Down the centuries, the locals hadn't been keen to take on the frightening heights dominating their lives; they had more pressing matters to attend to, scraping a meagre living. Sometimes rash explorers in search of rare Ecrins crystals did make foolhardy expeditions, and chamois-hunters took on the tough terrain. But it took outsiders to scale the heights more systematically. Mad military types and mappers were then followed by brave botanists and geologists.

Come the mid-19th century, plucky British men game for a mountaineering triumph began ticking off the Ecrins summits, notably the most famous of the lot, Edward Whymper. As an artist originally sent to the Dauphiné in 1860 to record the peaks in engravings, he rapidly turned to conquering them on foot. Local chamois-hunter Pierre Gaspard got rather put out by all these foreigners taking the glory for themselves. He did team up with outsiders to achieve the triumph, but in 1877, he became the figure most closely associated with the first successful ascent to the Grand Pic de la Meije. After that, he taught all six of his sons, his sons-in-law and his nephews to become proud mountain guides to the Ecrins. Nowadays, the range is among the most popular in France for hiking and mountaineering.

in summer as well as winter, their cool high altitude and sports facilities appreciated by many; summer skiing is even a possibility. **Les Deux-Alpes is** really like a modern town that's been transferred wholesale up into a long, spacious dead end in the mountains, although the **Musée Chasal Lento** at **Mont-de-Lans** along the way proves quite fascinating. **L'Alpe d'Huez**, in the Grandes Rousses range, is similar in feel to Les Deux-Alpes, but the sensational **Route Pastorale** you can take up to it from the valley **Lac du Chambon** seems to transport you into a different world. You pass the vestiges of a medieval silver mine lost way up in these mountains. Visit the open **archaeological site** at **Brandes-en-Oisans**, Besse's **Maison des Alpages de l'Isère**, or the little **Musée d'Huez et de l'Oisans** in the midst of L'Alpe d'Huez's mayhem of buildings, to focus on the history and traditions of the area.

A classic mountain road leads south of the Romanche, avoiding any large, modern resorts, up the glorious **Vénéon valley**. The road passes close to waterfalls and alongside the stream's turquoise waters. A network of hiking trails allows you to penetrate as far as you can go in the Oisans. One popular family hiking detour takes you up from the hamlet of **La Denchère** to the **Lac du Lauvitel**, the largest lake in the Ecrins, great waterfalls tumbling down to it.

Continuing up the Vénéon, stock up on woodwork, pottery, honey and silks at **Venosc**, just about the prettiest village in the range, all cobbled and cute, connected by cable car to Les Deux-Alpes.

Further up, **St-Christophe-en-Oisans** pays homage to Gaspard des Montagnes with a statue, and to exciting tales of summit fever and mountain conquests with its **Musée Mémoires d'Alpinisme**.

Reaching **La Bérarde**, you arrive at a legendary spot for mountaineers. You stand very close to the highest peak in the range, the **Barre des Ecrins**, soaring to 4,104m. The name of the **Pic Coolidge** to its side recalls the important part played by this American mountaineer in conquering the Dauphiné's peaks in the 1870s... along with his valiant aunt, and a faithful dog, Tshingel. Not all the walks from La Bérarde are impossibly difficult, and you're rewarded with fantastic views of the range's biggest summits, the glaciers crystal-clear on good summer days.

Back down in the Romanche valley bottom, **Le Bourg d'Oisans** is a lively place, packed with tourist shops, the gateway town into the area coming from Grenoble, accounting for the **Maison du Parc des Ecrins** based here. Up by the church, the **Musée des Minéraux et de la Faune** contains a stunning collection of Ecrins crystals, plus stuffed animals representing the range's wildlife.

The **Eau d'Olle valley** to the west is squeezed between the Grandes Rousses and Belledonne ranges. The river coming down from the Col de Glandon has been stopped in its tracks with the building of one of Europe's largest dams, **Grand-Maison**, in the late

## Sidebar

**Musée Chasal Lento**
*t 04 76 80 23 97,*
*www.les-2alpes.net;*
*open mid-Dec–April and late June–late Aug daily 10–12 and 3–7*

**Maison des Alpages de l'Isère**
*t 04 76 80 19 09; open July–Aug daily 10–12 and 3–7; by appt May–June and Sept–Oct plus school hols Thurs–Tues 9–12 and 2–6*

**Musée d'Huez et de l'Oisans**
*t 04 76 11 21 74,*
*www.musee.alpedhuez. com; open July–Aug and Dec–Mar Sun–Fri 10–12 and 3–7; adm*

 **Vénéon valley**

**Musée Mémoires d'Alpinisme**
*t 04 76 79 52 25, www. musee-alpinisme.com; open June–Sept daily 10–12 and 2–6; Oct–May school hols 2–7; adm*

**Musée des Minéraux et de la Faune**
*t 04 76 80 27 54, www. musee-bourgdoisans. com; open Jan–Oct summer daily 10–6; Nov–Dec daily 2–5; adm*

(i) **Eau d'Olle Valley**
*www.eau-dolle.com*

1970s. Before hydroelectricity, mining was briefly lucrative in these parts, after a local girl discovered deposits of valuable metals in 1767, at a mere 1,800m. The silver, nickel and cobalt were brought down by donkey to **Allemont**, where the grand 18th-century building now housing the tourist office was once the home of the director of the foundry that came into brief existence – the rush ended around 1800.

On the opposite bank, it's hard to resist a little detour to say that you've been off to see the village, the wonderful village of **Oz**. Close by, the well-presented **Hydrélec museum** fills you in on the big recent developments in the valley. Head up to **Vaujany** for the popular **Cascade de la Fare**, its impressive water-power natural.

Further up the Eau d'Olle, **Le Rivier d'Allemont**'s new little **Maison du Bouquetin** pays its respects not just to that lord of the Alps, the ibex, but also to a British group led by Air Chief Marshal Sir Trafford Leigh-Mallory, killed in a tragic air crash here in 1944. They were flying way off course, and mysteries remain over what happened.

Our last, long detour branching off the Romanche takes you up the splendid D526 and south along the wooded **Lignarre valley**. Out on a limb high on its western bank stands the village of **Oulles**, only linked to the main road by a track fit for cars since 1963. From its high hideout, it enjoys fabulous views across to the most magnificent Ecrins peaks. The other side of the valley, a ridiculously difficult road winds up at **Villard-Reymond**, abandoned in winter, but brought back to life by enthusiasts in summer. A daunting hiking track known as the *Sentier du Facteur*, the Postman's Path, links this perched mountain village with **Le Bourg-d'Oisans**.

Following the D526 south via the **Col d'Ornon**, along a path used down the centuries to bring produce up from Provence to these parts, you then descend through the **Malsanne valley**. Branch east along the dead-end roads up either the **Valsenestre** or **Bonne valleys**, allowing you once again to penetrate more deeply into the heart of the Ecrins. Only by walking can you reach the range's most fabulous, glacier-framed parts.

**Hydrélec museum**
*t 04 76 80 78 00,*
*www.musee-hydrelec.fr;*
*open mid-June–mid-*
*Sept daily 10–6; check*
*for rest of year*

**Maison du Bouquetin**
*t 04 76 79 83 06;*
*open June–Oct daily*
*10–6; adm*

ⓘ **Le Bourg d'Oisans**
*Quai Girard, 38520*
*Le Bourg d'Oisans,*
*t 04 76 80 03 25, infos@*
*bourgdoisans.com*

ⓘ **Allemont**
*La Fonderie, 38114*
*Allemont, t 04 76 80 71*
*60, www.allemont.com*

ⓘ **Vaujany**
*38114 Vaujany,*
*t 04 76 80 72 37,*
*www.vaujany.com*

ⓘ **Venosc/Vallée du Vénéon >**
*La Condamine, 38520*
*Venosc, t 04 76 80 06*
*82, www.venosc.com*

## Where to Stay and Eat in the Oisans

For places known mainly as ski resorts, see **Winter Sports** chapter.

### Venosc ✉ 38520
**\*Château de la Muzelle**, Bourg d'Arud, t 04 76 80 06 71 (€). Charming bargain hamlet mini-château, offering basic accommodation. Restaurant (€€–€) with broad terrace. Nice garden. *Open summer only, June–mid-Sept.*

**\*Les Amis de la Montagne**, Le Courtil, t 04 76 11 10 00, *www.hotel-venosc-deux-alpes.com* (€€). Dynamic, sweet family stop; some rooms are quite smart, spread out across several old village houses. Wide choice of menus (€€). Pool. *Closed mid-April–mid-June and early Sept–mid-Dec.*

### La Toussuire/St-Sorlin-sur-Arves/Valloire/L'Alpe d'Huez/Les Deux-Alpes
See **Winter Sports**.

# Winter Sports

*by Dave Watts*

*The Rhône-Alpes region includes the biggest ski areas and some of the best-known ski resorts in the world. It stretches from Châtel, Morzine and Avoriaz in the north to Alpe-d'Huez and Les Deux-Alpes in the south – with Val d'Isère, Courchevel and over 170 other resorts in between. No fewer than three Winter Olympics have been held in the Rhône-Alpes – in Chamonix in 1924, in Grenoble in 1968 and in Albertville in 1992. And no ski areas in the world come anywhere near to offering the extent and variety of, for example, the 600km of pistes of the Trois Vallées or the 650km of the Portes du Soleil.*

*This section of the book looks at the main ski areas in the Rhône-Alpes, how their slopes suit expert, intermediate and beginner downhill skiers and boarders, and at how the resorts that make them up differ in ambience and architecture.*

19

Whatever type of **resort** you want, you will find it here, from those based on traditional mountain villages such as La Clusaz, Les Contamines and Valloire, to ones which have been purpose-built in high, snowy wildernesses to allow you to ski straight from and right back to your accommodation. Prime examples of the latter include Flaine, La Plagne, Les Arcs and Le Corbier. You'll find chic expensive resorts with designer shops and fur coats, such as Megève and Courchevel 1850; ones aimed at the budget traveller such as Les Menuires and Brides-les-Bains; and resorts that firmly target the family market, like traffic-free Valmorel. You can even carry on skiing in summer, on glaciers high above resorts such as Tignes and Les Deux-Alpes.

The **ski areas** of the Rhône-Alpes are constantly improving and expanding. For example, the world's biggest double-decker **cable car** holding 200 people and covering 2km in less than four minutes opened for the 2004 season, linking the ski areas of Les Arcs and La Plagne to form a new joint area known as Paradiski with over 400km of pistes. At the same time, nine new lifts and five new pistes were built to link six existing resorts in the Maurienne valley with over 300km of pistes making up another new area known as Les Sybelles. The **lift systems** in the region include some of the most modern in the world, with state-of-the-art high-speed gondolas holding over 30 people in each cabin, six- and eight-seater chairlifts and fast underground funiculars as well as the cable car; queueing has largely become a thing of the past.

As well as downhill skiing terrain, most resorts also feature **cross-country skiing** (*see* p.396), which remarkably few British or North American guests try. They are missing out on a very different experience – skiing through winter-wonderland forests, around frozen lakes or on high plateaux makes a beautiful and peaceful change from the hurly-burly of crowded downhill pistes. But cross-country can also be a major aerobic workout – as you'll see from the Lycra-clad athletes hurtling past you. Some areas of the Rhône-Alpes, such as the Vercors and the Monts-Jura mountain ranges, have become renowned more for their extensive and compelling cross-country terrain than for their downhill slopes.

**Winter walking** on cleared mountain paths and **walking on snowshoes** makes the mountains accessible for those who don't want to ski, as well as being popular with skiers too. **Ice skating**, especially on an outdoor rink in the midst of a village, makes a jolly *après-ski* activity, as does **tobogganing** down dedicated runs that may be floodlit after dark. More sedately, you may be able to take a horse-drawn **sleigh ride**. **Parapenting** and **hang-gliding** have become hugely popular in many resorts and you can join a qualified instructor on a tandem flight from top to bottom of a mountain, soaring around on some thermals. For those of more nervous dispositions, **sightseeing flights** around the mountains are available in some resorts by either helicopter or small plane. **Snowmobiling** tours, **ice driving** courses, **go-karting** on snow and **ice-climbing** on frozen waterfalls or manmade pinnacles of ice may also be on offer. More specialized activities available include **ice diving** beneath a frozen lake (with a guide!) in Tignes, and trying out the Olympic **bobsleigh** run in La Plagne.

For maps covering the main winter sports regions, *see* pp.256, 284, 308 and 330.

# Haute Savoie

## Les Portes du Soleil: Avoriaz, Châtel, Les Gets, Morzine, La Chapelle d'Abondance – plus some Swiss resorts

**Portes du Soleil Ski Area**
*height of slopes*
*975m–2,465m*
*number of lifts 207*

**Pistes**
*650km*
*green 13%*
*blue 39%*
*red 38%*
*black 10%*

Local hero Jean Vuarnet, now of sunglasses fame, won the gold medal in the Men's Downhill at the Walt Disney-orchestrated 1960 Winter Olympics in Lake Tahoe, California. Shortly afterwards he was entrusted with the development of Avoriaz, one of the first French purpose-built ski resorts, which opened in 1966 high above the traditional mountain town of Morzine. It was Vuarnet's dream to build a cross-border ski area, linking the pistes of Avoriaz to those of Les Crosets and Champéry over the border in Switzerland – a dream that became a reality in 1968, when the **Portes du Soleil** ('Gateways to the Sun') ski area was born. Since then, development has been continuous, and Portes du Soleil now covers 14 resorts and claims 650km of pistes, over 200 lifts, 500 snow guns, more than 1,000 ski instructors and 100,000 beds. But each resort remains modest in size, and has a local ski area with distinct character that is not lost in a homogeneous whole.

The Portes du Soleil vies with the Trois Vallées (*see* p.367) for the crown of being the world's largest ski area. While the Trois Vallées claims 50km fewer pistes, they are truly linked by lifts and pistes, whereas in the Portes du Soleil you have to catch a bus or walk quite a distance in a few places – so a fair verdict might be a tie!

The area as a whole can be classed as an intermediate's paradise, with mile after mile of easy-cruising blue and red runs and an interesting mixture of snow-sure runs above the tree line and pretty runs through the woods below. The main Portes du Soleil circuit can be skied in either clockwise or anti-clockwise direction and takes in Avoriaz 1800 and Châtel in France and Morgins, Champoussin and Les Crosets in Switzerland (in that order if you go clockwise). It makes a wonderful day's skiing if the snow is good – and a full day's worth too, if you are tempted to linger over a long lunch at one of the many rustic mountain restaurants around. The circuit breaks down only at Châtel where, whichever direction you are travelling in, you need to take a short bus ride – the buses are frequent and free. The main disadvantage of the area is that it is relatively low for a big French ski area, with the slopes ranging from 975m to 2,465m (compared with 1,550m to 3,455m for L'Espace Killy). So the snow quality can suffer in warm or dry weather. But when snow conditions are good, the area is a delight.

The main French resorts all have good beginner slopes and easy green runs to progress to. But experts will find steep slopes in relatively short supply. Most are in the Avoriaz 1800 area and include four 'snowcross' runs – an excellent concept, where effectively off-piste runs are left ungroomed but are controlled for avalanches (and closed if dangerous) and patrolled. This is normal in North America but in Europe most off-piste is entirely uncontrolled and you risk being killed by an avalanche whenever you slide off the marked trails. Nicknamed the '**Swiss Wall**' because of its steepness and huge moguls, one (but not the only) piste down into Switzerland from above Avoriaz 1800 will challenge even the most expert – but the more timid can ride a chairlift down and chuckle at the carnage below on the way. Avoriaz also boasts three excellent terrain parks, including the main **Arare** park with its own drag lift which is often used for high profile pro-rider contests.

Morzine is just off the main Portes du Soleil circuit but has a gondola up into it (which you have to ride down as well). Its main local slopes are on the opposite side of the valley on gentle, wooded slopes that link up with those of Les Gets.

Perched above a dramatic, sheer rock face, **Avoriaz 1800** (the 1800 was added to the name in 2003 to emphasize its relatively high altitude) insists on cars being parked well outside the resort. From there, horse-drawn sleighs or snow-cats transport you and your luggage to your accommodation. Thankfully, the problem of horse mess has been cut since they now wear 'nappies' and staff on snowmobiles scoop up what escapes. A main snow-covered 'street', free of skiers and boarders as well as traffic, runs the length of the resort, and the cliff face behind, prettily lit at night, adds to the Alpine ambience. The angular, high-rise buildings, distinctly 1960s in style, fit in remarkably well with their mountain environment and their faded wood cladding adds a sense of age and style.

Eight hundred vertical metres below Avoriaz 1800, the traditional mountain town of **Morzine** is not unattractive, with nearly all buildings built in chalet style. But it sprawls on both sides of a river gorge and, if you are staying out of the centre, buses will be needed to reach both town and the lifts. Many UK chalet operators offer their own free minibus service to the lifts – worth looking for.

Just off the main road to Morzine and 6km away, the smaller old village of **Les Gets** makes a very atmospheric place to stay. The increasingly car-free centre, right by the slopes, has traditional

**Avoriaz 1800 Ski School**
*Avoriaz Alpine Ski School*, t 04 50 74 76 91, www.avoriaz alpineskischool.com: *British-run and very highly rated*

**Morzine Ski School**
*British Alpine Ski School*, t 04 50 74 78 59, www. britishskischool.com: *former British snowboard champion and top instructor Becci Malthouse is a partner*

**Les Gets Ski School**
*British Alpine Ski School*, t 04 50 79 85 42, www. britishskischool.com: the *original branch, still run by Scottish ski guru Hugh Monney*

chalet buildings and plenty of tempting restaurants and shops. An outdoor ice rink adds to the 'winter wonderland' charm and there's a mountain music museum with barrel organs, music boxes and guided tours in English. But it takes a long time to reach the main Portes du Soleil circuit on skis – you have to get to Morzine, cross the town and take the gondola up towards Avoriaz.

In the old village of **Châtel**, unpretentious newer chalet-style hotels and apartments rub shoulders with old farmhouses where cattle still live in winter. Like Morzine, it has expanded over the years and now sprawls along the road in from Lac Léman (Lake Geneva) and the diverging roads out – up the hillside towards Morgins in Switzerland and along the valley towards the lifts up to the link with Avoriaz 1800. The gondola up to **Super-Châtel** and the pistes to Switzerland starts right in the village centre.

Unspoiled **La Chapelle d'Abondance**, 5km from Châtel, has its own small ski area and a gondola that links with Torgon in Switzerland (excellent views of Lac Léman from there) and the slopes above Châtel. It is rather isolated, so best for those with cars.

**Châtel Ski School**
*International School,*
*t 04 50 73 31 92,*
*www.essi-chatel.com:*
*caters well for English-*
*speaking guests*

(i) **Avoriaz 1800** >
*t 04 50 74 02 11,*
*www.avoriaz.com*

(i) **Châtel**
*t 04 50 73 22 44,*
*www.chatel.com*

(i) **Les Gets**
*t 04 50 75 80 80,*
*www.lesgets.com*

(i) **Morzine**
*t 04 50 74 72 72,*
*www.morzine.com*

**19 Winter Sports | Haute Savoie: Les Portes du Soleil**

## Where to Stay in Les Portes du Soleil

### Avoriaz 1800
***Dromonts, t 04 94 97 91 91, www.christophe-leroy.com (€€€€€–€€€). Central and smartly renovated by celebrity chef Christophe Leroy, whose summer base is St-Tropez. Excellent food, and cookery courses.

### La Chapelle d'Abondance
**Cornettes, t 04 50 73 50 24, www.lescornettes.com (€€). Two-star rooms with four-star facilities (pool, sauna, steam, Jacuzzi), an excellent, great-value restaurant, and an atmospheric bar popular with locals. Family-run in idiosyncratic way (showcases with puppets and dolls, doors that unexpectedly open automatically).

### Apartments
Many in **Avoriaz 1800** are showing their age and in need of renovation. **Falaise**, near the top of the village, has some of the smartest.

### Catered Chalets
**Ski Total, t 08701 633 633.** Comfortable chalets in Les Gets.
**Snowline, t (020) 8870 4807.** Some very smart central chalets in Morzine.

**La Ferme de Montagne**, Les Gets, t 0800 072 3069. Gourmet cuisine, big rooms (most with sitting areas), and an outdoor Jacuzzi.
**The Farmhouse**, Morzine, t 04 50 79 08 26. The oldest building in Morzine, built in 1771, now beautifully renovated. Communal dining room. Minibus service to lifts.

## Eating Out in Les Portes du Soleil

### In the Resorts
**Avoriaz 1800: Hotel Dromonts** has inventive restaurant.
**Châtel: Vieux Four** does wonderful steaks and Savoyard specialities in a lovely rustic former farm building right in the centre.
**La Chapelle d'Abondance: Hôtel Cornettes** has great-value set menus.
**Morzine: La Taverne** in Hôtel Samoyede is highly regarded for lobster ravioli and truffle risotto.

### On the Mountain
**Avoriaz 1800:** Of the clutch of rustic chalets in the hamlet of Les Lindarets, **La Crémaillière** offers excellent steaks with chanterelle mushrooms and a reliable *plat du jour*. **La Grenouille du**

**Marais**, near the top of the gondola up from Morzine, has tasty food, lovely views and atmosphere.

**Morzine**: Don't miss **Chez Nannon**, near the top of the Troncs chair between Nyon and Chamossière – good Savoyard food, a fine terrace for sunny days and a rustic interior.

## Bars and Clubs in Les Portes du Soleil

**Avoriaz 1800: Yeti** is popular as the lifts close. **Tavaillon** has Sky TV

showing live sports. **Choucas** and **The Place** both have live bands.

**Châtel: Tunnel**, with a DJ or live music every night, is very popular with British guests. For an English-style pub, head for **Avalanche**. For a more French feel, try **Godille**.

**Morzine**: If dancing on tables in ski boots is your scene, head for **Crépu** when the lifts shut. For a quieter drink, try the **Boudha Café** with its Asian décor.

## Le Grand Massif: Les Carroz, Flaine, Morillon, Samoëns, Sixt

**Le Grand Massif Ski Area**
*height of slopes*
*700m–2,480m*
*number of lifts* 75

**Pistes**
*265km*
*green* 12%
*blue* 41%
*red* 38%
*black* 9%

Few ski areas contain such contrasting resorts as purpose-built, austere concrete-block Flaine (the first resort in the area to become popular on the UK market) and the ancient mountain village of Samoëns, the only winter sports resort in France to be classified a '*Monument Historique*' – complete with its pretty central square, medieval fountain and ancient church. But Flaine is about to undergo a renaissance, as Canadian ski resort developer Intrawest is building its second 'village' in the Alps here, and French company Immo Concepts is also building a tasteful new chalet and apartment development near the golf course practice green.

The Grand Massif resorts are among the easiest in France to get to, being an hour or less by car from Geneva airport, and they share one of the most underrated ski areas in the Rhône-Alpes: 265km of varied pistes plus some excellent off-piste. And, while the snow down towards the lower resorts can suffer if the weather is warm, the high bowl above Flaine often offers a paradise of fresh powder.

With almost 80 per cent of the area's pistes being classified blue or red, intermediates of all levels are guaranteed a great time. And if the snow is good throughout the area, cruising down to the valley villages can be a delight. One of the longest pistes in the Alps runs from above Flaine down to Sixt – the easy 14km picturesque **Cascades** blue takes you right away from the lift system and all signs of civilization, dropping over 1,700 vertical metres on the way. If you'd like to discover more about the local wildlife, don't miss the long green **Marvel run** to Morillon 1100, which has excellent signs along the way (in English as well as French) explaining all about the birds and animals you are likely to spot.

All the resorts have good nursery slopes (a lift ride above the villages in the cases of Samoëns and Morillon) for beginners, though Flaine's easy slopes do tend to have experienced skiers whizzing through them, which can be unnerving. Only Morillon has a good long, easy green to progress to (the Marvel run mentioned above). But there are plenty of easy blues.

All the black pistes on the map deserve their grading. The Gers drag lift serves great expert-only terrain, usually very quiet because of its position rather off the beaten track, outside the main Flaine bowl beyond **Tête Pelouse**. Two more serious black pistes run from **Tête des Saix** down towards Samoëns 1600 – most intermediates sensibly avoid these by taking the blue alternative.

Experts will love the area's **off-piste**. But beware: although much of it looks as if it can safely be explored without a local guide, this impression is mistaken. Ravines and potholes abound in the bowl above Flaine but are often hidden with a layer of snow, and the terrain should be treated with the same caution that you would use on a glacier. Touring is a possibility behind the **Grandes Platières**, and there are some scenic off-piste routes from which you can be retrieved by helicopter.

**Flaine Ski Schools**
*International School,*
*t 04 50 90 84 41,*
*www.flaine-*
*internationalskischool.*
*com: good reputation*
*for both group and*
*private lessons*

*Flaine Super Ski School,*
*t 04 50 90 82 88, www.*
*flainesuperski.com:*
*small school run by*
*two former French*
*ski team coaches and*
*specializing in sessions*
*for advanced and*
*expert skiers, offering*
*race training as well as*
*improvement courses*

When **Flaine** opened in 1968, its Bauhaus buildings designed by American architect Marcel Breuer, and intended to blend in with the rocks that surround it, met with great acclaim. But to many eyes they don't blend in at all – in winter, at least. Unusually for a ski resort, Flaine is approached over a high pass, and suddenly springs into view below – a mass of grey concrete blocks at the bottom of an impressively snowy bowl. You'll love it or hate it but, whatever your view on the architecture, it is compact and convenient. The main central square of **Flaine Forum**, the focal point of the resort, opens on one side to the slopes. Above it, connected by a lift that works day and night, **Flaine Forêt** has more apartments, shops and restaurants. The main gondola to the top of the Flaine bowl goes from Forum, and the eight-seater chair, which links to pistes leading to the other villages of the Grand Massif, goes from Forêt. A shuttle-bus ride away and with no direct access to lifts or pistes, the newer development of **Hameau-de-Flaine** has been built in a much more conventional chalet style. The new Intrawest and Immo Concepts developments will be near here.

If you prefer a more traditional village setting, try **Les Carroz**, on the road up from the valley to Flaine before you get to the pass. Set on a wide, sunny slope, this chalet-style resort has the lived-in feel of a real French village and life revolves around the village square with its pavement cafés, restaurants and interesting little shops. A choice of gondola or slow chairlift takes you up to the heart of the Grand Massif slopes – but they are a steep walk or shuttle-bus ride from some of the village centre.

The attraction of staying in the characterful old village of **Samoëns** increased dramatically from the 2003/4 season when a new eight-seater gondola, the Grand Massif Express, opened to whisk you from the edge of the village to the heart of the slopes at **Samoëns 1600** in just eight minutes. You ride the new gondola down as well, as there is no piste back to the village. It makes a pleasant change to stay in a real village with a life of its own outside skiing – with local bars, shops and restaurants. Samoëns was once a thriving centre for stonemasons, and their work is evident in ornate carvings around the village centre. Samoëns 1600 has excellent nursery slopes and some accommodation too.

**Morillon** is a small, pretty, rustic village with a gondola up to the mid-mountain, modern mini-resort of **Morillon 1100**, built in a quite attractive, low-rise style with slopes on your doorstep.

## Where to Stay in Le Grand Massif

**(i) Flaine >**
t 04 50 90 80 01,
www.flaine.com

**(i) Les Carroz >**
t 04 50 90 00 04,
www.lescarroz.com

**(i) Samoëns >**
t 04 50 34 40 28,
www.samoens.com

**(i) Morillon**
t 04 50 90 15 76,
www.ot-morillon.fr

### Flaine

There are no real hotels, but several club-hotels run by tour operators, including **Crystal, t** 0870 160 6040, which operates Hotel Totem.

### Les Carroz

**\*\*Bois de la Char, t** 04 90 06 18, www.hotel-boisdelachar.com (€€€–€). At the top of the resort right on the slopes with easy access to the gondola. Good food, friendly staff.

### Samoëns

**\*\*\*Neige et Roc, t** 04 50 34 40 72, www.neigeetroc.com (€€). A short walk from the centre and the gondola. Welcoming, with tasty food, a sauna, steam room, Jacuzzi and indoor pool.

### Apartments

**Flaine:** The **Forêt** and **Grand Massif** buildings are attractively woody inside and have hotel facilities such as a restaurant and bar.

**Les Carroz:** The **Fermes du Soleil** apartments have a pool and sauna.

**Samoëns:** The **Fermes de Samoëns** is one of the smartest, with a pool. Also try **La Maison de Fifine**, www.fifine.com, with apartments, chalets and chambres d'hôtes, pool and sauna.

## Eating Out in the Grand Massif

### In the Resorts

**Flaine:** The welcoming **Michet Chalet** at the foot of the pistes specializes in Savoyard food, and the smart **Perdrix Noire** in Forêt gets packed out.

**Samoëns: Pizzeria Louisiane** offers decent pizzas and some highly alcoholic ice creams, while **Chalet Fleurie** and **Chardon Bleu**, both a car ride away in Verchaix, are well worth the journey.

### On the Mountain

**Chalet du Lac de Gers** has a wonderfully isolated position overlooking the frozen lake, does simple, inexpensive food and is a real adventure, in that you use their phone part-way down the Cascades piste (next to a piste map sign) and they come down with a snowcat to tow you up while you hang on to a rope.

Above Morillon the rustic **Igloo** offers a reliable plat du jour. And the 200-year-old **Chalet les Molliets** near the bottom of the Molliets chair is charmingly rustic, with leather boots and old ski sticks decorating the walls, and features Savoyard food as well as steaks and other options.

## Bars and Clubs in Le Grand Massif

**Flaine:** The **White Pub** has a big screen TV, rock music and punters throwing drinks back in happy hour. Later on, you will find that the **Flying Dutchman** is the liveliest place, with live bands or karaoke.

**Other resorts:** Quieter, more typically French bars are the main option.

# The Chamonix Valley: Chamonix, Argentière, Les Houches (ski areas not linked), Vallée Blanche

**Chamonix Valley Ski Area**

*height of slopes*
*1,035m–3,840m*

*number of lifts 47*

**Pistes**

*155km*

*green 16%*
*blue 31%*
*red 36%*
*black 17%*

**Chamonix** could not be more different from the archetypal high-altitude purpose-built French resort, either in resort ambience or in the type of skiing on offer. The ancient town centre, steeped in the history of being a leading mountaineering centre for over 200 years (*see* p.41), oozes charm in a rugged way, with spectacular views from its cafés of tumbling glaciers and Europe's highest peaks which seem to rise perpendicular from the valley. As a first-time visitor you could be forgiven for wondering where on earth you could ski. The answer is much higher up and much further along the valley in both directions. The only run back to town (other than a nursery slope area at the bottom) is fearsomely steep and often closed and, although you can access ski slopes from near the town centre, a lot of the slopes are a bus or car ride away.

A gondola from near the centre heads up **Le Brévent** and links with **La Flégère**'s slopes, which can also be accessed by cable car from further up the valley. The sunny, largely south-facing pistes here have truly spectacular views over the valley to Mont Blanc, the **Aiguille du Midi** and numerous other memorable peaks. The spiky Aiguille du Midi itself is reached by a two-stage cable car which is a real feat of engineering and deposits you at a bone-chillingly cold altitude of 3,840m; wrap up well before you make the ascent and think hard before removing a glove to take a photo at the top. Lots of pedestrians make the trip just for the experience and the views, and those who intend to ski should not even dream of attempting to do so without a mountain guide – there is only off-piste here and the terrain is riddled with crevasses (known as 'slots').

## The Vallée Blanche

No competent intermediate or expert skier should go to Chamonix without tackling one of the world's epic runs. When there's enough snow on the lower slopes, the Vallée Blanche is 24km long and descends 2,800m vertically; often you have to stop 875m higher and catch the train down from Montenvers but even that curtailed version will be a day out to remember for the rest of your life.

The standard gentle and easy route – so flat in places that boarders will find it too tedious to enjoy – resembles a green run for much of its length; you do this run for the spectacular scenery rather than the challenge of the slope. The views of the crevasses and *séracs* (huge pillars of ice) – and the rugged rock spires beyond – are simply mind-blowing. The trickiest part is right at the top; after you emerge from the Aiguille du Midi cable car, a tunnel takes you to a narrow ridge with sheer drops on both sides which you have to walk down while carrying your skis, not something for those who suffer from vertigo to attempt. There is (usually) a fixed guide rope for you to hang on to, and many parties rope up to their mountain guides (the walk can be avoided completely by taking the lifts up from the Italian side of Mont Blanc instead). After that, the run seems very easy and you can concentrate on admiring the spectacular glacial surroundings. If you want more challenging slopes there are plenty of alternatives to the classic route, of varying difficulty and danger.

The classic route can get very busy at times with up to 2,500 people a day doing it; but do not attempt it without a qualified mountain guide – dangerous crevasses lurk to swallow those not in the know, and some of the snow bridges between them can be very narrow. Go early to avoid the crowds.

Back in the valley, head up it towards the Swiss border and you reach **Argentière**, whose local mountain, the **Grands Montets**, accesses some phenomenal off-piste for experts. Even further up the road towards Switzerland you come to **Le Tour** and a gondola into the largely intermediate slopes of **Col de Balme** (there's now also a gondola into this area from even further towards the Swiss border at Vallorcine). Down the valley, in the opposite direction from Chamonix, the slopes above **Les Houches** offer yet another substantial ski area and are home to Chamonix's World Cup Downhill course. With all these options, many involving fairly lengthy journeys, having a car rather than relying on local buses gives you a lot more flexibility. It also allows you to try out other resorts covered by the Mont Blanc area lift pass, which include Megève, Les Contamines and even Courmayeur in Italy, easily but expensively reached through the Mont Blanc tunnel.

Intermediates who like ski-in, ski-out convenience and mile after mile of perfectly groomed easy-cruising runs would be happier in many other resorts. But intermediates looking for something out of the ordinary, who relish the prospect of trying some steeper slopes or some off-piste and who fancy the prospect of exploring the whole Chamonix valley, can have a wonderful time here. Col de Balme at one end of the valley and Les Houches at the other both offer excellent blue and red intermediate pistes, the former above the tree line and ideal for sunny days, and the latter largely below the tree line and ideal for snowy ones. Le Brévent and La Flégère also have good cruising runs – but don't dream of trying the black runs down to the valley unless you are both competent and brave.

Beginners are catered for by various nursery slopes scattered along the valley floor. But they'd be better off learning elsewhere and saving Chamonix until they are experienced mountain people, when they can truly appreciate the splendours of the terrain here. Experts will love the place. Indeed many fall so head-over-heels in love that they never return home – or only for the time it takes to quit the job, sell up and move out here. It's the off-piste that attracts them; plus the powder, the scenic grandeur, the nightlife, and the food, of course. But the off-piste mainly. There's so much of it that no single run is worth describing here; suffice to say that you should hire a guide and explore, but do not explore *without* a guide – the terrain is riddled with dangers for the unwary. And options are plentiful; many top British mountain guides base themselves here and the local Compagnie des Guides, established over 150 years ago, is world-renowned.

**Chamonix** has expanded into quite a sizable town and, though the centre remains charming with its cobbled streets and squares, lovely old buildings, grand hotels, fast-flowing river and pedestrianized areas, the periphery has more than its fair share of tacky

**Chamonix
Ski Schools**

*Ecole de Ski Française,*
**t** *04 50 53 22 57,*
*www.esf-chamonix.*
*com: runs a great*
*programme of all-day*
*Ski Fun Tours, featuring*
*a different area daily*

*Compagnie des Guides,*
**t** *04 50 53 00 88, www.*
*cieguides-chamonix.*
*com: for days out on*
*the Vallée Blanche or*
*other glacier runs*

1960s and '70s architecture and traffic-choked streets. The choice of bars, restaurants and shops is large and varies from long-standing local enterprises to international chains. Staying centrally or way outside are the two best options, and both **Argentière** and **Les Houches** make smaller-scale alternatives: pleasant villages with enough bars and restaurants to create a friendly atmosphere. But neither is as centrally placed for exploring the whole valley.

## Where to Stay in the Chamonix Valley

There is a huge choice of hotels for a ski resort, especially of good-value two-stars.

(i) Chamonix >
t 04 50 53 00 24,
www.chamonix.com

### Chamonix

****Hameau Albert 1er**, t 04 50 53 05 09, *www.hameaualbert.fr* (€€€€€–€€€). The smartest place in town, a beautiful centrally situated 100-year-old chalet with some rooms in a separate farmhouse and chalet buildings in the grounds, indoor-outdoor pool, sauna, Jacuzzi, excellent restaurant with two Michelin stars.

**Arve**, t 04 50 53 02 31, *www.hotelarve-chamonix.com* (€€–€). Central, by the river, with small, newly decorated rooms, fitness facility, sauna, climbing wall.

(i) Argentière >
t 04 50 54 02 14,
www.chamonix.com

### Argentière

***Les Grands Montets**, t 04 50 54 06 66, *www.hotel-grands-montets.com* (€€€–€€). At the foot of the slopes by the lifts, with great views of Mont Blanc from some of the rooms, recently renovated, with lovely pool, sauna, steam and gym.

(i) Les Houches >
t 04 50 55 50 62,
www.leshouches.com

### Les Houches

***Hôtel du Bois**, t 04 50 54 50 35, *www.hotel-du-bois.com* (€€). Popular chalet-style hotel, with good views of Mont Blanc *massif* from half the rooms, pool and sauna. There's a minibus to take you to and from the slopes (and they do airport transfers).

### Apartments

There are plenty of the uninspiring cramped apartments typical of French ski resorts, but unusually also some very smart places. **Balcons du Savoy** on the slopes but close to the centre of Chamonix, **Ginabelle** near the train station, **Cristal d'Argentière** in the centre of Argentière and **Hauts de Chavants** near the slopes at Les Houches are all a cut above the norm, with relatively spacious well-furnished rooms and a swimming pool (some have saunas as well).

### Catered Chalets

A lot of small specialist Chamonix tour operators offer very high-quality personal service on top of comfortable accommodation, such as ferrying you around in minibuses and booking up mountain guides for you in advance. These include **Collineige**, t (01276) 24262; **Bigfoot**, t 0870 300 5874, **Huski**, t (020) 7938 4844, and **Les Chalets de Philippe**, *www.chamonixlocations.com.*

## Eating Out in the Chamonix Valley

### In the Resorts

**Chamonix**: For the best food in town head for the **Hameau Albert 1er**, which offers a *Maison de Savoie* fixed price menu as well as delicious *à la carte*. **L'Atmosphère** lives up to its name, a rustically furnished *auberge* by the river which serves traditional as well as local speciality dishes. The **Cabane** serves good-value classic dishes and there's a wide choice of ethnic food.

### On the Mountain

The beautiful old **Bergerie** at Planpraz on Le Brévent is by far the most attractive option in the area – with both self- and table-service sections, but it does get packed. The dull **Panoramic** at the top serves unremarkable food but has stunning views of Mont Blanc over the valley.

At Les Grands Montets, the attractive modern **Plan Joran** has decent food and table- and self-service options, and the rustic **Chalet-Refuge du Lognan** offers spectacular views of the Argentière glacier.

## Bars and Clubs in the Chamonix Valley

**Chamonix**: This is the place for the liveliest nightlife. Several bars in the centre get packed when the lifts close, including the **Choucas** video bar. Later on the partying crowd head for **The Pub**, **No Escape**, **Bar'd Up** and then on to night clubs and discos such as **Dick's T-Bar**. For a quieter drink try **Dérapage**.

**Argentière**: The **Office** bar is the focal point of the nightlife here.

## Evasion Mont-Blanc: Megève, St-Gervais, Combloux, St-Nicolas-de-Véroce

**Evasion Mont-Blanc Ski Area**
*height of slopes*
*850m–2,355m*
*number of lifts 113*

**Pistes**
*445km*
*green 16%*
*blue 27%*
*red 40%*
*black 17%*

In 1916 Megève was singled out by Baroness Rothschild as the resort to develop into the French equivalent of chic St-Moritz in Switzerland, and after her Mont d'Arbois Palace hotel opened in 1921 the resort boomed and attracted more European royalty than anywhere else in high season. For a time in the 1960s and '70s its reputation faded as newer, more snow-sure resorts were built. But now the beautiful people have returned, attracted by the charm of the exquisitely restored, traffic-free medieval centre with its cobbled streets, splendid church and designer shops. Together with St-Gervais it shares an extensive ski area, known as Evasion Mont-Blanc, of gentle, wooded slopes with stunning views, including wonderful close-up vistas of Mont Blanc. If only the town and slopes were 500m higher, Megève would fulfil many people's vision of the perfect ski resort. As it is, the price you pay for such an idyllic setting is the chance of poor snow; but when there's snow in the village and fresh powder on the slopes you could be forgiven for thinking you had died and gone to heaven.

Megève's pistes are perfect for its pampered clientele: mile after mile of well-groomed easy blue and red runs. Two of its three main mountains, **Mont d'Arbois** (which links with St-Gervais) and **Rochebrune**, can be reached from the centre of town and are linked by a cross-valley cable car but the third, **La Jaillet**, is a bus ride away. This third area, which links with runs above **Combloux**, was expanded from the 2004/5 season to link it with the slopes of **Le Torraz**, above La Giettaz, a tiny resort in the next valley on the road to La Clusaz. Timid intermediates will find easy cruising in all the sectors and there are gentle runs right from the top down to valley level. Those looking for more of a challenge can try the famous **Olympique** downhill run at Rochebrune – a wonderful undulating red run with snowmaking from top to bottom. And at **Côte 2000** the black **Stade Descente** piste is often groomed to racetrack perfection and open to all. Near the top of the Mont d'Arbois sector the **Epaule** chair accesses a fabulous red run along the ridge of the mountain, above the old village of **St-Nicolas-de-Véroce**, with jaw-dropping views of Mont Blanc in front of you, the whole of Megève's ski area to the left, and off-piste slopes leading down towards neighbouring Les Contamines to the right. The ski schools organize trips to ski the Vallée Blanche in Chamonix (*see* p.357) – competent intermediates who enjoy spectacular scenery should not miss this opportunity.

If the snow is good, beginners will find Megève perfect: nursery slopes both at valley level and at altitude on all three mountains, lots of very easy green and blue runs to progress to and patient instructors who are used to dealing with neophytes. Not renowned as an area for expert skiers, Megève has few steep pistes worthy of their black status, the toughest being those from **Mont-Joly** and **Epaule** on Mont d'Arbois and the black mentioned above at Côte 2000. But if the snow is good, there is worthwhile off-piste which remains untracked much longer than in many other resorts, as most Megève visitors have no desire to leave the perfectly manicured pistes. The steep wooded area under the second stage of the Princesse gondola on Mont d'Arbois and the more open bowls at Côte 2000 are especially worthy of exploration. If you hire a guide you can hike up from the top of the Mont-Joly chair and ski all the way down to the adjacent (but unlinked) resort of Les Contamines. And the Mont Blanc area lift pass which covers Megève also allows you to explore the steep runs and off-piste of Chamonix (an easy car journey and excursions are often laid on).

**Megève Ski School**
*International School,*
*t 04 50 58 78 88,*
*www.esimegeve.com:*
*long-established, and*
*more popular with*
*British guests than*
*the main ESF*

**Megève**'s beautiful and tranquil centre, based around the big church and open-air ice rink, contrasts sharply with its sprawling and traffic-choked outskirts. So it's best to stay in or close to the centre, where you can join the fur-coated and non-skiing crowd sipping coffee, window-shopping, taking rides in horse-drawn sleighs or just strolling around enjoying the ambience. Lunching is another major activity here and many of the mountain restaurants scattered around the ski areas can easily be accessed by non-skiers – some will even send snowcats to pick customers up from the top of the nearest gondola. The resort rivals Courchevel for its choice of swish four-star hotels and Michelin-starred restaurants and you can spend a fortune living the high life here, but there are plenty of more affordable options too.

For a much more down-to-earth holiday base, consider the handsome 19th-century spa town of **St-Gervais**, set in a narrow river gorge, halfway between Megève and Chamonix, at the entrance to the side-valley leading up to St-Nicolas-de-Véroce and Les Contamines. Interesting food shops, cosy bars, thermal baths and an Olympic skating rink make St-Gervais a pleasant place to explore. If you have a car and want to make full use of all the resorts covered by the Mont Blanc lift pass it makes a much more central base. It also has direct access to the Mont d'Arbois ski area via a 20-person gondola from just outside the town, and at the gondola mid-station a small collection of hotels, private chalets and apartments at **Le Bettex** are conveniently situated for the runs but have little evening animation. The other side of St-Gervais from the gondola, a rack-and-pinion railway takes you to the slopes of Les Houches (see 'Chamonix') – you catch the railway back or, given enough snow, can ski back to St-Gervais off-piste. When the railway was built in 1904 the original idea was for it to go all the way to the top of Mont Blanc but, not surprisingly, it didn't quite make it.

## Where to Stay in Evasion Mont-Blanc

### Megève

> **Megève** >
> t 04 50 21 27 28,
> www.megeve.com

****Fermes de Marie**, t 04 50 93 03 10, www. fermesdemarie.com (€€€€€–€€€€). Ten minutes' walk from the centre, beautifully converted former farm buildings based round a 16th-century vaulted cowshed. Spa with sauna, Jacuzzi, pool and fitness room.

***Ferme Hôtel Duvillard**, t 04 50 21 14 62, www.ferme-hotel.com (€€€€–€€€). Smartly restored farmhouse at the foot of the slopes right by the Mont d'Arbois gondola.

**Gai Soleil**, t 04 50 21 00 70, www. le-gai-soleil.fr (€€–€). Comfortable, family-run, five minutes from the centre and Rochebrune gondola. Savoyard cooking and a 'giant *tartiflette*' evening once a week.

### St-Gervais

> **St-Gervais** >
> t 04 50 47 76 08,
> www.st-gervais.net

> **Combloux** >
> t 04 50 58 60 49,
> www.combloux.com

La Ferme de Cupelin, t 04 50 93 47 30, www.ferme-de-cupelin.com (€€€). An ecologically built and run farm, with seven rooms and serving healthy but delicious natural pesticide-free food.

### Catered Chalets

****Hameau de Mavarin**, t 04 50 93 03 10, www.hameaudemavarin.com (€€€€€–€€€€). New luxury chalets and apartments in Megève, with spa, massages, pool and Jacuzzi.

**Stanford Skiing**, t (01223) 477 644, specializes in Megève, and its creaky old **Sylvana** chalet hotel makes a cheap and cheerful base near the cable car up to Rochebrune.

**Simon Butler Skiing**, t 0870 8730 001, another Megève chalet specialist, offers tuition-based holidays (Simon is a ski instructor).

## Eating Out in Evasion Mont-Blanc

### Megève

**La Ferme de Mon Père**, with three Michelin stars and 20 out of 20 from the Gault-Millau guide, is one of the very best restaurants in France, run by the famous chef Marc Veyrat who also has a wonderful restaurant in Annecy; it gets booked up weeks in advance. Exceptional food and wine but budget for a bill of a few hundred pounds a head.

For less astronomical prices and simpler food try **Brasserie Centrale**, **Flocons de Sel**, **Prieuré** and the **Bistrot**.

### On the Mountain

**Auberge du Côte 2000**, at the foot of the slopes so easily accessible to pedestrian trade, serves some of the finest (and priciest) lunchtime food in a former farmhouse owned by the Rothschild family. **Alpette**, on top of the Rochebrune ridge, runs a snowcat service from the top of the gondola for pedestrians to sample its refined fair. **La Ravière**, a tiny hut in the woods near the La Croix chair in the Mont d'Arbois area, does an excellent set menu daily. Above St-Nicolas, several charming chalets offer simpler food at much more modest prices.

## Bars and Clubs in Evasion Mont-Blanc

The **Club de Jazz Les Cinq Rues** in Megève opens from teatime till late, attracts some big-name musicians and serves excellent (if expensive) cocktails. The **Cocoon** is popular with British guests and the **Wake-Up** with the younger crowd.

19 Winter Sports | Haute Savoie: Les Contamines-Hauteluce

**L'Espace Diamant Ski Area**

*height of slopes*
*1,000m–2,070m*

*number of lifts 84*

**Pistes**

*175km*

*green 23%*
*blue 39%*
*red 30%*
*black 8%*

ⓘ **Val d'Arly**
*t 04 79 31 06 82,*
*www.valdarly-*
*montblanc.com*

ⓘ **Les Saisies**
*t 04 79 38 90 30,*
*www.lessaisies.com*

**Les Contamines-Hauteluce Ski Area**

*height of slopes*
*1,160m–2,485m*

*number of lifts 26*

**Pistes**

*120km*

*green 16%*
*blue 23%*
*red 40%*
*black 21%*

## L'Espace Diamant (partly in Savoie): Praz sur Arly, Flumet, Notre-Dame de Bellecombe, Crest-Voland-Cohennoz, Les Saisies

**Val d'Arly**'s small, traditional villages, very close to Megève, on the road towards Albertville, have now linked their main ski areas to those of **Crest-Voland-Cohennoz** and **Les Saisies** in Savoie to form **L'Espace Diamant**.

The combined area covers an impressive 175km of pistes, which suit intermediates and beginners best, with lots of green and gentle blue and red pistes and very few challenging runs. The area sprang to fame for the 1992 Albertville Winter Olympics when cross-country events were held at the **Mont Lachat** area, shared by Les Saisies and Crest-Voland-Cohennoz. The 80km of trails here form one of the premier **cross-country** areas in the French Alps, and other smaller loops dotted around the valley add variety.

## Les Contamines-Hauteluce

The charming unspoiled old village of **Les Contamines**, just a few kilometres from the macho slopes of Chamonix in one direction and the poodles and beautiful people of Megève in the other, makes a fine contrast to both. The compact centre, with pretty wooden chalets, ancient church and weekly market in the square, retains rural appeal, despite the resort as a whole having grown to spread thinly quite a distance over the valley. You can stay in the centre or near the lifts at **Le Lay**, a 1km bus ride away.

The resort's enviable snow record, said to be due to its proximity to Mont Blanc, together with a high proportion of shady northeast-facing slopes, means way above average snow reliability for a long season. Although the majority of the slopes (limited in extent compared with bigger-name resorts but still reasonably substantial) suit intermediate cruising best, experts can enjoy some decent off-piste and the Mont Blanc lift pass covers other resorts in the area, so you should not get bored if you are prepared to travel. For beginners, the nursery slopes at both the village and mid-mountain are fine, but there are few easy green runs to progress to.

Several rustic mountain restaurants add to the area's appeal for a relaxing time.

## Where to Stay in Les Contamines-Hauteluce

ⓘ **Les Contamines >**
*t 04 50 47 01 58,*
*www.lescontamines.com*

### Les Contamines

**\*\*\*Chemenaz**, t 04 50 47 02 44, *www.chemenaz.com* (€€–€). By the gondola in Les Contamines, a modern chalet, the only three-star place in town, with a sauna and a Jacuzzi.

# Les Aravis: La Clusaz, Le Grand-Bornand, St-Jean-de-Sixt (skiing not linked)

**La Clusaz Ski Area**

*height of slopes*
*1,100m–2,600m*
*number of lifts 55*

**Pistes**

*132km*

*green 28%*
*blue 36%*
*red 28%*
*black 8%*

**Le Grand-Bornand Ski Area**

*height of slopes*
*1,000m–2,100m*
*number of lifts 39*

**Pistes**

*82km*

*green 33%*
*blue 30%*
*red 30%*
*black 7%*

Few other major French ski resorts can claim to be based around what are still, essentially, genuine unpretentious mountain villages that exude rustic charm and Gallic atmosphere. And few others can be reached in an hour or so from Geneva airport via the beautiful lakeside town of Annecy or in a leisurely day's drive from the Channel ports. Combine these attractions with over 200km of largely intermediate slopes, above and below the tree line, spread over five linked sectors in La Clusaz and the separate Le Grand-Bornand area, and you can see why so many British families have decided to buy homes around here. If it weren't for the altitude, or rather the lack of it and therefore unreliable snow conditions, Les Aravis could attract many more winter visitors. Snowmaking has been installed in recent years and is continually increased, but of course it makes no difference in mild weather.

Most intermediates will love La Clusaz if the snow conditions are good. Early intermediates will delight in the gentle slopes at the top of **Beauregard** and over on **La Croix-Fry** at Manigod, with its network of tree-lined runs, and you can travel all over the area on gentle, green pistes. **L'Etale** and **L'Aiguille** have more challenging but wide blue runs, while more adventurous intermediates will prefer the steeper red pistes and good snow of the northwest-facing slopes of **La Balme** and the long red down **Combe du Fernuy** from L'Aiguille. Le Grand-Bornand is full of easy-cruising blue and red intermediate runs in both directions above Le Chinaillon.

For beginners, the nursery slope at village level in La Clusaz could not be more convenient, and the other, more snowsure ones up the mountain at the top of the Beauregard cable car and at **Crêt du Merle** are even better. The Beauregard area has lovely gentle blue runs to progress to, including one long run around the mountain right back to the village. Le Grand-Bornand and St-Jean-de-Sixt also feature good beginner slopes. The La Clusaz piste map doesn't seem to have much to offer experts, but most of the sectors offer decent off-piste, all the more attractive for being ignored by most visitors – don't miss the excellent run down **Combe de Borderan** from L'Aiguille and the **Combe de la Bellachat** reached from the top of La Balme. La Balme also has several fairly challenging pistes above mid-mountain, including the seriously steep black **Vraille** run, which leads to the speed skiing slope. The **Tetras** on L'Etale and the **Mur Edgar** run (named after local Olympic hero Edgar Grospiron) below Crêt du Loup on L'Aiguille have been reclassified as blacks, and rightly so. In Le Grand-Bornand the steepest runs, including the black **Noire du Lachat**, go from the top of **Le Lachat**.

**Cross-country** enthusiasts will also love Les Aravis, with around 70km of prepared trails to choose between, including a lovely sunny area at the top of the Beauregard cable car in La Clusaz and in the Vallée du Bouchet at Le Grand Bornand.

Built beside a fast-flowing stream at the junction of several wooded valleys, **La Clusaz**'s charming centre features old stone and wood buildings and a large church. Roads run from here in several directions, which is difficult to get to grips with initially, and the new buildings blend in well with the old. It has grown into quite a large sprawling place now, offering facilities such as a huge open-air swimming pool with fabulous views of the mountains. Every Monday evening a jolly welcome meeting in the main square allows you to mingle with locals and fellow guests and sample local cheeses and *vin chaud*. **Le Grand-Bornand,** a ten-minute free bus ride away, exudes the feel of remaining a quiet, unspoiled mountain village based around its Baroque church, despite having two gondolas up to the slopes. Much of the new development has taken place up the road at the chalet-style development of **Le Chinaillon,** served by chairlifts up into the skiing. Local farmers open their doors weekly to visitors, and Wednesday is market day, with a special wholesale market of local Reblochon cheese as well.

The small hamlet of **St-Jean-de-Sixt**, midway between La Clusaz and Le Grand Bornand, has a small slope for beginners and for tobogganing.

### La Clusaz Ski Schools

Sno-Academie, t 04 50 32 66 05, www.snowboard.com: smaller school providing good personal service

Aravis Challenge, t 04 50 02 81 29, www.aravischallenge.com: as above, but also includes off-piste and freestyle courses

### Le Grand-Bornand Ski School

Starski, t 04 50 27 04 69, www.esistarski.com: a small international school based in Chinaillon

ⓘ **La Clusaz >**
t 04 50 32 65 00, www.laclusaz.com

ⓘ **Le Grand-Bornand >**
t 04 50 02 78 00, www.legrandbornand.com

ⓘ **St-Jean-de-Sixt**
t 04 50 02 70 14, www.saintjeandesixt.com

## Where to Stay in Les Aravis

### La Clusaz

***Beauregard, t 04 50 32 68 00, www.hotel-beauregard.fr (€€€–€€).** Chalet-style buildings, with big pool, sauna, steam room, Jacuzzi and gym, on the fringe of the village. Good for families.

***Chalets de la Serraz, t 04 50 02 48 29, www.laserraz.com (€€€–€€)** wonderful old chalet beautifully converted to a small hotel, set in a peaceful position 4km from town, with a restaurant renowned for its excellent local cuisine.

### Le Grand-Bornand

**Le Chalet des Troncs, t 04 50 02 28 50, www.chaletdestroncs.com (€€€€).** A magnificent 18th-century chalet hotel with just 4 rooms, peaceful and beautifully decorated, with restaurant, pool and spa.

****Croix Saint-Maurice, t 04 50 02 20 05, www.hotel-lacroixstmaurice.com** (€€–€). Good-value chalet in the heart of the old town, right by the church and ski bus stop for La Clusaz.

### Catered Chalets

None of the big tour operators features Les Aravis, but plenty of private chalets are available, such as the old farmhouse out of town now run by **Aravis Alpine Retreat, t (020) 8878 8760.**

## Eating Out in Les Aravis

### In the Resorts

**La Clusaz: Les Chalets de la Serraz** (*see* left) has some of the best food in the region. In La Clusaz itself, the **Ecuelle** stands out for its Savoyard specialities.

**Le Grand-Bornand: La Ferme du Lormay** in the Vallée du Bouchet, 5km from Le Grand-Bornand, serves good-value local food with a heavy emphasis on cheese and polenta in an ancient Savoyard farmhouse.

### On the Mountain

The aptly named, creaky old **Vieux Chalet** just above La Clusaz near the top of the gondola is pleasant for a leisurely lunch, inside or out, and easily accessible for pedestrians too. The **Vieille Ferme** at Merdassier makes a splendid place for a serious lunch away from hustle and bustle.

### Bars and Clubs in Les Aravis

**La Clusaz**: It doesn't really get lively except at weekends. The **Caves du Paccaly** has live music, and **Pub Le Salto** Sky TV and draught Guinness. The **Ecluse** disco and **Club 18**, which often has live bands, liven up later.

## Savoie: The Tarentaise Valley

### Le Grand Domaine: Valmorel, Doucy-Combelouvière, St-François-Longchamp

**Le Grand Domaine Ski Area**

*height of slopes 1,250m–2,550m*

*number of lifts 56*

**Pistes**

*60km*

*green 33%*

*blue 39%*

*red 19%*

*black 9%*

If you have ever been to any of the Tarentaise resorts you will have driven past the turn-off to Valmorel, the major resort in the Grand Domaine ski area. That's what most people do, ignoring one of the most sympathetically designed French purpose-built ski resorts. It shares its slopes with two less popular and less attractive modern ski stations – St-François and Longchamp.

The ski area, though not as huge as its near neighbours, links the Tarentaise with the Maurienne valley and contains several distinct sectors divided by ridges and valleys either side of the **Col de la Madeleine**, which makes it interestingly varied and attractive to intermediates of all standards. The main **Planchamp** red run back to the village, lined with snow-guns, can be quite challenging towards the end of the day if the bumps have built up; for an easier option, take the alternative blue. Good intermediates should not miss the red and black in the **Gollet** sector and a day out to the far end of St-François-Longchamp and back. The area also provides lots of scope for trying a bit of off-piste between the main pistes.

Experts won't find many pistes to challenge them: those from the top of the **Mottet** chair and the nearby **Riondet** drag are some of the steepest and most interesting. But you'll find plenty of little-skied off-piste. To make the most of it, hire a guide and explore runs such as those along the fabulous north-facing valley from near the top of the **Lozière** chair, where the snow stays good for long after a fresh snowfall. You can also traverse from the top of the Gollet sector and ski down to the old village of **Les Avanchers**, way below Valmorel, passing through forests and over streams on the way.

Few resorts can boast anything as good for beginners as the excellent nursery slopes, isolated from better skiers racing through and yet right in the centre of the village. Speedy progress can be made here and on very easy green runs higher up.

**Valmorel**'s low-rise buildings, with liberal use of wood and coloured walls, and short traffic-free main street lined with shops and restaurants, give the resort a cheerful, family-friendly

**Valmorel Ski School**

*ESF, t 04 79 09 81 86, www.esf-valmorel.com: has an especially high reputation for teaching children and beginners*

## Where to Stay in Le Grand Domaine

(i) **Valmorel** >
*t 04 79 09 85 55,*
*www.valmorel.com*

(i) **Doucy-Combelouvière**
*t 04 79 22 94 17,*
*www.doucy-combelouvière.com*

(i) **St-François-Longchamp**
*t 04 79 59 10 56,*
*www.otsfl.com*

### Valmorel

**\*\*Hôtel du Bourg, t 04 79 09 86 66,**
*www.hoteldubourg.com* (€€–€).
A central position on the main street, with perfectly OK, good-value basic accommodation.

### Catered Chalets

**Valmorel: Neilson, t** 0870 333 3347, has a chalets targeted at families.

## Eating Out in Le Grand Domaine

**Valmorel:** The **Grange** is the place for Savoyard specialities, **Le Petit Prince** for pizzas and grills and **Jimbo Lolo** for tapas and Tex-Mex.

## Bars and Clubs in Le Grand Domaine

Don't come here for lively *après-ski*. The bar and restaurant terraces at the bottom of the main slope back to Valmorel are good for a beer. **Les Nuits Blanches** is the local disco.

atmosphere, with almost a Disneyesque feel to it. The main high-speed chairlift out and piste back are at one end of the main street, and at the other a step-on lift for pedestrians and skiers alike works until late to serve a number of higher accommodation 'hamlets' and the Pierrafort gondola. Below Valmorel, reached by a gentle blue and then even gentler green run and set prettily in the trees, **Doucy-Combelouvière** appeals to those looking for a quiet time. **St-François-Longchamp**, more starkly set just above the tree line, has more of a conventional purpose-built resort feel, with some chalet-style but mainly bigger, more block-like buildings (some of which are now being smartened up).

## Les Trois Vallées: Courchevel, La Tania, Méribel, Brides-les-Bains, St-Martin-de-Belleville, Les Menuires, Val-Thorens

**Les Trois Vallées Ski Area**
*height of slopes 1,260m–3,230m*
*number of lifts 182*

**Pistes**
*600km*
*green 17%*
*blue 34%*
*red 37%*
*black 12%*

Even the keenest skier or snowboarder will find that the 600km of linked pistes and 1,400 sq km of ski-able terrain **Les Trois Vallées** boasts will keep them busy for a week. Indeed, it would keep most people happy for a season. Nowhere else approaches this scale of ski *domaine*, where you have to take your skis or board off only to have lunch or ride the gondolas or cable cars among the 182 lifts that can carry 260,000 people an hour. While Les Portes du Soleil claims 650km of pistes and over 200 lifts, there are gaps between its pistes where you have to walk or take a bus.

The dream of linking the Saint-Bon, Allues and Belleville valleys from Courchevel at one end to Val-Thorens at the other began in 1925 but was not fully realized until 1975. Since then the ski area has expanded yet again, into the Maurienne valley beyond Val-Thorens, and should really be renamed Les Quatre Vallées, but that would be a waste of the millions francs and euros that have been ploughed into the marketing of this vast commercial enterprise.

From early December until late April, you can usually explore the whole area. But the 3,000m peaks and glaciers towering above Val-Thorens mean that this resort has one of the longest winter seasons in Europe, stretching from early November until May.

Intermediates of every standard will find the Trois Vallées a paradise, with over two-thirds of the pistes graded blue or red and most of them immaculately groomed every night. If you want to step out on to perfect corduroy-style pistes every morning without travelling 5,000 miles to the USA, this is the place to head for. The area seems to be on a mission to match the high standards of service in US ski areas in general, and Courchevel and Méribel have copied the useful US practice of having free maps available every morning showing which pistes have been groomed overnight. There is no point in picking out particular intermediate runs – suffice to say that, wherever you go, you won't be disappointed. Beginners are well-catered for too, at all the major resorts, with good nursery slopes and easy green runs to progress to.

Many experts deride the Trois Vallées as being simply for intermediates. It is true that only 12 per cent of the pistes are graded black. But among them are some real challenges. Courchevel offers the most steep black runs including the awesome **Grand Couloir**, near the top of the Saulire cable car, where the north-facing slope generally has excellent powder and is reached via a vertigo-inducing precipitous path. **Suisse** and **Chanrossa**, also near Saulire, are two of the longest, steepest mogul runs around. Lower down, leading to the lowest of Courchevel's villages, **Le Praz**, both **Jockeys** and **Jean Blanc** are entertaining blacks so long as the snow is good. In Méribel, head for the **Face**, which was created as the ladies downhill run for the 1992 Olympics, or for the **Combe de Vallon**, which is a real test of stamina despite being graded as a mere red. In Les Menuires, try the **La Masse** area where the steep blacks and reds usually have some of the best snow around because of their north-facing orientation. In Val-Thorens, for warp-speed cruising you can't beat the **Combe de Caron** run after it has been groomed – it will be well worth the wait for the cable car up, which is the only serious queue left in the Trois Vallées.

There is excellent off-piste to be explored with a guide – and most of it deserted compared with ski areas with a more macho image such as L'Espace Killy and Chamonix.

Nearly all the major resorts in the area, which between them have 140,000 beds, have been purpose-built – some with more panache and style than others. At the northern end, in the Saint-Bon valley, the highest of Courchevel's four main villages, **Courchevel 1850** is one of the chicest and most expensive ski resorts in Europe, with more four-star hotels than any city in France outside Paris. When you consider that they all have to make their

## Courchevel and Méribel Ski Schools

*New Generation*, **t** 04 79 01 03 18, www.skinewgen.com: highly rated and British-run, staffed largely by go-ahead young, highly qualified British instructors; started in Courchevel in the 1990s and opened in Méribel a few years later and generates rave reviews from most customers

*Magic in Motion*, **t** 04 79 01 01 81 (Courchevel), **t** 04 79 08 53 36 (Méribel), www. magicinmotion.co.uk: started in Méribel and expanded to Courchevel and other Trois Vallées resorts and also has a good reputation

money in a four-month season, it comes as no surprise that they charge sky-high prices. But the Paris jet set and *nouveau-riche* Russians happily pay them. British guests tend to stay in more affordable catered chalets or self-catering apartments. Most buildings here are no more than three or four storeys and had wood cladding and pitched roofs added to improve their appearance for the 1992 Olympics.

**Courchevel 1650**, with its old village square and friendly, less upmarket feel, has grown in a higgledy-piggledy fashion with different architectural styles either side of the road up to 1850. The food shops here are much better than in its upmarket neighbour, with an excellent butcher, baker and delicatessen. **Courchevel 1550** is set off the main road in a quiet position, but its square block-like buildings and absence of animation means it lacks character and focus. The same cannot be said of the lowest village, **Courchevel 1300** (more commonly called **Le Praz**), which still retains an old village with narrow cobbled paths at its heart – though it was expanded hugely for the 1992 Olympics, which also resulted in a huge ski-jump hill being built at the foot of the slopes. Gondolas are the main way out of each of the villages, though the rickety old pair from Le Praz badly need replacing (and hopefully will have been by the time you go).

**La Tania**
**Ski School**
*Magic in Motion,*
*t 04 79 01 07 85,*
*www.magicinmotion.*
*co.uk: the branch here*
*is specially highly*
*thought of for its*
*teaching of children*

Between Le Praz and Méribel, **La Tania** was built to house the press for the 1992 Olympics and its apartments and chalets, prettily set in the woods, now make a small, family-friendly resort with a traffic-free centre and an efficient gondola to the slopes.

There are few other resorts in the Alps that are as British as **Méribel** in the central Allues valley. Conceived and kick-started by Colonel Peter Lindsay in the 1930s and '40s, either side of the Second World War, many of its chalets are British-owned and the British population in winter appears to exceed the French. From the start, strict architectural guidelines were laid down limiting development to the traditional wooden chalet-style – so the resort escaped the architectural excesses that so many other French resorts suffered from. But the place has been allowed to expand hugely across the mountainside, with much of the newer development a bus ride from the slopes. **Méribel-Mottaret** is a rather soulless satellite a few kilometres up the valley with a traffic-free centre and convenient ski-in, ski-out accommodation.

Way below Méribel at an altitude of only 600m, the old spa town of **Brides-les-Bains** was very quiet in winter before a gondola was built linking it in 25 minutes to Méribel. It now makes a budget base from which to explore the slopes – but the last gondola back down leaves at around 5pm.

**St-Martin-**
**de-Belleville**
**Ski School**
*ESF, t 04 79 00 24 78,*
*www.esf-st-martin-*
*belleville.com*

The old village of **St-Martin-de-Belleville**, the administrative capital of the third (Belleville) valley, has a lovely 16th-century church, prettily floodlit at night. In 1950 it didn't even have running water or electricity and, while resorts around it developed in the 1960s and '70s, it wasn't until the 1980s that it was linked by a chairlift into the slopes – now replaced by a gondola. The resort has expanded slowly, with all new buildings in the original stone and wood style, and still retains a small and traditional village feel.

The next resort up the valley, **Les Menuires**, could not be in more stark contrast. The resort centre of **La Croisette** and its immediate neighbouring buildings are monstrous concrete blocks – some of them huge – with cheaply built apartments and a dark and tatty indoor shop and restaurant complex. But things have started to improve. The newest developments of **Reberty** and **Hameau des Marmottes** have been built in smart chalet style. And for several years they have been trying to smarten up the centre by different landscaping techniques; in November 2006 they even demolished one of the monstrous blocks, which will be replaced by another traditional chalet-style building due to open at Christmas 2008.

Further on up the road at the head of the valley, **Val-Thorens** (at 2,300m Europe's highest resort) forms the most snowsure part of the Trois Vallées. Despite its bleak setting, high above the tree line beneath towering peaks, this purpose-built resort has a more welcoming feel than Les Menuires, with smaller, mainly medium-rise and wood-clad buildings with car-free streets and squares and ski-in, ski-out convenience for most accommodation. When it's sunny here it makes an excellent base. When it's snowing hard, whiteout conditions can make it feel very inhospitable.

**Les Menuires Ski School**

*ESF, t 04 79 00 61 43, www.esf-lesmenuires. com*

**Val-Thorens Ski Schools**

*ESF, t 04 79 00 02 86, www.esf-valthorens. com: has a special group to explore the pistes and off-piste of the whole Trois Vallées – you can join just for a day or for the week*

*Prosneige, t 04 79 01 07 00, www.prosneige.fr: runs everything from beginner and children's classes to heli-skiing and a five-day off-piste course*

(i) **Courchevel** >
*t 04 79 08 00 29, www.courchevel.com*

(i) **Les Menuires** >>
*t 04 79 00 73 00, www.lesmenuires.com*

(i) **Brides-les-Bains**
*t 04 79 55 20 64, www.brides-les-bains.com*

(i) **Val-Thorens** >>
*t 04 79 00 08 08, www.valthorens.com*

(i) **Méribel** >
*t 04 79 08 60 01, www.meribel.net*

## Where to Stay in Les Trois Vallées

### Courchevel

You can spend a fortune staying in one of 16 plush four-star hotels, but there are cheaper options too.

****Mélézin**, t 04 79 08 01 33, *www.amanresorts.com* (€€€€€). On the piste just above the centre of 1850, extremely stylish and luxurious, with bathrooms overlooking superb views of the mountains. Pool, steam room, Jacuzzi, gym.

***Peupliers**, t 04 79 08 41 47, *www.lespeupliers.com* (€€€). Near the piste and lifts at 1300, a beautifully renovated and expanded old chalet with a good value, varied restaurant.

### Méribel

****Grand Cœur**, t 04 79 08 60 03, *www.legrandcoeur.com* (€€€€€–€€€€).

Wonderful old chalet just above the village centre near the piste, splendid comfortable lounge with grand piano, sauna, steam room, Jacuzzi, gym.

****Adray Télébar**, t 04 79 08 60 26, *www.telebar-hotel.com* (€€€). Lovely ancient chalet, peacefully positioned in the woods by the piste above the village, with a popular restaurant (lunchtime as well as evenings).

### Les Menuires

****Hôtel Kaya**, t 04 79 41 42 00, *www.hotel-kaya.com* (€€€€€–€€€). Big Japanese-styled luxury hotel on the piste, with a minimalist look in the rooms and the restaurant, Le K. Pool, sauna and relaxing spa treatments.

### Val-Thorens

****Fitz Roy**, t 04 79 00 04 78, *www.fitzroyhotel.com* (€€€€€–€€€€). Sumptuous modern Relais et Châteaux chalet on the slopes in

**ⓘ St-Martin-de-Belleville**
*t 04 79 00 20 00,*
*www.st-martin-belleville.com*

**ⓘ La Tania**
*t 04 79 08 40 40,*
*www.latania.com*

the centre of the resort, with superb piste-side terrace, pool, sauna, salon.

**\*\*\*Sherpa, t 04 79 00 00 70, *www.lesherpa.com* (€€€–€€).** Smart, friendly new chalet near top of resort, with special offers for children sharing parents' room. Sauna, Jacuzzi.

### Apartments
**Courchevel**: High-quality apartments include the **Forum** in the centre of 1850 and the **Montagnettes** in 1650.

**Les Menuires**: **Montagnettes** and **Alpages**, both in Reberty and the latter with a pool, are smart newish developments, far superior to the dire apartments in the central La Croisette area.

**Méribel**: The **Fermes de Méribel Village** at the bottom of a chairlift in a new development 2km from Méribel centre are well furnished with lots of beams and wood, good views, pool, sauna, steam room and gym.

**Val-Thorens**: A huge choice of smart apartments – some of the best include **Oxalys** (with pool, sauna, steam room, Jacuzzi and excellent restaurant), **Montagnettes**, **Balcons de Val-Thorens** and **Village Montana**.

### Catered Chalets
The Trois Vallées is the catered chalet capital of the world. Huge numbers of UK tour operators have chalets in all the main resorts (over 50 feature Méribel, for example).

**Courchevel 1850**: Full of luxury chalets; tour operators who specialize in them include **Flexiski, t 0870 9090 754**, **Supertravel, t (020) 7962 9933**, and **Scott Dunn, t (020) 8682 5050**.

**Courchevel 1650**: **Le Ski, t 0870 7544 444**, has a varied selection of conveniently located, mid-market options.

**Méribel**: Check the position of chalets carefully – some are a long way from lifts and pistes (though many tour operators have minibuses to shuttle guests to and fro). **Meriski, t (01285) 648 515**, has specialized in upmarket Méribel chalets for over 20 years. Other deluxe options include **Descente International, t (020) 7384 3854**, **Supertravel, t (020) 7962 9933**, **Scott Dunn, t (020) 8682 5050**, **Snowline, t (020) 8870 4807**, and **VIP, t (020) 8875 1957**. **Bonne Neige**,

**t (01270) 256 966**, **Purple Ski, t (01494) 488 633**, **Ski Blanc, t (020) 8502 9082** and **Ski Total, t 0871 633 633**, all have good chalets. **Mark Warner, t 0870 7704 226**, has a big chalet-hotel right on the piste at Méribel-Mottaret.

**St-Martin-de-Belleville**: The **Alpine Club, t 07977 465285**, has two chalets with good food. **Chalets de St-Martin, t (01202) 473 255**, features self-catered apartments and chalets as well as a catered chalet.

## Eating Out in Les Trois Vallées

### In the Resorts
**Courchevel 1850**: The **Bateau Ivre** and **Chabichou** in 1850 both have two Michelin stars and prices to match. The cosy **La Saulire** (also known as **Chez Jacques**) is more affordable and offers Savoyard specialities, while **La Locomotive** with its railway-themed décor has a big, varied menu and the **Potinière** is a budget option for pizza, steak or pasta.

**Courchevel 1850**: The **Petit Savoyard**, **Montagne** and **Eterlou** are close together and do good steaks as well as Savoyard specialities.

**Courchevel 1300**: The **Peupliers** (*see* 'Where to Stay') has built a good reputation since its refurbishment.

**Méribel**: **Croix Jean-Claude** down in Les Allues, a taxi-ride from the centre, serves good honest local food such as rabbit and lake fish in a pleasant rustic dining room, away from the bustle of the main resort. In Méribel itself, the **Grand Cœur** (*see* 'Where to Stay') has the highest reputation for *haute cuisine*, **Chez Kiki** is famous for charcoal-grilled meats, **Cro-Magnon** specializes in fondue, raclette and pizza.

**St-Martin-de-Belleville**: People come from miles around to the excellent cuisine of the prettily presented, traditonal *auberge* of **La Bouitte** in nearby St-Marcel, which is famous for its *foie gras*, veal, cheeses and dessert trolley and has a Michelin star.

**Val-Thorens**: **L'Oxalys** opened for the 2002/3 season and thoroughly deserves its recently awarded

Michelin star (the highest restaurant in France to have one): it serves the best classic French cuisine in town and has superb views from its piste-side terrace. **Galoubet** is excellent for Savoyard specialities such as *pierrade* and *tartiflette*. For Tex-Mex, try **El Gringo's**.

## On the Mountain

**Courchevel:** Beware of the **Chalet de Pierres** and **Cap Horn**, two of the most expensive mountain restaurants in the Alps. Much better value are the **Soucoupe** (table- and self-service) near the top of the Verdons gondola, and the simple menu (including excellent *omelette savoyarde*) and sunny three-tier terrace of **Bel Air** at the top of the gondola from 1650.

**Méribel:** The **Altibar** has a lovely peaceful sun terrace and a varied menu, the **Altiport hotel terrace** serves an excellent buffet and *steak tartare*, and the **Chardonnet**, at the mid-station of the Mottaret-Saulire gondola, is a wonderful suntrap. For a cheaper, quicker option try **Rond Point**, just below the mid-station of the Rhodos gondola, for the tasty paninis.

**Les Menuires:** The old chalet of **L'Etoile**, on the piste just above the resort, with a rustic interior and sunny terrace, features waiters in traditional costume.

**Val-Thorens:** **Bar de la Marine**, on the Dalles piste, does good grills and *plat du jour*, has a decent wine list and a nautical theme.

## Bars and Clubs in Les Trois Vallées

**Courchevel:** If you want lots of nightlife, head for 1850. **Jump**, at the bottom of the main pistes, is popular when the lifts close. Later on, the exclusive **Caves** nightclub, with top Paris cabaret acts and sky-high prices, and **Kalico**, with DJs and cocktails, get busy. The **Bergerie** does themed evenings of food, music and entertainment. Down in 1650, the **Bubble** and **Rocky's** bars are the focal points, with a largely British clientele.

**Méribel:** **Rond Point** by the piste gets packed as the lifts close and often has live music; the **Taverne** and **Pub** in the main square and **Rastro** and **Downtown** at Mottaret attract the crowds too. Later on, **Scott's**, in the main square, and **Dick's Tea Bar**, on the road below the centre, have late dancing.

**St-Martin-de-Belleville:** **Pourquoi Pas?** piano bar with log fire and comfy sofas is a great contrast to **Brewski's**, the other main bar with its wooden chairs and tables, photos of 1960s and '70s rock groups and occasional live bands – both are British-run.

**Val-Thorens:** The **Frog and Roastbeef** attracts a lot of British customers with its cut-price beer and often a live band at teatime, and claims to be the highest pub in Europe. The **Red Fox** has teatime karaoke and also attracts the crowds. Later on, the **Underground** nightclub and **Malaysia** cellar bar are the places to head for.

## Paradiski: Les Arcs, La Grande Plagne, Peisey Vallandry

**Paradiski Ski Area**
*height of slopes*
*1,200m–3,225m*
*number of lifts 137*

**Pistes**
*425km*
*green 5%*
*blue 55%*
*red 28%*
*black 12%*

The world's largest cable car – a double-decker called the Vanoise Express which holds 200 people – opened in December 2003 to link two already famous ski areas. Spanning the 2km between **Montchavin** on the La Plagne slopes and **Plan Peisey** on the Les Arcs side in less than four minutes, it whisks you smoothly along, with stunning views towards the Plan Peisey side – be sure to face that way. The resulting joint ski *domaine*, called Paradiski, leapt into the record books as one of the biggest in the world. Only the Trois Vallées and the Portes du Soleil can legitimately claim significantly more than Paradiski's 425km of pistes and 137 lifts. Arguably, in terms of total skiing terrain including off-piste potential, Paradiski beats them both.

Both La Plagne and Les Arcs are classic examples of 1960s purpose-built ski resort development on previously deserted, high snowfields. Over the last 40 years, they have both developed big networks of ideal intermediate cruising runs, perfectly suited to the mass-market clientele they have aimed to attract. Plenty of beginners learn their skiing and snowboarding skills happily here, though once you progress from the nursery slopes there are no really easy long green runs to move on to, which is less than ideal. For experts, black runs near the top of both La Plagne and Les Arcs present worthwhile challenges; and don't miss one of the longest pistes in the Alps from the top of Les Arcs' **Aiguille Rouge** cable car down to **Villaroger** – a total vertical descent of over 2,000m.

Because most visitors to these resorts are intermediates, off-piste in both areas tends to be deserted and becomes tracked out much less quickly that in more macho resorts such as Val d'Isère. Good skiers willing to hire a guide will love epic off-piste runs such as the north face of **Bellecôte** and the run over the **Col du Nant** glacier to **Champagny-le-Haut** through the Vanoise National Park (both starting from the La Plagne area) and the **Combe de l'Anchette** from the Grand Col above Les Arcs to Villaroger.

None of **Les Arcs'** three oldest purpose-built traffic-free villages, unimaginatively named after their heights, can be described as attractive. Many of the big wood-clad apartment blocks do, however, offer the convenience of allowing you to ski to and from their doors. **Arc 1600**, the original Arc which opened in 1968, has the friendliest feel because of its setting in the trees and its fine views along the valley and towards Mont Blanc; it is also where the funicular up from Bourg-St-Maurice in the valley below arrives. By far the largest, with the widest variety of shops and restaurants, **Arc 1800** is the liveliest place to stay. **Arc 2000** sits bleakly on a shelf, way above the tree line, and consists of little more than a few giant blocks, including a Club Med. The newest village, **Arc 1950**, is completely different: it is the first European village to be created by Canadian resort developer Intrawest, who specialize in building attractive resort villages. True to form, Arc 1950's low-rise, chalet-

## Les Arcs Ski Schools

*New Generation,*
*t 04 79 01 03 18,*
*www.skinewgen.com:*
*this highly rated*
*British-run company*
*started a school based*
*in Vallandry in 2003/4*
*after establishing*
*itself in Courchevel*
*and Méribel*

*Spirit 1950, t 04 79 04*
*25 72, www.spirit1950.*
*com: with bilingual*
*instructors, based in Arc*
*1950, this has rapidly*
*built a good reputation*

*Arc Aventures, t 04 79*
*07 41 28, www.arc-*
*aventures.com:*
*the previous main*
*international school*

## High-speed Thrills

In 1992, Olympic athletes hurtled down the bobsleigh run in La Plagne. Now you can experience the thrills of reaching over 100kph and negotiating the 19 banked bends of the 1.5km track, which is opened and floodlit several times a week. You have the choice of a solo mono-bob, an Olympic 4-man bob with you sandwiched between the fully-trained driver and brakeman, or a slightly slower padded bob-raft where four tourists go it alone.

In Les Arcs, the 1992 Olympians hit speeds of well over 200kph in the speed skiing event. Now anyone with the nerve can try the famous 'flying kilometre' here – an immaculately groomed steep slope above Arc 2000 reserved specially for the event. You'll be supplied with special long, straight skis, a helmet and goggles, and win a bronze medal for hitting 110kph (nearly everyone does), silver for 130kph and gold for 150kph.

style curved buildings made from local wood and stone, set around a cobbled pedestrian street, offer a much more pleasant environment than the other Arc villages. But the apartments themselves are disappointingly small and cramped. Set just below Arc 2000 and linked by gondola lift till late at night, Arc 1950 opened its first phase for winter 2003/4 and is due to be complete by 2008.

The cable-car link to La Plagne, at the western end of the Les Arcs ski area, prompted rapid development (of low-rise chalet-style buildings) in that area too. **Plan Peisey** and **Vallandry** are side by side, with the latter having more of a focal point, with a pedestrianized square of shops and restaurants – a friendly, quiet place to stay and ideal for exploring the whole Paradiski area. For a more rustic base, the old village of **Peisey**, below here, is linked by lift but not piste and is still a largely unspoiled mountain village with few tourist trappings except a couple of restaurants.

At the **La Plagne** end of the cable-car link, the genuine old farming village of **Montchavin** has expanded in sympathetic style and makes a peaceful place to stay, with a fair choice of shops and restaurants around its car-free centre. Just above it, the new development of **Les Coches** has been built in similarly attractive chalet style. The contrast between these and the hideous cheap, purpose-built original high-altitude La Plagne accommodation centre of **Plagne-Centre**, with its claustrophobic underground shopping malls and restaurants, could not be starker. Two of the other high-altitude 'villages', **Plagne-Bellecôte** and **Aime La Plagne**, give a similar impression of being slung up to provide budget accommodation with little regard for the environment – huge apartment blocks are what you see and what you get. **Belle-Plagne** is the most attractive of the purpose-built villages, with low-rise buildings built to resemble typical Savoyard architecture.

At the southern end of the La Plagne ski area, furthest from the link to Les Arcs and way down in the valley at 1,250m (compared with the 2,000m or so of the purpose-built villages), **Champagny-en-Vanoise** makes another attractive place to stay. Like Montchavin it is based around an old mountain village, but it doesn't have quite the same rural feel to it, perhaps because it has developed along a winding approach road. A powerful gondola whisks you up to snow-sure slopes, but you may have to ride it down as well, because the runs home are often closed, as the snow suffers from their south-facing aspect and they have no snowmaking.

**La Plagne
Ski Schools**
*Evolution 2,
Montchavin,*
t 04 79 07 81 85,
*www.evolution2.com:
good personal service*

*Oxygène, Plagne-Centre,* t 04 79 09 03 99, *www.oxygene-ski.com: also good personal service*

*El Pro, Belle-Plagne,* t 04 79 09 11 62, *www.elpro.fr: also good personal service*

ⓘ **Les Arcs** >>
t 04 79 07 12 57,
*www.lesarcs.com*

## Where to Stay in Paradiski

There are very few hotels; most accommodation is apartments and chalets.

**Les Arcs**

\*\*\*Grand Hotel Paradiso (Arc 1800), t 04 79 07 65 00, *www.grand-hotel-lesarcs.com* (€€€). Relatively new and modern, locally judged to be worth four stars.

(i) **Peisey-Vallandry**
*t 04 79 07 94 28, www.
peisey-vallandry.com*

(i) **La Plagne** >
*t 04 79 09 79 79,
www.la-plagne.com*

(i) **Montchavin-les-Coches**
*t 04 79 07 82 82,
www.la-plagne.com*

(i) **Plagne Montalbert**
*t 04 79 09 77 33,
www.la-plagne.com*

(i) **Champagny-en-Vanoise**
*t 04 79 55 06 55,
www.la-plagne.com*

**L'Espace San Bernardo Ski Area**
*height of slopes
1,175m–2,650m
number of lifts 38*

**Pistes**
*150km*
*green 12%*
*blue 36%*
*red 35%*
*black 17%*

**\*\*Vanoise** (Plan-Peisey), **t** 04 79 07 92 19, *www.hotel-la-vanoise.com* (€€). Modern rooms, friendly staff, great views from restaurant, close to the cable-car to La Plagne.

## La Plagne
**\*\*Glières** (Champagny-en-Vanoise), **t** 04 79 55 05 52, *www.hotel-glieres. com* (€€). Rustic, varied rooms, friendly welcome, 100m from the gondola.

### Apartments
There are thousands to choose from in each resort. **Erna Low, t** 0870 7506 820, is the official UK representative for both Les Arcs and La Plagne.

**Les Arcs:** Arc 1950's smart new development and MGM's **Alpages de Chantel** above Arc 1800 and **Orée des Cîmes** in Peisey-Vallandry have access to pools, saunas and gyms.

**La Plagne: Montagnettes** in Belle-Plagne and MGM in Aime La Plagne are spacious and well-furnished, with views. In Champagny-en-Vanoise the **Alpages de Champagny** is an impressive chalet-style development, new for 2006/07 with a pool and sauna.

### Catered Chalets
**Peisey-Vallandry: Ski Olympic, t** (01302) 328 820, has a big chalet-hotel; **Ski Beat, t** (01243) 780 405 has attractive new chalets; and family-specialist **Esprit Ski, t** (01252) 618 300, has similar chalets and a nursery.

**La Plagne: Ski Beat, t** (01243) 780 405 has a wide selection throughout the resort; **Finlays, t** (01573) 226 611, has 5 smart chalets in or near Les Coches.

## Eating Out in Paradiski

### In the Resorts
**Les Arcs:** In 2000, **Chez Eux** is the place to go for Savoyard food. In 1800 the **Petit Zinc** restaurant in the Golf hotel has *haute cuisine* and high prices, and **Chalet Bouvier** and **Chalet de Millou** both have good French

food. In Peisey village, a 5min taxi-ride below Peisey-Vallandry, **L'Ancolie** is a delightful traditional *auberge* which serves generous portions of the best local produce, such as duck breast and rabbit, and offers good-value menus.

**La Plagne:** The **Refuge** in Plagne-Centre, decorated with bobsleigh memorabilia, claims to be the oldest restaurant in La Plagne (from 1961) and serves a wide-ranging menu. At Aime La Plagne the **Cave**, buried deep in the main block, is worth searching out for its excellent cuisine.

### On the Mountain
**Les Arcs:** The charmingly rustic 500-year-old **Belliou la Fumée** at Pre-St-Esprit below Arc 2000 boasts a lovely log fire in the centre of the main dining room and a varied menu. **Chalets de l'Arc**, above Arc 2000, though quite large and only a few years old, has been built in traditional style and features interesting *plats du jour*, such as chicken in vinegar.

**La Plagne: Chez Pat du Sauget**, above Montchavin, and **Au Bon Vieux Temps**, just below Aime La Plagne, are both small, rustic huts – very cosy and jolly on a snowy day. **Roc des Blanchets** at the top of the Champagny gondola has beautiful views to Courchevel and often offers free *Viperine* (a local liquor with a dead viper in the bottle) at the end of your meal.

## Bars and Clubs in Paradiski

**Les Arcs:** In 1800 the **Red Hot Saloon** and **Jungle Café** both have live music and the **Fairway** disco rocks till 4am.

**La Plagne:** The **Tête Inn** in Belle-Plagne resembles an English pub, **No Bl'm Café** in Plagne-Centre gets packed and has a huge TV and occasional live music, **Mine** in Plagne-1800 attracts lots of Brits and boasts an old train and mining artefacts.

## L'Espace San Bernardo/Sud Mont-Blanc: La Rosière and La Thuile (Italy)
Perched far above the most dramatic bend in the Isère valley, La Rosière occupies a sensational location with stunning views over to the slopes of the Les Arcs ski area on the other side of the

gorge. Its attractive, purpose-built, chalet-style buildings, set among trees on sunny slopes, give it a very friendly feel and make the least well-known and smallest of the major Tarentaise resorts particularly appealing to families. Kids also love the friendly St Bernard dogs kept at the far end of the resort – a dead end in winter, but open in summer when it forms the start of the Petit-St-Bernard pass over to Italy. Cross-border skiing to La Thuile in Italy forms another of the winter attractions and the joint area is now known as Espace San Bernardo.

**La Rosière** Ski Schools
*Evolution 2,*
*t 04 79 40 19 80,*
*www. evolution2.com:*
*receives high praise and*
*also organizes*
*heli-ski groups*

**La Rosière**'s own slopes are south-facing, which is unusual for a major French resort. But they can cope with the battering they get from the sun because of the unusually large amounts of snow they receive from storms funnelled up the Isère valley from the south-west. **La Thuile** in Italy, just over the Col de la Traversette, frequently gets much less snow – though what it does get stays in good condition because of the slopes being predominantly north-facing. But it is not unusual in cold weather to find hard, icy slopes in Italy and deep, soft snow in La Rosière. In warm weather, heading for Italy may be the best bet to avoid slush.

These cross-border options make La Rosière a good resort for intermediates. The top half of La Rosière's own slopes boast some fairly steep and challenging red runs, while the lower half are mainly gentle blues and greens. Over in Italy, you'll be struck by how crazy it is not to have a standardized piste-grading system between countries (in fact, there isn't even one between resorts in the same country, but that's a different story). Most of La Thuile's red runs would be blue elsewhere and most of its blues would be green; virtually the whole of the top half of the mountain on the Italian side is very easy cruising. Only the pistes down from mid-mountain to La Thuile village offer a significant challenge – a lovely red through the woods and a couple of genuinely steep blacks.

Nursery slopes both in the village centre and at the rapidly developing area of **Les Eucherts**, with a green run near the village and some gentle blues on the lower half of the mountain to progress to, make La Rosière a convenient resort for beginners. They'll enjoy the sun and the wonderful views over the valley, too.

Experts will find little excitement in La Rosière. The steepest pistes are on the lowest slopes where the snow quality can suffer badly from the sun, down the Marcassin run to Le Vaz and down the Ecudets and Eterlou runs to **Les Ecudets**. The black runs down to La Thuile usually have decent snow and certainly offer a challenge. But all this doesn't add up to much. The real attraction for experts is the **heli-skiing** on offer from Italy (heli-skiing is not allowed from the French side). You can be dropped (with a guide, of course) on the Ruitor glacier for a splendid 20km off-piste run that ends up near Ste-Foy, a short taxi-ride from La Rosière. The upper

## Where to Stay in L'Espace San Bernardo

**(i) La Rosière >**
*t 04 79 06 80 51,
www.larosiere.net*

### La Rosière

****Hôtel Matsuzaka, t** 04 79 07 53 13 (€€€€€). New luxury chalet-hôtel in Japanese style, at the foot of the piste, with seven rooms in two styles – Japanese or Savoyard – plus suites. An outside Japanese hot tub and sauna complete the elegant picture.

**Plein Soleil, t** 04 79 06 80 43 (€€–€). A cheerful little hotel in the centre with small, cosy rooms and restaurant and great views.

### Apartments

**La Rosière**: The best places are newly built, away from the centre at the rapidly developing area of Les Eucherts. The **Cimes Blanches** has an attractive pool, Jacuzzi and sauna and the **Balcons** offers smart accommodation for larger groups in spacious apartments, some with wood-burning stoves and all with Jacuzzis.

### Catered Chalets

**La Rosière**: For years **Ski Olympic**, **t** (01302) 328 820, was the only British chalet operator in La Rosière, and it now has four chalets and a chalet-hotel. Family specialist **Esprit Ski**, **t** (01252) 618 300, has eight chalets, all fairly central and all with access to reliable and comprehensive childcare facilities. **Crystal, t** 0870 160 6040, has five chalet-apartments in two separate buildings, one of which also houses its own crèche run by British nannies. Sister company **Thomson**, **t** 0870 606 1470, also has chalet-apartments in the same buildings and shares the child-care facilities. **Ski Beat** moved into the resort for its first season in 2006/7 and has seven chalet-apartments and its own childcare facilities in the same building at Les Eucherts.

## Eating Out and Bars in L'Espace San Bernardo

Many people come down the mountain for lunch, where **Relais du Petit St-Bernard** and **P'tit Relais** are popular (evenings as well as lunch).

Of the handful of bars, **Arpins** has karaoke, but the *après-ski* is generally quite quiet here.

part of this takes you through open powder fields with stunning views of crags and glaciers and the lower part meanders through the woods by a stream with summer dwellings dotted around.

La Rosière's buildings start along the winding road up from the valley town of **Séez** and culminate in the tiny resort 'centre' – which is actually the top of the approach road and foot of the main slopes. There isn't more to it than a few shops, bars, restaurants and hotels at the village centre, with more now being built, along with accommodation at the alternative base of Les Eucherts, served by its own chairlift onto the slopes. The small scale of the resort and the pleasant, low-rise architecture contrast hugely with the hustle and bustle and big block-like buildings of nearby Tignes and La Plagne, for example.

*Ste-Foy-Tarentaise
Ski Area
height of slopes
1,550m–2,620m
number of lifts 5*

**Pistes**
*30km
green 8%
blue 15%
red 54%
black 23%*

### Ste-Foy-Tarentaise

Despite a recent building boom, Ste-Foy-Tarentaise is still one of the great undiscovered gems of the Rhône-Alpes. Tucked away just a short drive from big name resorts such as Val d'Isère, Les Arcs, Tignes and La Plagne, Ste-Foy offers some of the most deserted off-piste terrain in the region. Ski instructors and mountain guides from the bigger resorts come here on their days off and bring their favourite clients to find untracked powder, days after the last snowfall. If you want to see it in its pristine form, go now.

You'll see the valley village of **Ste-Foy-Tarentaise** on the approach to Tignes and Val d'Isère, where a tiny road branches off for Villaroger and a chairlift link up towards Les Arcs. Carry on a short distance and you'll come across La Thuile; turn left here and you are on the approach road up to the Ste-Foy lift base (also known as Bonconseil) and the brand new resort village (it has all been built in chalet-style using local wood and stone in the last few years).

**Ste-Foy-Tarentaise
Ski Schools**

*ESF, t 04 79 06 96 76,
www.saintefoy.net/
esf-a.htm: the only
school here; organizes
off-piste groups*

*Guides Office of Ste-Foy,
t 06 14 62 90 24,
www.guide-montagne-
tarentaise.com: for off-
piste and heli-skiing*

Three successive quad chairlifts take you up to **Col de l'Aiguille** over the handful of deserted pistes on offer. The 2006/7 season saw the resort's first high-speed chairlift open up more terrain and two more pistes in an area previously reachable only by traversing and hiking. Despite the recent development, it still counts as a busy day in Ste-Foy if you see someone else on a chairlift in front of you, and the few people who do come here don't normally do so for the pistes. If you want to stick to the marked trails, you'll end up skiing the same delightfully uncrowded slopes. The 1,000m vertical of empty red runs is ideal for confidence-building and high-speed carving, while a couple of black runs and one blue add a bit of variety. Keen intermediates, though, will probably be champing at the bit to spend some time at one of the nearby mega-resorts.

While not the best place for beginners, Ste-Foy now has a moving carpet on the nursery slopes at the base and a new children's area. There's a green run to progress to from the top of the first chairlift and a couple of gentle blues from the top of the second.

Expert skiers and boarders will love the off-piste. You can see endless possibilities on the front face from the chairlifts as you ride up and much of this is good for trying off-piste terrain for the first time. But local guides will show you wonderful, long runs from the top which take you away from all signs of civilization. One classic run takes you down through the ruined old village of **Le Monal** and ends up on the road between Ste-Foy and Val d'Isère. Another starts with a hike up to **Pointe de la Foglietta**, and descends through trees and over a stream to the tiny village of **Le Crot**. The possibilities are enormous – but you will need a guide.

The first chalets were completed at the foot of the slopes in time for winter 2001/2. Since then, the first phase of development of 1,700 beds in attractively built chalets and chalet-style apartments has been completed, including some with access to a pool and leisure facilities. There is also a handful of restaurants and bars, a supermarket and a few other shops. The focus for new building has now shifted to the other side of the lift base area. Despite the recent development, it's still a good idea to have a car or to stay at one of the chalets which have minibuses to shuttle you around to the scattered restaurants and nearby resorts.

## Where to Stay in Ste-Foy-Tarentaise

ⓘ Ste-Foy-
Tarentaise ›
*t 04 79 06 95 19,
www.saintefoy.net*

### Ste-Foy-Tarentaise

**La Ferme du Baptieu**, t 04 79 06 97 52, *www.lafermedubaptieu.com* (€€€). A beautifully restored 18th century farmhouse, at 1,100m, with great views, five rooms and a suite, and a Jacuzzi.

**Auberge sur la Montagne**, t 04 79 06 95 83, *www.auberge-montagne.co.uk* (€€). Just above the turn off at La Thuile, run by British owners Sue and Andy Mac, with lots of old wooden beams, wholesome French food, recently refurbished bedrooms. Sauna and outdoor Jacuzzi.

**Le Monal**, t 04 79 06 90 07, *www.le-monal.com* (€). In the valley hamlet of Ste-Foy-Tarentaise, basic rooms, bar popular with locals, two restaurants.

### Apartments

Lots of smart places are now available at the slopes, bookable through the tourist office – see its website.

### Catered Chalets

**Ste-Foy-Tarentaise: Première Neige**, t 07092 000 300, and **Gîte de Sainte Foy-station**, t 04 79 06 97 18, both have several smart chalets and apartments, with catered and self-catered options. The former will also transport you around to different ski areas. Luxurious **Yellow-Stone Chalet**, t 04 79 06 96 06, has a huge living room with a big stone fireplace, six double bedrooms, sauna and a Jacuzzi with panoramic valley views.

## Eating Out in Ste-Foy-Tarentaise

### In the Resort

A few places have opened in the resort of Ste-Foy itself, the most upmarket of which is the **Bergerie** (which offers a delivery service as well as eat-in). **Chez Mérie** in the hamlet of Le Miroir is delightfully rustic with a varied menu from steaks to local specialities. The **Grange** in Hôtel Le Monal has built a fine reputation.

### On the Mountain

At Plan Bois at the top of the first chairlift, **Chez Léon** has Savoyard specialities, a charcoal grill and a terrace, and **Brevettes** does good simple food including omlettes.

## Bars and Clubs in Ste-Foy-Tarentaise

Don't come here for lively *après-ski*. At the ski station, the **Iceberg** piano bar is popular and the **Pitchouli** has table football and live music. The **Hôtel Le Monal bar** is popular with locals and typically French – a refreshing change from many of the bars packed with Brits and Scandinavians in nearby Val d'Isère.

## L'Espace Killy: Val d'Isère and Tignes

**L'Espace Killy
Ski Area**
*height of slopes
1,550m–3,455m
number of lifts 90*

**Pistes**
*300km
green 15%
blue 40%
red 28%
black 17%*

Local hero Jean-Claude Killy gained demigod status by winning three gold medals at the 1968 Grenoble Winter Olympics, went on to spearhead the organization of the 1992 Albertville Winter Olympics, and was appointed President of the Coordination Commission for the 2006 Turin Winter Olympics. Between times he received the ultimate accolade of having one of Europe's best and most snow-sure ski areas named after him. Val d'Isère has now been chosen to host the 2009 World Ski Championships.

With Val d'Isère at 1,850m, Tignes at 2,100m and slopes (including two glaciers) going up to 3,455m, L'Espace Killy boasts a longer season than virtually any other ski area in France, lasting from November till May. The **Grande Motte** glacier in Tignes also opens for summer skiing and boarding; in winter the snow normally remains delightfully light and powdery here. Constant improvement of the lift system has generally made lift queues a thing of the past. Powerful gondolas whisk you out of both Val d'Isère and Tignes-le-Lac, and high-speed underground funiculars run from Val d'Isère to the top of Bellevarde and from Tignes-Val-Claret to the Grande Motte. High-speed chairlifts abound, and one of the world's first eight-seater chairs serves the Tovière link from Val d'Isère to Tignes.

The 300km of pistes suit intermediates best. But beware: grading is inconsistent and you'll come across blues that would be reds elsewhere and reds that would be black. The runs at the top of all the sectors, but especially the **Le Fornet** and **Solaise** areas of Val d'Isère, offer the easiest cruising, whereas the runs back down to the valley tend to be the steepest of all. The long reds and blues from the Grande Motte to Tignes-Val-Claret and **L'Aiguille Percée** to Tignes-les-Brévières are delightful for good intermediates, who should also consider exploring some of the easy off-piste throughout the area with the help of a guide.

Only the brave should tackle the serious black runs, especially the Face run from the top of **Bellevarde** to Val d'Isère, which is often covered in huge moguls for much of its length. The **Face** was the venue for the 1992 Olympic downhill and judged by the racers to be too steep and dangerous (so the World Cup Première Neige downhill held in Val d'Isère every December reverted to the old OK piste from Bellevarde to La Daille).

Experts will love the steep on-piste challenges but, even more so, some of the best and most extensive lift-served off-piste terrain in the world. This extends right from one end of the ski area to the other with, at the Val d'Isère end, the fabulous **Col Pers** run from near the top of the **Pissaillas glacier** above Le Fornet which, if the snow is good, ends in the **Gorges de Malpasset**, where you ski over the frozen Isère river back to the Le Fornet cable car. At the Tignes end, as well as lots of routes off the Grande Motte glacier you can ski from **Col du Palet** all the way over the back and through the Vanoise National Park to Champagny, part of the La Plagne ski area.

For beginners, neither resort is ideal. Both may have good nursery slopes, largely free of through-traffic of accomplished skiers and boarders, but Tignes offers no easy green runs to progress to and Val d'Isère no easy runs back down to the village – you'll have to catch the lifts back.

The two resorts contrast sharply in character. Set in a deep valley, way below the source of the Isère river and the Col de l'Iseran, one of highest passes in the Alps (shut in winter of course), **Val d'Isère** first developed as a ski resort in the early 1930s. Although the old village and an 11th-century church still form its heart, a huge amount of more modern construction has gone on, with largely

## Val d'Isère Ski Schools

*Snow Fun, t 04 79 06 19 79, www.valfun.com: one of the first ski schools here to cater specifically for English-speakers and now has over 60 instructors*

*Mountain Masters, t 04 79 06 05 14, www.mountain-masters.com: has a mixture of highly qualified British and French instructors*

*The Development Centre, t 06 15 55 31 56, www.tdcski.com: started for the 2002/3 season by four top young British instructors and has quickly built a good reputation*

*New Generation, t 04 79 01 03 18, www.skinewgen.com: another British-run school that started up recently*

*Alpine Experience, t 04 79 06 28 81, www.alpineexperience.com: specializes in off-piste guiding, organizes groups each morning and offers lessons in the afternoons*

*Top Ski, t 04 79 06 14 80, www.topskival.com: as Alpine Experience*

*Misty Fly, t 04 79 40 08 74, www.mistyflyvaldisere.com: a specialist snowboard school (and shop)*

ribbon development along the access road and by the '*front de neige*' (edge of the slopes). At the entrance to the village stands **La Daille**, an uncompromising area of high-rise blocks built of grey concrete and stone 'to blend in with the mountains in summer' but to many a horrendous eyesore. After that the buildings become largely low-rise, wood-clad and much easier on the eye. The tasteful, central, pedestrian-only **Val Village** area, built of local wood and stone before the 1992 Olympics, features some smart shops and hotels and restaurants competing for attention by the nursery slopes. The resort has one of the most efficient free bus systems in the ski world (called the Train Rouge), which shuttles continuously along the main road and between all the major lift stations; it is also becoming more pedestrian-friendly year-by-year as more and more traffic restrictions are introduced.

But don't expect to practise your French much in Val d'Isère. In winter the place often seems to be dominated by British guests and workers. Over 60 UK tour operators feature Val d'Isère in their programmes and between them run hundreds of catered chalets here – staffed largely by young British people wanting to spend the winter in the Alps. Many of the ski schools, shops, restaurants and bars are owned or staffed by Britons too.

**Tignes Ski School**
*Evolution 2,*
*t 04 79 06 86 94,*
*www.evolution2.com:*
*has a good reputation*

**Tignes** has a much more French feel to it. The main parts – **Tignes-le-Lac** and **Tignes-Val-Claret**, a few hundred metres apart and separated by a lake (frozen in winter and used for cross-country, ice diving and even kite skiing) – were built largely in the 1960s and '70s, high above the tree line in a spacious, open bowl surrounded by spectacular peaks and glaciers. There have been attempts to smarten up the original stark, block-like buildings which were thrown up to allow functional, affordable, ski-in, ski-out vacations rather than aesthetic pleasure and many now have wood cladding. Traffic has been rerouted or sent underground to make it less intrusive, and newer developments – such as in the **Les Almes** area of Le Lac – are built in a more attractive traditional wooden chalet style. The old village of **Tignes-les-Brévières**, at 1,550m the lowest point in the Espace Killy, has been renovated to provide a much more atmospheric place to stay.

*19 Winter Sports | Savoie: The Tarantaise Valley: L'Espace Killy*

## Where to Stay in L'Espace Killy

**ⓘ Val d'Isère >**
*t 04 79 06 06 60,*
*www.valdisere.com*

**ⓘ Tignes >>**
*t 04 79 40 04 40,*
*www.tignes.net*

### Val d'Isère

****Barmes de L'Ours**, t 04 79 41 37 00, *www.hotel-les-barmes.com* (€€€€€) Recently built, the best in town, with rooms in different style on each floor, three restaurants and an excellent pool and spa.

****Blizzard**, t 04 79 06 02 07, *www. hotelblizzard.com* (€€€€€–€€€). Right in the centre with pool and good food.

***Samovar**, t 04 79 06 13 51, *www. lesamovar.com* (€€€–€) By the gondola and funicular at La Daille, traditional and family-run with good food.

### Tignes

***Campanules**, t 04 79 06 34 36, *www.campanules.com* (€€€–€€).

Smartly rustic chalet in upper Le Lac, with good spa (including an outdoor pool) and restaurant.

***Village Montana**, t 04 79 40 01 44, *www.vmontana.com* (€€€–€€). Stylish new complex with outdoor pool above Le Lac.

****Arbina**, t 04 79 06 34 78, *www.arbina.net* (€€–€). Right by the lifts in Le Lac, with busy lunchtime terrace and *après-ski* bar and good restaurant.

### Apartments

**Val d'Isère**: Pierre & Vacances' rustic-style, well furnished **Chalets du Laisinant** are peacefully set at the bottom of a piste from Solaise, near a new high-speed chairlift onto the slopes; its **Val d'Isère Centre** apartments, near the shops and nightlife, have a sauna, fitness room and outdoor pool. **Chalets de Solaise** (with outdoor pool) and **Alpina Lodge** are also comfortable and central. Local agency **Val d'Isère Agence**, t 04 79 06 73 50, *www.valdisere-agence.com*, has a large selection of places.

**Tignes**: MGM's **Ecrin des Neiges** in Tignes-Val-Claret has a welcoming reception with open fire, comfortable apartments and an indoor 'aquatonic' centre with spectacular views, sauna and steam room (separate fee). **Village Montana** (*see* 'Where to Stay') has apartments as well as hotel rooms.

### Catered Chalets

**Val d'Isère**: There's a huge variety. Operators specializing in luxury chalets include **Supertravel**, t (020) 7962 99 33, **Scott Dunn Ski**, t (020) 8682 5050, and **VIP**, t (020) 8875 1957. **Finlays**, t (01573) 226 611, has a varied selection across the price range, as does Val d'Isère specialist **YSE**, t (020) 8871 5117. **Le Ski**, t 0870 754 4444, has a great-value group of chalets just off the main street, and **Ski Beat**, t (01243) 780 405, has a smart five-unit chalet at La Daille. **Mark Warner**, t 0870 7704 226, offers four chalet-hotels, including one with a rooftop outdoor pool.

**Tignes**: More are coming on the market each year. **Total Ski**, t (08701) 633 633, **Ski Olympic**, t (01302) 328 820, and **Neilson**, t 9870 9099 099, each have several; and **Esprit Ski**, t (01252) 618 300, runs a chalet-hotel with childcare facilities as well as chalets. See also **Chalet Colinn**, *www.chaletcolinn.com*, an isolated place with charm on the road to Val d'Isère.

## Eating Out in L'Espace Killy

### In the Resorts

**Val d'Isère**: For an expensive gastronomic delight head for the **Table de l'Ours** with its Michelin star in the Barmes de L'Ours hotel. The **Grand Ours**, by the nursery slope, and **Les Clochetons**, out in the Manchet valley (with its own free minibus service to pick guests up and drop them home), are top-notch and much cheaper. **Perdrix Blanche** in the centre of town is a busy brasserie with a wide-ranging menu.

**Tignes**: **Campanules** in Le Lac has a smart restaurant with good service, as is the **Caveau** in Val-Claret. **Pizza 2000** has reasonable prices and caters well for large parties (e.g. chalet staff's night off).

### On the Mountain

Surprisingly for such a well-known area, good, atmospheric mountain restaurants are sparse but the choice is gradually improving.

**Val d'Isère**: **La Fruitière** at the top of the gondola from La Daille has long been regarded the best up the mountain, with table service and decorated with artefacts from a dairy in the valley. But the pleasantly woody **Edelweiss**, above Le Fornet, is now a serious rival. **Trifollet**, halfway down the run to La Daille, is reasonably priced with varied food and a good *plat du jour*. Down at the bottom of La Daille the cheaper **Les Tufs** does good pizza and, on the first floor, an excellent buffet.

**Tignes**: The **Alpage** (self-service) and **Lo Soli** (table-service and excellent food) at the top of the Chaudannes chair on the eastern slopes both have excellent views over to the Grande Motte. On the western side, try the **Chalet de Bollin**, just above Val Claret.

## Bars and Clubs in L'Espace Killy

**Val d'Isère: Bananas**, at the bottom of Bellevarde, with a sunny terrace and cosy wooden interior, beckons at the end of the day for a (relatively) quiet drink, with the basement bar of **Taverne d'Alsace** an attractive alternative. Later on, **Dick's T-Bar** springs into life as the main disco; **Petit Danois** is somewhat less frenetic. **Tignes**: The **Crowded House** and **Fish Tank** in Val Claret, the **Arbina** in Le-Lac and **Censored** in Le Lavachet (near Le Lac) are popular.

# Savoie: The Maurienne Valley

## Les Sybelles: Le Corbier, La Toussuire, Les Bottières, St-Jean-d'Arves, St-Sorlin-d'Arves, St-Colomban-des-Villards, Les Albiez

**Les Sybelles Ski Area**
*height of slopes*
*1,300m–2,620m*
*number of lifts 73*

**Pistes**
*310km*
*green 18%*
*blue 40%*
*red 36%*
*black 6%*

**Albiez-Montrond Ski Area**
*18 lifts and 18 pistes*

For the 2003/4 season a major new ski area was formed by the building of nine new lifts and five new pistes linking the modern, purpose-built resorts of Le Corbier and La Toussuire via the L'Ouillon summit with the traditional old villages of St-Sorlin-d'Arves on one side of it and St-Colomban-des-Villards on the other. In terms of piste mileage, Les Sybelles, with 310km, rivals L'Espace Killy with a mere 300km. But the similarity ends there. Les Sybelles has pistes that are almost entirely suited to beginners and early intermediates. Unusually for such an extensive ski area, there is hardly a seriously challenging slope in sight.

Early and unadventurous intermediates can cruise the whole area on gentle blue pistes and almost as gentle reds, most of which are immaculately groomed each night. More adventurous types will soon tire of the lack of steeper slopes, so don't come here expecting another Les Arcs, Trois Vallées or L'Alpe d'Huez or the variety they offer. About the steepest long run, **Vallée Perdue**, down the valley between La Toussuire and Le Corbier and graded black, justifies no more than a red grading for steepness. The highest point in the area, **Les Perrons** above St-Sorlin-d'Arves, has some excellent long reds on both sides of the summit.

It is difficult to think of any ski area whose slopes are as well suited to beginners as Les Sybelles. All the main resorts have good nursery slopes and long, easy greens and blues to progress to. Experts should cross Les Sybelles off their shortlist, however, unless they want to rely on fresh snow making the easy off-piste near the pistes a powder playground. It simply lacks any on-piste challenge.

**Le Corbier's** eight tower blocks, typical of 1960s design, dominate the resort and reach as high as 19 storeys above underground walkways and shopping malls. But the traffic-free nature of the core of the resort at the foot of the slopes makes it very family-friendly – indeed it runs a French Family Championship each year with teams made up of mother, father and one child.

**Les Sybelles Ski Schools**
*the local ESF is the only option in all the resorts except La Toussuire, where the International School, t 04 79 56 77 74, www.esi-toussuire.com, offers an alternative*

Neighbouring **La Toussuire** just up the road grew up over a somewhat longer period, with many more low-rise buildings built in a hotch-potch of styles. The pedestrian-only main street, lined with shops, bars, restaurants and apartments, has the slopes behind one side, traffic behind the other and music and announcements from the radio station in the tourist office building piped out constantly through loudspeakers on the lampposts.

Slopes from above Le Corbier lead down towards **St-Jean-d'Arves** and a tasteful development of new chalet-style buildings near the lift base at **La Chal**. The original old village lies over the valley and has bus links to both here and the more substantial old village of **St-Sorlin-d'Arves** at the head of the valley. St-Sorlin has grown in ribbon-development fashion in the confined valley floor near the piste which runs along most of its length and has interesting local shops, a Baroque church and a year-round life outside the ski industry. At the opposite end of the ski area, a series of slow chairs and drags connect the tiny old village of **St-Colomban-des-Villards** to **L'Ouillon** and the rest of the ski area. The roadside hamlet of **Les Bottières** below La Toussuire is even smaller.

ⓘ **Albiez-Montrond**
*t 04 79 59 30 48, www. albiez-montrond.com*

The separate small ski area of **Albiez-Montrond** is also part of Les Sybelles.

ⓘ **Les Sybelles**
*www.les-sybelles.com*

ⓘ **La Toussuire** ›
*t 04 79 83 06 06, www.la-toussuire.com*

ⓘ **St-Sorlin-d'Arves** ›
*t 04 79 59 71 77, www. saintsorlindarves.com*

ⓘ **Le Corbier**
*t 04 79 83 04 04, www.le-corbier.com*

ⓘ **St-Colomban-des-Villards**
*t 04 79 56 24 53, www. saint-colomban.com*

ⓘ **Les Bottières**
*t 04 79 83 27 09, www. bottieres-jarrier.com*

ⓘ **St-Jean-d'Arves**
*t 04 79 59 73 30, www. saintjeandarves.com*

## Where to Stay in Les Sybelles

### La Toussuire
***Soldanelles**, t 04 79 56 75 29, *www. hotelsoldanelles.com* (€€–€). Two minutes from the main street, with simple rooms, pool, Jacuzzi and sauna.

### St-Sorlin-d'Arves
**La Balme**, t 04 79 59 70 21, *www. hotel-balme.com* (€€). At the top of the resort near the piste: basically furnished rooms, lovely views.

### Apartments
The main option in all these resorts. St-Jean and St-Sorlin-d'Arves: **Crystal**, t 0870 1606 040, and **Thomson**, t 0870 606 1470, both feature new apartments, including some with pool and sauna.

### Catered Chalets
Le Corbier: **Equity**, t (01273) 298 298, runs a chalet-hotel near the centre with a popular bar and prices which include lift pass, equipment hire and insurance.

## Eating Out in Les Sybelles

### In the Resorts
Le Corbier: **Le Grillon**, 3km away in the Villarembert, makes a pleasant rustic change from Le Corbier's blocks, with traditional French food like *magret de canard* and *gratin dauphinois*.

St-Sorlin-d'Arves: **Table de Marie** features local specialities.

La Toussuire: **Envol**, in a rustic hut near the entrance to town, specializes in Savoyard cuisine.

### On the Mountain
St-Sorlin-d'Arves: The **Bergerie** at the top of the main chair out of town has a big sunny terrace with great views, a rustic interior, and good prices.

## Bars and Clubs in Les Sybelles
This is not the area to come to for lively nightlife.
Le Corbier: **Roches Blanches** restaurant in the centre includes a cosy bar area

with comfortable seating and an open fire. For dancing, the **Président** gets busy only on peak holiday periods.

**St-Jean** and **St-Sorlin-d'Arves**: The **Irish Pub** in St-Jean lives up to its name; for

a more traditional French atmosphere head for the **Godille** in St-Sorlin.

**La Toussuire**: The **Alpen Rock** night-club, next to the Envol restaurant, can get lively in peak periods. The **Tonneau** is one of several bars that sells food.

**Les Karellis Ski Area**
*height of slopes*
*1,600m–2,520m*
*number of lifts 17*

**Pistes**
*60km*
*green 14%*
*blue 40%*
*red 32%*
*black 14%*

ⓘ **Les Karellis**
*t 04 79 59 50 36,*
*www.les-karellis.com*

# Les Karellis

Set at a lofty 1,600m, the modern, purpose-built resort of Les Karellis consists of little more that a clutch of block-like, flat-roofed apartment buildings with little in the way of charm. But what it lacks in that department is to some extent made up for by its interestingly varied, snowsure slopes with fine views of the Maurienne range. These offer more challenging intermediate runs than nearby Valloire and Valmeinier and a day trip to here, if you are staying at those resorts and have a car, is worth considering.

**Valloire-Valmeinier Ski Area**
*height of slopes*
*1,430m–2,600m*
*number of lifts 33*

**Pistes**
*150km*
*green 22%*
*blue 25%*
*red 43%*
*black 10%*

# Valloire-Valmeinier

The old mountain villages of Valloire and Valmeinier 1500 and the tastefully designed, modern purpose-built resort of Valmeinier 1800 share the most extensive slopes in the Maurienne valley, and their contrasting characters adds considerable interest to the ski area. All are reached by a long, winding road which eventually splits into two, high above the austere valley town of **St-Michel-de-Maurienne**.

Two gondolas from different parts of town access Valloire's two linked mountains. The **Setaz sector**'s shady slopes, the lower part tree-lined and the upper section open, generally have the best snow and the toughest slopes. The broad, open, west-facing slopes of **Crey du Quart** offer a choice of routes to link to the Valmeinier valley. A gentle blue heads down from Grand Plateau to Valmeinier 1800, while an even gentler blue or green leads to the Armera chairlift which goes down and then up to Valmeinier 1500. The open, west-facing slopes above and between the two Valmeiniers, like the Crey du Quart slopes, get full afternoon sun, so snow quality can suffer.

The vast majority of the slopes are ideal for intermediates of all standards. For easy cruising, head for the Crey du Quart and Valmeinier sectors, which have gentle blues and almost-as-gentle reds everywhere. The often deserted long, gentle **Armera** blue winds its way delightfully through the trees down from Crey du Quart towards Valmeinier 1500 and the **Neuvache** blue along the valley from Valmeinier 1800 is flat enough to be a green. The rather out-of-the-way red **Praz Violette** piste from the top of the Combe lift can be a wonderful cruise away from the crowds. For more of a challenge, head over to **Cretaz** and try the highest runs, including the **Cascade** black which often has excellent snow.

All the resorts suit beginners well, with nursery slopes both at village level and up the mountain at the top of both Valloire's gondolas, followed by very easy green runs to progress to. Experts will find the area limited. The long **Grandes Droze** black run can present a challenge when the bumps build up, and the areas beyond Valmeinier 1800 served by the Inversins chairlift and from Crey du Quart down into the Valmeinier valley have some decent off-piste if the snow is good.

The six day lift pass allows a cut-price day in the Trois Vallées (the Val-Thorens sector can be accessed easily by gondola from Orelle in the Maurienne valley, around 30 minutes away by bus).

**Valloire** still feels like a real mountain village, with a year-round population of 1,000, an old church and square in the centre, *crêperies*, *fromageries* and reasonably priced restaurants. Various events such as street markets and ice-carving competitions add to its lively ambience and because the Col du Galibier pass beyond it closes in winter the place is mercifully free of through traffic; its one-way system is there only because of its narrow streets.

The much smaller old village of **Valmeinier 1500** has less life, while its purpose-built satellite of **Valmeinier 1800** attracts most of the tourists. Started in 1986, its low-rise chalet-style buildings line the bottom and side of the main slope and fit in well with their surroundings.

**Valloire Ski School**
*International School, t 04 79 59 05 18, www.esivalloire.free.fr: has now been going over 20 years; an alternative to the ESF*

**Valmeinier Ski School**
*ESF, t 04 79 59 20 10, www.esf-valmeinier. com: the only option*

ⓘ **Valloire >**
*t 04 79 59 03 96, www.valloire.net*

ⓘ **Valmeinier**
*t 04 79 59 53 69, www.valmeinier.com*

## Where to Stay in Valloire-Valmeinier

### Valloire
***Aux Oursons**, t 04 79 59 01 37, *www.hotel-les-oursons.com* (€€€–€€). Near the centre, comfortable, friendly, pretty dining room, teddy bears (*ourson* means teddy bear), small pool, Jacuzzi and sauna.

### Apartments
**Valloire:** The **Galibier** (1km from the centre but close to the piste and a chairlift) and central Valmonts apartments both have a pool, sauna and steam room.

**Valmeinier 1800:** The **Pierre & Vacances** apartments are above average for the chain, right on the piste, with an outdoor pool and sauna.

## Eating Out in Valloire-Valmeinier

**Valloire: Bistrot Chez Fred** serves reasonably priced brasserie food and gets so packed that they erect a canvas awning on the balcony to fit more people in. The **Grange** *crêperie* resembles a barn, and the **Asile des Fondues** serves what you'd expect from the name, in a beautiful old building with stone walls.

## Bars and Clubs in Valloire-Valmeinier

**Valloire:** Few of the mountain restaurants are memorable and neither resort is the place to go for lively nightlife, though the **Touring Bar** attracts teens and 20s with table football, a pool table and loud music.

# Valfréjus

**Valfréjus Ski Area**
*height of slopes*
*1,550m–2,735m*
*number of lifts 12*

**Pistes**
*52km*
*green 20%*
*blue 50%*
*red 10%*
*black 20%*

ⓘ **Valfréjus**
*t 04 79 05 33 83,*
*www.valfrejus.com*

Tucked away in the woods above the valley town of Modane on the site of the old hamlet of Charmaix, the purpose-built resort of Valfréjus and its small ski area offer a peaceful alternative to more frenetic bigger places. The compact resort includes a couple of hotels, several apartment blocks, a handful of bars, restaurants and shops, all pleasantly built in local wood and stone in chalet style and centred around the foot of the gondola and chairlifts which take you up to the main focus of the ski area at **Plateau d'Arrondaz**, 2,200m, 650m higher than the village.

The mainly open bowls above Plateau d'Arrondaz and the tree-lined runs back down to the village offer lots of different blue run options, ideal for intermediate cruising. You can ski off both the front and the back of the top ridge and a wonderful long blue from the top at **Punta Bagna**, served by the second stage of the gondola, takes you right away from all the lifts amid scenic splendour and all the way down to the village, a descent of almost 1,200m vertical. The main drawback for keen piste-bashers is the limited extent of the area – but the lift pass covers La Norma too, and buses run between the two resorts Monday to Friday. Experts will find the area of limited interest, apart from two steep, bumpy blacks down the front from Punta Bagna and some off-piste potential. Beginners are catered for by nursery slopes at both village and mid-mountain level, with a few green runs to move on to.

# La Norma

**La Norma Ski Area**
*height of slopes*
*1,350m–2,750m*
*number of lifts 20*

**Pistes**
*65km*
*green 30%*
*blue 22%*
*red 41%*
*black 7%*

ⓘ **La Norma**
*t 04 79 20 31 46,*
*www.lanorma.com*

La Norma, with its wood-clad low-rise buildings offering traffic-free ski-in, ski-out convenience, makes a quiet, family-friendly destination for those not looking for much of a challenge on the slopes. If you get bored with the local mainly easy intermediate pistes, the six-day lift pass covers a day at nearby Valfréjus and a cut-price day pass for the Trois Vallées (accessed by gondola from Orelle in the Maurienne valley). There are bus links to each of these once a week, on different days.

# Val Cenis

**Val Cenis Ski Area**
*height of slopes*
*1,400m–2,800m*
*number of lifts 19*

**Pistes**
*80km*
*green 21%*
*blue 23%*
*red 42%*
*black 14%*

The two traditional, unspoilt old villages of **Lanslebourg** and **Lanslevillard** have joined together for marketing purposes as Val Cenis, set by a road that in summer links over the **Col de l'Iseran** pass to mighty Val d'Isère. The contrast between sleepy little Val Cenis and brash and bustling Val d'Isère is sharp.

While Lanslebourg spreads along Route Nationale 6 (a dead end in winter, when the road over the Col du Mont Cenis becomes a piste), Lanslevillard, 100m higher and set off the road further up the valley, with an ice rink and swimming pool, exudes more charm and convenience for the slopes. Thanks to strict controls in both

ⓘ Val Cenis >
t 04 79 05 23 66
(Lanslebourg),
t 04 79 05 99 10
(Lanslevillard),
www.valcenis.com

## Where to Stay in Val Cenis

Specialist tour operator **MGS**, t (01799) 525984, has a selection of apartments to rent. Contact them if you want somewhere to stay in this area.

villages, no buildings of over three storeys exist, and all exhibit a traditional style in stone or wood. Between them they have 11 mainly two-star hotels and 25 restaurants.

One lift from Lanslebourg and three from Lanslevillard take you into the shared slopes, which are reasonably snow-sure due to their north-facing aspect, snowmaking on the lower runs, and top height of 2,800m. Above mid-mountain a good variety of blue and red runs suit intermediates best, and a top-to-bottom descent of 1,400m covers an impressive amount of vertical for a relatively small ski area. Although the wooded lower half of the mountain includes a few red runs, most are easy blues and greens, including Europe's longest green run, the 10km **L'Escargot**, ideal for beginners to try out once they are off the village nursery slopes.

The **Termignon** ski area, 10 minutes away by bus and covered by the 6-day lift pass (which also entitles you to reduced price day passes at other resorts in the Maurienne valley), provides another 35km of mainly gentle intermediate and beginner terrain.

# Isère

### Les Grandes Rousses: L'Alpe-d'Huez, Auris-en-Oisans, Oz-en-Oisans, Vaujany, Villard-Reculas

**Les Grandes Rousses Ski Area**
*height of slopes*
*1,220m–3,320m*
*number of lifts* 87

**Pistes**
*230km*
*green 35%*
*blue 27%*
*red 25%*
*black 13%*

L'Alpe-d'Huez sprang to fame as one of the venues used for the 1968 Grenoble Winter Olympics, the Games when French hero Jean-Claude Killy won all three Alpine skiing event gold medals. After that it quickly in a seemingly unplanned way, and its buildings come in all designs. Four other main villages at lower altitudes and with very different characters offer other bases to explore the large ski area (known as the Grandes Rousses, though this name is not well-known in the UK), one of the few in the Alps that is equally good for beginners, intermediates and expert skiers.

It advertises itself as the 'Island in the Sun' because so many of its slopes face south or southwest. In cold, wintry conditions this makes for great skiing and a wonderful suntan, but when the weather is warmer the direct sun can turn the slopes slushy later in the day and icy first thing. Extensive snowmaking covers around a quarter of the slopes and helps keep these in good condition as long as it is cold enough at night to use it. And the high Sarenne glacier and shady slopes above Vaujany and at Signal de l'Homme almost always offer good snow.

With just over half the 230km of pistes classified blue or red, intermediates can cruise around the whole area easily. The main **Couloir** blue run from the top of the DMC gondola out of L'Alpe-d'Huez will please early intermediates so long as it isn't too crowded, as will the gentle blues from **Signal** and above **Vaujany**; all offer delightfully easy cruising. Many of the red runs in the area, such as those accessed from the **Lièvre Blanc** chair and the runs down to Oz and Vaujany, present serious challenges that suit more ambitious or confident intermediates best. They will also enjoy the 16km-long **Sarenne** run (*see* box, below) and being able to brag about it in the pub back home.

A large area of very gentle green slopes immediately above L'Alpe-d'Huez, served by 11 lifts covered by a special beginners' lift pass, makes the resort almost ideal for beginners. Sadly, despite this whole area being declared a slow skiing zone, many better skiers and boarders still flash through it too quickly. Above Vaujany, a much smaller but good beginner area serves people staying locally.

Although L'Alpe-d'Huez lacks a macho image, experts will find plenty to keep them entertained – long and challenging black runs, some reds that ought to be black and serious off-piste options. A 300m tunnel below the top of the **Pic Blanc** cable car leads to three long blacks on the front side of the mountain, usually impressively mogulled, sometimes made even more tricky by the effects of the sun and with a start that requires nerve. The Fare run down to below Vaujany now has snowmaking, and its north-facing aspect means the snow can be good despite its lack of altitude. If you hire a guide, excellent off-piste can be found all over the area, including descents starting over glaciers and ending around 2,000 vertical metres lower.

**L'Alpe-d'Huez Ski School**

*Masterclass, t 04 76 80 93 83: highly acclaimed, run by British instructor Stuart Adamson*

**L'Alpe-d'Huez** spreads across an open mountainside, its hotch-potch of buildings including a futuristic church dating from the 1960s. If you had to pick a focal point, it would be the Avenue des Jeux near the centre, where you'll find the big outdoor swimming pool, ice-skating rink and some of the shops, bars and restaurants. A bus service (free with a lift pass) runs through the resort and a slow bucket lift is handy for getting you from much of the accommodation to the big DMC gondola at the top.

## The World's Longest Black Run

Starting at 3,330m from the top of the Pic Blanc cable car, the black Sarenne piste descends 2,000m vertical over its 16km length, making it one of the Alps' classic runs and the longest black run in the world. It gains its black grading because of its steep upper section, with stunning views and a section of seriously huge moguls that can be avoided by taking a recently created easier option. The bottom half flattens out into what could be classed as an easy green with the spectacular rock faces of the Sarenne gorge rising up above you. Competent and adventurous intermediates will find the whole run well within their capabilities but boarders beware: you are likely to face a tiring scoot or walk out along the flat final section.

19 Winter Sports | Isère: Les Grandes Rousses

Pleasantly situated close to the most forested part of the area, a series of wood-clad, chalet-style apartment blocks and a few shops, bars and restaurants make up **Auris-en-Oisans**. Its peaceful setting makes it a good family resort, and easy access by car makes it good for drivers who want to try out other resorts such as Les Deux-Alpes and Serre Chevalier which are included on a six-day lift pass.

Purpose-built **Oz-en-Oisans** station, above the attractive old village of Oz-en-Oisans, has two powerful gondolas onto the slopes – one arrives above L'Alpe-d'Huez, the other above Vaujany, making it a very convenient place to stay. While still quiet, Oz has developed into a fair-sized place with attractive chalet-style buildings of wood and stone and a skating rink as well as a choice of restaurants, bars and sports shops.

**Vaujany Ski School**
*ESF, t 04 76 80 71 80, www.esf-vaujany.com: has had excellent reports*

The old mountain hamlet of **Vaujany** suddenly found itself rich beyond its wildest dreams when a hydroelectric power operation was built on its land in the 1980s. It spent some of this new-found wealth on a huge cable car (at the time the world's biggest) towards L'Alpe-d'Huez and a two-stage gondola to its local slopes – and the local bed base is small enough to mean that you'll never find a queue. The village has two sections, built at different levels up the steep mountainside facing the ski area. The top section, high above, is a pleasant mix of the original rustic village and traditional-style additions. It's linked to the lower village by an impressive glass-domed escalator, and is the hub of the resort in the evenings. It has a pedestrianized main street with the village's only supermarket (small), several restaurants, a play area, the tourist office and some apartments. The lower section, called **Le Village**, has been built in traditional style around the cable car and gondola stations. It is a large pedestrianized complex of spacious, mid-range apartments, with a good ski shop, pizzeria, bakery, bar, café and a sports centre with a big swimming pool.

A high-speed chairlift built a few years ago to Signal, above L'Alpe-d'Huez, resulted in the rustic old village of **Villard-Reculas** gradually being renovated and developed into a resort. A few new apartment blocks have been built and cowsheds and barns converted to join a couple of bars and restaurants and a small hotel. But it remains essentially a quiet and peaceful backwater.

ⓘ **L'Alpe-d'Huez >**
*t 04 76 11 44 44, www.alpedhuez.com*

ⓘ **Vaujany >>**
*t 04 76 80 72 37, www.vaujany.com*

## Where to Stay in Les Grandes Rousses

### L'Alpe-d'Huez
****Royal Ours Blanc, t 04 76 80 35 50, www.eurogroup-vacances.com (€€€€€–€€€). Central, luxurious, excellent fitness centre with Jacuzzi, pool and sauna.

### Vaujany
**Rissiou, t 04 76 80 71 00 (€€–€). Run by British tour operator Ski Peak (see 'Catered Chalets'). Simple rooms, good food, nice bar popular with locals.

### (i) Auris-en-Oisans

t 04 76 80 13 52, www.auris-en-oisans.com

### (i) Oz-en-Oisans

t 04 76 80 78 01, www.oz-en-oisans.com

### (i) Villard-Reculas

t 04 76 80 45 69, www.villard-reculas.com

## Apartments

L'Alpe-d'Huez: Pierre & Vacances' attractive Quartier des Bergers apartments with pool and sauna are set near the Marmottes gondola.

## Catered Chalets

Vaujany: Ski Peak, t (01428) 608 070, pioneered Vaujany on the UK market and now have several chalets, some quite luxurious, in Vaujany and also in the hamlet of La Villette up the valley at the mid-station of the gondola. They have minibuses to shuttle you around.

## Eating Out in Les Grandes Rousses

### In the Resorts

Crémaillère, Au P'tit Creux and Génépi in L'Alpe-d'Huez are all worth a look.

## On the Mountain

The cosy Chalet du Lac Besson, peacefully set by a cross-country trail north of the DMC gondola mid-station and reached by the blue Boulevard des Lacs piste, has a sunny terrace and some of the best food on the mountain. La Bergerie, on the red run down to Villard-Reculas, has a log fire, good food and friendly service.

## Bars and Clubs in Les Grandes Rousses

L'Alpe-d'Huez is the liveliest place. British tour operators run bars such as the Underground in Neilson's Hôtel Chamois and the Crowded House in Crystal's Hermitage – both get packed, along with Smithy's. The Igloo disco livens up later on. For a more French atmosphere, head for the Zoo bar, a four-star hotel bar, or choose one of the lower villages.

## Les Deux-Alpes (linked to La Grave)

**Les Deux-Alpes Ski Area**

height of slopes 1,300m–3,600m

number of lifts 51

### Pistes

200km

green 26%
blue 44%
red 17%
black 13%

As far as the skiing is concerned, Les Deux-Alpes would be more appropriately named *'Une Alpe et Un Peu'* ('An Alp and a Bit'). The main slopes rise up steeply along the eastern edge of the long, sprawling, narrow resort village and culminate in the Glacier du Mont de Lans, which reaches 3,570m. Now that's a real Alp. The other side of the main road the second ski area of Pied Moutet reaches a mere 2,100m, less than 500m above the resort itself. Most people stick to the eastern side, itself linked at the top by snowcat to the cult resort of La Grave, where virtually all the slopes are off-piste. Les Deux-Alpes welcomes large numbers of British guests and its glacier opens for business in summer as well as winter, attracting lots of snowboarders who love its terrain-park and half-pipe. Many come on special 'camps' where tuition is included in the package.

The main ski area resembles the village in that its shape is long (high) and narrow. The main Jandri Express gondola is followed by the Dôme Express underground funicular to take you almost 1,800m vertical above the village. But this is no Trois Vallées, Espace Killy or even L'Alpe-d'Huez: instead of opening up a huge playground of lifts and pistes as in these bigger resorts, your choices are restricted to heading down again or playing on a handful of 'spur' lifts that take you to one side or the other of the main route. At one point the mountain narrows down to form essentially just a single run, which can become extremely crowded.

Intermediates who don't mind skiing the same runs repeatedly can have a good time here. The higher runs generally have good snow and some great fast cruising, especially on the mainly north-facing pistes served by the chairlifts off to the sides, where you can often pick gentle or steeper terrain as you wish. But avid piste-bashers will explore all there is to offer in a couple of days and many visitors take the opportunity of excursions to other resorts covered for a day on the six-day lift pass, such as L'Alpe-d'Huez (to which there's a helicopter as well as a bus link) and Serre-Chevalier. Less confident intermediates will love the quality of the snow and the gentleness of most of the runs on the upper mountain. Their problem might lie in finding the pistes too crowded, especially if poor snow in other resorts results in people being bussed in. At the end of the day, you can ride the Jandri Express down or take the long winding green back to town. Unless you are competent, confident and enjoy icy or slushy moguls, beware of the more direct short black runs back home, except on the rare occasion when one has been groomed.

A string of drag lifts (some of them free to use even without a lift pass) and one chairlift line the bottom of the slope by the village and serve an excellent spacious and gentle area for beginners. After that, beginners can head for the glacier and its fine array of very easy slopes – but bad weather can close these top lifts, and novices might find the blue runs on mid-mountain intimidating because of better skiers and boarders flashing past them at speed.

The most challenging black pistes include the aptly named **Super Diable** and the **Grand Couloir** from **Tête Moute**, plus the runs down to town (where you can often see those not up to it tumbling long distances without their skis). But off-piste opportunities form the area's main attraction for experts. The **Chalence** itineraries from just below the top of the Jandri Express to the Fée chairlift can be great fun in good snow, as can the area between the Fée and Thuit chairs. More serious routes that end well outside the lift network, with verticals of over 2,000m, can be tackled with a guide, including outings across the glacier to the awesome slopes of La Grave and down to the small valley village of **St-Christophe**.

Although no Alpine beauty, **Les Deux-Alpes** has avoided the worst excesses of many purpose-built resorts: rather than being planned, it gives the impression of having grown haphazardly over the years, with a wide range of building styles, from old chalets through 1960s blocks to more sympathetic recent developments. It looks better as you leave than as you arrive along the road from the north, because all the balconies face the southern end of town. Hotels, apartments, bars and shops line the busy main street and the parallel one that completes the one-way traffic system, although the village does lack a real centre.

### Les Deux-Alpes Ski Schools

*ESF, t 04 76 79 21 21, www.esf2alpes.com: this branch has a better reputation than most*

*Primitive snowboard school, t 06 07 90 71 35: teaches advanced riders half-pipe and off-piste skills, plus beginner/ intermediate classes*

The area around the tourist office and the Jandri Express, near the middle of the resort, boasts an outdoor ice rink and some good restaurants and bars. The village straggles north from here, becoming less convenient the further you go, though a free shuttle-bus saves some very long walks from one end of town to the other. **Alpe de Venosc**, at the southern end, has many of the best bars and nightspots, the most character, the fewest cars, the best shops and the Diable gondola up to the tough terrain around Tête Moute. The resort is one of the liveliest in France for *après-ski*, which goes on until the early hours.

Another gondola from the Alpe de Venosc end of town descends steeply down the side of the Vénéon valley to the old village of **Venosc**, where craft shops and studios line the cobbled streets (*see* p.347).

## Where to Stay in Les Deux-Alpes

ⓘ **Les Deux-Alpes >**
*t 04 76 79 22 00,*
*www.les2alpes.com*

### Les Deux-Alpes
***Chalet Mounier, t 04 76 80 56 90, *www.chalet-mounier.com* (€€€–€€). Smartly modernized old farm building at southern end of town near the Diable gondola. Extras include a swimming pool, sauna, steam room, Jacuzzi, gym and a splendid Michelin-rosetted restaurant.

### Apartments
**Cortina**, at the southern end of town, is now the smartest in town, with 15 brand new spacious apartments and a sauna, steam room and hot-tubs. The **Alpina Lodge**, right by the slopes near the ski school meeting place, is also nice.

### Catered Chalets
**Mark Warner, t** 0870 770 4226, now runs what was the smartest hotel in town (the Bérangère) as a chalet-hotel; it is right by the piste at the less convenient north end of resort, with a pool, sauna and steam room.

## Eating Out in Les Deux-Alpes

### In the Resort
The **Chalet Mounier** is one of the best places for fine French food (*see*

'Where to Stay'). At the other end of the price scale try the **Vetrata**, **Spaghetteria** or **Smokey Joe's** (which also does a good English breakfast).

### On the Mountain
The table-service **Diable au Cœur** at the top of the Diable gondola serves the best food on the mountain – not surprising as it is run by the Chalet Mounier owners. **Chalet de la Toura** with its big terrace and efficient table-service near the Toura chair, and the table-service **Panoramic** nearby, are worth trying.

## Bars and Clubs in Les Deux-Alpes

There's no shortage of lively places. The **Secret** is one of the most popular with live music most nights and satellite TV with four screens. **Santa Fee** has daily happy hours from 5pm to 7pm, **Rodéo Saloon** attracts crowds of rowdy *après-ski*-ers who like watching people being flung off the mechanical bucking bronco, the **Windsor Pub** sells a wide selection of beers and whiskies, **Smithy's** features live bands and DJs, **Corrigans Irish Pub** is popular and the **Lounge** is the place to go before heading for **L'Opera** nightclub, which livens up later on.

## Belledonne: Chamrousse and Les-Sept-Laux (skiing not linked)

**Chamrousse Ski Area**
*height of slopes*
*1,400m–2,250m*
*number of lifts 39*

**Pistes**
*92km*
*green 17%*
*blue 43%*
*red 20%*
*black 20%*

ⓘ **Chamrousse**
*t 04 76 89 92 65,*
*www.chamrousse.com*

Jean-Claude Killy hurtled to victory in the 1968 Olympic men's downhill in the resort of **Chamrousse** in the Belledonne *massif*, just to the southeast of Grenoble. This functional family resort, popular with day-trippers from Grenoble, boasts a wide variety of terrain within its limited area. The slopes above **Chamrousse 1750** (also known as **Roche Béranger**) suit early intermediates and beginners best, with easy blue cruising runs, a few green runs and an area of nursery slopes right by the village. From the upper part of the mountain more challenging red runs head down towards the other main village of **Chamrousse 1650** (also known as Le Recoin), some of which are floodlit for night skiing. On the cable-car ride from Chamrousse 1650 to the summit of **Croix de Chamrousse**, you look down on the area's black runs, including the famous Olympic pistes, which offer interesting challenges for experts, among them fairly long runs of 850m vertical down to **Casserousse** at 1,400m. Cross-country enthusiasts can try the 40km of attractive trails on the **Plateau de l'Areselle** at 1,500m.

**Les-Sept-Laux/ Prapoutel Ski Area**
*height of slopes*
*1,350m–2,400m*
*number of lifts 25*

**Pistes**
*100km*
*green 11%*
*blue 38%*
*red 43%*
*black 8%*

ⓘ **Les-Sept-Laux**
*t 04 76 08 17 86,*
*www.les7laux.com*

The other major downhill resort in the Belledonne, **Les-Sept-Laux**, with a slightly larger piste network, lacks the same extent of challenging black runs but is popular with intermediates and beginners. Most accommodation, shops, bars and restaurants have been purpose-built at **Prapoutel**, at the western end of the ski area, where the slopes benefit from the afternoon and evening sun. From there slopes spread along the mountain eastwards to **Le Pleynet** where the slopes attract the morning sun, with **Pipay** in the centre being a popular base for day-trippers from Grenoble, with chairlift access to the heart of the pistes. Intermediates will find pistes to suit them throughout the area – the easy route marked on the piste map in yellow will help you explore from one end to the other. The main interest for experts lies in the off-piste.

## Vercors: Villard-de-Lans/Corrençon-en-Vercors, Lans-en-Vercors, Méaudre and Autrans (skiing not linked)

**Villard/Corrençon Ski Area**
*height of slopes*
*1,050m–2,050m*
*number of lifts 28*

**Pistes**
*125km*
*green 20%*
*blue 30%*
*red 24%*
*black 26%*

ⓘ **Villard-de-Lans**
*t 04 76 95 10 38,*
*www.villarddelans.com*

Unspoilt villages in the beautiful Parc Naturel Régional du Vercors, just to the southwest of Grenoble, turn into winter wonderlands from December to March and offer skiing holidays with a quieter pace and more genuinely French countryside feel to them than the big resorts of the Alps; prices here are much lower too. **Cross-country** is as important and more extensive than downhill skiing, and for downhillers the area is best for those who are looking for a peaceful, relaxing holiday rather than clocking up as much mileage on the snow as possible.

The biggest downhill resort, the charming old market town of **Villard-de-Lans** which, together with its smaller rustic neighbour

**ⓘ Corrençon-
en-Vercors**
*t 04 76 95 81 75,
www.villarddelans.com*

**Lans-en-Vercors
Ski Area**
*height of slopes
1,020m–1,810m*
*number of lifts 14*

**Pistes**
*40km*

*green 35%*
*blue 41%*
*red 24%*

**ⓘ Lans-en-Vercors**
*t 04 76 95 42 62,
www.ot-lans-en-
vercors.com*

**Méaudre Ski Area**
*height of slopes
1,010m–1,600m*
*number of lifts 10*

**Pistes**
*18km*

*green 38%*
*blue 31%*
*red 23%*
*black 8%*

**ⓘ Meaudre**
*t 04 76 95 20 68,
www.meaudre.com*

**Autrans Ski Area**
*height of slopes
1,050m–1,650m*
*number of lifts 11*

**Pistes**
*19km*

*green 52%*
*blue 11%*
*red 31%*
*black 6%*

**ⓘ Autrans**
*t 04 76 95 30 70,
www.autrans.com*

**ⓘ Monts-Jura**
*t 04 50 20 91 43,
www.monts-jura.com*

Corrençon-en-Vercors shares a very respectable 130km of pistes, took off as a tourist destination early last century with the popularity of its 'clean air and milk' health cures; the milk came from the local Villarde breed of cows. Skiing started here in 1925 and it hosted the World Skiing Championships in 1931 and part of the Winter Olympics in 1968. The area's latest hero, local girl Carole Montillet, became the first Frenchwoman to win an Olympic gold medal in the prestigious downhill event in Salt Lake City in 2002.

Intermediates will find plenty of blues and greens to keep them interested and wonderful views, especially over the **Lac du Pré** above Villard-de-Lans and of the Alps and Mont Blanc from the top of the highest lifts. Beginners have ideal nursery slopes right by Corrençon-en-Vercors and at **Les Glovettes** above Villard-de-Lans. Experts can enjoy no fewer than eight black runs, mainly on the higher slopes above Corrençon-en-Vercors, and some off-piste.

The 160km of tracks on the **High Vercors Nordic Site**, which includes what in summer is an 18-hole golf course, has become one of the leading **cross-country** areas in France. There's even a Nordic ski adventure park, with bumps, ridges, jumps and bends, popular with experienced and beginner Nordic skiers, and a 30km Royal Chrono circuit where you can compare your time with, say, Olympic champion Raphaël Poirée.

A huge amount of money has been invested in recent years in snowmaking machinery to ensure good snow (so long as it's cold enough) in both the downhill and cross-country areas.

On the road from Grenoble to Villard-de-Lans, you pass through the village of **Lans-en-Vercors**, with the second largest downhill ski area in the Regional Park, though with only 40km of pistes it is hardly huge and it has no black runs. Its two cross-country areas offer 68km of trails. **Méaudre**, a tiny, charmingly unspoilt village just to the north of Villard-de-Lans, and **Autrans**, larger and a little further north again, both have even smaller areas of downhill slopes but their main claims to fame are their cross-country facilities. Méaudre's two areas, one right by the village and the other 300m higher at **Les Narces**, total 100km, and Autrans' varied trails total 160km. Autrans is famous for cross-country skiing, especially thanks to the great January race, the Foulée Blanche.

# Ain

## Monts-Jura: Mijoux/La Faucille, Lélex/Crozet (skiing not linked)

Just to the northwest of Geneva, the unspoilt Monts-Jura resorts offer a relaxingly low-key winter holiday with magnificent views over Lac Léman and towards Mont Blanc. The two neighbouring

**Monts-Jura
Ski Area**
*height of slopes
900m–1,680m*
*number of lifts 28*

**Pistes**
*50km*
*green 37%*
*blue 30%*
*red 22%*
*black 11%*

resorts of **Mijoux** and **Lélex** sit at the foot of their small and separate downhill ski areas, **Mijoux-La Faucille** and **Lélex-Crozet**, with gentle slopes which suit beginners and intermediates best. Neither is high (with a maximum altitude of 1,680m and the valley at 900m) which means that the snow can suffer in times of shortage and in warm weather, though snowmaking on Lélex-Crozet helps.

The 120km of **cross-country** trails in both the Valserine valley and on the more snow-sure La Vattay plateau are more than double the length of the downhill pistes and make the area a popular destination with cross-country enthusiasts. Other popular activities here include **snowshoeing** and **dogsledding**.

## Cross-country (Nordic) Skiing

Because most British and non-European skiers usually learn downhill skiing when they first visit the Alps and then visit the mountains for only one or two weeks a year, very few try cross-country skiing. Those who do frequently become hooked by the peace and tranquillity of it, compared with downhill, as it allows you to get away from the crowds and the lift systems and into the forests, on and around frozen lakes and onto high plateaux. Compared with downhill, cross-country skiing also appeals to those in search of an aerobic work-out; while the ski lifts take a lot of the effort out of downhill skiing, it's your own energy that gets you up the hills of a cross-country trail. The lightness of the skis and the comfortable shoes you wear compared with the heavy skis and bindings and stiff plastic boots of downhill equipment form another attraction for many people.

There are two main types of cross-country skiing (which is increasingly becoming known as '*ski nordique*' rather than '*ski de fond*' in France). The most common one involves gliding along in grooves in the snow, one for each ski, that have been prepared by special machines – it looks at first sight rather like walking on skis but in practice there's much more to it than that, and lessons to teach you the basics are a must if you are to get the most out of the sport. The other main style is more like skating on skis on tracks that have been prepared specially for that purpose – that's the type you see on TV for most of the main Nordic competitive races and biathlons.

With over 200 special Nordic skiing areas and 11,000km of prepared and secured pistes, cross-country is booming in France. While most ski resorts have some cross-country facilities, a few specialize in this activity. In the Rhône-Alpes, these include: Vercors, Monts-Jura, Le Grand Bornand with Les Confins in Les Aravis, Plateau des Glières and Praz de Lys in Haute Savoie, Domaine d'Agy (Morillon and Les Carroz) and Les Saisies. As well as skiing, most Espace Nordique areas also offer other activities such as walking paths, dogsledding and snowshoeing, have detailed maps showing all the trails and their own ski pass. In the Rhône-Alpes, area passes are available allowing you to try cross-country throughout the region – for example, throughout Savoie or Haute Savoie. The Espace Nordique areas also offer original tours and courses with the local ESF.

For more information about Nordic skiing, visit *www.ski-nordic-france.com*, where you'll find details of Nordic areas including piste maps, costs and links to the relevant resort websites. For contact details on Vercors, Monts-Jura, the biggest Nordic areas in Rhône-Alpes, and Les Saisies (Espace Cristal), see the relevant chapters.

### Other Nordic Skiing Areas

**Les Glières Plateau:** Cross-country skiing centre at Thorens-Glières, **t** 04 50 22 45 63.
**La Clusaz Les Confins Plateau:** Nordic area centre at La Clusaz, **t** 04 50 02 47 43.
**Agy/Les Carroz:** Agy Nordic Centre at St-Sigismond, **t** 04 50 34 27 53.
**Praz de Lys:** Nordic Centre at Taninges, **t** 04 50 34 25 05.
**Le Semnoz:** Nordic Ski Centre at Leschaux, **t** 04 50 01 16 48.
**Savoie:** Grand Revard, **t** 04 79 25 80 49.

# Language

Everywhere in France the same level of politeness expected: use *monsieur*, *madame* or *mademoiselle* when speaking to everyone (including waiters), from your first *bonjour* to your last *au revoir*.

*See* pp.47–50 for a menu vocabulary.

## Pronunciation

The stress usually falls on the last syllable except when the word ends with an unaccented *e*.

### Vowels

*a, à, â* between *a* in 'bat' and 'part'
*é, er, ez* at end of word as *a* in 'plate' but a bit shorter
*e* at end of word not pronounced
*e* at end of syllable or in one-syllable word pronounced weakly, like *er* in 'mother'
*i* as *ee* in 'bee'
*o* as *o* in 'pot'
*ô* as *o* in 'go'
*u, û* between *oo* in 'boot' and *ee* in 'bee'

### Vowel Combinations

*ai* as *a* in 'plate'
*aî* as *e* in 'bet'
*ail* as *i* in 'kite'
*au, eau* as *o* in 'go'
*ei* as *e* in 'bet'
*eu, œu* as *er* in 'mother'
*oi* between *wa* in 'swam' and *u* in 'swum'
*oy* in middle of words as 'why'; otherwise as 'oi', above
*ui* as *wee* in 'twee'

### Nasal Vowels

Vowels followed by an *n* or an *m* have a nasal sound.
*an, en* as *o* in 'pot' + nasal sound
*ain, ein, in* as *a* in 'bat' + nasal sound
*on* as *aw* in 'paw' + nasal sound
*un* as *u* in 'nut' + nasal sound

## Consonants

Many French consonants are pronounced as in English, but there are some exceptions:
*c* followed by *e, i* or *y* and *ç* as *s* in 'sit'
*c* followed by *a, o* or *u* as *c* in 'cat'
*g* followed by *e, i* or *y* as *s* in 'pleasure'
*gn* as *ni* in 'opinion'
*j* as *s* in 'pleasure'
*ll* as *y* in 'yes'
*qu* as *k* in 'kite'
*s* between vowels as *z* in 'zebra'
*s* otherwise as *s* in 'sit'
*w* except in English words as *v* in 'vest'
*x* at end of word as *s* in 'sit'
*x* otherwise as *x* in 'six'

## Vocabulary

The nouns in the list below are marked as either masculine *(m)* or feminine *(f)*.

If masculine, 'the' is *le*, or *l'* if the word begins with a vowel; and 'a' is *un*. 'Some' or 'any' is *du*. For example, *'A quelle heure part le train pour Montpellier?/Je voudrais un oreiller/du savon.'*

If feminine, 'the' is *la*, or *l'* if the word begins with a vowel; and 'a' is *une*. 'Some' or 'any' is *'de la'*. For example, *'Je cherche la sortie/une pharmacie/Je voudrais de l'aspirine.'*

If plural, 'the' is *les*, and 'some' or 'any' is *des*. For example, *'Où sont les toilettes/Est-ce que vous avez des cartes postales?'*

## General

**hello** *bonjour*
**good evening** *bonsoir*
**good night** *bonne nuit*
**goodbye** *au revoir*
**please** *s'il vous plaît*
**thank you (very much)** *merci (beaucoup)*
**yes** *oui*
**no** *non*
**good / bad** *bon (bonne) / mauvais*

**excuse me** *pardon, excusez-moi*
**Can you help me?** *Pourriez-vous m'aider?*
**My name is...** *Je m'appelle...*
**What is your name?** *Comment t'appelles-tu?*
(informal), *Comment vous appelez-vous?*
(formal)
**How are you?** *Comment allez-vous?*
**Fine** *Ça va bien*
**I don't understand** *Je ne comprends pas*
**I don't know** *Je ne sais pas*
**Speak more slowly** *Pourriez-vous parler plus lentement?*
**How do you say ... in French?** *Comment dit-on ... en français?*
**Help!** *Au secours!*
**Where is...?** *Où se trouve ...?*
**Is it far?** *C'est loin?*
**left / right** *à gauche / à droite*
**straight on** *tout droit*
**entrance / exit** *entrée (f) / sortie (f)*
**open / closed** *ouvert(e) / fermé(e)*
**WC** *toilettes (fpl)*
**men** *hommes*
**ladies** *dames* or *femmes*
**doctor** *médecin (m)*
**hospital** *hôpital (m)*
**emergency room/A&E** *salle des urgences (f)*
**police station** *commissariat de police (m)*

## Months and Days

**January / February** *janvier / février*
**March /April** *mars / avril*
**May / June** *mai / juin*
**July / August** *juillet / août*
**September / October** *septembre / octobre*
**November / December** *novembre / décembre*

**Monday / Tuesday** *lundi / mardi*
**Wednesday** *mercredi*
**Thursday / Friday** *jeudi / vendredi*
**Saturday / Sunday** *samedi / dimanche*

## Accommodation

**single room** *chambre pour une personne (f)*
**twin room** *chambre à deux lits (f)*
**double room** *chambre pour deux personnes (f)/chambre double (f)*
**bed** *lit (m)*
**blanket** *couverture (f)*
**cot (child's bed)** *lit d'enfant (m)*
**pillow** *oreiller (m)*
**soap** *savon (m)*
**towel** *serviette (f)*

**booking** *réservation (f)*
**I would like to book a room** *Je voudrais réserver une chambre*

## Shopping and Services

**How much is it?** *C'est combien?*
**Do you have...?** *Est-ce que vous avez...?*
**It's too expensive** *C'est trop cher*
**bank** *banque (f)*
**money** *argent (m)*
**change** *monnaie (f)*
**credit card** *carte de crédit (f)*
**traveller's cheque** *chèque de voyage (m)*
**post office** *la poste*
**stamp** *timbre (m)*
**postcard** *carte postale (f)*
**public phone** *cabine téléphonique (f)*
**shop** *magasin (m)*
**central food market** *halles (fpl)*
**tobacconist** *tabac (m)*
**pharmacy** *pharmacie (f)*
**aspirin** *aspirine (f)*
**condoms** *préservatifs (mpl)*
**insect repellent** *anti-insecte (m)*
**sun cream** *crème solaire (f)*
**tampons** *tampons hygiéniques (mpl)*

## Transport

**airport** *aéroport (m)*
**go on foot** *aller à pied*
**bicycle** *bicyclette (f) / vélo (m)*
**mountain bike** *vélo tout terrain, VTT (m)*
**bus** *autobus (m)*
**bus stop** *arrêt d'autobus (m)*
**coach station** *gare routière (f)*
**railway station** *gare (f)*
**train** *train (m)*
**platform** *quai (m)/voie (f)*
**date-stamp machine** *composteur (m)*
**timetable** *horaire (m)*
**seat** *place (f)*
**left-luggage locker** *consigne automatique (f)*
**car** *voiture (f)*
**to hire** *louer*
**taxi** *taxi (m)*
**ticket office** *guichet (m)*
**ticket** *billet (m)*
**single to...** *un aller* (or *aller simple*) *pour...*
**return/round trip** *aller et retour (m)*
**What time does the ... leave?** *A quelle heure part...?*
**delayed / on time** *en retard / à l'heure*

# Glossary

*ardoise* slate

*aven* swallow hole (vertical hole in the rock)

*basse-cour* (for château) outer courtyard; (for farm) farmyard

*bastide* a new town founded in the Middle Ages; usually rectangular, with a grid of streets and an arcaded central square; sometimes circular in plan

*bien national* property of the state

*cachot* prison cell; dungeon

*castrum* a rectangular Roman army camp, which often grew into a permanent settlement

*cave* or *caveau* wine cellar

*chemin* path

*chemin de ronde* parapet walk, wall walk, rampart walk

*clé* (or *clef*) *de voûte* keystone or boss (architecturally speaking)

*clocher-mur* the west front of a church that rises high above the roofline for its entire width to make a bell tower

*col* pass

*collégiale* collegiate church

*commune* in the Middle Ages, the government of a free town or city; today, the smallest unit of local government, encompassing a town or village

*(les) communs* outbuildings

*corps de logis* main building

*côte* coast; on wine labels *côte, coteaux* and *costières* mean 'hills' or 'slopes'

*cour* court; courtyard (a *cour d'honneur* is the principal courtyard of a château)

*cours* wide main street, like an elongated main square

*donjon* castle keep

*fabrique* folly (more commonly, manufacture or factory)

*gîte* self-catering accommodation

*gîte d'étape* basic shelter for walkers

*grange* farm

*grotte* cave

*historié* historiated (decorated with flowers or figures or animals, often telling a story

*hôtel (particulier)* originally the town residence of the nobility; by the 18th century became more generally used for any large, private residence; also a hotel

*hôtel de ville* town hall

*lavoir* communal fountain, usually covered, for the washing of clothes

*mairie* town hall

*la maison* ordinary word for a house, but also a euphemism for a château, which it would be too vulgar to refer to directly

*maquis* Mediterranean scrub; also used as a term for the French Resistance in hiding during the Second World War

*Parlement* a regional law court before the Revolution, with members appointed by the king; by the late Ancien Régime, parlements exercised a great deal of influence over political affairs

*presqu'île* peninsula

*puy* high point (also pujol)

*retable* a carved or painted altarpiece

*rez-de-chaussée* (rc) ground floor (US first floor)

*romain* Roman (note difference from roman)

*roman* Romanesque (10th-12th century architectural style characterized by rounded arches); as a noun, a novel

*sens de la visite* generally not sense of the visit, but direction to follow on the visit

*sens interdit* no entry

*sens unique* one way

*transi* in a tomb, a relief of the decomposing cadaver

*tympanum* semicircular panel over a church door; often the occasion for the most ambitious ensembles of medieval sculpture

*vieille ville* historic, old quarter of town

*village perché* hilltop or hillside village

*visite libre* unaccompanied visit, not free visit (which would be *visite gratuite*)

# Index

Main page references are in **bold**. Page references to maps are in *italics*.

## Author's Acknowledgements

For this second edition, Isabelle Faure of the Comité Régional du Tourisme Rhône-Alpes was immensely kind and helpful. The press officers for the region's eight *départements* also greatly assisted me with information and my itineraries; they and the people who looked after me at the tourist offices and sights were a joy. All these people are too numerous to mention here, but I must single out Corinne, Céline and Gérard for plying me with Savoie wine, then sending me plunging over a cliff for my first-ever paragliding experience, over Lac d'Aiguebelette – the most exhilarating of many memorable moments updating this book. My parents as ever looked after me wonderfully at their heavenly home in the Drôme. Back in England, John Lotherington was a fantastic support.

## About the Contributor

Ski enthusiast **Dave Watts**, specialist author of the **Winter Sports** chapter, is editor of *Where to Ski and Snowboard*, Britain's leading annual guidebook to winter sports worldwide, and editor-in-chief of *Daily Mail Ski & Snowboard*, Britain's biggest-selling winter sports magazine.

## 2nd edition Published 2007

**Cadogan Guides**
2nd Floor, 233 High Holborn,
London WC1V 7DN
info@cadoganguides.co.uk
www.cadoganguides.com

**The Globe Pequot Press**
246 Goose Lane, PO Box 480, Guilford,
Connecticut 06437–0480

Copyright © Philippe Barbour 2004, 2007
Cover photographs: Château d'Yvoire by Lac Léman
© Philippe Barbour; grapes © OLIVIA
Introduction photographs: © OLIVIA; © Philippe
Barbour; © Aline Perrier
Maps © Cadogan Guides, drawn by
Maidenhead Cartographic Services Ltd

Art Director: Sarah Gardner
Editor: Linda McQueen
Assistant Editor: Nicola Jessop
Proofreading: Dominique Shead
Indexing: Isobel McLean

Printed in Italy by Legoprint
A catalogue record for this book is available
from the British Library
ISBN: 978-186011-357-4

The author and publishers have made every effort to ensure the accuracy of the information in this book at the time of going to press. However, they cannot accept any responsibility for any loss, injury or inconvenience resulting from the use of information contained in this guide.

Please help us to keep this guide up to date. We have done our best to ensure that the information in this guide is correct at the time of going to press. But places and facilities are constantly changing, and standards and prices in hotels and restaurants fluctuate. We would be delighted to receive any comments concerning existing entries or omissions. Authors of the best letters will receive a Cadogan Guide of their choice.

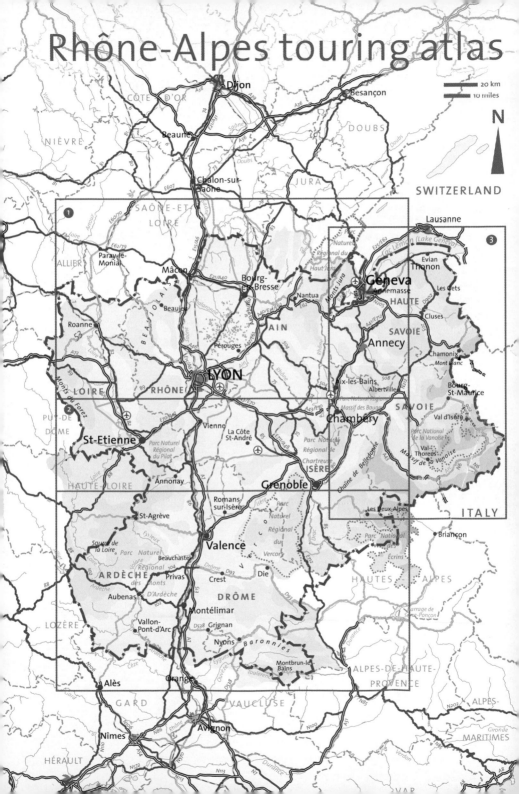

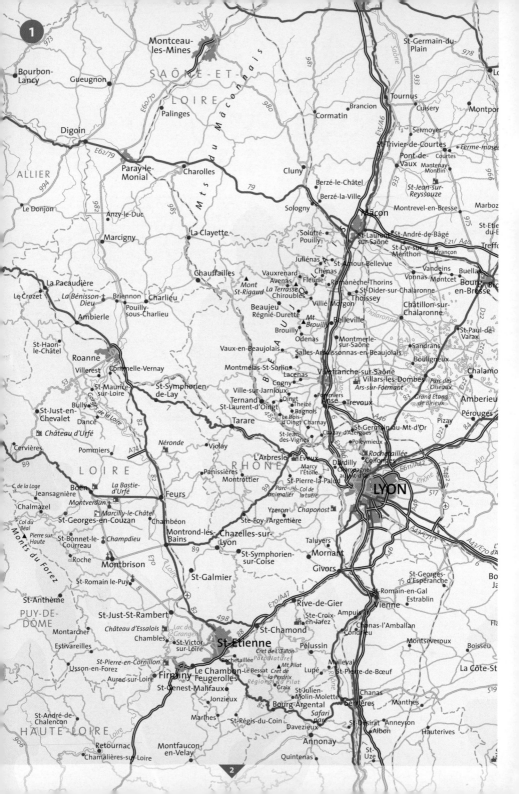

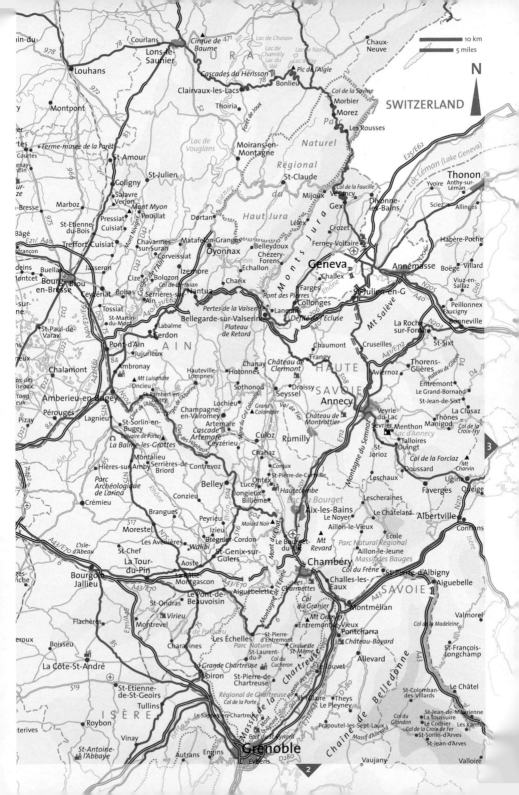

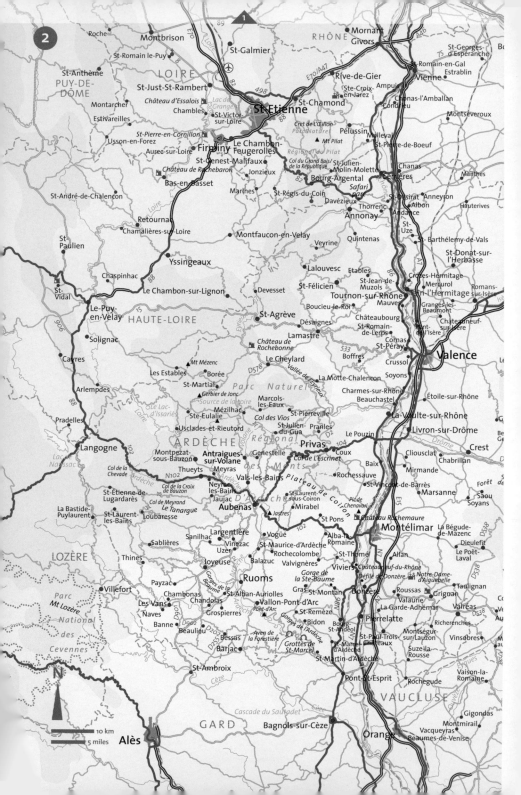

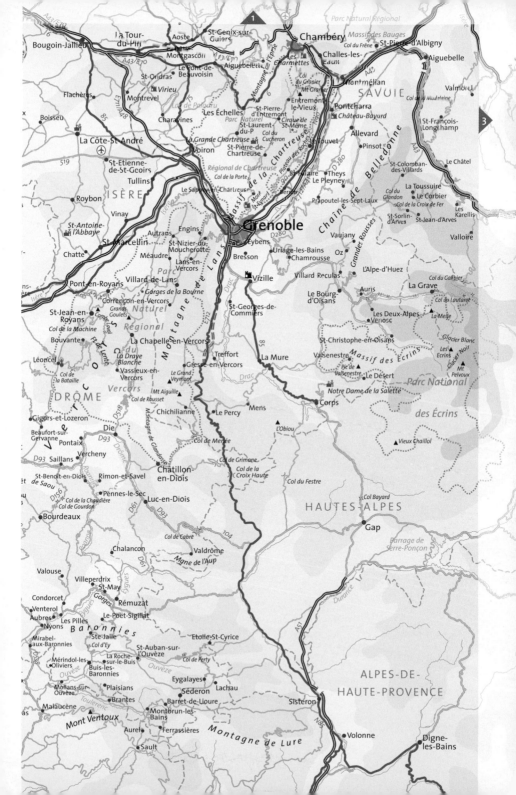

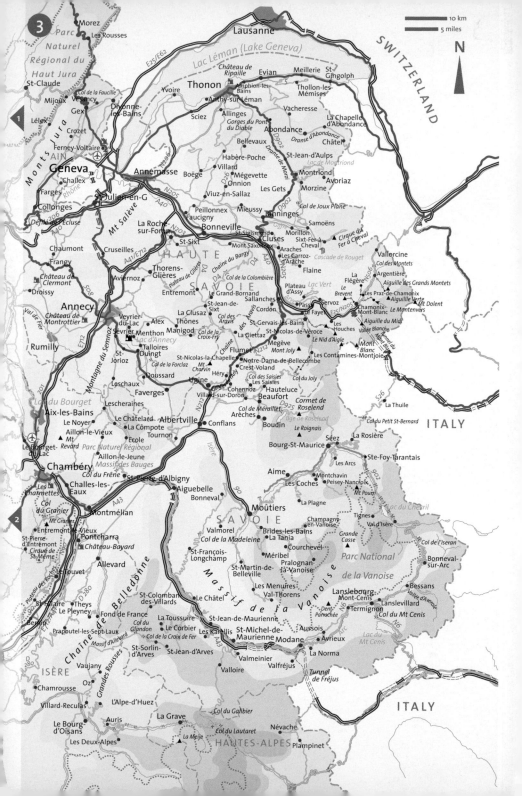

# Buying a property

'An in-depth look at buying and living... everything from employment law to etiquette'

*Ideal Home* Magazine